Productivity growth is the key driver of sustainable income growth and poverty reduction. Its effects on human welfare are enormous. While economists agree on the importance of productivity, its measurement and drivers remain elusive. We sometime refer to productivity as a "residual" or even as a "measure of our ignorance." This important book analyzes the trends and drivers of productivity growth, with a special focus on emerging and developing countries. It uses state-of-the-art econometric techniques and brings together the analysis of a wide range of productivity drivers which, so far, have been analyzed in isolation. It also discusses the impact of COVID-19 on productivity growth. Reading this book will help in reducing our ignorance on the most important driver of human well-being.

Ugo Panizza
Pictet Chair in Finance and Development
The Graduate Institute, Geneva
and Vice President, CEPR (Center for Economic and Policy Research)

This study is valuable in providing a very timely overview of recent developments in productivity growth around the world. The global shock of COVID-19 is placed in the context of pre-existing trends, with the slowdown in productivity growth across all groups of countries as the dominant development. The perspective on emerging market and developing economies is likewise valuable as their convergence to living standards seen in advanced economies today is conditional on (strong) productivity growth. This study provides several useful perspectives on these crucial topics with policy-relevant findings, including on the importance of stimulating structural transformation in emerging market and developing economies.

Robert Inklaar
Professor
University of Groningen

The impact of the COVID-19 pandemic on the global economy is yet to be fully comprehended. This timely and comprehensive book explores the experience of productivity growth across countries, across sectors, and across time. Key issues explored include what drives productivity growth, what harms productivity growth, what is the experience of productivity convergence across countries, and what policies can enhance productivity performance. Importantly in the context of the current crisis, the book explores the impact of natural disasters and economic disruption on productivity growth. With its focus on data and empirical evidence organized through a historical lens for a wide range of countries, this book is a valuable resource for researchers and policy makers who are interested in the changing nature of productivity growth.

Warwick McKibbin
Professor and Director of the Centre for
Applied Macroeconomic Analysis
Australian National University

T0350834

This is a very comprehensive assessment on the global slowing of productivity growth that now extends over a full decade. It is a book of unusual breadth examining recent developments in both advanced and emerging market economies together with an extensive amount of sectoral and firm-level analysis. It highlights many of the common causes including a near-universal slowing of capital accumulation and markedly lower rates of total factor productivity in countries at widely differing stages of economic development. Many researchers will also be drawn to the very up-to-date appraisal of the empirical literature.

Barry Bosworth
Senior Fellow
Robert V. Roosa Chair in International Economics
Brookings Institution

This study is a must read for policy makers, academics, and those in industry who are interested in the drivers and challenges of low productivity growth and its policy implications, including the impact of technological change. The comprehensive look at productivity drivers in emerging markets and developing economies is also a very welcome contribution and will inform policies that can foster sustainable economic growth.

Joshua Meltzer
Senior Fellow
Brookings Institution

This book is one of the most comprehensive studies of recent trends in productivity. Especially in its research covering emerging and developing economies, it breaks new ground in analytical breadth and depth. Its analysis of the impact of shocks, such as the COVID-19 pandemic, makes this work even more valuable and timely. With its emphasis on drawing implications for policy, the book is useful reading for researchers and practitioners alike.

Zia Qureshi
Visiting Fellow
Brookings Institution

This book is possibly the most comprehensive and global empirical analysis of the drivers of long-term productivity growth. By using a variety of data sets and methodologies, it provides the reader with a variety of novel insights. This is particularly true for emerging market economies as previous studies have been too focused on advanced economies. A must read for academics and policy makers interested in designing growth-friendly policies.

Antonio Fatas
Portuguese Council Chaired Professor of European Studies
and Professor of Economics
INSEAD

Global Productivity

Global Productivity

Trends, Drivers, and Policies

Editor

Alistair Dieppe

 **WORLD BANK GROUP**

Summary of Contents

Contents

Boxes

Figures

Tables

Foreword

The COVID-19 (coronavirus disease 2019) pandemic has plunged the global economy into its deepest recession since World War II. Per capita incomes declined in more than 90 percent of countries in 2020, the largest fraction since 1870. The pandemic may leave lasting economic scars through multiple channels, including lower investment, erosion of human capital because of unemployment and loss of schooling, and a retreat from global trade and supply linkages. These effects may also lower productivity and limit the ability of economies to raise real incomes in the long term.

Worryingly, the pandemic has occurred on the heels of a steep, broad-based slowdown in productivity growth after the 2007-09 global financial crisis. The postcrisis slowdown was widespread, affecting about 70 percent of advanced economies and emerging market and developing economies (EMDEs) and more than 80 percent of the global extreme poor. Productivity growth slowed in all EMDE regions. In EMDEs, which have a history of recurring multiyear productivity growth surges and setbacks, the productivity growth deceleration after the global financial crisis was the steepest, longest, and broadest in recent decades.

The slowdown in productivity growth is concerning because productivity growth is the main source of lasting per capita income growth, which in turn is the primary driver of poverty reduction. Most cross-country differences in per capita incomes have been attributed to differences in productivity. Whereas the one-quarter of EMDEs with the fastest labor productivity growth during 1981-2015 reduced their extreme poverty rates by an average of more than 1 percentage point per year, poverty rates rose in EMDEs with labor productivity growth in the lowest quartile.

This book presents the first comprehensive study of the evolution, sources, and drivers of productivity growth during the past decades, including at the regional level. It studies the impact of major adverse events, such as natural disasters, wars, and financial crises, on productivity. It provides analysis that disentangles long-term and short-term productivity fluctuations. It examines how sectoral reallocation has contributed to productivity growth trends. And, importantly, it discusses a range of policy options to rekindle productivity.

The book offers three main conclusions:

First, there are multiple reasons for the global productivity growth slowdown. Since the global financial crisis, improvements in several key correlates of productivity growth have slowed or gone into reverse. Working-age population growth has decelerated, educational attainment has stabilized, and the pace of expansion into more diverse and complex forms of production has lost momentum as the growth of global value chains has stalled. At the same time, reallocation of labor across and between economic sectors has slowed. The COVID-19 pandemic may compound these trends. Although they are less frequent than climate-related disasters, historically, pandemics and epidemics have had significant and persistent adverse impacts on productivity.

Second, the productivity growth slowdown since the global financial crisis, compounded by the impacts of COVID-19, may have profound impacts on progress toward development goals. Since the global financial crisis, the pace of EMDEs' convergence to advanced economy productivity levels has slowed. At recent productivity growth rates, it would take more than a century to halve the productivity gap between EMDEs and advanced economies. Moreover, the manufacturing- and export-led approach to increasing productivity growth taken by EMDEs that converged rapidly to productivity levels in advanced economies before the global financial crisis may move further out of reach as automation increases and the world retreats from global value chains.

Finally, a proactive policy approach is needed to boost productivity growth. Policy makers will need to facilitate investment in physical and human capital. Resources will need to be reallocated toward more productive sectors and enterprises, including through strengthening competition. Firms' capabilities to reinvigorate technology adoption and innovation will need to be reinvigorated, including through ensuring that workers possess appropriate skills to transition to new sectors and that they are adequately covered by social protections.

A stable macroeconomic environment and growth-friendly institutional environment will increase the effectiveness of these approaches. Although the productivity growth slowdown is common to a large number of countries, the policy initiatives to boost productivity must be well targeted. Individual country characteristics and the interactions between policy measures need to be taken into account.

The COVID-19 pandemic is a once-in-a-century crisis that presents extraordinary challenges to policy makers around the world. In addition to the immediate challenges associated with the health and economic crises, there are formidable long-term developmental challenges magnified by the pandemic. The global community's significant progress on poverty reduction in recent decades will likely be partly reversed. It will also be more difficult to achieve broader development goals by the end of this decade.

However, every crisis presents new opportunities. For example, major economic disruptions such as those caused by the pandemic can usher in structural changes that may improve productivity within certain sectors. A sustained shift toward teleworking or the onshoring of the production, with greater capital intensity, of certain essential products could be direct results of the COVID-19 recession with important consequences for productivity and welfare. Rapid technological changes triggered by the pandemic may result in large productivity gains.

EMDEs need to urgently put in place the necessary preconditions to seize the potential opportunities offered by the disruptions caused by the COVID-19 pandemic. Skills building and labor flexibility could help spread the gains from any COVID-19-induced technology improvements more evenly. Fostering investment in digital connectivity could broaden access to quality online schooling and training. Better-targeted social safety nets could prevent the school dropouts that are associated with long-term income losses.

Streamlined government regulations and robust bankruptcy codes that ensure prompt and efficient resolution of failing firms could facilitate labor reallocation from low-productivity firms and sectors to higher-productivity ones. These policies would also form part of a comprehensive package to address the challenges of informality that could, over time, shrink the large part of the economy that is particularly vulnerable to disruptions.

Many questions remain about the impact of COVID-19 on prospects for global growth. Policy makers now need to get ahead of the health crisis with bold, timely, and comprehensive measures. Once the crisis abates, they need to look forward and explore policy interventions to build back their economies better and lay the foundations for sustainable and equitable growth.

Ceyla Pazarbasioglu
Former Vice President
Equitable Growth, Finance and Institutions
World Bank Group

Acknowledgments

This book is a product of the Prospects Group in the Equitable Growth, Finance and Institutions (EFI) Vice Presidency, formerly led by Ceyla Pazarbasioglu. The project was managed by Alistair Dieppe, under the general guidance of M. Ayhan Kose. Ayhan's constant support, thoughtful questioning, insights, and dedication immeasurably raised the quality of the book. The book also benefited from the vast experience and outstanding advice of Franziska Ohnsorge.

The core team underlying the project included Neville Francis, Atsushi Kawamoto, Sinem Kilic Celik, Gene Kindberg-Hanlon, Hideaki Matsuoka, Yoki Okawa, Cedric Okou, and Jonathan Temple. The book reflects their original insights, analytical depth, and exemplary work ethic. The chapter on regional dimensions of productivity was prepared by Gene Kindberg-Hanlon, Rudi Steinbach, Temel Taskin, Ekaterine T. Vashakmadze, Dana Vorisek, Collette Mari Wheeler, and Lei Sandy Ye, who brought their extensive regional knowledge to the subject.

Many colleagues in the Prospects Group provided detailed comments and feedback, including Carlos Arteta, Justin Damien Guenette, Jongrim Ha, Ergys Islamaj, Sergiy Kasyanenko, Patrick Alexander Kirby, Csilla Lakatos, Peter Stephen Oliver Nagle, Franz Ulrich Ruch, Rudi Steinbach, Marc Stocker, Naotaka Sugawara, Temel Taskin, Dana Vorisek, Collette Mari Wheeler, and Shu Yu.

We owe a particular debt of gratitude to Graham Hacche, who painstakingly edited all the chapters, and to John Fernald, from whom we received valuable feedback and had extensive discussions. We also benefited from early discussions with Simona Manu and Peter McAdam, Filippo di Mauro, and Markus Eberhardt. We are thankful to the participants at a workshop held in September 2019, who provided valuable early feedback: Davide Furceri, Charles Hulten, Chris Papageorgiou, Zia Qureshi, and Robert Vigfusson. We are particularly grateful to the colleagues who provided extensive comments on the drafts: Cesar Calderon, Kevin Clinton, Hali J. Edison, Antonio Fatas, Stephane Hallegatte, Annabelle Mourougane, Ugo Panizza, Zia Qureshi, Ashley Taylor, Chris Towe, and Guillermo Javier Vuletin.

We also received useful comments from Kevin Carey, Ana Paula Cusolito, Erik Feyen, James Hamilton, Ivailo V. Izvorski, Andrei Levchenko, Norman Loayza, William Maloney, Valerie Ramey, and Hans Timmer. In addition, many World Bank Group colleagues provided extensive feedback at different stages of the project, including during the institution-wide review of our work featured in the January 2020 *Global Economic Prospects* report.

The foundation of this project was built upon the support of Khamal Antonio Clayton, Aygul Evdokimova, Awais Khuhro, Yi Li, Kaltrina Temaj, Xinyue Wang, and Xi Zhang, who along with Fuda Jiang, Julia Renee Roseman Norfleet, Ipek Ceylan Oymak, Vasiliki Papagianni, Shijie Shi, Jingran Wang, and Heqing Zhao provided outstanding research assistance. Bala Bhaskar Naidu Kalimili and Charles Yao Kouadio Kouame helped compile the sectoral database, and Jorge Luis Rodriguez Meza provided firm total factor productivity data.

We are indebted to colleagues who supported us in the production process: Maria Hazel Macadangdang for guiding us through the steps from beginning to completion of the book; Adriana Maximiliano for designing and typesetting; Graeme B. Littler for editorial and website support; and Paulina M. Flewitt, Rebecca Martin, Quinn John Sutton, and Agnes R. Yaptenco for assisting with logistics. Abdennour Azeddine provided excellent technology support. We also appreciate the great support we received from many colleagues in communication, including Alejandra Viveros and Mark Edgar Felsenthal.

The Prospects Group gratefully acknowledges financial support from the Policy and Human Resources Development (PHRD) Fund provided by the Government of Japan.

Authors

Alistair Dieppe, Lead Economist, World Bank

Neville Francis, Professor of Economics, University of North Carolina

Atsushi Kawamoto, Senior Economist, World Bank

Sinem Kilic Celik, Economist, World Bank

Gene Kindberg-Hanlon, Economist, World Bank

Hideaki Matsuoka, Economist, World Bank

Yoki Okawa, Economist, World Bank

Cedric Okou, Economist, World Bank

Rudi Steinbach, Senior Economist, World Bank

Temel Taskin, Economist, World Bank

Jonathan Temple, Freelance Economist

Ekaterine T. Vashakmadze, Senior Economist, World Bank

Dana Vorisek, Senior Economist, World Bank

Collette Mari Wheeler, Economist, World Bank

Lei Sandy Ye, Economist, World Bank

Abbreviations

AEs	advanced economies
ASEAN	Association of Southeast Asian Nations
BMA	Bayesian model averaging
COVID-19	coronavirus disease 2019
COW	Correlates of War Database
CPI	consumer price index
DTF	distance to frontier
EAP	East Asia and Pacific
EASD	Expanded Africa Sector Database
ECA	Europe and Central Asia
ECI	Economic Complexity Index
EM	expectation maximization
EM-DAT	Emergency Events Database
EMDEs	emerging market and developing economies
ES	Enterprise Surveys (World Bank)
EU	European Union
FCV	fragility, conflict, and violence
FDI	foreign direct investment
GCC	Gulf Cooperation Council
GDP	gross domestic product
GFC	global financial crisis
GGDC	Groningen Growth Development Center
GST	Goods and Services Tax
GVC	global value chains
HCI	Human Capital Index
HGFs	high-growth firms
ICP	International Comparison Program
ICRG	International Country Risk Guide
ICT	information and communication technology
ILO	International Labour Organization
IMF	International Monetary Fund
IRFs	impulse response functions
LAC	Latin America and the Caribbean
LICs	low-income countries
LPM	local projection method
MNA	Middle East and North Africa
MER	market exchange rate
MERS	Middle East respiratory syndrome
MIMIC	multiple indicators multiple causes (model)

MINE	manufacturing of other non-metallic mineral products
NatCat	Natural Catastrophe Database
OECD	Organisation for Economic Co-operation and Development
PIPs	posterior inclusion probabilities
PPP	purchasing power parity
PRIO	Peace Research Institute Oslo
PS	Phillips and Sul
PWT	Penn World Table
RHS	right-hand side
R&D	research and development
SAR	South Asia
SARS	severe acute respiratory syndrome
SMEs	small and medium-sized enterprises
SOEs	state-owned enterprises
SSA	Sub-Saharan Africa
SVAR	structural vector autoregression model
TED	Total Economy Database
TFP	total factor productivity
TFPQ	markups-corrected total factor productivity
TFPR	revenue-based total factor productivity
VAR	vector autoregression
WDI	World Development Indicators
WGI	Worldwide Governance Indicators

If sustained, low productivity growth would have profound, adverse implications for progress in global living standards.

Maurice Obstfeld (2018)

Class of 1958 Professor of Economics,
University of California, Berkeley

Productivity isn't everything, but in the long run it is almost everything.

Paul Krugman (1990)

Distinguished Professor of Economics,
City University of New York

Introduction

Motivation

The COVID-19 (coronavirus disease 2019) pandemic has plunged the global economy into its deepest recession since the Second World War. Per capita incomes are expected to decline in about 90 percent of countries in 2020, the largest fraction in recorded economic history, and many millions will be tipped into poverty (World Bank 2020a). The pandemic is also likely to leave lasting scars through multiple channels, including lower investment, erosion of human capital because of unemployment and loss of schooling, and a possible retreat from global trade and supply linkages. These effects may lower productivity and limit the ability of economies to generate growth of real incomes in the long term.

The likely adverse impact of the pandemic on productivity would be a worrisome outcome, because the growth of labor productivity is the main source of lasting per capita income growth, which in turn is the primary driver of poverty reduction. Most cross-country differences in per capita incomes have been attributed to differences in labor productivity.[1] Whereas the one-fourth of emerging market and developing economies (EMDEs) with the fastest labor productivity growth during 1981-2015 reduced their extreme poverty rates by an average of more than 1 percentage point per year, poverty rates rose in EMDEs with labor productivity growth in the lowest quartile (figure 1).

The pandemic struck the global economy after a decade that witnessed a broad-based decline in productivity growth. The productivity slowdown before the pandemic affected about 70 percent of advanced economies and EMDEs. In advanced economies, the prolonged deceleration in productivity growth before the pandemic sparked an intense debate on how it would evolve in the future.[2] Some innovations that had held the promise of considerable productivity gains, including digital technologies and automation of production processes, seemed to have been disappointing in this regard.

Meanwhile, EMDEs experienced the steepest, longest, and most synchronized productivity slowdown over recent decades. In these economies, decelerating productivity growth has put at risk hard-won gains in terms of catch-up with advanced

---

[1] Cross-country differences in growth outcomes have been attributed to differences in human capital, physical capital, and productivity (Caselli 2005; Hall and Jones 1999).

[2] Some have attributed the weakness in productivity growth to waning technological progress. Others argued that the slowdown reflects the delay of incorporation of new technologies in production processes. Another strand of the literature suggests it is due to deficient demand (for details, see Brynjolfsson, Rock, and Syverson 2020, Cowen 2011; Fernald 2015; Gordon 2012; Summers 2015).

FIGURE 1 Productivity, EMDEs vs. other economies, 1981-2015

Between 1981 and 2015 poverty declined in EMDEs with the fastest pace of productivity growth and rose in economies with the lowest pace. Since the global financial crisis, there has been a broad-based slowdown in productivity growth. Productivity levels in EMDEs remain less than 20 percent of the advanced economy average. The productivity deceleration reflects smaller gains from sectoral reallocation, a slowdown in improvements in many drivers of productivity growth, and an increase in frequency of adverse shocks.

A. Annual change in the poverty rate

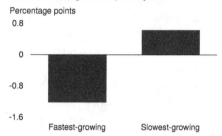

B. Global, AE, and EMDE productivity growth

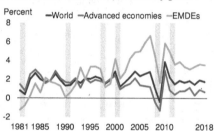

C. Share of economies with 2013-18 productivity growth below historical averages

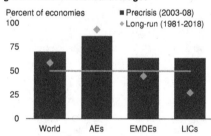

D. Labor productivity, 2010-18 average

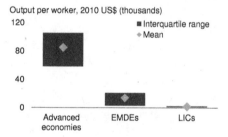

E. Within- and between-sector contributions to productivity growth

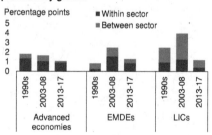

F. Decline in labor productivity in EMDEs, after natural disasters, wars, and financial crises

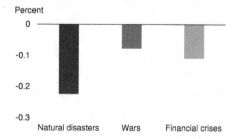

Sources: Correlates of War (COW); Emergency Events Database (EM-DAT); Laeven and Valencia (2018); Peace Research Institute Oslo (PRIO); Penn World Table; The Conference Board; World Bank (PovcalNet, World Development Indicators).

Note: Productivity is defined as output per worker in U.S. dollars. GDP-weighted averages (at 2010 prices and exchange rates), unless otherwise noted. AEs = advanced economies; EMDEs = emerging market and developing economies; LICs = low-income countries.

A-C. Sample of 29 advanced economies and 74 EMDEs, including 11 LICs.

A. Unweighted averages using annual data over 1981-2015. Fastest-growing EMDEs are those in the top quartile by productivity growth; slowest-growing EMDEs are those in the bottom quartile of labor productivity growth. Poverty rate defined as the share of the population living on less than $1.90 a day (2011 purchasing power parity).

B. Shaded areas indicate global recessions and slowdowns (1982, 1991, 1998, 2001, 2009, and 2012) as defined in Kose, Sugawara, and Terrones (2020) and Kose and Terrones (2015).

C. Share of economies for which average productivity growth during 2013-18 was lower than the long-run (1981-2018) average or the precrisis (2003-08) average. For advanced economies, precrisis growth is calculated as the average during 2003-07.

D. Simple average of sample that includes 35 advanced economies and 126 EMDEs, of which 27 are LICs.

E. Median contribution based on 54 countries during 1975-95, 94 countries during 1995-99, and 103 countries during 2003-17.

F. The average impact of the event, that is, the effect of an event multiplied by the probability of the event occurring in EMDEs.

economies achieved before the 2007-09 global financial crisis (GFC). Labor productivity gaps with advanced economies remain substantial, with workers in the average EMDE producing less than 20 percent of the output of those in advanced economies.

Against this backdrop, this book presents the first comprehensive study of the evolution and drivers of productivity growth and policy options to rekindle it. It makes several contributions to a large literature.

Comprehensive assessment. The book examines a wide range of topics that the literature has typically analyzed in isolated studies for smaller groups of countries: trends and prospects for productivity growth; global, regional, domestic, and sectoral drivers of productivity, including factor reallocation and technological change; the effects of natural disasters and economic disruptions on productivity; and international productivity convergence.

EMDE emphasis. The literature focuses largely on productivity developments in groups of countries, such as advanced economies or Organisation for Economic Co-operation and Development countries, or in specific economies or regions.[3] This book is the first to provide both an overarching global view of productivity developments and an in-depth view of productivity in EMDEs, including extensive regional analysis. It uses a comprehensive data set that provides several measures of productivity growth for up to 35 advanced economies and 129 EMDEs, including 24 low-income countries (LICs), for 1981-2018. A new, comprehensive sectoral database for 103 economies allows a detailed analysis of sectoral productivity developments in six EMDE regions.[4]

Analysis of the implications of COVID-19. In analyzing the likely implications of COVID-19 for productivity, the book discusses the critical role of human capital accumulation, investment, and global integration in sustaining productivity growth—and documents how these factors were weakening already before the pandemic struck. It sheds light on the effects of COVID-19 on productivity by examining severe disasters (including epidemics, climate disasters, and wars) since 1960. Although the current pandemic constitutes a truly exceptional shock, the book documents that even relatively milder health crises, such as past epidemics, were followed by lasting investment and labor productivity losses. The book also recognizes the possibility that the pandemic could unleash a boost to productivity and discusses the need for complementary policies to enhance potential productivity gains. Although the gains from such a boost may be unequally distributed, policy interventions can mitigate such unintended distributional consequences.

Multiple approaches. The book synthesizes findings from macroeconomic, sectoral, and firm-level data on productivity. Previous studies have typically focused on only one of

---

[3] For some recent studies considering specific groups of countries, see ADB (2017); Adler et al. (2017); Cusolito and Maloney (2018); Dabla-Norris et al. (2015); Fernald (2012); OECD (2015); and World Bank (2018b, 2019).

[4] The six regions are East Asia and Pacific (EAP), Europe and Central Asia (ECA), Latin America and the Caribbean (LAC), the Middle East and North Africa (MNA), South Asia (SAR), and Sub-Saharan Africa (SSA).

these three dimensions.[5] It combines these dimensions with a comprehensive review of the literature in each area and state-of-the-art empirical methodologies that have in most cases previously been applied only to advanced economies.

Throughout the book, unless otherwise indicated, productivity refers to real gross domestic product (GDP) per worker. To ensure as large and comparable a sample as possible over time and across countries, this book uses the number of people employed rather than the number of hours worked as the measure of labor input. A second measure, total factor productivity (TFP), is also examined. TFP measures the efficiency with which factor inputs are combined; in "growth accounting" exercises, estimates of TFP growth are often used to proxy the rate of technological progress.

Key findings and policy messages

Using multiple data sets assembled expressly for this study, the book examines trends in productivity growth since the 1980s. The analysis shows that productivity growth has become more synchronized, with steeper declines and shallower recoveries, and that cyclical factors have played a large role in driving these trends. The study of cross-country sectoral data establishes that the slowdown in productivity growth after the 2007-09 GFC has partly reflected fading reallocation gains due to the increased role of employment in some services sectors, where productivity tends to be lower than in the industrial sector. It concludes that labor productivity growth has been driven by innovation, better education, and investment in physical capital. It also finds that adverse shocks—such as natural disasters, epidemics, wars, and financial crises—have weakened productivity growth.

A recurring theme of the book is the long-standing and broad-based nature of the productivity growth slowdown that began before the COVID-19 pandemic. This highlights that any policy package to rekindle productivity growth needs to be similarly broad-based. A comprehensive approach is needed to facilitate investment in physical and human capital; encourage reallocation of resources toward more productive sectors and enterprises; foster firm capabilities to reinvigorate technology adoption and innovation; and promote an inclusive, sustainable, and growth-friendly macroeconomic and institutional environment. Within this comprehensive approach, specific policy priorities will depend on country circumstances.

A decade of slowing productivity growth

Before the outbreak of the COVID-19 pandemic, the global economy featured a broad-based decline in productivity growth. Global labor productivity growth slowed from its peak of 2.8 percent in 2007, just before the GFC, to a postcrisis trough of 1.4 percent in 2016 and remained below 2.0 percent a year in 2017-18 (figure 1). The

---

[5] For macroeconomic analysis, see Adler et al. (2017) and Kim and Loayza (2019). For sectoral analysis, see McMillan, Rodrik, and Sepulveda (2017) and McMillan, Rodrik, and Verduzco-Gallo (2014). For firm-level analysis, see Cirera and Maloney (2017); Cusolito and Maloney (2018); and Fuglie et al. (2020).

postcrisis slowdown was widespread, affecting about 70 percent of advanced economies and EMDEs and countries including over 80 percent of the global extreme poor; and it affected all EMDE regions. In EMDEs, which have a history of recurring multiyear productivity growth surges and setbacks, the productivity growth deceleration from peak (6.6 percent in 2007) to trough (3.1 percent in 2015) was the steepest, longest, and most synchronized multiyear slowdown in recent decades. Labor productivity in LICs was just 2 percent of the advanced economy average over 2010-18.

Estimates of the sources of labor productivity growth, based on the growth-accounting decomposition framework, suggest that the slowdown stemmed from both weaker investment and a deceleration in TFP growth, in approximately equal measures (chapter 1). Most of the labor productivity growth decline in advanced economies and EMDEs over 2013-18 reflected lasting trends beyond cyclical factors.

As a result of the slide in productivity growth during the post-GFC period, the pace of catch-up to advanced economy productivity levels slowed in Europe and Central Asia (ECA), and productivity fell further behind advanced economy levels in Latin America and the Caribbean (LAC), the Middle East and North Africa (MNA), and Sub-Saharan Africa (SSA). In the regions that suffered the steepest slowdowns in productivity convergence, Europe and Central Asia (ECA) and SSA, catch-up and productivity were affected by slowing investment growth, financial market disruptions, and a major commodity price slide.

Many sources of the slowdown

Over the past decade, the global economy has been buffeted by a series of shocks that undermined productivity growth, of which COVID-19 is only the latest. These shocks have compounded the erosion caused by an undercurrent of weakening fundamental drivers of productivity growth, associated with slowing progress achieved in convergence toward advanced economy productivity levels.

Weakening fundamental drivers of productivity growth. Since the GFC, improvements in many key correlates of productivity growth have slowed or gone into reverse. Working-age population growth has decelerated, educational attainment has stabilized, and the pace of expansion into more diverse and complex forms of production has lost momentum as the growth of global value chains stalled (chapter 2). A new finding is the increasing importance over time of economic complexity, urbanization, and innovation, as well as of demographic factors, and that many drivers of productivity have been stabilizing or declining over time. In addition, technology-driven gains in productivity have tended to displace workers in the short run. The COVID-19 pandemic and associated severe recession have increased the risk of further slowing in the pace of improvements in the long-term correlates of productivity growth.

A major feature of the current global recession has been the collapse of global trade, at more than twice the rate of decline in global output in 2020. This may be followed by an extended period of weak trade growth, particularly if concerns about the reliability of global supply chains lead countries to retreat from them. This would be particularly damaging to productivity growth prospects in EMDEs, where integration into global value chains has served to boost technological innovation and more effective management processes, and where export-oriented firms are usually the most productive. EMDEs would lose a critical engine of productivity growth if the loss of momentum of global trade growth were sustained.

Slowing reallocation within and between sectors. At the sectoral level, labor reallocation toward higher-productivity sectors has historically accounted for about two-fifths of overall productivity growth in EMDEs. This mechanism of structural change has also weakened since the GFC. Fading productivity gains from labor reallocation have accounted for about one-third of the postcrisis productivity slowdown in EMDEs (chapter 7). The COVID-19 pandemic may compound this trend. Health crises, such as epidemics and pandemics, restrict the mobility of people, which slows geographical and sectoral labor reallocation.[6]

Adverse shocks to productivity growth. Natural disasters, wars, and major economic disruptions such as financial crises and deep recessions tend to be accompanied by a large and protracted decline in labor productivity. Natural disasters—70 percent of which are climate-related—account for the vast majority of these adverse events. The number of natural disasters in 2000-18 was nearly double that of the preceding two decades. Health crises, such as pandemics and epidemics, have occurred less frequently than climate disasters—during 2000-18, the world experienced four major epidemics in addition to the swine flu (2009-10) pandemic: SARS (severe acute respiratory syndrome, 2002-03), MERS (Middle East respiratory syndrome, 2012), Ebola (2014-15), and Zika (2015-16). Nonetheless, these epidemics left lasting scars on labor productivity and output by 4 percent cumulatively after three years, mainly through their adverse effects on investment due to elevated uncertainty (chapter 3).

The COVID-19 pandemic has hit the global economy at a time of heightened vulnerability, with debt at record highs (Kose et al. 2020). This may aggravate the productivity losses from the pandemic. In general, the long-term productivity losses associated with adverse shocks have tended to be larger and more protracted in economies with larger debt vulnerabilities (chapters 3 and 6). This may have reflected highly indebted economies' constraints in supporting demand and activity through fiscal and monetary policies.

Implications of COVID-19 for productivity

As noted above, there are multiple channels through which COVID-19 could have a negative impact on productivity.

---

[6] For earlier work on the sectoral effects, see Burda (2008); Cusolito and Maloney (2018); Timmer, de Vries, and de Vries (2015); and Fuglie et al. (2020). In the context of COVID-19, specifically, restrictions imposed on the mobility of people affect some sectors more than others and can make it difficult for agricultural workers to move to other sectors (Brinca, Duarte, and Faria-e-Castro 2020; Hale et al. 2020; OECD 2020; Siu and Wong 2004).

- *Weaker investment and trade.* Uncertainty about the duration of the pandemic, and the global economic landscape that eventually emerges from it, may discourage investment (Bloom 2014). Concerns about long-term viability and resilience of operations may lead to a retreat from global value chains—which would choke off an important channel for international technology transmission—and may discourage foreign investment that is often related to such production processes (World Bank 2019). Investment and trade play important roles in promoting productivity growth (chapter 2).

- *Erosion of human capital and shifts in labor markets.* Steep income losses and disruptions to schooling, which have affected more than 90 percent of the world's children, could increase dropout rates and set back human capital accumulation for a generation of children (World Bank 2020b). Education remains a critical driver of productivity growth (chapter 2).

- *Slowing momentum in labor reallocation.* Since 1995, the reallocation of labor from low-productivity to higher-productivity sectors has accounted for about two-fifths of overall productivity growth in EMDEs (chapter 7). Mobility restrictions may slow the reallocation of workers away from low-productivity firms and sectors to higher-productivity ones, which often involves relocation from rural to urban areas (di Mauro and Syverson 2020). Pandemic-induced job losses may fall disproportionately on those previously employed in lower-paying services and informal sector jobs, possibly widening income inequality and eroding human capital.

- *Heavy debt burden.* Governments and corporations entered the COVID-19 pandemic with already-stretched debt burdens (Kose et al. 2020). Corporate balance sheets may eventually buckle in COVID-19-induced recessions, straining bank balance sheets to an extent that could trigger financial crises. This would lead to obsolescence of capital as well as large losses of employment (World Bank 2020c). Lasting productivity losses from financial crises are well-documented and confirmed in new event studies in chapter 3.

At the same time, the pandemic may also create offsetting productivity-enhancing opportunities—for those countries that employ complementary policies to seize them. Whereas major natural disasters, wars, and financial crises were typically associated with lasting productivity losses, major recessions sometimes encouraged the adoption of new technologies in certain sectors. COVID-19 could accelerate the automation of production, particularly in manufacturing, as well as the incorporation of digital technologies more broadly. These productivity gains may be unevenly distributed, causing employment losses in some sectors (chapter 6).

- *Organizational and technological changes.* The COVID-19 pandemic may trigger lasting organizational and technological changes to the way businesses operate if the pandemic becomes a source of "cleansing" effects that eliminate the least efficient firms and encourages the adoption of more efficient production technologies

(Barrero, Bloom, and Davis 2020; Caballero and Hammour 1994; Foster, Grim, and Haltiwanger 2016).

- *Diverse and resilient supply chains.* Supply chains may be restructured in ways that increase their diversity and improve resilience. In countries with strong or credibly improving business climates and governance, this could be a new opportunity to join global value chains that promote trade, foreign direct investment (FDI), and knowledge transfer and ultimately support productivity growth (World Bank 2019).

- *Improvements in education.* Where reliable and widespread internet access exists but education systems are weak, the pandemic could improve utilization of higher-quality online schooling and training.

- *Financial development.* Digital technologies tested in the pandemic may expand access to finance in the poorest countries, enable more effective government service delivery, and accelerate the trend toward the automation of some routine occupations.[7]

Profound implications for development outcomes

The broad-based productivity growth slowdown since the GFC, potentially compounded by protracted productivity losses due to COVID-19, is likely to impede progress toward development goals (Sheiner and Yilla 2020). The acceleration of EMDE productivity growth before the GFC reduced the gap between productivity levels in advanced economies and EMDEs; however, since the GFC, the pace of convergence has slowed (chapter 4). Output per worker in EMDEs remains less than one-fifth of that in advanced economies. In LICs, the corresponding figure is just one-fiftieth. At recent productivity growth rates, it would require over a century to halve the productivity gap between EMDEs and advanced economies.[8] If productivity losses materialize similar to those after past epidemics, convergence could be further set back by COVID-19.

Before the GFC, a subset of EMDEs with a strong foundation of education provision, institutional strength, and deepening economic complexity transitioned to higher-productivity convergence "clubs," with rapid convergence to advanced economy productivity levels. However, the manufacturing and export-led approach to increasing productivity growth taken by many of these economies has faced challenges because of increased automation and a retreat from global value chains. Even if improvements in production technologies drive a sustained boost to productivity, they can lower employment and increase income inequality in the short and medium term (chapter 6).

---

[7] On how automation changed following recent recessions, see Hershbein and Kahn (2018); Jaimovich and Siu (2020); and Leduc and Liu (2020).

[8] Despite the slow pace of convergence, absolute growth in many LICs improved ahead of the crisis, resulting in falling global poverty rates in recent decades. This helped reduce the proportion of the world's population living in extreme poverty from 36 percent in 1990 to 10 percent in 2015 (World Bank 2018a).

No silver policy bullet

Immediate policy measures to address the challenges related to COVID-19 include support for health care systems and measures to mitigate the short-term adverse impact of the pandemic on activity and employment. These measures include fiscal, monetary, and financial sector policies to contain the devastating economic and social effects of the pandemic (World Bank 2020b).

Yet it is also important to implement reforms that would enhance potential productivity gains as the pandemic recedes. The multiple sources of the broad-based labor productivity growth slowdown, combined with potential implications of the pandemic, suggest that a multipronged policy approach is needed to lift productivity.

Policies to stimulate investment and improve human capital in order to raise labor productivity economy-wide. Boosting investment is particularly key in South Asia (SAR) and SSA, where infrastructure gaps remain large, and in LAC, where investment has been persistently subdued or contracting on a region-wide basis in recent years (chapter 5). In terms of human capital development, initiatives that improve educational attainment could boost productivity in SAR and SSA. In East Asia and Pacific (EAP), ECA, LAC, and MNA, where educational attainment is already substantially closer to the level of advanced economies, productivity gains could be reaped from improving the quality of education and job training.

Policies that facilitate the mobility and reallocation of resources toward more productive and more diverse sectors. Given the vulnerability of energy and metals production to price declines in international markets that can have temporary and long-lasting impacts on productivity, economic diversification has long been on the policy agenda in regions with a large number of commodity-exporting economies (ECA, LAC, MNA, and SSA). Sectoral reallocation could also be accelerated by strengthening competition (EAP and LAC), promoting intersectoral linkages such as from the information and communication technology sector to the remainder of the services sector (SAR), and reducing barriers to factor mobility (LAC and SSA).

Policies to boost productivity growth at the firm level. The structural slowdown in TFP growth in EMDEs suggests a need to reinvigorate technology adoption and innovation. Among the EMDE regions, strengthening intellectual property rights (EAP); reducing state ownership (ECA); revamping rigid labor regulations (LAC); improving access to finance, especially for small and medium-size enterprises; and leveraging technology, digital or otherwise (SSA), could reduce bottlenecks to firm productivity. In regions that are relatively closed to trade (LAC, MNA, SAR, and SSA), reduction of formal trade barriers and further integration into global value chains could spur higher firm productivity. In all EMDE regions, productivity gains could stem from encouraging the formalization of informal firms, including through lowering barriers to entry or aligning tax systems with international standards.

Supportive measures to manage technology-driven labor market disruptions. These measures need to ensure that workers possess skills that complement new production techniques and mitigate the negative effects on transitioning workers through adequate social protections. To be effective, these policies also need to be set in the context of a stable macroeconomic and growth-friendly institutional environment.

Building back better after the pandemic. Better education and more room for dynamic labor relocation could help spread the likely gains from pandemic-induced technology improvements more evenly. Where learning outcomes are poor, government investment in widespread internet access could broaden access to quality online schooling and training. Better-targeted social safety nets could prevent the school dropouts that are associated with long-term income losses (UNPD 2015). A better-educated labor force would be less likely to be replaced by automation (chapter 6).

In addition, streamlined government regulations and insolvency systems that ensure prompt and efficient resolution of failing firms could strengthen incentives for, and reduce barriers to, labor reallocation from low-productivity firms and sectors to higher-productivity ones (Djankov et al. 2008; Leroy and Grandolini 2016; World Bank 2020a). These policies would also form part of a comprehensive package to address the challenges of informality that could, over time, shrink the large part of the economy that is particularly vulnerable to economic disruptions such as health and financial crises (World Bank 2019).

Within these broad strands, specific priorities will depend on country characteristics. For example, countries with large unmet public investment needs may want to prioritize expanding fiscal resources to achieve more and better public investment. Countries with anemic private investment may want to prioritize business climate and institutional reforms, reduce support for state-owned enterprises, and broaden access to finance. Countries with predominantly low-skilled workers may want to improve health care and the provision of education and training for workers and managers alike. Countries with lethargic innovation may want to expose their private sectors to foreign knowledge and technologies through greater openness to trade and FDI.

Given the low level of productivity in EMDE agricultural sectors, and agriculture's role as the primary source of jobs in LICs, policies to raise agricultural productivity, such as boosting infrastructure and land property rights, would likely pay significant dividends. Furthermore, many high-value-added service sectors—including finance, information and communication technologies, accounting, and legal services—provide opportunities for rapid productivity catch-up growth. Facilitating the reallocation of resources toward more productive and more diversified sectors and enterprises by reducing distortions that prevent the efficient allocation of resources can yield significant gains.

In addition to these policies to strengthen the underlying, long-term drivers of productivity growth, steps are needed to limit the long-term damage of adverse events. Countries with ample fiscal space and transparent governance are better able to pursue reconstruction activities, and to use policy efficiently and in a timely manner as well as to help vulnerable sectors that can in turn support productivity growth. Well-designed and enforced policies and regulations concerning the prudent management of financial institutions, construction, and environmental protection can help reduce the likelihood and impact of adverse shocks.

When pursuing these policy steps, it is important to keep in mind that their interactions, as well as the preexisting policy frameworks, can lead to unintended consequences. For instance, on the one hand, trade liberalization can increase the exposure of private sector firms to foreign knowledge and frontier technologies, thus boosting productivity. On the other hand, however, trade liberalization could be associated with greater informality in the short term if labor markets are not flexible, thus counteracting policies that aim at facilitating the reallocation of resources toward more productive sectors (Bosch, Goni, and Maloney 2007; World Bank 2019; Wu et al. 2019). Such potential interactions underscore how policy reforms complement each other, which needs to be taken into account when designing a country's appropriate policy mix.

Synopsis

The remainder of this introduction presents a summary of each chapter. After presenting the motivation of the chapter, each summary explains the main questions, contributions to the literature, and analytical findings. After these summaries, a brief discussion of future research directions is presented.

Part I: Productivity Trends and Explanations

Part I examines the evolution of productivity growth, as well as its main drivers and implications. Chapter 1 documents the evolution of productivity over the past four decades, globally and across various country groups. In particular, it highlights the broad-based productivity growth slowdown over the past decade. Chapter 2 explores the role of a large number of long-term correlates of productivity growth in this productivity growth slowdown. Chapter 3 focuses on the role of short-term adverse events in depressing productivity growth. Chapter 4 shows the implications of the productivity growth slowdown for income convergence.

Chapter 1: Global Productivity Trends

In chapter 1, Dieppe, Kilic Celik, and Kindberg-Hanlon show that a broad-based slowdown in labor productivity was already under way before the collapse in global activity due to the COVID-19 pandemic (figure 2). In EMDEs, the slowdown that followed the GFC set back progress toward Sustainable Development Goals. The pace of convergence slowed even as labor productivity gaps with advanced economies remained substantial, with workers in the average EMDE producing less than one-fifth of the output of those in advanced economies.

FIGURE 2 **Productivity trends**

Labor productivity increased in EMDEs before the global financial crisis, but during the crisis suffered the steepest, most broad-based, and most prolonged decline yet. This slowdown reflected, in equal measure, investment weakness and slowing TFP growth.

A. EMDE productivity growth

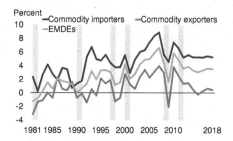

B. Magnitude and extent of multiyear productivity slowdowns and recoveries

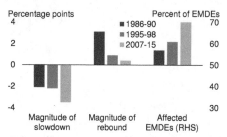

C. Economies with 2013-18 productivity growth below historical averages

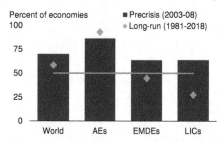

D. EMDE productivity growth, before and after the crisis

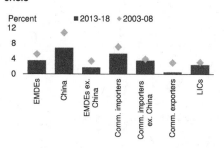

E. Contributions to productivity growth in EMDEs

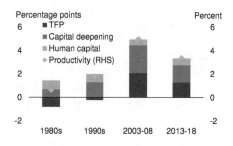

F. Synchronization of productivity measures across EMDEs

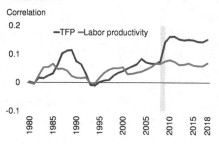

Sources: Penn World Table; The Conference Board; World Bank, World Development Indicators.

Note: Productivity is defined as output per worker in U.S. dollars (at 2010 prices and exchange rates). Data are from a balanced sample between 1981 and 2018 that includes 29 AEs and 74 EMDEs, including 11 LICs, as of 2019 World Bank classifications, 52 commodity exporters and 22 commodity importers. GDP-weighted averages (at 2010 prices and exchange rates), unless otherwise noted. AEs = advanced economies; EMDEs = emerging market and developing economies; LICs = low-income countries; TFP = total factor productivity.

A. Shaded regions indicate global recessions and slowdowns (1982, 1991, 1998, 2001, 2009, and 2012), as defined in Kose, Sugawara, and Terrones (2020) and Kose and Terrones (2015).

B. "Magnitude of slowdown" is the cumulative decline in EMDE productivity growth from the peak of the episode to the trough for episodes lasting more than two years. "Magnitude of rebound" is the cumulative increase in EMDE productivity growth from the trough (end) of the episode to three years later. "Affected EMDEs" is the share of EMDEs that experienced a slowdown.

C. Share of economies for which average productivity growth during 2013-18 was lower than the long-run (1981-2018) average or the precrisis (2003-08) average. For advanced economies, precrisis growth is calculated as the average during 2003-07, due to the earlier crisis-related impact on productivity growth (-0.4 percent in 2008, while EMDE productivity growth remained over 4 percent).

F. Figure shows 10-year rolling correlations. Simple average across all bilateral pairs of economies for each measure of productivity.

The synchronized nature of the productivity slowdown over the past decade raises questions about the role of common factors or spillovers, and the extent to which they will again operate during the pandemic-driven recession beginning in 2020. The nature of the slowdown of the past decade and its drivers has proved controversial. Some have attributed the weakness in productivity growth to waning technological progress as innovations regarded as "low-hanging fruit" have already been developed, leaving only innovations with lower marginal gains (Gordon 2012; Gordon and Sayed 2019). Others regard the slowdown in productivity growth as a "pause," given the time delay between radical new digital technologies being developed and then incorporated into production processes (Brynjolfsson, Rock, and Syverson 2020). A third argument is that the broad-based weakness has been driven by deficient demand (Summers 2015).

As context for the remainder of this book, chapter 1 presents a comprehensive examination of the evolution of productivity over the past four decades, with an emphasis on developments over the past decade and ahead of what could be a major decline in global productivity growth due to COVID-19. Productivity growth is decomposed into contributions from factor inputs and TFP, as well as sectoral growth and reallocation. The productivity slowdown over the past decade, along with the synchronized nature of global productivity fluctuations, is attributed to demand and other factors.

Specifically, chapter 1 addresses the following questions:

- How has productivity growth evolved over the last four decades?

- What factors explain developments in productivity and, in particular, the slowdown since the 2007-09 global financial crisis?

- How synchronized are productivity developments?

Contribution. The chapter makes several contributions to the literature and policy debate on labor productivity. First, the chapter introduces an EMDE focus. Thus far, the literature has focused on trends in subsets of countries such as advanced economies, Organisation for Economic Co-operation and Development economies, or specific regions. This chapter is the first to provide both an overarching global and in-depth EMDE view of productivity developments, with a particular focus on the decline in productivity growth over the past decade.

Second, the chapter systematically decomposes productivity into its cyclical and structural sources for the broadest sample of countries yet. This chapter also identifies the sources of the productivity growth slowdown over the past decade—capital deepening, human capital, and TFP—over a broad set of countries.

Third, this chapter is the first to assess the synchronization of productivity growth across a broad range of countries for multiple measures of productivity. It disentangles the role of cyclical productivity drivers in generating broad-based global productivity developments from other drivers. The existing literature has focused on advanced economy synchronization, whereas this chapter study also considers EMDEs (Imbs 1999; Levchenko and Pandalai-Nayar 2018).

Main findings. The following findings emerge from the chapter. First, the chapter documents a diverse range of productivity trends. Global productivity growth has been resilient, in general, over the past four decades. While experiencing several surges and declines, global productivity growth averaged 1.8 percent in the 1980s and 1990s and the post-GFC period. However, this masks divergent trends among advanced economies and EMDEs. Advanced economy labor productivity growth has halved since the 1980s, in a declining trend that was accelerated by the GFC. In contrast, EMDE productivity growth accelerated rapidly in the runup to the GFC following the stagnation of the 1980s. The GFC ended a period of rising productivity growth, and the ensuing slump risks becoming an entrenched deceleration.

Second, global labor productivity growth declined sharply and the recovery was subdued following the GFC. The labor productivity growth decline following the GFC was the steepest, longest, and broadest multiyear productivity slowdown yet. The post-GFC slowdown has been broad-based, affecting 70 percent of economies and over 80 percent of the global extreme poor as well as reaching all EMDE regions. Commodity-exporting EMDEs—which account for almost two-thirds of EMDEs—have been the worst affected. Synchronized declines in productivity growth have become steeper and recoveries shallower since 1980, pointing to risks ahead of what is expected to be the largest contraction in global output since World War II due to COVID-19 (World Bank 2020a).

Third, investment weakness accounted for the lion's share of the slowdown in productivity growth over the past decade in advanced economies but not in EMDEs. In EMDEs, subdued investment and slowing TFP growth accounted, in approximately equal measure, for the productivity growth slowdown since the GFC. Fading gains from factor reallocation toward more productive sectors also played a role. The long-run consequences of weak investment growth on productivity point to a need for robust support from public investment and to create the conditions for increased private investment.

Fourth, there has been a large role for cyclical factors in cross-country productivity synchronization. The synchronization of productivity across countries increased sharply during the GFC. After removing cyclical factors from labor productivity growth, however, the correlation across economies was negligible during the GFC. Common productivity developments are therefore largely a business cycle phenomenon. This pattern is likely to be repeated as a result of the COVID-19 crisis, given the magnitude of the cyclical and demand-driven factors at play.

Having documented the productivity growth slowdown over the last four decades and established its main sources, the book examines the role of long-term drivers of productivity growth in chapter 2. These have been identified in a large literature on the correlates of productivity.

Chapter 2: What Explains Productivity Growth

Long-term labor productivity growth rates have varied enormously across EMDEs. In 1960, labor productivity—output per worker—in China was $423 in 2010 U.S. dollars, slightly lower than Burkina Faso's $427. By 2018, productivity in China had increased to $13,919, eight times higher than Burkina Faso's $1,641. There are many differences between the two countries: for example, in 1960 the share of the population with primary school education was 26.0 percent in China compared to 0.7 percent in Burkina Faso. China also invested substantially more: gross investment in China averaged 37 percent of GDP over 1960-2018, about double that of Burkina Faso.

In chapter 2, Dieppe, Kawamoto, Okawa, Okou, and Temple explore the drivers of long-term productivity growth and how their roles have varied over time, with a focus on the recent slowdown. Many factors have influenced productivity growth over the past 60 years. In the long term, labor productivity growth relies on innovation, physical capital investment, and investment in human capital. These proximate drivers are shaped by the environment in which firms operate: market structures, infrastructure, the institutional framework, and the quality of governance.

Key drivers of productivity growth—such as investment in human capital through primary and secondary education—have seen major improvements over the last 60 years in EMDEs (figure 3). They have even improved more than in advanced economies and contributed to strong productivity growth before the GFC. Nonetheless, in many cases, wide gaps between EMDEs and advanced economies remain. At the same time, reflecting the structural changes that economies have undergone over the last 60 years, the roles of various drivers have changed, with some increasing in importance and others decreasing.

The recent evolution of these drivers helps to explain why global productivity growth has weakened over the past decade. Some changes can be linked directly to the crisis, such as increased uncertainty and slower investment growth. The COVID-19 pandemic will be a further blow to growth prospects around the world, disrupting trade and FDI, causing investments to be postponed or canceled, and weakening government finances. Other changes reflect separate, long-term trends. For example, the pace of improvement in some drivers of productivity in EMDEs has naturally slowed as the distance to the best-practice frontier has diminished.

The COVID-19 pandemic threatens to weigh on longer-run trends that could impede productivity growth in EMDEs. Over the past decade, the prospects for further trade integration have diminished, and the expansion of global value chains has lost momentum. Sharp declines in global trade and investment amid the pandemic could accelerate these trends. For many countries, they will mean subdued activity, instability, and new pressures on governments.

In the latter decades of the twentieth century, many countries benefited from a rising share of the working-age population. This is now leading to aging populations and at least a partial reversal of the earlier demographic dividend. In other areas, past

FIGURE 3 Productivity growth performance and initial conditions

Productivity growth was 1 to 3 percentage points higher in countries with strong macroeconomic fundamentals and favorable demographic trends. Gaps in drivers of productivity between advanced economies and EMDEs widened in tertiary education, life expectancy at age 50, financial development indexes, and GVC participation.

A. Improvement in productivity growth with favorable initial conditions

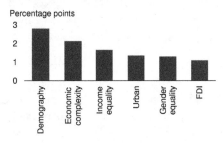

B. Improvement in productivity growth with favorable initial conditions, continued

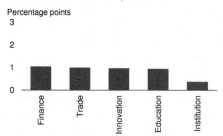

C. Average level of drivers over time

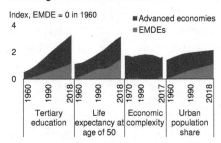

D. Average level of drivers over time, continued

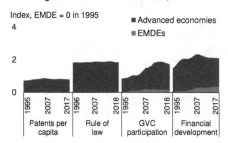

E. Quartiles of productivity drivers and average EMDE productivity growth, 1995-2008

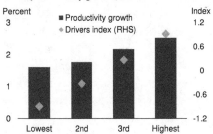

F. Share of EMDEs with a slowdown in productivity drivers in 2008-18 relative to 1998-2007

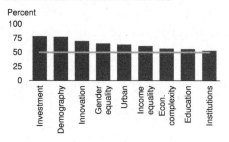

Source: World Bank.
Note: EMDEs = emerging market and developing economies; FDI = foreign direct investment; GVC = global value chain.
A-D. Unbalanced panel of 111 countries.
A.B. The difference in average labor productivity growth between the highest 25 percent and lowest 25 percent of the distribution of initial levels of key correlates of productivity growth. See chapter 2 for details.
C.D. Simple average of drivers over time, by income level. Variables are normalized so that the average value for EMDEs in 1960 is zero and standard deviation is one. Data are five-year moving averages for economic complexity, and are three-year moving averages for patents per capita, rules of law, GVC participation, and financial development.
E. Average level of productivity growth and "index of drivers" in each quartile over 1995-2008. "Index of drivers" created by weighting normalized levels of each potential driver in panels A and B by its estimated impact on productivity growth.
F. Share of economies where improvements in each driver of productivity during 2008-18 was lower than those in the precrisis period of 1998-2007. The following variables correspond to each concept (sample in parentheses): Investment (69) = investment-to-GDP ratio, Demography (75) = share of working-age population, Innovation (27) = patents per capita, Gender equality = ratio of years of schooling of female to male, Urban (75) = Urban population (percent total), Income equality (73) = (-1)*Gini coefficient, Econ. complexity (56) = Economic Complexity Index as defined in Hidalgo and Hausmann (2009), Education (52) = years of schooling, Institutions (75) = World Governance Indicators Government Effectiveness Index.

improvements will be difficult to replicate. Further progress in health and education can contribute to growth, but it will be hard to match the major gains of the last 60 years. Meanwhile, investments could be further damaged by the lasting impacts of COVID-19. On a more positive tone, new technologies could yet reinvigorate productivity growth, and some of the improvements in drivers already achieved should continue to support growth over the next few decades.

Against this backdrop, chapter 2 examines the following questions:

- What have been the main factors associated with long-term productivity growth?

- How much have the main factors individually contributed to long-term productivity growth?

- What are the factors behind recent trends in productivity?

- What policy options are available to boost productivity?

Contributions. The chapter makes several contributions to the literature and policy debates. First, the chapter reviews past research on the correlates of productivity growth, motivating the selection of drivers for investigation. It explores the channels through which various drivers operate, while recognizing that they cannot be considered in isolation. As some previous research acknowledges, drivers can interact in ways that strengthen or weaken their effects. The chapter also reviews the literature on sources of growth in TFP at the firm level.

Second, the chapter presents new empirical findings that go beyond previous work, partly by examining a range of potential drivers over a longer time period, using a Bayesian approach to combine information from many different models. The analysis allows the importance of drivers to change over time, whereas the choice of priors recognizes that several candidate variables may represent the same underlying driver.

Third, the chapter presents new stylized facts on developments in key productivity drivers: whether drivers in EMDEs have been converging with those in advanced economies over the long run, their paths over the past decade, and the prospects for improvement. The chapter also discusses policy options to support the main drivers and thereby raise productivity growth.

Main findings. The following findings emerge. First, historically, labor productivity growth has been driven by innovation, better education, and investment in physical capital. Innovation and private sector investment require a growth-friendly environment, with supportive institutions and policies, including policies that promote macroeconomic stability and the rule of law. Productivity growth also seems to benefit from expertise in producing relatively complex and sophisticated exports, which is associated with international technology diffusion. This finding complements past research and supports the argument that "what you export matters" (Hausmann, Hwang, and Rodrik 2007).

Second, the effects of different drivers on productivity growth have changed over time. Innovation and experience with economic complexity, related to participation in global value chains and cross-border technology transfer, seem to have increased in importance. So have demographic factors, notably changes in population age structures. In contrast, the importance of urbanization, related to the sectoral shift from agriculture to manufacturing and services, has weakened. These findings complement those of Bruns and Ioannidis (2020), as well as recent evidence on the changing effects of economic complexity, urbanization, and innovation.

Third, many productivity drivers in EMDEs fall short of advanced economy conditions, despite remarkable improvements over the last 60 years in key human capital indicators such as the provision of primary education and infant mortality rates. The chapter documents these gaps in a systematic way. For some productivity drivers, including ones that are essential to innovative economies—tertiary education, financial development, and patents per capita—the gaps have widened. Improvements in other drivers, such as institutions and economic complexity, have stalled. In addition, many drivers of productivity growth have faltered, including those that had previously supported strong productivity growth. Working-age population growth has slowed, along with growth in average educational attainment. As the expansion of global value chains has lost momentum, so has the movement toward more diverse and complex forms of production.

Fourth, the COVID-19 pandemic has made the near-term outlook for productivity growth even more challenging. Weaker investment and trade, erosion of human capital, slower labor reallocation, heavier public and private debt burdens, and widening inequality could push down on productivity growth. Yet the pandemic may also create productivity-enhancing opportunities such as lasting organizational and technological changes for business and education, diversifying global value chains, and changing social norms.

Fifth, the recent slowdown in productivity growth has multiple sources; therefore, action on a range of fronts will be needed. Governments seeking to raise productivity growth can increase public investment and stimulate private investment; improve human capital; foster firm productivity, partly through on-the-job training and upgraded management capabilities; increase the exposure of firms to international trade and foreign investment; enable the reallocation of resources toward more productive sectors; and seek to diversify production. The benefits of many productivity-friendly policies could be enhanced by improving the macroeconomic and institutional environment.

Chapter 2 has explored the long-term drivers of productivity. However, the past decade has been buffeted by a series of adverse shocks. Chapter 3 examines the implications of such shocks for productivity.

Chapter 3: What Happens to Productivity during Major Adverse Events

As chapter 1 showed, the global economy has witnessed a broad-based slump in labor productivity growth over the past decade. In chapter 3, Dieppe, Kilic Celik, and Okou show that this follows a typical pattern associated with adverse events such as natural disasters, wars, and financial crises. These events often result in protracted economic losses through declines in both the level and growth rate of output, as well as persistent losses in labor productivity. Among natural disasters, the COVID-19 pandemic—a major epidemiological disaster—is an adverse event on a massive global scale that could have a large and persistent impact on global productivity.

The damage from adverse events comes through a variety of channels. Natural disasters and wars may damage key infrastructure and disrupt value chains (Acevedo et al. 2018; Cerra and Saxena 2008). Financial crises increase uncertainty, damage confidence, impede access to finance, and lower corporate earnings—all developments that are likely to reduce investment. More generally, adverse events can dampen labor productivity by causing a loss of skills, reducing the efficiency of job matching, as well as by disrupting knowledge creation, transfer, and acquisition. The growth of labor productivity is therefore likely to be impeded by declines in both the growth of TFP and capital deepening.

Severe global biological disasters such as COVID-19 can damage labor productivity by affecting both supply and demand. Adverse supply-side effects can occur through the depletion of the labor force, the tightening of financial conditions, and the disruption of supply chains, which are an important measure for the diffusion of innovation. The COVID-19 pandemic is also weighing sharply on aggregate demand by depressing consumer demand for goods and services, eroding business confidence and investment, and raising financing costs (Baker et al. 2020; Ludvigson, Ma, and Ng 2020; Ma, Rogers, and Zhou 2020). Weaker aggregate demand can reduce the incentives for product innovation and quality improvement, slow technological progress, and lower productivity. Furthermore, these negative impacts can be amplified by other factors such as cross-border spillovers, lingering financial vulnerabilities, and the compounding effects of recessions. An analysis of economic developments around previous, smaller-scale epidemiological disasters can provide a framework for understanding the channels through which productivity could be affected by COVID-19, and the potential persistence of its effects.

The productivity losses that result from adverse events in EMDEs can reduce the rate of convergence to the advanced economy technology frontier. However, the effects of adverse events on labor productivity and output hinge not only on their magnitude, duration, and frequency but also on country characteristics and circumstances, including the policy response and the pre-shock buffers established by policy makers. Large-scale and severe disasters are typically more damaging to labor productivity and output. LICs and countries that are already affected by fragile and conflict-affected situations (FCS) have generally been less able than other countries to cope with wars and climate disasters such as droughts. If sufficiently severe, natural disasters can trigger financial crises—particularly in countries with high levels of debt—or lead to conflicts and wars.

Policies should be geared toward both reducing the likelihood of adverse shocks and alleviating their impacts. Depending on available policy space, countercyclical macroeconomic policies can help counter negative effects on investment and labor markets. Successful examples include the fiscal and monetary stimulus undertaken in the GFC and, in 2020, in the COVID-19 pandemic by many advanced economies and EMDEs and the international assistance provided for reconstruction in the aftermath of recent natural disasters in some FCS countries. Structural policy frameworks—such as the quality of governance and business climates—can facilitate faster adjustment, protect vulnerable groups, and mitigate long-lasting damage to productivity.

Chapter 3 examines a wide range of adverse events to assess the extent to which they have had protracted effects on labor productivity and TFP. The chapter aims to shed light on the following questions:

- How frequently and through what channels have adverse events affected productivity?

- How have adverse events differed in the scale of their impact on productivity?

- What policies can help to mitigate the impact of adverse events on productivity?

Contributions. This chapter makes several contributions to an expanding literature on the impact on productivity of adverse events. First, it is the first to undertake a systematic study of the effects of a broad range of adverse events—natural disasters (with a focus on large epidemics), wars, and financial crises—on alternative productivity measures across a wide range of advanced economies, EMDEs, and LICs.

Second, it explores both short-term and long-term effects of these events on productivity. One key aspect of the effects of adverse events on productivity is their persistence. Several studies have documented protracted losses in output or productivity following business cycle downturns, recessions, or financial crises. This chapter builds on and broadens previous work (Easterly et al. 1993; Kilic Celik et al., forthcoming; Mourougane 2017; Noy 2009) by assessing the channels, the magnitude of the losses, and the speed of recovery across a wide range of different types of adverse events.

Third, it offers a comprehensive discussion of supportive policy frameworks. This chapter analyzes feasible policies to mitigate the corrosive effects of negative shocks. It discusses the role of structural policies and reforms that can support productivity following adverse shocks. It also highlights the importance of fiscal space in building a cushion that can be used to counter productivity losses in a country hit by adverse events.

Main findings. The estimated results, broadly consistent with the literature, include the following. First, natural disasters have occurred more often than wars or financial crises, and their frequency has increased since 2000 (figure 4). Natural disasters can be subdivided into several distinct types: climate disasters such as floods and cyclones, biological disasters such as epidemics or insect infestations, and geophysical disasters such as earthquakes and volcanoes. During 1960-2018, the number of episodes of natural disasters was 25 times that of wars and 12 times that of financial crises. Climate-related events were the most frequent type of natural disaster, with a doubling of their frequency after 2000. LICs, particularly in SSA, were most affected by natural disasters. Biological and geophysical episodes are less frequent and are often more geographically contained.

Second, severe disasters have lasting effects on productivity. Although wars inflict particularly severe and long-lasting damage to both capital and TFP, the high frequency of climate disasters increases their importance as a source of damage to productivity. On average during 1960-2018, climate disasters reduced annual contemporaneous labor productivity by about 0.5 percent—about one-fifth of the impact of a typical war episode. However, climate disasters have occurred 25 times as frequently as wars, meaning their cumulative negative effects on productivity are larger. Moreover, severe disasters have strong negative effects on productivity. After three years, severe climate disasters lower labor productivity by about 7 percent, mainly through weakened TFP. Severe disasters can also trigger other types of adverse events such as financial crises and wars, thus compounding the corrosive effects on productivity.

Third, severe biological disasters can cause persistent damage to productivity. Four epidemics since 2000 (SARS, MERS, Ebola, and Zika) had significant and persistent negative effects on productivity. They lowered productivity by 4 percent after three years. Amid elevated uncertainty, epidemics have reduced labor productivity through their adverse effects on investment and the labor force. The COVID-19 pandemic may be significantly worse than most past disasters because of its global reach and the unprecedented social distancing and containment measures put in place to slow the spread of the virus.

Fourth, productivity is highly vulnerable to financial stress, especially when accompanied by a rapid buildup of debt. Financial crises weigh heavily on productivity growth through a wide range of channels. During debt accumulation episodes associated with financial crises, cumulative productivity gains three years into the episode were 2 percentage points lower than in episodes without crises in EMDEs. The rapid buildup of debt in EMDEs over the past decade increases vulnerabilities to financial crises and limits the ability of countries to cope with other types of adverse events. The current COVID-19 pandemic is likely to exacerbate those vulnerabilities by further stretching public and private balance sheets.

Fifth, policies can help to prevent and to mitigate the effects of adverse events. A rapid policy response to adverse events, including countercyclical macroeconomic policies and reconstruction spending when appropriate, can help to mitigate the negative effects on productivity. Improving institutions and the business climate can also help increase the pace of recovery following an adverse event. Appropriate policies and regulations with respect to finance, construction, and environmental protection can help reduce the frequency of adverse events. Fiscal space allows economies to fund recovery efforts after natural disasters, and sound fiscal policies tend to limit the likelihood of a financial crisis. Fiscal stimulus also helps cushion the severity of large adverse events such as severe biological disasters.

FIGURE 4 Productivity after major adverse events

In 1960-2018, natural disaster episodes occurred 25 times more frequently than wars, and 12 times more frequently than financial crises. Climate disasters accounted for nearly 70 percent of all disasters. However, natural disasters were typically shorter than financial crises or wars. Previous epidemics (SARS, MERS, Ebola, and Zika) caused lasting labor productivity losses of about 4 percent after three years, mainly through weakened investment.

A. Average number of episodes per year

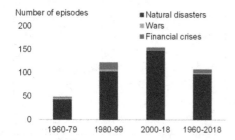

B. Episodes by type of natural disaster, worldwide, 1960-2018

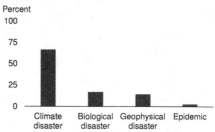

C. Average duration of adverse events

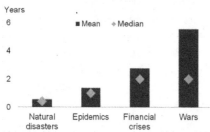

D. Effects of epidemics on labor productivity

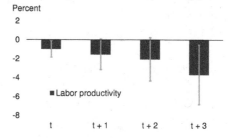

E. Contemporaneous impacts of adverse events episodes on labor productivity, scaled by frequency of event types

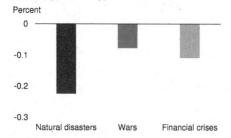

F. Contemporaneous impacts of climate, banking, and currency episodes on labor productivity

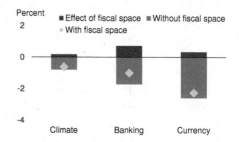

Sources: Correlates of War (COW); Emergency Events Database (EM-DAT); Laeven and Valencia (2018); Peace Research Institute Oslo (PRIO); World Bank.

Note: Natural disasters include climate, biological, and geophysical disasters (EM-DAT). Wars include intrastate and external (extrastate and interstate) wars (COW and PRIO). Financial crises include banking, currency, and sovereign debt crises (Leaven and Valencia 2018). An episode dummy is set to 1 if the event occurs at least once (≥1) in a year and 0 otherwise. The sample includes 35 advanced economies and 135 are EMDEs, including 27 LICs. EMDEs = emerging market and developing economies; LICs = low-income countries; MERS = Middle East respiratory syndrome; SARS = severe acute respiratory syndrome.

A. Average number of episodes per year for each type of adverse event.

C. The five pandemics and epidemics are SARS (2002-03), Swine flu (2009), MERS (2012), Ebola (2014-15), and Zika (2015-16).

D. Bars show the estimated impacts of the four most severe biological epidemics on labor productivity levels. The four epidemics considered are SARS (2002-03), MERS (2012), Ebola (2014-15). See chapter 3 for details.

E. The average impact of the event, which is the effect of an event multiplied by the probability of the event occurring in EMDEs.

F. Blue bars indicate the impact of having fiscal space on the effect of the adverse events on labor productivity (effect of fiscal space); red bars represent the gross effect of adverse events on labor productivity without the fiscal space impact (without fiscal space); and orange markers show the average net effect of adverse events for the countries that have fiscal space (with fiscal space).

Chapter 4: Productivity Convergence: Is Anyone Catching Up?

In chapter 4, Kindberg-Hanlon and Okou show that labor productivity in EMDEs is less than 20 percent of the level in advanced economies, whereas in LICs it is just 2 percent of advanced economy levels. The unconditional convergence hypothesis states that productivity catch-up growth will tend to occur where productivity differentials exist and that these will decline over time. However, this type of convergence may fail to occur for reasons such as the existence of international barriers to technology transfer and differences in saving and investment behavior. Conditional convergence is more restrictive, as catch-up productivity growth may depend on characteristics of economies beyond their initial productivity levels. For example, only economies with characteristics such as high institutional quality or education levels may be able to converge to the frontier.

The large productivity gap between EMDEs and the frontier implies that there is a potential for substantial income gains in EMDEs if either of these two hypotheses holds. Historically, productivity gaps have remained stubbornly ingrained, with the bulk of evidence pointing away from unconditional convergence (Johnson and Papageorgiou 2020). However, falling global poverty rates in recent decades have been an encouraging sign that economies near the bottom of the distribution have made productivity and income gains, helping reduce the proportion of the world's population living in extreme poverty from 36 percent in 1990 to 10 percent in 2015 (World Bank 2018a). Most of the fall is concentrated in SAR and in EAP, the two regions with the highest rates of productivity growth among EMDEs.

Faster EMDE productivity growth in recent decades does not itself imply convergence toward the advanced economy frontier, which has also continued to expand. In addition, if the unconditional convergence hypothesis holds, the gains in productivity should be broad-based. More complex dynamics of productivity growth could instead support the convergence club hypothesis, with different clubs of economies converging toward different productivity levels depending on their characteristics.

Finally, productivity growth in EMDEs has slowed following the GFC and faces headwinds from the COVID-19 crisis. The pandemic-driven global recession is occurring during a period of heightened debt vulnerabilities, whereas previous epidemics and other major natural disasters have been followed by prolonged declines in labor productivity growth and investment. Commodity prices have also collapsed, adding negative pressure on investment in the large number of commodity-reliant EMDEs, and will remain weak in the event the global recovery is drawn out. There are further risks to EMDE convergence if countries adopt inward-looking policies that result in the fragmentation of global trade—integration into global value chains has been a key vehicle for the adoption of more advanced production processes in EMDEs.

Against this backdrop, this chapter examines the following questions:

- How has productivity convergence evolved over the past five decades?

- Are there "clubs" of economies following different convergence trajectories?

- What separates those economies in successful and unsuccessful clubs?

- What are the policy implications?

Contribution. This chapter makes several contributions to the literature. First, it expands a reinvigorated literature on *income per capita* convergence by examining *labor productivity* convergence. The existing literature, which began empirically assessing income convergence in the mid-1980s, has generally found broad-based support for convergence that is conditional on country characteristics, but little support for the unconditional convergence hypothesis. The surge in EMDE growth in the 2000s has reignited this debate (Patel, Sandefur, and Subramanian 2018). The majority of the literature has focused on convergence in income per capita (Barro 2015; Caselli 2005; Mankiw, Romer, and Weil 1992). In contrast, the focus in this chapter is on labor productivity convergence, the main driver of lasting per capita income convergence.

Second, this chapter highlights important nonlinearities captured by "convergence clubs" following different convergence paths. The existing literature on convergence clubs thus far has not taken account of the large increase in EMDE productivity growth since 2000 (Battisti and Parmeter 2013; Pesaran 2007; Phillips and Sul 2009). This chapter updates this literature and identifies important changes in the membership of convergence clubs that have occurred in recent decades.

Third, this chapter utilizes multiple methodologies and common data sets—previous studies have been hampered by data differences that have made conclusions non-comparable (Johnson et al. 2013). It is also the only recent study of convergence that measures labor productivity at market exchange rates as opposed to measures adjusted by purchasing power parity, noting that the latter can be problematic in assessing club convergence.

Fourth, this chapter is one of the few studies examining the drivers of convergence club membership and transitions, and the only one applied to a global set of economies. Existing studies focus on either European economies (Bartkowska and Riedl 2012; Von Lyncker and Thoennessen 2017) or regions within China (Tian et al. 2016) and do not assess the causes of changing club membership over time. In contrast, this study identifies the drivers of convergence club membership and transitions between clubs among 97 economies during 1970-2018.

Main findings. The following findings emerge from the analysis in this chapter. First, there are large gaps between EMDE and advanced economy productivity. On average since 2010, labor productivity in EMDEs was just under 20 percent of that in advanced economies, and in LICs it is a mere 2 percent (figure 5). EMDE productivity gaps relative to advanced economies widened during the 1970s, 1980s, and 1990s but began to narrow in the 2000s.

Second, there has been some convergence in productivity levels since 2000. Examples of economies converging from low levels of labor productivity all the way to the frontier were rare in the latter half of the twentieth century. Since 2000, productivity growth has exceeded the advanced economy average in about 60 percent of EMDEs. However, the

FIGURE 5 Unconditional, conditional, and club productivity convergence

On average, labor productivity in EMDEs is less than one-fifth of the advanced economy average. These EMDE productivity gaps widened during the 1970s, 1980s, and 1990s but narrowed from 2000 onward. Since the late 1990s, productivity growth has been higher in economies with lower initial levels of productivity. However, the implied pace of convergence is small, suggesting that it will take more than 100 years to halve the gap (on average). Sixteen EMDEs have transitioned to the highest-productivity convergence club since the 2000s and made the largest productivity gains. Those transitioning EMDEs benefited from high average levels of education, diverse and complex production capabilities, strong institutions, and above-average FDI inflows.

A. Labor productivity in EMDEs by commodity exporter status, 2010-18 average

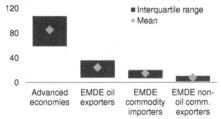

B. Share of EMDEs with a narrowing productivity gap with advanced economies

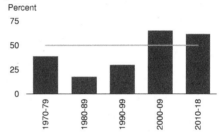

C. Unconditional convergence rate

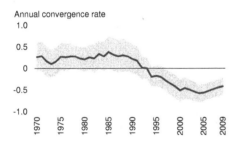

D. Conditional annual convergence rate: all economies

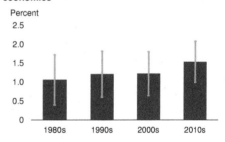

E. Productivity, by convergence club, 1970s-2010s

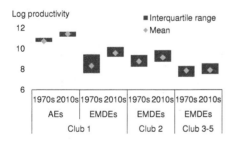

F. The effect of covariates on the probability of EMDE joining high-productivity convergence club

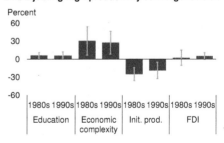

Sources: Penn World Table; The Conference Board; World Bank, World Development Indicators.
Note: Productivity defined as output per worker in U.S. dollars (at 2010 prices and exchange rates). See chapter 4 for details. AEs = advanced economies; EMDEs = emerging market and developing economies; FDI = foreign direct investment.
A. Simple average of sample that includes 35 advanced economies and 126 EMDEs, of which 27 are oil exporters, 47 are commodity-importing EMDEs, and 52 are non-oil commodity-exporting EMDEs.
B. Based on a sample of 29 advanced economies and 74 EMDEs for a consistent sample since 1970. Share of EMDEs with average productivity growth above average advanced economy productivity growth in each decade.
C. Gray shaded area indicates 95 percent confidence intervals.
D. Annual convergence rate implied by a cross-sectional β-regression in each decade.
E. Based on convergence clubs estimated as in Phillips and Sul (2009). Unweighted average log productivity levels during 1970-79 and 2010-18. Blue bars show interquartile range.
F. Marginal effect of a one-unit increase in the covariates on the probability of an EMDE joining the fast productivity growth convergence Club 1. Init. prod = initial productivity.

productivity gap declined at just 0.5 percent per year, on average, and convergence rates have begun to slow. Even at this peak rate, it would take more than 100 years to halve the initial productivity gap between economies. Although the average rate of convergence has been low, convergence rates for economies with good characteristics are substantially higher—new evidence suggests that the conditional convergence rate has accelerated in recent decades.

Third, since 1970, countries have fallen into five distinct convergence clubs. The first club of countries, converging to the highest productivity levels, includes all advanced economies and several middle-income EMDEs that have experienced sustained long periods of robust growth since the 1990s. The second club includes the majority of upper-middle-income EMDEs, and the third through fifth clubs include lower-middle- and low-income countries.

Fourth, transition to higher-productivity convergence clubs has been associated with successful policies. Increasing numbers of EMDEs have moved into the highest-level productivity club in recent decades, in contrast to older assessments of club convergence that found few positive convergence club transitions. These countries are found to have had a foundation of systematically better initial education levels and greater political stability, which has helped them deepen the complexity of their economies, with diversified production across a broad range of sectors outside of their original comparative advantage. Several country case studies highlight the importance of export-promotion, global value chain integration, and FDI in transitioning to higher-productivity convergence clubs.

Fifth, the environment for switching to higher convergence paths is becoming more challenging. EMDEs that have successfully shifted into higher-level productivity clubs have often relied upon manufacturing-led development—efforts to enhance the complexity and diversity of exports can prove to be high-reward but have also frequently been costly failures. This strategy faces increasing challenges due to falling global manufacturing employment and slower trade growth. In addition, a weak outlook for commodity prices and slow improvements in many key covariates of productivity growth, such as institutional quality, urbanization, and educational attainment, pose further headwinds to both new and continuing transitions to high productivity levels. The global recession due to COVID-19 has the potential to amplify many of these headwinds. Risks include persistently subdued commodity prices, global value chain fragmentation if governments pursue inward-looking policies, and lasting damage to human capital development from the widespread closure of education institutions due to social distancing measures and erosion of skills due to unemployment.

Part II. Regional Dimensions of Productivity

As part I established, the productivity growth slowdown over the past decade was broad-based and reached all EMDE regions. That said, its extent, its sources and drivers, and its implications for convergence differed considerably across EMDE regions. Part II explores these regional differences.

Chapter 5: Regional Productivity

In chapter 5, Vorisek, Kindberg-Hanlon, Steinbach, Taskin, Vashakmadze, Wheeler, and Ye draw out differences in regional productivity trends and policy priorities. Specifically, it addresses the following questions:

- How has the evolution of productivity varied across the six EMDE regions?

- What factors have been associated with productivity growth?

- What policies should be prioritized in order to boost productivity growth?

Contributions. The chapter makes several contributions to the literature and policy debate on productivity at the regional level. First, the chapter uses a larger, more diverse sample of EMDEs relative to previous studies and to other chapters in this book.[9] It starts with a discussion of the evolution, sources, and bottlenecks of productivity growth across the six EMDE regions.

Second, for each of the six regions, the chapter decomposes productivity growth into contributions from human capital, physical capital, and TFP. For some regions, this analysis is extended to include natural capital.

Third, using a nine-sector database, the chapter measures within-sector and between-sector contributions to productivity growth in each region and calculates the contribution of each sector to productivity growth, employment, and value added.

Fourth, the chapter contains a detailed discussion of the policy options for boosting productivity growth, including some of the policies that may be effective in offsetting the adverse effects of the COVID-19 pandemic on productivity.

Main findings. The chapter offers several key findings. First, although the post-GFC productivity slowdown affected all EMDE regions, it was most pronounced in EAP, ECA, and SSA amid slowing investment growth, financial market disruptions, and a major commodity price slide. The recent productivity growth slowdown occurred in the context of already weak productivity growth in some regions (figure 6). Productivity growth in LAC and MNA, already sluggish before the GFC, was stagnant in the post-GFC period, reflecting political uncertainty, episodes of financial stress in major economies, falling commodity prices, and ongoing market distortions.

Second, as a result of the productivity growth slowdown during the post-GFC period, the pace of catch-up to advanced economy productivity levels slowed in most EMDE regions, and fell further behind advanced economy levels in LAC, MNA, and SSA. This means that in these regions, it will now take longer to reach the level of productivity, or GDP per worker, observed in advanced economies, all else equal. In MNA, labor productivity averaged 40 percent of the advanced economy level in the post-GFC

---

[9] This chapter uses a sample of 129 EMDEs, compared to 74 EMDEs in other chapters. Unless otherwise indicated, region-wide productivity statistics are GDP-weighted averages.

FIGURE 6 Regional productivity developments

The slowdown in productivity growth following the GFC affected all regions, but was particularly severe in EAP, ECA, and SSA. Productivity levels fell further behind advanced economy levels in some regions during the post-GFC period. In all regions, TFP contributed less to productivity growth in the post-GFC period. Since the GFC, productivity gains from sectoral reallocation have faded in most regions.

A. Productivity growth

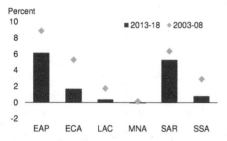

B. Productivity levels

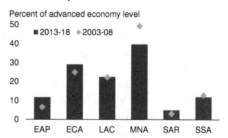

C. Factor contributions to regional productivity growth: EAP, ECA, LAC

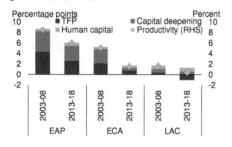

D. Factor contributions to regional productivity growth: MNA, SAR, SSA

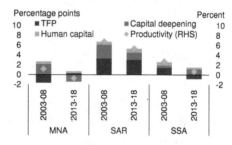

E. Within- and between-sector contributions to regional productivity growth: EAP, ECA, LAC

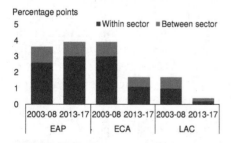

F. Within- and between-sector contributions to regional productivity growth: MNA, SAR, SSA

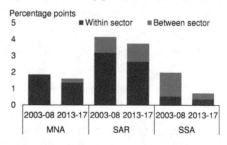

Sources: Asian Productivity Organization Productivity Database; Barro and Lee (2015); The Conference Board; Groningen Growth Development Center database; Haver Analytics; International Labour Organization ILOSTAT; International Monetary Fund; Organisation for Economic Co-operation and Development Structural Analysis Database; Penn World Table; World KLEMS; World Bank (World Development Indicators).

Note: Productivity is defined as real GDP per worker (at 2010 market prices and exchange rates). Country group aggregates for a given year are calculated using constant 2010 U.S. dollar GDP weights. Data for multiyear spans show simple averages of the annual data. EAP = East Asia and Pacific; ECA = Europe and Central Asia; EMDEs = emerging market and developing economies; GFC = global financial crisis; LAC = Latin America and the Caribbean; MNA = Middle East and North Africa; SAR = South Asia; SSA = Sub-Saharan Africa.

A.B. Sample includes 16 economies in EAP, 21 in ECA, 26 in LAC, 14 in MNA, 7 in SAR, and 45 in SSA.

C.D. Sample includes 93 EMDEs, including 8 in EAP, 21 in ECA, 20 in LAC, 12 in MNA, 2 in SAR, and 30 in SSA.

E.F. Median contribution for each region. "Within sector" shows the contribution of initial real value added-weighted productivity growth rate of each sector and "between sector" shows the contribution arising from changes in sectoral employment shares. Sample includes 69 EMDEs, of which 9 are in EAP, 11 in ECA, 17 in LAC, 6 in the MNA, 4 in SAR, and 22 in SSA.

period, down from 49 percent before GFC. In SSA and LAC, productivity relative to that in advanced economies stalled at 12 and 22 percent respectively.

Third, despite the relatively stable contribution of human capital to productivity growth, capital deepening contributed less to productivity growth in the post-GFC period compared to the pre-GFC period in all regions except SSA. All regions experienced a weaker contribution from TFP—especially LAC and SSA, where TFP contracted after the GFC.

Fourth, productivity gains from the reallocation of labor between sectors faded in four regions (EAP, ECA, LAC, and SSA) during the post-GFC period. LAC and SSA were particularly affected. Yet within-sector productivity enhancements also slowed. Only one region, EAP, achieved within-sector productivity gains during the post-GFC period.

Finally, a well-targeted reform agenda is needed to reignite productivity growth, especially in light of the possible persistent effects of COVID-19 on productivity. In particular, policies are needed to address key obstacles common across multiple regions, such as lack of economic diversification, weak governance and institutions, widespread informality, shortcomings in education, and lack of integration through trade.

Part III: Technological Change and Sectoral Shifts

Having established the broad productivity trends, drivers, and implications across the world, large country groups, and EMDE regions in parts I and II, part III delves into specific long-term drivers of productivity: technology and structural transformation.

Chapter 6 disentangles long-term shocks, which are interpreted as technology shocks, from short-term shocks, which are interpreted as demand shocks, to productivity. It documents that both types of shocks have long-term consequences for productivity. Chapter 7 moves away from shocks and instead focuses on structural transformation, in particular the productivity gains that can be derived from reallocation of factors of production from lower-productivity to higher-productivity sectors. The chapter shows that this process has been an important source of productivity gains since the 1990s but has recently begun to fade.

Chapter 6: Technology, Demand, and Employment Trade-Offs

In chapter 6, Dieppe, Francis, and Kindberg-Hanlon show the many surges and declines that productivity growth has historically gone through, usually coinciding with economic upswings and slowdowns respectively. Such short-term swings often reflect cyclical fluctuations in labor and capacity utilization (Basu, Fernald, and Kimball 2006; Fernald and Wang 2016).

The COVID-19 pandemic, for example, is likely dealing a severe blow to labor productivity growth by triggering the deepest global recession since the Second World War. If past recessions are any guide, labor productivity is likely to rebound in a cyclical upturn as the global economy recovers but to remain below the prepandemic trend for many years to come. The global recession resulting from the shock of the COVID-19 pandemic in 2020 is likely to drive a larger decline in productivity growth even than that experienced in the wake of the GFC (World Bank 2020a).

The COVID-19 pandemic may trigger lasting organizational and technological changes to the way businesses operate. These could adversely affect productivity growth if they erode capital or disrupt the accumulation of physical or human capital. However, pandemic-induced structural changes could also have productivity-enhancing effects, such as a "cleansing" effect, eliminating the least efficient firms and encouraging the adoption of more efficient production technologies (Caballero and Hammour 1994). Although such effects could result in faster overall per capita income gains, they might well increase income inequality, especially if they reduce the need for labor.

Against this backdrop, this chapter reports research that disentangles long-term productivity changes from short-term, cyclical productivity fluctuations using structural vector autoregressions (SVARs). Throughout this chapter, the long-term drivers of productivity growth will be referred to as "technology," as is common in the literature, and encompass changes to TFP as well as investment that embeds new technologies.[10] Changes in technology, in this sense, may occur not only as a result of technical innovations but also when there are organizational or institutional changes to the production process.

This chapter addresses the following questions:

- How much do long-term changes and business cycle fluctuations each contribute to changes in labor productivity growth?

- What are the effects of long-term changes in labor productivity growth on employment?

- What are the lasting effects of demand-driven cyclical fluctuations in labor productivity growth?

- What are the policy implications?

Contribution to the literature. This chapter makes various contributions to a literature that has primarily focused on advanced economies. First, this chapter is the first study to identify "technology" drivers of labor productivity growth in a comprehensive cross-country sample of 30 advanced economies and 96 EMDEs.[11] Other studies have restricted themselves to a decomposition of labor productivity growth into its growth

---

[10] More specifically, they are referred to as "technology shocks," or unanticipated changes in labor productivity. For example, changes in taxation could persistently alter the degree of capital deepening, leading to higher or lower productivity over long horizons. See also Chen and Wemy (2015), Fisher (2006), and Francis and Ramey (2005).

[11] Previous studies have focused on a small subset of advanced economies. For example, Galí (1999) and Rujin (2019) apply long-run restriction-identified SVARs only to Group of Seven economies.

accounting components, or have only examined the role of cyclically adjusted TFP growth or econometrically identified measures of changes in technology in a small number of advanced economies (Coibion, Gorodnichenko, and Ulate 2017; Fernald 2015; Goodridge, Haskel, and Wallis 2018; OECD 2015; World Bank 2018c).

Second, this chapter is the first study to estimate the effects of technological change on aggregate employment across a broad range of EMDEs and advanced economies. It is also the first to examine the extent of technology-driven job losses outside the Group of Seven (G7) economies (Canada, Japan, France, Germany, Italy, the United Kingdom, and the United States) and to determine the correlates of their scale and persistence, in contrast to earlier studies that focused on a narrower set of advanced economies.[12]

Third, this chapter is the first study to illustrate the persistent effects of demand shocks on labor productivity and its components in a wide range of EMDEs and advanced economies. Previous studies have examined a smaller subset of productivity growth drivers over shorter time horizons or have used data for fewer and mostly advanced economies (Aslam et al. 2016; Dabla-Norris et al. 2015; Fornero, Kirchner, and Andres 2014). This complements the analysis of chapter 3, which explores a set of specific adverse events, some of which also constitute demand shocks.

Main findings. The chapter reports several novel findings. First, long-term, "technological" drivers of productivity accounted for a large portion of labor productivity variation in the period 1980-2018: for about 40 percent of the one-year-ahead forecast error variance of labor productivity and 60-75 percent of the five- to ten-year-ahead forecast error variance of labor productivity (figure 7). The cyclical, nontechnological component of productivity growth accounts for the remainder and largely reflected volatile TFP growth.

Second, in about 75 percent of EMDEs and 90 percent of advanced economies, employment fell initially after technology-driven productivity improvements. These employment losses were larger but less persistent in advanced economies than in EMDEs. Such employment losses were also larger in economies with larger increases in industry's share of employment since the 1990s, possibly because industry is particularly amenable to labor-saving innovations such as automation.

Third, this chapter highlights the persistent effects that cyclical developments driven by demand shocks can have on productivity.[13] Although such developments may unwind faster than technology shocks, their impact on productivity can last well beyond the typical two- to eight-year duration of a cyclical upswing or downswing. Demand-driven fluctuations in productivity growth have historically been considered to be neutral in the

---

[12] Some studies have examined the link between productivity growth and employment growth in a reduced-form framework in a broad set of economies including some EMDEs, but have not separately identified the differential impact of technology- and demand-driven changes in productivity (Beaudry and Collard 2003; Boulhol and Turner 2009).

[13] Many studies have documented the persistent negative output effects of financial, currency, and political crises (Cerra and Saxena 2008; Jordà, Schularick, and Taylor 2013; Reinhart and Rogoff 2009).

FIGURE 7 **Employment and technological change**

Innovations in production technologies lead to higher income but can come at the cost of lower employment, particularly in the short term. This effect is found in over one-third of economies. Economies with higher productivity levels and higher industrial employment shares since 1990 have experienced larger employment losses from new production technologies. Demand-driven changes in labor productivity are generally less persistent than those driven by new production technologies.

A. Response of employment to technology shock that boosts labor productivity by 1 percent

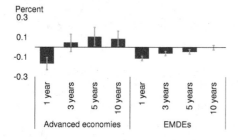

B. Share of economies with negative employment impact in year 1

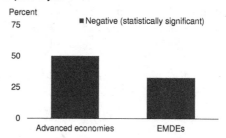

C. Covariates of employment impact in year 1

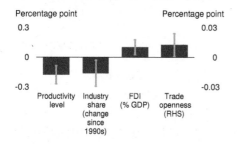

D. Employment impact of technology in EMDEs

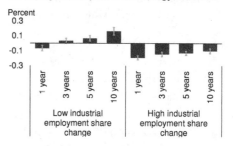

E. The response of labor productivity to demand shocks: Advanced economies

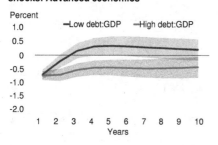

F. The response of labor productivity to demand shocks: EMDEs

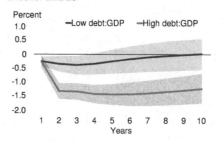

Source: World Bank.

Note: See chapter 6 for details. EMDEs = emerging market and developing economies; FDI = foreign direct investment; IRF = impulse response function; VAR = vector autoregression.

A. Panel VAR estimates of IRFs from a technology shock identified using the Spectral VAR methodology. Panel estimations with fixed effects are performed separately for advanced economies and EMDEs. IRFs are scaled to the size of the impact on labor productivity.

B. Based on individual VAR estimations. The share of economies where the 84th percentile is below zero in year 1.

C. Coefficient estimated in a regression of the correlates of the employment impact of a technology innovation at the 1-year horizon. Productivity level is measured in log units of output per worker measured in U.S. dollars at 2010 prices and exchange rates; industry share shows the effect of a 10-percentage-point increase in the share of industrial sector employment between 1990-99 and 2010-18.

D. Panel VAR estimation of the employment impact of a technology innovation in two separate groups. "High industrial employment share change" are EMDEs in the top quartile of changes in employment share in industry between 1990-99 and 2010-18, while "Low industrial employment share change" are those in the bottom quartile. IRFs are scaled to reflect the employment impact per percentage point increase in the level of labor productivity at each horizon.

E.F. Sample includes 30 advanced economies and 95 EMDEs, using the top and bottom quartile for the 1990-2018 average government debt-to-GDP ratio. The panel VAR is estimated for each group, producing an IRF for labor productivity in response to the dominant driver of business cycle frequency investment fluctuations. Shaded areas reflect 68 percent confidence bands.

long run, with rising efficiency of production in cyclical upswings reversed in downswings. This chapter's contrasting finding is in line with a growing literature uncovering persistent effects on productivity in advanced economies from a range of demand-side developments.[14]

Fourth, policy options are available to promote the equitable sharing across the economy of gains from technology-driven productivity growth. These include measures to ensure that technological change does not lead to prolonged unemployment and measures that encourage diversification of skills. Training and retraining can encourage the accumulation of worker skills that complement new technologies, including in sectors conducive to automation. Adequate social protection provisions can help temporarily displaced workers transition to new sectors.

Chapter 6 complements the production function decomposition employed in chapter 1 with a decomposition of long-term and short-term shocks to productivity that is agnostic about its sources in human or physical capital or TFP. Chapter 7 explores yet another angle of labor productivity—a sectoral decomposition.

Chapter 7: Sectoral Sources of Productivity Growth

Factor reallocation toward higher-productivity sectors has long been recognized as one of the most powerful drivers of aggregate productivity growth (Baumol 1967). It has been identified as an important driver of productivity growth in EMDE regions as diverse as EAP and SSA (Cusolito and Maloney 2018; de Vries, Timmer, and de Vries 2015). Especially in EAP, the move out of agriculture into higher-productivity industry and services has been credited with rapid productivity growth (Helble, Trinh, and Le 2019).

After several decades of sectoral reallocation away from agriculture, only 30 percent of EMDE employment is accounted for by agriculture—compared with 50 percent of employment less than two decades earlier—and less than 10 percent of value added. LICs, however, are an exception, with agriculture still accounting for over 60 of employment. This partly explains the low aggregate productivity observed in LICs (Caselli 2005; Restuccia, Yang, and Zhu 2008).

The services sector has been the main source of productivity growth over the past decade, accounting for almost two-thirds of productivity growth in the average EMDE (compared with one-fifth accounted for by industry) and more than nine-tenths in the average LIC (figure 8). Despite this rapid growth, the sector still accounts for only about 40 percent of employment in EMDEs compared with 75 percent of employment in advanced economies.

---

[14] Bachmann and Sims (2012) and Jordà, Singh, and Taylor (2020) find evidence that monetary and fiscal policy-induced expansions and contractions have had long-lasting effects on advanced economy productivity, in contrast to traditional assumptions of neutrality at long horizons.

FIGURE 8 Sectoral productivity developments

During the post-GFC period, aggregate productivity growth slowed among the EMDEs, reflecting weakness in manufacturing, finance, and agriculture in LICs. EMDEs are characterized by large, albeit narrowing, productivity gaps across sectors. Agriculture remains the largest source of employment in LICs. Sectoral reallocations to more productive sectors have accounted for a sizable proportion of EMDE productivity growth, but have been fading since the GFC.

A. Contributions to productivity growth between 2003-08 and 2013-17

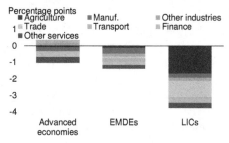

B. Average productivity gap: Advanced economies and EMDEs

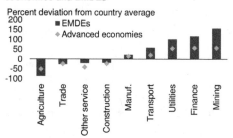

C. Within- and between-sector contributions to productivity growth

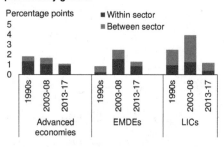

D. Employment share

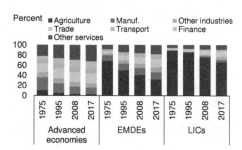

Sources: Asian Productivity Organization; Expanded Africa Sector Database; Groningen Growth Development Center; International Labour Organization; national sources; Organisation for Economic Co-operation and Development; United Nations; World Bank; World KLEMS.

Note: EMDEs = emerging market and developing economies; GFC = global financial crisis; LICs = low-income countries.

A. Based on samples of 54 countries during 1975-95, 94 countries during 1995-99, and 103 countries during 2003-17. "Other industries" includes mining, utilities, and construction; "Finance" includes business services; "Other services" includes government and personal services.

B. Average labor productivity is value added per worker in 2017, based on 103 countries. "Finance" includes business services; "Other service" includes government and personal services.

C. Median contribution based on 54 countries during 1975-95, 94 countries during 1995-99, and 103 countries during 2003-17.

D. Based on samples of 94 countries during 1995-99 and 103 countries during 2003-17.

Productivity gains through such factor reallocation between sectors have slowed over the past decade, contributing to the steepest and most prolonged slowdown in productivity growth since the 1980s (chapter 1). The COVID-19 pandemic may slow this process further. In addition, the widespread restrictions that have been introduced to combat the COVID-19 pandemic may damage within-sector productivity through its impacts on health, business models, and workplace practices (World Bank 2020a).

Against this backdrop, this chapter addresses the following questions:

- How large are productivity gaps across sectors?

- What has been the role of sectoral reallocation in aggregate labor productivity growth?

- How might government policies help raise sectoral productivity growth?

Contributions. This chapter extends the literature in two dimensions. First, the chapter employs the most comprehensive data set of sectoral labor productivity available, with data for nine sectors. Past analysis had limited country or time coverage.[15] The updated time coverage also allows for an analysis of developments since the GFC more than a decade ago.

Second, the rich sectoral detail allows an analysis of the heterogeneity of industrial and services subsectors within and across countries, as well as within-sector and between-sector developments that are sensitive to aggregation bias (de Vries et al. 2012; Üngör 2017). This sectoral analysis is complemented by firm-level analysis that points to drivers of within-sector productivity growth.

Findings. The chapter offers several novel findings. First, the chapter documents large productivity gaps across the nine sectors and also across countries within each of the nine sectors. In the average EMDE, productivity in agriculture, the lowest-productivity sector, is 85 percent lower than the average productivity. In advanced economies, the corresponding difference is considerably narrower. Agriculture accounts for less than 10 percent of value added and about 30 percent of employment in EMDEs. The gap between EMDE and advanced economy productivity is particularly wide in agriculture, with EMDEs less than 20 percent as productive as advanced economies. This partly reflects slow technology adoption in the agriculture sector in some of the poorest EMDEs. Within manufacturing, productivity is highest among firms with a high share of exports in output. Those that operate in a conducive business environment are also closer to the global technology frontier.

Second, sectoral reallocation accounted for two-fifths of overall productivity gains between 1995 and 2017. This shift lost momentum after the GFC. This slowing sectoral reallocation accounted for two-fifths of the productivity growth slowdown in EMDEs between 2013 and 2017. By curtailing labor mobility as well as economic activity, the COVID-19 pandemic may further slow sectoral reallocation.

Third, policies can both rekindle sectoral reallocation and boost productivity in low-productivity sectors. Policies to support labor mobility and capital investment include improving the quality of, and access to, education; promoting good governance and reducing the costs of doing business; strengthening institutional and managerial capabilities; reducing distortions, such as anticompetitive regulations and subsidies; supporting research and development; and removing infrastructure bottlenecks. Given

---

[15] Diao, McMillan, and Rodrik (2017) and McMillan, Rodrik, and Verduzco-Gall (2014) employ 39 and 38 countries; Martins (2019) uses 7 sectors and 169 countries; IMF (2018) uses 10 sectors and 62 countries; and McCullough (2017) has 16 sectors for the United States and 10 European Union members.

the low productivity of EMDE agricultural sectors and agriculture's role as the primary employer in LICs, policies to raise productivity in this sector, such as actions to strengthen infrastructure and improve land property rights, could pay particularly significant dividends.

Future research directions

The study presents new analytical work on productivity but also points toward several avenues for future research.

Adverse shocks and the COVID-19 pandemic. Evidence that adverse events are likely to cause lasting productivity and output losses opens new research avenues for a more in-depth analysis of propagation channels and socioeconomic impacts (chapter 3). This is particularly important in light of the COVID-19 pandemic. Future research could refine the analysis of the intensity of the adverse events by constructing severity indexes for different types of events. In addition, a more detailed empirical assessment of the transmission channels is warranted. This could be explored by studying the effects of adverse shocks on different economic sectors as well as on consumption, investment, and FDI. This can also enable an assessment of the distributional and developmental implications of adverse events. Finally, more in-depth analysis of how policies explain differences in impacts, responses, and resilience to adverse shocks across countries would help prevent and mitigate future disasters.

Medium-term drivers of productivity growth. The broad-based slowdown of productivity growth has raised many questions on what is causing it. The research highlighted in chapter 2 has shown there are many drivers and correlates of productivity but that the main long-term drivers have changed over time, with some becoming more prominent and others less prominent as the structures of economies evolve. The analysis could be expanded to better understand the medium-term dynamics of productivity and how they may vary both within and across countries. Medium-term analysis can also help quantify the implications of COVID-19 on productivity growth.

Understanding convergence club transitions. Additional scrutiny of the drivers of transitions of economies into convergence clubs with higher productivity convergence trajectories can provide useful insights for policy makers about the conditions necessary for faster productivity growth. However, methodologies to isolate the period of transition, used in chapter 4, are currently underdeveloped and generally rely on comparing results over different estimation samples. Future research could place more focus on estimating more precise transition points between convergence clubs. Further research is required into strategies that could be used by EMDEs to develop capabilities in more advanced and complex sectors while safeguarding employment.

The future of automation in EMDEs. The analysis of the loss of employment from new productivity-improving technologies in chapter 6 is based on historical trends, during a period in which automation has primarily been concentrated in certain sectors in advanced economies. Future research could examine the role of cross-country wage differentials in limiting the adoption of these technologies in EMDEs. In addition, future research should examine the extent to which jobs in the service sector, which have increasingly driven EMDE productivity growth and job creation, are at risk.

Underlying drivers of sectoral reallocation. Chapter 7 employs a detailed shift-share approach that decomposes aggregate labor productivity growth into within- and between-sector components. However, this approach does not fully account for the endogeneity of sectoral allocation. For example, within-sector growth could also directly affect sector reallocation—an improvement in agricultural productivity could reduce agriculture's share of employment and facilitate between-sector productivity growth, and hence the contribution of the agricultural productivity could be larger and that of sectoral reallocation could be smaller. Further research using the nine-sector database could take into account endogeneity and provide greater insights into which underlying forces are driving sectoral contributions to productivity growth and convergence.

References

Acevedo, S. M., M. Mrkaic, N. Novta, E. Pugacheva, and P. Topalova. 2018. "The Effects of Weather Shocks on Economic Activity: What Are the Channels of Impact?" IMF Working Paper 18/144, International Monetary Fund, Washington, DC.

ADB (Asian Development Bank). 2017. *Asian Development Outlook: Transcending the Middle-Income Challenge.* Manila: Asian Development Bank.

Adler, G., R. Duval, D. Furceri, S. Kilic Celik, K. Koloskova, and M. Poplawski-Ribeiro. 2017. "Gone with the Headwinds: Global Productivity." IMF Staff Discussion Note 17/04, International Monetary Fund, Washington, DC.

Aslam, A., S. Beidas-Strom, R. Bems, O. Celasun, S. Kilic Celik, and Z. Koczan. 2016. "Trading on Their Terms? Commodity Exporters in the Aftermath of the Commodity Boom." IMF Working Paper 16/27, International Monetary Fund, Washington, DC.

Bachmann, R., and E. R. Sims. 2012. "Confidence and the Transmission of Government Spending Shocks." *Journal of Monetary Economics* 59 (3): 235–49.

Baker, S. R., N. Bloom, S. J. Davis, and S. J. Terry. 2020. "Covid-Induced Economic Uncertainty." NBER Working Paper 26983, National Bureau of Economic Research, Cambridge, MA.

Barrero, J. M., N. Bloom, and S. J. Davis. 2020. "COVID-19 Is Also a Reallocation Shock." *SSRN Electronic Journal.* SSRN: https://ssrn.com/abstract=3592953.

Barro, R. J. 2015. "Convergence and Modernisation." *Economic Journal* 125 (585): 911–42.

Basu, S., J. G. Fernald, and M. S. Kimball. 2006. "Are Technology Improvements Contractionary?" *American Economic Review* 96 (5): 1418–48.

Bartkowska, M., and A. Riedl. 2012. "Regional Convergence Clubs in Europe: Identification and Conditioning Factors." *Economic Modelling* 29 (1): 22–31.

Battisti, M., and C. F. Parmeter. 2013. "Clustering and Polarization in the Distribution of Output: A Multivariate Perspective." *Journal of Macroeconomics* 35 (March): 144–62.

Baumol, W. J. 1967. "Macroeconomics of Unbalanced Growth: The Anatomy of Urban Crisis." *American Economic Review* 57 (3): 415–26.

Beaudry, P., and F. Collard. 2003. "Recent Technological and Economic Change among Industrialized Countries: Insights from Population Growth." *Scandinavian Journal of Economics* 105 (3): 441–63.

Bloom, N. 2014. "Fluctuations in Uncertainty." *Journal of Economic Perspectives* 28 (2): 153–76.

Bosch, M., E. Goni, and W. F. Maloney. 2007. "The Determinants of Rising Informality in Brazil: Evidence from Gross Worker Flows." Policy Research Working Paper 4375, World Bank, Washington, DC.

Boulhol, H., and L. Turner. 2009. "Employment-Productivity Trade-Off and Labour Composition." OECD Economics Department Working Papers 698, Organisation for Economic Co-operation and Development, Paris.

Brinca, P., J. B. Duarte, and M. Faria-e-Castro. 2020. "Measuring Sectoral Supply and Demand Shocks During COVID-19." Working Paper 2020-011, Federal Reserve Bank of St. Louis.

Bruns, S. B., and J. P. A. Ioannidis. 2020. "Determinants of Economic Growth: Different Time Different Answer?" *Journal of Macroeconomics* 63 (March): 103–85.

Brynjolfsson, E., D. Rock, and C. Syverson. 2020. "The Productivity J-Curve: How Intangibles Complement General Purpose Technologies." NBER Working Paper 25148, National Bureau of Economic Research, Cambridge, MA.

Burda, M. C. 2008. "What Kind of Shock Was It? Regional Integration and Structural Change in Germany after Unification." *Journal of Comparative Economics* 36 (4): 557–67.

Caballero, R. J., and M. L. Hammour. 1994. "The Cleansing Effect of Recessions." *American Economic Review* 84 (5): 1350–68.

Caselli, F. 2005. "Accounting for Cross-Country Income Differences." In *Handbook of Economic Growth 1A*, edited by P. Aghion and S. N. Durlauf, 679–741. Amsterdam: North-Holland.

Cerra, V., and S. C. Saxena. 2008. "Growth Dynamics: The Myth of Economic Recovery." *American Economic Review* 98 (1): 439–57.

Cerra, V., and S. C. Saxena. 2017. "Booms, Crises, and Recoveries: A New Paradigm of the Business Cycle and Its Policy Implications." IMF Working Paper 17/250, International Monetary Fund, Washington, DC.

Chen, K., and E. Wemy. 2015. "Investment-Specific Technological Changes: The Source of Long-Run TFP Fluctuations." *European Economic Review* 80: 230–52.

Cirera, X., and W. F. Maloney. 2017. *The Innovation Paradox: Developing-Country Capabilities and the Unrealized Promise of Technological Catch-Up*. Washington, DC: The World Bank.

Coibion, O., Y. Gorodnichenko, and M. Ulate. 2017. "The Cyclical Sensitivity in Estimates of Potential Output." NBER Working Paper 23580, National Bureau of Economic Research, Cambridge, MA.

Cowen, T. 2011. *The Great Stagnation: How America Ate All the Low-Hanging Fruit of Modern History, Got Sick, and Will (Eventually) Feel Better*. New York: Dutton.

Cusolito, A. P., and W. F. Maloney. 2018. *Productivity Revisited: Shifting Paradigms in Analysis and Policy*. Washington, DC: Washington, DC.

Dabla-Norris, E., S. Guo, V. Haksar, M. Kim, K. Kochhar, K. Wiseman, and A. Zdzienicka. 2015. "The New Normal: A Sector-Level Perspective on Productivity Trends in Advanced Economies." IMF Staff Discussion Note 15/03, International Monetary Fund, Washington, DC.

de Vries, G. J., A. A. Erumban, M. P. Timmer, I. Voskoboynikov, and H. X. Wu. 2012. "Deconstructing the BRICs: Structural Transformation and Aggregate Productivity Growth." *Journal of Comparative Economics* 40 (2): 211–27.

de Vries, G., M. Timmer, and K. de Vries. 2015. "Structural Transformation in Africa: Static Gains, Dynamic Losses." *Journal of Development Studies* 51 (6): 674–88.

di Mauro, F. and C. Syverson. 2020. "The COVID Crisis and Productivity Growth." Vox CERP Policy Portal, April 16, 2020. https://voxeu.org/article/covid-crisis-and-productivity-growth.

Diao, X., M. McMillan, and D. Rodrik. 2017. "The Recent Growth Boom in Developing Economies: A Structural Change Perspective." NBER Working Paper 23132, National Bureau of Economic Research, Cambridge, MA.

Djankov, S., O. Hart, C. McLiesh, and A. Shleifer. 2008. "Debt Enforcement Around the World." *Journal of Political Economy* 116 (6): 1105–50.

Easterly, W., M. Kremer, L. Pritchett, and L. H. Summers. 1993. "Good Policy or Good Luck? Country Growth Performance and Temporary Shocks." *Journal of Monetary Economics* 32 (3): 459–83.

Fernald, J. 2012. "A Quarterly, Utilization-Adjusted Series on Total Factor Productivity." Working Paper 2012-19, Federal Reserve Bank of San Francisco.

Fernald, J. 2014. "Productivity and Potential Output before, during, and after the Great Recession." *NBER Macroeconomics Annual* 29 (1): 1–51.

Fernald, J. G., and J. C. Wang. 2016. "Why Has the Cyclicality of Productivity Changed? What Does It Mean?" *Annual Review of Economics* 8: 465–96.

Fisher, J. D. M. 2006. "The Dynamic Effects of Neutral and Investment-Specific Technology Shocks." *Journal of Political Economy* 114 (3): 413–51.

Fornero, J., M. Kirchner, and Y. Andres. 2014. "Terms of Trade Shocks and Investment in Commodity-Exporting Economies." Series on Central Banking Analysis 22, Central Bank of Chile, Santiago.

Foster, L., C. Grim, and J. Haltiwanger. 2016. "Reallocation in the Great Recession: Cleansing or Not?" *Journal of Labor Economics* 34: 293–331.

Francis, N., and V. A. Ramey. 2005. "Is the Technology-Driven Real Business Cycle Hypothesis Dead? Shocks and Aggregate Fluctuations Revisited." *Journal of Monetary Economics* 52 (8): 1379–99.

Fuglie, K., M. Gautam, A. Goyal, and W. F. Maloney. 2020. *Harvesting Prosperity: Technology and Productivity Growth in Agriculture.* Washington, DC: World Bank.

Galí, J. 1999. "Technology, Employment, and the Business Cycle: Do Technology Shocks Explain Aggregate Fluctuations?" *American Economic Review* 89 (1): 249–71.

Goodridge, P., J. Haskel, and G. Wallis. 2018. "Accounting for the UK Productivity Puzzle: A Decomposition and Predictions." *Economica* 85 (339): 581–605.

Gordon, R. J. 2012. "Is U.S. Economic Growth Over? Faltering Innovation Confronts the Six Headwinds." NBER Working Paper 18315, National Bureau of Economic Research, Cambridge, MA.

Gordon, R. J., and H. Sayed. 2019. "The Industry Anatomy of the Transatlantic Productivity Growth Slowdown." NBER Working Paper 25703, National Bureau of Economic Research, Cambridge, MA.

Hale, T., A. Petherick, T. Phillips, and S. Webster. 2020. "Variation in Government Responses to COVID-19." 2020/031. BSG Working Paper Series 2020/032, University of Oxford, Oxford.

Hall, R. E., and C. I. Jones. 1999. "Why Do Some Countries Produce So Much More Output Per Worker than Others?" *The Quarterly Journal of Economics* 114 (1): 83–116.

Hausmann, R., J. Hwang, and D. Rodrik. 2007. "What You Export Matters." *Journal of Economic Growth* 12 (1): 1–25.

Helble, M., L. Trinh, and T. Le 2019. "Sectoral and Skill Contributions to Labor Productivity in Asia." Asian Development Bank Institute Working Paper 929, Asian Development Bank, Manila.

Hershbein, B., and L. B. Kahn. 2018. "Do Recessions Accelerate Routine-Biased Technological Change? Evidence from Vacancy Postings." *American Economic Review* 108 (7): 1737–72.

Hidalgo, C., and R. Hausmann. 2009. "The Building Blocks of Economic Complexity." CID Working Paper 186, Harvard Kennedy School, Cambridge, MA.

Hulten, C. R. 1992. "Growth Accounting When Technical Change Is Embodied in Capital." *American Economic Review* 82 (4): 964–80.

Imbs, J. M. 1999. "Technology, Growth and the Business Cycle." *Journal of Monetary Economics* 44 (1): 65–80.

IMF (International Monetary Fund). 2018. *World Economic Outlook: Cyclical Upswing, Structural Change.* Washington, DC: International Monetary Fund.

Jaimovich, N., and H. E. Siu. 2019. "Job Polarization and Jobless Recoveries." *Review of Economics and Statistics* 102 (1): 129–47.

Johnson, P., and C. Papageorgiou. 2020. "What Remains of Cross-Country Convergence?" *Journal of Economic Literature* 58 (1): 129–75.

Johnson, S., W. Larson, C. Papageorgiou, and A. Subramanian. 2013. "Is Newer Better? Penn World Table Revisions and Their Impact on Growth Estimates." *Journal of Monetary Economics* 60 (2): 255–74.

Jordà, Ò., M. Schularick, and A. M. Taylor. 2013. "When Credit Bites Back." *Journal of Money, Credit and Banking* 45 (s2): 3–28.

Jordà, Ò., S. R. Singh, and A. M. Taylor. 2020. "The Long-Run Effects of Monetary Policy." NBER Working Paper 26666, National Bureau of Economic Research, Cambridge, MA.

Kilic Celik, S., M. A. Kose, F. Ohnsorge, and M. Some. Forthcoming. "A Cross-Country Database of Potential Growth." Policy Research Working Paper, World Bank, Washington, DC.

Kim, Y. E., and N. V. Loayza. 2019. "Productivity Growth: Patterns and Determinants across the World." Policy Research Working Paper 8852, World Bank, Washington, DC.

Kose, A., P. Nagle, F. Ohnsorge, and N. Sugawara. 2020. *Global Waves of Debt: Causes and Consequences.* Washington, DC: World Bank.

Kose, M. A,. N. Sugawara, and M. Terrones. 2020. "Global Recessions." Policy Research Working Paper 9172, World Bank, Washington, DC.

Kose, M. A., and M. Terrones. 2015. "Collapse and Revival: Understanding Global Recessions and Recoveries." Washington, DC: International Monetary Fund, 2015.

Krugman, P. 1994. *The Age of Diminishing Expectations: U.S. Economic Policy in the 1990s.* Cambridge, MA: MIT Press.

Laeven, L. And F. Valencia. 2018. "Systemic Banking Crises Revisited." IMF Working Paper 18/206, International Monetary Fund, Washington, DC.

Leduc, S., and Z. Liu. 2020. "Can Pandemic-Induced Job Uncertainty Stimulate Automation?" Working Paper 2020–19, Federal Reserve Bank of San Francisco.

Levchenko, A., and N. Pandalai-Nayar. 2018. "Technology and Non-Technology Shocks: Measurement and Implications for International Comovement." Conference proceedings, ECB-CBRT Conference, the Federal Reserve Board, UT-Austin, and the NBER-IFM, Cambridge, MA.

Leroy, A. M., and G. M. Grandolini. 2016. *Principles for Effective Insolvency and Creditor and Debtor Regimes.* Washington, DC: World Bank.

Ludvigson, S. C., S. Ma, and S. Ng. 2020. "COVID-19 and the Macroeconomic Effects of Costly Disasters." NBER Working Paper 26987, National Bureau of Economic Research, Cambridge, MA.

Ma, C., J. H. Rogers, and S. Zhou. 2020. "Global Economic and Financial Effects of 21st Century Pandemics and Epidemics." *SSRN Electronic Journal*, March. http://dx.doi.org/10.2139/ssrn.3565646.

Mankiw, N. G., D. Romer, and D. N. Weil. 1992. "A Contribution to the Empirics of Economic-Growth." *Quarterly Journal of Economics* 107 (2): 407–37.

Martins, P. M. G. 2019. "Structural Change: Pace, Patterns and Determinants." *Review of Development Economics* 23 (1): 1–32.

McCullough, E. B. 2017. "Labor Productivity and Employment Gaps in Sub-Saharan Africa." *Food Policy* 67 (2017): 133–52.

McMillan, M., D. Rodrik, and C. Sepulveda. 2017. "Structural Change, Fundamentals and Growth: A Framework and Case Studies." NBER Working Paper 23378, National Bureau of Economic Research, Cambridge, MA.

McMillan, M., D. Rodrik, and Í. Verduzco-Gallo. 2014. "Globalization, Structural Change, and Productivity Growth, with an Update on Africa." *World Development* 63 (2014): 11–32.

Mourougane, A. 2017. "Crisis, Potential Output and Hysteresis." *International Economics* 149 (May): 1–14.

Noy, I. 2009. "The Macroeconomic Consequences of Disasters." *Journal of Development Economics* 88 (2): 221–31.

Obstfeld, M. 2018. "Can Accommodative Monetary Policies Help Explain the Productivity Slowdown?" Remarks to joint BIS-IMF-OECD conference, "Weak Productivity: The Role of Financial Factors and Policies." January 10. Organization for Economic Co-Operation and Development, Paris.

OECD (Organisation for Economic Co-operation and Development). 2015. *The Future of Productivity.* Paris: OECD.

OECD (Organisation for Economic Co-operation and Development). 2020. *OECD Economic Outlook: Double Hit Scenario.* Paris: OECD.

Patel, D., J. Sandefur, and A. Subramanian. 2018. "Everything You Know about Cross-Country Convergence Is (Now) Wrong." *Center for Global Development* (blog), October 15, 2018. https://www.cgdev.org/blog/everything-you-know-about-cross-country-convergence-now-wrong.

Pesaran, H. 2007. "A Pair-Wise Approach to Testing for Output and Growth Convergence." *Journal of Econometrics* 138 (1): 312–55.

Phillips, P., and D. Sul. 2009. "Economic Transition and Growth." *Journal of Applied Econometrics* 24 (7): 1153–85.

Reinhart, C. M., and K. S. Rogoff. 2009. "The Aftermath of Financial Crises." *American Economic Review* 99 (2): 466–72.

Restuccia, D., D. T. Yang, and X. Zhu. 2008. "Agriculture and Aggregate Productivity: A Quantitative Cross-Country Analysis." *Journal of Monetary Economics* 55 (2): 234–50.

Rujin, S. 2019. "What Are the Effects of Technology Shocks on International Labor Markets?" Ruhr Economic Paper 86, RWI, North Rhine-Westphalia, Germany.

Sheiner, L., and K. Yilla. 2020. "The ABCs of the Post-COVID Economic Recovery." *Up Front* (blog), May 4, 2020. https://www.brookings.edu/blog/up-front/.

Siu, A., and Y. C. R. Wong. 2004. "Economic Impact of SARS in Hong Kong Economic." *Asian Economic Papers* 3 (1): 62–83.

Summers, L. H. 2015. "Demand Side Secular Stagnation." *American Economic Review* 105 (5): 60–65.

Tian, X., X. Zhang, Y. Zhou, and X. Yu. 2016. "Regional Income Inequality in China Revisited: A Perspective from Club Convergence." *Economic Modelling* 56 (August): 50–58.

Timmer, M., G. de Vries, and K. de Vries. 2015. "Patterns of Structural Change in Developing Countries." GGDC Research Memorandum 149, University of Gronigen, Groningen, Netherlands.

UNDP (United Nations Development Programme). 2015. "Confronting the Gender Impact of Ebola Virus Disease in Guinea, Liberia, and Sierra Leone." *UNDP Africa Policy Note* 2 (1): 1–9.

Üngör, M. 2017. "Productivity Growth and Labor Reallocation: Latin America versus East Asia." *Review of Economic Dynamics* 24 (March): 25–42.

Von Lyncker, K., and R. Thoennessen. 2017. "Regional Club Convergence in the EU: Evidence from a Panel Data Analysis." *Empirical Economics* 52 (2): 525–53.

Wang, G., Y. Zhang, J. Zhao, J. Zhang, and F. Jiang. 2020. "Mitigate the Effects of Home Confinement on Children During the COVID-19 Outbreak." *The Lancet* 395 (10228): 945–47.

World Bank. 2018a. *Piecing Together the Poverty Puzzle.* Washington, DC: World Bank.

World Bank. 2018b. *Global Economic Prospects: Broad Based Upturn, but for How Long?* January. Washington, DC: World Bank.

World Bank. 2018c. *Africa's Pulse: An Analysis of Issues Shaping Africa's Economic Future.* October. Washington, DC: World Bank.

World Bank. 2019. *Global Economic Prospects: Darkening Skies.* January. Washington, DC: World Bank.

World Bank. 2020a. *Global Economic Prospects.* June. Washington, DC: World Bank.

World Bank. 2020b. *The COVID-19 Pandemic: Shocks to Education and Policy Responses.* Washington, DC: World Bank.

World Bank. 2020c. *Africa's Pulse: Assessing the Economic Impact of COVID-19 and Policy Responses in Sub-Saharan Africa.* April. Washington, DC: World Bank.

Wu, M., J. Ul-Haq., N. Zafar, H. Sun, and J. Jiang. 2019. "Trade liberalization and informality nexus: Evidence from Pakistan." The Journal of International Trade & Economic Development 28(6): 732–54.

PART I

Productivity: Trends and Explanations

Both theory and evidence support the belief that significant long-run gains, even if not permanent changes in the growth rate, can be achieved by increased investment in the broadest sense, including human capital, technological knowledge, and industrial plant and equipment.

Robert Solow (1992)
Nobel Prize Winner in Economic Sciences

Increasing jobs more than output implies a fall in productivity and standards of living. That surely cannot be our goal.

Alan Greenspan (2011)
Former Chairman of
the Board of Governors of the Federal Reserve

CHAPTER 1
Global Productivity Trends

Since the 1980s, labor productivity growth in emerging market and developing economies (EMDEs) has undergone various surges and declines, each of increasing magnitude over time. The COVID-19 (coronavirus disease 2019) pandemic threatens a further fall of EMDE produc-tivity growth, which could be the largest and most broad-based yet and would compound a trend slowdown in labor productivity growth that was already under way after the 2007-09 global financial crisis (GFC). Multiple decomposition methodologies provide insights into the causes of the deceleration of productivity growth. Globally, investment weakness accounted for the majority of the slowdown after the GFC; in EMDEs, it reflected weak investment and total factor productivity growth in broadly equal measure, as well as fading gains from factor reallocation toward more productive sectors. Cyclical factors explain a substantial share of the synchronized productivity slowdown during the GFC. However, the degree of post-GFC scarring on productivity varies significantly across EMDEs, suggesting a role for policy. Previous global recessions suggest that both advanced economies and EMDEs are likely to face a further decline in labor productivity growth due to the COVID-19 shock.

Introduction

Even before the collapse in global activity due to the COVID-19 (coronavirus disease 2019) pandemic, a broad-based slowdown in labor productivity was under way. In emerging market and developing economies (EMDEs), the slowdown that followed the 2007-09 global financial crisis (GFC) made achieving the Sustainable Development Goals more difficult. The pace of convergence slowed as labor productivity gaps with advanced economies remained substantial, with workers in the average EMDE producing less than one-fifth of the output of those in advanced economies.

The synchronized nature of the productivity slowdown after the GFC raises questions about the role of common factors or spillovers, and the extent to which they will again operate during the pandemic-driven recession in 2020. The nature of the post-GFC slowdown and its drivers has proved controversial. Some have attributed the weakness in productivity growth to waning technological progress as innovations regarded as "low-hanging fruit" have already been developed, leaving only innovations with lower marginal gains (Gordon 2012; Gordon and Sayed 2019). Others regard the slowdown in productivity growth as a "pause," given the time delay between radical new digital technologies being developed and then incorporated into production processes

Note: This chapter was prepared by Alistair Dieppe, Sinem Kilic Celik, and Gene Kindberg-Hanlon. Research assistance was provided by Khamal Clayton, Aygul Evdokimova, Yi Li, Awais Qureshi, and Xinyue Wang.

(Brynjolfsson, Rock, and Syverson 2018). A third argument is that the broad-based weakness has been driven by deficient demand (Summers 2015).

Against this backdrop, this chapter presents a comprehensive examination of the evolution of productivity over the past four decades, with an emphasis on the scarring effects of the GFC, in order to take stock of productivity developments ahead of what could be a major decline in global productivity growth due to COVID-19. Productivity growth is decomposed into contributions from factor inputs and total factor productivity (TFP), as well as from sectoral growth and reallocation. This chapter also examines the role of demand influences in driving the post-GFC productivity slowdown and their role in driving synchronized global productivity fluctuations. More generally, this chapter provides context for the analysis in the remainder of the book, which will more closely examine the primary drivers of productivity growth and convergence, assess the risks to productivity growth from a range of shocks, and explore the likely long-run impacts of the COVID-19 crisis.

Specifically, the chapter addresses the following questions:

- How has productivity growth evolved over the last four decades?

- What factors explain developments in productivity and, in particular, the slowdown since the 2007-09 global financial crisis?

- How synchronized are productivity developments?

Contribution and framework

The chapter makes several contributions to the literature and policy debate on labor productivity.

- *EMDE focus.* Thus far, the literature has focused on trends in subsets of countries such as advanced economies, OECD economies, or specific regions.[1] This chapter is the first to provide both an overarching global and an in-depth EMDE view of productivity developments, with a particular focus on the decline in productivity growth following the GFC.

- *Productivity decompositions.* This chapter undertakes a thorough assessment of the sources of the slowdown since the GFC across a broad range of countries by decomposing productivity into factor inputs—capital deepening, human capital, and TFP. This chapter is the first to remove cyclical and other demand-side components from labor productivity for a broad range of economies.

- *Synchronization.* This chapter is the first to assess the synchronization of productivity growth across a broad range of countries for multiple measures of

---

[1] For examples of such literature, see ADB (2017), Adler et al. (2017), Cusolito and Maloney (2018), Dabla-Norris et al. (2015), Fernald (2012), Fernald and Inklaar (2020), OECD (2015), and World Bank (2018a).

productivity. In addition, it documents the role of cyclical productivity drivers in generating broad-based global productivity developments. The existing literature has focused on synchronization in advanced economies, whereas this chapter study also considers EMDEs (Imbs 1999; Levchenko and Pandalai-Nayar 2018).

Main findings

The following findings emerge from the chapter:

- *Diverse range of productivity trends.* Global labor productivity growth has been resilient, in general, over the past four decades. While experiencing several surges and declines, global productivity growth averaged 1.8 percent in the 1980s and 1990s and the post-GFC period. However, this masks divergent trends among advanced economies and EMDEs. Advanced economy labor productivity growth has halved since the 1980s, in a declining trend that was accelerated by the GFC. In contrast, EMDE productivity growth accelerated rapidly in the run-up to the GFC following the stagnation of the 1980s. The GFC ended a period of rising productivity growth, and the ensuing slump risks becoming an entrenched deceleration.

- *Sharp decline and subdued recovery following the GFC.* The labor productivity growth decline following the GFC was the steepest, longest, and broadest multiyear productivity slowdown yet. The post-GFC slowdown has been broad-based, affecting 70 percent of economies and over 80 percent of the global extreme poor as well as reaching all EMDE regions. Commodity-exporting EMDEs—which account for almost two-thirds of EMDEs—have been the worst affected.[2] Synchronized declines in productivity growth have become steeper, and recoveries shallower since 1980, pointing to risks ahead of what is expected to be the largest contraction in global output since World War II due to COVID-19 (World Bank 2020).

- *Accounting for the post-GFC slowdown.* Investment weakness accounted for the lion's share of the post-GFC (2013-18) slowdown in productivity growth in advanced economies from pre-GFC averages (2003-08). In EMDEs, subdued investment and slowing TFP accounted, in approximately equal measure, for the post-GFC productivity growth slowdown. Fading gains from factor reallocation toward more productive sectors also played a role. The long-run consequences of weak investment growth on productivity point to a need for robust support from public investment and to create the conditions for increased private investment.

- *Large role for cyclical factors in productivity synchronization.* The synchronization of productivity across countries increased sharply during the GFC. After removing

---

[2] In commodity-exporting EMDEs, annual productivity growth slowed by 4.0 percentage points between 2010 and 2015, compared with 2.2 percentage points in commodity-importing EMDEs.

cyclical factors from labor productivity growth, the correlation across economies is negligible during the GFC. Common productivity developments are therefore largely a business cycle phenomenon. This pattern is likely to be repeated as a result of the COVID-19 crisis, given the magnitude of the cyclical and demand-driven factors at play. The ultimate scale of the slowdown following the GFC varied widely across EMDEs, highlighting the important roles that cross-country differences in the fundamental drivers of productivity, such as education and institutional quality, have played in generating productivity growth (chapters 2 and 4). Reinvigorating these underlying drivers of productivity growth will therefore be key in limiting long-term damage from the pandemic-driven recession in 2020.

Concepts. Throughout this chapter, productivity is defined as output (gross domestic product [GDP]) per input of a unit of labor. To ensure as large and comparable a sample as possible over time and across countries, this chapter uses the number of people engaged rather than the number of hours worked as the measure of labor input.[3] A second measure, TFP, is also featured in the chapter; it measures the efficiency with which factor inputs are combined and is often used to proxy technological progress (box 1.1). As a result, this chapter includes annual labor productivity, TFP, and capital services data for 103 economies, of which 74 are EMDEs and 29 are advanced economies, for 1981-2018.

Evolution of productivity

Since 1980, global productivity growth has gone through a series of peaks and troughs. In all cases, the troughs for productivity growth have coincided with global recessions or slowdowns (figure 1.1). In advanced economies, these surges and declines have centered around a declining trend, which was accelerated by the GFC. However, in EMDEs, although the surges and declines have been larger, until the GFC they were accompanied by a rising trend. The GFC, the largest and most synchronized downturn since World War II, therefore marked a significant turning point for global labor productivity growth.

Global productivity. From its pre-GFC peak in 2007, global productivity growth slowed drastically in 2009 to -0.4 percent. The GFC resulted in lasting damage to global productivity growth, which remains 1.0 percentage point below its precrisis peak, at 1.8 percent in 2018, below both precrisis and longer-run averages (figure 1.1). This post-GFC slowdown from pre-GFC averages was broad-based, affecting two-thirds of economies, both among advanced economies and EMDEs. Those economies with slower post-GFC productivity growth than during the pre-GFC period account for 90 percent of global GDP and of the global extreme poor.

Advanced economies. The slowdown following the GFC in advanced economy productivity growth continues a trend that has been under way since the late 1990s,

---

[3] Number of people engaged includes employees and self-employed. Alternative measures such as hours per worker might better capture labor input but have insufficient coverage for EMDEs (box 1.1). In countries with large informal sectors, both employment and output may be subject to sizable measurement error.

FIGURE 1.1 **Evolution of global productivity growth**

In advanced economies, productivity growth has experienced a long-run decline over the past 40 years, while in general, EMDE labor productivity growth has trended up over the same horizon until the global financial crisis (GFC). In EMDEs, labor productivity growth has declined from precrisis levels in the longest and most broad-based multiyear decline since the 1980s. EMDE commodity exporters have had the weakest average productivity growth since 2013. Productivity growth in commodity importers and LICs has been more resilient, although the postcrisis slowdown has affected all regions.

A. Global, AE, and EMDE productivity growth

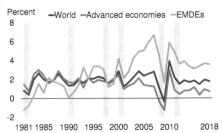

B. EMDE productivity growth

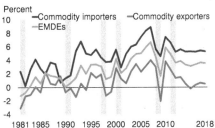

C. Share of economies with 2013-18 productivity growth below historical averages

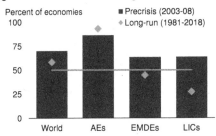

D. Magnitude and extent of multiyear EMDE productivity slowdowns and recoveries

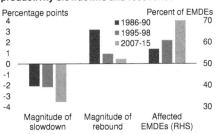

E. EMDE productivity growth, pre- and postcrisis

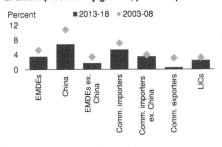

F. Productivity growth in EMDE regions

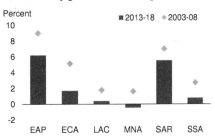

Sources: Conference Board; Penn World Table; World Bank, World Development Indicators.

Note: Productivity is defined as output per worker in U.S. dollars (at 2010 prices and exchange rates). Sample of 29 advanced economies (AEs) and 74 emerging market and developing economies (EMDEs), including 11 low-income countries (LICs), as of 2019 World Bank classifications, 52 commodity exporters and 22 commodity importers. Aggregate growth rates are GDP-weighted at constant 2010 prices and exchange rates.

A.B. Shaded regions indicate global recessions and slowdowns (1982, 1991, 1998, 2001, 2009, and 2012), as defined in Kose, Sugawara and Terrones (2020) and Kose and Terrones (2015).

C. Share of economies for which average productivity growth during 2013-18 was lower than the long-run (1981-2018) average or the precrisis (2003-2008) average. For advanced economies, the precrisis growth is calculated as the average during 2003-07.

D. "Magnitude of slowdown" is the cumulative decline in EMDE productivity growth from the peak of the episode to the trough for episodes lasting more than two years. "Magnitude of rebound" is the cumulative increase in EMDE productivity growth from the trough (of the episode to three years later. "Affected EMDEs" is the share of EMDEs that experienced a slowdown.

F. Sample of 8 EMDEs in East Asia and Pacific (EAP),10 EMDEs in Europe and Central Asia (ECA), 18 EMDEs in Latin America and the Caribbean (LAC), 10 EMDEs in the Middle East and North Africa (MNA), 2 EMDEs in South Asia (SAR), and 26 EMDEs in Sub-Saharan Africa (SSA).

following a brief resurgence from an even longer-running declining trend. The slowdown has been attributed to a declining contribution from information and communication technology (ICT) intensive sectors in the United States, and slow adoption of ICT technologies, and to restrictive product market regulations in parts of Europe.[4] During the GFC, productivity growth in advanced economies plunged and never recovered to precrisis levels. At 0.8 percent on average during 2013-18, it was one-half its long-term average and 0.7 percentage points below its precrisis average. This slowdown relative to long-run averages affected about 90 percent of advanced economies.

EMDEs. Productivity growth in EMDEs has slowed sharply from its 2007 peak of 6.6 percent to a low of 3.1 percent in 2015 and, since then, has inched up to 3.5 percent in 2018. The post-GFC slowdown from precrisis averages affected over 60 percent of EMDEs, and, in nearly half of EMDEs, productivity growth has fallen below its long-term (1981-2018) average. The slowdown has been particularly pronounced in China, where a policy-guided decline in public investment growth has been under way for several years, and in commodity exporters, which have been hit hard by the commodity price plunge of 2014-16. Weak post-GFC productivity growth follows on the heels of a major productivity surge during 2003-08 when EMDE productivity growth more than doubled from 1990s averages.

Whereas EMDE productivity growth has always slowed sharply during global recessions and slowdowns, previous *multiyear* slowdowns—in 1986-90 and 1995-98—preceded global recessions (1991) or global slowdowns and EMDE crises (1998). However, the multiyear slowdown since 2007 has been the most prolonged, steepest, and broadest-based yet (figure 1.1).[5] In contrast to previous episodes, the current productivity slowdown has persisted.

Large differences in the scale of slowdown. Aggregate EMDE productivity growth in 2018 remained above its average in the 1980s and 1990s. However, the scale of the post-GFC slowdown has varied significantly across regions, highlighting different degrees of vulnerability and resilience to major shocks. In commodity-importing EMDEs, average productivity growth in 2013-18 has remained more than twice its 1980s average and one-quarter above its 1990s average. Excluding China, labor productivity growth in commodity importers has slowed by just 0.4 percentage point relative to the pre-GFC period. In commodity-exporting EMDEs, the post-GFC commodity price plunge has

---

[4] For a summary of the effects of the ICT slowdown on U.S. productivity in the 2000s, see Duval, Hong, and Timmer (2017), and Jorgenson, Ho, and Stiroh (2008). In Europe, the trend decline in productivity has been ascribed to sectoral misallocation due to cheap credit in southern Europe (Gopinath et al. 2017), a failure to adopt ICT and associated technology to the same extent as the United States (van Ark, O'Mahony, and Timmer 2008), and restrictive product market regulations (Haltiwanger, Scarpetta, and Schweiger 2014).

[5] The most recent slowdown in productivity growth has lasted eight years—compared with the four years of 1986-90 and the three years of 1995-98—and, from peak to trough, has been 50 percent steeper than the slowdowns in the late 1980s and the late 1990s. It has affected over 70 percent of EMDEs, more than the slowdown in the 1990s (61 percent) and 1980s (57 percent).

reduced productivity growth from 2.9 percent to just 0.5 percent, rates which are only just above the growth rates of the 1980s. The forecast plunge in global output due to COVID-19, therefore, presents a heightened risk in these economies of returning to the poor performance of the 1980s, particularly if it increases the likelihood of financial distress and lower-for-longer commodity prices (World Bank 2020).

Low-income countries. Over one-half of low-income countries (LICs)—and especially the larger ones among them—have productivity growth that remains above long-run averages. On average, LIC productivity growth has fallen only modestly to 2.4 percent during 2013-18, substantially above the negative rates of the 1980s and the 1990s.

Regions. Productivity growth decelerated in all EMDE regions during 2013-18 from their pre-GFC (2003-08) averages (chapter 5). The most pronounced slowdown (by 3.4 percentage points to 1.7 percent in 2013-18) occurred in Europe and Central Asia (ECA), where the GFC and subsequent euro area debt crisis caused severe economic disruptions. Productivity growth also fell steeply in Latin America and the Caribbean (LAC), the Middle East and North Africa (MNA), and Sub-Saharan Africa (SSA), to below 1 percent. All four regions have major energy exporters that were negatively affected by the 2014-16 oil price collapse. Productivity growth declined substantially in East Asia and Pacific (EAP) and to a smaller extent in South Asia (SAR) from precrisis levels, but it continued to be robust in both regions, remaining above 5 percent.

Missed opportunities. The one-quarter of EMDEs with the fastest productivity growth have reduced their extreme poverty rates by an average of more than 1 percentage point per year since 1981, whereas poverty rates rose in EMDEs in the lowest quartile of productivity growth (figure 1.2). The steep productivity growth slowdown since the GFC implies considerable output losses relative to a counterfactual of productivity growth continuing at its pre-GFC trend and therefore a missed opportunity for more rapid poverty reduction. Output per worker in advanced economies would be 9 percent higher today had productivity growth continued at its average pace ahead of the GFC (2003-08). Losses relative to the exceptionally high rate of productivity growth in EMDEs ahead of the GFC are closer to 14 percent, and higher still at 19 percent for EMDE commodity exporters. The further decline in productivity growth that will likely be driven by the COVID-19 pandemic will lead to further losses and decelerate the pace of poverty reduction.

Productivity gaps remain. The slowdown in productivity growth in EMDEs since the GFC and the renewed threat to productivity growth from COVID-19 are particularly disappointing in the context of large outstanding productivity gaps with advanced economies. EMDE productivity levels are less than one-fifth of the advanced economy average, falling to just 2 percent of the advanced economy average in LICs (figure 1.2). In some large EMDEs, such as China and India, productivity is growing substantially faster than in advanced economies, resulting in productivity catch-up. However, on average, EMDE productivity growth is just half a percentage point faster than in advanced economies, requiring more than a century to halve outstanding productivity gaps (chapter 4).

FIGURE 1.2 Poverty, productivity, and missed opportunities

Poverty declined by more than 1 percentage point on average per year in the one-quarter of EMDEs with the highest productivity growth during 1981-2015, whereas poverty rose in EMDEs with the lowest productivity growth. The slowdown in productivity growth relative to pre-GFC (global financial crisis) trends presents a large missed opportunity for further poverty reduction. EMDE productivity growth remains far below the levels at the advanced economy frontier and will require significantly stronger growth to rapidly close this gap. On average, productivity in EMDEs is less than one-fifth of the advanced economy average, and in LICs it is just 2 percent.

A. Annual change in the poverty rate in EMDEs, by productivity growth

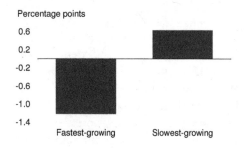

B. Cumulative labor productivity losses relative to pre-GFC trend

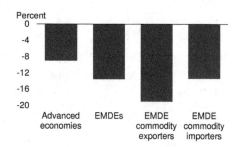

C. EMDE labor productivity levels, 2013-18

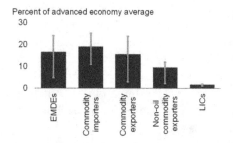

D. Labor productivity relative to advanced economies by region, 2013-18

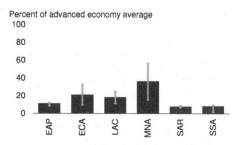

Sources: Conference Board; Penn World Table; PovcalNet; World Bank; World Development Indicators.

Note: Labor productivity is defined as output per worker in U.S. dollars (at 2010 prices and exchange rates). Unless otherwise indicated, data are from a sample of 29 advanced economies and 74 EMDEs (emerging market and developing economies).

A. Unweighted averages using annual data during 1981-2015. Fastest-growing EMDEs are those in the top quartile by productivity growth; slowest-growing EMDEs are those in the bottom quartile of labor productivity growth. Poverty rate defined as the share of the population living on less than $1.90 a day (2011 purchasing power parity [PPP]).

B. Percent fall in productivity level by 2018 relative to a counterfactual scenario where productivity continued to grow at its 2003-07 average growth from 2008 onwards for advanced economies, and 2003-08 average for EMDEs from 2009 onwards.

C. The samples include 22 commodity-importing EMDEs and 52 commodity-exporting EMDEs. Blue bars indicate the unweighted average output per worker during 2013-18 relative to the advanced economy average. Whiskers indicate interquartile range relative to the advanced economy average.

D. Unweighted average productivity during 2013-18 relative to the average advanced economy by region (2013-18). Includes 8 EMDEs in East Asia and Pacific (EAP), 10 EMDEs in Europe and Central Asia (ECA), 18 EMDEs in Latin America and the Caribbean (LAC), 10 EMDEs in the Middle East and North Africa (MNA), 2 EMDEs in South Asia (SAR), and 26 EMDEs in Sub-Saharan Africa (SSA).

Sources of the slowdown in labor productivity growth after the GFC

Aggregate labor productivity growth can be decomposed into (1) factor inputs and the efficiency of their use, or (2) sectoral contributions. These decompositions help to diagnose the sources of the post-GFC productivity growth slowdown in EMDEs.

Factor inputs and the efficiency of their use

Approach. In the first step, productivity growth is decomposed into contributions from individual factor inputs (physical capital and human capital) and the effectiveness of their use (total factor productivity), assuming a Cobb-Douglas production function (box 1.1). Capital deepening directly increases labor productivity, while human capital improvements (for example, education and training) enhance the quality of labor input and therefore the resulting quantity of output produced. TFP measures the efficiency with which all factors are employed and is often considered a proxy for the technology behind the production process.[6]

Factor inputs vs. the effectiveness of their use. Globally, the post-GFC (2013-18) slowdown in labor productivity growth from pre-GFC (2003-07/08) averages amounted to half of a percentage point, the majority of which was a result of a slowdown in capital accumulation (both public and private; World Bank 2019b; figure 1.3). In advanced economies, TFP contributed only marginally to the decline in labor productivity growth after the GFC, in part due to a structural slowdown before the GFC.[7] In EMDEs, however, it accounted for about one-half of the slowdown in labor productivity growth.

- *Advanced economies.* Investment weakness accounted for virtually all of the slowdown (0.7 percentage point) in productivity growth from pre-GFC averages in advanced economies. From 2008, investment growth slowed sharply in response to weak and highly uncertain growth prospects, heightened policy uncertainty, and credit constraints in the aftermath of the GFC (see Duval, Hong, and Timmer 2017; Ollivaud, Guillemette, and Turner 2016). Investment contracted by an average of 6 percent per year between 2008 and 2009. Although investment growth has recovered close to pre-GFC rates, it has been accompanied by strong rates of employment growth, such that the growth of capital per worker has remained subdued (ECB 2017). TFP growth had already declined in the 1990s and pre-GFC

---

[6] The decomposition above is an accounting framework that does not control for dynamic interactions between TFP and investment growth. However, there is evidence that weak underlying TFP and investment growth reinforce each other, which could have amplified the postcrisis productivity slowdown.

[7] The finding of a longer-running decline in TFP growth is largely due to a long-run decline in Europe. In the United States, TFP growth enjoyed a brief resurgence due to the ICT boom during 1996-2004 (Adler et al. 2017; Fernald et al. 2017).

FIGURE 1.3 Growth accounting decomposition

Almost three-quarters of the postcrisis slowdown in global productivity growth from precrisis averages—and virtually all in advanced economies—reflected a slowdown in capital deepening. The postcrisis slowdown in EMDE productivity growth from precrisis averages reflected, in approximately equal measure, investment weakness and slowing TFP growth. In LICs, strong investment has supported postcrisis output and productivity growth.

A. Contributions to productivity growth in advanced economies

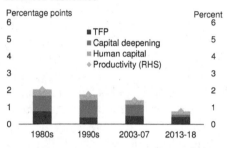

B. Contributions to productivity growth in EMDEs

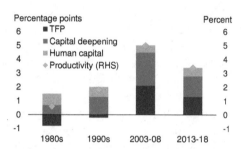

C. Contributions to productivity growth in EMDE commodity exporters and importers

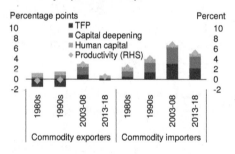

D. Contributions to productivity growth in LICs

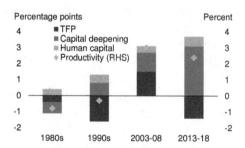

E. Contributions to regional productivity growth: EAP, ECA, LAC

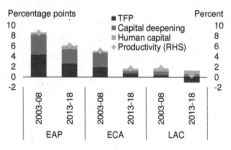

F. Contributions to regional productivity growth: MNA, SAR, SSA

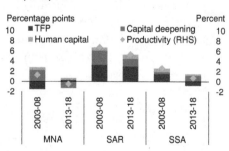

Sources: Barro and Lee (2015); International Monetary Fund; Penn World Table; United Nations; World Bank; World Development Indicators.

Note: Productivity defined as output per worker in U.S. dollars (at 2010 prices and exchange rates). Growth accounting decomposition methodology described in box 1.1. Aggregate growth rates calculated using constant 2010 U.S. dollar weights. The sample includes 29 advanced economies, and 74 EMDEs including 11 LICs, 52 commodity exporters, 22 EMDE commodity importers, 8 East Asia and Pacific (EAP), 10 Europe and Central Asia (ECA), 18 Latin America and the Caribbean (LAC), 10 Middle East and North Africa (MNA), 2 South Asia (SAR), and 26 Sub-Saharan Africa (SSA) economies. EMDE = emerging market and developing economy; LIC = low-income country; TFP = total factor productivity.

BOX 1.1 Productivity: Conceptual considerations and measurement challenges

Concepts. There are two primary ways of measuring productivity: labor productivity and total factor productivity (TFP). Throughout this book, productivity is defined as output (gross domestic product [GDP]) per input of a unit of labor. To ensure as large and comparable a sample as possible over time and across countries, this book uses the number of people engaged rather than the number of hours worked as the measure of labor input.[a] Also featured in this book is a second measure, TFP, which measures the efficiency with which factor inputs are combined and is often used to proxy technological progress. TFP may also incorporate wider factors such as organizational and institutional characteristics. This box reviews definitions and conceptual considerations, and different techniques and challenges of these different productivity measures, and explains how they are tackled in this study.

Labor productivity. For the purposes of this book, labor productivity is measured as output per worker, with the number of employees used as the unit of labor input. This has the advantage of wide availability across countries. Its disadvantage rests in the failure to account for the quality and intensity of labor input:

- *Comprehensiveness.* Labor input is intended to capture all of those involved in the production process. Thus, total employment figures include self-employment, which accounts for a large proportion of informal employment in emerging market and developing economies (EMDEs) (World Bank 2019a). However, difficulties in measurement of the informal sector create uncertainty and increase the potential for inconsistency across countries around the productivity level, particularly in EMDEs with high shares of informal employment (Fajnzylber, Maloney, and Montes-Rojas 2011).[b] Nonetheless, many national statistics offices estimate the size of the informal sector and adjust their GDP estimates accordingly (Charmes 2012; SNA 2008; UNECE 2008).

- *Quality of labor input.* The effectiveness of labor input may be influenced by the level of education, training, and health of workers. These aspects of human capital can be addressed by estimating the average years of schooling of the workforce and life expectancy to proxy workforce health. However, the quality of formal education and health, and the effects of on-the-job training provided outside of the education system, is difficult to measure consistently.

Note: This box was prepared by Sinem Kilic Celik. Research assistance was provided by Yi Li.

a. Number of people engaged includes both employees and self-employed. Alternative measures such as hours per worker might better capture labor input but have insufficient coverage for EMDEs. In countries with large informal sectors, both employment and output may be subject to sizable measurement error.

b. The direction of the bias depends on how national statistics offices adjust their employment and official GDP to cover the informal sector, which may vary across countries (UNECE 2008).

BOX 1.1 Productivity: Conceptual considerations and measurement challenges (*continued*)

- *Intensity of labor input.* The number of people involved in the production process does not consider different work arrangements that vary the intensity of labor input. The intensity of labor input is, for example, better captured by hours worked, but these data are not available for many countries.

Total factor productivity. One of the most commonly used measures of technological enhancement to the production process is TFP growth. The standard growth accounting approach is one of the most common methodologies in the literature to estimate TFP. Following Caselli (2005), labor productivity is decomposed into contributions from several factor inputs: [c]

$$Labor\ productivity = Y_t/L_t = A_t (K_t/L_t)^{(1-\alpha)} H_t^{\alpha},$$

where Y is output, L is labor input, H is human capital level, and A is TFP. Following Solow (1957), a Cobb-Douglas production function with constant returns to scale is assumed. By taking log differences, labor productivity growth can be decomposed into the following factor inputs

$$\Delta LP_t = (1-\alpha)\Delta k_t + \alpha \Delta h_t + \Delta a_t,$$

where $k_t = \log(K_t/L_t)$ and $h_t = \log(H_t)$, and a_t is the log of TFP, calculated here as a residual of labor productivity growth after subtracting the change in capital deepening and human capital indexes, weighted by their respective shares in the production function [$(1-\alpha)$ and α].

This approach is appealing for its simple nature and its ease of interpretation. Being estimated as a residual, TFP depends on the assumed functional form of the production function, and is vulnerable to measurement error for factor input estimates.

- *Functional form.* TFP is defined as "a shift in the production function." Its calculation assumes the existence of a well-behaved and stable production function, which also accurately describes the technology in use (Baqaee and Farhi 2018). One of the commonly used functional forms is Cobb-Douglas with constant returns to scale and unitary elasticities of substitution between capital and labor. If the assumption of constant returns to scale is not valid, TFP estimations may be biased (Dribe et al. 2017).

- *Capital measurement.* Physical capital is difficult to asses accurately. Its value depends on the longevity of assets (*short-lived assets* such as computers vs.

---

c. Another way of decomposition is level accounting where the labor productivity level is decomposed into physical and human capital intensities (Hsieh and Klenow 2010; Klenow and Rodríguez-Clare 1997).

BOX 1.1 Productivity: Conceptual considerations and measurement challenges (*continued*)

long-lived assets such as roads) and the nature of capital (*intangible* capital such as research and development or marketing expenditures). A common way of measuring the capital stock is to apply the perpetual inventory methodology to the flow of expenditure on assets and their depreciation rates. Because data for the initial capital stock are usually not available, assumptions are made on capital-to-output ratio of the initial year, but this ratio can be highly country-specific (Feenstra, Inklaar, and Timmer 2015). Data on capital services are from the Penn World Table (PWT) 9.1 (Feenstra, Inklaar, and Timmer 2015). In contrast to previous versions of PWT, this edition utilizes capital *services* as a measure of capital inputs instead of capital *stocks* (Inklaar, Woltjer, and Gallardo 2019). Capital services methodology allows us to relax the assumption of homogeneity of different assets by attributing appropriate weights to different types of assets (less to the short-lived assets, for example) while aggregating the capital input up.

- *Factor utilization.* Because TFP is measured as a residual, it estimates not only technological change but also any mismeasurement of capital and labor inputs (Basu, Fernald, and Kimball 2006). Capital services is a measure of the total physical capital available for production without necessarily considering how much of the existing capital is used actively in the production process (capital utilization). Similarly, labor input, even if it is finely measured as total working hours, does not account for variable labor effort. This may lead to an overly cyclical measure of productivity. One way of obtaining a "technology" series, cleaned of variable utilization of the factors of production (and other demand-driven cyclical components), is by using structural vector autoregressions (SVARs), which assume that changes in the underlying technology behind production are longer-term phenomena (chapter 6). SVAR-derived measures of the contribution of technology to productivity, and other lasting factors such as organizational and institutional change, are included in this chapter.

Human capital (H_t). The human capital index from the PWT 9.1 is used throughout the book. This measure uses average years of schooling of the working-age population in combination with an estimate of the global returns to education. [d]

Labor share estimates. The output-labor elasticity (α), proxied by the labor income share, is estimated using the labor compensation-to-output ratio for each

---

d. As one of the determinants of human capital, health should ideally be included in the human capital index but the lack of long consistent series provides a constraint (Kraay 2018; World Bank 2018b).

BOX 1.1 Productivity: Conceptual considerations and measurement challenges (*continued*)

country, including adjustments to take account of mixed-income and wages from self-employment (from PWT 9.1). This analysis uses constant labor shares over time, defined as the long-term average of labor share data from PWT 9.1.

Natural capital (N_t). In resource-rich regions and countries, natural resources are an important input to production (chapter 5). Without taking into account natural capital in the production function, the function might be misspecified. Assume a natural capital-augmented production function:

$$Y_t = A_t K_t^{1-\alpha-\gamma} N_t^{\gamma} (H_t L_t)^{\alpha},$$

where N_t is capital based on natural resources and γ is the ratio of the output using natural capital in the whole economy. Using the production function above, labor productivity growth can be decomposed into the following:

$$\Delta LP_t = (1-\alpha-\gamma)\Delta k_t + \gamma \Delta n_t + \alpha \Delta h_t + \Delta a_t,$$

where n_t is equal to the log ratio of natural resources to labor inputs. γ is the ratio of natural resources in the total economy and measured by total natural resources rent as a percent of GDP, obtained from the World Bank's World Development Indicators. Therefore, TFP growth measures, which ignore the contribution of natural resources, are upward biased when the ratio of physical capital to labor in an economy is higher than the ratio of inputs of natural resources to labor and vice versa. Although including natural capital in growth accounting makes a nonnegligible difference in TFP growth calculations in resource-abundant countries, it is not the basic focus of the chapter because the difference is not substantial in aggregate for EMDEs (figure B1.1.1).

New technologies and output mismeasurement. There have been concerns that quality improvements in information and communication technology (ICT) have not been accurately captured in national accounts measures of output. Official national accounts may have underestimated quality improvements of new devices, leading price deflators for ICT to understate the true price declines in these assets, while nonmarket technologies such as search engines and social media provide consumer benefit without contributing to output (Brynjolfsson and Collis 2019; Hatzius et al. 2016). Mismeasurement of new ICT products could, therefore, explain some of the slowdown in measured productivity growth that has occurred since the global financial crisis. Some studies find evidence of mismeasurement in both the pre- and postcrisis periods, such that mismeasurement explains little of the slowdown in measured productivity (Byrne, Fernald, and Reinsdorf 2016). Others find evidence of sizable mismeasurement and attribute part of the U.S. productivity slowdown to measurement biases, particularly due to the increasing share of the services sector

BOX 1.1 Productivity: Conceptual considerations and measurement challenges (*continued*)

FIGURE B1.1.1 Labor productivity decomposition and natural capital in EMDEs

The decomposition of labor productivity without taking natural capital into account could be misleading, especially for resource-rich countries. However, because the bias in TFP can be either positive or negative depending on the relative growth rates of physical and natural capital, the difference becomes very small when aggregating the decomposition up for large country groups such as EMDEs.

A. Decomposition without natural capital

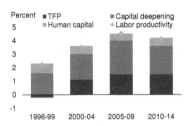

B. Decomposition with natural capital

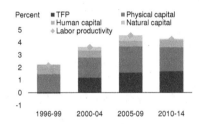

Source: World Bank.
Note: Aggregate growth rates are GDP-weighted at constant 2010 prices and exchange rates. EMDE = emerging market and developing economy; TFP = total factor productivity.
A. B. Sample consists of 74 EMDEs for the period 1996-2014.

in output (Brynjolfsson and McAfee 2014; Feldstein 2017). Overall, despite some evidence for mismeasurement, it is unlikely that a significant part of the broad-based slowdown in productivity growth since the global financial crisis can be explained by mismeasurement alone (Cerra and Saxena 2017; Syverson 2016). Where mismeasurement has been uncovered, it has been found to be present in larger, or equally significant, scale in earlier periods.

Delayed adoption. A further view is that the wave of new digital technologies that have been developed can take extended periods of time to incorporate into production processes, suggesting that productivity is likely to pick up rapidly in the future. This view notes that the industrial revolution in the early nineteenth century and the electrification of production in the early twentieth century took decades to result in a material improvement in measured productivity, particularly TFP (David 1990). Current intangible investment in ICT technologies may, therefore, be undercounted in current national accounts and then subsequently overaccounted for as these technologies return higher production efficiency as they are incorporated into production on a broad basis (Brynjolfsson, Rock, and Syverson 2018).

period (2003-07) to low levels relative to the 1980s, primarily due to a slowdown in European economies, and had recovered to grow close to its longer-term pre-GFC average (0.4 percent over 1998-2007).[8]

- *EMDEs.* The post-GFC slowdown in EMDE productivity growth reflected, in approximately equal measure, investment weakness and slowing TFP growth. In commodity exporters, the contribution of capital accumulation faded almost entirely, after having accounted for about half of productivity growth before the GFC. This was compounded by contracting TFP growth, which had accounted for most of the remainder of pre-GFC productivity growth. Investment stalled or contracted in commodity exporters during the commodity prices collapse of 2011- 16 (Aslam et al. 2016; World Bank 2017). In commodity importers, capital deepening has slowed since the GFC, reflecting diminishing growth prospects and heightened uncertainty. In the early 2000s, TFP was boosted by reforms that allowed greater foreign direct investment (FDI) inflows in the 1990s and China's World Trade Organization accession in 2001, which unleashed a productivity boom in China and its trading partners, while a decade of reforms oriented to the service sector boosted productivity in India in the 1990s and 2000s (Bosworth and Collins 2008; He and Zhang 2010; Tuan, Ng, and Zhao 2009).

- *LICs.* In LICs, public infrastructure investment and business climate improvements supported post-GFC output and productivity growth (World Bank 2019b). This followed on the heels of a decade of heavy investment into mines and oil fields amid surging precrisis commodity prices. As a result, continued post-GFC strength in productivity growth reflected increased capital accumulation. Modest improvements in human capital partly offset increasingly negative TFP growth in these economies. A continued concentration in the agricultural and extractives sectors has led to low technological progress, with additional negative shocks from conflict and high levels of debt in the 1980s and 1990s also contributing to frequently negative TFP growth (Claessens et al. 1997; IMF 2014).

- *EMDE regions.* Capital accumulation accounted for virtually all of the post-GFC slowdown in productivity growth in MNA, where oil-exporting EMDEs suffered stalled or contracting investment amid the oil price collapse of 2014-16 (Stocker et al. 2018). It also accounted for most of the slowdown in ECA, whose banking systems were hard-hit by the euro area crisis and the subsequent retreat from the region of European Union-headquartered banks (Arteta and Kasyanenko 2019). In EAP, a deliberate policy-guided public investment slowdown in China has been under way and slower capital accumulation accounted for about two-fifths of the slowdown in post-GFC productivity growth. In SSA, which hosts most LICs, and

---

[8] Much of the recent discussion of advanced economy TFP growth has focused on the slowdown in the United States, where TFP weakened further after the crisis following a surge from the mid-1990s to 2000s (Fernald et al. 2017; Gordon 2018). In contrast, average TFP growth was much lower in the precrisis period in major European economies such as France and Germany (0.3-0.4), and even negative in Italy (-0.7), such that the postcrisis TFP slowdown is much less pronounced for advanced economies in aggregate.

in LAC, the slowdown was entirely driven by declining TFP growth. In contrast to other EMDE regions, TFP growth strengthened in MNA, from negative pre-GFC rates amid heavy resource investment, and was stable in SAR, which was less affected than other regions by the disruptions of the GFC.

Natural capital. In many resource-rich countries, natural resources are an important input into production. In these cases, without taking into account the inputs of natural resources, the decomposition of labor productivity may be misleading. Although the aggregate effects of natural capital for EMDEs are small, effects are larger for some resource-rich economies (box 1.1; chapter 5).

Sectoral productivity growth

Approach. Higher aggregate productivity growth in EMDEs in the pre-GFC period was associated with a reallocation of resources toward more productive sectors in addition to productivity growth within sectors (Diao, McMillan, and Rodrik 2017). More recently, pre-GFC gains from such reallocation appear to have faded. This is illustrated in a decomposition of economy-wide labor productivity growth into within- and between-sector productivity growth for up to 103 economies during 1995-2017 (chapter 7).

Post-GFC slowdown broad-based across sectors. The post-GFC slowdown in manufacturing productivity growth in EMDEs was the largest among the nine sectors (figure 1.4). However, the slowdown in EMDEs affected most sectors. The service sectors have grown rapidly over the past two decades, supporting aggregate productivity growth in EMDEs alongside rapid manufacturing growth. However, there has been a slowing contribution to aggregate productivity growth since the crisis, particularly from the finance and transport service sectors. LICs suffered even more than other EMDEs from a productivity slowdown in their agriculture sector, which coincided with a broad-based decline in commodity prices since 2011.

Fading gains from factor reallocation in EMDEs. In EMDEs, about one-half of the post-GFC (2013-17) slowdown in productivity growth from pre-GFC (2003-08) averages reflected fading gains from resource reallocation toward more productive sectors (figure 1.4). In the 1990s and before the GFC, such resource reallocation had accounted for more than two-fifths of average labor productivity growth, in line with earlier findings (Diao, McMillan, and Rodrik 2017). Productivity gains from such a reallocation were particularly large in Sub-Saharan Africa, where they accounted for more than half of productivity growth during 2003-08, amid a large fall in the share of agricultural employment.

After the GFC, the contribution of reallocation to aggregate productivity growth fell to one-third on average in EMDEs. To some degree as countries reach middle- to high-income status, sectoral reallocation tends to become a less important driver of productivity growth (Mason and Shetty 2019; Nicola, Kehayova, and Nguyen 2018). In addition, technological and knowledge spillovers between sectors may also be diminishing (Foerster et al. 2019). However, productivity gaps between sectors in

FIGURE 1.4 **Sectoral contributions to the postcrisis productivity slowdown**

During the postcrisis period, aggregate productivity growth slowed among EMDEs. About half of the weakness reflected slower within-sector productivity growth in manufacturing and financial services. In LICs, the slowdown was concentrated in agriculture. In addition to weaker within-sector growth, fading gains from resource reallocation toward more productive sectors have accounted for about one-third of the postcrisis slowdown in productivity growth. Within-sector productivity growth has also slowed.

A. Contribution to productivity growth between 2003-08 and 2013-17

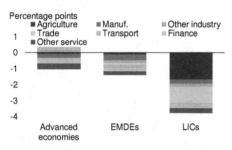

B. Within- and between-sector contributions to productivity growth

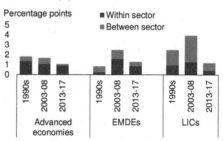

Source: World Bank.
Note: Based on samples of 54 countries during 1975-95, 94 countries during 1995-99, and 103 countries during 2003-17. EMDEs = emerging market and developing economies; LICs = low-income countries.
A. "Other industry" includes mining, utilities, and construction; "Finance" includes business services; "Other service" includes government and personal services. For advanced economies, the precrisis growth is calculated as the average during 2003-07, due to the earlier crisis-related impact on productivity growth.
B. Growth within sector shows the contribution of initial real value-added weighted productivity growth rate and structural change effect given the contribution arising from changes in the employment share. Median of the country-specific contributions.

EMDEs remain substantial, suggesting that potential gains from further reallocation remain sizable.

Fading gains from reallocation away from agriculture in LICs. In LICs, agriculture accounts for 60 percent of employment, on average, but agricultural productivity is low (Cusolito and Maloney 2018). As a result, a reallocation of employment, especially from agriculture, to higher-productivity sectors accounted for almost two-thirds of LIC productivity growth before the GFC (chapter 7). Since then, this engine of LIC productivity growth appears to have stalled. In part, this is due to a collapse in global industrial commodity prices having discouraged further growth in employment in the mining and extraction sectors, which have above-average productivity levels in LICs. Despite having high productivity levels, the mining and extraction sectors often offer limited scope for expanding employment outside of commodity booms, and therefore few opportunities for sustainable sectoral reallocation.

Drivers of productivity growth synchronization

Limitations of growth accounting. The standard growth accounting framework has limitations. TFP growth can be affected not only by factors such as technological and organizational changes but also by changing levels of capital and labor utilization, which are frequently associated with demand-side drivers (Basu, Fernald, and Kimball 2006;

Fernald and Wang 2016).[9] Therefore traditional estimates of TFP may over- or understate the true change in the influence of supply-side drivers on productivity. Factor inputs can be adjusted using observable proxies for factor utilization, but data requirements for this approach—in particular, annual data on the sectoral distribution of hours worked, employment, and capital—are prohibitive for most EMDEs.[10]

Methodology. A complementary approach to the growth accounting decomposition is to estimate the underlying drivers of labor productivity having removed cyclical or demand-led components of productivity growth. Using structural vector auto-regressions (SVARs), *persistent* or *permanent* variations in productivity can be identified (chapter 6).[11] These are assumed to reflect lasting influences on productivity, such as changing production technologies, in contrast to changing factor utilization. As it is common in the literature, these components will henceforth be referred to as "technology." However, this is a generic term that reflects new technologies and can also include a range of other persistent factors such as improved resource allocation driven by organizational or institutional changes (Chen and Wemy 2015; Fisher 2006; Francis and Ramey 2005).

Removing cyclical factors from the labor productivity collapse of 2007-09. Cyclical factors such as changing factor utilization explain about half or more of the slowdown in advanced economies and EMDEs during the collapse in labor productivity growth during 2007-09 (figure 1.5). In the years ahead of the GFC, EMDEs experienced a large surge in productivity growth, which suddenly receded, particularly in 2009. In the longer term, the slowdown has become dominated by noncyclical factors. The finding that the longer-term productivity slowdown following the GFC is a largely structural phenomenon has been observed in utilization-adjusted measures of TFP in the United States and several major European economies (Byrne, Fernald, and Reinsdorf 2016; Comin et al. 2019; Goodridge, Haskel, and Wallis 2018). In some cases, weaker demand due to crises has been found to generate slower technological progress over the medium to long term. In addition to the lasting effects of weaker investment and capital deepening, costly development and adoption of technology may be delayed or reduced, generating further scarring effects (Adler et al. 2017; Anzoategui et al. 2019). However, the extent of the fall across regions and EMDE commodity importers and exporters has varied widely.

---

[9] In the United States, one-half of TFP growth variability has been attributed to demand-driven factors (Basu, Fernald, and Kimball 2006).

[10] Adler et al. (2017); Basu, Fernald, and Kimball (2006); Comin et al. (2019); Duval et al. (2020); and Levchenko and Pandalai-Nayar (2018) have implemented these for advanced economies other than the United States, but not for EMDEs. A second difficulty with this approach is the possibility of a wide range of structural relationships between different inputs to production, preventing the application of this methodology on a broad basis. For example, labor markets may be inflexible around the number of hours worked, making it a poor proxy for utilization.

[11] Importantly, this identification does not impose the condition that no other shocks can have permanent impacts on productivity, as is the case with long-run identifications. A similar methodology has been used to assess shocks that drive business cycle movements in a range of macroeconomic variables, which allows the identification of demand drivers of the macroeconomy (Angeletos, Collard, and Dellas 2018).

FIGURE 1.5 Role of cyclical factors in the GFC productivity slowdown

Cyclical factors such as changing factor utilization explain one-half or more of the labor productivity slowdown during the global financial crisis (GFC), and a proportion of the postcrisis slowdown (about one-third). A measure of labor productivity that removes the effects of changing utilization of factor inputs (and other less persistent demand-side drivers of productivity), "technology," has declined significantly since the GFC but by different magnitudes across EMDE regions, suggesting different degrees of scarring from the crisis.

A. Labor productivity growth change 2007-09: Advanced economies and EMDEs

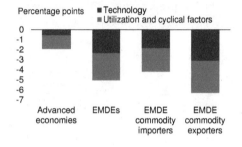

B. Labor productivity growth change 2007-09: EMDE regions

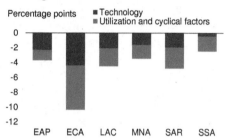

C. Slowdown 2013-18 relative to precrisis period: Advanced economies and EMDEs

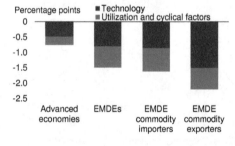

D. Productivity growth 2013-18 relative to precrisis period: EMDE regions

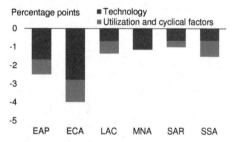

Source: World Bank.
Note: The "technology" contribution to labor productivity growth consists of the contribution of the Spectral SVAR-identified technology shock in addition to the contribution from the constant and initial condition in the SVAR, which can also be considered long-term processes. Utilization and cyclical factor contributions are defined as the residual of the contribution of "technology" and labor productivity growth. See annex 1A for further details. Sample of 32 advanced economies and 96 EMDEs, including 65 commodity exporters and 31 commodity importers. EAP = East Asia and Pacific; ECA = Europe and Central Asia; EMDEs = emerging market and developing economies; GFC = global financial crisis; LAC = Latin America and the Caribbean; MNA = Middle East and North Africa; SAR = South Asia; SSA = Sub-Saharan Africa; SVAR = structural vector autoregression.
A.B. Contributions to labor productivity slowdown during 2007-09.
C.D. Precrisis period defined as 2003-07 for advanced economies, and 2003-08 for EMDEs.

Role of cyclical factors in productivity synchronization

The broad-based decline in productivity growth since the GFC in both advanced economies and EMDEs in all regions suggests the presence of common factors or spillovers. A large literature has already documented the comovement of output across economies (Francis, Owyang, and Savascin 2017; Francis, Owyang, and Soques 2019; Kose, Otrok, and Whiteman 2003). The strong correlation between output growth and labor productivity growth (70 percent on average) raises the possibility of common determinants of productivity developments across economies. The cross-country synchronization of labor productivity growth, and the extent to which it is driven by demand or supply-side factors, has so far been underexplored. The literature that does exist has focused on advanced economy synchronization and has found some comovement in cyclical drivers of productivity but little in longer term developments, such as the pace of technological change. This contrasts with expectations of increasingly rapid diffusion of new production technologies and techniques through trade and the development of global value chains, FDI, and other global financial flows along with the increased presence of multinational corporations and the internet.

Evidence on cross-country productivity comovement. Evidence on the comovement of productivity across countries has so far focused on the synchronization of TFP, and not yet explored the degree to which labor productivity is synchronized across countries. In advanced economies, although unadjusted measures of TFP are correlated, utilization-adjusted TFP, a similar measure to the SVAR-identified technology, is found to be uncorrelated across countries (Huo, Levchenko, and Pandalai-Nayar 2019; Imbs 1999). Finally, in a factor modeling framework, TFP growth is shown to be one of the most important correlates of common developments in GDP growth (Abate and Serven 2019; Crucini, Kose, and Otrok 2011). These studies have therefore concluded that changes in productivity are a key correlate of cross-country business cycle synchronization.

Evidence of spillovers. SVARs point to the presence of cointegration between TFP in the United States and other economies but with slow and limited spillovers (Mandelman et al. 2011; Miyamoto and Nguyen 2017). In a broader data set, utilization-adjusted U.S. TFP has been found to have spillover effects on TFP growth in other advanced economies but only at very gradual rates (Adler et al. 2017). An alternative and growing strand of the literature has highlighted the role of slow technological diffusion between leading and lagging firms across advanced economies (Andrews, Criscuolo, and Gal 2015; Cirera and Maloney 2017; OECD 2015). Long lags in the adoption and intensity of use of new technologies have been found to explain a material proportion of cross-country income divergence (Comin and Hobijn 2010; Comin and Mestieri 2018). Both approaches, based on firm- and country-level data, emphasize that structural improvements in productivity can diffuse across borders primarily over long time lags, implying that structural measures of productivity synchronization are low.

Methodology. Cross-country correlations provide an insight into the extent to which different measures of productivity are synchronized. This approach is applied to labor productivity growth, TFP growth, and the SVAR-identified technology measure. Average correlations provide a summary statistic of synchronization within groups of economies (IMF 2013).[12]

---

[12] An alternative approach to assessing the synchronization of different measures of productivity would be to estimate the contribution of common factors to productivity variation. However, common factors may explain a large proportion of the variance of productivity, while at the same time having opposite effects on different economies (productivity growth can rise in one country and fall in another). Correlation analysis is a better tool to assess the extent to which common directional variation is prevalent across economies.

Results—cyclical contribution to labor productivity synchronization. The average 10-year rolling correlation between all bilateral pairs of economies for each measure of productivity growth suggests that global synchronization of productivity was very low before the onset of the GFC (figure 1.6). During the GFC and its immediate aftermath, correlations rose for all measures of productivity growth. Correlations between those measures with sizable demand-driven cyclical components (labor productivity and TFP growth) were considerably higher than those for the SVAR-identified technology shocks, which exclude these components. This result is consistent with previous findings for advanced economies (Huo, Levchenko, and Pandalai-Nayar 2019; Imbs 1999). Using a shorter rolling sample window, the correlations of labor productivity and TFP have also returned close to zero shortly after the GFC, adding further evidence that the decline was a largely cyclical phenomenon (figure 1.7).

Slow pace of technology diffusion. According to these correlations, productivity synchronization in both advanced economies and EMDEs appears to be a largely cyclical phenomenon. Advanced economies featured higher cross-country correlations of labor productivity and TFP than EMDEs over this period. Since 2005, LIC productivity growth has been largely unsynchronized even during the GFC, plausibly reflecting limited trade integration and the effects of idiosyncratic shocks. Low average correlations of the SVAR-identified technology measure do not rule out transfers of productivity-enhancing technology across countries over the long-term. However, low synchronization of structural measures of productivity growth supports findings of very low average rates of productivity convergence for most EMDEs with advanced economies, suggesting slow or nonexistent levels of technology adoption (chapter 5).

Sizable cyclical productivity spillovers. The high degree of cyclical comovement of TFP and labor productivity growth during the GFC suggests a sizable labor productivity and TFP growth slowdown could occur during the COVID-19 recession. Some of these factors are likely to have scarring effects through a reduction in investment and endogenous technology adoption. However, a more complex set of headwinds and country-specific characteristics has influenced the extent of the longer-term post-GFC slowdowns in advanced economies and EMDEs, which have varied widely across regions and economies, limiting their synchronization.

Conclusion

The weakness in productivity growth during and after the GFC is estimated to stem from both a common cyclical demand shock and a wide range of structural headwinds. To prevent lasting negative effects from an additional synchronized negative shock due to COVID-19, EMDEs will require a range of policy actions.

Weakening investment. The postcrisis period has been characterized by pronounced investment weakness reflecting adverse terms-of-trade shocks for commodity exporters, slowing FDI inflows for commodity importers, spillovers from growth weakness in advanced economies, heightened policy uncertainty, and private debt burdens (World

FIGURE 1.6 Synchronization of productivity measures: 10-year rolling correlations

Globally, TFP and labor productivity have shown a material pickup in synchronization since the global financial crisis. However, a large proportion of this synchronization reflects nontechnology spillovers from factors such as demand developments—SVAR-identified technology developments, which exclude business cycle factors, have remained uncorrelated. A similar pattern emerges in the synchronization within advanced economies, and EMDEs, which show a lower average level of cross-country correlation for all measures. In contrast, the synchronization of all productivity measures has remained subdued in LICs since the early 2000s.

A. Average correlation: World

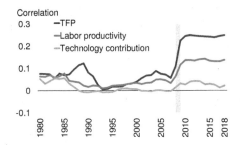

B. Average correlation: Advanced economies

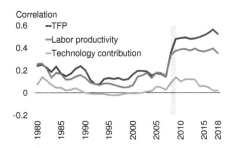

C. Average correlation: EMDEs

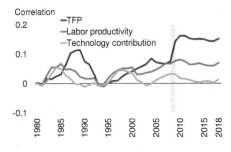

D. Average correlation: LICs

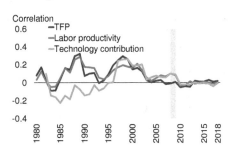

Source: World Bank.
Note: EMDE = emerging market and developing economy; LIC = low-income country; SVAR = structural vector autoregression; TFP = total factor productivity.
A.-D. Ten-year rolling correlations. Simple average across all bilateral pairs of economies for each measure of productivity. The "technology" measure is the contribution of "technology" drivers to productivity growth. This measure removes cyclical components that are present in labor productivity and TFP growth. Sample includes 24 advanced economies and 74 EMDEs, including 6 LICs, with data available for all measures since at least 1981.

Bank 2017). The legacy of weak investment since the GFC and the diminishing long-term outlook for investment growth raise concerns about future productivity growth (World Bank 2019b). Moreover, subdued investment growth, especially in sectors dependent on research and development, can hinder technological progress and TFP growth through weaker capital-embodied technological change (Adler et al. 2017). A range of policies to encourage public sector investment and foster private sector investment can spur labor productivity growth (chapter 4). Major financial crises, pandemics, and commodity price shocks have been found to have lasting negative consequences for labor productivity, particularly through the capital deepening channel,

FIGURE 1.7 Synchronization of productivity measures: Five-year rolling correlations

A smaller rolling window for correlations is more volatile, but shows that the increase in correlations of measures of productivity containing cyclical components faded shortly after the global financial crisis.

A. Average correlation: World

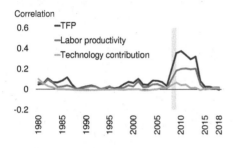

B. Average correlation: Advanced economies

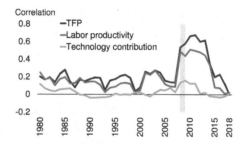

C. Average correlation: EMDEs

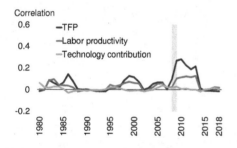

D. Average correlation: LICs

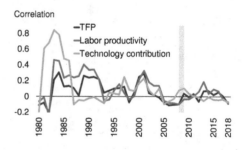

Source: World Bank.
Note: EMDE = emerging market and developing economy; LIC = low income country; SVAR = structural vector autoregression; TFP = total factor productivity.
A.-D. Five-year rolling correlations. Simple average across all bilateral pairs of economies for each measure of productivity. The "technology" measure is the contribution of "technology" drivers to productivity growth. This measure removes cyclical components that are present in labor productivity and TFP growth. Sample includes 24 advanced economies and 74 EMDEs, including 6 LICs, with data available for all measures since at least 1981.

highlighting the importance of countercyclical policy to counteract the effects of the global recession driven by COVID-19 (chapters 2 and 5).

Slower sectoral transformation. Sectoral reallocation from agriculture to manufacturing has historically been an important driver of growth, particularly for EMDEs. However, this transformation has slowed since the GFC. The rising complexity and automation of the manufacturing sector and sectoral distortions have made it increasingly difficult for employment to switch to high-productivity sectors. Nonetheless, there remain opportunities for EMDEs to raise productivity in agriculture, which remains the most important sector for many countries, and to shift activity toward high-productivity service sectors (chapter 7).

Slower growth at the technology frontier. There has been a broad-based slowdown in both labor productivity and TFP growth in advanced economies since the 1990s, with limited signs of an impending upturn. However, there are mixed views on the prospects of groundbreaking technological progress that could return growth to historical norms and spill over to EMDEs. On the one hand, the impact on productivity growth of modern innovations seems to be reduced compared to those of the twentieth century (Fernald 2015; Gordon 2016). On the other, recently introduced new digital technologies and those on the horizon such as artificial intelligence and innovations in ICT sectors may begin to feed through to measured productivity (Cusolito and Maloney 2018). Some of these innovations may require time to be widely adopted into production processes, resulting in an acceleration of productivity growth only after a long lag (Brynjolfsson, Rock, and Syverson 2018). This process may be accelerated as some innovations have been utilized and adopted more intensively because of social distancing measures to restrain COVID-19.

Cyclical drivers dominate synchronized labor productivity developments. Global recessions and slowdowns are generally accompanied by sharp declines in labor productivity and TFP growth. The demand-driven component of productivity growth was the dominant driver of the synchronized nature of the slowdown during the GFC, but the degree of synchronization faded shortly after the crisis. The longer-term degree of slowing productivity growth, and the changing pace of convergence, has varied widely across EMDE commodity exporters and importers, and EMDE regions. More generally, low average synchronization of labor productivity growth outside of cyclical downturns and recoveries suggests a weak and delayed degree of technology transfer and adoption across economies. EMDEs may foster trade integration, FDI, and economic flexibility so they can benefit to a greater extent from technology spillovers, which currently appear to be limited in many economies (chapter 4).

Broad range of productivity growth trends across EMDE regions. Longer-term developments in productivity growth have been highly diverse across advanced economies, EMDEs, and EMDE regions. Commodity exporters have experienced substantially lower average rates of labor productivity growth over the past 40 years, and have proved less resilient in the aftermath of the GFC than more diversified economies. Many EMDEs have continued to foster positive climates for investment growth and technology adoption, albeit at a reduced pace relative to the pre-GFC period. The importance of a range of correlates for driving cross-country differentials in long-run productivity growth is further explored in chapter 2 and chapter 4. These hold important lessons that could limit permanent damage from the COVID-19 pandemic.

Future research. The dynamics in global productivity growth around the GFC—with an appreciable acceleration beforehand, followed by a sustained slump thereafter—merits further study. In particular, future research could dig more deeply into the extent that pre-GFC productivity growth in EMDEs was linked to favorable external conditions, as embodied in rising exports and high commodity prices, and the extent that it was the result of domestic reforms. In particular, positive developments can be shaped by a set of drivers, which are examined in the next chapter.

ANNEX 1A Cyclical and technology-driven labor productivity developments

This annex describes the SVAR used to separate supply (technology) and demand-side influences on labor productivity growth. The methodology used to identify supply-side "technology" drivers of labor productivity uses a Spectral identification. "Technology" shocks are identified as those that explain the majority of productivity fluctuations at frequencies longer than 10 years—this approach disregards fluctuations at higher (shorter) frequencies and is robust to contamination in economies where productivity is affected by many other factors such as demand shocks. This approach identifies long-lasting innovations to labor productivity, assuming that these highly persistent changes are likely to consist of structural supply-side factors. The methodology is further explored in chapter 6.

Estimation

Each SVAR is estimated using annual data and consists of the natural log-difference of labor productivity, the log-level of employment, the share of investment and separately consumption in GDP, the consumer price inflation rate, and, where available, the short-term policy interest rate. Table 1A.1 provides summary statistics on the data length available in each income group.

TABLE 1A.1 Median sample periods

	Labor productivity	TFP	Spectral
AEs	1962-2018	1951-2018	1973-2018
EMDEs	1972-2018	1971-2018	1981-2018
LICs	1981-2018	1981-2018	1981-2018

Source: World Bank.
Note: AEs = advanced economies; EMDEs = emerging market and developing economies; LICs = low-income countries; TFP = total factor productivity.

Shock decomposition

The decomposition for each region or income grouping is based on individual estimations which are aggregated using GDP weights on GDP at 2010 U.S. dollar prices and exchange rates.

Historical decompositions of labor productivity growth, Y_t, can be written as a function of the structural shocks identified through the Spectral identification ϵ_t, initial condition X_0 (which accounts for the lack of data before the start of the sample), and the constant, C:

$$Y_t = \sum_{i=0}^{t-1} F^i \epsilon_{t-i} + A^t X_0 + \sum_{i=0}^{t-1} F^i C.$$

In the decompositions shown in figure 1.5, the identified technology shock, initial condition, and constants are included in the "technology" category, given that they reflect average rates of growth and persistent effects from initial conditions, such as long-run trends. The effects of all other shocks are included in the nontechnology category. The estimation used for the historical decomposition includes labor productivity in growth rates. This is because the effects of initial conditions can be substantial in unit-root or highly persistent processes such as labor productivity levels. In the estimation on growth rates, the change in the contribution of the initial condition over time is minimal given the stationary nature of productivity growth.

References

Abate, G. D., and L. Serven. 2019. "Adding Space to the International Business Cycle." Policy Research Working Paper 8786, World Bank, Washington, DC.

ADB (Asian Development Bank). 2017. *Asian Development Outlook: Transcending the Middle-Income Challenge*. Manila: Asian Development Bank.

Adler, G., R. Duval, D. Furceri, S. Kilic Celik, K. Koloskova, and M. Poplawski-Ribeiro. 2017. "Gone with the Headwinds: Global Productivity." IMF Staff Discussion Note 17/04, International Monetary Fund, Washington, DC.

Andrews, D., C. Criscuolo, and P. Gal. 2015. "Frontier Firms, Technology Diffusion and Public Policy: Micro Evidence from OECD Countries." Organisation for Economic Co-operation and Development, Paris.

Angeletos, G.-M., F. Collard, and H. Dellas. 2018. "Business Cycle Anatomy." NBER Working Paper 24875, National Bureau of Economic Research, Cambridge, MA.

Anzoategui, D., D. Comin, M. Gertler, and J. Martinez. 2019. "Endogenous Technology Adoption and R&D as Sources of Business Cycle Persistence." *American Economic Journal: Macroeconomics* 11 (3): 67–110.

Arteta, C., and S. Kasyanenko. 2019. "Financial Market Developments." In *A Decade after the Global Recession: Lessons and Challenges for Emerging and Developing Economies*, edited by M. A. Kose and F. Ohnsorge. Washington, DC: World Bank.

Aslam, A., S. Beidas-Strom, R. Bems, O. Celasun, S. Kilic Celik, and Z. Koczan. 2016. "Trading on Their Terms? Commodity Exporters in the Aftermath of the Commodity Boom." IMF Working Paper 16/27, International Monetary Fund, Washington, DC.

Baqaee, D., and E. Farhi. 2018. "The Microeconomic Foundations of Aggregate Production Functions." NBER Working Paper 2593, National Bureau of Economic Research, Cambridge, MA.

Barro R., and J. Lee. 2015. *Education Matters: Global Schooling Gains from the 19th to the 21st Century*. New York: Oxford University Press.

Basu, S., J. G. Fernald, and M. S. Kimball. 2006. "Are Technology Improvements Contractionary?" *American Economic Review* 96 (5): 1418–48.

Bosworth, B., and S. M. Collins. 2008. "Accounting for Growth: Comparing China and India." *Journal of Economic Perspectives* 22 (1): 45–66.

Brynjolfsson, E., and A. Collis. 2019. "How Should We Measure the Digital Economy?" *Harvard Business Review* 97(6): 140–48.

Brynjolfsson, E., and A. McAfee. 2014. *The Second Machine Age: Work, Progress, and Prosperity in a Time of Brilliant Technologies*. New York: W.W. Norton & Co.

Brynjolfsson, E., D. Rock, and C. Syverson. 2018. "The Productivity J-Curve: How Intangibles Complement General Purpose Technologies." NBER Working Paper 25148, National Bureau of Economic Research, Cambridge, MA.

Byrne, D. M., J. G. Fernald, and M. B. Reinsdorf. 2016. "Does the United States Have a Productivity Slowdown or a Measurement Problem?" *Brookings Papers on Economic Activity* (Spring): 109–15.

Caselli, F. 2005. "Accounting for Cross-Country Income Differences." In *Handbook of Economic Growth*, edited by Philippe Aghion and Steven N. Durlauf, 1:679–741. Amsterdam,: Elsevier.

Cerra, V., and S. C. Saxena. 2017. "Booms, Crises, and Recoveries: A New Paradigm of the Business Cycle and Its Policy Implications." IMF Working Paper 17/250, International Monetary Fund, Washington, DC.

Charmes, J. 2012. "The Informal Economy Worldwide: Trends and Characteristics." *Margin: The Journal of Applied Economic Research* 6 (2): 103–32.

Chen, K., and E. Wemy. 2015. "Investment-Specific Technological Changes: The Source of Long-Run TFP Fluctuations." *European Economic Review* 80 (November): 230–52.

Cirera, X., and W. F. Maloney. 2017. *The Innovation Paradox: Developing-Country Capabilities and the Unrealized Promise of Technological Catch-Up*. Washington, DC: World Bank.

Claessens, S., E. Detragiache, R. Kanbur, and P. Wickham. 1997. "HIPCs' Debt Review of the Issues." *Journal of African Economies* 6 (2): 231–54.

Comin, D., and B. Hobijn. 2010. "An Exploration of Technology Diffusion." *American Economic Review* 100 (5): 2031–59.

Comin, D., and M. Mestieri. 2018. "If Technology Has Arrived Everywhere, Why Has Income Diverged?" *American Economic Journal: Macroeconomics* 10 (3): 137–78.

Comin, D., J. Quintana, T. Schmitz, and A. Trigari. 2019. "A New Measure of Utilization-Adjusted TFP Growth for European Countries." FRAME Final Policy Conference, Centre for Economic Policy Research, London.

Crucini, M. J., M. A. Kose, and C. Otrok. 2011. "What Are the Driving Forces of International Business Cycles?" *Review of Economic Dynamics* 14 (1): 156–75.

Cusolito, A. P., and W. F. Maloney. 2018. *Productivity Revisited—Shifting Paradigms in Analysis and Policy*. Washington, DC: World Bank.

Dabla-Norris, E., S. Guo, V. Haksar, M. Kim, K. Kochhar, K. Wiseman, and A. Zdzienicka. 2015. "The New Normal: A Sector-Level Perspective on Productivity Trends in Advanced Economies." IMF Staff Discussion Note 15/03, International Monetary Fund, Washington, DC.

David, P. A. 1990. "The Dynamo and the Computer: An Historical Perspective on the Modern Productivity Paradox." *American Economic Review* 80 (2): 355–61.

Diao, X., M. McMillan, and D. Rodrik. 2017. "The Recent Growth Boom in Developing Economies: A Structural Change Perspective." NBER Working Paper 23132, National Bureau of Economic Research, Cambridge, MA.

Dribe, M., M. Breschi, A. Gagnon, D. Gauvreau, H. A. Hanson, T. N. Maloney, S. Mazzoni, et al. 2017. "Socio-Economic Status and Fertility Decline: Insights from Historical Transitions in Europe and North America." *Population Studies* 71 (1): 3–21.

Duval, R., D. Furceri, S. Kilic Celik, and M. Poplawski-Ribeiro. 2020. "Productivity Spillovers in Advanced Economies." IMF Working Paper, International Monetary Fund, Washington, DC.

Duval, R., G. H. Hong, and Y. Timmer. 2017. "Financial Frictions and the Great Productivity Slowdown." IMF Working Papers 17/129, International Monetary Fund, Washington, DC.

ECB (European Central Bank). 2017. "The Slowdown in Euro Area Productivity in a Global Context." ECB Economic Bulletin 3/2017, European Central Bank, Frankfurt.

Fajnzylber, P., W. F. Maloney, and G. V. Montes-Rojas. 2011. "Does Formality Improve Micro-Firm Performance? Evidence from the Brazilian SIMPLES Program." *Journal of Development Economics* 94 (2): 262–76.

Feenstra, R. C., R. Inklaar, and M. P. Timmer. 2015. "The Next Generation of the Penn World Table." *American Economic Review* 105 (10): 3150–82.

Feldstein, M. 2017. "Underestimating the Real Growth of GDP, Personal Income, and Productivity." *Journal of Economic Perspectives* 31(2): 145-64.

Fernald, J. 2012. "A Quarterly, Utilization-Adjusted Series on Total Factor Productivity." Working Paper 2012–19, Federal Reserve Bank of San Francisco.

Fernald, J. 2015. "Productivity and Potential Output before, during, and after the Great Recession." Working Paper 2014-15, Federal Reserve Bank of San Francisco.

Fernald, J., R. E. Hall, J. H. Stock, and M. W. Watson. 2017. "The Disappointing Recovery Of Output after 2009." NBER Working Paper 23543, National Bureau of Economic Research, Cambridge, MA.

Fernald J., and R. Inklaar. 2020. "Does Disappointing European Productivity Growth Reflect a Slowing Trend? Weighing the Evidence and Assessing the Future." *International Productivity Monitor, Centre for the Study of Living Standards* 38 (Spring): 104–35.

Fernald, J., and J. C. Wang. 2016. "Why Has the Cyclicality of Productivity Changed? What Does It Mean?" *Annual Review of Economics* 8 (1): 465–96.

Fisher, J. D. M. 2006. "The Dynamic Effects of Neutral and Investment-Specific Technology Shocks." *Journal of Political Economy* 114 (3): 413–51.

Foerster, A., A. Hornstein, P.-D. Sarte, and M. Watson. 2019. "Aggregate Implications of Changing Sectoral Trends." Working Paper 2019-16, Federal Reserve Bank of San Francisco.

Francis, N., M. T. Owyang, and O. Savascin. 2017. "An Endogenously Clustered Factor Approach to International Business Cycles." *Journal of Applied Econometrics* 32 (7): 1261–76.

Francis, N., M. T. Owyang, and D. Soques. 2019. "Business Cycles Across Space and Time." Working Paper 2019-010A, Federal Reserve Bank of St. Louis.

Francis, N., and V. A. Ramey. 2005. "Is the Technology-Driven Real Business Cycle Hypothesis Dead? Shocks and Aggregate Fluctuations Revisited." *Journal of Monetary Economics* 52 (8): 1379–99.

Goodridge, P., J. Haskel, and G. Wallis. 2018. "Accounting for the U.K. Productivity Puzzle: A Decomposition and Predictions." *Economica* 85 (339): 581–605.

Gopinath, G., Ş. Kalemli-Özcan, L. Karabarbounis, and C. Villegas-Sanchez. 2017. "Capital Allocation and Productivity in South Europe." *Quarterly Journal of Economics* 132 (4): 1915–67.

Gordon, R. J. 2012. "Is U.S. Economic Growth Over? Faltering Innovation Confronts the Six Headwinds." NBER Working Paper 18315, National Bureau of Economic Research, Cambridge, MA.

Gordon, R. J. 2016. *The Rise and Fall of American Growth: The U.S. Standard of Living since the Civil War*. New Jersey: Princeton University Press.

Gordon, R. J. 2018. "Why Has Economic Growth Slowed When Innovation Appears to Be Accelerating?" NBER Working Paper 24554, National Bureau of Economic Research, Cambridge, MA.

Gordon, R. J., and H. Sayed. 2019. "The Industry Anatomy of the Transatlantic Productivity Growth Slowdown." NBER Working Paper 25703, National Bureau of Economic Research, Cambridge, MA.

Greenspan, A. 2011. "Should Jobs Matter in the U.S. Trade Debate?" *The Globalist*. July 7, 2020. https://www.theglobalist.com/globalist-interview-with-alan-greenspan-should-jobs-matter-in-the-u-s-trade-debate/

Haltiwanger, J., S. Scarpetta, and H. Schweiger. 2014. "Cross Country Differences in Job Reallocation: The Role of Industry, Firm Size and Regulations." *Labour Economics* 26 (January): 11–25.

Hatzius, J., Z. Pandl, A. Phillips, D. Mericle, E. Pashtan, D. Struyven, K. Reichgott, and A. Thakkar. 2016. "Productivity Paradox v2.0 Revisited." *U.S. Economics Analyst*, Goldman Sachs Economic Research, New York.

He, D., and W. Zhang. 2010. "How Dependent Is the Chinese Economy on Exports and in What Sense Has Its Growth Been Export-Led?" *Journal of Asian Economics* 21 (1): 87–104.

Hsieh, C. T., and P. J. Klenow. 2010. "Development Accounting." *American Economic Journal: Macroeconomics* 2 (1): 207–23.

Huo, Z., A. Levchenko, and N. Pandalai-Nayar. 2019. "The Global Business Cycle: Measurement and Transmission." NBER Working Paper 25978, National Bureau of Economic Research, Cambridge, MA.

Imbs, J. M. 1999. "Technology, Growth and the Business Cycle." *Journal of Monetary Economics* 44 (1): 65–80.

IMF (International Monetary Fund). 2013. "Dancing Together? Spillovers, Common Shocks, and the Role of Financial and Trade Linkages." In *World Economic Outlook: Transitions and Tensions*, 81–112. Washington, DC: International Monetary Fund.

IMF (International Monetary Fund). 2014. "Sustaining Long-Run Growth and Macroeconomic Stability in Low-Income Countries—the Role of Structural Transformation and Diversification—Background Notes." IMF Policy Paper, International Monetary Fund, Washington, DC.

Inklaar, R., P. Woltjer, and D. Gallardo. 2019. "The Composition of Capital and Cross-Country Productivity Comparisons." The Fifth World KLEMS Conference 36, University of Groningen, Netherlands.

Jorgenson, D. W., M. S. Ho, and K. J. Stiroh. 2008. "A Retrospective Look at the U.S. Productivity Growth Resurgence." *Journal of Economic Perspectives* 22 (1): 3–24.

Keller, W. 2010. "International Trade, Foreign Direct Investment, and Technology Spillovers." *Handbook of the Economics of Innovation* 2: 793–829.

Klenow, P. J., and A. Rodríguez-Clare. 1997. "The Neoclassical Revival in Growth Economics: Has It Gone Too Far?" In *NBER Macroeconomics Annual. Vol. 12*, edited by B. S. Bernake and J. Rotemberg, 73–114. Cambridge, MA: MIT Press.

Kose, M. A., C. Otrok, and C. H. Whiteman. 2003. "International Business Cycles: World, Region, and Country-Specific Factors." *American Economic Review* 93 (4): 1216–39.

Kose, M. A., and M. Terrones. 2015. "Collapse and Revival: Understanding Global Recessions and Recoveries." Washington, DC: International Monetary Fund, 2015.

Kose, M. A,. N. Sugawara, and M. Terrones. 2020. "Global Recessions." Policy Research Working Paper 9172, World Bank, Washington, DC.

Kraay, A. 2018. "Methodology for a World Bank Human Capital Index." Policy Research Working Paper 8593, World Bank, Washington, DC.

Levchenko, A., and N. Pandalai-Nayar. 2018. "Technology and Non-Technology Shocks: Measurement and Implications for International Comovement." Conference proceedings, ECB-CBRT Conference, the Federal Reserve Board, UT-Austin, and the NBER-IFM, Cambridge, MA.

Mandelman, F. S., P. Rabanal, J. F. Rubio-Ramírez, and D. Vilán. 2011. "Investment-Specific Technology Shocks and International Business Cycles: An Empirical Assessment." *Review of Economic Dynamics* 14 (1): 136–55.

Mason, A. D., and S. Shetty. 2019. *A Resurgent East Asia: Navigating a Changing World.* Washington, DC: World Bank.

Miyamoto, W., and T. L. Nguyen. 2017. "Understanding the Cross-Country Effects of U.S. Technology Shocks." *Journal of International Economics* 106 (May): 143–64.

Nicola, F. de, V. Kehayova, and H. Nguyen. 2018. "On the Allocation of Resources in Developing East Asia and Pacific." Policy Research Working Paper 8634, World Bank, Washington, DC.

OECD (Organisation for Economic Co-operation and Development). 2015. *The Future of Productivity.* Paris: OECD.

Ollivaud, P., Y. Guillemette, and D. Turner. 2016. "The Links between Weak Investment and the Slowdown in OECD Productivity and Potential Output Growth." OECD Working Paper 1304, Organisation for Economic Co-operation and Development, Paris.

SNA (System of National Accounts). 2008. *System of National Accounts.* New York: Commission of the European Communities, International Monetary Fund, Organisation for Economic Co-operation and Development, United Nations, World Bank.

Solow, R. M. 1957. "Technical Change and the Aggregate Production Function." *The Review of Economics and Statistics* 39 (3): 312–20.

Solow, R. M. 1992. "Policies for Economic Growth." *De Economist* 140: 1–15.

Stocker, M., J. Baffes, Y. M. Some, D. Vorisek, and C. M. Wheeler. 2018. "The 2014–16 Oil Price Collapse in Retrospect: Sources and Implications." Policy Research Working Paper 8419, World Bank, Washington, DC.

Summers, L. H. 2015. "Demand Side Secular Stagnation." *American Economic Review* 105 (5): 60–65.

Syverson, C. 2016. "Challenges to Mismeasurement Explanations for the U.S. Productivity Slowdown." NBER Working Paper 21974, National Bureau of Economic Research, Cambridge, MA.

Tuan, C., L. F. Y. Ng, and B. Zhao. 2009. "China's Post-Economic Reform Growth: The Role of FDI and Productivity Progress." *Journal of Asian Economics* 20 (3): 280–93.

UNECE (United Nations Economic Commission for Europe). 2008. *Non-Observed Economy in National Accounts*. Geneva: UNECE.

van Ark, B., M. O'Mahony, and M. P. Timmer. 2008. "The Productivity Gap between Europe and the United States: Trends and Causes." *Journal of Economic Perspectives* 22 (1): 25–44.

World Bank. 2017. *Global Economic Prospects: Weak Investment in Uncertain Times*. January. Washington, DC: World Bank.

World Bank. 2018a. *Global Economic Prospects: Broad Based Upturn, but for How Long?* January. Washington, DC: World Bank.

World Bank. 2018b. *The Human Capital Project*. Washington, DC: World Bank.

World Bank. 2019a. *Global Economic Prospects: Darkening Skies*. January. Washington, DC: World Bank.

World Bank. 2019b. *Global Economic Prospects: Heightened Tensions, Subdued Investment*. June. Washington, DC: World Bank.

World Bank. 2020. "Pandemic, Recession: The Global Economy in Crisis." In *Global Economic Prospects*, June. Washington, DC: World Bank.

Productivity depends on many factors, including our workforce's knowledge and skills and the quantity and quality of the capital, technology, and infrastructure that they have to work with.

Janet Yellen (2015)
United States Secretary of the Treasury

Knowledge is power. Information is liberating. Education is the premise of progress, in every society, in every family.

Kofi Annan (1997)
Former Secretary-General of the United Nations

CHAPTER 2

What Explains Productivity Growth

Long-term productivity growth is driven by innovation, investment in physical capital, and enhanced human capital. This requires a growth-friendly environment, with supportive institutions and macroeconomic stability. The effects of some drivers on productivity growth have changed over time. Innovation, cross-border technology transfer, and expertise in producing complex and sophisticated exports have increased in importance, along with demographic factors. Despite remarkable improvements over the past 60 years in schooling and health outcomes, gaps between emerging market and developing economies and advanced economies remain. Some gaps have even widened, in areas such as tertiary education, financial development, and patents per capita. Furthermore, improvements in key drivers of productivity growth—including education, urbanization, and institutions—have slowed since the global financial crisis and are expected to remain subdued in the years ahead, not least in the aftermath of the COVID-19 (coronavirus disease 2019) pandemic. To rekindle productivity growth, a comprehensive approach is needed to stimulate investment in physical and human capital, and to promote a growth-friendly macroeconomic and institutional environment.

Introduction

Long-term labor productivity growth rates have varied enormously across emerging market and developing economies (EMDEs). In 1960, labor productivity—output per worker—in China was $423 in 2010 U.S. dollars, slightly lower than Burkina Faso's $427. By 2018, productivity in China had increased to $13,919, eight times higher than Burkina Faso's $1,641. There were many differences between the two countries that led to these productivity outcomes: for example, in 1960 the share of the population with primary school education was 26 percent in China compared to 0.7 percent in Burkina Faso. China has also invested substantially more: gross investment in China averaged 37 percent of gross domestic product (GDP) over 1960-2018, about double that of Burkina Faso.

This chapter explores the drivers of long-term productivity growth and how their roles have varied over time, with a focus on the recent slowdown. Many factors have influenced productivity growth over the past 60 years.[1] In the long term, labor productivity growth relies on innovation, physical capital investment, and investment in human capital. These proximate drivers are shaped by the environment in which firms operate: market structures, infrastructure, the institutional framework, and the quality of governance.

Note: This chapter was prepared by Alistair Dieppe, Atsushi Kawamoto, Yoki Okawa, Cedric Okou, and Jonathan Temple. Research assistance was provided by Yi Li.

[1] For discussions of these factors, see Bruns and Ioannidis (2020); Durlauf (2009); Durlauf, Johnson, and Temple (2005); Kataryniuk and Martínez-Martín (2019); Kim and Loayza (2019); and Rockey and Temple (2016).

Key drivers of productivity growth—such as investment in human capital through primary and secondary education—have seen major improvements over the last 60 years in EMDEs. They have even improved more than in advanced economies and contributed to strong productivity growth before the global financial crisis (GFC). Nonetheless, in many cases, wide gaps between EMDEs and advanced economies remain. At the same time, reflecting the structural changes that economies have undergone over the last 60 years, the roles of various drivers have changed, with some increasing in importance and others decreasing.

The recent evolution of these drivers helps to explain why global productivity growth has weakened since the GFC. Some changes can be linked directly to the crisis, such as increased uncertainty and slower investment growth. The COVID-19 (coronavirus disease 2019) pandemic will be a further blow to growth prospects around the world, disrupting trade and foreign direct investment, causing investments to be postponed or canceled, and weakening government finances. Other changes reflect separate, long-term trends. For example, the pace of improvements in some drivers of productivity in EMDEs has naturally slowed as the distance to the best-practice frontier has diminished.

The COVID-19 pandemic threatens to weigh on longer-run trends that could impede productivity growth in EMDEs. Over the past decade, the prospects for further trade integration have diminished, and the expansion of global value chains has lost momentum. Sharp declines in global trade and investment, amid the pandemic, could accelerate these trends. For many countries, they will mean subdued activity, instability, and new pressures on governments.

In the latter decades of the twentieth century, many countries benefited from a rising share of the working-age population. This is now leading to aging populations and at least a partial reversal of the earlier "demographic dividend." In other areas, past improvements will be difficult to replicate. Further progress in health and education can contribute to growth, but it will be hard to match the major gains of the last 60 years. Meanwhile, investments could be further damaged by the lasting impacts of COVID-19. On a more positive note, new technologies could yet reinvigorate productivity growth, and some of the improvements in drivers already achieved should continue to support growth over the next few decades.

Against this backdrop, the chapter examines the following questions:

- What have been the main factors associated with long-term productivity growth?

- How much have the main factors individually contributed to long-term productivity growth?

- What are the factors behind recent trends in productivity?

- What policy options are available to boost productivity?

Contributions

The chapter makes several contributions to the literature and policy debates:

- The chapter reviews past research on the correlates of productivity growth, motivating the selection of drivers for investigation. It explores the channels through which various drivers operate, while recognizing that they should not be considered in isolation. As some previous research acknowledges, drivers can interact in ways that strengthen or weaken their effects. The chapter also reviews the literature on sources of growth in total factor productivity (TFP) at the firm level.

- The chapter presents new empirical findings that go beyond previous work, partly by examining a range of potential drivers over a longer time period, using a Bayesian approach to combine information from many different models. The analysis allows the importance of drivers to change over time, while the choice of priors recognizes that several candidate variables may represent the same underlying driver.

- The chapter presents new stylized facts on developments in key productivity drivers: whether drivers in EMDEs have been converging with those in advanced economies over the long run, their paths since the GFC, and the prospects for improvement. The chapter presents the likely implications of COVID-19 for productivity drivers and discusses policy options to raise productivity growth.

Main findings

The following findings emerge:

- *Key long-run drivers.* Historically, labor productivity growth has been driven by innovation, better education, and investment in physical capital. Innovation and investment by the private sector require a growth-friendly environment, with supportive institutions and policies, including policies that promote macroeconomic stability and the rule of law. Productivity growth also seems to benefit from expertise in producing relatively complex and sophisticated exports, which is associated with international technology diffusion. This finding complements past research on familiarity with complex production, and supports the argument that "what you export matters" (Hausmann, Hwang, and Rodrik 2007).

- *Changing contribution to productivity growth of drivers.* The effects of different drivers on productivity growth have changed over time. Innovation and experience with economic complexity, related to participation in global value chains and cross-border technology transfer, seem to have increased in importance. So have demographic factors, notably changes in population age structures. In contrast, the importance of urbanization, related to the sectoral shift from agriculture to manufacturing and services, has weakened. These findings complement those of Bruns and Ioannidis (2020), as well as recent evidence on the changing effects of economic complexity, urbanization, and innovation.

- *Widening or persistent gaps in many drivers.* Many productivity drivers in EMDEs fall short of advanced economy conditions, despite remarkable improvements over the last 60 years in key human capital indicators such as the provision of primary education and infant mortality rates. The chapter documents these gaps in a systematic way. For some productivity drivers, including ones that are essential to innovative economies—tertiary education, financial development, and patents per capita—the gaps have widened. Improvements in other drivers, such as institutions and economic complexity, have stalled. Over the past decade, many drivers of productivity growth have faltered, including those that had previously supported strong productivity growth. Working-age population growth has slowed, along with growth in average educational attainment. As the expansion of global value chains has lost momentum, so has the movement toward more diverse and complex forms of production.

- *Challenging prospects with the impact of COVID-19 on drivers.* The COVID-19 pandemic has made the near-term outlook for productivity growth even more challenging. Weaker investment and trade, erosion of human capital, slower labor reallocation, heavier public and private debt burden, and widening inequality could push down the productivity growth. Yet the pandemic may also create productivity-enhancing opportunities such as lasting organizational and technological changes for business and education, reshaping global value chains toward higher diversification, and changing social norms.

- *Policy priorities.* The recent slowdown in productivity growth has multiple sources, and action on a range of fronts will be needed. Governments seeking to raise productivity growth can increase public investment and stimulate private investment; improve human capital; foster firm productivity, partly through on-the-job training and upgraded management capabilities; increase the exposure of firms to international trade and foreign investment; enable the reallocation of resources toward more productive sectors; and seek to diversify production. The benefits of many productivity-friendly policies could be enhanced by improving the macroeconomic and institutional environment.

Long-run drivers

This section reviews the literature and presents new stylized facts. It considers theory and evidence on the links between productivity drivers and growth, and draws attention to differences across income groups and regions, and over time.

Sustained economic growth ultimately requires technological progress and higher TFP, because growth cannot rely indefinitely on expanding the quantity of inputs (Easterly and Levine 2001; Solow 1956). Drawing on growth theory and economic history, the empirical literature has identified many potential drivers of labor productivity growth.[2]

---

[2] For discussions of various drivers, see Acemoglu and Dell (2010); Barro (1996); Barro and Sala-i-Martin (2004); Isaksson (2007); Kim and Loayza (2019); and Pritchett (2000).

For the purpose of this chapter, these can be classified into three broad categories: [3]

1. Proximate sources: innovation, physical capital, and the quality of the labor force

2. The supporting environment: institutions, infrastructure, policies, and social conditions

3. Improvements in firm-level factors: innovation capabilities, input quality, and regulations acting at the firm or market level

Proximate sources of growth

Innovation and technology transfer. In the long run, growth relies on innovation. Firms innovate by introducing new products and better ways to produce existing goods and services. As a result, overall productivity is likely to rise (Hall, Mairesse, and Mohnen 2010).

The role of research and development (R&D) activity in EMDEs differs compared to countries already at the technological frontier. New patents, one measure of R&D outcomes, tend to be more closely associated with productivity growth in countries with highly educated and skilled workers. But, even when human capital is less developed, improvements in productivity can be achieved, albeit slowly (Chen and Dahlman 2004; Furman and Hayes 2004; World Bank 2018a). Gradual improvements in production processes and product quality have been reported across all income levels (Goñi and Maloney 2017). In addition, R&D activity can enhance the absorptive capacities of firms and their ability to assimilate new technology (Cohen and Levinthal 1989, 1990).

EMDEs can benefit from the diffusion of technologies across national borders. Buera and Oberfield (2020) use a calibrated model to show that trade-induced technology diffusion can greatly increase the gains from trade. This can help to explain past instances of sustained growth, in which countries such as China and the Republic of Korea have rapidly integrated with the world economy. In other cases, though, the diffusion of technology may be slow (chapter 1).

EMDEs invest much less than advanced economies in formal R&D (figure 2.1; Acemoglu and Zilibotti 2001; Goñi and Maloney 2017). The gap between EMDEs and advanced economies narrowed after 2000, mainly because of more innovation-related activity in China. For EMDEs excluding China, patent applications per capita and R&D spending as a share of GDP barely increased between 2000 and 2017. In Latin America and the Caribbean (LAC), South Asia (SAR), and Sub-Saharan Africa (SSA), the number of patent applications per capita remains relatively low, and lags advanced economies.

Physical capital. Since Solow (1956), standard growth models have linked the height of the long-run growth path to the rate of investment. In many economies in East Asia and

---

[3] As some concepts overlap, there could be alternative classifications that focus on other concepts, such as competition, geography, and social fragmentation.

FIGURE 2.1 Innovation

Economies characterized by formal innovation activities—such as more patents per capita and R&D expenditure—tend to grow faster after controlling for the initial productivity level. Measures of innovation are lower in EMDEs than in advanced economies—the number of new patents per capita was six times larger in advanced economies than EMDEs in 2017. Although the gap between advanced economies and EMDEs has been narrowing since 2000, the convergence in patents per capita and R&D expenditure is largely driven by China.

A. Productivity growth by innovation activity

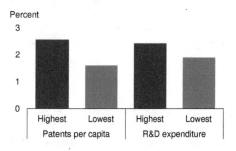

B. Innovation activities

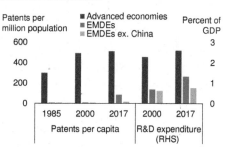

Sources: United Nations Educational, Scientific and Cultural Organization; World Bank.
Note: EMDEs = emerging market and developing economies; R&D = research and development.
A. Average annualized labor productivity growth grouped by the initial level of each indicator. "Highest"/"Lowest" group contains countries whose indicator is in top/bottom 25 percent. The effect of initial productivity has been partialled out. See annex 2A for detail. "Patents per capita" is the number of new patent applications per capita. The samples include 32 advanced economies and 74 EMDEs for patents per capita from 1995 to 2018, and 31 advanced economies and 49 EMDEs for R&D expenditures from 2000 to 2018.
B. Aggregates are calculated using GDP weights at 2010 prices and market exchange rates. The samples include 23 advanced economies and 37 EMDEs for patents per capita, and 26 advanced economies and 40 EMDEs for R&D expenditures.

Pacific (EAP), rapid output growth has been closely linked to high investment. In the empirical literature, there is a robust cross-section association between the investment rate and labor productivity, which may even have strengthened over time (Beaudry, Collard, and Green 2005). Research based on the nonparametric estimation of global production frontiers, tracking their movement over time, also finds a major role for capital accumulation in productivity growth (Kumar and Russell 2002).

Most private sector firms rely on services provided by infrastructure. Investment in infrastructure can complement new technologies, and raise productivity and well-being.[4] Infrastructure needs in EMDEs remain high and relate to transport, water and sanitation, power, and telecommunications. Achieving infrastructure-related Sustainable Development Goals in low-income and middle-income countries will require average yearly investment of 2 to 8 percent of GDP during 2015-30 (Rozenberg and Fay 2019; Vorisek and Yu 2020). The contribution of capital accumulation to output growth has been higher for EMDEs than for advanced economies (chapter 1).

The quality of labor. The productivity of an economy depends partly on the quality of its labor force, which can be improved in several ways. Other things being equal, a

---

[4] For a discussion of infrastructure investment, see, for example, Aschauer (1989); Calderón, Moral-Benito, and Servén (2015); Martins (2019); Melo, Graham, and Brage-Ardao (2013); and Pereira and Andraz (2013).

better-educated and healthier labor force will contribute more to economic activity. Education can enhance not only skills but also the ability to adopt new technologies. In the long term, education may have wider positive effects, on the nature of civil society and the effectiveness of governments.

- *Education.* Workers who are more educated, better trained, and more highly skilled are better placed to contribute to technological advances and to help absorb new technologies, including ones from abroad (Benhabib and Spiegel 2003; Im and Rosenblatt 2015; Romer 1990). For EMDEs, investment in education is likely to shift patterns of comparative advantage toward more complex and higher-value products.[5] It should encourage shifts in resources, toward sectors that draw more intensively on education and skills (chapter 7).

  Since the 1960s, there has been a substantial increase in average years of schooling in EMDEs, from 3.5 to 8.6 years.[6] Primary education is now almost universal. Gaps between EMDEs and advanced economies in the provision of secondary education have steadily narrowed, but the overall gap with advanced economies remains at four years, reflecting a divergence in tertiary education (figure 2.2). Over the last 60 years, tertiary education has expanded faster in advanced economies than in EMDEs.

- *Health.* Better health raises labor productivity. Healthy workers tend to be more efficient, faster learners, and more committed to improving their skills (Benhabib and Spiegel 2003; Knowles and Owen 1995; World Bank 2018b). Good health complements education, reinforcing the supply of high-quality labor (Bloom, Canning, and Sevilla 2004; Knowles and Owen 1995). Evidence is mixed on the size of these effects, however. Acemoglu, Johnson, and Robinson (2003) and Acemoglu and Johnson (2007) find against large effects of health improvements on growth, but this has been contested.[7]

  Over the last 60 years, infant mortality rates in EMDEs have converged on those in advanced economies, whereas mortality rates for older ages have diverged for some EMDE regions (figure 2.3). The infant mortality rate in EMDEs in 2018 was one-tenth that of 1960. Across all regions, the infant mortality gap between EMDEs and advanced economies has narrowed. In contrast, life expectancy at age 50 has risen faster in advanced economies. These differences are likely to reflect variation in non-communicable disease rates (UNDP 2019).

Demographic factors. One demographic factor affecting labor productivity is the age composition of the labor force. New technologies may be adopted faster in economies with younger labor forces: compared to more experienced workers, their expertise is less tied to older technologies. Evidence suggests that economies with higher young or

---

[5] A measure of product complexity will be discussed in the latter part of this section.

[6] Quality of education also matters. See, for example, World Bank (2018c).

[7] For examples, see the discussion in Acemoglu and Johnson (2014) and in Bloom, Canning, and Fink (2014).

FIGURE 2.2 **Education**

Productivity in economies with a higher level of education grew about 1 percentage point faster than in economies with lower education levels, after controlling for initial productivity levels. The average years of schooling for EMDEs more than doubled over the last 50 years. Despite catch-up in primary and secondary education, the difference in education levels between advanced economies and EMDEs is only slowly narrowing as gaps widen in tertiary education.

A. Productivity growth by education level, 1960-2018

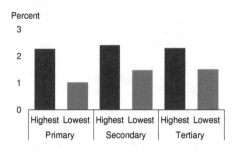

B. Years of schooling

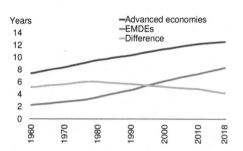

C. Share of education in EMDEs

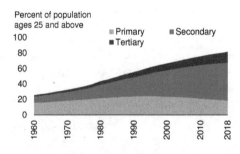

D. Differences in education shares between advanced economies and EMDEs

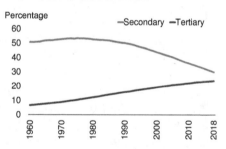

Sources: Wittgenstein Center for Demography and Global Human Capital; World Bank.
Note: EMDEs = emerging market and developing economies.
A. Average annualized productivity growth from 1960 to 2018, grouped by the level of education as a share of the adult population in 1960. "Highest"/"Lowest" group contains countries whose indicator is in top/bottom 25 percent. The effect of initial productivity has been partialled out. See annex 2A for detail. The samples include 26 advanced economies and 51 EMDEs.
B-D. Aggregates are calculated using GDP weights at 2010 prices and market exchange rates.
B. Total years of schooling. "Difference" shows the gap in years of schooling between advanced economies and EMDEs. The samples include 26 advanced economies and 75 EMDEs.
C.D. Share of the population age 25 or above with specified education levels. The samples include 26 advanced economies and 82 EMDEs.

working-age population shares adapt more readily to new technologies, skills, and organizational structures (Liu and Westelius 2017; Maestas, Mullen, and Powell 2016).

Working-age population shares in EMDEs increased between 1969 and their peak in 2015 (figure 2.3). In advanced economies, the share peaked in 1990 and fell by 3 percentage points between 2008 and 2018. This decline reflects aging workforces, which have been associated with lower productivity growth (Aiyar, Ebeke, and Shao 2016; Aksoy et al. 2019; Feyrer 2008; Jones 2010; Liu and Westelius 2017; Maestas, Mullen, and Powell 2016).

FIGURE 2.3 **Health and demography**

The survival rate at age five was significantly lower in EMDEs than in advanced economies in 1960, but has been converging to advanced economy levels since then. For life expectancy at age 50, which is related to the control of noncommunicable diseases, advanced economies made more progress than EMDEs, which has widened the gap in 2017 compared to 1960. Furthermore, the improvement is slowest in SSA, whose initial level was low, suggesting divergence within EMDEs. Productivity growth is positively associated with the working-age population share, which has increased over the last 50 years in EMDEs as fertility rates have declined. However, the working-age population share peaked in 1990 for advanced economies and in 2015 for EMDEs.

A. Age five survival rate

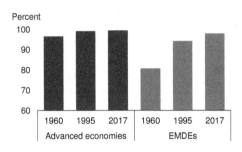

B. Life expectancy at age 50

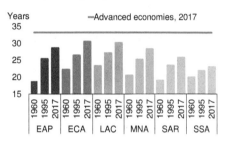

C. Productivity growth by working-age population share

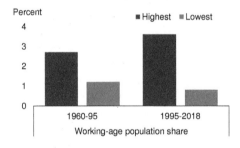

D. Age structure

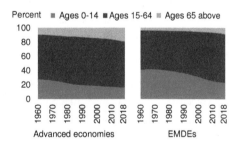

Sources: United Nations; World Bank.
Note: EMDEs = emerging market and developing economies; EAP = East Asia and Pacific; ECA = Europe and Central Asia; LAC = Latin America and the Caribbean; MNA = Middle East and North Africa; SAR = South Asia; SSA = Sub-Saharan Africa.
A.-B. Aggregates are calculated using GDP weights at 2010 prices and market exchange rates. The samples include 26 advanced economies and 85 EMDEs.
C. Average annualized labor productivity growth grouped by the initial level of working-age population share. "Highest"/"Lowest" group contains countries whose indicator is in top/bottom 25 percent. The effect of initial productivity has been partialled out. See annex 2A for detail. The samples include 26 advanced economies and 52 EMDEs from 1960 to 1995 and 32 advanced economies and 127 EMDEs from 1995 to 2018.
D. Share of the population for each age group. Aggregates are calculated using GDP weights at 2010 prices and market exchange rates. The samples include 26 advanced economies and 85 EMDEs.

The supporting environment

Institutions. North (1991) defined institutions as "the humanly devised constraints that structure political, economic and social interaction. They consist of both informal constraints (sanctions, taboos, customs, traditions, and codes of conduct), and formal rules (constitutions, laws, property rights)." Institutions include the rule of law, the legal system, and regulatory barriers to the creation and operation of firms. Political institutions include the system of government. Institutional considerations are often invoked to explain why TFP and labor productivity vary across countries, including differences between EMDEs and advanced economies.

Economists often regard the rule of law as an especially important determinant of productivity (Acemoglu, Johnson, and Robinson 2001; Acemoglu and Johnson 2005; Barro 1996; Bazzi and Clemens 2013). The rule of law can mitigate violence, secure property rights, preserve institutional checks and constraints on government, and limit state capture and corruption. The control of corruption may be one of the most important channels (Haggard and Tiede 2011; Kaufmann, Kraay, and Mastruzzi 2007).

Productivity growth is positively associated with institutional quality, proxied by a rule of law index, after controlling for the initial level of productivity (figure 2.4). Productivity growth in economies with relatively good institutions also tends to be more stable than where institutions are weaker. In EMDEs, this measure of institutional quality remains significantly lower than in advanced economies, across all regions, with little improvement over the last 20 years.

Transitions to democracy seem to have positive effects on productivity growth in subsequent years, as in the findings of Papaioannou and Siourounis (2008). A more recent study finds that democratic transitions could raise productivity by about 20 percent over the subsequent 25 years (Acemoglu et al. 2019). However, some other work finds no effect of democracy on growth (Ruiz Pozuelo, Slipowitz, and Vuletin 2016).

Macroeconomic stability. This chapter uses two proxies for macroeconomic stability: low inflation and a low black market exchange rate premium. Macroeconomic instability can form a binding constraint, which limits the benefits of other drivers. Uncertainty in the macroeconomic environment can deter investment and cause capital outflows (Gramacy, Malone, and Ter Horst 2014). There is also evidence that, in stable macroeconomic environments, the effect of investment on output is stronger, conditional convergence is faster, and measures of institutional quality have more explanatory power as determinants of productivity growth (Sirimaneetham and Temple 2009).

The aftermath of the COVID-19 pandemic is likely to place government finances under new pressure, risking instability for many EMDEs. Even for countries with ample buffers, financial instability can be contagious. Monetary and fiscal policy frameworks still lag behind best practices in many EMDEs (Kose and Ohnsorge 2019). Nevertheless, trends in inflation have been favorable in recent decades. In advanced economies, inflation rates have trended downward since the early 1980s. For some EMDEs, inflation spiked in the 1990s, when financial and currency crises were relatively common. Inflation in the Europe and Central Asia (ECA) region was especially high in the mid-1990s, as transition economies adjusted. But inflation in EMDEs has moderated since then. The median annual inflation rate in EMDEs has recently been about 3 percent, down from 12 percent in the 1990s (figure 2.4).

FIGURE 2.4 **Institutional quality and price stability**

Productivity growth is positively related to institutional quality, proxied by the rule of law index, after controlling for the initial level of productivity. Productivity growth in economies with good institutions tends to be more stable than in economies with low institutional quality. In EMDEs, however, this measure of institutional quality remains significantly lower than in advanced economies across all regions, with little improvement over the last 20 years. Inflation rates have been trending down in advanced economies, and have moderated in EMDEs following a spike in the 1990s. The number of financial crisis episodes rose during the commodity price collapse in 2011-16.

A. Productivity growth and rule of law, 1996-2018

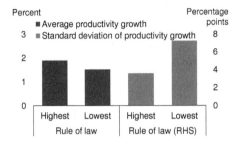

B. Rule of law

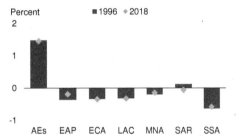

C. Inflation

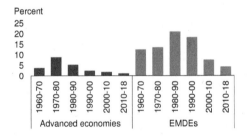

D. Financial crisis

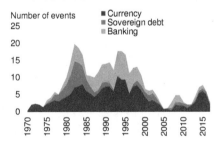

Sources: International Monetary Fund, International Financial Statistics; Laeven and Valencia (2018); World Bank, World Governance Indicators.

Note: AEs = advanced economies; EMDEs = emerging market and developing economies; EAP = East Asia and Pacific; ECA = Europe and Central Asia; LAC = Latin America and the Caribbean; MNA = Middle East and North Africa; SAR = South Asia; SSA = Sub-Saharan Africa.

A. Average productivity growth from 1996 to 2018. Countries are grouped by average values during the period. "Highest" shows the average productivity growth of countries in the fourth quartile; "Lowest" shows the average productivity growth of countries in the first quartile. The effect of initial productivity has been partialled out. Standard deviations are calculated across time for each country. Calculated standard deviations are aggregated using simple averages.

B. Aggregates of index are calculated using GDP weights at 2010 prices and market exchange rates.

C. Average annual consumer price index inflation rate during each period. Aggregates are calculated using GDP weights at 2010 prices and market exchange rates.

D. The number of financial crises defined in chapter 3 for EMDEs by type. Three-year moving averages.

Income inequality. Most empirical studies that link growth to income inequality find that inequality has an adverse effect.[8] The literature has considered several mechanisms: higher fertility, lower provision of schooling, and greater political and social instability, including pressures for redistribution (Perotti 1996).

---

[8] A nonexhaustive list includes Alesina and Rodrik (1994), Berg et al. (2018), Clarke (1995), Deininger and Squire (1998), Herzer and Vollmer (2012), Perotti (1996), and Persson and Tabellini (1994).

Some work has questioned the relative importance of these mechanisms and the overall effect of inequality (Alvaredo et al. 2018; Herzer and Vollmer 2012). A few studies report no relationship (Panizza 2002) or even a positive relationship (Forbes 2000; Frank 2009). The effect may vary with the level of development (Barro 2000) and depend on precisely where inequality arises within the income distribution (Voitchovsky 2005). It has also been argued that changes in inequality, rather than its level, could affect growth (Banerjee and Duflo 2003). A more recent study finds that lower inequality (after taxes and transfers) is associated with faster and more durable growth, and that redistribution does not have an adverse effect on growth unless it is extreme (Berg et al. 2018).

Recent trends in inequality have varied across EMDE regions. Between 1995 and 2015, the income share of the poorest 10 percent of the population declined in EAP and ECA, remained virtually unchanged in the Middle East and North Africa (MNA), SSA, and SAR, and increased in LAC (figure 2.5).

Gender equality. Disparities between women and men—in access to education, health care, and earning opportunities—can lower overall productivity and national income. Improved earning opportunities for women can increase human capital and physical capital investment, through higher income and higher returns to the human capital of women (Galor and Weil 1996; Klasen and Santos Silva 2018). Improved female access to education and earning opportunities will also tend to lower fertility, and fewer children per family can mean that each child receives better education and health care. Improved female education can contribute to the health of civil society and social participation. It can also broaden perspectives in decision making, contributing to better outcomes (Gallen 2018; Loko and Diouf 2014; Schober and Winter-Ebmer 2011). In Italy, teams with a higher proportion of women have been found to be more innovative (Díaz-García, González-Moreno, and Sáez-Martínez 2013).

The productivity of women in farming can be constrained by unequal access to finance and weaker property rights protection. Female farmers have been found to be less productive than men in several countries, including Burkina Faso, Ethiopia, Ghana, Paraguay, and Zimbabwe (Croppenstedt, Goldstein, and Rosas 2013). The gender difference disappears after controlling for access to farmer education and factor inputs, such as fertilizer usage. This suggests routes through which female farmers could become more productive.

The average gender gap in tertiary schooling remains larger in EMDEs than in advanced economies but narrowed significantly between 1960 and 2020 (figure 2.5). The range of gender gaps also narrowed significantly in this period across advanced economies, which have achieved near-universal gender equality in tertiary education. However, gender gaps in some EMDEs remain substantial. There are 20 EMDEs where average years of tertiary education are more than 50 percent higher for men than women, whereas the gap is less than 10 percent in all advanced economies.

Trade. Most of the evidence on trade indicates that relatively open economies are more productive (Alcala and Ciccone 2004; De Loecker 2013; Frankel and Romer 1999; Hall

FIGURE 2.5 **Income and gender equality**

Productivity growth is positively associated with income equality, after controlling for initial productivity levels. The evolution of income equality varies across EMDE regions, with notable declines in EAP and ECA, but is almost unchanged for MNA, SAR, and SSA, and has increased in LAC. Productivity growth is correlated with gender equality in education in the 1995-2018 period. The gender gap in schooling is larger in EMDEs than in advanced economies but has narrowed significantly on average, albeit with wide variation for EMDEs.

A. Productivity growth by income equality, 1995-2018

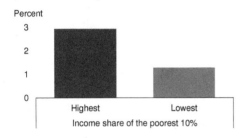

B. Poorest 10 percent income share

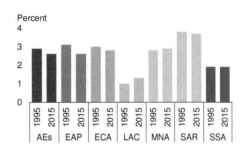

C. Productivity growth by gender equality, 1995-2018

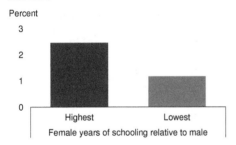

D. Interquartile range for female ratio for tertiary education

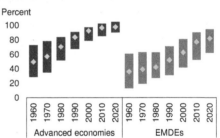

Sources: United Nations; Wittgenstein Center for Demography and Global Human Capital; World Bank.
Note: AEs = advanced economies; EMDEs = emerging market and developing economies; EAP = East Asia and Pacific;
ECA = Europe and Central Asia; LAC = Latin America and the Caribbean; MNA = Middle East and North Africa; SAR = South Asia;
SSA = Sub-Saharan Africa.
A.C. "Highest"/"Lowest" group contains countries whose indicator is in top/bottom 25 percent. The effect of initial productivity has been partialled out. See annex 2A for details.
A. Average annualized labor productivity growth grouped by the share of the bottom 10 percent in income distribution. The samples include 30 advanced economies and 109 EMDEs from 1995 to 2018.
B. Data are the median income share of the poorest 10 percent for each country group. Data are inter/extrapolated as necessary when data are unavailable. The samples include 10 advanced economies and 64 EMDEs.
C. Average annualized labor productivity growth grouped by the initial level of the ratio of the female years of schooling to male years of schooling. The samples include 32 advanced economies and 123 EMDEs from 1995 to 2018.
D. Ratio of female share of population with tertiary education to male share of population with tertiary education, as a percentage: 100 indicates perfect equality and less than 100 indicates gender bias toward men. Bars show the interquartile range. Diamonds show the median. The samples include 26 advanced economies and 77 EMDEs.

and Jones 1999).[9] Trade liberalizations in the 1980s and 1990s were often followed by significant productivity gains (Irwin 2019). In addition to gains through exploiting comparative advantage, participation in global markets can enable knowledge diffusion

---

[9] A few studies find only a weak relationship between trade and productivity, or trade and growth (Bosworth and Collins 2003; Rodríguez and Rodrik 2000; Rodrik, Subramanian, and Trebbi 2004).

and technology transfer. Imports of sophisticated machinery can directly improve labor productivity at the firm, sector, and country level (Casacuberta, Fachola, and Gandelman 2004; Fernandes 2007; Mayer 2001; Xu and Wang 1999).

Exporting firms are often relatively productive, but evidence on the role of exports is complicated by self-selection: other things equal, productive firms are more likely to be competitive and choose to export (Clerides, Lach, and Tybout 1998; Dercon et al. 2004; Graner and Isaksson 2009). Some evidence from Kenya and Korea accounts for self-selection and finds that exporting does increase productivity (Aw, Chung, and Roberts 2000; Graner and Isaksson 2009). "Learning-by-exporting" effects may depend on the development levels of importers or exporters, with learning gains that are larger when the exporter and importer are at similar development levels, or when the importer has high human capital (Aw, Chung, and Roberts 2000; Blalock and Gertler 2004; Graner and Isaksson 2009; Keller 2004).

EMDE participation in global value chains declined after the GFC, partly reflecting the shift to domestic production within China (figure 2.6). This may reduce cross-border transfers of technology. In the longer term, supply chains could be restructured in ways that increase their diversity and improve resilience (World Bank 2020b).

Economic complexity. Complexity reflects diversification and production capabilities, and may be linked with higher productivity or greater scope for future growth (Diao, McMillan, and Rodrik 2019; Jarreau and Poncet 2012). Producing more complex goods may also promote technological diffusion and convergence (Goodfriend and McDermott 1998).

Hidalgo and Hausmann (2009) introduced the Economic Complexity Index as a holistic measure of the productive capabilities of a country. The index reflects the diversity, sophistication, and relative knowledge manifested in a country's exports; it is constructed by comparing a country's sectoral export shares with the respective shares of the corresponding sectors in world trade. Measured complexity will be higher when a country exports more complex goods, such as ceramic-metal composites and compound semiconductors, produced by relatively few economies (Hausmann et al. 2014). EMDEs generally remain behind advanced economies in the complexity of their exports, but with significant regional variation. Complexity in the EAP region is now close to advanced economy levels, but other regions remain significantly behind. Complexity in the SSA region fell further behind advanced economies between 1970 and 2017 (figure 2.6).

Foreign direct investment. Inflows of foreign direct investment (FDI) can promote convergence in productivity, through improved organizational structures and management practices, as well as advanced technology (Griffith, Redding, and Simpson 2004; Keller and Yeaple 2009). As a source of capital, FDI should raise labor productivity and wages, especially for host countries with a high development level and high-quality institutions (Isaksson 2007; Kose, Prasad, and Terrones 2009). The positive relationship between FDI and labor productivity may, however, be weaker for

FIGURE 2.6 **Trade and foreign direct investment**

Productivity growth is positively correlated with measures related to external openness, such as global value chain participation, complexity of export goods, and share of foreign direct investment (FDI) as percentage of GDP, after controlling for the initial productivity level. Global value chain participation declined in EMDEs after the global financial crisis, partly reflecting the shift to domestic production in China. Economic complexity, which measures the relative sophistication of the domestic manufacturing sector, reached the advanced economy level in EAP, whereas other regions remained significantly below the advanced economy level. In particular, relative economic complexity declined in SSA from 1970 to 2017. Inward FDI to EMDEs stalled after the financial crisis.

A. Productivity growth by trade-related measures

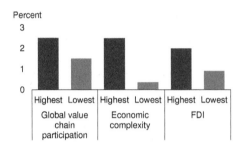

B. Global value chain participation

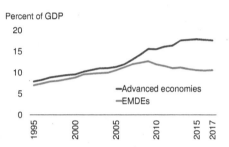

C. Economic complexity

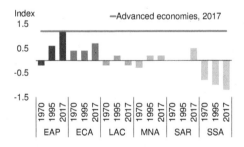

D. Inward FDI share of GDP

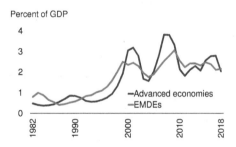

Sources: United Nations Conference on Trade and Development; World Bank, World Development Indicators; World Trade Organization.

Note: EMDEs = emerging market and developing economies; EAP = East Asia and Pacific; ECA = Europe and Central Asia; FDI = foreign direct investment. LAC = Latin America and the Caribbean; MNA = Middle East and North Africa; SAR = South Asia; SSA = Sub-Saharan Africa.

A. Average annualized labor productivity growth grouped by the initial level of drivers. "Highest"/"Lowest" group contains countries whose indicator is in top/bottom 25 percent. The effect of initial productivity has been partialled out. See annex 2A for detail. The samples include 32 advanced economies and 113 EMDEs from 1995 to 2018 for global value chain participation as a share of GDP, 23 advanced economies and 59 EMDEs from 1970 to 2018 for economic complexity, and 25 advanced economies and 101 EMDEs from 1995 to 2018 for FDI.

B. The total amount of intermediate goods in imports and exports, as a percentage of GDP. Three-year moving averages. Aggregates are calculated using GDP weights at 2010 prices and market exchange rates.

C. The Economic Complexity Index (ECI+) of Albeaik et al. (2017), extended with an economic complexity index using the methodology of Hidalgo and Hausmann (2009). Aggregates are calculated using GDP weights at 2010 prices and market exchange rates. The samples include 23 advanced economies and 68 EMDEs.

D. Three-year moving averages of total inward FDI flow as a share of nominal GDP.

EMDEs (Keller and Yeaple 2009). In some countries, the cost of subsidies used to attract FDI may exceed the productivity benefits (Görg and Greenaway 2004; Haskel, Pereira, and Slaughter 2007). Inward FDI to EMDEs stalled after the GFC (figure 2.6) and is likely to be under new pressure after the COVID-19 pandemic.

Urbanization. Agglomeration, through urbanization and higher population density, tends to raise productivity (Combes and Gobillon 2015; Duranton and Puga 2004). Agglomeration benefits include knowledge spillovers, deeper markets for workers and local services, and better matching between the skills of workers and the needs of firms. Densely populated areas bring people and firms closer together, making it easier to share ideas, exchange information, invent new technologies, design new projects, engage in partnerships, and start new businesses (Abel, Dey, and Gabe 2014). Urban populations are steadily increasing in EMDEs and, in aggregate, first exceeded the rural population in 2017 (figure 2.7). Nevertheless, the difference between the shares of urban populations in advanced economies and EMDEs has remained almost unchanged over the last 60 years.

Finance. Financial depth is often linked with higher labor productivity (Buera, Kaboski, and Shin 2011) and faster productivity growth (Aghion, Howitt, and Mayer-Foulkes 2005; King and Levine 1993). For countries with a given level of initial productivity, greater financial depth is associated with faster subsequent productivity growth (figure 2.7). Well-developed financial markets can improve the efficiency of capital allocation and enable firms to make productivity-enhancing investments (Fisman and Love 2003; Levine 1997). They may also allow firms to diversify investment risk and increase liquidity, and to stimulate entrepreneurship (Beck, Levine, and Loayza 2000a, 2000b; Demirgüç-Kunt and Levine 1996).

There is generally a wide gap between EMDEs and advanced economies in financial development, reflecting the fact that many EMDEs lack developed capital markets, and financial products are not easy to access for much of their populations (Sahay et al. 2015). This can be seen in an index based on financial depth and the quality of institutions related to financial markets. Measured by the index, progress from 1995 to 2017 was slower in LAC, MNA, and SSA than in advanced economies, but faster in EAP, ECA, and SAR. SSA remains behind in financial depth and had the slowest rate of improvement between 1995 and 2017. But financial sector reform is not without risks, because mismanaged deregulation can lead to unsustainable lending booms and banking crises. For this reason, poorer countries may benefit less from financial sector reforms (Prati, Onorato, and Papageorgiou 2013).

Firm productivity

In most markets, highly productive firms are likely to have an edge. They will tend to innovate more and grow faster, and are more likely to survive than less productive competitors (Goñi and Maloney 2017). There are both internal and external factors that help to shape firm productivity:

Internal drivers. The internal drivers include productivity-enhancing organizational features and practices that shape firms' capabilities.

- *Technological progress.* A firm's TFP hinges on its ability to create, acquire, and use advanced technology. Technological innovation, driven partly by R&D and

FIGURE 2.7 **Urbanization and financial development**

The urban population is steadily increasing in EMDEs, exceeding the rural population by 2017. Higher productivity growth is associated with a large urban population share. Financial development varied across EMDE regions, and progress has been slowest in SSA. Long-term productivity growth is correlated with financial development, after controlling for initial productivity levels.

A. Productivity growth by urban population share, 1960-2018

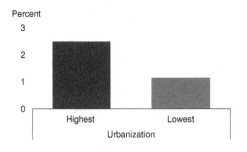

B. Rural and urban population

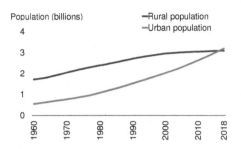

C. Financial development, by region

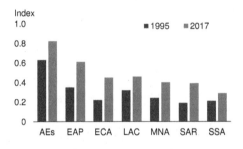

D. Productivity growth and financial development, 1995-2018

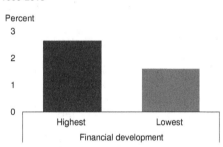

Sources: International Monetary Fund; World Bank, World Development Indicators.
Note: AEs = advanced economies; EAP = East Asia and Pacific; ECA = Europe and Central Asia; EMDEs = emerging market and developing economies; LAC = Latin America and the Caribbean; MNA = Middle East and North Africa; SAR = South Asia; SSA = Sub-Saharan Africa.
A. Average annualized productivity growth from 1960 to 2018, grouped by the level of urban population share in 1960. "Highest"/"Lowest" group contains countries whose indicator is in top/bottom 25 percent. The effect of initial productivity has been partialled out. See annex 2A for detail. The samples include 26 advanced economies and 52 EMDEs.
B. Total rural and urban population in EMDEs from 1960 to 2018. The sample includes 159 EMDEs.
C. Aggregates are calculated using GDP weights at 2010 prices and market exchange rates. The financial development index is a relative ranking of countries on the depth, access, and efficiency of their financial markets from the International Monetary Fund. The samples include 32 advanced economies and 124 EMDEs.
D. Average annualized productivity growth from 1995 to 2018, grouped by the level of financial development in 1995. "Highest"/"Lowest" group contains countries whose indicator is in top/bottom 25 percent. The effect of initial productivity has been partialled out. See annex 2A for details. The samples include 32 advanced economies and 124 EMDEs.

complemented by physical capital and workers' skills, will boost labor productivity and output (Cohen and Levinthal 1990). New production techniques allow firms to improve product quality and expand the range of marketed products (Bernard, Redding, and Schott 2010). An increase in patenting and the variety of products can also strengthen firm productivity (Balasubramanian and Sivadasan 2011).

• *Input quality.* Higher-quality labor and capital can raise a firm's labor productivity measured as output per worker or per worker hour. Better-educated, well-trained, and experienced workers tend to be more productive (Fox and Smeets 2011). New capital goods enable faster productivity growth, through embodied technical progress (Sakellaris and Wilson 2004).

- *Management.* Good management can improve the efficiency of production. The best managerial practices include setting clear targets, monitoring progress, and rewarding performance (Bloom and Van Reenen 2010; Lazear 2000). Incentives for team production, cross-training, work experience, and frequent employee-manager communication can also raise firm productivity (Bandiera, Barankay, and Rasul 2011).

External drivers. Outside forces influence productivity within and between firms. These external factors can allow each firm to improve its efficiency (the "within" effect) and stimulate more efficient firms to grow faster than others (the "between" effect).

- *Regulatory and operating environments.* Institutions and regulations influence firm productivity partly through incentives to invest in human and physical capital, and to acquire technology (Bartelsman and Doms 2000; Kouamé and Tapsoba 2018). Firm productivity tends to be lower in poorly regulated markets: weaker enforcement of competition laws can allow a large inefficient firm to drive productive competitors out of the market by abusing its market power; higher barriers of entry can prevent creative destruction (Goldberg et al. 2010). Private firms may be reluctant to undertake costly R&D when competitors, especially those in the informal sector, can infringe intellectual property rights (Amin and Islam 2015; Amin, Ohnsorge, and Okou 2019). The enforcement of property rights, and public-private partnerships to create technology extension centers in sectoral clusters, can increase firm participation in global value chains and raise productivity (Cirera and Maloney 2017). Improvements in the business environment and conducive regulatory practices—fair competition, increased business freedom—support growth of TFP and labor productivity.

- *Spillovers and input markets.* The presence of highly productive firms can have spillover effects and raise the productivity of other firms. These spillovers occur as knowledge and innovation are transferred through trade, FDI, and agglomeration channels (Aitken and Harrison 1999; Combes and Gobillon 2015). Flexible and integrated capital and labor markets can promote the reallocation of inputs toward the most productive firms (Bartelsman, Haltiwanger, and Scarpetta 2013).

Box 2.1 reviews the literature on firm-level TFP in more detail.

Summary of stylized facts

In summary, there are positive associations between several drivers and labor productivity growth, after controlling for the initial productivity level (figure 2.8). Growth of labor productivity has been faster in countries that began with a larger working-age population share, greater economic complexity, lower income inequality, more patents per capita, deeper financial markets, higher educational attainment, higher

FIGURE 2.8 **Productivity growth performance and key initial conditions**

Growth was faster for countries that began with a higher working-age population share, higher economic complexity, lower income inequality, more patents per capita, deeper financial markets, higher education, larger FDI per GDP, greater gender equality in education, higher global GVC participation, larger share of urban population, and better institutions. Gaps in average levels of drivers between advanced economies and EMDEs are widening in tertiary education, life expectancy at age 50, financial development index, and GVC participation. Gaps remain almost constant for economic complexity, urban population share, patents per capita, and rule of law.

A. Improvement in productivity growth with favorable initial conditions

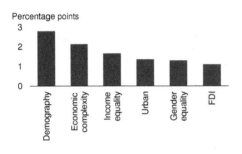

B. Improvement in productivity growth with favorable initial conditions (cont.)

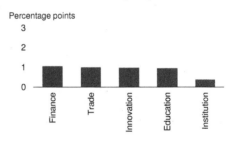

C. Average level of drivers over time

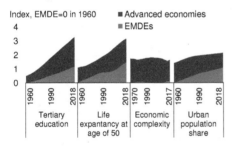

D. Average level of drivers over time (cont.)

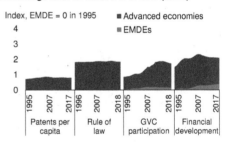

Source: World Bank.
Note: EMDEs = emerging market and developing economies; FDI = foreign direct investment; GVC = global value chain.
A.B. The difference in productivity growth between the highest 25 percent and lowest 25 percent of the distribution of initial levels of key correlates of productivity growth. The following variables correspond to each concept (sample years in parentheses): Demography = working-age population share (1995-2018); Economic complexity = Economic Complexity Index of Hidalgo and Hausmann (2009) and Albeaik et al. (2017) (1970-2018); Income equality = income share of poorest 10 percent (1995-2018); Innovation = patents per capita (1995-2018); Finance = financial development index (1995-2018); Education = share of population with secondary education and above (1960-2018); FDI = inward FDI as a percent of GDP (1995-2018); Gender equality = the ratio of the female years of schooling to male (1995-2018); Trade = GVC participation (total amount of intermediate goods in imports and exports, as a percentage of GDP) (1995 to 2018); Urban = urban population share (1960-2018); Institution = rule of law index (1996-2018). See figures 2.1-2.7 for detail.
C.D. Simple average of drivers over time, by income level. Variables are normalized so that average value for the EMDEs in the starting year is zero and standard deviation in the starting year is one. Economic complexity is a five-year moving average, and patents per capita, rule of law, GVC participation, and financial development are three-year moving averages.

FDI relative to GDP, lower gender inequality, greater global value chain participation, a higher urban population share, and better institutions. These associations are only indicative and should not be seen as causal effects.

Between 1960 and 2018, most drivers in EMDEs improved. However, the gaps between EMDEs and advanced economies have widened for some drivers, including ones that are essential to innovative economies—tertiary education, financial development, patents

TABLE 2.1 **Recent developments in productivity drivers**

	Driver	Are EMDEs approaching advanced economies?
Proximate sources	Innovation	Partially. Divergence in innovation measures excluding China.
	Capital	Partially. Higher investment ratio in EMDEs; divergence in financial development indicators.
	Education	Partially. Convergence in secondary education and divergence in tertiary education.
	Health	Partially. Convergence in infant mortality and divergence in old age life expectancy.
	Demography[a]	No. Working-age population share in EMDEs has started to decline.
Supporting environment	Institutions	Partially. Significant improvements in rule-based fiscal and monetary policy, but limited improvement in institutional measures.
	Macroeconomic stability	Yes. Milder inflation and fewer financial crises compared to 1980-90s.
	Gender inequality	Partially. Gender gaps are narrowing except in some regions.
	Income inequality[a]	No clear uniform trend in the last 25 years.
Market development	Trade/Complexity	Stalled. Divergence of GVC participation. No convergence in economic complexity, with a few exceptions.
	FDI[a]	Stalled. No increase in FDI.
	Urban	No. Continued large gap in urbanization rate.

Sample period is the longest available: typically, 1960-2018, but significantly shorter for some drivers.

Source: World Bank.
Note: EMDEs = emerging market and developing economies; FDI = foreign direct investment; GVC = global value chain.
a. These drivers are not necessarily lower in EMDEs than in advanced economies. The answers in the row are about absolute improvements, rather than improvements relative to advanced economies.

per capita—and in EMDEs improvements in other drivers, such as institutions and economic complexity, have stalled (table 2.1).

Analyzing the effects of drivers

Thus far, the analysis has considered individual drivers in isolation. This section considers them together: it examines the partial correlations between productivity growth and various drivers, and how they have changed over time.

Methods. To study the role of drivers in productivity growth, cross-country regressions are used. These regressions are useful for uncovering associations between initial conditions and later growth. The sample comprises 60 countries, including 38 EMDEs, observed from 1960 to 2018. The time span is longer than in many previous studies and should ensure that the results are not confounded by short-run or cyclical effects. The use of initial values of the drivers, rather than averages or changes during the sample period, helps to address potential concerns over reverse causality. Nevertheless,

FIGURE 2.9 **Impact of drivers on productivity growth**

Productivity in economies with favorable initial conditions grew faster than other economies, after controlling for interactions among drivers. The scale of these effects varies over time. In 1960, the importance of innovation and economic complexity was lower in EMDEs. Demography and economic complexity have become increasingly important determinants of EMDE productivity growth in recent decades. Productivity growth is 0.78 percentage points higher for an economy with a 7.1-percentage-point higher working-age population share.

A. Effects of drivers on productivity growth, 1960-2018, EMDEs vs. world

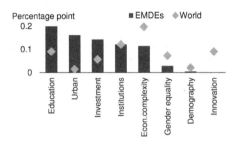

B. Effects of drivers on EMDE productivity growth, 1960-2018 vs. 1995-2018

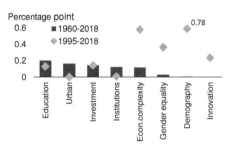

Source: World Bank.
Note: EMDEs = emerging market and developing economies.
A.B. Estimated marginal contribution to annual long-term productivity growth if a driver improves from the 25th percentile to the 75th percentile. The samples include 59 economies, 38 of which are EMDEs. Groups that are not significant in both 1960-2018 and 1995-2018 (finance, income equality, and health) are excluded from the chart. The following variables correspond to each concept: Institutions = International Country Risk Guide rule of law index; Geography = share of nontropical area; Innovation = patents per capita; Investment = investment to GDP ratio; Income equality = (-1)*Gini coefficient; Urbanization = urban population (% total); Econ. complexity = Economic Complexity Index of Hidalgo and Hausmann (2009); Education = years of schooling; Demography = share of working-age population; Gender equality = ratio of years of schooling of female to male. See annex 2B for details.
B. Marginal contribution of demography for 1995-2018 is 0.78 percentage points.

significant pitfalls remain, and it should be remembered that causality is hard to establish.[10]

In early growth studies, researchers often carried out inference as if the identity of the true model was known with certainty. This approach was heavily criticized, because many findings were sensitive to changes in model specification (Levine and Renelt 1992). Following the more recent literature, this chapter uses a Bayesian approach that combines information from a wide range of models, while favoring simple models with high explanatory power. This approach is used to identify key correlates of productivity growth from a pool of 29 candidate variables. It recognizes that some variables overlap and may reflect the same underlying driver, with implications for the appropriate structure of the priors. The details of the approach are discussed in annex 2B.

Key initial conditions. The results indicate that, other things equal, countries with favorable initial conditions subsequently experienced faster productivity growth (figure 2.9). More specifically, higher productivity growth rates between 1960 and 2018 were associated with the following conditions in 1960: higher investment as a share of GDP,

---

[10] A discussion of causality and other qualifications to the results is included in annex 2B.

BOX 2.1 Review of recent firm-level total factor productivity literature

A large literature identifies various sources of firm total factor productivity (TFP) growth, which has slowed over the last decade. Enhancing firm capabilities, easing the efficient reallocation of input factors, and fostering the net entry of high-productivity firms are key to raising TFP growth.

Introduction

The literature on firm productivity is extensive (Bloom et al. 2010). This box reviews the literature on total factor productivity (TFP), a measure of efficiency in translating a combination of inputs into value added (Cusolito et al. 2018). It addresses the following questions:

- How has firm-level TFP varied over time and across countries?

- What factors drive firm TFP growth?

Firm TFP patterns

Research provides a range of empirical findings on firm TFP growth patterns (Dall'Olio et al. 2014; di Mauro et al. 2018).

Longitudinal evidence. The post-GFC slowdown in productivity reignited the debate on firm-level drivers of TFP growth. In the United States, TFP growth has slowed since the 2000s, reflecting a loss of momentum in job reallocation and entrepreneurship, exacerbated by adverse shocks from the crisis (Cardarelli and Lusinyan 2015; Decker et al. 2016). Japan has experienced a longer-term decline in TFP growth since the early 1990s, with headwinds from an aging population and a gradual reduction in the statutory workweek (Hayashi and Prescott 2002). In EMDEs, TFP growth has also slowed down, though by less than in the advanced economies (Cusolito and Maloney 2018; Papa, Rehill, and O'Connor 2018).

Cross-sectional evidence. Variation in aggregate TFP is often found to account for nearly half the variation in output per capita across economies (Bartelsman, Haltiwanger, and Scarpetta 2013). Studies of firm-level TFP in Organisation for Economic Co-operation and Development (OECD) member countries reveal dispersion between the frontier and lagging firms.[a] This is true as well within particular sectors and across firms in advanced economies and EMDEs (Bartelsman and Doms 2000). The typical "frontier firm" is more productive, more innovative, more capital intensive, with larger sales revenue, and more

---

Note: This box was prepared by Cedric Okou.

a. At the firm level, revenue-based productivity measures use total sales as a proxy for output.

**BOX 2.1 Review of recent firm-level total factor productivity literature
(continued)**

likely to benefit from cross-border technology transfers via multinational
networks (Andrews, Criscuolo, and Gal 2016).

In the U.S. manufacturing sector, the top 10 percent of firms ranked by TFP
levels are twice as productive as the bottom 10 percent of firms, for given inputs
(Syverson 2004, 2011). The TFP gap between the top 10 percent and the
bottom 10 percent of firms is even more pronounced in emerging economies,
with a ratio of more than 5 to 1 in China and India (Hsieh and Klenow 2009).
The dispersion of firm-level TFP is typically skewed, with more firms below the
average than above (Bernard, Redding, and Schott 2011). The dispersion can
matter for policy, because interventions may affect firms differently, depending
on where they are within the productivity distribution (di Giovanni, Levchenko,
and Mejean 2018).

Regional evidence. Market frictions, stringent regulations, and weak institutions
lower productivity. This has been especially apparent in Sub-Saharan Africa
(World Bank 2017). Harmonized and simplified regulation through integrated
regional markets can remedy these challenges and help diffuse knowledge and
accelerate technology adoption (Acemoglu and Autor 2011; Autor and Dorn
2013; Dutz, Almeida, and Packard 2018). Connectivity-led productivity
improvements have been documented in Europe and Central Asia, East Asia and
Pacific, and South Asia through global value chains, foreign direct investment,
communication, transport, and migration (Gould 2018; Lopez-Acevedo,
Medvedev, and Palmade 2017; World Bank 2019c).

Bottlenecks. Unfair privileges insulate certain firms with deep political
connections from competition and discourage other firms from innovating
(Schiffbauer et al. 2015). Reforms that remove benefits for vested interest groups
and promote fairer competition can raise TFP and labor productivity (Araujo,
Vostroknutova, and Wacker 2017; EBRD, EIB, and World Bank. 2016).
Informality is pervasive in many economies, especially in Latin America and the
Caribbean and Sub-Saharan Africa, and is associated with low productivity
(Amin, Ohnsorge, and Okou 2019). Addressing informality may lead to
improvements in productivity. Moreover, technology adoption can be slower in
economies with high agricultural employment and low levels of numeracy and
literacy. Low-skill-biased technologies can be leveraged to upgrade skills and
boost firm productivity (Dutz, Almeida, and Packard 2018; Fuglie et al. 2020;
Nguimkeu and Okou 2019).

Measurement challenges. Conceptual and measurement issues complicate the
analysis of firm-level TFP (Cusolito and Maloney 2018; Goldberg et al. 2010).
Data limitations mean that standard microeconomic measures of productivity

---

BOX 2.1 Review of recent firm-level total factor productivity literature *(continued)*

and distortions can be misleading. Good measures should account for the effects of markups, market power, adjustment costs, quality differences, and investment risk (Cusolito et al. 2018; Foster et al. 2008, 2017; Hsieh and Klenow 2009; Restuccia and Rogerson 2013; Syverson 2011).

Drivers of firm TFP growth

Rules and regulations shape the business environment and TFP dynamics within and between firms (Goldberg et al. 2010).

Within-firm TFP growth and internal capabilities. Firms can achieve "more from less" (McAfee 2019) by strengthening their internal capabilities. These include innovation and absorption capacities, workforce quality, and managerial skills (Cusolito and Maloney 2018). The accumulation of knowledge, experience, and research and development can support innovation, upgrade product quality, improve production methods, and raise TFP.[b] Firm size plays a role: larger firms can benefit from a richer set of new ideas and expertise, and invest more in research and development (Isaksson 2007; World Bank 2019a). Skilled workers are better placed to create and adopt new technologies. Targeted educational programs can be used to develop cognitive skills through on-the-job training and tertiary education (Danquah, Moral-Benito, and Ouattara 2014; World Bank 2018c). Managers matter, because they coordinate the production process and influence its efficiency. Managerial and organizational styles vary across firms because of competition, location, ownership, and trade ties (Collard-Wexler and De Loecker 2015; Del Carpio and Taskin 2019). Interventions to improve management practices can raise productivity by more than 10 percent (Bloom and Van Reenen 2010; Van Reenen 2011).

Between-firm TFP growth, efficient allocation, and input quality. Economy-wide productivity depends partly on the market shares of productive firms compared to less productive firms, and their respective factor usage (Autor et al. 2020). Poor rules and regulations—weak legal systems, corruption, and unfair competition—sometimes obstruct the reallocation of factors to more productive firms (Cirera, Fattal Jaef, and Gonne 2017; Dias, Marques, and Richmond 2020). Addressing market distortions, through fairer competition, greater product and labor market flexibility, and trade liberalization, can aid reallocation and raise aggregate TFP (Goñi and Maloney 2017; Maloney and Nayyar 2018).

TFP dispersion across firms can arise from differences in the quality of labor and capital (Isaksson 2007; Syverson 2011). Labor force quality, or human capital,

---

b. For examples in the literature, see Atkin, Khandelwal, and Osman (2017); Yahmed and Dougherty (2012); Brynjolfsson and Hitt (1995); Goldberg et al. (2010); Nelson (1981); Romer (1990); Syverson (2004); and Wolitzky (2018).

BOX 2.1 Review of recent firm-level total factor productivity literature (continued)

may vary because of health, education, training, and experience (Acemoglu 1996; Acemoglu and Dell 2010; Gamberoni, Giordano, and Lopez-Garcia 2016). Variation across firms in the distribution of capital vintages can help to explain disparities in capital-embodied technical progress (Nguyen, Taskin, and Yilmaz 2016; Restuccia and Rogerson 2013).

Net entry of high-productivity firms. Entry of high-productivity firms and exit of low-productivity ones should lead to aggregate TFP gains (Decker et al. 2016). In some developing countries, High-growth firms (HGFs) make up less than 20 percent of firms in manufacturing and services, yet account for 80 percent of output and job creation.[c] They generate spillovers for other businesses through gains in agglomeration, innovation, value chains, skill upgrading, and managerial experience.

In practice, it may be difficult to identify HGFs in their early stages, and predicting firm success has proved challenging (Grover Goswami, Medvedev, and Olafsen 2019). Rather than relying on guesswork to identify HGFs, policies should aim at removing entry and exit barriers (Cirera, Fattal Jaef, and Gonne 2017; Decker et al. 2016).

Conclusion

For individual firms, TFP can benefit from enhanced firm capabilities. Workforce quality and managerial skills complement technological innovations and absorption capacity. Across firms, aggregate TFP growth can benefit from flexible labor and product markets that enable the reallocation of inputs. When highly productive firms enter, they can increase their market share relative to less productive incumbents, thereby raising overall productivity.

---

c. HGFs can be defined either in absolute terms, on the basis of average annualized employment or revenue growth of more than, say, 20 percent over a three-year period, or in relative terms, as firms above, say, the 90th percentile in employment and sales growth.

---

a better-educated workforce (proxied by average years of schooling), stronger institutions (proxied by the rule of law), greater innovation (proxied by a higher number of patents per capita), higher urbanization, and lower inflation. A positive association was also found between productivity growth and the initial value of the Economic Complexity Index of Hidalgo and Hausmann (2009).

The effects of key initial conditions: differences between EMDEs and advanced economies. The estimated effects of the productivity drivers differ between EMDEs and advanced economies. The effects of average years of schooling and the investment rate are higher for EMDEs than for advanced economies, indicating the relative importance of these proximate sources of growth for EMDEs. The extent of urbanization also has a larger impact on productivity growth in EMDEs than in advanced economies. This could reflect reallocation of workers from agriculture to manufacturing and service sectors, where productivity may be higher at the margin (chapter 7).

Changing importance of drivers. The changing importance of productivity growth drivers can be highlighted by comparing results for 1960-2018 with results for 1995-2018, updating the initial conditions. In EMDEs, the role of economic complexity seems to have strengthened since the mid-1990s (Diao, McMillan, and Rodrik 2019; Hausmann and Hidalgo 2010; Jarreau and Poncet 2012). Experience in complex production can assist in knowledge diffusion and raise productivity growth (Kraay, Soloaga, and Tybout 2004; Schor 2004). In EMDEs, the role of complexity may reflect experience gained through participation in global value chains and the hosting of FDI, in addition to an increasingly important role in innovation. Knowledge transfer via foreign investment could lead to diversified and more sophisticated exports (World Bank 2020a).

Demographic forces—in the form of changes in the working-age share of populations—supported growth in the latter half of the twentieth century in EMDEs and advanced economies. More recently, population aging has become a potential headwind for many economies, working against further productivity growth. In a related Bayesian study, using a rolling sample, Bruns and Ioannidis (2020) also find that the importance of demographic variables has increased over time, although their work emphasizes population growth and the fertility rate.

Developments in drivers of productivity

This section examines how drivers have developed in the recent past, and relates these changes to the post-GFC slowdown in productivity growth. The prospects for some of the drivers are also assessed.

Pre-GFC improvements. Before the financial crisis, there had been major improvements in many drivers of productivity growth, and improvements in EMDEs were often larger than in advanced economies (figure 2.10). Using the cross-country regression results, the drivers considered here can be aggregated into a single index, weighted by their relative estimated effects. The analysis suggests that demographics, economic complexity, the number of patents filed per capita, and low inflation were key determinants of productivity growth over this period. Between 1995 and 2008, the quarter of EMDEs with the most favorable initial conditions experienced productivity increases 23 percent larger, on average, than the quarter of EMDEs with the least favorable initial conditions. Among low-income countries, the differential between the two groups was even larger, at 52 percent.

Post-GFC slowdown in improvements. After the financial crisis, some of the drivers most strongly associated with productivity growth in EMDEs have seen slower

FIGURE 2.10 **Pre-GFC developments in productivity drivers and productivity growth**

Drivers of productivity growth in EMDEs, except for innovation, gender equality, and institutions, improved more than in advanced economies during the pre-GFC period, helping to narrow the productivity gap with advanced economies. There was a strong link between drivers and productivity growth—those economies with better initial conditions in the 1990s grew at faster rates.

A. EMDEs with faster improvements relative to advanced economies, 1995-2008

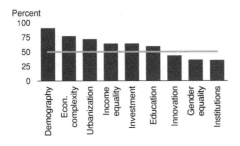

B. Productivity drivers and average EMDE productivity growth 1995-2008

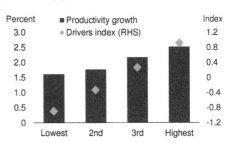

Sources: Barro and Lee (2015); International Monetary Fund; Observatory of Economic Complexity; Penn World Table; World Bank.
Note: EMDEs = emerging market and developing economies; GFC = global financial crisis.
A. Share of EMDE countries whose improvement in drivers are larger than average changes for advanced economies. The following variables correspond to each concept: Institutions = Worldwide Governance Indicators Government Effectiveness Index; Innovation = patents per capita; Investment = investment-to-GDP ratio; Income equality = (-1)*Gini coefficient; Urbanization = urban population (% total); Econ. complexity = Economic Complexity Index of Hidalgo and Hausmann (2009); Education = years of schooling; Demography = share of working-age population; Gender equality = ratio of years of schooling of female to male. The samples include 30 advanced economies and 61 EMDEs.
B. Average level of productivity growth and "index of drivers" in each quartile over 1995-2008. Index of drivers created by weighting normalized levels of each potential driver in panel A by its estimated impact on productivity growth (figure 2.9; annex 2B).

improvement, or even reversals. This is consistent with the slowdown in productivity growth in this period (figure 2.11). Investment growth in EMDEs faltered, reflecting weaker activity in advanced economies, subdued growth in demand for primary commodities, and political uncertainty. Demographic trends that had previously been favorable in many EMDEs waned, as populations aged. Other factors that spurred EMDE productivity growth before the crisis have also weakened. As the expansion of global value chains lost momentum after 2008, so did the trend toward broadening and diversifying production and the movement into upstream stages of the value chain (World Bank 2020a). Neither institutional quality nor income inequality has shown significant improvement. Before the crisis, gains in price stability improved operating environments for firms, but such gains have more recently slowed (Ha, Kose, and Ohnsorge 2019). At the same time, however, EMDEs have seen faster growth than advanced economies in educational attainment, measured by average years of schooling.

Outlook

Even before the COVID-19 pandemic, several fundamental drivers of productivity growth had faltered in the wake of the 2008 GFC (figure 2.11). The pandemic will further undermine a number of drivers, perhaps especially in the short run, but with

FIGURE 2.11 **Post-GFC slowdown of the drivers of productivity growth**

In EMDEs, improvements in a broad range of productivity drivers slowed after 2008. Investment growth slowed to one-third of its pre-GFC rate in EMDEs. Working-age population shares are expected to contract in coming years. The growth of educational attainment has also slowed.

A. EMDEs with a slowdown in productivity drivers in the post-GFC period

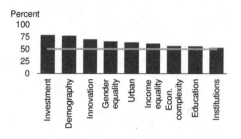

B. Average investment growth

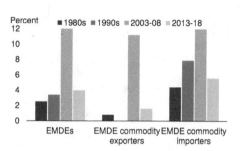

C. Change in working-age population shares

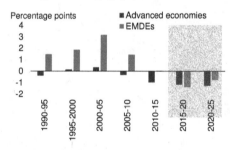

D. Average growth in educational attainment

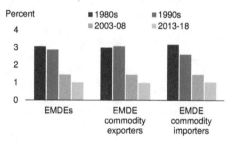

Sources: Barro and Lee (2015); International Monetary Fund; Observatory of Economic Complexity; Penn World Table; World Bank, World Development Indicators; IMF World Economic Outlook; United Nations; Wittgenstein Centre for Demography and Global Human Capital.

Note: EMDEs = emerging market and developing economies; GFC = global financial crisis.

A. Share of economies where improvements in each driver of productivity during 2008-18 are lower than those in the pre-GFC period 1998-2007. The following variables correspond to each concept (sample in parentheses): Institutions (75) = Worldwide Governance Indicators Government Effectiveness Index; Innovation (27) = patents per capita; Investment (69) = investment-to-GDP ratio; Income equality (73) = (-1)*Gini coefficient; Urbanization (75) = Urban population share; ECI (56) = Economic Complexity Index of Hidalgo and Hausmann (2009);

Education (52) = years of schooling; Gender equality = ratio of years of schooling of female to male; Demography (75) = share of working-age population.

B. GDP-weighted average annual investment (gross fixed capital formation) growth.

C. Five-year average percentage point changes in the share of the working-age population (aged 15-64).

D. GDP-weighted average changes in years of education.

scope for longer-term effects also (table 2.2). This section sketches how preexisting trends and the pandemic will shape the outlook for productivity growth, while acknowledging that many effects remain uncertain.

Lasting impact of COVID-19. Many productivity drivers are expected to be negatively affected by the pandemic. Uncertainty about the duration of the pandemic and the global economic landscape may discourage investment (Bloom 2014). Concerns about their long-term viability and resilience may lead to a retreat from global value chains—which would choke off an important channel for international technology transmission—and discourage foreign investment that is often related to such production processes (World Bank 2019a). FDI could see a 30-40 percent fall in the short run (UNCTAD 2020). Steep income losses and disruptions to schooling, which have taken place in countries accounting for 90 percent of global GDP, could increase dropout rates and set back human capital accumulation for a generation of children (World Bank 2020b).

Pandemic-caused job losses could disproportionally affect the income and labor participation of low-skill workers and push 70 million to 100 million into poverty (Chetty et al. 2020; Lakner et al. 2020; Mahler et al. 2020; Sumner, Hoy, and Ortiz-Juarez 2020). Such job loss may affect poor women more than educated men, possibly widening income inequality.

A few consequences of the pandemic may be less negative. The experience of past crises suggests that some forms of human capital investment are more likely to be undertaken, which could partially offset the negative impact of school closures. History also suggests that some institutional reforms, including in the financial sector, may become more likely in the aftermath of a crisis. Supply chains could be restructured in ways that increase their diversity and improve resilience (World Bank 2020b). This could yet promote trade, FDI, and knowledge transfer for economies not well integrated in existing global value chains.

Weaker investment. Investment growth has been slower in the post-GFC period. This reflects adverse terms-of-trade shocks for primary commodity exporters, slowing FDI for commodity importers; heightened policy uncertainty; lower growth in advanced economies; and private debt burdens (World Bank 2017). Uncertainty related to the pandemic seems likely to further reduce investment over the coming years (chapter 3). As well as the direct effect on labor productivity growth, subdued investment may slow capital-embodied technical change, especially in R&D-dependent sectors (Adler et al. 2017; Hulten 1992).

Slower growth at the frontier. Since the early 2000s, there has been a broad-based slowdown in productivity growth in advanced economies, with few signs of an upturn even before the dislocation of the pandemic. These developments may limit the future role of FDI in transferring technologies to EMDEs (Görg and Strobl 2001; Wooster and Diebel 2010).

Views are divided on the growth prospects for advanced economies over the next few decades, and on whether productivity growth will return to historical norms, with spillovers for EMDEs. On the one hand, the innovations of recent decades seem to have benefited productivity growth less than those of the twentieth century (Cowen 2011; Fernald 2015; Gordon 2016). On the other hand, new digital technologies, such as artificial intelligence and other information technology innovations, may soon feed through to productivity (Cusolito and Maloney 2018). As with earlier "general purpose technologies," major innovations often require organizational and operational changes that delay some of their benefits for productivity (Brynjolfsson, Rock, and Syverson, forthcoming).

TABLE 2.2 Possible impacts of COVID-19 on drivers of productivity growth

	Damaging	Offsetting
Innovation	A retreat from global value chains and FDI could undermine technology transfer and R&D spending (UNCTAD 2020). Subdued investment growth, especially in R&D-dependent sectors, could slow technological progress and total factor productivity growth, partly through weaker capital-embodied technological change (Adler et al. 2017). Labor reallocation to productive firms could slow during severe recession (Foster, Grim, and Haltiwanger 2016). Large-scale government intervention in the economy could create "zombie firms" limiting the entrance and expansion of high-productivity firms (di Mauro and Syverson 2020).	Low investment and accelerated capital depreciation due to an event such as the COVID-19 pandemic could lead to faster adoption of new technologies in the near future (Caballero and Hammour 1994; Caballero 2008). Some sectors, such as health care and pharmaceutical industries, communications, and e-distribution, could experience a boost in R&D.
Investment	Past epidemics have been associated with lower investment, in part due to heightened uncertainty (chapter 3). Given its global reach and the unprecedented containment measures, COVID-19 may erode investment more than prior epidemics.	In addition to higher public investment through fiscal support policies in response to the crisis, shifts in sector composition can spur new investment (chapter 7). Investments in pandemic-critical sectors, such as health care, medical supplies, pharmaceutical industries, communications, and e-distribution, are likely to increase.
Education and human capital	There could be lasting setbacks to education and human capital accumulation because of school closures and persistent unemployment (Protopsaltis and Baum 2019; World Bank 2020c).	Economic crisis lowers opportunity costs of learning, and human capital accumulation accelerated in some cases (Dellas 2003; Heylen and Pozzi 2007). Improved utilization of online learning could expand access to education (Ichino and Winter-Ebmer 2004; Psacharopoulos et al. 2020).
Institutions	Economies could get more politically polarized and fractionalized following economic crises and slow structural reforms (Mian, Sufi, and Trebbi 2014).	Major crises could accelerate the pace of some structural reforms (Ostry, Prati, and Spilimbergo 2009).
Macroeconomic stability	The pandemic could exacerbate macroeconomic imbalances, especially fiscal and external vulnerabilities. Countries that entered the COVID-19 crisis with elevated debt levels and limited policy space could risk financial stress (World Bank 2020b).	The risk of a financial crisis may encourage reforms to strengthen macroeconomic policy frameworks, to return to fiscal sustainability and preserve price stability. Financial market reforms tend to happen more often during crises or in their wake (Ostry, Prati, and Spilimbergo 2009).
Income equality	Pandemic-caused job losses could disproportionally affect the income and labor participation of low-skill workers and push 70 million to 100 million into poverty (Chetty et al. 2020; Lakner et al. 2020; Mahler et al. 2020; Sumner, Hoy, and Ortiz-Juarez 2020). Epidemics tend to hurt employment prospects for workers with basic education compared to those with higher education (Furceri et al. 2020). Higher inequality can negatively affect both social stability and human capital accumulation.	In some EMDE regions, such as SSA, inequality could decrease during recessions, perhaps reflecting a larger decline in income for relatively affluent households compared to low-income households (Camacho and Palmieri 2019).

TABLE 2.2 Possible impacts of COVID-19 on drivers of productivity growth (continued)

	Damaging	Offsetting
Gender	COVID-19 could increase caretaking burdens and unemployment for women and raise informality (World Bank 2020b). Differences across firms in implementing flexible work arrangements may lock workers into particular jobs and reduce labor mobility, particularly for women (James 2014).	Shifts toward flexible work arrangements, and changes in social norms as more men take primary responsibility for childcare, could promote gender equality (Alon et al. 2020).
Trade and FDI	Global trade is likely to see its worst contraction since World War II, at least in the short run (World Bank 2020b). FDI could see a 30-40 percent fall in the short run (UNCTAD 2020). Lower trade and FDI will narrow the path for achieving knowledge diffusion and technology transfer.	Supply chains could be restructured in ways that increase their diversity and improve resilience (World Bank 2020b). In countries with strong or credibly improving business climates and governance, this could be a new opportunity to attract FDI and participate in global value chains, which could boost knowledge and technological transfer (World Bank 2019c).
Urbanization	Agglomeration in urban areas could be less, and urbanization could be slower (Florida et al. 2020). Less agglomeration could limit knowledge exchange and the depth of markets in labor and services markets.	COVID-19 could spur improvements in urban design and functionality, based on incentivizing better access to core services, smarter cities, shorter commutes, and greener spaces. Home-based working for workers in middle- to high-income economies could boost performance (Bloom et al. 2010).

Source: World Bank.
Note: The effects of the COVID-19 pandemic are highly uncertain, and many are not yet visible in official data at the time of writing. The possible implications described above have partly been inferred from research on past crises, such as World War II, the Great Depression, and the global financial crisis. Which effects prove most important in practice could differ significantly from those described in the table. COVID-19 = coronavirus disease 2019; EMDE = emerging market and developing economy; FDI = foreign direct investment; R&D = research and development; SSA = Sub-Saharan Africa.

Fewer opportunities for technology transfer through trade and investment. At first glance, the fact that EMDEs remain behind the technology frontier seems to indicate scope for rapid growth. The paths to technology transfer may be narrowing, however. As noted earlier, the rapid expansion of global value chains before 2007 lost momentum with the GFC (World Bank 2020b). It will be weakened further by the effect of the COVID-19 pandemic as well as recent moves toward protectionism. Low absorption capacity in some firms in EMDEs will continue to limit adoption of new technologies, without more progress in the quality of education and training, including management training (Cirera and Maloney 2017).

Limited progress in governance indicators. According to survey measures of perceptions of government effectiveness, the control of corruption, the rule of law, and political stability, there has been only limited progress since the 1990s (figure 2.4). Across EMDEs, the total number of people exposed to fragile and conflict-affected situations has doubled since 1990. There are few signs of renewed institutional progress in

EMDEs. Although these developments may be seen as discouraging, they also indicate continuing potential for major productivity gains if the right reforms are implemented.

Climate change and agriculture. Climate change is expected to continue to adversely affect productivity, partly because natural disasters have become more common (chapter 3). The agriculture sector may be particularly affected if higher temperatures decrease crop yields in some countries (Fuglie et al. 2020). Agriculture currently accounts for 32 percent of GDP in low-income countries, compared to just 9 percent in EMDEs excluding low-income countries. In 2018, agriculture accounted for half of all employment in SSA and 44 percent in SAR.

Less favorable demographics. The share of the working-age population rose by 13 percentage points between 1995 and 2008 in MNA, and by 3.0 percentage points in SSA. In the coming years, populations in these regions are set to age. From 2018 to 2030 the share of the working-age population is expected to decline by 4.0 percentage points in advanced economies and 2.5 percentage points in EMDEs (figure 2.11). In EAP and ECA, the share of the working-age population is expected to decline by 3-4 percentage points by 2030, the reversal of a previous demographic dividend. In other regions—LAC, MNA, SAR, and SSA—the share is expected to be broadly stable.

Increased macroeconomic crisis risk. The COVID-19 pandemic could increase the vulnerability of many EMDEs to a macroeconomic crisis, perhaps linked to sovereign and private sector debt (World Bank 2020b; chapter 3). New pressures on the financial sector could also play a role. Previously, from the mid-1990s onward, EMDEs had made progress in achieving low inflation and macroeconomic stability (figure 2.4). In most cases, the scope for further improvement is limited (Ha, Kose, and Ohnsorge 2019). More EMDEs have adopted floating exchange rates and inflation targeting. Output volatility has declined in many countries (Ćorić 2014, 2019). It may be difficult to maintain that lower volatility given the pandemic, and, more generally, productivity gains from greater stability may be even harder to achieve.

Policy priorities

The new analysis presented in this chapter, and its review of the literature, suggests that a comprehensive policy approach is needed to raise productivity growth. Such an approach could have three main strands, recognizing that the productivity slowdown of the past decade has multiple sources.

First, governments should aim to stimulate private and public investment, and improve human capital. Second, policies should be designed to ensure a growth-friendly macroeconomic and institutional environment (Cirera and Maloney 2017). Third, governments should promote productivity growth at the firm level, by ensuring that enterprises are appropriately exposed to trade and foreign investment, and encouraging investment in human capital, including management as well as technical training.

Within these three strands, priorities will depend on the context. Countries with large unmet needs for infrastructure could seek to expand fiscal resources to finance more and better public investment. Countries with low private investment could implement institutional reform and other measures to improve the business climate, reduce support for state-owned enterprises, and improve access to finance, to enable private investment to flourish. Countries with skill shortages and many unskilled workers could seek to improve education and training. Countries where technological innovation is lacking may want to expose their private sectors to foreign knowledge and technologies, through greater openness to trade and FDI.

The design of policies for individual countries should consider the scope for them to interact and the potential unintended consequences. For instance, although liberalizing trade can increase the exposure of domestic firms to frontier technologies, increased competition with foreign firms can increase underemployment and the size of the informal sector, especially where labor markets are not flexible. This could counteract the reallocation of resources toward more productive sectors (Bosch, Goñi, and Maloney 2007; Goldberg and Pavcnik 2007; World Bank 2019a).

Improving the proximate sources of growth

Meet infrastructure investment needs. Among the forces explaining why growth has slowed, the weaker pace of capital deepening seems the largest contributor in several regions (ECA, MNA, SAR). Major investment needs remain. Better infrastructure—transport, power, telecommunications—can boost productivity (Aschauer 1989; Calderón, Moral-Benito, and Servén 2015; Martins 2019). In South Africa, a range of infrastructure investments in road and telecommunications networks was found to raise TFP (Bogetic and Fedderke 2009). Poor infrastructure, such as power supply problems, has constrained manufacturing TFP in Bangladesh (Fernandes 2008).

One practical challenge is to set priorities, because not all needs can be met. Where fiscal space allows, governments should fund projects especially likely to generate high social returns. It has been estimated that, to meet the infrastructure-related Sustainable Development Goals by 2030, EMDEs would need to spend between 2 and 8 percent of GDP on new infrastructure each year (Rozenberg and Fay 2019).[11] The region with the largest infrastructure deficit, relative to the Sustainable Development Goals, is SSA (figure 2.12). In EMDEs, annual investment of 2.5 percent of GDP in new infrastructure could raise the growth rate by three-tenths of a percentage point (Rozenberg and Fay 2019).

Remove private sector investment constraints. Productivity growth can be promoted by improving the business environment, corporate governance, and the functioning of labor and product markets (Richter 2006; World Bank 2019b). Financial depth is also relevant, because credit constraints can hold back private investment. Efforts are needed

---

[11] This is based on Sustainable Development Goal targets for universal access to safely managed water, sanitation, and hygiene services; improved irrigation infrastructure to improve food supplies; universal access to electricity; and improved transport infrastructure.

FIGURE 2.12 **EMDE infrastructure and education gaps**

Infrastructure needs to meet the Sustainable Development Goals are highest in SSA. While education gaps, measured as years of schooling, are closing in many regions, they remain large in SAR and SSA. The gaps with advanced economy levels are even larger after adjusting for educational quality.

A. Infrastructure gaps

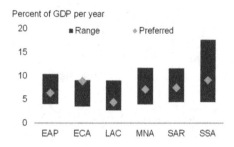

B. Years of schooling and learning-adjusted years of schooling

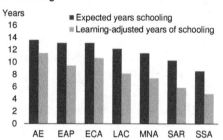

Sources: Rozenberg and Fay (2019); World Bank, Human Capital Project.

Note: AE = advanced economy; EMDEs = emerging market and developing economies; EAP = East Asia and Pacific; ECA = Europe and Central Asia; LAC = Latin America and the Caribbean; MNA = Middle East and North Africa; SAR = South Asia; SSA = Sub-Saharan Africa.

A. Investment and maintenance needs based on the Sustainable Development Goals as set out in Rozenberg and Fay (2019) including both new investment and maintenance of the existing capital stock. Infrastructure investment includes investment in electricity, transport, water supply and sanitation, flood protection, and irrigation. Preferred is defined as the infrastructure "pathway that limits stranded assets, has a relatively high per capita consumption due to electric mobility, and invests mostly in renewable energy and storage."

B. GDP-weighted expected years of schooling and learning-adjusted years of schooling from the World Bank's Human Capital Project. Learning-adjusted years of schooling use harmonized cross-country test scores to adjust average years of schooling.

to encourage the use of financial technology ("fintech") products in regions where few adults have access to traditional banking products and sources of finance (figure 2.13; IMF and World Bank 2019).

Invest in human capital. Educational gaps with advanced economies are largest in SAR and SSA. Compared to advanced economies, average years of schooling are three years lower in SAR and five years lower in SSA. On adjusting for differences in the quality of education, these gaps increase to eight and nine years, respectively (figure 2.12). This suggests that public schooling reform should be a priority in these regions. Tailored interventions could be used to improve school attendance, provide student grants and prizes, support nutrition programs for early childhood development, upgrade teacher training, foster teacher accountability and incentivize performance. If EMDEs were to close half the gap in educational attainment between them and advanced economies, that could raise the annual growth rate by about 0.2 percentage points (figure 2.14).

Better health also increases human capital. By 2017, average life expectancy at birth in EMDEs had risen to 70 years, from 50 years in 1960. This is striking progress, yet average EMDE life expectancy remains about 10 years below the average for advanced economies (81 years). Continued improvements in access to clean water, adequate sanitation, and health care would improve well-being substantially as well as raise

FIGURE 2.13 **Developments in financial and government technology**

Economies with large "unbanked" populations have also seen the biggest increases in financial technology innovations in payment systems and other financial services. These systems are critical to improving access to finance to make productivity-enhancing investments. EMDE government transparency still lags advanced economies. New information and communication technology can facilitate the rapid dissemination of information within and outside government to monitor performance and service shortfalls.

A. Access to banking services and mobile money accounts

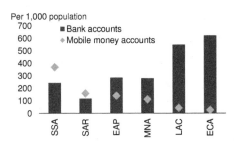

B. Information openness: National government data availability

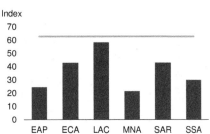

Sources: GSM Association (GSMA), Open Knowledge Foundation, World Bank.
Note: EAP = East Asia and Pacific; ECA = Europe and Central Asia; LAC = Latin America and the Caribbean; MNA = Middle East and North Africa; SAR = South Asia; SSA = Sub-Saharan Africa.
A. Mobile money accounts based on a sample of 16 EMDEs in EAP, 7 EMDEs in ECA, 18 EMDEs in LAC, 9 EMDEs in MNA, 7 EMDEs in SAR, and 40 EMDEs in SSA. Bank accounts, defined as depositors at commercial banks, based on a sample of 22 EMDEs in EAP, 24 EMDEs in ECA, 32 EMDEs in LAC, 19 EMDEs in MNA, 8 EMDEs in SAR, and 48 EMDEs in SSA.
B. Global Open Data Index is a proxy for the availability of open national government data at large. GDP weighted average. 2016/7 data. It is based on a sample of 27 advanced economies, 14 EMDEs in ECA, 6 EMDEs in EAP, 25 EMDEs in LAC, 2 EMDEs in the MNA, 6 EMDEs in SAR, and 12 EMDEs in SSA.

productivity. Such policies as improved training and performance-based payments for service providers could improve access to good-quality health care (World Bank 2012, 2018b).[12]

Creating a growth-friendly environment

Strengthen institutions and government effectiveness. Over the long term, institutional quality plays a crucial role in growth. Productivity gains can stem from policies that limit market power and promote fair competition, more even-handed contract enforcement, simplified and transparent legal systems, and governance reforms that lower political risk (Acemoglu et al. 2019; Rodrik 1999; Rodrik, Subramanian, and Trebbi 2004). Governments can also promote productivity growth by lowering transaction costs and increasing trust in institutions (Knack and Keefer 1997; World Bank 2019a).[13]

---

[12] Efforts to create a transparent and easily understandable metric of human capital might also help address the issue, especially considering the time needed for the benefits of human capital investment to materialize in the form of productivity growth (Kraay 2018; World Bank 2018a).

[13] In Rwanda, civil service reform between 1999 and 2009 increased the share of civil servants with a university degree from 6 percent to 79 percent and coincided with faster growth after 2000.

FIGURE 2.14 **Effects of reforms in EMDEs**

Governance reform spurts have been associated with increased potential TFP and investment growth. Setbacks, where perceptions of the quality of governance decline sharply, are associated with slowing investment and TFP growth. A reform package that combines filling investment needs, boosting human capital, and improving the adoption of new technologies could lift productivity growth by about 1 percentage point.

A. Effects of governance reform/setback

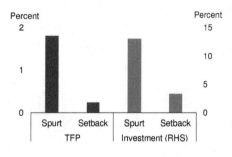

B. Simulated policy impact

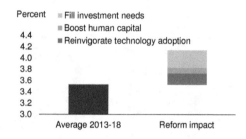

Source: World Bank.

Note: EMDEs = emerging market and developing economies; TFP = total factor productivity.

A. TFP growth refers to potential TFP growth, as estimated in Kose and Ohnsorge (2019). Potential TFP and investment growth during reform spurts and setbacks (minus simple average potential TFP and investment growth outside such episodes) using the Worldwide Governance Indicators. Based on an event study of 305 reform events—defined as two-standard-error changes in one of four Worldwide Governance Indicators—for 150 EMDEs and 36 advanced economies. Data are from 1996-2017.

B. Annual average labor productivity growth in EMDEs and the long-run effect on labor productivity growth based on the reform scenario assuming the following: "fill investment needs" means that the investment share of GDP increases by 4.5 percentage points each year as in the Rozenberg and Fay (2019) preferred infrastructure scenario; "boost human capital" means that the education attainment gap between advanced economies and EMDES is reduced by half; "reinvigorate technology adoption" means that the economic complexity gap between advanced economies and EMDES is reduced by half.

Simple comparisons suggest that better governance is associated with faster productivity growth (figure 2.4).[14] In the years ahead, governments can use new information and communication technologies ("govtech") to disseminate information more rapidly within and beyond government. This should enable better monitoring of performance and service shortfalls, and contribute to greater transparency (figure 2.13; World Bank 2018a).

Promote gender equality. Improvements in gender equality could raise productivity and income per capita (figure 2.5). Other things equal, reducing gender differentials in education and labor force participation would enhance the human capital available for production and management, and increase the ratio of workers to population, thereby raising productivity and income. As noted earlier, in many countries, declining fertility means that the share of the working-age population will fall in the coming years. Aging populations may be one headwind restraining growth, but steps to improve female participation could partially offset this (World Bank 2018d).

---

[14] These spurts are defined as those that raise at least one of four Worldwide Governance Indicators (government effectiveness, control of corruption, rule of law, and regulatory quality) by at least two standard deviations over two years, as in Didier et al. (2016). Setbacks are similarly defined.

Boosting productivity at the firm level

Foster capabilities of firms. Governments could promote international and domestic knowledge diffusion, and enhance the absorptive capacities of firms to support domestic innovation (Visscher, Eberhardt, and Everaert 2020). Firm-level analysis indicates that trade integration and economic flexibility can support economy-wide productivity growth (box 2.1). Efforts to increase market integration include regional trade agreements such as the African Continental Free Trade Area, which includes economies in MNA and SSA. Countries that reduce trade restrictions and invest in schooling and training can diversify their exports, becoming less reliant on primary commodities (Giri, Quayyum, and Yin 2019). Bangladeshi textile exporters, after gaining tariff-free access to European Union markets in 2001, saw increases in their productivity. There were also gains to productivity in domestically focused firms, suggesting the presence of spillovers (World Bank 2020a). Enhanced technology adoption in EMDEs—say, closing half the gap with advanced economies in product complexity—could increase the annual growth rate by a tenth of a percentage point (figure 2.14).

Management skills matter for high-quality R&D and innovation. In India, an intervention that provided firms with training on management practices saw productivity rise by 17 percent (Bloom et al. 2013). Participation in global value chains can improve management, partly through the diffusion of good practices. Moreover, the use of public-private partnerships to create technology extension centers in sectoral clusters can increase firm participation in global value chains and raise productivity (Cirera and Maloney 2017).[15] However, private firms may be reluctant to undertake costly R&D or develop market niches when competitors can free-ride on research or cost discovery (Hausmann and Rodrik 2003). This underscores the importance of enforcing patents and property rights, but these are only partial solutions.

Address informality. Informal sectors account for about 70 percent of employment in EMDEs, with especially high concentrations in SSA and SAR (World Bank 2019a). Informal enterprises are often small, inefficient, and relatively unproductive (La Porta and Shleifer 2014). Reallocating capital and workers from relatively unproductive informal enterprises to formal firms could boost aggregate productivity (Amin and Islam 2015; Amin, Ohnsorge, and Okou 2019; Ulyssea 2018). This reallocation could be achieved by limiting rent-seeking bureaucracy and improving the even-handedness of regulation and tax enforcement. Measures to raise productivity and skills could look beyond the formal sector, to address enterprises and unskilled workers and managers in the informal sector (Benhassine et al. 2018; Nguimkeu and Okou 2019).

Conclusion

Labor productivity growth has been driven by innovation, better education, and investment in physical capital. They are complemented by supportive institutions and

---

[15] Technology extension centers generate and transfer new foreign and domestic technologies, for local users, tailored to a country's specific needs.

policies, including measures that promote macroeconomic stability and enhance the rule of law. Productivity growth also benefits from expertise in producing relatively complex and sophisticated exports, linked to international technology diffusion. The effects of some of these drivers may have changed over time. Innovation and experience with economic complexity seem to have increased in importance. So have demographic factors, notably changes in population age structures.

Despite remarkable improvements over the last 60 years in key human capital indicators, such as the provision of primary education and infant mortality rates, many gaps between EMDEs and advanced economies remain. Moreover, since the GFC, many drivers of productivity growth have faltered, including those that had previously supported strong productivity growth. Some of these adverse trends are likely to be amplified and reinforced by the global effects of the COVID-19 pandemic.

The recent slowdown in productivity growth has multiple sources, and action on a range of fronts will be needed. Governments seeking to raise productivity growth can increase public investment and stimulate private investment; improve human capital; foster firm productivity, partly by promoting on-the-job training and upgrading management capabilities; increase the exposure of firms to international trade and foreign investment; enable the reallocation of resources toward more productive sectors; and seek to diversify production. The benefits of many productivity-friendly measures could often be enhanced by improving the macroeconomic and institutional environment.

Future research. Examining the effectiveness and the optimal design of policy measures attempting to boost labor productivity in different countries would be fruitful. In particular, analysis of the relative importance of specific aspects of the institutional environment that are conducive to productivity growth is needed. It is also critical to identify alternative sources of productivity growth capable of offsetting the fading impact of traditional drivers such as demographics, education, and global value chains. In light of the likely damage that COVID-19 is inflicting on long-term growth, implementing the appropriate structural reforms is critical, especially for EMDEs that are aiming to catch up with advanced economies. The next chapter focuses on the impact of unexpected adverse events and examines them in detail.

ANNEX 2A **Partial correlations**

Many drivers discussed in this chapter, such as patents per capita, are strongly correlated with the initial productivity level. The effect of initial productivity should be allowed for before analyzing the relationship between drivers and productivity growth. To remove the linear effect of the initial productivity level, consider the following equations:

$$dy_i = \beta_0 + \beta_1 y_{0,i} + e_{y,i},$$

$$x_i = \alpha_0 + \alpha_1 y_{0,i} + e_{x,I},$$

where dy_i is the long-term productivity growth rate of country i, $y_{0,i}$ is the initial log productivity level, x_i is the level of a driver, and $e_{y,i}$, $e_{x,i}$ are residuals. $e_{y,I}$ contains information about productivity growth after partialling out the (linear) effect of the initial productivity level. $e_{x,i}$ contains information about the driver after partialling out the effect of initial productivity.

In several of the charts, the average levels of $e_{y,i}$ for different subgroups of economies, grouped by the level of the $e_{x,i}$, are presented. Because $e_{y,i}$ is mean zero by construction, average dy_i are added to $e_{y,i}$ to recover the original average productivity growth.

ANNEX 2B **Long-run regressions**

For the growth regressions, the dependent variable is the log difference in labor productivity between the end and start years. Version 9.1 of the Penn World Table is used to construct labor productivity data. Data on drivers are mainly obtained from the World Development Indicators (table 2B.1). Following Barro and Sala-i-Martin (2004), independent variables are taken from the start year or the year closest to the start year.

Bayesian Model Averaging. Model uncertainty is inherent in growth regressions because there are many potential drivers and hence many potential specifications (Brock and Durlauf 2001; Durlauf, Kourtellos, and Tan 2008; Fernández, Ley, and Steel 2001). As of 2005, more than 140 variables had been identified as growth determinants in the empirical literature (Durlauf, Johnson, and Temple 2005). Bayesian model averaging can address model uncertainty formally, by recognizing that the identity of the true model is unknown and that it may be preferable to combine evidence from many different models. In the work for this chapter, a hyper-g prior is used for each coefficient, following Feldkircher and Zeugner (2012), which may achieve greater robustness than the priors used in the earlier literature. Priors on the inclusion probabilities are discussed below.

Grouping variables. Multiple variables can represent the same broad concepts; for example, both years of primary schooling and years of secondary schooling can proxy for educational attainment. Bayesian approaches should be designed to take this into account (Durlauf, Kourtellos, and Tan 2008; Ghosh and Ghattas 2015). In the analysis underlying this chapter, variables that represent common concepts are grouped together following Durlauf, Kourtellos, and Tan (2008). As in their work, a group is deemed relevant if the posterior probability of including at least one variable from the group exceeds the prior inclusion probability. To account for the dependency within groups, the prior inclusion probability of each variable is defined as

$$m_j^i = 1 - (1 - p_j)^{\frac{1}{K_j}},$$

where m_j^i, p_j, and K_j are the prior inclusion probability of variable i in group j, the total probability of inclusion for group j, and the number of variables in group j, respectively. m_j^i is set so that the prior probability of including at least one variable out of the K_j variables in the group is equal to p_j. The quantity p_j is set to 0.5 for all j, so there is no specific prior knowledge on the probability of a group's inclusion. Posterior distributions of the coefficients of the variables obtained from Bayesian model averaging are aggregated to the group level (tables 2B.2 and 2B.3). The marginal impact of a group is defined as follows:

$$\beta_j^G = \sum_{i \in \text{Group } j} \beta_i \, PIP_i \delta_{j,i},$$

where β_j^G is the marginal impact of the group j, β_i is a posterior mean of variable i given inclusion of the variable, PIP_i is a posterior inclusion probability of variable i, and $\delta_{j,i}$ is the factor loading of variable i in group j. A factor of group j is defined as the variable within a group whose coefficient posterior mean multiplied by the posterior inclusion probability is the highest. $\delta_{j,i}$ is the coefficient from the linear regression of variable i on the factor. β_j^G can be interpreted as the marginal impact of the factor, accounting for the correlations of the variables within groups. It can also be interpreted as the hypothetical posterior mean when including only one variable per group. In a linear regression, the factor-loading weighted sum of the coefficients is identical to the coefficient obtained by another regression that includes one variable per group.

Cross-section analysis. The empirical specification is based on the prediction of conditional convergence made by neoclassical growth models. In Mankiw, Romer, and Weil (1992), the conditional convergence dynamics are described by the following equation:

$$\ln(y_{t,j}) - \ln(y_{0,j}) = (1 - e^{-\lambda t}) \ln(y_j^*) - (1 - e^{-\lambda t}) \ln(y_{0,j}),$$

where $y_{t,j}$ is output per worker for country j at time t, y_j^* is steady-state output per worker, and λ is the rate of convergence.

The steady-state output per worker depends on a linear combination of the various drivers X_j:

$$\ln(y_j^*) = X_j \beta + \varepsilon_j.$$

Using $e^{-\lambda t} \approx 1 - \lambda t$ for small λt, the conditional convergence equation becomes

$$\frac{\ln(y_{T,j}) - \ln(y_{0,j})}{T} = -\lambda \ln(y_{0,j}) + X_j \gamma + \tilde{\varepsilon}_j,$$

where $\gamma = \beta \lambda$ and $\tilde{\varepsilon}_j = \varepsilon_j \lambda$. This is the equation used in the empirical work for this chapter. The dependent variable is annualized long-run productivity growth. In addition to the initial level of log productivity (y_0), other regressors (X_0)—discussed in the literature and measured at the beginning of the period—are included.

The vector γ captures how the covariates ($X_{0,j}$) drive long-run productivity growth and/ or the steady-state productivity level (the height of the growth path). The empirical literature often distinguishes between determinants suggested by the Solow model—the log of initial GDP per worker, the investment rate, and the population growth rate— and additional drivers such as education, demography, institutions, geography, innovation, and trade. The selection of these drivers is sometimes based on alternative

TABLE 2B.1 **Variables included in the regressions and their sources**

Group	Variable	Source
Financial development	Ratio of domestic credit to GDP	**WDI**
Investment	**Ratio of gross fixed capital formation to GDP**	**WDI**
Education	**Years of schooling**	**Barro and Lee (2015), UN**
	Human capital	UNDP
	Years of tertiary schooling	Barro and Lee (2015), UN
	Years of primary and secondary schooling	Barro and Lee (2015), UN
Economic Complexity	**Economic Complexity Index**	**Economic Observatory**
	(Exports + Imports)/GDP	WDI
Innovation	**Patents per capita**	**WDI**
	Patents per capita * years of tertiary schooling	WDI
Equality	**100 - Gini coefficient**	**UNU WIDER database**
Institutions	Political Rights Index	Freedom House
	Civil Rights Index	Freedom House
	Rule of Law Index	**International Country Risk Guide, PRS**
	Ratio of government consumption to GDP	WDI and various other sources
Urban	**Share of population in urban areas**	**WDI**
	Population density	WDI
Health	**Survival rate after 5 years per 1,000 births = 1,000-Infant mortality rate**	**WDI**
	Life expectancy at birth	WDI
Demography	**Share of population aged 15-64**	**WDI**
	Share of population aged below 15	WDI
Gender	**Ratio of years of schooling of female to male**	**Barro and Lee (2015), UN**
	Ratio of years of primary schooling of female to male	Barro and Lee (2015), UN
	Ratio of labor participation rate of female to male	WDI
Geography	Dummy for landlocked countries	WDI
	Share of land in tropical regions	**WDI**
	EMDE energy exporter dummy	World Bank
Stability	**(-1) * CPI Inflation Rate**	**WDI**
	Black market exchange rate relative to the official rate	WDI

Source: World Bank.
Note: List and sources of candidate variables used in Bayesian model averaging. For each category, variables with the highest posterior probability of inclusion are shown in bold. CPI = consumer price index; EMDE = emerging market and developing economy; PRS = The PRS Group; UN = United Nations; UNDP = United Nations Development Programme; UNU WIDER = United Nations University World Institute for Development Economics Research; WDI = World Development Indicators.

growth theories, or augmented versions of the Solow model (Mankiw, Romer, and Weil 1992).

Robustness and caveats. The empirical analysis of growth and aggregate productivity raises major challenges. The growth literature has sought to address these, but the small number of countries available for analysis is a major constraint. Discussions of various issues arising in the study of growth can be found in Brock and Durlauf (2001); Durlauf, Johnson, and Temple (2005); Durlauf, Kourtellos and Tan (2008); Kim and Loayza (2019); and Temple (1999).

TABLE 2B.2 **Estimates of PIPs and posterior means**

	PIP	Posterior mean	Group	Group marginal effects
Initial productivity	1.00	-0.01	Initial productivity	-0.01
Domestic credit	0.33	0.07	Finance	0.02
Investment ratio	0.47	0.09	Investment	0.04
Years of schooling	0.38	0.38		
Years of tertiary schooling	0.24	0.01	Education	0.07
Years of primary/secondary schooling	0.32	-0.26		
ECI+	0.61	0.32	Complexity	0.20
Trade openness	0.21	-0.01	Trade	0.00
Patents per capita	0.37	0.14		
Patents per capita* years of tertiary schooling	0.25	-0.03	Innovation	0.07
R&D expenditure	0.35	0.08		
Gini *(-1)	0.33	0.05	Equality	0.02
Government consumption share	0.25	0.02		
Political rights	0.23	0.00	Institution	0.09
Civil rights	0.22	-0.01		
Rule of law	0.52	0.17		
Urban population	0.60	-0.28	Urban	0.01
Population density	0.37	0.06		
Infant survival rate	0.36	0.10	Health	0.04
Working-age population share	0.25	-0.07	Demography	0.02
Population share less than 15	0.29	-0.11		
Female/male labor market participation rate relativeto male labor market participatin rate	0.23	-0.01	Gender	0.05
Female years of schooling ratio	0.34	-0.01		
Female years of primary schooling ratio	0.35	0.16		
Water access	0.19	0.01		
Share of land in tropical region	0.69	0.26	Geography	0.18
Oil exporter	0.21	0.01		
Inflation *(-1)	0.21	0.00	Stability	-0.03
Black market premium *(-1)	0.92	-0.33		

Source: World Bank.
Note: ECI = Economic Complexity Index; PIP = posterior inclusion probability; R&D = research and development.

Endogeneity. The Bayesian approach used in the chapter can help to overcome ad hoc variable selection and the arbitrary omission of variables. Issues of interpretation remain, because many candidate explanatory variables—innovation, democracy, rule of law, trade, education, health, investment, and so on—are best seen as equilibrium outcomes. Because growth and the explanatory variables are jointly determined, it is hard to draw conclusions about causal effects, and persuasive instrumental variables are hard to find.

TABLE 2B.3 **Estimated group marginal effects**

Group	1960-2018		1995-2018	
	Full	EMDEs	Full	EMDEs
Finance	0.022	0.112	-0.001	-0.006
Investment	0.042	0.105	0.023	0.084
Education	0.067	0.147	0.445	0.095
Complexity	0.196	0.085	0.961	0.372
Trade	-0.002	-0.002	0.015	0.000
Innovation	0.067	0.000	-0.007	0.153
Equality	0.016	0.010	-0.004	-0.010
Institution	0.090	0.089	0.050	0.005
Urban	0.011	0.119	-0.036	-0.006
Health	0.036	0.000	-0.005	-0.139
Demography	0.015	0.003	0.233	0.617
Gender	0.053	0.021	-0.004	0.142
Geography	0.179	0.049	0.087	0.032
Stability	-0.030	-0.020	0.015	0.165

Source: World Bank.
Note: EMDEs = emerging market and developing economies.

Some candidate variables may be best viewed as outcomes of growth, rather than (or as well as) drivers of growth. To limit this problem, the analysis summarized in the chapter is based on the use of initial conditions. Nevertheless, interpretation of the findings should be cautious.

References

Abel, J. R., I. Dey, and T. M. Gabe. 2014. "Productivity and the Density of Human Capital." *Journal of Regional Science* 52 (4): 562–86.

Acemoglu, D. 1996. "A Microfoundation for Social Increasing Returns in Human Capital Accumulation." *Quarterly Journal of Economics* 111 (3): 779–804.

Acemoglu, D., and D. Autor. 2011. "Skills, Tasks and Technologies: Implications for Employment and Earnings." In *Handbook of Labor Economic, Vol. 4*, edited by D. Card and O. Ashenfelter, 1043–171. Amsterdam: Elsevier.

Acemoglu, D., and M. Dell. 2010. "Productivity Differences between and within Countries." *American Economic Journal: Macroeconomics* 2 (1): 169–88.

Acemoglu, D., and S. Johnson. 2005. "Unbundling Institutions." *Journal of Political Economy* 113 (5): 949–95.

Acemoglu, D., and S. Johnson. 2007. "Disease and Development: The Effect of Life Expectancy on Economic Growth." *Journal of Political Economy* 115 (6): 925–85.

Acemoglu, D., and S. Johnson. 2014. "Disease and Development: A Reply to Bloom, Canning, and Fink." *Journal of Political Economy*.122 (6): 1367–75.

Acemoglu, D., S. Johnson, and J. A. Robinson. 2001. "The Colonial Origins of Comparative Development: An Empirical Investigation." *American Economic Review* 91 (5): 1369–401.

Acemoglu, D., S. Johnson, and J. A. Robinson. 2003. "Disease and Development in Historical Perspective." *Journal of the European Economic Association* 1 (2–3): 397–405.

Acemoglu, D., S. Naidu, P. Restrepo, and J. A. Robinson. 2019. "Democracy Does Cause Growth." *Journal of Political Economy* 127 (1): 47–100.

Acemoglu, D., and F. Zilibotti. 2001. "Productivity Differences." *Quarterly Journal of Economics* 116 (2): 563–606.

Adler, G., R. Duval, D. Furceri, S. Kilic Celik, K. Koloskova, and M. Poplawski-Ribeiro. 2017. "Gone with the Headwinds: Global Productivity." IMF Staff Discussion Note 17/04, International Monetary Fund, Washington, DC.

Aghion, P., P. Howitt, and D. Mayer-Foulkes. 2005. "The Effect of Financial Development on Convergence: Theory and Evidence." *Quarterly Journal of Economics* 120 (1): 173–224.

Aitken, B. J., and A. E. Harrison. 1999. "Do Domestic Firms Benefit from Direct Foreign Investment? Evidence from Venezuela." *American Economic Review* 89 (3): 605–18.

Aiyar, S., C. Ebeke, and X. Shao. 2016. "The Impact of Workforce Aging on European Productivity." IMF Working Paper 16/238, International Monetary Fund, Washington, DC.

Aksoy, Y., H. S. Basso, R. P. Smith, and T. Grasl. 2019. "Demographic Structure and Macroeconomic Trends." *American Economic Journal: Macroeconomics* 11 (1): 193–224.

Albeaik, S., M. Kaltenberg, M. Alsaleh, and C. A. Hidalgo. 2017. "Improving the Economic Complexity Index." Cornell University, Ithaca, New York. https://arxiv.org/abs/1707.05826.

Alcala, F., and A. Ciccone. 2004. "Trade and Productivity." *Quarterly Journal of Economics* 119 (2): 613–46.

Alesina, A., and D. Rodrik. 1994. "Distributive Politics and Economic Growth." *Quarterly Journal of Economics* 109 (2): 465–90.

Alon, T. M., M. Doepke, J. Olmstead-Rumsey, and M. Tertilt. 2020. "The Impact of COVID-19 on Gender Equality." NBER Working Paper 26947, National Bureau of Economic Research, Cambridge, MA.

Alvaredo, F., L. Chancel, T. Piketty, E. Saez, and G. Zucman. 2018. "The Elephant Curve of Global Inequality and Growth." *AEA Papers and Proceedings* 108: 103–8.

Amin, M., and A. Islam. 2015. "Are Large Informal Firms More Productive than Small Informal Firms? Evidence from Firm-Level Surveys in Africa." *World Development* 74 (October): 374–85.

Amin, M., F. Ohnsorge, and C. Okou. 2019. "Casting a Shadow: Productivity of Formal Firms and Informality." Policy Research Working Paper 8945, World Bank, Washington, DC.

Annan, K. 1997. Speech at World Bank Conference: Global Knowledge 97, Toronto, June 22. https://www.un.org/press/en/1997/19970623.sgsm6268.html.

Andrews, D., C. Criscuolo, and P. Gal. 2016. "The Best versus the Rest: The Global Productivity Slowdown, Divergence across Firms and the Role of Public Policy." OECD Productivity Working Paper 05, Organisation for Economic Co-operation and Development, Paris.

Araujo, J. T., E. Vostroknutova, and K. Wacker. 2017. "Productivity Growth in Latin America and the Caribbean: Exploring the Macro-Micro Linkages." Discussion Paper 19, World Bank, Washington, DC.

Aschauer, D. A. 1989. "Is Public Expenditure Productive?" *Journal of Monetary Economics* 23 (2): 177–200.

Atkin, D., A. K. Khandelwal, and A. Osman. 2017. "Exporting and Firm Performance: Evidence from a Randomized Experiment." *Quarterly Journal of Economics* 132 (2): 551–615.

Autor, D. H., and D. Dorn. 2013. "The Growth of Low-Skill Service Jobs and the Polarization of the U.S. Labor Market." *American Economic Review* 103 (5): 1553–97.

Autor, D. H., D. Dorn, L. F. Katz, C. Patterson, and J. Van Reenen. 2020. "The Fall of the Labor Share and the Rise of Superstar Firms." *Quarterly Journal of Economics* 135 (2): 645–709.

Aw, B. Y., S. Chung, and M. J. Roberts. 2000. "Productivity and Turnover in the Export Market: Micro-level Evidence from the Republic of Korea and Taiwan (China)." *World Bank Economic Review* 14 (1): 65–90.

Balasubramanian, N., and J. Sivadasan. 2011. "What Happens When Firms Patent? New Evidence from U.S. Economic Census Data." *Review of Economics and Statistics* 93 (1): 126–46.

Bandiera, O., I. Barankay, and I. Rasul. 2011. "Field Experiments with Firms." *Journal of Economic Perspectives* 25 (3): 63–84.

Banerjee, A. V., and E. Duflo. 2003. "Inequality and Growth: What Can the Data Say?" *Journal of Economic Growth* 8 (3): 267–99.

Barro, R. J. 1996. "Determinants of Economic Growth: A Cross-Country Empirical Study." NBER Working Paper 5698, National Bureau of Economic Research, Cambridge, MA.

Barro, R. J. 2000. "Inequality and Growth in a Panel of Countries." *Journal of Economic Growth* 5 (1): 5–34.

Barro, R. J., and J. W. Lee. 2015. *Education Matters: Global Schooling Gains from the 19th to the 21st Century.* New York: Oxford University Press.

Barro, R. J., and X. Sala-i-Martin. 2004. *Economic Growth.* Cambridge, MA: MIT Press.

Bartelsman, E. J., and M. Doms. 2000. "Understanding Productivity: Lessons from Longitudinal Microdata." *Journal of Economic Literature* 38 (3): 569–94.

Bartelsman, E. J., J. Haltiwanger, and S. Scarpetta. 2013. "Cross-Country Differences in Productivity: The Role of Allocation and Selection." *American Economic Review* 103 (1): 305–34.

Bazzi, S., and M. A. Clemens. 2013. "Blunt Instruments: Avoiding Common Pitfalls in Identifying the Causes of Economic Growth." *American Economic Journal: Macroeconomics* 5 (2): 152–86.

Beaudry, P., F. Collard, and D. A. Green. 2005. "Changes in the World Distribution of Output Per Worker, 1960–1998: How a Standard Decomposition Tells an Unorthodox Story." *Review of Economics and Statistics* 87 (4): 741–53.

Beck, T., R. Levine, and N. Loayza. 2000a. "Finance and the Sources of Growth." *Journal of Financial Economics* 58 (1–2): 261–300.

Beck, T., R. Levine, and N. Loayza. 2000b. "Financial Intermediation and Growth: Causality and Causes." *Journal of Monetary Economics* 46 (1): 31–77.

Benhabib, J., and M. M. Spiegel. 2003. "Human Capital and Technology Diffusion." Working Paper 2003-02, Federal Reserve Bank of San Francisco.

Benhassine, N., D. McKenzie, V. Pouliquen, and M. Santini. 2018. "Does Inducing Informal Firms to Formalize Make Sense? Experimental Evidence from Benin." *Journal of Public Economics* 157 (January): 1–14.

Berg, A., J. D. Ostry, C. G. Tsangarides, and Y. Yakhshilikov. 2018. "Redistribution, Inequality, and Growth: New Evidence." *Journal of Economic Growth* 23 (3): 259–305.

Bernard, A. B., S. J. Redding, and P. K. Schott. 2010. "Multiple-Product Firms and Product Switching." *American Economic Review* 100 (1): 70–97.

Bernard, A. B., S. J. Redding, and P. K. Schott. 2011. "Multiproduct Firms and Trade Liberalization." *Quarterly Journal of Economics* 126 (3): 1271–318.

Blalock, G., and P. J. Gertler. 2004. "Learning from Exporting Revisited in a Less Developed Setting." *Journal of Development Economics* 75 (2): 397–416.

Bloom, N. 2014. "Fluctuations in Uncertainty." *Journal of Economic Perspectives* 28 (2): 153–76.

Bloom, D. E., D. Canning, and G. Fink. 2014. "Disease and Development Revisited." *Journal of Political Economy* 122 (6): 1355–66.

Bloom, D. E., D. Canning, and J. Sevilla. 2004. "The Effect of Health on Economic Growth: A Production Function Approach." *World Development* 32 (1): 1–13.

Bloom, N., B. Eifert, A. Mahajan, D. McKenzie, and J. Roberts. 2013. "Does Management Matter? Evidence from India." *Quarterly Journal of Economics* 128 (1): 1–51.

Bloom, N., A. Mahajan, D. J. McKenzie, and J. Roberts. 2010. "Why Do Firms in Developing Countries Have Low Productivity?" *American Economic Review* 100 (2): 619–23.

Bloom, N., and J. Van Reenen. 2010. "Why Do Management Practices Differ across Firms and Countries?" *Journal of Economic Perspectives* 24 (1): 203–24.

Bogetic, Z., and J. W. Fedderke. 2009. "Infrastructure and Growth in South Africa: Direct and Indirect Productivity Impacts of 19 Infrastructure Measures." *World Development* 37 (9): 1522–39.

Bosch, M., E. Goñi, and W. Maloney. 2007. "The Determinants of Rising Informality in Brazil: Evidence from Gross Worker Flows." Policy Research Working Paper 4375, World Bank, Washington, DC.

Bosworth, B., and S. M. Collins. 2003. "The Empirics of Growth: An Update." *Brookings Papers on Economic Activity* 2003 (2): 113–206.

Brock, W. A., and S. N. Durlauf. 2001. "Growth Empirics and Reality." *World Bank Economic Review* 15 (2): 229–74.

Bruns, S. B., and J. P. A. Ioannidis. 2020. "Determinants of Economic Growth: Different Time Different Answer?" *Journal of Macroeconomics* 63 (March): 103–85.

Brynjolfsson, E., and L. Hitt. 1995. "Information Technology as a Factor of Production: The Role of Differences among Firms." *Economics of Innovation and New Technology* 3 (3–4): 183–99.

Brynjolfsson, E., D. Rock, and C. Syverson. Forthcoming. "The Productivity J-Curve: How Intangibles Complement General Purpose Technologies." *American Economic Journal: Macroeconomics*.

Buera, F. J., J. P. Kaboski, and Y. Shin. 2011. "Finance and Development: A Tale of Two Sectors." *American Economic Review* 101 (5): 1964–2004.

Buera, F. J., and E. Oberfield. 2020. "The Global Diffusion of Ideas." *Econometrica* 88 (1): 83–114.

Caballero, R. J. 2008. "Creative Destruction." In *The New Palgrave Dictionary of Economics, 2nd edition*, edited by S. N. Durlauf and L. E. Blume. London: Palgrave Macmillan.

Caballero, R. J., and M. L. Hammour. 1994. "The Cleansing Effect of Recessions." *American Economic Review* 84 (5): 1350–68.

Calderón, C., E. Moral-Benito, and L. Servén. 2015. "Is Infrastructure Capital Productive? A Dynamic Heterogeneous Approach." *Journal of Applied Econometrics* 30 (2): 177–98.

Camacho, M., and G. Palmieri. 2019. "Do Economic Recessions Cause Inequality to Rise?" *Journal of Applied Economics* 22 (1): 304–20.

Cardarelli, R., and L. Lusinyan. 2015. "U.S. Total Factor Productivity Slowdown: Evidence from the U.S. States." IMF Working Paper 15/116, International Monetary Fund, Washington, DC.

Casacuberta, C., G. Fachola, and N. Gandelman. 2004. "The Impact of Trade Liberalization on Employment, Capital, and Productivity Dynamics: Evidence from the Uruguayan Manufacturing Sector." *The Journal of Policy Reform* 7 (4): 225–48.

Chen, D. H. C., and C. J. Dahlman. 2004. "Knowledge and Development: A Cross-Section Approach." Policy Research Working Paper 3366, World Bank, Washington, DC.

Chetty, R., J. N. Friedman, N. Hendren, M. Stepner, and Opportunity Insights. 2020. "How Did COVID-19 and Stabilization Policies Affect Spending and Employment? A New Real-Time Economic Tracker Based on Private Sector Data." NBER Working Paper 27431, National Bureau of Economic Research, Cambridge, MA.

Cirera, X., R. Fattal Jaef, and N. Gonne. 2017. "High-Growth Firms and Misallocation in Low-Income Countries: Evidence from Côte d'Ivoire." World Bank, Washington, DC.

Cirera, X., and W. F. Maloney. 2017. *The Innovation Paradox: Developing-Country Capabilities and the Unrealized Promise of Technological Catch-Up.* Washington, DC: World Bank.

Clarke, G. R. G. 1995. "More Evidence on Income Distribution and Growth." *Journal of Development Economics* 47 (2): 403–27.

Clerides, S. K., S. Lach, and J. R. Tybout. 1998. "Is Learning by Exporting Important? Micro-Dynamic Evidence from Colombia, Mexico, and Morocco." *Quarterly Journal of Economics* 113 (3): 903–47.

Cohen, W. M., and D. A. Levinthal. 1989. "Innovation and Learning: The Two Faces of R&D." *Economic Journal* 99 (397): 569.

Cohen, W. M., and D. A. Levinthal. 1990. "Absorptive Capacity: A New Perspective on Learning and Innovation." *Administrative Science Quarterly* 35 (1): 128.

Collard-Wexler, A., and J. De Loecker. 2015. "Reallocation and Technology: Evidence from the U. S. Steel Industry." *American Economic Review* 105 (1): 131–71.

Combes, P., and L. Gobillon. 2015. "The Empirics of Agglomeration Economies." In *Handbook of Regional and Urban Economics*, edited by G. Duranton, V. Henderson, and W. Strange, 247–348. Amsterdam: Elsevier.

Ćorić, B. 2014. "The Global Extent of the Great Moderation." *Oxford Bulletin of Economics and Statistics* 74 (4): 493–509.

Ćorić, B. 2019. "Variations in Output Volatility: Evidence from International Historical Data." *Economics Letters* 178 (May): 102–5.

Cowen, T. 2011. *The Great Stagnation: How America Ate All the Low-Hanging Fruit of Modern History, Got Sick, and Will (Eventually) Feel Better.* New York: Dutton.

Croppenstedt, A., M. Goldstein, and N. Rosas. 2013. "Gender and Agriculture, Inefficiencies, Segregation, and Low Productivity Traps." *World Bank Research Observer* 28 (1): 79–109.

Cusolito, A. P., D. C. Francis, N. Karalashvili, and J. R. Meza. 2018. "Firm Level Productivity Estimates." Methodological Note, World Bank, Washington, DC.

Cusolito, A. P., and W. F. Maloney. 2018. *Productivity Revisited: Shifting Paradigms in Analysis and Policy.* Washington, DC: World Bank.

Dall'Olio, A., M. Iootty, N. Kanehira, and F. Saliola. 2014. "Enterprise Productivity: a Three-Speed Europe." ECB Working Paper Series 1748, European Central Bank, Frankfurt.

Danquah, M., E. Moral-Benito, and B. Ouattara. 2014. "TFP Growth and Its Determinants: A Model Averaging Approach." *Empirical Economics* 47 (1): 227–51.

Decker, R. A., J. Haltiwanger, R. S. Jarmin, and J. Miranda. 2016. "Where Has All the Skewness Gone? The Decline in High-Growth (Young) Firms in the U.S." *European Economic Review* 86 (July): 4–23.

Deininger, K., and L. Squire. 1998. "New Ways of Looking at Old Issues: Inequality and Growth." *Journal of Development Economics* 57 (2): 259–87.

Del Carpio, X., and T. Taskin. 2019. "Quality of Management of Firms in Turkey." Jobs Working Paper 27, World Bank, Washington, DC.

Dellas, H. 2003. "On the Cyclicality of Schooling: Theory and Evidence." *Oxford Economic Papers* 55 (1): 148–72.

De Loecker, J. 2013. "Detecting Learning by Exporting." *American Economic Journal: Microeconomics* 5 (3): 1–21.

Demirgüç-Kunt, A., and R. Levine. 1996. "Stock Markets, Corporate Finance, and Economic Growth: An Overview." *World Bank Economic Review* 10 (2): 223–39.

Dercon, S., M. Fafchamps, C. Pattillo, R. Oostendorp, J. Willem Gunning, P. Collier, A. Zeufack, et al. 2004. "Do African Manufacturing Firms Learn from Exporting?" *Journal of Development Studies* 40 (3): 115–41.

Diao, X., M. McMillan, and D. Rodrik. 2019. "The Recent Growth Boom in Developing Economies: A Structural-Change Perspective." In *The Palgrave Handbook of Development Economics: Critical Reflections on Globalization and Development,* edited by M. Nissanke and J. A. Ocampo. London: Palgrave Macmillan.

Dias, D. A., C. R. Marques, and C. Richmond. 2020. "A Tale of Two Sectors: Why Is Misallocation Higher in Services than in Manufacturing?" *Review of Income and Wealth* 66 (2): 361–93.

Díaz-García, C., A. González-Moreno, and F. J. Sáez-Martínez. 2013. "Gender Diversity within R&D Teams: Its Impact on Radicalness of Innovation." *Innovation: Management, Policy and Practice* 15 (2): 149–60.

Didier, T., M. A. Kose, F. Ohnsorge, and L. (Sandy) Ye. 2016. "Slowdown in Emerging Markets: Rough Patch or Prolonged Weakness?" *SSRN Electronic Journal.* https://papers.ssrn.com/sol3/papers.cfm?abstract_id=2723326.

di Giovanni, J., A. A. Levchenko, and I. Mejean. 2018. "The Micro Origins of International Business-Cycle Comovement." *American Economic Review* 108 (1): 82–108.

di Mauro, F., B. Mottironi, G. Ottaviano, and A. Zona-Mattioli. 2018. "Living with Lower Productivity Growth: Impact on Exports." Working Paper 18-10, Peterson Institute for International Economics, Washington, DC.

di Mauro, F. and C. Syverson. 2020. "The COVID Crisis and Productivity Growth." Vox CERP Policy Portal, April 16, 2020. https://voxeu.org/article/covid-crisis-and-productivity-growth.

Duranton, G., and D. Puga. 2004. "Micro-Foundations of Urban Agglomeration Economies." In *Handbook of Regional and Urban Economics,* edited by J.V. Henderson and J. F. Thisse, 2063–117. Amsterdam: Elsevier.

Durlauf, S. N. 2009. "The Rise and Fall of Cross-Country Growth Regressions." *History of Political Economy* 41 (Suppl 1): 315–33.

Durlauf, S. N., P. A. Johnson, and J. R. W. Temple. 2005. "Growth Econometrics." In *Handbook of*

Economic Growth 1A, edited by P. Aghion and S. N. Durlauf, 555–677. Amsterdam: North Holland Publishing.

Durlauf, S. N., A. Kourtellos, and C. M. Tan. 2008. "Are Any Growth Theories Robust?" *Economic Journal* 118 (527): 329–46.

Dutz, M. A., R. K. Almeida, and T. G. Packard. 2018. *The Jobs of Tomorrow: Technology, Productivity, and Prosperity in Latin America and the Caribbean.* Directions in Development Series. Washington, DC: World Bank.

Easterly, W., and R. Levine. 2001. "What Have We Learned from a Decade of Empirical Research on Growth? It's Not Factor Accumulation: Stylized Facts and Growth Models." *World Bank Economic Review* 15 (2): 177–219.

EBRD (European Bank for Reconstruction and Development), EIB (European Investment Bank), and World Bank 2016. *What's Holding Back the Private Sector in MENA? Lessons from the Enterprise Survey.* Washington, DC: World Bank.

Feldkircher, M., and S. Zeugner. 2012. "The Impact of Data Revisions on the Robustness of Growth Determinants—A Note on 'Determinants of Economic Growth: Will Data Tell?'" *Journal of Applied Econometrics* 27 (4): 686–94.

Fernald, J. 2015. "Productivity and Potential Output before, during, and after the Great Recession." In *NBER Macroeconomics Annual 2014, vol. 29,* edited J. A. Parker and M. Woodford, 1–51. Chicago: University of Chicago Press.

Fernandes, A. M. 2007. "Trade Policy, Trade Volumes and Plant-Level Productivity in Colombian Manufacturing Industries." *Journal of International Economics* 71 (1): 52–71.

Fernandes, A. M. 2008. "Firm Productivity in Bangladesh Manufacturing Industries." *World Development* 36 (10): 1725–44.

Fernández, C., E. Ley, and M. F. J. Steel. 2001. "Model Uncertainty in Cross-Country Growth Regressions." *Journal of Applied Econometrics* 16 (5): 563–76.

Feyrer, J. 2008. "Aggregate Evidence on the Link between Age Structure and Productivity." *Population and Development Review* 34 (2008): 78–99.

Fisman, R., and I. Love. 2003. "Financial Development and the Composition of Industrial Growth." NBER Working Paper 9583, National Bureau of Economic Research, Cambridge, MA.

Florida, R., E. Glaeser, M. M. Sharif, K. Bedi, T. J. Campanella, C. H. Chee, D. Doctoroff, et al. 2020. "How Life in Our Cities Will Look after the Coronavirus Pandemic." *Foreign Policy*, May 1, 2020.

Forbes, K. J. 2000. "A Reassessment of the Relationship between Inequality and Growth." *American Economic Review* 90 (4): 869–87.

Foster, L., C. Grim, and J. Haltiwanger. 2016. "Reallocation in the Great Recession: Cleansing or Not?" *Journal of Labor Economics* 34 (S1): S293–S331.

Foster, L., C. A. Grim, J. C. Haltiwanger, and Z. Wolf. 2017. "Macro and Micro Dynamics of Productivity: From Devilish Details to Insights." NBER Working Paper 23666, National Bureau of Economic Research, Cambridge, MA.

Foster, L., J. Haltiwanger, C. Syverson, B. Lucia Foster, S. Basu, J. Chevalier, S. Davis, K. Murphy, and D. Neal. 2008. "Reallocation, Firm Turnover, and Efficiency: Selection on Productivity or Profitability?" *American Economic Review* 98 (1): 394–425.

Fox, J. T., and V. Smeets. 2011. "Does Input Quality Drive Measured Differences in Firm Productivity?" *International Economic Review* 52 (4): 961–89.

Frank, M. W. 2009. "Inequality and Growth in the United States: Evidence from a New State-Level Panel of Income Inequality Measures." *Economic Inquiry* 47 (1): 55–68.

Frankel, J. A., and D. Romer. 1999. "Does Trade Cause Growth?" *American Economic Review* 89 (3): 397–98.

Fuglie, K., M. Gautam, A. Goyal, and W. F. Maloney. 2020. *Harvesting Prosperity: Technology and Productivity Growth in Agriculture.* Washington, DC: World Bank.

Furceri, D., P. Loungani, J. D. Ostry, and P. Pizzuto. 2020. "Will Covid-19 Affect Inequality? Evidence from Past Pandemics." *Covid Economics* 12: 138–57.

Furman, J. L., and R. Hayes. 2004. "Catching up or Standing Still? National Innovative Productivity among 'Follower' Countries, 1978–1999." *Research Policy* 33 (9): 1329–54.

Gallen, Y. 2018. "Motherhood and the Gender Productivity Gap." *SSRN Electronic Journal.* https://papers.ssrn.com/sol3/papers.cfm?abstract_id=3198356.

Galor, O., and D. N. Weil. 1996. "The Gender Gap, Fertility, and Growth." *American Economic Review* 86 (3): 374–87.

Gamberoni, E., C. Giordano, and P. Lopez-Garcia. 2016. "Capital and Labour (Mis)Allocation in the Euro Area: Some Stylized Facts and Determinants." Working Paper 1981, European Central Bank, Frankfurt.

Ghosh, J., and A. E. Ghattas. 2015. "Bayesian Variable Selection under Collinearity." *The American Statistician* 69 (3): 165–73.

Giri, R., S. N. Quayyum, and R. J. Yin. 2019. "Understanding Export Diversification: Key Drivers and Policy Implications." IMF Working Paper 19/105, International Monetary Fund, Washington, DC.

Goldberg, P. K., A. K. Khandelwal, N. Pavcnik, and P. Topalova. 2010. "Multi-Product Firms and Product Turnover in the Developing World: Evidence from India." *Review of Economics and Statistics* 92 (4): 1042–49.

Goldberg, P. K., and N. Pavcnik. 2007. "Distributional Effects of Globalization in Developing Countries." *Journal of Economic Literature* 45 (1): 39–84.

Goñi, E., and W. F. Maloney. 2017. "Why Don't Poor Countries Do R&D? Varying Rates of Factor Returns across the Development Process." *European Economic Review* 94 (May): 126–47.

Goodfriend, M., and J. McDermott. 1998. "Industrial Development and the Convergence Question." *American Economic Review* 88 (5): 1277–89.

Gordon, R. J. 2016. *The Rise and Fall of American Growth: The U.S. Standard of Living since the Civil War.* Princeton, New Jersey: Princeton University Press.

Görg, H., and D. Greenaway. 2004. "Much Ado about Nothing? Do Domestic Firms Really Benefit from Foreign Direct Investment?" *World Bank Research Observer* 19 (2): 171–97.

Görg, H., and E. Strobl. 2001. "Multinational Companies and Productivity Spillovers: A Meta-Analysis." *Economic Journal* 111 (475): F723–39.

Gould, D. M. 2018. *Critical Connections: Promoting Economic Growth and Resilience in Europe and Central Asia.* Europe and Central Asia Studies. Washington, DC: World Bank.

Gramacy, R. B., S. W. Malone, and E. Ter Horst. 2014. "Exchange Rate Fundamentals, Forecasting, and Speculation: Bayesian Models in Black Markets." *Journal of Applied Econometrics* 29 (1): 22–41.

Graner, M., and A. Isaksson. 2009. "Firm Efficiency and the Destination of Exports: Evidence from Kenyan Plant-Level Data." *Developing Economies* 47 (3): 279–306.

Griffith, R., S. Redding, and H. Simpson. 2004. "Convergence and Foreign Ownership at the Establishment Level." IFS Working Paper 02/22, Institute for Fiscal Studies, London.

Grover Goswami, A., D. Medvedev, and E. Olafsen. 2019. *High-Growth Firms: Facts, Fiction, and Policy Options for Emerging Economies.* Washington, DC: World Bank.

Ha, J., M. A. Kose, and F. Ohnsorge, eds. 2019. *Inflation in Emerging and Developing Economies: Evolution, Drivers, and Policies.* Washington, DC: World Bank.

Haggard, S., and L. Tiede. 2011. "The Rule of Law and Economic Growth: Where Are We?" *World Development* 39 (5): 673–85.

Hall, B. H., J. Mairesse, and P. Mohnen. 2010. "Measuring the Returns to R&D." In *Handbook of the Economics of Inovation* 2, edited by B. H. Hall and N. Rosenberg, 1033–84. Amsterdam: North Holland Publishing.

Hall, R. E., and C. I. Jones. 1999. "Why Do Some Countries Produce So Much More Output per Worker than Others?" *Quarterly Journal of Economics* 114 (1): 83–116.

Haskel, J. E., S. C. Pereira, and M. J. Slaughter. 2007. "Does Inward Foreign Direct Investment Boost the Productivity of Domestic Firms?" *Review of Economics and Statistics* 89 (3): 482–96.

Hausmann, R., and C. Hidalgo. 2010. "Country Diversification, Product Ubiquity, and Economic Divergence." CID Working Paper 201, Harvard Kennedy School, Cambridge, MA.

Hausmann, R., C. A. Hidalgo, S. Bustos, M. Coscia, S. Chung, J. Jimenez, A. Simoes, et al. 2014. *The Atlas of Economic Complexity: Mapping Paths to Prosperity.* Cambridge, MA: MIT Press.

Hausmann, R., J. Hwang, and D. Rodrik. 2007. "What You Export Matters." *Journal of Economic Growth* 12 (1): 1–25.

Hausmann, R., and D. Rodrik. 2003. "Economic Development as Self-Discovery." *Journal of Development Economics* 27 (2): 603–33.

Hayashi, F., and E. C. Prescott. 2002. "The 1990s in Japan: A Lost Decade." *Review of Economic Dynamics* 5 (1): 206–35.

Herzer, D., and S. Vollmer. 2012. "Inequality and Growth: Evidence from Panel Cointegration." *Journal of Economic Inequality* 10 (4): 489–503.

Heylen, F., and L. Pozzi. 2007. "Crises and Human Capital Accumulation." *Canadian Journal of Economics* 40 (4): 1261–85.

Hidalgo, C., and R. Hausmann. 2009. "The Building Blocks of Economic Complexity." CID Working Paper 186, Harvard Kennedy School, Cambridge, MA.

Hsieh, C., and P. J. Klenow. 2009. "Misallocation and Manufacturing TFP in China and India." *Quarterly Journal of Economics* 124 (4): 1403–48.

Hulten, C. R. 1992. "Growth Accounting when Technical Change Is Embodied in Capital." *American Economic Review* 82 (4): 964–80.

Ichino, A., and R. Winter-Ebmer. 2004. "The Long-Run Educational Cost of World War II." *Journal of Labor Economics* 22 (1): 57–86.

Im, F. G., and D. Rosenblatt. 2015. "Middle-Income Traps: A Conceptual and Empirical Survey." *Journal of International Commerce, Economics and Policy* 6 (3): 1–39.

IMF and World Bank. 2019. *Fintech: The Experience So Far—Executive Summary.* Washington, DC: International Monetary Fund.

Irwin, D. 2019. "Does Trade Reform Promote Economic Growth? A Review of Recent Evidence." NBER Working Paper 25927, National Bureau of Economic Research, Cambridge, MA.

Isaksson, A. 2007. "Determinants of Total Factor Productivity: A Literature Review." UNIDO Staff Working Paper 02/2007, United Nations Industrial Development Organization, Vienna.

Jarreau, J., and S. Poncet. 2012. "Export Sophistication and Economic Growth: Evidence from China." *Journal of Development Economics* 97 (2): 281–94.

James, A. 2014. "Work–Life 'Balance' and Gendered (Im)Mobilities of Knowledge and Learning in High-Tech Regional Economies." *Journal of Economic Geography* 14 (3): 483–510.

Jones, B. F. 2010. "Age and Great Invention." *Review of Economics and Statistics* 92 (1): 1–14.

Kataryniuk, I., and J. Martínez-Martín. 2019. "TFP Growth and Commodity Prices in Emerging Economies." *Emerging Markets Finance and Trade* 55 (10): 2211–29.

Kaufmann, D., A. Kraay, and M. Mastruzzi. 2007. "Worldwide Governance Indicators Project: Answering the Critics." Policy Research Working Paper 4149, World Bank, Washington, DC.

Keller, W. 2004. "International Technology Diffusion." *Journal of Economic Literature* 42 (3): 752–84.

Keller, W., and S. R. Yeaple. 2009. "Multinational Enterprises, International Trade, and Productivity Growth: Firm-Level Evidence from the United States." *Review of Economics and Statistics* 91 (4): 821–31.

Kim, Y. E., and N. V. Loayza. 2019. "Productivity Growth: Patterns and Determinants across the World." Policy Research Working Paper 8852, World Bank, Washington, DC.

King, R. G., and R. Levine. 1993. "Finance and Growth: Schumpeter Might Be Right." *Quarterly Journal of Economics* 108 (3): 717–37.

Klasen, S., and M. Santos Silva. 2018. "Gender Inequality as a Barrier to Economic Growth: A Review of the Theoretical Literature." Working Paper 252, Courant Research Center on Poverty, University of Göttingen, Germany.

Knack, S., and P. Keefer. 1997. "Does Social Capital Have an Economic Payoff? A Cross-Country Investigation." *Quarterly Journal of Economics* 112 (4): 1251–88.

Knowles, S., and P. D. Owen. 1995. "Health Capital and Cross-Country Variation in Income per Capita in the Mankiw-Romer-Weil Model." *Economics Letters* 48 (1): 99–106.

Kose, M. A., and F. Ohnsorge. 2019. *A Decade after the Global Recession: Lessons and Challenges for Emerging and Developing Economies.* Washington, DC: World Bank.

Kose, M. A., E. S. Prasad, and M. E. Terrones. 2009. "Does Openness to International Financial Flows Raise Productivity Growth?" *Journal of International Money and Finance* 28 (4): 554–80.

Kouamé, W. A., and S. J. Tapsoba. 2018. "Structural Reforms and Firms' Productivity: Evidence from Developing Countries." IMF Working Paper 18/63, International Monetary Fund, Washington, DC.

Kraay, A. 2018. "Methodology for a World Bank Human Capital Index." Policy Research Working Paper 8593, World Bank, Washington, DC.

Kraay, A., I. Soloaga, and J. Tybout. 2004. "Product Quality, Productive Efficiency, and International Technology Diffusion: Evidence from Plant-Level Panel Data." Policy Research Working Paper 2759, World Bank, Washington, DC.

Kumar, S., and R. R. Russell. 2002. "Technological Change, Technological Catch-up, and Capital Deepening: Relative Contributions to Growth and Convergence." *American Economic Review* 92 (3): 527–48.

La Porta, R., and A. Shleifer. 2014. "Informality and Development." *Journal of Economic Perspectives* 28 (3): 109–26.

Laeven, L. And F. Valencia. 2018. "Systemic Banking Crises Revisited." IMF Working Paper 18/206, International Monetary Fund, Washington, DC.

Lakner, C., D. G. Mahler, M. Negre, and E. B. Prydz. 2020. "How Much Does Reducing Inequality Matter for Global Poverty?" Global Poverty Monitoring Technical Note 13, World Bank, Washington, DC.

Lazear, E. P. 2000. "Performance Pay and Productivity." *American Economic Review* 90 (5): 1346–61.

Levine, R. 1997. "Financial Development and Economic Growth: Views and Agenda." *Journal of Economic Literature* 35 (2): 688–726.

Levine, R., and D. Renelt. 1992. "A Sensitivity Analysis of Cross-Country Growth Regressions." *American Economic Review* 82 (4): 942–63.

Liu, Y., and N. Westelius. 2017. "The Impact of Demographics on Productivity and Inflation in Japan." *Journal of International Commerce, Economics and Policy* 8 (2): 1–16.

Loko, B., and M. A. Diouf. 2014. "Revisiting the Determinants of Productivity Growth: What's New?" IMF Working Paper 09/225, International Monetary Fund, Washington, DC.

Lopez-Acevedo, G., D. Medvedev, and V. Palmade. 2017. *South Asia's Turn: Policies to Boost Competitiveness and Create the Next Export Powerhouse.* Washington, DC: World Bank.

Maestas, N., K. Mullen, and D. Powell. 2016. "The Effect of Population Aging on Economic Growth, the Labor Force and Productivity." Working Paper 1063, RAND Labor & Population, Santa Monica, CA.

Mahler, D. G., C. Lanker, R. A. C. Aguilar, and H. Wu. 2020. "Updated Estimates of the Impact of COVID-19 on Global Poverty." *Data Blog,* June 8, 2020. https://blogs.worldbank.org/opendata.

Maloney, W. F., and G. Nayyar. 2018. "Industrial Policy, Information, and Government Capacity." *World Bank Research Observer* 33 (2): 189–217.

Mankiw, N. G., D. Romer, and D. N. Weil. 1992. "A Contribution to the Empirics of Economic Growth." *Quarterly Journal of Economics* 107 (2): 407–37.

Martins, P. M. G. 2019. "Structural Change: Pace, Patterns and Determinants." *Review of Development Economics* 23 (1): 1–34.

Mayer, J. 2001. "Technology Diffusion, Human Capital and Economic Growth in Developing Countries." UNCTAD Discussion Papers 154, United Nations Conference on Trade and Development, Geneva.

McAfee, A. 2019. *More from Less: The Surprising Story of How We Learned to Prosper Using Fewer Resources and What Happens Next.* New York: Scribner.

Melo, P. C., D. J. Graham, and R. Brage-Ardao. 2013. "The Productivity of Transport Infrastructure Investment: A Meta-Analysis of Empirical Evidence." *Regional Science and Urban Economics* 43 (5): 695–706.

Mian, A., A. Sufi, and F. Trebbi. 2014. "Resolving Debt Overhang: Political Constraints in the Aftermath of Financial Crises." *American Economic Journal: Macroeconomics* 6 (2): 1–28.

Nelson, R. R. 1981. "Research on Productivity Growth and Productivity Differences: Dead Ends and New Departures." *Journal of Economic Literature* 19 (3): 1029–64.

Nguimkeu, P., and C. Okou. 2019. "Informality." In *The Future of Work In Africa: Harnessing the Potential of Digital Technologies for All,* edited by J. Choi, M. Dutz, and Z. Usman, 107–39. Washington, DC: World Bank.

Nguyen, H., T. Taskin, and A. Yilmaz. 2016. "Resource Misallocation in Turkey." Policy Research Working Paper 7780, World Bank, Washington, DC.

North, D. C. 1991. "Institutions." *Journal of Economic Perspectives* 5 (1): 97–114.

Ostry, J. D., A. Prati, and A. Spilimbergo. 2009. "Structural Reforms and Economic Performance in Advanced and Developing Countries." IMF Occasional Papers, International Monetary Fund, Washington, DC.

Panizza, U. 2002. "Income Inequality and Economic Growth: Evidence from American Data." *Journal of Economic Growth* 7 (1): 25–41.

Papa, J., L. Rehill, and B. O'Connor. 2018. "Patterns of Firm Level Productivity in Ireland." OECD Productivity Working Paper 15, Organisation for Economic Co-operation and Development, Paris.

Papaioannou, E., and G. Siourounis. 2008. "Democratisation and Growth." *Economic Journal* 118 (532): 1520–51.

Pereira, A. M., and J. M. Andraz. 2013. "On the Economic Effects of Public Infrastructure Investment: A Survey of the International Evidence." Working Paper 108, College of William and Mary, Williamsburg, VA.

Perotti, R. 1996. "Growth, Income Distribution, and Democracy: What the Data Say." *Journal of Economic Growth* 1 (2): 149–87.

Persson, T., and G. Tabellini. 1994. "Is Inequality Harmful for Growth? Theory and Evidence." *American Economic Review* 84 (3): 600–21.

Prati, A., M. G. Onorato, and C. Papageorgiou. 2013. "Which Reforms Work and under What Institutional Environment? Evidence from a New Data Set on Structural Reforms." *Review of Economics and Statistics* 95 (3): 946–68.

Pritchett, L. 2000. "Understanding Patterns of Economic Growth: Searching for Hills among Plateaus, Mountains, and Plains." *World Bank Economic Review* 14 (2): 221–50.

Protopsaltis, S., and S. Baum. 2019. "Does Online Education Live Up to Its Promise? A Look at the Evidence and Implications for Federal Policy." George Mason University. http://mason.gmu.edu/~sprotops/OnlineEd.pdf.

Psacharopoulos, G., H. Patrinos, V. Collis, and E. Vegas. 2020. "The COVID-19 Cost of School Closures." *Education and Development* (blog), April 29, 2020. https://www.brookings.edu/blog/education-plus-development.

Restuccia, D., and R. Rogerson. 2013. "Misallocation and Productivity." *Review of Economic Dynamics* 16 (1): 1–10.

Richter, K. 2006. "Thailand's Growth Path: From Recovery to Prosperity." Policy Research Working Paper 3912, World Bank, Washington, DC.

Rockey, J., and J. Temple. 2016. "Growth Econometrics for Agnostics and True Believers." *European Economic Review* 81 (January): 86–104.

Rodríguez, F., and D. Rodrik. 2000. "Trade Policy and Economic Growth: A Skeptic's Guide to the Cross-National Evidence." In *NBER Macroeconomics Annual* 15: 261–338.

Rodrik, D. 1999. "Where Did All the Growth Go? External Shocks, Social Conflict, and Growth Collapses." *Journal of Economic Growth* 4 (4): 385–414.

Rodrik, D., A. Subramanian, and F. Trebbi. 2004. "Institutions Rule: The Primacy of Institutions over Geography and Integration in Economic Development." *Journal of Economic Growth* 9 (2): 131–65.

Romer, P. M. 1990. "Endogenous Technological Change." *Journal of Political Economy* 98 (5): S71–S102.

Rozenberg, J., and M. Fay. 2019, eds. *Beyond the Gap: How Countries Can Afford the Infrastructure They Need while Protecting the Planet*. Washington, DC: World Bank.

Ruiz Pozuelo, J., A. Slipowitz, and G. Vuletin. 2016. "Democracy Does Not Cause Growth: The Importance of Endogeneity Arguments." IDB Working Paper 694, Inter-American Development Bank, Washington, DC.

Sahay, R., M. Cihak, P. N'Diaye, R. B. Barajas, D. Ayala, Y. Gao, A. Kyobe, et al. 2015. "Rethinking Financial Deepening: Stability and Growth in Emerging Markets." Staff Discussion Note 15/08, International Monetary Fund, Washington, DC.

Sakellaris, P., and D. J. Wilson. 2004. "Quantifying Embodied Technological Change." *Review of Economic Dynamics* 7 (1): 1–26.

Schiffbauer, M., A. Sy, S. Hussain, H. Sahnoun, and P. Keefer. 2015. *Jobs or Privileges: Unleashing the Employment Potential of the Middle East and North Africa*. Washington, DC: World Bank.

Schober, T., and R. Winter-Ebmer. 2011. "Gender Wage Inequality and Economic Growth: Is There Really a Puzzle?—A Comment." *World Development* 39 (8): 1476–84.

Schor, A. 2004. "Heterogeneous Productivity Response to Tariff Reduction. Evidence from Brazilian Manufacturing Firms." *Journal of Development Economics* 75 (2): 373–96.

Sirimaneetham, V., and J. R. W. Temple. 2009. "Macroeconomic Stability and the Distribution of Growth Rates." *World Bank Economic Review* 23 (3): 443–79.

Solow, R. 1956. "A Contribution to the Theory of Economic Growth." *Quarterly Journal of Economics* 70 (1): 65–94.

Sumner, A., C. Hoy, and E. Ortiz-Juarez. 2020. "Estimates of the Impact of COVID-19 on Global Poverty." WIDER Working Paper 43, United Nations University World Institute for Development Economics Research (WIDER), Helsinki.

Syverson, C. 2004. "Product Substituability and Productivity Dispersion." *Review of Economics and Statistics* 86 (2): 534–50.

Syverson, C. 2011. "What Determines Productivity?" *Journal of Economic Literature* 49 (2): 326–65.

Temple, J. 1999. "The New Growth Evidence." *Journal of Economic Literature* 37 (1): 112–56.

Ulyssea, G. 2018. "Firms, Informality, and Development: Theory and Evidence from Brazil." *American Economic Review* 108 (8): 2015–47.

UNCTAD (United Nations Conference on Trade and Development). 2020. "Impact of the COVID-19 Pandemic on Global FDI and GVCs. Updated Analysis." Investment Trends Monitor, March.

UNDP (United Nations Development Programme). 2019. *Human Development Report 2019: beyond Income, beyond Averages, beyond Today: Inequalities in Human Development in the 21st Century*. New York: UNDP.

Van Reenen, J. 2011. "Does Competition Raise Productivity through Improving Management Quality?" *International Journal of Industrial Organization* 29 (3): 306–16.

Visscher, S. D., M. Eberhardt, and G. Everaert. 2020. "Estimating and Testing the Multicountry Endogenous Growth Model." *Journal of International Economics* 125 (July): 103325.

Voitchovsky, S. 2005. "Does the Profile of Income Inequality Matter for Economic Growth?" *Journal of Economic Growth* 10 (3): 273–96.

Vorisek, D., and S. Yu. 2020. "Understanding the Cost of Achieving the Sustainable Development Goals." Policy Research Working Paper 9146, World Bank, Washington, DC.

Wolitzky, A. 2018. "Learning from Others." *American Economic Review* 108 (10): 2763–801.

Wooster, R. B., and D. S. Diebel. 2010. "Productivity Spillovers from Foreign Direct Investment in Developing Countries: A Meta-Regression Analysis." *Review of Development Economics* 14 (3): 640–55.

World Bank. 2012. *World Development Report: Gender Equality and Development.* Washington, DC: World Bank.

World Bank. 2017. *World Development Report 2017: Governance and the Law.* Washington, DC: World Bank.

World Bank. 2018a. *Improving Public Sector Performance: Through Innovation and Inter-Agency Coordination.* Washington, DC: World Bank.

World Bank. 2018b. *The Human Capital Project.* Washington, DC: World Bank.

World Bank. 2018c. *World Development Report 2018: Learning to Realize Education's Promise.* Washington, DC: World Bank.

World Bank. 2018d. *Global Economic Prospects: Broad-Based Upturn, but for How Long?* January. Washington, DC: World Bank.

World Bank. 2019a. *Global Economic Prospects: Darkening Skies.* January. Washington, DC: World Bank.

World Bank. 2019b. *World Development Report: The Changing Nature of Work.* Washington, DC: World Bank.

World Bank. 2019c. *East Asia and Pacific Economic Update: Managing Headwinds.* April. Washington, DC: World Bank.

World Bank. 2020a. *World Development Report 2020: Trading for Development in the Age of Global Value Chains.* Washington, DC: World Bank.

World Bank. 2020b. *Global Economic Prospects.* June. Washington, DC: World Bank.

World Bank. 2020c. *The COVID-19 Pandemic: Shocks to Education and Policy Responses.* Washington, DC: World Bank.

Xu, B., and J. Wang. 1999. "Capital Goods Trade and R&D Spillovers in the OECD." *Canadian Journal of Economics/Revue Canadienne d'Economique* 32 (5): 1258–74.

Yahmed, S. B., and S. Dougherty. 2014. "Import Competition, Domestic Regulation and Firm-Level Productivity Growth in the OECD." OECD Economic Department Working Papers 980. Organisation for Economic Co-operation and Development, Paris.

Yellen, J. L. 2015. "The Outlook for the Economy." Speech to Providence Chamber of Commerce, Providence, RI, May 22. https://www.bis.org/review/r150528a.pdf.

Coming out of crisis is not just about winning the war, but also establishing the peace. If you only focus on ending the crisis, without building the future you end up more vulnerable than before.

Mohamed El-Erian *(2020)*
Chief Economic Advisor at Allianz

CHAPTER 3

What Happens to Productivity during Major Adverse Events

Since 2000, there have been three major global slowdowns, with the latest and most pronounced episode triggered by the COVID-19 (coronavirus disease 2019) pandemic. At the same time, many countries have faced major adverse events including natural disasters, wars, and financial crises, all of which can lead to long-lasting harm to productivity. Wars inflict particularly severe damage to productivity, and financial crises also lead to substantial losses, especially accompanied by a rapid buildup of debt. The greater frequency of natural disasters, especially climate disasters, means that they have the largest aggregate impact on productivity; natural disasters have occurred most often, and their frequency has doubled since 2000. Global adverse events—such as an epidemiological disaster of the magnitude of the COVID-19 pandemic—can have large sustained negative effects on productivity through a dislocation of labor, a tightening of credit, a disruption of value chains, and a decline in innovation. Policies to counter the negative consequences of adverse shocks include accommodative fiscal policies such as reconstruction spending on resilient infrastructure, transparent governance, efficient use of relief funds, and growth-friendly structural reforms. Appropriate policies and regulations concerning finance, construction, and environmental protection can help reduce the frequency of adverse shocks.

Introduction

The aftermath of the 2007-09 global financial crisis (GFC) witnessed a broad-based slowdown in labor productivity growth lasting over a decade (chapter 1). This follows a typical pattern associated with adverse events such as natural disasters, wars, and financial crises. These events often result in protracted economic losses through declines in both the level and the growth rate of output, as well as persistent losses in labor productivity.[1] Among natural disasters, the COVID-19 (coronavirus disease 2019) pandemic—a major epidemiological disaster— is an adverse event on a massive global scale and could have a large and persistent impact on global productivity.

The damage from adverse events comes through a variety of channels. Natural disasters and wars may damage key infrastructure and disrupt value chains (Acevedo et al. 2018; Cerra and Saxena 2008). Financial crises increase uncertainty, damage confidence, impede access to finance, and lower corporate earnings—all developments that are likely to reduce investment. More generally, adverse events can dampen labor productivity by

---

Note: This chapter was prepared by Alistair Dieppe, Sinem Kilic Celik, and Cedric Okou. Research assistance was provided by Khamal Clayton, Xinyue Wang, and Xi Zhang.

[1] Discussion of these topics can be found in, for example, Cerra and Saxena (2008); Blanchard, Cerutti, and Summers (2015); Cerra and Saxena (2017); Furceri and Mourougane (2012b); Jordà, Schularick, and Taylor (2013); Kilic Celik et al. (forthcoming); and Ray and Esteban (2017).

causing a loss of skills and by reducing the efficiency of job matching, as well as by disrupting knowledge creation, transfer, and acquisition. The growth of labor productivity is therefore likely to be impeded by declines in both the growth of total factor productivity (TFP) and capital deepening.[2]

Severe global biological disasters such as COVID-19 can damage labor productivity by affecting both supply and demand (chapter 6). Adverse supply-side effects can occur through the depletion of the labor force, the tightening of financial conditions, and the disruption of supply chains, which are an important measure for the diffusion of innovation. The COVID-19 pandemic is also weighing sharply on aggregate demand by depressing consumer demand for goods and services, eroding business confidence and investment, and raising financial costs (Baker et al. 2020; Ludvigson, Ma, and Ng 2020; Ma, Rogers, and Zhou 2020). Weaker aggregate demand can reduce the incentives for product innovation and quality improvement, slow technological progress, and lower productivity. Furthermore, these negative impacts can be amplified by other factors such as cross-border spillovers, lingering financial vulnerabilities, and the compounding effects of recessions. An analysis of economic developments around previous, smaller-scale epidemiological disasters can provide a framework for understanding the channels through which productivity could be affected by COVID-19, and the potential persistence of its effects (box 3.1).

The productivity losses that result from adverse events in emerging market and developing economies (EMDEs) can reduce the rate of convergence to the advanced economy technology frontier (chapter 4). However, the effects of adverse events on labor productivity and output hinge not only on their magnitude, duration, and frequency, but also on country characteristics and circumstances, including the policy response and the pre-shock buffers established by policy makers. Large-scale and severe disasters are typically more damaging to labor productivity and output. Low-income countries (LICs) and countries that are already affected by fragile and conflict-affected situations (FCS) have generally been less able than other countries to cope with wars and climate disasters such as droughts. If sufficiently severe, natural disaster can trigger financial crises—particularly in countries with high levels of debt—or lead to conflicts and wars.

Policies should be geared toward both reducing the likelihood of adverse shocks and alleviating their impacts. Depending on available policy space, countercyclical macroeconomic policies can help counter negative effects on investment and labor markets. Successful examples include the fiscal and monetary stimulus undertaken after

---

[2] TFP growth captures growth in production not explained by increases in factor inputs (essentially capital and labor). Under a standard growth accounting decomposition, which relies on a number of special assumptions, TFP growth may be computed as a residual of labor productivity growth after deduction of the estimated contribution of the growth of capital per unit of labor (capital deepening). Labor productivity growth is prone to measurement issues, especially in countries where the services, government, or informal sectors account for large shares of the economy. Estimates of TFP growth depend additionally on a number of special assumptions, including that factors of production (labor and capital) are paid their marginal products, presumably under conditions of perfect competition and constant returns to scale (See annex 3B and chapter 1).

the GFC and the COVID-19 pandemic in 2020 by many advanced economies and EMDEs, and the international assistance provided for reconstruction in the aftermath of recent natural disasters in some FCS countries.[3] Structural policy frameworks—such as the quality of governance and business climates—can facilitate faster adjustment, protect vulnerable groups, and mitigate long-lasting damage to productivity.

This chapter examines a wide range of adverse events to assess the extent to which they have had protracted effects on labor productivity and TFP. The chapter aims to shed light on the following questions:

- How frequently and through what channels have adverse events affected productivity?

- How have adverse events differed in the scale of their impact on productivity?

- What policies can help to mitigate the impact of adverse events on productivity?

Contributions

This chapter makes several contributions to an expanding literature on the impact on productivity of adverse events.

Systematic cross-country evaluation of adverse events on productivity. This chapter is the first to undertake a systematic study of the effects of a broad range of adverse events—natural disasters (with a focus on large epidemics), wars, and financial crises—on alternative productivity measures across a wide range of advanced economies, EMDEs, and LICs.

Comprehensive explorations of persistent effects on productivity. One key aspect of the effects of adverse events on productivity is their persistence. Several studies have documented protracted losses in output or productivity following business cycle downturns, recessions, or financial crises (Blanchard, Cerutti, and Summers 2015; Cerra and Saxena 2008; Hall 2014). This chapter builds on and broadens previous work (Easterly et al. 1993; Kilic Celik et al. forthcoming; Mourougane 2017; Noy 2009), by assessing the channels, the magnitude of the losses, and the speed of recovery across a wide range of different types of adverse events.

Comprehensive discussion of supportive policy framework. This chapter analyzes feasible policies to mitigate the corrosive effects of negative shocks. It discusses the role of structural policies and reforms that can support productivity following adverse shocks.

---

[3] The effectiveness of such assistance depends on the government's ability to efficiently spend the relief money where it is needed. Designing and deploying a disaster-response infrastructure with well-defined rules and procedures before disasters hit improves resilience and boosts the effectiveness of reconstruction efforts (Hallegatte and Rentschler 2018).

It also highlights the importance of fiscal space in building a cushion that can be used to counter productivity loss in a country hit by adverse events.

Main findings

The estimated results, broadly consistent with the literature, include the following:

- *Natural disasters have occurred more often than wars or financial crises, and their frequency has increased since 2000.* Natural disasters can be subdivided into several distinct types: climate disasters such as floods and cyclones, biological disasters such as epidemics or insect infestations, and geophysical disasters such as earthquakes and volcanoes. In the period 1960-2018, the number of episodes of natural disasters was 25 times that of wars and 12 times that of financial crises. Climate-related events were the most frequent type of natural disaster, with a doubling of their frequency after 2000. LICs, particularly in Sub-Saharan Africa (SSA), were most affected by natural disasters. Biological and geophysical episodes are less frequent and are often more geographically contained.[4]

- *Severe disasters have lasting effects on productivity.* Although wars inflict particularly severe and long-lasting damage to both capital and TFP, the high frequency of climate disasters increases their importance as a source of damage to productivity. On average during 1960-2018, climate disasters reduced annual contemporaneous labor productivity by about 0.5 percent—about one-fifth of the impact of a typical war episode. However, climate disasters have occurred 25 times as frequently as wars, meaning their cumulative negative effects on productivity are larger. Moreover, although the frequency of severe natural disasters has stabilized since 2000, they have strong negative effects on productivity. After three years, severe climate disasters lower labor productivity by about 7 percent, mainly through weakened TFP. Severe disasters can also trigger other types of adverse events such as financial crises and wars, thus compounding the corrosive effects on productivity.

- *Severe epidemics such as COVID-19 can cause persistent damage to productivity.* Four epidemics since 2000 (SARS [severe acute respiratory syndrome], MERS [Middle East respiratory syndrome], Ebola, and Zika) had significant and persistent negative effects on productivity.[5] They lowered productivity by 4 percent after three years. Amid elevated uncertainty, epidemics have reduced labor productivity through their adverse effects on investment and the labor force. The COVID-19 pandemic may be significantly worse than most past disasters because of its global reach and the unprecedented social distancing and containment measures put in place to slow the spread of the virus.

---

[4] The COVID-19 pandemic is one of the very rare pandemics which has affected almost every country and region. This might be a signal of the severity of future pandemics with increasing international mobility of people (Jordà, Singh, and Taylor 2020).

[5] Swine flu (H1N1, 2009-10) is excluded because it coincided with the 2008-09 GFC.

- *Productivity is highly vulnerable to financial stress, especially when accompanied by a rapid buildup of debt.* Financial crises weigh heavily on productivity growth through a wide range of channels. During debt accumulation episodes associated with financial crises, cumulative productivity gains three years into the episode were 2 percentage points lower than in episodes without crises in EMDEs. The rapid buildup of debt in EMDEs since the GFC increases vulnerabilities to financial crises and limits the ability of countries to cope with other types of adverse events. The current COVID-19 pandemic is likely to exacerbate those vulnerabilities by further stretching public and private balance sheets.

- *Appropriate policies can help to prevent and to mitigate the effects of adverse events.* A rapid policy response to adverse events, including countercyclical macroeconomic policies and reconstruction spending when appropriate, can help to mitigate the negative effects on productivity. Improving institutions and the business climate can also help increase the pace of recovery following an adverse event. Appropriate policies and regulations with respect to finance, construction, and environmental protection can help reduce the frequency of adverse events. Fiscal space allows economies to fund recovery efforts after natural disasters, and sound fiscal policies tend to limit the likelihood of a financial crisis. Fiscal stimulus also helps cushion the severity of large adverse events such as severe biological disasters.

The remainder of this chapter is organized as follows. The next section reviews the literature and seeks to identify the stylized facts relating to the effects of adverse events and the channels through which natural disasters, wars, and financial crises have affected productivity. The third section describes the results of new research into the negative impacts of these adverse events on productivity across different groups of countries. The fourth section discusses the policy options available to counter the corrosive effects of adverse events on productivity. The chapter concludes with a summary of the findings. Box 3.1 focuses on the effects of epidemics on productivity.

Adverse events: Literature and stylized facts

This section reviews the literature on the economic effects of adverse events and documents their main features. It focuses on three main types of adverse events: natural disasters (climate, biological, and geophysical), wars (intrastate and external) and financial crises (banking, debt, and currency). The definitions of the events are provided in annex 3A. Globally in the period 1960-2018, countries were far more frequently hit by natural disasters than by financial crises or wars (figure 3.1). However, the frequency of big and severe natural disasters—defined respectively as causing losses of life exceeding 10 and 100 people per million—stabilized after 2000, perhaps reflecting better mitigation policies in some countries as they have confronted climate change (figure 3.1).

An episode is defined if a specific type of event occurs at least once in a country in a year. Therefore, there are typically more occurrences than episodes. The remainder of

FIGURE 3.1 Global occurrence of major adverse events, 1960-2018

In 1960-2018, countries were hit more frequently by natural disasters than by financial crises or wars. The occurrence of natural disasters per year rose steeply until 2000 and then leveled off; in 2000-18 their average occurrence per year was nearly double that of the preceding 20 years. The occurrences of big and severe climate disasters stabilized after 2000, perhaps reflecting better mitigation policies. The frequency of financial crises spiked in the 1980s and 1990s, and fell by 70 percent after 2000. The frequency of wars declined by 50 percent in 2000-18 relative to 1980-99.

A. Number of occurrences per year

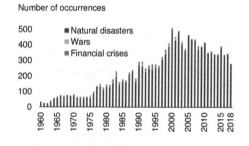

B. Average number of occurrences for big natural disasters and big wars per year

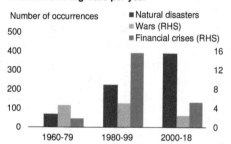

C. Average number of events per year

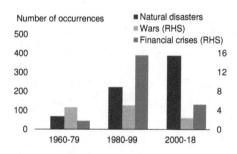

D. Average number of occurrences for severe natural disasters and severe wars per year

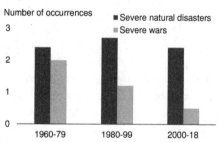

Sources: Correlates of War (COW); Emergency Events Database (EM-DAT); Laeven and Valencia (2018); Peace Research Institute Oslo (PRIO); World Bank.
Note: Financial crises include banking, currency, and sovereign debt crises (Laeven and Valencia 2018). Natural disasters include climate, biological, and geophysical disasters (EM-DAT). Wars include intrastate, extrastate, and interstate wars (COW and PRIO). Definitions are in annex 3A. A specific type of event can have multiple occurrences in a country-year pair. Big natural disasters and big wars are defined as events that led to at least 10 deaths per million population. Severe natural disasters and severe wars are defined as events that led to at least 100 deaths per million population. The sample includes 170 economies: 35 advanced economies and 135 emerging market and developing economies, of which 27 are low-income countries.

this chapter focuses on the impacts of episodes of natural disasters, wars, and financial crises. The three broad types of adverse events are now explored in more detail.

Natural disasters

Three types of natural disasters are considered: climate events (such as storms, floods, droughts, and periods of extreme temperature), biological events (such as epidemics and insect infestations), and geophysical events (such as earthquakes and volcanoes). Natural disasters, unlike financial crises, are typically measured in terms of the number of deaths and casualties, the number of people otherwise affected, and property damage.[6] Natural disasters can affect productivity through various channels:

- *Erosion of human capital.* The human cost of natural disasters can be substantial. They often lead to many fatalities and large population displacements. They also tend to degrade hygiene conditions in affected areas, increase the risk of large-scale outbreaks of infectious diseases and epidemics, and aggravate health challenges. In the case of a global pandemic such as COVID-19, the disruption of labor supply is exacerbated by containment measures that make it difficult for workers to get to their places of employment or to work in close physical proximity with each other. Moreover, prolonged natural disasters can disrupt schooling, undermine learning conditions, and erode human capital through degraded work environments, sickness, and so on (Acevedo et al. 2018; IMF 2017; Thomas and López 2015).

- *Destruction and misallocation of physical capital.* Natural disasters can destroy critical physical assets, damage major infrastructures, cut supply lines, and discourage private investment (Kunreuther 2006; Sawada, Tomoaki, and Bhattacharyay 2011). For the period 2000-12, the annual cost of natural disasters worldwide has been estimated to have exceeded $100 billion (Kousky 2014).[7] Moreover, major pandemics such as COVID-19 hinder capital accumulation because of a substantial increase in uncertainty (World Bank 2020d). Natural disasters tend to reduce and degrade the capital stock and can lead to a misallocation of the residual capital, because undamaged roads or offices (residual capital) often cannot be readily used in the way they had been, or are used to replace or repair other damaged assets such as bridges or factories. This misallocation of capital weighs on labor productivity (Hallegatte and Vogt-Schilb 2019).

- *Disruption of innovation.* Beyond the immediate loss of lives and damage to physical assets, natural disasters can lead to delayed or canceled investments in new technologies. The disruption of global value chains can also impede the creation, transfer, and adoption of new technologies (ADB 2019; Bloom et al. 2010). This was exemplified by COVID-19 containment measures that have limited mobility, compressed trade, and to some extent restricted the diffusion of innovation. Conversely, effective reconstruction efforts can boost investment and enhance productivity via upgraded capital, health improvements, and widespread use of new technologies.[8]

---

[6] The number of people affected (excluding those killed) is usually considered to be the sum of people injured, made homeless, and otherwise requiring immediate assistance. Property damage includes damage to crops and livestock as well as real estate (annex 3A).

[7] In assessing the economic cost of a disaster, it is important to avoid double-counting losses: the value of the damaged machine and the subsequent lost production should not both be counted as a loss.

[8] The overall impact of a natural disaster depends partly on initial economic conditions. A disaster may be more economically damaging in periods of high employment and capacity utilization because the increase in output needed for reconstruction may not be feasible, and the increase in demand generated may induce inflation. By contrast, a disaster that occurs when the economy is depressed may cause less economic damage because the stimulus effect of reconstruction will activate unused resources (Benson and Clay 2004; Cuaresma, Hlouskova, and Obersteiner 2008; Hallegatte and Vogt-Schilb 2019; Skidmore and Toya 2002).

TABLE 3.1 **Number of episodes, by type of event**

	AEs	EMDEs	LICs	World
Natural disasters	**1,031**	**4,699**	**1,098**	**5,730**
Climate disasters	843	3,054	651	3,897
Biological disasters	50	953	369	1,003
Geophysical disasters	138	692	78	830
Wars	**45**	**191**	**55**	**236**
Intrastate wars	0	123	46	123
External wars	45	68	9	113
Financial crises	**54**	**390**	**83**	**444**
Systemic banking crisis	34	113	27	147
Currency crisis	18	208	44	226
Sovereign debt crisis	2	69	12	71

Sources: Correlates of War (COW); Emergency Events Database (EM-DAT); Laeven and Valencia (2018); Peace Research Institute Oslo (PRIO); World Bank.
Note: Natural disasters include climate, biological, and geophysical disasters (EM-DAT). Wars include intrastate and external (extrastate and interstate) wars (COW and PRIO). Financial crises include banking, currency, and sovereign debt crises (Laeven and Valencia 2018). Sample is restricted to the observations where labor productivity growth data exist for the period 1960-2018. For each country-year pair, the episode dummy of a specific type of event is 1 if the event occurs at least once (≥1), 0 otherwise. The total number of episodes (in bold) for each group of events (all financials, all disasters, all wars) may include events that occur simultaneously. The events are defined in annex 3A. AEs = advanced economies; EMDEs = emerging market and developing economies (including LICs); LICs = low-income countries.

In addition to supply effects, because of the many unknowns, epidemics and pandemics can weigh on productivity through demand-side channels, by raising uncertainty, eroding consumer and business confidence, weakening investment, and depressing demand (box 3.1).

Increase in frequency of climate and other natural disasters. Climate disasters accounted for about 70 percent of natural disasters during 1960-2018, occurring twice as often as biological and geophysical disasters combined (table 3.1, figure 3.2). From 1960-79 to 2000-18, there was a large increase in the number of natural disaster episodes.[9] Increases occurred in all three categories but most markedly in climate disasters, the frequency of which tripled between 1960-79 and 2000-18.[10] Over 2000-18, natural disasters affected some 200 million people, costing on average more than 60,000 lives each year (Ritchie and Roser 2020). In 2000-18, the average number of climate disaster episodes per year doubled relative to 1980-99, and the frequency of biological and geophysical disaster episodes increased by 40 and 10 percent, respectively (figure 3.2). Also in 2000-18, a natural disaster was 80 percent more likely to occur in LICs, and 35 percent more likely to occur in EMDEs, than in advanced economies.

---

[9] To some degree, the increase in the number of recorded events may reflect improved measurement of natural disasters, particularly for small events.

[10] Climate disasters refer to extreme weather events. Exposure to an adverse weather event will depend on the size of the population and total asset value located in at-risk areas. Vulnerabilities materialize when weather events hit exposed populations and assets, leading to economic losses (Cavallo and Noy 2011; Costanza and Farley 2007).

FIGURE 3.2 **Episodes of natural disaster**

Climate disasters were the most frequent type of natural disaster in the full sample period. The annual frequency of climate-related episodes nearly doubled after 2000, and the frequency of biological and geophysical disaster episodes increased by 40 and 10 percent, respectively. Since 2000, the frequency of big and severe natural disasters has leveled off. After 2000, a natural disaster was 80 percent more likely to occur in an LIC and 35 percent more likely in an EMDE than in an advanced economy. Among EMDE regions, SSA experienced the steepest increase in the frequency of natural disasters after 2000 relative to 1980-99.

A. Average number of natural disaster episodes per year, by type

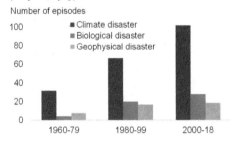

B. Average number of natural disaster episodes per country per year

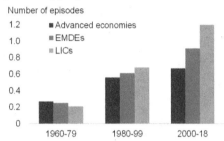

C. Average number of big natural disaster episodes per year, by type

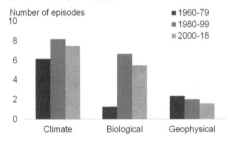

D. Average number of severe natural disaster episodes per year, by type

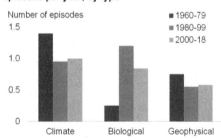

E. Share of natural disasters, by region

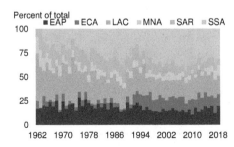

F. Average number of natural disaster episodes per year, by region

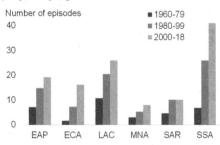

Sources: Emergency Events Database (EM-DAT); World Bank.
Note: Natural disasters include climate, biological, and geophysical disasters (EM-DAT). An episode dummy for a specific type of event is 1 if the event occurs at least once (≥1) in a country-year pair and 0 otherwise. Big natural disasters and big wars are events that led to at least 10 deaths per million population. Severe natural disasters and severe wars are events that led to at least 100 deaths per million population. The sample includes 170 economies: 35 advanced economies and 135 EMDEs, of which 27 are LICs.
AEs=advanced economies; EMDEs=emerging market and developing economies (including LICs); LICs = low-income countries; EAP = East Asia and Pacific; ECA = Europe and Central Asia; LAC = Latin America and the Caribbean; MNA = Middle East and North Africa; SAR = South Asia; SSA = Sub-Saharan Africa.

Pandemics. Global pandemics such as COVID-19 (2019-21) are rare events. There were only a few pandemics in the twentieth century, including the Spanish flu (1918-19), Asian flu (1957-58), Hong Kong flu (1968-69), and HIV/AIDS (1980s). Since the 2000s, the major epidemics were SARS (2002-03), swine flu (2009-10), MERS (2012), Ebola (2014-15), and Zika (2015-16), which affected over 115 EMDEs and advanced economies (box 3.1). The COVID-19 (2019-21) outbreak has affected virtually all countries around the world and led to a sudden stop of the global economy.

Regional distribution. SSA seems to be more exposed to natural disasters than other EMDE regions. In both 1980-99 and 2000-18, SSA had the highest frequency of natural disasters among EMDE regions. And, in 2000-18, SSA experienced the largest increase in the frequency of natural disaster episodes relative to 1980-99. East Asia and Pacific (EAP) and Latin America and the Caribbean (LAC) were hit by at least 20 natural disaster episodes per year over 2000-18 (figure 3.3). Although climate events were relatively more frequent in EAP, LAC, and SSA, historically, the largest number of biological disasters such as epidemic outbreaks occurred in SSA. The region least frequently affected by natural disasters was the Middle East and North Africa (MNA).[11]

Exposure to frequent natural disasters is correlated with lower productivity. While the number of natural disaster episodes tripled between 1960-89 and 1990-2018, labor productivity growth halved in advanced economies and slowed in EMDEs other than LICs. Thus, more frequent natural disasters were correlated in this period with weaker labor productivity growth. The annual frequency of natural disasters and TFP growth are also negatively correlated in advanced economies. Moreover, severe natural disasters, especially severe biological disasters, are associated with weaker labor productivity and TFP in EMDEs. Three years into a severe natural disaster episode, median labor productivity was about 8 percent lower in the countries affected, and TFP was 7 percent lower than in unaffected countries (figure 3.3).

Wars

Apart from their direct toll on human life and welfare, wars can have major adverse effects on output and productivity (Abadie and Gardeazabal 2003; Cerra and Saxena 2008). Two types of wars are considered: intrastate and external armed conflicts (which include extrastate and interstate wars).[12] The destruction, disruption, and diversion effects of wars can cause sharp reductions in the labor force and physical capital, and dampen productive investment and innovation (Becker and Mauro 2006; Collier 1999; Easterly et al. 1993; Field 2008; Raddatz 2007; Rodrik 1999).

- *Reduced and disrupted labor forces.* Conflict-related losses of lives, coupled with population displacements, dampen output directly and disrupt the functioning of

---

[11] Regions with large geographical areas can be exposed to more natural disasters than regions with small geographical areas.

[12] Intrastate wars are conducted between a state and a group within its borders. Extrastate wars take place between a system member and a nonstate entity (not a system member). Interstate wars are conducted between members of the interstate system.

FIGURE 3.3 **Correlations between natural disaster frequency and productivity growth**

On average comparing 1960-89 with 1990-2018, the number of natural disaster episodes per country per year correlates negatively with labor productivity growth in advanced economies and EMDEs—these correlations are weak for LICs. The correlations between the frequency of these events and TFP growth are negative for advanced economies but mixed for EMDEs and LICs. In EMDEs, severe natural disasters, especially severe biological disasters, are associated with lower labor productivity and TFP.

A. Average number of natural disaster episodes per country per year and average labor productivity growth

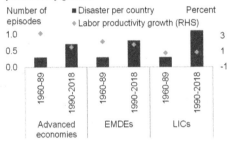

B. Average number of natural disaster episodes per year and average TFP growth

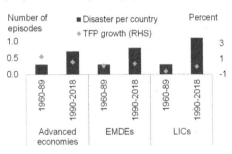

C. Effects of severe natural disaster episodes on labor productivity in EMDEs

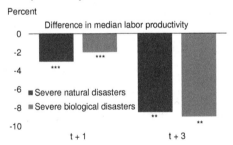

D. Effects of severe natural disasters on TFP in EMDEs

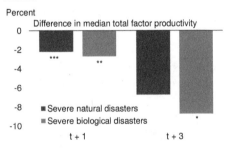

Sources: Emergency Events Database (EM-DAT); World Bank.
Note: Natural disaster episodes include climate, biological, and geophysical hazards (EM-DAT; annex 3A). An episode dummy for a specific type of event is 1 if the event occurs at least once (≥1) in a country-year pair and 0 otherwise. Severe natural disasters and severe biological disasters are events that led to at least 100 deaths per million population. The sample includes 170 economies: 35 advanced economies and 135 EMDEs, of which 27 are LICs. EMDEs = emerging markets and developing economies (including LICs); LICs = low-income countries; TFP = total factor productivity.
A.B. Correlations between the average number of natural disaster episodes per country per year and (A) average growth of labor productivity (output per worker), and (B) average growth of TFP over two 30-year periods (1960-89 and 1990-2018).
C.D. ***, ** and * indicate 1, 5, and 10 percent significance levels.

labor markets (Field 2019; Ksoll, Macchiavello, and Morjaria 2010; Mueller 2013).[13] Worldwide, about 68.5 million people—or 1 percent of the world's population—were in forcibly displaced situations in 2017 because of conflicts

---

[13] For instance, during the 2007 postelection violence in Kenya, the labor force in the affected areas was reduced by as much as half owing to deaths, injuries, and lack of security for workers; as a result, wages rose by 70 percent (Ksoll, Macchiavello, and Morjaria 2010).

BOX 3.1 **How do epidemics affect productivity?**

Epidemics that have occurred since 2000 are estimated to have lowered labor productivity by a cumulative 4 percent after three years, mainly through their adverse impact on investment and the labor force. Given its global nature, COVID-19 (coronavirus disease 2019) may lead to sizeable adverse cross-border spillovers and weaken global value chains, which will further damage productivity. The immediate policy focus is to address the health crisis, but policy makers also need to introduce reforms to rekindle productivity growth once the health crisis abates.

Introduction

Prior to the emergence of COVID-19, there were already concerns about the prospects for long-term productivity growth in emerging market and developing economies (EMDEs) and the achievement of development goals, especially the reduction of poverty. COVID-19 has put these goals in even greater jeopardy (World Bank 2020a). In less than half a year since its start, COVID-19 already ranks as a major disaster (figure B3.1.1). Because pandemics are rare events, this box sheds light on the effects of COVID-19 on labor productivity by examining epidemics since 1960.

Natural disasters such as biological, climate, and geophysical events have caused significant economic damage.[a] Past severe disasters (more than 100 deaths per million people) are relevant for gauging the likely effects of COVID-19 on labor productivity and understanding the channels through which disasters may affect the economy. This box examines the following questions:

- What are the main channels through which epidemics and pandemics affect productivity?

- What are the frequency and extent of epidemics and pandemics?

- What are the likely implications of epidemics and pandemics for productivity?

Channels through which severe epidemics affect productivity

Epidemics and pandemics can affect productivity and long-term economic growth through both supply- and demand-side channels.

Note: This box was prepared by Alistair Dieppe, Sinem Kilic Celik, and Cedric Okou, with research assistance by Yi Li, Kaltrina Temaj, and Xinyue Wang.

a. Natural disasters include climate (floods, cyclones), biological (epidemics, insect infestation), and geophysical disasters (earthquakes, volcanoes), and follow Emergency Events Database (EM-DAT) definitions.

BOX 3.1 How do epidemics affect productivity? *(continued)*

FIGURE B3.1.1 Severity of pandemics, epidemics, and climate disasters

COVID-19 already ranks as a major disaster. In the most severely affected countries, its impact may be as large as those from a severe climate disaster. Climate disasters were the most frequent type of natural disaster in 1960-2018, accounting for nearly 70 percent of all disasters. Epidemics and wars are much rarer but longer-lived. About 20 percent of biological disasters that have affected EMDEs and LICs have been severe.

A. Global mortality rates for selected pandemics

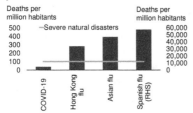

B. Global mortality rates for recent epidemics

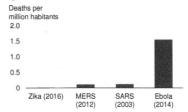

C. Mortality rates for severe climate events, pandemics, and epidemics for affected countries

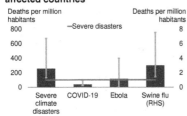

D. Number of biological and epidemic episodes, 1960-2018

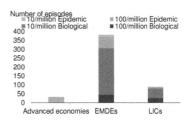

E. Episodes by type of natural disaster, worldwide, 1960-2018

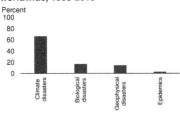

F. Average duration of natural disasters and epidemics

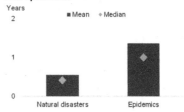

Sources: Centers for Disease Control and Prevention; Emergency Events Database (EM-DAT); Johns Hopkins University; OurWorldInData.org; United Nations; World Bank; World Health Organization.

Note: COVID-19 = coronavirus disease 2019; EMDEs = emerging market and developing economies; LICs = low-income countries; MERS = Middle East respiratory syndrome; SARS = severe acute respiratory syndrome.

A-B. Cumulative deaths per million population worldwide. Last observation of death toll for COVID-19 is May 14, 2020. Severe climate disasters are defined as events that led to at least 100 deaths per million population.

C. Blue bars indicate the medians of mortality rates across affected countries. The bottom (top) of the yellow line represents the 1st (3rd) quintile. Red marker indicates 100 deaths per million habitants.

D-F. Natural disasters include climate (floods, cyclones), biological (epidemics, insect infestation), and geophysical (earthquakes, volcanoes) disasters, and follow EM-DAT definitions. The sample includes 170 economies: 35 advanced economies and 135 EMDEs, of which 27 are LICs.

E. Biological disasters include epidemics.

F. The five pandemics and epidemics considered are SARS (2002-03), MERS (2012), Swine flu (2009), Ebola (2014-15), and Zika (2015-16).

BOX 3.1 How do epidemics affect productivity? *(continued)*

Epidemics and pandemics can impact **supply** through the following channels:

- *Depleted labor forces.* Major epidemics can reduce the labor supply by causing widespread sickness and fatalities. Mitigation efforts such as workplace closures, social distancing, and lockdowns to contain the spread of infectious diseases can also disrupt the functioning of labor markets. These disruptions undermine the productivity of those remaining in the workforce owing to the loss of complementary skills, among others.[b]

- *Weakened physical capital.* Severe epidemics typically damage the outlook for economic activity and profitability because of heightened uncertainty. This epidemic-driven uncertainty can lead to idle physical capital, tighten credit conditions, and trigger capital outflows—especially in EMDEs. These effects are likely to hold back capital accumulation. (Claessens et al. 1997; Claessens and Kose 2017, 2018; Collier 1999; Hutchinson and Margo 2006).

- *Disrupted supply chains and innovation.* Major epidemics can freeze and damage global value chains (Collier 1999; Reynaerts and Vanschoonbeek 2018; Rodrik 1999). They also undermine the incentives to invest in research and development, and new technologies, including by weakening property rights and increasing costs of doing business. Capital outflows tend to be associated with drops in inward foreign direct investment, which can be an important source of technology transfer.[c] Containment efforts during epidemics—such as workplace closures and quarantines—can further limit the diffusion of technologies.

Epidemics and pandemics can affect **demand** through the following:

- *Lower business investment.* Short-term projections of demand and economic activity tend to be scaled back and business uncertainty tends to increase sharply following major epidemics. These typically cause a sharp drop in investment demand, which can be amplified by the disruption to value chains. The duration of the disaster is essential to its impact on the economy via its effect on investment. A more prolonged epidemic, even at the same magnitude, results in higher uncertainty. This causes firms to delay or deter investments and thereby compounds the negative economic effects of

---

b. Unexpected adverse events that affect large geographic areas have been shown to have lasting consequences on human capital (health, education, and nutrition outcomes) regardless of the income group. See Acevedo et al. (2018); Akbulut-Yuksel (2009); Alderman, Hoddinott, and Kinsey (2006); IMF (2017); Maccini and Yang (2009); and Thomas and López (2015). Biological epidemics can also disproportionally affect low-skilled workers and raise inequality (Furceri et al. 2020).

c. The COVID-19 pandemic is projected to lower foreign direct investment by 20 percent in EMDEs during 2020-21 (UNCTAD 2020).

BOX 3.1 How do epidemics affect productivity? *(continued)*

disasters (Baker, Bloom, and Terry 2019; Bloom 2014; Bloom et al. 2018). The more severe the epidemic, the larger the uncertainty (Ludvigson, Ma, and Ng 2020). Model-based estimates by Baker, Bloom, and Davis (2020) suggest that increased uncertainty accounts for half of the output loss in the U.S. economy in early 2020.

- *Weaker consumer demand.* Job losses, reduced income, increased cost of debt service, higher uncertainty, the forced closure of marketing outlets, and, in the case of diseases, fear of infection, all tend to cause consumers to reduce their spending on goods and services and to increase saving rates. Furthermore, effects on consumer behavior could be long-lasting—for example, a pandemic could cause households to reduce their demand, over an extended period, for travel, tourism, eating out, entertainment, and other activities involving human interaction, and to increase their saving in the absence of close substitutes.

Frequency and short-term effects of disasters

Pandemics and epidemics are rare events although they last longer than other types of disasters. Other biological disasters (such as insect infestation) and geophysical disasters are more common. Climate disasters (such as storms, floods, droughts, and periods of extreme temperature) occur more often but typically last for less than six months. All these events are associated with weaker productivity over long time spans.

Pandemics. The Spanish flu (1918-19) had an unusually high death toll and mortality rate, killing between 20 million and 100 million people globally. Other, more recent, pandemics had far lower mortality rates. They included the Hong Kong flu (1968-69) and the Asian flu (1957-58), with nearly 300 and 400 deaths per million, respectively. They were followed by swine flu (2009-10), with 11 deaths per million globally (figure B3.1.1). COVID-19 is the most severe pandemic since the Hong Kong flu, despite the unprecedented mitigation efforts that have been implemented.

Epidemics since the 2000s. During 2000-18, the world experienced SARS (severe acute respiratory syndrome, 2002-03), MERS (Middle East respiratory syndrome, 2012), Ebola (2014-15), and Zika (2015-16). The increased frequency of epidemics increases the likelihood that pandemics will break out. There were over 250 episodes of biological disasters with losses of life of over 10 per million population in the countries affected since 1960. Low-income countries have been disproportionally affected by these types of disasters whereas advanced economies were not affected. The frequency of such biological episodes has been increasing over time, but they have mostly been contained in size and

BOX 3.1 How do epidemics affect productivity? *(continued)*

FIGURE B3.1.2 Severe disasters and productivity

In EMDEs, severe natural disasters, especially severe biological disasters, are associated with lower labor productivity. Severe biological disasters are also correlated with lower investment, possibly reflecting a sizable increase in uncertainty that holds off new spending.

A. Labor productivity

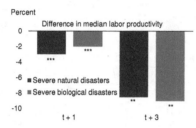

B. Total factor productivity

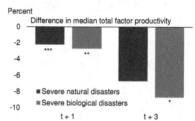

C. Investment

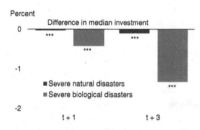

D. Output

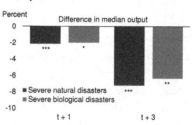

Sources: Emergency Events Database (EM-DAT); World Bank

Note: EMDEs = emerging market and developing economies; MERS = Middle East respiratory syndrome; SARS = severe acute respiratory syndrome.

A.-D. Natural disasters include climate (floods, cyclones), biological (epidemics, insect infestation), and geophysical (earthquakes, volcanoes) disasters, and follow EM-DAT definitions. An episode dummy for a specific type of event is 1 if the event occurs at least once (≥1) in a country-year pair and 0 otherwise. Severe natural disasters and severe biological disasters are defined as events that led to at least 100 deaths per million population. The sample includes 170 economies: 35 advanced economies and 135 EMDEs, of which 27 are low-income countries.

Bars show the difference between the median growth of macroeconomic indicators in EMDEs with and without severe biological disasters (red) and severe natural disasters (blue; including climate, biological, geophysical disasters). A Fisher's test is used to test if medians in two subsamples (with and without disasters) are equal. The four biological disasters considered are SARS (2002-03), MERS (2012), Ebola (2014-15), and Zika (2015-16). Swine flu (2009), which coincided with the 2008-09 global financial crisis, is excluded to limit possible confounding effects. ***, ** and * indicate 1, 5, and 10 percent significance levels.

severity. Furthermore, climate disasters tend to be short-lived compared to epidemics, which on average last twice as long.

Severe disasters. With a rising death toll and possible subsequent infection waves, the COVID-19 pandemic is potentially a severe biological disaster. Compared to unaffected countries, severe biological disasters are associated with 9 percent lower median labor productivity and 8 percent lower total factor productivity (TFP) three years after the shock (figure B3.1.2). Severe natural disasters

BOX 3.1 How do epidemics affect productivity? *(continued)*

(including climate and biological disasters) also correlate with weaker labor productivity and TFP compared to countries not suffering such disasters. In EMDEs, three years into a severe natural disaster episode median labor productivity was about 8 percent lower in the countries affected, and TFP was 7 percent lower than in countries unaffected whereas investment remained virtually unchanged, which could reflect large-scale reconstruction investment offsetting other negative effects.

Investment effects. Median investment growth remained virtually the same in both affected and unaffected countries in natural disasters. This could suggest that large-scale reconstruction investment after a natural disaster roughly offset declines in investment in other activities due to uncertainty. For severe biological disasters, however, the effects on investment are negative, reflecting the longer duration of the disaster and increased uncertainty.

Long-term effects of epidemics

To help draw inferences on the possible effects of COVID-19, this section examines the extent to which epidemics have lasting negative effects on labor productivity. Epidemics are particularly damaging to productivity, lowering it by 4 percent after three years.

Methodology. The local projection method (LPM) is used to provide a reduced-form estimate of the response of labor productivity to adverse events over various horizons (Jordà, 2005; Jordà, Schularick, and Taylor 2013; annex 3C). It allows the identification of key transmission channels through output, investment, and TFP.

Adverse effects of epidemics. Results suggest that four epidemics since 2000 (SARS, MERS, Ebola, and Zika) had significant and persistent negative effects on productivity (swine flu is excluded because it coincided with the global financial crisis).[d] These estimates indicate that epidemics led, on average, to a contemporaneous loss of productivity equal to about 1 percent (figure B3.1.3). After three years, such epidemics lowered labor productivity by a cumulative amount of about 4 percent. Over the same horizon, investment declined by nearly 9 percent, reflecting heightened uncertainty and risk aversion.

---

d. Jordà, Singh, and Taylor (2020) consider major pandemics and find long-lasting effects on output. Barro and Ursúa (2008) report that the macroeconomic impact of the Great Influenza Pandemic of 1918 is substantial. Sustained low levels of demand, and excess capacity during disasters, including pandemics, can have persistent effects on productivity (Dieppe, Francis, and Kindberg-Hanlon, forthcoming). Ma, Rogers, and Zhou (2020), also focusing on of the same set of epidemics in 210 countries, find that real GDP in EMDEs is about 2 percent lower on average in the first year and decreases to 4 percent below after five years.

BOX 3.1 How do epidemics affect productivity? *(continued)*

FIGURE B3.1.3 **Impact of epidemics**

SARS, MERS, Ebola, and Zika left lasting scars on labor productivity with declines of about 4 percent after three years and larger effects on investment, whereas estimates suggest that TFP hardly declined. The impact of swine flu too was probably large, but impossible to assess because the epidemic overlapped with the 2008-09 global financial crisis.

A. Effects of epidemics on labor productivity and TFP

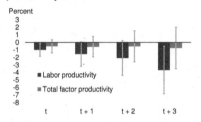

B. Effects of epidemics on investment and output

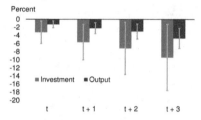

Sources: Emergency Events Database (EM-DAT); World Bank.
Note: Orange lines display the range of the estimates with 90th percentile significance. An episode dummy for a specific type of event is 1 if the event occurs at least once (≥1) in a country-year pair and 0 otherwise. EMDEs = emerging market and developing economies; MERS = Middle East respiratory syndrome; SARS = severe acute respiratory syndrome; TFP = total factor productivity.
A.B. Bars show the estimated impacts of the four most severe biological epidemics on output, labor productivity, TFP, and investment levels relative to unaffected EMDEs. The four epidemics considered are SARS (2002-03), MERS (2012), Ebola (2014-15), Zika (2015-16). Swine flu (2009), which coincided with the 2008-09 global financial crisis, is excluded to limit possible confounding effects. The sample includes 116 economies: 30 advanced economies and 86 EMDEs.

Conclusion

The COVID-19 pandemic raises questions about its effects on productivity. Pandemics and epidemics are rare events in comparison to climate disasters, but they have had adverse and persistent effects on productivity. Adverse impacts on productivity increase more than proportionately with the severity and duration of these types of disasters. Epidemics that have occurred since 2000 have lowered labor productivity by a cumulative 4 percent after three years, because of elevated uncertainty and mainly through their adverse effects on investment and the labor force.

The COVID-19 pandemic may have a significantly worse impact on productivity than most previous natural disasters for the following reasons:

- *Global reach.* The COVID-19 pandemic appears to have considerably broader reach—in terms of numbers of both countries and people affected— than other disasters since 1960. The increased integration of the global economy, through trade and financial linkages, will amplify the adverse impact of COVID-19.

BOX 3.1 How do epidemics affect productivity? *(continued)*

- *Contagion prevention and physical distancing.* As long as strict social distancing is required, some activities will not be viable. In the hospitality sector, where close socialization is part of the product, the capital stock will become obsolete. Even in less directly affected sectors, severe capacity under-utilization lowers TFP while restrictions to stem the spread of the pandemic remain in place. Disruptions to employment, schooling, and other education while restrictions remain in place—or, in the event of severe income losses, even once restrictions are lifted—will also lower human capital and labor productivity (World Bank 2020b).

- *Compounding financial stress.* Financial crises tend to result in especially protracted labor productivity losses (Benson and Clay 2004; Blanchard, Cerutti, and Summers 2015; Celiku and Kraay 2017; Cerra and Saxena 2008, 2017; World Bank 2020c).[e] Larger disasters are more likely to cause a cascade of business and household bankruptcies and hence a systemic financial crisis. Although only a few disasters have been associated with financial crises, governments and private sectors entered the COVID-19 pandemic with already-stretched debt burdens (Kose et al. 2020). These have since increased further and heighten risk of a financial crisis should financial conditions tighten further (Ludvigson, Ma, and Ng 2020).

Mitigating factors. In some dimensions, pandemics and epidemics can accelerate productivity-enhancing changes. They can encourage investment in new and more technologically advanced capital and training of more highly skilled workers (Bloom 2014). They may also lead to new opportunities for green growth with environmentally friendly new investment, especially if it is induced by structural reforms (Strand and Toman 2010). The mitigation measures of COVID-19, including social distancing, may encourage investment in more efficient business practices, including robotics and other digital technologies such as artificial intelligence (Hallward-Driemeier and Nayyar 2017; Hsiang 2010; Skidmore and Toya 2002; Strobl 2011).[f]

Structural reforms. The negative outlook ahead means that, after addressing the immediate health crisis, countries need to make productivity-enhancing reforms a priority. These include facilitating investment in human and physical capital, as

---

e. During 1990-2018, the number of financial crises—sovereign debt, banking, and currency—nearly doubled compared to 1960-89. Over the past three decades, labor productivity growth halved in advanced economies and slowed, albeit less markedly, in EMDEs.

f. The accompanying job losses are likely to be lower-skilled and less productive (Lazear, Shaw, and Stanton 2013). To the extent vulnerable groups are particularly exposed to economic losses from disasters, policies to protect these groups are needed (OECD 2020).

BOX 3.1 **How do epidemics affect productivity?** *(continued)*

well as in research and development; encouraging reallocation of resources toward more productive sectors; fostering technology adoption and innovation; and promoting a growth-friendly macroeconomic and institutional environment (World Bank 2020c). In addition, raising the quality and effectiveness of governance and improving the business climate can encourage a faster rebound from disasters. Governments that improved labor and product market flexibility, strengthened legal systems and property rights, fostered effective competition, and addressed inequality set the foundations for more effective adjustment to adverse events (Anbarci, Escaleras, and Register 2005).

(UNHCR 2018). Moreover, many displaced persons are relatively well educated and skilled.

- *Weakened capital deepening.* Violent conflict destroys physical assets, holds back productive investment, provokes capital flight, and causes capital and finance to be diverted to less productive uses, including expenditure on armaments (Collier 1999; Hutchinson and Margo 2006). In the 1980s, wars are estimated to have lowered the ratio of investment to GDP in Eastern Europe by about 5 percent over 1986-90 (Knight, Loayza, and Villanueva 1996).

- *Hindered innovation.* Wars can have adverse effects on innovation and the adoption of technology.[14] They can lead to large-scale institutional disfunction, weakening of property rights, and sharp reductions in research and development (R&D) investment; wars can also impede global value chains. All these effects can slow technological progress (Collier 1999; Rodrik 1999; Reynaerts and Vanschoonbeek 2018). Wars can be particularly pernicious in LICs and FCS countries, partly because of weak R&D capacity in those countries.

Intrastate wars in EMDEs, external wars in advanced economies. Between 1980-99 and 2000-18, the number of intrastate and external wars fell by almost 70 percent and 25 percent, respectively (figure 3.4). EMDEs and LICs were mainly hit by intrastate conflicts, whereas advanced economies mainly experienced external wars (table 3.1). A typical LIC was twice as likely to experience any kind of conflict as a typical EMDE. In 2000-18, the frequency of wars dropped in all regions. In 1960-2018, intrastate armed conflicts mainly occurred in SSA, whereas external wars mainly occurred in EAP and MNA.

---

[14] In some cases, such as the Manhattan Project undertaken during World War II, conflicts can stimulate innovation and R&D.

FIGURE 3.4 **Episodes of war**

Intrastate conflicts were the most frequent type of wars over the full sample. The frequency of war episodes in total dropped after 2000. Since 2000, there were almost 70 percent fewer intrastate and 25 percent fewer external (extra- and interstate) war episodes per year compared to the 1980s and 1990s. A typical LIC was twice as likely to be hit by a war as a typical EMDE (including LICs) and 10 percent more likely than an advanced economy after 2000. Intrastate conflicts mainly occurred in SSA, whereas external wars mainly occurred in EAP and MNA. The frequency of wars dropped in all regions in 2000-18 relative to 1980-99.

A. Average number of war episodes per year, by type

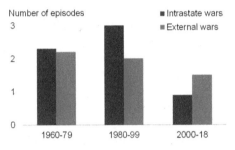

B. Average number of war episodes per country per year

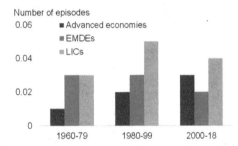

C. Share of war episodes, by region, 1960-2018

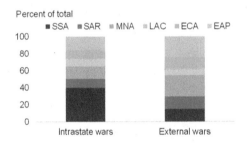

D. Average number of war episodes per year, by region

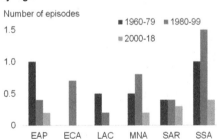

Sources: Correlates of War (COW); Peace Research Institute Oslo (PRIO); World Bank.
Note: Wars include intrastate and external (interstate and extrastate) wars (COW and PRIO; annex 3A). An episode dummy for a specific type of event is 1 if the event occurs at least once (≥1) in a country-year pair and 0 otherwise. The sample includes 170 economies: 35 advanced economies and 135 EMDEs, of which 27 are LICs. EMDEs = emerging market and developing economies; LICs = low-income countries; EAP = East Asia and Pacific; ECA = Europe and Central Asia; LAC = Latin America and the Caribbean; MNA = Middle East and North Africa; SAR = South Asia; SSA = Sub-Saharan Africa.

Wars in advanced economies have been accompanied by weaker productivity growth. In advanced economies, the number of wars tripled while labor productivity and TFP growth halved from 1960-89 to 1990-2018. These associations appear weak in EMDEs and LICs (figure 3.5).

Financial crises

Financial crises sharply raise borrowing costs and worsen balance sheets. They have often led to severe economic contractions, with lasting corrosive effects on productivity levels

FIGURE 3.5 Correlations between war frequency and productivity growth

In advanced economies, an increased annual frequency of wars from 1960-89 to 1990-2018 was accompanied by lower labor productivity growth; corresponding correlations seem weak for EMDEs and LICs. The correlations between the frequency of war episodes and TFP growth appear negative for advanced economies and EMDEs, but they are mixed for LICs.

A. Average number of war episodes per country per year and average labor productivity growth

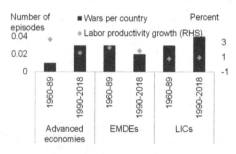

B. Average number of war episodes per country per year and average TFP growth

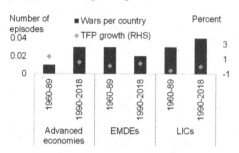

Sources: Correlates of War (COW); Peace Research Institute Oslo (PRIO); World Bank.
Note: War episodes include intrastate, interstate and extrastate armed conflicts (COW and PRIO; annex 3A). An episode dummy for a specific type of event is 1 if the event occurs at least once (≥1) in a country-year pair and 0 otherwise. The sample includes 170 economies: 35 advanced economies and 135 EMDEs, of which 27 are LICs. EMDEs = emerging market and developing economies; LICs = low-income countries; TFP = total factor productivity.
A.B. Correlations between the average number of war episodes per country per year and (A) average growth of labor productivity (output per worker), and (B) average growth of TFP over two 30-year periods (1960-89 and 1990-2018).

and, in some cases, productivity growth (Blanchard, Cerutti, and Summers 2015; Cerra and Saxena 2008, 2017). In the years since the GFC and subsequent global recession, a broad range of countries has experienced significant and sustained slowdowns of productivity growth (Kose et al. 2020). Financial crises have often originated from the excessive accumulation of public or private sector debt and the associated development of mismatches in balance sheets. Debt accumulation increases risks to productivity growth not only by increasing the risk of crises in the short term but also by tending to lead to the misallocation of resources toward low-productivity sectors and depressing investment and technological innovation in the long term (Blanchard and Wolfers 2000; Bulow and Rogoff 1989; Hall 2014; Schnitzer 2002).

Three broad types of financial crises are considered: sovereign debt crises, banking crises, and currency crises (annex 3A). This section emphasizes the role of government debt accumulation, financial crises, and productivity losses, because of concerns about elevated debt levels in many countries.

Sovereign debt crises. These can be particularly detrimental to output and productivity. They generally originate from the excessive accumulation of government debt. Before a crisis occurs, higher government debt tends to increase the burden of interest payments in the government budget and to raise borrowing costs, which may crowd out private investment (Kose et al. 2020; Oulton and Sebastiá-Barriel 2017; Reinhart and Rogoff 2010). Excessive growth of government debt erodes the country's ability to borrow, degrades private as well as public creditworthiness, and often leads to a curtailment of credit from institutional investors (Aguiar and Gopinath 2006; Arellano 2008; Sandri 2015). Elevated government debt can affect productivity growth through several channels:

- *Increased probability of financial crises.* Rising government debt will increase the risk of a financial crisis when it raises doubts about its sustainability. One of the ways this may occur is that higher debt may lead governments to adopt lower-cost but higher-risk debt management practices, including issuing debt with shorter maturities or denominated in foreign currency (Kalemli-Özcan, Laeven, and Moreno 2018). Such practices can sharply raise risk premia on government debt, increasing borrowing costs and the risk of crisis (Aguiar and Gopinath 2006; Arellano 2008; Sandri 2015). Moreover, high sovereign debt constrains the ability of governments to exercise countercyclical fiscal policy (Eberhardt and Presbitero 2015; Reinhart and Rogoff 2010). Given the close interconnectedness between sovereign, banking, and foreign exchange sectors, sovereign debt crises can precipitate (or be caused by) banking and currency crises, compounding the damage to output and productivity (Aghion, Bacchetta, and Banerjee 2000; Aghion et al. 2009; Kalemli-Özcan, Laeven, and Moreno 2018; Morris and Shin 1998).

- *Misallocation of resources.* If used to fund productive investments with high rates of return, debt can have positive effects on productivity and growth (Poirson, Pattillo, and Ricci 2004; Reinhart and Rogoff 2010). However, debt accumulation can impede productivity if it is associated with a misallocation of resources toward projects that yield only short-term returns or purely political gains (Checherita-Westphal and Rother 2012; Poirson, Pattillo, and Ricci 2002). Such misallocation is more likely if projects are being funded on unrealistic, possibly politically biased, expectations of rapid future growth (Claessens et al. 1997; Claessens and Kose 2017, 2018).

- *Policy uncertainty.* High government debt can increase uncertainty about prospects for economic growth (Kose et al. 2020). For investors, the fear may be that high debt could eventually compel the government to hike taxes (including taxes on future investment returns), curtail growth-enhancing spending, crowd out productive investment (debt overhangs), or delay reforms that could support innovation and productivity growth (IMF 2018; Kumar and Woo 2010).[15]

- *Productivity losses during rapid debt accumulation episodes.* Long-term productivity gains during rapid debt accumulation episodes have been considerably lower when these debt accumulation episodes were accompanied by financial crises. In a debt

---

[15] With regard to private sector debt, at the firm level, a large outstanding debt stock can weigh on investment and, hence, the productivity that technology embedded in this investment can generate (Borensztein and Ye 2018; Bulow and Rogoff 1989; Ridder 2017). At the government level, debt service on high debt may crowd out other productivity-enhancing spending, including for education, health, or infrastructure (Kose and Ohnsorge 2019).

accumulation episode preceding a crisis, the cumulative growth rate of median productivity three years into the episode was 3 percent (figure 3.6). This is statistically significantly less than the median increase during a debt accumulation episode that was not associated with a crisis (5 percent). The difference may be interpreted as a measure of the short-term damage to productivity from financial crises.

Banking and currency crises. Other types of financial crises, including systemic banking crises and currency crises, can also do lasting damage to productivity (Blanchard, Cerutti, and Summers 2015; Cerra and Saxena 2008, 2017; Oulton and Sebastiá-Barriel 2017). The disruptions to financial intermediation that occur in banking crises impede investment, curb the funding of productivity-enhancing technologies, and typically trigger recessions (De Ridder 2017). In periods of protracted economic weakness, prolonged and elevated unemployment erodes human capital (Ball 2009; Blanchard and Wolfers 2000; Bustos et al. 2016; Furceri and Mourougane 2012a; Hall 2014). Because of their shorter duration, currency crises are typically less harmful to productivity than other financial crises (Cerra and Saxena 2008).

Frequent financial crises erode productivity. Compared to 1960-89, the number of financial crises episodes nearly doubled in 1990-2018, while labor productivity growth halved in advanced economies and slowed, albeit less markedly, in EMDEs (figure 3.7). This negative correlation is also observed between the annual frequency of financial crises and TFP growth.

Comparing across types of adverse events

Climate disasters are the most frequent. Globally, natural disasters accounted for more than 90 percent of the recorded adverse events in 1960-2018 (table 3.1). Over this entire sample, natural disaster episodes were about 25 times more frequent than wars despite the decline in natural disasters over the last 10 years (figures 3.1 and 3.8). Financial crises occurred twice as frequently as wars. Severe natural disasters—that caused at least 100 deaths per million population—occurred twice as often as severe wars (figure 3.8). Epidemics and pandemics are rare events.

Wars are typically protracted. The average duration of wars was almost six years. Nearly half of financial crises last for more than two years. Natural disasters are typically much more short-lived (figure 3.8). Some climate disasters last for just a few days whereas others, such as droughts, can last for several months. The cumulative loss of productivity can be larger if the adverse events last for a more extended period of time or if reconstruction efforts are delayed (Sawada 2007; Cerra and Saxena 2008).[16]

---

[16] Reconstruction pace may be slowed by financial, physical, and transaction constraints (Hallegatte and Rentschler 2018).

FIGURE 3.6 **Episodes of financial crisis**

The frequency of financial crises spiked in the 1980s and 1990s. In 2000-18, there were on average six financial crisis episodes a year. Financial crises were markedly more likely to occur in a typical EMDE or LIC than in a typical advanced economy in 1980-99; their frequency declined in EMDEs and LICs after 2000. In 2000-18, ECA, LAC, and SSA were more frequently hit by financial crises than other EMDE regions. About 40 percent of episodes of rapid accumulation of total (government and private) debt were associated with financial crises. During those episodes, productivity gains were significantly lower than during other episodes.

A. Average number of financial crisis episodes per year, by type (World)

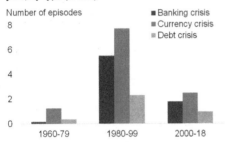

B. Average number of financial crisis episodes per country per year

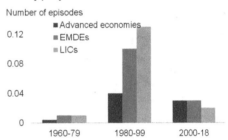

C. Share of financial crisis episodes, by region, 1960-2018

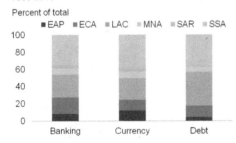

D. Average number of financial crisis episodes per year, by region

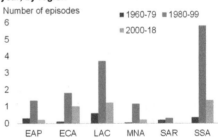

E. Total debt accumulation episodes around crises

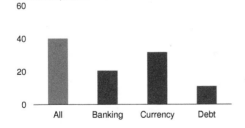

F. Cumulative productivity gains during episodes of rapid debt accumulation

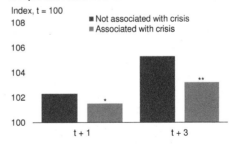

Sources: Laeven and Valencia (2018); World Bank.
Note: Financial crisis episodes include banking, currency, and sovereign debt crises (Laeven and Valencia 2018; annex 3A).
An episode dummy for a specific type of event is 1 if the event occurs at least once (≥1) in a country-year pair and 0 otherwise.
The sample includes 170 economies: 35 advanced economies and 135 EMDEs, of which 27 are LICs. EMDEs = emerging market and developing economies; LICs = low-income countries; EAP = East Asia and Pacific; ECA = Europe and Central Asia; LAC = Latin America and the Caribbean; MNA = Middle East and North Africa; SAR = South Asia; SSA = Sub-Saharan Africa.
A-D. Debt crisis refers to sovereign debt crisis.
E. Share of total (government and private) debt accumulation episodes associated with financial (banking, currency, debt) crises.
F. ** and * indicate 5 and 10 percent significance levels.

FIGURE 3.7 Correlations between financial crisis frequency and productivity growth

Advanced economies and EMDEs that experienced more financial crisis episodes per year tended to have lower labor productivity growth; these correlations are weak for LICs. The correlations between the frequency of these events and TFP growth are negative for advanced economies but mixed for EMDEs and LICs.

A. Average number of financial crisis episodes per country per year and average labor productivity growth

B. Average number of financial crisis episodes per country per year and average TFP growth

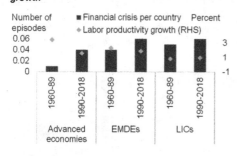
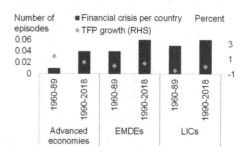

Sources: Laeven and Valencia (2018); World Bank.
Note: Financial crisis episodes include banking, currency, and sovereign debt crises (Laeven and Valencia 2018; annex 3A). An episode dummy for a specific type of event is 1 if the event occurs at least once (≥1) in a country-year pair and 0 otherwise. The sample includes 170 economies: 35 advanced economies and 135 EMDEs, of which 27 are LICs. EMDEs = emerging market and developing economies; LICs = low-income countries; TFP = total factor productivity.
A.B. Correlations between the average number of financial crisis episodes per country per year and (A) average growth of labor productivity (output per worker), and (B) average TFP growth, in 1960-89 and 1990-2018.

Measuring the impact of adverse events on productivity

This section analyzes the effects of natural disasters, wars, and financial crises on both labor productivity and TFP.[17]

Methodological approach. To assess the effects of adverse events on productivity, the local projection method (LPM) is used, with country productivity level estimates as the dependent variables (Jordà 2005; Jordà, Schularick, and Taylor 2013). For a specific type of event, the explanatory variable of interest is an episode, which equals 1 if the event occurred at least once in a particular country in a year and 0 otherwise. The LPM approach provides an estimate of the response of labor productivity (and TFP) to adverse events over various horizons (annex 3C). It also helps to identify key transmission channels, assess how countries' resilience to adverse events has changed over time, and analyze the role of policies in mitigating their effects. The advantage of this approach is that it avoids the problem of dimensionality inherent in other approaches such as vector autoregressions.[18] However, it does not directly take into account the severity of the adverse event.

---

[17] See chapter 1 for details on the derivation of TFP.

[18] Vector autoregressions approaches entails modeling and estimating a large number of time series, whereas LPM focuses on the dynamics of the variable of interest—productivity in this case.

FIGURE 3.8 **Episodes across different types of events**

In 1960-2018, natural disaster episodes occurred 25 times more frequently than wars, and 12 times more frequently than financial crises. Severe natural disasters occurred twice as often as severe wars. However, on average, wars lasted for about six years, twice as long as financial crises, with natural disasters the shortest-lived.

A. Average number of episodes per year

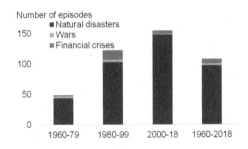

B. Average number of severe natural disaster and severe war episodes per year

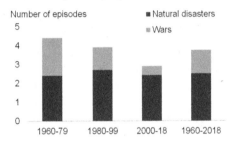

C. Average number of episodes per year in EMDEs

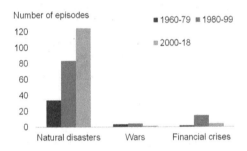

D. Average number of episodes per year in AEs

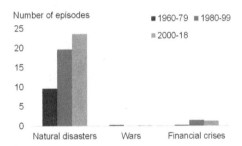

E. Average number of episodes per year in LICs

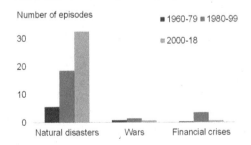

F. Average duration

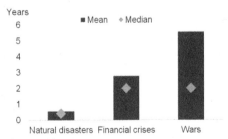

Sources: Correlates of War (COW); Emergency Events Database (EM-DAT); Laeven and Valencia (2018); Peace Research Institute Oslo (PRIO); World Bank.

Note: Natural disasters include climate, biological, and geophysical disasters (EM-DAT). Wars include intrastate and external (extrastate and interstate) wars (COW and PRIO). Financial crises include banking, currency, and sovereign debt crises (Laeven and Valencia 2018). Definitions are in annex 3A. An episode dummy for a specific type of event is 1 if the event occurs at least once (≥1) in a country-year pair and 0 otherwise. Severe natural disasters and severe wars are events that led to at least 100 deaths per million population. The sample includes 170 economies: 35 advanced economies and 135 EMDEs, of which 27 are LICs. EMDEs = emerging market and developing economies; LICs = low-income countries.

B. Severe natural disasters and severe wars are defined as events that led to at least 100 deaths in million population.

In some cases, weak productivity accompanied by a sharp decline in output can trigger financial crises and wars. To guard against such possible endogeneity or reverse causation between productivity and the event, lagged productivity is used as a control. Also, the explanatory variables are lagged—which helps to attenuate the potential endogeneity bias caused by contemporaneous interactions between productivity and crises. The regressions are estimated separately for natural disasters, wars, and financial crises over 1960-2018.

Impacts of natural disasters

Natural disasters can lead to significant contemporaneous losses in labor productivity in both advanced economies and EMDEs (figure 3.9). The estimates indicate that, immediately after a natural disaster, labor productivity tended to decline by 0.5 and 0.3 percent in advanced economies and EMDEs, respectively. These results are consistent with those found in the literature (Dell, Jones, and Olken 2012; Fomby, Ikeda, and Loayza 2013; Strömberg 2007). As well as the destruction of the capital stock, which weakens labor productivity, natural disasters also adversely affect TFP (Noy and Nualsri 2011; Skidmore and Toya 2002; Strobl 2011). However, the magnitude of the estimated effect of natural disasters on TFP may be expected to be smaller than that on labor productivity, because of the effect on the latter of the loss of physical capital. Indeed, the estimates indicate that natural disasters led to a 0.3 percent decline in TFP in advanced economies, in the first year of the disaster, with no significant effect in EMDEs. This may reflect possible offsetting productivity gains resulting from investment by governments and firms in new and more technologically advanced capital—investment induced by the natural disaster—leading to improvements in both TFP and labor productivity (Hallegatte and Dumas 2009; Hsiang 2010; Skidmore and Toya 2002; Strobl 2011).

Climate disasters. Among the different types of natural disasters, climate disasters have been particularly detrimental in terms of lost labor productivity. The estimates for both advanced economies and EMDEs indicate that climate disasters contemporaneously reduced labor productivity by about 0.5 percent and have persistent effects in both advanced economies and EMDEs. For EMDEs however, the estimated longer-term drag on productivity is smaller and subject to a wider margin of error. In fact, many previous studies have found that economies hit by climate disasters have been able to recover, especially after smaller-scale events (Hallegatte, Hourcade, and Dumas 2007; Loayza et al. 2012).

Threshold effects and severe climate disasters. Previous studies have distinguished among natural disasters in terms of their scale, using different thresholds, and found that the estimated effects on productivity and output are dependent on the size of the natural disaster (annex 3A).[19] Larger natural disasters have been found to have more severe immediate negative consequences for the economy (Fomby, Ikeda, and Loayza 2013).

---

[19] Data from the Emergency Events Database (EM-DAT) can suffer from selection biases leading to a non-linear link between physical intensity and (direct) asset losses (Felbermayr and Gröschl 2014b).

FIGURE 3.9 **Estimated effects of natural disaster episodes on productivity**

Episodes of natural disasters are estimated to have led to significant losses in productivity, especially labor productivity. Climate disasters, especially severe ones, have been particularly detrimental to productivity, although public and private investment have tended to increase in the short term, reflecting the shorter duration of the shock and reconstruction.

A. Contemporaneous effect of natural disaster episodes on labor productivity and TFP

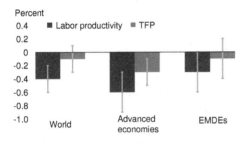

B. Effect of climate disaster episodes on labor productivity

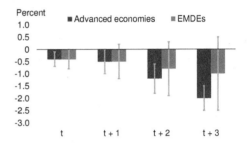

C. Effects of severe climate disaster episodes on labor productivity and TFP

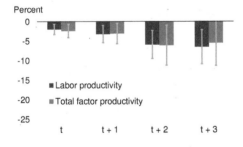

D. Effects of severe climate disaster episodes on labor investment and output

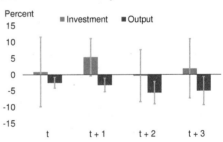

Sources: Emergency Events Database (EM-DAT); World Bank.
Note: EMDEs = emergency market and developing economies; TFP = total factor productivity.
A-D. Natural disasters include climate, biological, and geophysical disasters (EM-DAT; annex 3A) An episode dummy for a specific type of event is 1 if the event occurs at least once (≥1) in a country-year pair and 0 otherwise. Blue (and red) bars indicate the average impact of the event for each group, and orange lines represent the 90 percent significance range.
C-D. Severe climate disasters are defined as events that led to at least 100 deaths in million population.

Smaller events have been shown to have less persistent effects and even positive effects over the longer term (Cavallo et al. 2013a; Loayza et al. 2012). The literature finds that severe disasters have disproportionately larger economic impacts because of nonlinear effects on labor force participation and human capital, particularly among younger workers (Cavallo et al. 2013; Hallegatte and Przyluski 2010; Loayza et al. 2012). Furthermore, the cumulative loss of productivity tends to be larger if the disaster lasts for a more extended period—as is the case with biological disasters—or if reconstruction efforts are delayed (Cerra and Saxena 2008; Sawada 2007).[20] Some studies suggest that

---

[20] The pace of reconstruction may be slowed by financial, physical, and transaction constraints (Hallegatte and Rentschler 2018).

the long-run costs of natural disasters are mainly driven by uninsured losses, subsequent institutional instability, or regime changes.[21] This is supported by the analysis here, which suggests that larger shocks can have a positive effect on productivity in advanced economies, which likely benefit from better emergency response, more effective reconstruction plans, and deeper insurance markets (annex 3A).

In the analysis here, severe climate disasters are defined as those that caused at least 100 deaths per one million inhabitants. The results support the intuition that severe climate disasters have larger and more persistent effects on productivity in EMDEs than less severe ones. Labor productivity fell initially by about 2 percent and more than 7 percent below baseline, three years after a severe climate disaster (figure 3.9). The estimates show that lower labor productivity is mainly accounted for by weaker TFP rather than reduced investment.[22] On the one hand, this could be because after a severe disaster firms delay or trim down R&D spending, which impedes the creation, transfer, and adoption of new technologies, and hinders global value chains. On the other hand, overall investment may remain more resilient as reconstruction spending partly offsets some reduction in other types of capital spending.

The effects of biological and geophysical events are found to be not statistically significant. However, the estimates are for the average event, which could be localized or for other reasons affect only a limited number of people. Large biological or geophysical events may have large negative effects on productivity, including by constraining economic activity and human interaction, disrupting global value chains, and depressing demand, as exemplified by the COVID-19 outbreak.

Effects of epidemics. Epidemics lead to large and lasting negative effects on labor productivity.[23] There were five epidemics during the period 2000-18: SARS (2002-03), Swine flu (2009), MERS (2012), Ebola (2014-15), and Zika (2015-16). These four major epidemics (to avoid compounding effects, the Swine flu is excluded because it coincided with the GFC) lowered labor productivity initially by 1 percent, and by 4 percent cumulatively after three years (box 3.1). These severe epidemics seem to adversely affect labor productivity primarily through investment, which declined by 9 percent after three years because of increased uncertainty.

Cascade effects. Natural disasters can trigger other types of adverse events such as debt crises and wars, thus compounding the effects on productivity (Benson and Clay 2004; Celiku and Kraay 2017). Studies show that countries hit by major disasters can experience a sharp widening of the budget deficit, which can then increase the likelihood of a sovereign debt crisis (Benson and Clay 2004). Moreover, natural disasters can widen

---

[21] For example, some have found that the adverse macroeconomic effects of natural disasters dissipate after five years and that climate disasters explain a very small portion of the variance in real per capita GDP (Noy and Nualsri 2007; Peter, Von Dahlen, and Saxena 2012; Raddatz 2007).

[22] The impact on investment can be noisy because of possible mismeasurements in capital stock (chapter 1, box 1.1).

[23] Epidemics are different than typical biological disasters in the sense that they last longer and are accompanied by elevated uncertainty.

inequalities and exacerbate political tensions in affected countries. Besley and Persson (2011) estimate, for a sample of 97 countries in the period 1950-2005, that natural disasters increased the probability of wars by about 4 percentage points.

LICs. Fragile states and LICs are among the countries most exposed to natural disasters (table 3A.3, figures 3.2 and 3.3).[24] Although land-locked LICs have tended to experience fewer natural disasters than non-land-locked LICs, the impacts of such events on LICs have generally been considerably larger than in other income group economies, with more deaths as a percentage of the population and larger losses of output (Gaiha, Hill, and Thapa 2012; Noy 2009). This is partly because larger proportions of workers are in primary sectors—agriculture and mining—which are more susceptible to natural disasters. Moreover, infrastructure in LICs tends not to be as robust as in advanced economies. LICs also often lack the ability to quickly cope with natural disasters and thus tend to suffer additional losses stemming from disease and displacement (Benson and Clay 2004; Ghesquiere and Mahul 2010; Kahn 2005). LICs that are more often hit by natural disasters tend to have lower labor productivity and TFP levels than LICs that are less frequently hit by them. The disruptive effects of natural disasters may substantially delay—or even derail—the convergence process in LICs (chapter 4).

Impacts of wars

The analysis here focuses on the effects of wars on EMDEs.[25]

Intrastate wars. On average, EMDEs that experienced intrastate wars are estimated to have suffered a reduction in labor productivity of roughly 5 percent three years after the beginning of the war (figure 3.10).[26] Significant negative effects on TFP occurred with more of a time lag. Other research suggests that the loss of TFP may have been partly the result of negative effects on health, especially of children; disruptions to education; and weakened trade (Ades and Chua 1997; Akresh et al. 2012; Collier and Hoeffler 2004). The decline in TFP reaches about 6 percent three years after the beginning of the war.

External wars. These refer to interstate and extrastate wars combined. The losses from these two kinds of external wars have been much more pronounced than those from intrastate wars. This may be accounted for partly by the fact that international trade and foreign direct investment have been found to decline more in times of external conflict (Bayer and Rupert 2004; Busse and Hefeker 2007). Three years after the onset of an external war in an EMDE, the estimated decline in labor productivity exceeds 12

---

[24] There are 41 natural disasters episodes per country in LICs compared to 34 in EMDEs in the whole sample (table 3A.3).

[25] The focus here is on EMDEs because there have in recent years been no civil wars in advanced economies and the estimates suggest that the effects of external wars for advanced economies are ambiguous.

[26] Easterly et al. (1993) found, for 80 countries during the 1970s and 1980s, that the number of war-related casualties per capita is correlated significantly negatively (-0.3) with GDP per capita growth. Rodrik (1999) extended this study and found larger declines in GDP per capita growth for countries with high ethnolinguistic fragmentation.

FIGURE 3.10 **Estimated effects of war episodes on productivity in EMDEs**

Episodes of wars are estimated to have led to the steepest productivity losses among all types of events. The effects of war episodes on labor productivity have occurred immediately after the onset of wars, but their effects on TFP have mainly occurred one to two years later. Although the damage to productivity from internal wars has tended to be apparent immediately after the onset of the wars, longer-term losses from external wars have been much more pronounced.

A. Effects of war episodes on labor productivity

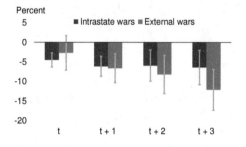

B. Effects of war episodes on TFP

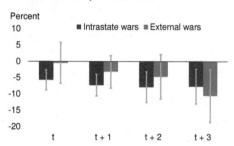

Sources: Correlates of War (COW); Peace Research Institute Oslo (PRIO); World Bank.
Note: EMDEs = emerging market and developing economies; TFP = total factor productivity.
A.B. Wars include intrastate and external (extrastate and interstate) wars (COW and PRIO; annex 3A). An episode dummy for a specific type of event is 1 if the event occurs at least once (≥1) in a country-year pair and 0 otherwise. Blue and red bars indicate the average effect of the event for each horizon, and orange lines represent the 90 percent significance range.

percent on average. The estimated negative effects on TFP are, not surprisingly, somewhat smaller than on labor productivity given that labor productivity, but not TFP, is affected by the loss of capital (Hutchinson and Margo 2006). The estimated decline in TFP after three years is 10 percent, with only a modest subsequent recovery (figure 3.10).

Impacts of financial crises

Financial crises tend to lead to large and long-lasting productivity losses. The estimates indicate that, in the year of the onset of a financial crisis, labor productivity globally has declined on average by about 2 percent (figure 3.11). The estimated decline three years later is 4 percent. The estimated effects are more modest for EMDEs than for advanced economies. For advanced economies, the decline in labor productivity three years after the onset of the crisis is about 6 percent, compared to about 3 percent in EMDEs. The larger productivity fall in advanced economies could reflect the larger size and economic importance of financial markets in these economies. The large initial productivity losses associated with financial crises are consistent with the literature (Ball 2014; Cerra and Saxena 2008; Furceri and Mourougane 2012b; Hutchison and Noy 2002). The estimates showing sustained damage to productivity are consistent with the years of subpar growth since the 2008-09 global recession, as well of the sharp reduction of economic growth and investment in Asia following the region's 1997-98 financial crisis (Barro 2009; Cecchetti, Kohler, and Upper 2010; Cerra and Saxena 2008).

FIGURE 3.11 **Estimated effects of financial crisis episodes on labor productivity**

Episodes of financial crises are estimated to have led to large and persistent losses in labor productivity. The estimated effects are smaller in EMDEs than in advanced economies. Financial crises (except for currency crises) are estimated to have been more detrimental to labor productivity than to TFP. Sovereign debt crises have led to more severe losses in productivity, especially labor productivity, than have other types of financial crisis.

A. Effects of financial crisis episodes on labor productivity, world

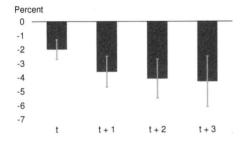

B. Effects of financial crisis episodes on labor productivity

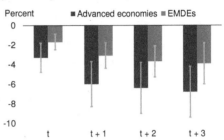

C. Change in labor productivity three years after financial crisis episodes

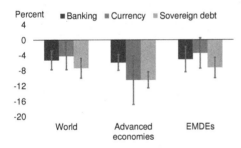

D. Change in TFP three years after financial crisis episodes

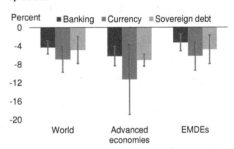

Sources: Laeven and Valencia (2018); World Bank.
Note: Financial crisis episodes include banking, currency, and sovereign debt crises (Laeven and Valencia 2018; annex 3A). An episode dummy for a specific type of event is 1 if the event occurs at least once (≥1) in a country-year pair and 0 otherwise. EMDEs = emerging market and developing economies (including low-income countries); TFP = total factor productivity.
A.B. Blue bars indicate the average impact of the event for each horizon, and orange lines represent the 90 percent significance range.
C.D. Blue, red, and orange bars indicate the average impact of the event for each financial crisis three years after the onset of the crises; and gray lines represent the 90 percent significance range.

Sovereign debt crises have typically been associated with falls in labor productivity and TFP of about 7.5 percent and 4.5 percent, respectively, three years after a default or debt restructuring.

Banking and currency crises have tended to be associated with subsequent reductions in labor productivity of between 5 percent and 7 percent in EMDEs after three years. This is consistent with other studies in the literature, although some suggest that the effects of banking crises are often short-lived (Barro 2001; Crafts 2013; Demirgüç-Kunt, Detragiache, and Gupta 2006; Morris and Shin 1998; Obstfeld 1996; Reinhart and

Rogoff 2009). These adverse effects on productivity appear to be larger in advanced economies, again possibly because of their larger and more economically important financial markets. However, advanced economies may have more competitive banking systems, which may reduce the likelihood of experiencing a financial crisis relative to EMDEs (Beck, Demirgüç-Kunt, and Levine 2006; Demirgüç-Kunt and Levine 2001).

Compounding effects of twin crises. Consistent with some of the literature, currency crises in EMDEs were found to lead to smaller labor productivity losses than debt and banking crises. However, sovereign debt crises can exacerbate the effects of currency or banking crises (Kapp and Vega 2014). Thus, the current estimates for EMDEs find that the effect of twin crises, consisting of simultaneous banking and currency crises, has been more severe than the sum of the effects of separate banking and currency crises.[27] Whereas banking crises have been associated with a contemporaneous decline in labor productivity of about 2 percent and currency crises with a decline of 0.2 percent, twin banking-currency crises have been associated with a 3.5 percent decrease, suggesting that in a combined crisis interaction substantially compounds the harm that ensues.

Comparison across different types of events

From a public policy perspective, the allocation of budgetary resources to disaster prevention efforts should depend on the relative costs of the expected output losses and other problems associated with the events, as well as the effectiveness of the mitigation efforts. However, comparing the costs of different types of shocks is challenging, because the identification of events depends on the threshold used for metrics such as the size of financial losses and the number of casualties. Moreover, the impact of future events may differ from past ones of the same type because of changing socioeconomic environments.

In EMDEs, according to the estimates, wars have been about 10 times more detrimental to productivity on impact than natural disasters, and 1.5 times more detrimental than financial crises. An average financial crisis has thus tended to reduce productivity much more than a typical natural disaster (figure 3.12). The results, which are broadly in line with the literature, show that on average financial crises induce a loss of about 2 percent in output per capita one year after their onset. This is twice the magnitude of the one-year productivity loss following an average natural disaster.

Over a longer horizon, according to estimates from the literature, wars appear to be most disruptive at the five-year horizon, reducing output per capita by an average of about 9 percent. However, there is a wide range of estimates, with some as high as 20 percent (Barro 2009). This may stem from differences in the criteria used to identify adverse events such as definitions, thresholds for damage and casualties, country coverage, the sample period, and estimation approach (for example, counterfactual analysis, panel regressions, and local projection).

---

[27] Cerra and Saxena (2008), Kapp and Vega (2014), and Kaminsky and Reinhart (1999) find larger effects. However, Hutchison and Noy (2005) find no additional (marginal) negative impacts above and beyond the combined effect of the two crises.

FIGURE 3.12 **Comparison of estimated effects in EMDEs**

An average financial crisis has been associated with much more damage to labor productivity than an average natural disaster, but wars have been the most damaging events. The findings of this chapter are consistent with the literature, which finds that one year after their onset, financial crises have tended to reduce output by about 2 percent, twice the adverse impact of natural disasters. Natural disasters have led to declines in output per capita of about 3 percent after five years, pointing to long-run corrosive effects. The peak of the damage to productivity from war appears to occur about five years after the event.

A. Initial impacts of natural disaster, war, and financial crisis episodes on EMDE productivity

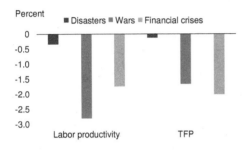

B. Estimated effects of natural disasters, wars, and financial crises on output per capita from the literature

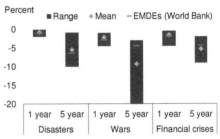

Sources: Correlates of War (COW); Emergency Events Database (EM-DAT); Laeven and Valencia (2018); Peace Research Institute Oslo (PRIO); World Bank.
Note: Natural disasters include climate, biological, and geophysical disasters (EM-DAT). Wars include intrastate and external (extrastate and interstate) wars (COW and PRIO). Financial crises include banking, currency, and sovereign debt crises (Laeven and Valencia 2018). Definitions are in annex 3A. An episode dummy for a specific type of event is 1 if the event occurs at least once (≥1) in a country-year pair and 0 otherwise. EMDEs = emerging market and developing economies; TFP = total factor productivity.
A. Blue, red, and orange bars indicate the average contemporaneous effect of the event.
B. The range of estimates is from the literature.

When estimating the overall impact of different types of disasters and considering policy design, it is critical to consider not only the average impact of an average shock but also the frequency of different events (figure 3.13). Although climate disasters tend to have small effects on productivity, they are much more frequent than financial shocks or wars; they also typically affect the poorest countries most. Because of the relatively high frequency of climate disasters in EMDEs, the expected annual loss of labor productivity resulting from them is well above the expected loss from financial crises. In contrast, wars and epidemics tend to be infrequent and to affect only a few countries, so that the average expected losses are small. However, the effects of infrequent wars and epidemics on the countries affected tend to be severe, which underscores the importance of implementing proactive policies to address tail risk events. These results are useful to gauge where risks are relatively high and provide guidance to prioritize mitigation policies.

Severe adverse events

Rare and severe events may have disproportionately large impacts on the afflicted countries compared to the small and frequent ones (Hallegatte and Przyluski 2010; Loayza et al. 2012). Large-scale natural disasters tend to cause larger damage to capital,

FIGURE 3.13 **Productivity loss in EMDEs, scaled by event frequency**

Despite the differences in average estimated effects among different types of adverse events, the estimated average effects scaled by the different frequencies of the types of event are more similar, with the exception of external wars, where the adjusted effect is smaller. The expected losses are bigger over longer horizons because of the compounding effect.

A. Contemporaneous impacts of natural disaster, war, and financial crisis episodes on labor productivity

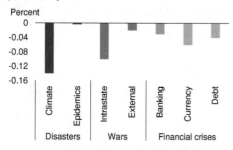

B. Contemporaneous impacts of natural disaster, war, and financial crisis episodes on TFP

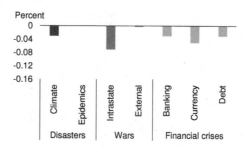

C. Average cumulative loss of labor productivity, three years after natural disaster, war, and financial crisis episodes

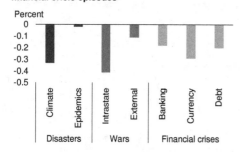

D. Average cumulative loss of TFP, three years after natural disaster, war, and financial crisis episodes

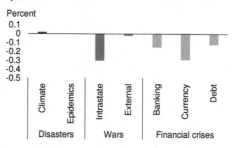

Sources: Correlates of War (COW); Emergency Events Database (EM-DAT); Laeven and Valencia (2018); Peace Research Institute Oslo (PRIO); World Bank.
Note: Natural disasters include climate, biological, and geophysical disasters (EM-DAT). Wars include intrastate and external (extrastate and interstate) wars (COW and PRIO). Financial crises include banking, currency, and sovereign debt crises (Laeven and Valencia 2018). Definitions are in annex 3A. An episode dummy for a specific type of event is 1 if the event occurs at least once (≥1) in a country-year pair and 0 otherwise. EMDEs = emerging market and developing economies; TFP = total factor productivity.
A-D. Blue, red and orange bars indicate the average impact of the event, which is the effect of event multiplied by the probability of that particular event in EMDEs.

employment, and output. Severe wars and intense armed conflicts with large death tolls also cause outsized damage to physical capital, labor, and output (Hutchinson and Margo 2006). The negative effects of severe events on labor force participation and human capital are particularly more acute among the most vulnerable population groups such as women and younger workers.

Global adverse events

Some large-scale adverse events affect many countries simultaneously. The effects of these global shocks have been amplified through various propagation channels—financial markets, value chains, transport services, and trade—as economies have become more integrated. This was exemplified by the 2008 GFC, which started in the U.S. subprime sector, spilled over to global financial markets and economies around the world, and was followed by a global productivity slowdown (chapter 1). Large-scale natural disasters such as the COVID-19 pandemic will likely leave deep scars on productivity and output via a dislocation of labor, a tightening of credit, a disruption of value chains, and a decline in innovation in addition to triggering financial crisis (box 3.1).

The recent policies implemented in response to COVID-19 show that quick intervention by international, national, and local authorities with various policies is essential because global adverse events are likely to occur in the future and have lasting negative effects on productivity. They underscore the need for countries to be better prepared to cope with global shocks. Policy support can help to mitigate some of the scarring effects of these global shocks.

What policies can mitigate the effects of adverse events?

Policies can help to reduce the risks of some natural disasters, including through actions to tackle global warming, better protect vulnerable areas and populations, and reduce the likelihood of wars and financial crises. Mitigation policies are likely to require adequate fiscal space and involve appropriate structural reforms.

Addressing vulnerabilities and mitigating the effects of adverse events. In the aftermath of large-scale destructive events like the COVID-19 pandemic, wars, and natural disasters, emergency response and reconstruction can help prevent lasting productivity losses. Countries vulnerable to natural disasters could bolster investment in resilient infrastructure, strengthen health care systems, and foster climate-friendly innovation.[28] They could also strengthen social safety nets. In LICs, in particular, fiscal buffers might be limited, so foreign aid flows could help by complementing domestic resources (Raddatz 2009). If appropriate, populations and critical infrastructures could be relocated to areas less prone to natural disasters. Regulatory reforms and macroprudential policies to monitor and address, in a timely manner, systemic banking risks, and debt and external vulnerabilities, can reduce the likelihood of financial crises.

Improving institutions and the business climate. Structural reforms that raise the quality and effectiveness of governance and improve the business climate can reduce the likelihood of some adverse events and also help to limit the damage caused by those that occur. Governments that have improved labor and product market flexibility, strengthened legal systems and property rights, fostered effective competition, and addressed inequality will have laid the foundations for more effective private sector adjustment to adverse events (Anbarci, Escaleras, and Register 2005). Good regulations

---

[28] Reducing those vulnerabilities is efficient in economic terms because each dollar invested in resilience tends to generate four dollars in benefits (Hallegatte, Rentschler, and Rozenberg 2019).

and institutions can improve risk sharing and the prevention and mitigation of financial crises and some natural disasters. They can also reduce the probability of wars, which can be rooted in inequalities, unresolved grievances, and greed (Collier and Hoeffler 2004). Reform-driven productivity gains critically depend on the sustainability, timing, size, mix, and duration of such interventions.

Building fiscal space. Emergency responses and reconstruction efforts after wars or natural disasters can be costly. Deep financial crisis may require a sizable fiscal response as well—several advanced economies and EMDEs implemented fiscal stimulus to counter the negative consequences of the 2008 GFC. This underscores the importance of having adequate fiscal buffers to be able to counter negative shocks as well as effective, transparent governance to ensure that funds are spent effectively and in appropriate amounts (Hallegatte and Rentschler 2018; Oulton and Sebastiá-Barriel 2017; Reinhart and Rogoff 2010).[29] Fiscal space may be defined as a government's ability to fund expansionary fiscal policies without undermining sustainability of public finances. When the previously described LPM regressions were amended to introduce an estimate of fiscal space as a variable (Duval and Furceri 2018; Jordà 2005), it was found that countries with positive fiscal space tended to experience smaller detrimental effects on productivity after banking or currency crises, or climate disasters (figure 3.14). The estimates suggest that positive fiscal space provides support to productivity of about 0.9 percent in the case of currency crises, and 0.8 percent in banking crises. Positive fiscal space is also estimated to help alleviate the detrimental effects of climate disasters on productivity, although to a smaller degree. There are similar effects on TFP. In addition, fiscal space is found to help reduce the likelihood of adverse financial events.

Conclusion

Major adverse events—natural disasters, wars, and financial crises—can have long-lasting negative effects on productivity. This chapter has presented a comprehensive analysis of the effects of adverse events on labor productivity and TFP. It explored the channels through which events can erode productivity, how different types of events affect productivity differently, and the extent to which they have larger effects on EMDEs and LICs. The chapter also explored the role that policies can play in mitigating these adverse effects.

The results suggest that wars tend to be highly damaging to productivity. In addition to their human toll, wars destroy physical capital and disrupt production and trade. Intrastate and external wars are estimated to have lowered labor productivity after three years by about 6 and 12 percent, respectively. The estimated effect of natural disasters on labor productivity and TFP is smaller, but such events are the most frequent and are therefore a substantial hindrance to productivity. Negative effects from natural disasters have varied by type and also across countries, with LICs particularly vulnerable, so that

---

[29] Not only do needs for emergency and reconstruction expenditures rise after natural disasters but also government revenues tend to fall (Noy and Nualsri 2011).

FIGURE 3.14 **Productivity loss, taking account of fiscal space in EMDEs**

Positive fiscal space is associated with a modestly smaller detrimental impact on productivity after financial crisis episodes, especially in the case of currency crises. Countries with positive fiscal space saw a smaller decline in labor productivity after financial crises, with an estimated benefit from the fiscal space of 0.8 percent for banking crises and 0.3 percent for currency crises. Similarly, countries with positive fiscal space benefit by 0.5 and 0.7 percent, in terms of decline in TFP, after the banking and currency crises, respectively. Having fiscal space makes it more feasible to help alleviate the detrimental effects of climate disasters on productivity. Declines in labor productivity and TFP immediately after the onset of a climate disaster have been 0.2 and 0.1 percent smaller, respectively, in countries having a fiscal buffer.

A. Contemporaneous impacts of climate, banking, and currency episodes on labor productivity

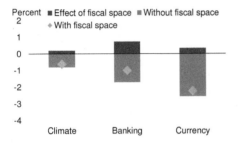

B. Contemporaneous impacts of climate, banking, and currency episodes on TFP

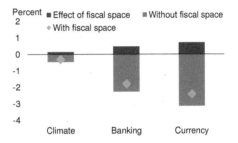

Sources: Emergency Events Database (EM-DAT); Laeven and Valencia (2018); World Bank.
Note: Climate disasters (EM-DAT), banking and currency crises (Laeven and Valencia 2018) are defined in annex 3A. An episode dummy for a specific type of event is 1 if the event occurs at least once (≥1) in a country-year pair and 0 otherwise. EMDEs = emerging market and developing economies; TFP = total factor productivity.
A.B. Blue bars indicate the impact of having a fiscal space on the effect of the adverse events on productivity (effect of fiscal space); red bars represent the gross effect of adverse events on productivity without the fiscal space impact (without fiscal space); orange diamonds show the average net effect of adverse events for the countries that have fiscal space (with fiscal space).

there have been important adverse effects on poverty. Productivity is also highly vulnerable to financial stress, particularly when accompanied by a rapid buildup of government debt. Severe disasters, such as the COVID-19 pandemic, not only dislocate labor and supply chains but can also trigger financial stress with severe lasting effects on productivity. Epidemics that occurred since 2000 have lowered labor productivity by a cumulative 4 percent after three years, mainly through their adverse impact on investment and the labor force. In contrast, severe climate disasters were shorter-lived and reduced labor productivity by a cumulative 7 percent after three years, mainly through weakened TFP. The COVID-19 pandemic is likely to have a significantly worse impact on productivity than most previous natural disasters because of its global reach and the widespread disruptions to production and transportation, unprecedented measures to control it, and changes to consumer behavior that it has caused. If not properly addressed, the negative effects of adverse disasters on productivity can delay or even derail the convergence of EMDEs to the advanced economy technology frontier and may undermine hard-won gains in poverty reduction in LICs and FCS countries.

Macroeconomic and other policies are important tools to counter the adverse effects of natural disasters, financial crises, and wars. Policies are warranted to reduce the pace of global warming and to better protect vulnerable areas and populations against natural hazards, as well as to encourage relocation from, and hazard-resistant building in, disaster-prone areas. Enhanced regulatory frameworks can help to reduce the likelihood of financial crises, as well as to mitigate their harm. Appropriate institutional and business climates, including good governance, can also alleviate the initial effects of adverse events and increase the pace of economic recovery. Fiscal space and transparent governance enable reconstruction efforts, after a natural disaster or armed conflict, to get under way in a timely and effective fashion as well as help to prevent financial crises.

Future research could explore in greater detail the relationship between country characteristics and vulnerability to adverse events. This chapter found that countries with rising government debt tend to suffer more from financial crises. A deeper dive could reveal more information about the importance of characteristics such as governance, infrastructure quality, and regulatory quality for mitigating the impact of disasters, and could provide insights to build greater resilience to these types of negative shocks.

Unexpected adverse events are generally considered short-term shocks to the economy. However, longer-term productivity is also affected, especially by repeated events, which will impede the convergence of economies, as examined in the next chapter.

ANNEX 3A Data, sources, and definitions

Identification of natural disasters. The data are taken from the Emergency Events Database (EM-DAT) for the period 1960-2018. There are two main categories in the EM-DAT database: (1) natural and (2) technological or human-caused hazards. Our analysis is solely based on natural disasters. Natural disasters are split into six categories in EM-DAT. Two of these are used as defined in EM-DAT: (1) biological (diseases and epidemics) and (2) geophysical (earthquakes, tsunamis, and volcanic activity) disasters. Three are used as one combined climate category in our analysis: (1) climatological (extreme heat and cold, droughts), (2) hydrological (floods), and (3) meteorological (cyclones and storms). The sixth category of natural disasters is not included in our analysis because of limited observations: extraterrestrial, defined as hazards caused by asteroids, comets, or meteoroids, or changes in interplanetary conditions that affect the earth's magnetosphere, ionosphere, and thermosphere. The following inclusion criteria are used: (1) 10 or more people reported killed, (2) 100 or more people affected, (3) an official declaration of a state of emergency, or (4) a call for international assistance.[30] Seventy percent of natural disasters were climate disasters, whereas biological and geophysical disasters were much less frequent (tables 3A.1 through 3A.3, figure 3A.1). There were 3,897 climate, 1,003 biological, and 830 geophysical disasters over 1960-

---

[30] These selection criteria may, to some extent, bias the estimates toward natural disasters with larger socioeconomic impacts. The number of affected people is determined by the sum of injured, homeless, and those who required immediate assistance during the state of emergency.

FIGURE 3A.1 Time series of number of occurrences, by income group

Disasters, especially climate-related hazards, were the most frequent events in advanced economies, EMDEs, and LICs. Over the last three decades, the number of natural disaster occurrences per year has more than tripled. In LICs, climate and biological disaster occurrences have increased sharply in the last 30 years.

A. Number of occurrences in EMDEs

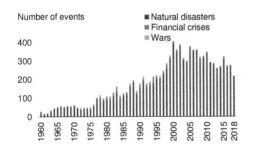

B. Number of natural disaster occurrences in EMDEs

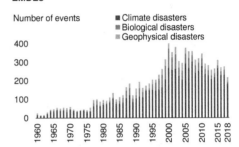

C. Number of occurrences in advanced economies

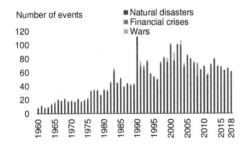

D. Number of natural disasters in advanced economies

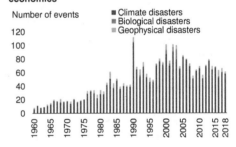

E. Number of occurrences in LICs

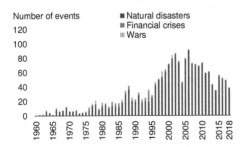

F. Number of natural disaster occurrences in LICs

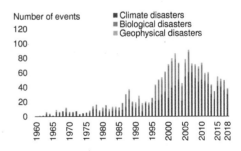

Sources: Correlates of War (COW); Emergency Events Database (EM-DAT); Laeven and Valencia (2018); Peace Research Institute Oslo (PRIO); World Bank.

Note: Financial crises include banking, currency, and sovereign debt crises (Laeven and Valencia 2018). Natural disasters include climate, biological, and geophysical disasters (EM-DAT). Wars include intrastate, extrastate, and interstate wars (COW and PRIO). Definitions are in annex 3A. A specific type of event can have multiple occurrences in a country-year pair. The sample includes 170 economies: 35 advanced economies and 135 EMDEs, of which 27 are EMDEs. EMDEs = emerging market and developing economies (including LICs); LICs = low-income countries.

A-F. Times series of the total number of events in advanced economies, EMDEs, and LICs.

2018.[31] The results are sensitive to the thresholds on the number of deaths that are applied to identify a natural disaster. For severe natural disasters with a threshold of one death per million inhabitants, the number of natural disasters declines substantially to 1,730, 576, and 256 for climate, biological, and geophysical, respectively.

Comparability of natural disaster databases. Despite substantial improvements in the collection of systematic and harmonized natural disaster data, identifying these events remains challenging. Recorded data differ across different international natural disaster databases because of different methodologies and definitions. EM-DAT uses a threshold of at least 10 deaths, or 100 people affected, or a declaration of state emergency, or a call for international assistance at the country level; this definition discards small-scale disasters. By contrast, the DesInventar data set, maintained by the United Nations Office for Disaster Risk Reduction, uses a lower threshold of at least one death or one dollar of economic loss and, therefore, has a greater number of recorded events than EM-DAT (Moriyama, Sasaki, and Ono 2018). Other databases such as NatCat, maintained by Munich Reinsurance Company, and Sigma, maintained by Swiss Reinsurance Company, use different criteria based on the number of deaths or cost of property damages. Comparing the data from EM-DAT, NatCat, and Sigma, only 26 percent of the total events reported during 1985-99 for four countries (Honduras, India, Mozambique, and Vietnam) were common across three data sets (Guha-Sapir and Below 2002). NatCat and Sigma suggest an increase of natural catastrophes worldwide over the last decade, likely reflecting that they are better at capturing less severe events. NatCat finds the number of severe events has been stable for the last decade, suggesting better mitigation policies.

Challenges to the assessment of the economic costs of natural disasters. From an economic perspective, natural disasters are events that cause a shock to the functioning of the economic system, with significant negative impacts on assets, production factors, output, employment, and consumption (Hallegatte and Przyluski 2010). Natural disasters have direct and indirect economic effects. Direct effects include the immediate reduction in output caused by the natural disaster, whereas indirect effects pertain to losses not provoked by the natural disaster itself, but by its consequences. Consider a hurricane or tornado in a country dependent on tourism revenue: besides the direct effects of damage caused by the hurricane, a resulting smaller number of tourists will tend to dampen output growth until reconstruction of facilities is completed and memories of the disaster dissipate.

The literature suggests that the impact of natural disasters on productivity and output tends to be negative.[32] However, it is difficult to compare results across various studies because of different methods and metrics (Felbermayr and Gröschl 2014; Fomby,

---

[31] Felbermayr and Gröschl (2014) show that natural disaster information obtained from the EM-DAT data set suffers from selection bias because the magnitude of destruction depends on GDP per capita, which leads to upwards-biased estimates.

[32] For surveys of the literature, see Cavallo and Noy (2011); Dell, Jones, and Olken (2014); and Kousky (2014). Recent papers include Pigato (2019) and Batten (2018).

Ikeda, and Loayza 2013; Loayza et al. 2012; Noy 2009; Raddatz 2009). Cumulative net effects of natural disasters on productivity and output depend on the magnitude and type of natural disaster, and on income level.

- *Magnitude.* Large or multiple natural disasters have sizable negative effects on productivity, in both the short and long term.[33] In contrast, the effects of small or moderate natural disasters are ambiguous. In the short run, the direct effects of these natural disasters include an immediate loss of output (Cashin, Mohaddes, and Raissi 2017; Cavallo et al. 2013a; Noy and Nualsri 2011; Raddatz 2007, 2009; Strobl 2011). However, reconstruction activities can subsequently boost growth, innovation, and productivity (Benson and Clay 2004; Cuaresma, Hlouskova, and Obersteiner 2008; Skidmore and Toya 2002).

- *Type.* The impacts of natural disasters on output and productivity can vary substantially across types of disasters (Hochrainer 2009; Loayza et al. 2012). Climate disasters tend to be negative for growth, whereas other natural disasters have more variable impacts (Felbermayr and Gröschl 2014; Raddatz 2009).[34] This might reflect the negative disruptive effects of the natural disasters being offset by the positive effects of reconstruction as governments and aid agencies provide investment.

- *Income level.* More generally, advanced economies suffer smaller negative effects on output growth (Noy 2009). This could be because they have the resources, human capital, and institutions to mitigate the direct effects of adverse events through reconstruction and investment. In addition, the impacts of natural disasters on productivity and output growth can also vary substantially across economic sectors (Loayza et al. 2012). Given the larger role of agricultural activity in LICs, weather events are likely to have more pernicious effects on productivity (Acevedo et al. 2018) than in advanced economies.

Identification of wars. Wars are identified using the World Bank's Correlates of War (COW) database. In this data set, wars are defined as conflicts with at least 1,000 battle-related deaths over the entire episode (Singer and Small 1994). The COW database covers 1816-2007 and is updated from 2008 to 2018 using the Peace Research Institute Oslo (PRIO) data (Pettersson, Högbladh, and Öberg 2019).[35] Three types of wars are considered in this study: (1) intrastate wars, which involve a government in opposition to one or more rebel groups within a state; (2) extrastate wars, which are armed conflicts

---

[33] For example, Cavallo, Powell, and Becerra (2010) estimate that the earthquake that hit Haiti on January 12, 2010, caused damage to Haiti's economy equivalent to 100 percent of the country's GDP (Cavallo and Noy 2011; Fomby, Ikeda, and Loayza 2013; Von Peter, Von Dahlen, and Saxena 2012).

[34] Even within the category of climatic disasters the effects can differ. Fomby, Ikeda, and Loayza (2013) and Loayza et al. (2012) find that the effects of droughts are negative. In contrast, Cunado and Ferreira (2014) find that floods can lead to a positive effect in advanced economies, as the additional rainfall could boost crop production in the following years.

[35] To extend the COW database beyond 2007, the number of battle-related deaths for each conflict in the PRIO database is aggregated over the whole episode.

between a state outside its own territory and a nonstate group; and (3) interstate wars, in which both sides are states in the Gleditsch and Ward membership system (Gleditsch et al. 2002). Among the different types of wars, 123 intrastate, 29 extrastate, and 84 interstate wars are identified for 1960-2018 (table 3A.1). Virtually all intrastate wars take place in EMDEs and 37 percent of intrastate wars happen in LICs.

Identification of financial crises. Data for financial crises are based on the Laeven and Valencia (2018) database for the period 1960-2018.

- *Banking crises* are recorded as having started in a given year if one of the following three conditions is met: (1) the share of nonperforming loans is above 20 percent of total loans, (2) bank closures reach at least 20 percent of banking system assets, or (3) the costs of restructuring of the banking system exceeds 5 percent of GDP. The sample contains 147 episodes of banking crises for which labor productivity estimates are available. About 23 percent of these episodes occurred in 29 advanced economies, 59 percent in 64 EMDEs excluding LICs, and 18 percent in 21 LICs.

- *Currency crises* are defined to have occurred if the following two conditions are met simultaneously: (1) local currency depreciates by at least 30 percent (from the year earlier), and (2) the magnitude of the depreciation is at least 10 percentage points larger than occurred in the previous year. There are 226 currency crises in our sample for which labor productivity estimates are available. Nearly 8 percent of these currency crises occurred in 13 advanced economies, 72 percent in 75 EMDEs excluding LICs, and 20 percent in 23 LICs. About 10 percent of currency crises were accompanied by banking crises.

- *Sovereign debt crises* are defined as the occurrence of a sovereign debt default or restructuring. In the case of a restructuring of public debt without default, the crisis year is the year of restructuring. There are 71 sovereign debt default events in our sample for which labor productivity estimates are available. Fewer than 3 percent of these episodes occurred in two advanced economies, 80 percent in 44 EMDEs excluding LICs, and about 17 percent in 12 LICs (tables 3A.1-3A.3).

- *A rapid debt accumulation* episode is defined as an expansion from trough to peak of total debt-to-GDP ratios by more than one standard deviation, with troughs and peaks identified using the Harding and Pagan (2002) algorithm. This yields 190 episodes. Almost half of the debt accumulation episodes were associated with financial crises.

Decline in financial crisis frequency, rising debt risk. Over the 58-year sample period, currency crises occurred more often than banking and debt crises (figure 3.6). The frequency of financial crises was three times greater in the 1980s and 1990s than in the post-1990 period. After 2000, there were on average three currency crises, two banking crises, and one debt crisis each year. Although the frequency of financial crises declined after 2008, concerns have risen about elevated debt and exchange rate pressures in several countries in recent years (Kose et al. 2020; Sandri 2015). Over the last 30 years, a financial crisis was 50 percent more likely to occur in EMDEs or LICs than in advanced economies (figure 3.6). The regions most affected by financial crises were SSA and LAC, with Europe and Central Asia (ECA) experiencing a large increase. Countries in ECA and SSA were markedly more affected by adverse financial events during 2000-18, reflecting their economic links to advanced economies and spillovers from the euro area debt crisis.[36]

TABLE 3A.1 **Number of episodes**

	AEs	EMDEs	LICs	EAP	ECA	LAC	MNA	SAR	SSA	World
All financial crises	54	390	83	37	57	109	28	10	149	444
Systemic banking crisis	34	113	27	9	22	30	8	4	40	147
Currency crisis	18	208	44	25	26	52	16	6	83	226
Sovereign debt crisis	2	69	12	3	9	27	4	0	26	71
All disasters	1,031	4,699	1,098	799	481	1,114	313	481	1,510	5,730
Disasters (climate)	843	3,054	651	512	355	788	211	300	887	3,897
Disasters (biological)	50	953	369	98	39	124	32	94	566	1,003
Disasters (geophysical)	138	692	78	189	87	202	70	87	57	830
All wars	45	191	55	37	21	16	35	23	59	236
Internal wars	0	123	46	20	12	11	18	13	49	123
External wars	45	68	9	17	9	5	17	10	10	113

Sources: Correlates of War (COW); Emergency Events Database (EM-DAT); Laeven and Valencia (2018); Peace Research Institute Oslo (PRIO); World Bank.
Note: An episode dummy for a specific type of event is 1 if the event occurs at least once (≥1) in a country-year pair and 0 otherwise. The sample is restricted to the observations where labor productivity growth data exist for the period 1960-2018. The total number of episodes (in bold) for each group of events (all financials, all disasters, all wars) may include events that occur simultaneously. The events are defined in annex 3A. AEs = advanced economies; EMDEs = emerging market and developing economies (including LICs); LICs = low-income countries; EAP = East Asia and Pacific; ECA = Europe and Central Asia; LAC = Latin America and the Caribbean; MNA = Middle East and North Africa; SAR = South Asia; SSA = Sub-Saharan Africa.

---

[36] In the postcrisis period, 2010-18, adverse financial shocks, mainly currency and debt shocks, were more frequent in EMDEs and LICs than in advanced economies (Arizala, Bellon, and Macdonald 2018; Bussière, Fidrmuc, and Schnatz 2005).

TABLE 3A.2 Number of countries experiencing at least one episode

	AEs	EMDEs	LICs	EAP	ECA	LAC	MNA	SAR	SSA	World
All financial crises	31	133	27	18	21	26	16	7	45	164
Systemic banking crisis	29	85	21	7	17	18	8	4	31	114
Currency crisis	13	98	23	11	14	20	8	5	40	111
Sovereign debt crisis	2	56	12	3	8	18	4	0	23	58
All disasters	34	137	27	18	21	27	16	8	46	171
Disasters (climate)	33	134	27	18	21	27	15	7	45	167
Disasters (biological)	20	109	27	15	12	18	10	8	46	129
Disasters (geophysical)	19	79	15	12	16	18	8	8	17	98
All wars	13	69	17	9	12	10	13	5	20	82
Internal wars	0	54	15	9	9	8	7	5	16	54
External wars	13	37	6	6	6	5	9	3	8	50

Sources: Correlates of War (COW); Emergency Events Database (EM-DAT); Laeven and Valencia (2018); Peace Research Institute Oslo (PRIO); World Bank.
Note: An episode dummy for a specific type of event is 1 if the event occurs at least once (≥1) in a country-year pair and 0 otherwise. The sample is restricted to the observations where labor productivity growth data exist for the period 1960-2018. For each group of events (all financials, all disasters, all wars), the total number of countries affected (in bold) may be smaller than the sum of countries affected by each type of event because a country can be hit by different events at the same time. The events are defined in annex 3A. AEs = advanced economies; EMDEs = emerging market and developing economies (including LICs); LICs = low-income countries; EAP = East Asia and Pacific; ECA = Europe and Central Asia; LAC = Latin America and the Caribbean; MNA = Middle East and North Africa; SAR = South Asia; SSA = Sub-Saharan Africa.

TABLE 3A.3 Number of episodes per country

	AEs	EMDEs	LICs	EAP	ECA	LAC	MNA	SAR	SSA	World
All financial crises	2	3	3	2	3	4	2	1	3	3
Systemic banking crisis	1	1	1	1	1	2	1	1	1	1
Currency crisis	1	2	2	2	2	3	2	1	2	2
Sovereign debt crisis	1	1	1	1	1	2	1	0	1	1
All disasters	30	34	41	44	23	41	20	60	33	34
Disasters (climate)	26	23	24	28	17	29	14	43	20	23
Disasters (biological)	3	9	14	7	3	7	3	12	12	8
Disasters (geophysical)	7	9	5	16	5	11	9	11	3	8
All wars	3	3	3	4	2	2	3	5	3	3
Internal wars	0	2	3	2	1	1	3	3	3	2
External wars	3	2	2	3	2	1	2	3	1	2

Sources: Correlates of War (COW); Emergency Events Database (EM-DAT); Laeven and Valencia (2018); Peace Research Institute Oslo (PRIO); World Bank.
Note: An episode dummy for a specific type of event is 1 if the event occurs at least once (≥1) in a country-year pair and 0 otherwise. The sample is restricted to the observations where labor productivity growth data exist for the period 1960-2018. For each type of event, the number of episodes per country is computed by dividing the number of episodes by the number of countries affected. The events are defined in annex 3A. AEs = advanced economies; EMDEs = emerging market and developing economies (including LICs); LICs = low-income countries; EAP = East Asia and Pacific; ECA = Europe and Central Asia; LAC = Latin America and the Caribbean; MNA = Middle East and North Africa; SAR = South Asia; SSA = Sub-Saharan Africa

ANNEX 3B **Robustness**

Mismeasurement caveats. The literature has identified several issues surrounding the reporting of adverse events. Natural disasters, physical damages, and the number of deaths may be underestimated in areas with limited natural disaster monitoring systems or overreported to secure foreign aid (Albala-Bertrand 1993). In addition, there are well-known measurement issues—particularly for LICs—pertaining to the effects of the informal sector (Jennings 2011; Kousky 2014), the lack of accounting of reconstruction (Raddatz 2009), or the effects of insurance (Felbermayr and Gröschl 2014). However, measurement has been improved by increasingly sophisticated methods for reporting natural disasters, including advanced satellite imagery (Voigt et al. 2007).

Productivity is prone to measurement issues as well. Any measurement issues in variables used in the estimation of labor productivity (output and employment) and TFP (output, employment, and capital) would be reflected in those productivity measures. It is especially important in countries where services and government sectors account for a large share of the economy because of the difficulties in appropriate measurements of those sectors. Data quality, especially in EMDEs, might include imputed estimations and may be poor beyond the general measurement issues such as the difficulty in taking into account various work arrangements in measuring labor input (Brandolini and Viviano 2018; Katz and Krueger 2016). Measurement of capital inputs is complicated because of its large heterogeneity in various aspects such as tangible vs. intangible, short lived vs. long-lived assets (Hulten 2010). The capital input measure used in this study is from Penn World Table 9.1 and accounts for different types of assets on the basis of their life span (Inklaar, Woltjer, and Gallardo 2019).

Endogeneity and simultaneity between events. An adverse event may be triggered by other negative shocks. This raises endogeneity concerns when estimating the impact of an adverse event on productivity. Natural disasters can fuel political unrest and conflicts, further damaging the productive capabilities of affected countries (Brancati 2007; Cavallo et al. 2013b; Nel and Righarts 2008). Financial crises and adverse external shocks, such as sharp declines in trade or commodity prices, can precipitate conflicts and wars, and lead to severe productivity and output losses (Reynaerts and Vanschoonbeek 2018). Both wars and natural disasters can lead to rapid debt accumulation, which is often associated with financial crisis (Kose et al. 2020). Among the three types of events explored in this chapter, natural disasters seem the most immune to these endogeneity issues.

Endogeneity with productivity. Natural disasters are in all likelihood not caused by changes in productivity.[37] However, endogeneity concerns may arise in the analysis of financial crises and wars. Subdued productivity growth may contribute to a financial

---

[37] Even though economic activity is linked to greenhouse gas emissions and climate change, the global spatial and long temporal scale means that productivity has no impact on climate over the time scales considered in this chapter.

crisis or lead to an armed conflict through feeble output growth. Weakening productivity growth can lead to underperforming loans as it becomes harder for firms to meet their financial commitments. On a large scale, these underperforming loans can cause substantial deterioration in the balance sheets of financial institutions and trigger financial crises (Aghion, Bacchetta, and Banerjee 2000; Kalemli-Özcan, Laeven, and Moreno 2018). Moreover, low output growth because of weaker productivity growth may lead to lower wealth, increased inequality, heightened social tensions, and polarized communities, and consequently trigger political instability. This reverse causal effect may not be immediate but is likely to materialize after only a few years.

ANNEX 3C **Methodology**

This chapter mainly uses a local projection methodology (Jordà 2005). This methodology enables the identification of the effects of events on labor productivity and TFP while controlling for endogeneity or reverse causation. Another advantage of using this methodology is that it can help identify whether specific country characteristics matter and bolster recovery.

Local projection method. The dependent variable is the cumulative change between labor productivity or TFP (log) levels between horizons $t - 1$ and $t + h$, denoted as $y_{t+h,j} - y_{t-1,j}$. The explanatory variables include the event dummy and controls. The baseline model is given by

$$y_{t+h,j} - y_{t-1,j} = \alpha_{(h),j} + \tau_{(h),t} + \beta_{(h)} E_{t,j} + \Sigma_{s=1}^{p} \gamma_{l(h),s} E_{t-s,j}$$
$$+ \Sigma_{s=1}^{h-1} \gamma_{f(h),s} E_{t+h-s,j} + \Sigma_{s=1}^{p} \delta_{(h),s} \Delta y_{t-s,j} + u_{(h)t,j},$$

where $h = 0,\ldots,5$ is the horizon, $\alpha_{(h),j}$ and $\tau_{(h),t}$ are country j and time fixed effects, and $u_{(h)t,j}$ is an error term. The coefficient of interest $\beta_{(h)}$ captures the dynamic multiplier effect (impulse response) of the dependent variable with respect to the event dummy variable $E_{t,j}$. The number of lags for each variable is denoted by p and set to 1 for the estimation. The specification controls for (1) country-specific trends, (2) lagged event dates, (3) future values of the event dummy between time t and $t + h - 1$ to correct for possible forward bias (Teulings and Zubanov 2014), and (4) past changes $\Delta y_{t-s,j}$. Additional controls for country-specific interactions and nonlinear effects may also be included.

References

Abadie, A., and J. Gardeazabal. 2003. "The Economic Costs of Conflict: A Case Study of the Basque Country." *American Economic Review* 93 (1): 113–32.

Acevedo, S. M., M. Mrkaic, N. Novta, E. Pugacheva, and P. Topalova. 2018. "The Effects of Weather Shocks on Economic Activity: What Are the Channels of Impact?" IMF Working Papers 18/144, International Monetary Fund, Washington, DC.

ADB (Asian Development Bank). 2019. *Asian Development Outlook: Strengthening Disaster Resilience.* Manila: Asian Development Bank.

Ades, A., and H. B. Chua. 1997. "Thy Neighbor's Curse: Regional Instability and Economic Growth." *Journal of Economic Growth* 2 (3): 279–304.

Aghion, P., P. Bacchetta, and A. Banerjee. 2000. "A Simple Model of Monetary Policy and Currency Crises." *European Economic Review* 44 (4–6): 728–38.

Aghion, P., P. Bacchetta, R. Rancière, and K. Rogoff. 2009. "Exchange Rate Volatility and Productivity Growth: The Role of Financial Development." *Journal of Monetary Economics* 56 (4): 494–513.

Aguiar, M., and G. Gopinath. 2006. "Defaultable Debt, Interest Rates and the Current Account." *Journal of International Economics* 69 (1): 64–83.

Akbulut-Yuksel, M. 2009. "Children of War: The Long-Run Effects of Large-Scale Physical Destruction and Warfare on Children." *Journal of Human Resources* 49 (3): 634–62.

Akresh, R., S. Bhalotra, M. Leone, and U. O. Osili. 2012. "War and Stature: Growing up during the Nigerian Civil War." *American Economic Review* 102 (3): 273–77.

Albala-Bertrand, J. M. 1993. "Natural Disaster Situations and Growth: A Macroeconomic Model for Sudden Disaster Impacts." *World Development* 21 (9): 1417–34.

Alderman, H., J. Hoddinott, and B. Kinsey. 2006. "Long Term Consequences of Early Childhood Malnutrition." *Oxford Economic Papers* 58 (3): 450–74.

Anbarci, N., M. Escaleras, and C. A. Register. 2005. "Earthquake Fatalities: The Interaction of Nature and Political Economy." *Journal of Public Economics* 89 (9–10): 1907–33.

Arellano, C. 2008. "Default Risk and Income Fluctuations in Emerging Economies." *American Economic Review* 98 (3): 690–712.

Arizala, F., M. Bellon, and M. Macdonald. 2018. "Regional Spillovers in Sub-Saharan Africa: Exploring Different Channels." *Spillover Note,* August. International Monetary Fund, Washington, DC.

Baker, S. R., N. Bloom, S. J. Davis, and S. J. Terry. 2020. "Covid-Induced Economic Uncertainty." NBER Working Paper 26983, National Bureau of Economic Research, Cambridge, MA.

Baker, S. R., N. Bloom, and S. J. Terry. 2019. "Does Uncertainty Reduce Growth? Using Disasters as Natural Experiments." NBER Working Paper 19475, National Bureau of Economic Research, Cambridge, MA.

Ball, L. 2009. "Hysteresis in Unemployment: Old and New Evidence." NBER Working Paper 14818, National Bureau of Economic Research, Cambridge, MA.

Ball, L. 2014. "Long-Term Damage from the Great Recession in OECD Countries." *European Journal of Economics and Economic Policies: Intervention* 11 (2): 149–60.

Barro, R. J. 2001. "Economic Growth in East Asia before and after the Financial Crisis." NBER Working Paper 8330, National Bureau of Economic Research, Cambridge, MA.

Barro, R. J. 2009. "Rare Disasters, Asset Prices, and Welfare Costs." *American Economic Review* 99 (1): 243–64.

Barro, R. J., and J. F. Ursúa. 2008. "Macroeconomic Crises since 1870." *Brookings Papers on Economic Activity* 39 (Spring): 255–350.

Batten, S. 2018. "Climate Change and the Macro-Economy: A Critical Review." Staff Working Paper 706, Bank of England, London.

Bayer, R., and M. C. Rupert. 2004. "Effects of Civil Wars on International Trade, 1950-92." *Journal of Peace Research* 41 (6): 699–713.

Beck, T., A. Demirgüç-Kunt, and R. Levine. 2006. "Bank Concentration, Competition, and Crises: First Results." *Journal of Banking and Finance* 30 (5): 1581–603.

Becker, T., and P. Mauro. 2006. "Output Drops and the Shocks That Matter." IMF Working Paper 06/172, International Monetary Fund, Washington, DC.

Benson, C., and E. J. Clay. 2004. *Understanding the Economic and Financial Impacts of Natural Disasters.* Disaster Risk Management Series No. 4. World Bank, Washington, DC.

Besley, T., and T. Persson. 2011. "The Logic of Political Violence." *Quarterly Journal of Economics* 126 (3): 1411–45.

Blanchard, O., E. Cerutti, and L. Summers. 2015. "Inflation and Activity – Two Explorations and Their Monetary Policy Implications." NBER Working Paper 21726, National Bureau of Economic Research, Cambridge, MA.

Blanchard, O., and J. Wolfers. 2000. "The Role of Shocks and Institutions in the Rise of European Unemployment: The Aggregate Evidence." *The Economic Journal* 110 (462): 1–33.

Bloom, N. 2014. "Fluctuations in Uncertainty." *Journal of Economic Perspectives* 28 (2): 153–76.

Bloom, N., M. Floetotto, N. Jaimovich, I. Saporta-Eksten, and S. J. Terry. 2018. "Really Uncertain Business Cycles." *Econometrica* 86 (3): 1031–65.

Bloom, N., A. Mahajan, D. J. McKenzie, and D. J. Roberts. 2010. "Why Do Firms in Developing Countries Have Low Productivity?" *American Economic Review* 200 (2): 619–23.

Borensztein, E., and S. L. Ye. 2018. "Corporate Debt Overhang and Investment: Firm-Level Evidence." Policy Research Working Paper 8553, World Bank, Washington, DC.

Brancati, D. 2007. "Political Aftershocks: The Impact of Earthquakes on Intrastate Conflict." *Journal of Conflict Resolution* 51 (5): 715–43.

Brandolini, A., and E. Viviano. 2018. "Measuring Employment and Unemployment: Should Statistical Criteria for Measuring Employment and Unemployment Be Re-Examined?" IZA World of Labor 445, Institute of Labor Economics, Bonn.

Bulow, B. J., and K. Rogoff. 1989. "Sovereign Debt: Is to Forgive to Forget?" *American Economic Review* 79 (1): 43–50.

Busse, M., and C. Hefeker. 2007. "Political Risk, Institutions and Foreign Direct Investment." *European Journal of Political Economy* 23 (2): 397–415.

Bussière, M., J. Fidrmuc, and B. Schnatz. 2005. "Trade Integration of Central and Eastern European Countries: Lessons from a Gravity Model." ECB Working Paper 545, European Central Bank, Frankfurt.

Bustos, P., B. Caprettini, J. Ponticelli, D. Atkin, F. Buera, V. Carvalho, G. Gancia, et al. 2016. "Agricultural Productivity and Structural Transformation: Evidence from Brazil." *American Economic Review* 106 (6): 1320–65.

Cashin, P., K. Mohaddes, and M. Raissi. 2017. "Fair Weather or Foul? The Macroeconomic Effects of El Niño." *Journal of International Economics* 106 (May): 37–54.

Cavallo, E., S. Galiani, I. Noy, and J. Pantano. 2013. "Catastrophic Natural Disasters and Economic Growth." *The Review of Economics and Statistics* 95 (5): 1549–61.

Cavallo, E., and I. Noy. 2011. "Natural Disasters and the Economy – A Survey." *International Review of Environmental and Resource Economics* 5 (1): 63–102.

Cavallo, E., A. Powell, and O. Becerra. 2010. "Estimating the Direct Economic Damages of the Earthquake in Haiti." *The Economic Journal* 120 (546): F298–F312.

Cecchetti, S. G., M. Kohler, and C. Upper. 2010. "The Financial Crisis and Economic Activity." NBER Working Paper 15379, National Bureau of Economic Research, Cambridge, MA.

Celiku, B., and A. Kraay. 2017. "Predicting Conflict." Policy Research Working Paper 8075, World Bank, Washington, DC.

Cerra, V., and S. C. Saxena. 2008. "Growth Dynamics: The Myth of Economic Recovery." *American Economic Review* 98 (1): 439–57.

Cerra, V., and S. C. Saxena. 2017. "Booms, Crises, and Recoveries: A New Paradigm of the Business Cycle and Its Policy Implications." IMF Working Paper 17/250, International Monetary Fund, Washington, DC.

Checherita-Westphal, C., and P. Rother. 2012. "The Impact of High Government Debt on Economic Growth and Its Channels: An Empirical Investigation for the Euro Area." *European Economic Review* 56 (7): 1392–405.

Claessens, S., E. Detragiache, R. Kanbur, and P. Wickham. 1997. "HIPCs' Debt Review of the Issues." *Journal of African Economies* 6 (2): 231–54.

Claessens, S., and M. A. Kose. 2017. "Asset Prices and Macroeconomic Outcomes: A Survey." BIS Paper 676, Bank for International Settlements, Basel.

Claessens, S., and M. A. Kose. 2018. "Frontiers of Macrofinancial Linkages." BIS Paper 95, Bank for International Settlements, Basel.

Collier, P. 1999. "On the Economic Consequences of Civil War." *Oxford Economic Papers* 51 (1): 168–83.

Collier, P., and A. Hoeffler. 2004. "Greed and Grievance in Civil War." *Oxford Economic Papers* 56 (4): 563–95.

Costanza, R., and J. Farley. 2007. "Ecological Economics of Coastal Disasters: Introduction to the Special Issue." *Ecological Economics* 63 (2–3): 249–53.

Crafts, N. 2013. "Long-Term Growth in Europe: What Difference Does the Crisis Make?" *National Institute Economic Review* 224 (1): 14–28.

Cuaresma, C. J., J. Hlouskova, and M. Obersteiner. 2008. "Natural Disasters as Creative Destruction? Evidence from Developing Countries." *Economic Inquiry* 46 (2): 214–26.

Cunado, J., and S. Ferreira. 2014. "The Macroeconomic Impacts of Natural Disasters: The Case of Floods." *Land Economics* 90 (1): 149–68.

Dell, M., B. F. Jones, and B. A. Olken. 2012. "Temperature Shocks and Economic Growth: Evidence from the Last Half Century." *American Economic Journal: Macroeconomics* 4 (3): 66–95.

Dell, M., B. F. Jones, and B. A. Olken. 2014. "What Do We Learn from the Weather? The New Climate-Economy Literature." *Journal of Economic Literature* 52 (3): 740–98.

Demirgüç-Kunt, A., E. Detragiache, and P. Gupta. 2006. "Inside the Crisis: An Empirical Analysis of Banking Systems." *Journal of International Money and Finance* 25 (5): 702–18.

Demirgüç-Kunt, A., and R. Levine. 2001. *Financial Structure and Economic Growth: Perspectives and Lessons,* edited by Asli Demirgüç-Kunt and Ross Levine. Cambridge, MA: MIT Press.

De Ridder, M. 2017. "Investment in Productivity and the Long-Run Effect of Financial Crises on Output." CESifo Working Paper 6243, Center for Economic Studies and Ifo Institute, Cambridge, U.K.

Dieppe, A., N. Francis, and G. Kindberg-Hanlon. Forthcoming. "Productivity Dynamics across Emerging and Developed Countries." World Bank, Washington, DC.

Duval, R., and D. Furceri. 2018. "The Effects of Labor and Product Market Reforms: The Role of Macroeconomic Conditions and Policies." *IMF Economic Review* 66 (1): 31–69.

Easterly, W., M. Kremer, L. Pritchett, and L. H. Summers. 1993. "Good Policy or Good Luck? Country Growth Performance and Temporary Shocks." *Journal of Monetary Economics* 32 (3): 459–83.

Eberhardt, M., and A. F. Presbitero. 2015. "Public Debt and Growth: Heterogeneity and Non-Linearity." *Journal of International Economics* 97 (1): 45–58.

El-Erian, M. 2020. "A Shock Like No Other: The Way Forward for Developing Countries." Speech in World Bank Panel. June 3, 2020.

Felbermayr, G., and J. Gröschl. 2014. "Naturally Negative: The Growth Effects of Natural Disasters." *Journal of Development Economics* 111: 92–106.

Field, A. J. 2008. "The Impact of the Second World War on US Productivity Growth." *Economic History Review* 61 (3): 672–94.

Field, A. J. 2019. "The Productivity Impact of World War II Mobilization in the United States." https://ssrn.com/abstract=3110832.

Fomby, T., Y. Ikeda, and N. V. Loayza. 2013. "The Growth Aftermath of Natural Disasters." *Journal of Applied Econometrics* 28 (1): 412–34.

Furceri, D., P. Loungani, J. D. Ostry, and P. Pizzuto. 2020. "Will Covid-19 Affect Inequality? Evidence from Past Pandemics." *Covid Economics* 12: 138–57.

Furceri, D., and A. Mourougane. 2012a. "How Do Institutions Affect Structural Unemployment in Times of Crises?" *Panoeconomicus* 59 (4): 393–419.

Furceri, D., and A. Mourougane. 2012b. "The Effect of Financial Crises on Potential Output: New Empirical Evidence from OECD Countries." *Journal of Macroeconomics* 34 (3): 822–32.

Gaiha, R., K. Hill, and G. Thapa. 2012. "Have Natural Disasters Become Deadlier?" ASARC Working Paper 2012/03, Australia South Asia Research Centre, The Australian National Univesity, Canberra.

Ghesquiere, F., and O. Mahul. 2010. "Financial Protection of the State against Natural Disasters: A Primer." Policy Research Working Paper 5429, World Bank, Washington, DC.

Gleditsch, N. P., P. Wallensteen, M. Eriksson, M. Sollenberg, and H. Strand. 2002. "Armed Conflict 1946-2001: A New Dataset." *Journal of Peace Research* 39 (5): 615–37.

Guha-Sapir, D., and R. Below. 2002. "The Quality and Accuracy of Disaster Data: A Comparative Analyses of Three Global Data Sets." Working Paper 191, prepared for the ProVention Consortium and the Disaster Management Facility, World Bank.

Hall, R. E. 2014. "Quantifying the Lasting Harm to the U.S. Economy from the Financial Crisis." NBER Working Paper 20183, National Bureau of Economic Research, Cambridge, MA.

Hallegatte, S., and P. Dumas. 2009. "Can Natural Disasters Have Positive Consequences? Investigating the Role of Embodied Technical Change." *Ecological Economics* 68 (3): 777–86.

Hallegatte, S., J. C. Hourcade, and P. Dumas. 2007. "Why Economic Dynamics Matter in Assessing Climate Change Damages: Illustration on Extreme Events." *Ecological Economics* 62 (2): 330–40.

Hallegatte, S., and V. Przyluski. 2010. "The Economics of Natural Disasters: Concepts and Methods." Policy Research Working Paper 5507, World Bank, Washington, DC.

Hallegatte, S., and J. Rentschler. 2018. "The Last Mile: Delivery Mechanisms for Post-Disaster Finance." World Bank, Washington, DC.

Hallegatte, S., J. Rentschler, and J. Rozenberg. 2019. *Lifelines: The Resilient Infrastructure Opportunity.* Washington, DC: World Bank.

Hallegatte, S., and A. Vogt-Schilb. 2019. "Are Losses from Natural Disasters: More than Just Asset Losses?" In *Advances in Spatial and Economic Modeling of Disaster Impacts*, edited by Y. Okuyama and R. Adam, 15–42. Cham, Switzerland: Springer.

Hallward-Driemeier, M., and G. Nayyar. 2017. *Trouble in the Making? The Future of Manufacturing-Led Development.* Washington, DC: World Bank.

Harding, D., and A. Pagan. 2002. "Dissecting the Cycle: A Methodological Investigation." *Journal of Monetary Economics* 49 (2): 365–81.

Hochrainer, S. 2009. "Assessing The Macroeconomic Impacts of Natural Disasters: Are There Any?" Policy Research Working Paper 4968, World Bank, Washington, DC.

Hsiang, S. M. 2010. "Temperatures and Cyclones Strongly Associated with Economic Production in the Caribbean and Central America." In *Proceedings of the National Academy of Sciences of the United States of America* 107 (35): 15367–72.

Hulten, C. R. 2010. "Growth Accounting." In *Handbook of the Economics of Innovation, Vol. 2*, edited by B. H. Hall and N. Rosenberg, 987–1031. Amsterdam: Elsevier.

Hutchinson, W., and R. A. Margo. 2006. "The Impact of the Civil War on Capital Intensity and Labor Productivity in Southern Manufacturing." *Explorations in Economic History* 43 (4): 689–704.

Hutchison, M. M., and I. Noy. 2002. "Output Costs of Currency and Balance of Payments Crises in Emerging Markets." *Comparative Economic Studies* 44 (2–3): 27–44.

Hutchison, M. M., and I. Noy. 2005. "How Bad Are Twins? Output Costs of Currency and Banking Crises." *Journal of Money, Credit and Banking* 37 (4): 725–52.

IMF (International Monetary Fund). 2017. "The Effects of Weather Shocks on Economic Activity: How Can Low-Income Countries Cope?" Chapter 3 in *World Economic Outlook October 2017: Seeking Sustainable Growth: Short-Term Recovery, Long-Term Challenges.* Washington, DC: International Monetary Fund.

IMF (International Monetary Fund). 2018. "Macroeconomic Developments and Prospects in Low-Income Developing Countries—2018." IMF Policy Paper, International Monetary Fund, Washington, DC.

Inklaar, R., P. Woltjer, and D. Gallardo. 2019. "The Composition of Capital and Cross-Country Productivity Comparisons." The Fifth World KLEMS Conference 36, University of Groningen, Netherlands.

Jennings, S. 2011. "Time's Bitter Flood: Trends in the Number of Reported Natural Disasters." May. Oxfam GB Research Report, Oxford, U.K.

Jordà, Ò. 2005. "Estimation and Inference of Impulse Responses by Local Projections." *American Economic Review* 95 (1): 161–82.

Jordà, Ò., M. Schularick, and A. M. Taylor. 2013. "When Credit Bites Back." *Journal of Money, Credit and Banking* 45 (2): 3–28.

Jordà, Ò., S. R. Singh, and A. M. Taylor. 2020. "The Long-Run Effects of Monetary Policy." FRBSF Working Paper 2020-01, Federal Reserve Bank of San Francisco.

Kahn, M. E. 2005. "The Death Toll from Natural Disasters: The Role of Income, Geography and Institutions: Comment." *Review of Economics and Statistics* 87 (2): 271–84.

Kalemli-Özcan, S., L. Laeven, and D. Moreno. 2018. "Debt Overhang, Rollover Risk, and Corporate Investment: Evidence from the European Crisis." NBER Working Paper 24555, National Bureau of Economic Research, Cambridge, MA.

Kaminsky, G. L., and C. M. Reinhart. 1999. "The Twin Crises: The Causes of Banking and Balance-of-Payments Problems." *American Economic Review* 89 (3): 473–500.

Kapp, D., and M. Vega. 2014. "Real Output Costs of Financial Crises: A Loss Distribution Approach." *Cuadernos de Economía (Spain)* 37 (103): 13–28.

Katz, L. F., and A. B. Krueger. 2016. "The Rise and Nature of Alternative Work Arrangements in the United States, 1995-2015." NBER Working Paper 22667, National Bureau of Economic Research, Cambridge, MA.

Kilic Celik, S., M. A. Kose, F. Ohnsorge, and M. Some. Forthcoming. "A Cross-Country Database of Potential Growth." Policy Research Working Paper, World Bank, Washington, DC.

Knight, M., N. Loayza, and D. Villanueva. 1996. "The Peace Dividend: Military Spending Cuts and Economic Growth." Policy Research Working Paper 1577, World Bank, Washington, DC.

Kose, A., and F. Ohnsorge. 2019. *A Decade after the Global Recession: Lessons and Challenges for Emerging and Developing Economies.* Washington, DC: World Bank.

Kose, A., P. Nagle, F. Ohnsorge, and N. Sugawara. 2020. *Global Waves of Debt: Causes and Consequences.* Washington, DC: World Bank.

Kousky, C. 2014. "Informing Climate Adaptation: A Review of the Economic Costs of Natural Disasters." *Energy Economics* 46 (November): 576–92.

Ksoll, C., R. Macchiavello, and A. Morjaria. 2010. "The Effect of Ethnic Violence on an Export-Oriented Industry." CEPR Discussion Paper 8074, Centre for Economic Policy Research, London.

Kumar, M. S., and J. Woo. 2010. "Public Debt and Growth." IMF Working Paper 10/174, International Monetary Fund, Washington, DC.

Kunreuther, H. 2006. "Disaster Mitigation and Insurance: Learning from Katrina." *The Annals of the American Academy of Political and Social Science* 604 (1): 208–27.

Laeven, L., and F. Valencia. 2018. "Systemic Banking Crises Revisited." IMF Working Paper 18/206, International Monetary Fund, Washington, DC.

Lazear, E. P., K. L. Shaw, and C. Stanton. 2013. "Making Do With Less: Working Harder during Recessions." *Journal of Labor Economics* 34 (S1): S333–60.

Loayza, N. V., E. Olaberría, J. Rigolini, and L. Christiaensen. 2012. "Natural Disasters and Growth: Going beyond the Averages." *World Development* 40 (7): 1317–36.

Ludvigson, S. C., S. Ma, and S. Ng. 2020. "Covid19 and the Macroeconomic Effects of Costly Disasters." NBER Working Paper 26987, National Bureau of Economic Research, Cambridge, MA.

Ma, C., J. H. Rogers, and S. Zhou. 2020. "Global Economic and Financial Effects of 21st Century Pandemics and Epidemics." *SSRN Electronic Journal*, March. http://dx.doi.org/10.2139/ssrn.3565646.

Maccini, S., and D. Yang. 2009. "Under the Weather: Health, Schooling and Economic Consequences of Early-Life Rainfall." *American Economic Review* 99 (3): 1006–26.

Moriyama, K., D. Sasaki, and Y. Ono. 2018. "Comparison of Global Databases for Disaster Loss and Damage Data." *Journal of Disaster Research* 13 (6): 1007–14.

Morris, S., and H. S. Shin. 1998. "Unique Equilibrium in a Model of Self-Fulfilling Currency Attacks." *American Economic Review* 88 (3): 587–97.

Mourougane, A. 2017. "Crisis, Potential Output and Hysteresis." *International Economics* 149 (May): 1–14.

Mueller, H. 2013. "The Economic Cost of Conflict." Working Paper, International Growth Centre, London.

Nel, P., and M. Righarts. 2008. "Natural Disasters and the Risk of Violent Civil Conflict." *International Studies Quarterly* 52 (1): 159–85.

Noy, I. 2009. "The Macroeconomic Consequences of Disasters." *Journal of Development Economics* 88 (2): 221–31.

Noy, I., and A. Nualsri. 2007. "What Do Exogenous Shocks Tell Us about Growth Theories." Working Paper 200728, University of Hawaii at Manoa.

Noy, I., and A. Nualsri. 2011. "Fiscal Storms: Public Spending and Revenues in the Aftermath of Natural Disasters." *Environment and Development Economics* 16 (1): 113–28.

Obstfeld, M. 1996. "Models of Currency Crises with Self-Fulfilling Features." *European Economic Review* 40 (95): 1037–47.

OECD (Organisation for Economic Co-operation and Development). 2020. "OECD Policy Brief: Women at the Core of the Fight against COVID-19." OECD, Paris.

Oulton, N., and M. Sebastiá-Barriel. 2017. "Effects of Financial Crises on Productivity, Capital and Employment." *Review of Income and Wealth* 63 (February): S90–112.

Peter, G. Von, S. Von Dahlen, and S. Saxena. 2012. "Unmitigated Disasters? New Evidence on the Macroeconomic Cost of Natural Catastrophes." BIS Working Paper 394, Bank for International Settlements, Basel.

Pettersson, T., S. Högbladh, and M. Öberg. 2019. "Organized Violence, 1989–2018 and Peace Agreements." *Journal of Peace Research* 56 (4): 589–603.

Pigato, M. A. 2019. "Benefits Beyond Climate: Environmental Tax Reform." In *Fiscal Policies for Development and Climate Action*, edited by M. A. Pigato, 155–86. Washington, DC: World Bank.

Poirson, H., C. Pattillo, and L. Ricci. 2002. "External Debt and Growth." IMF Working Paper 02/69, International Monetary Fund, Washington, DC.

Poirson, H., C. Pattillo, and L. Ricci. 2004. "What Are the Channels through Which External Debt Affects Growth?" IMF Working Paper 04/15, International Monetary Fund, Washington, DC.

Raddatz, C. 2007. "Are External Shocks Responsible for the Instability of Output in Low-Income Countries?" *Journal of Development Economics* 84 (1): 155–87.

Raddatz, C. 2009. "The Wrath of God: Macroeconomic Costs of Natural Disasters." Policy Research Working Paper 5039, World Bank, Washington, DC.

Ray, D., and J. Esteban. 2017. "Conflict and Development." *Annual Review of Economics* 9: 263–93.

Reinhart, C. M., and K. S. Rogoff. 2009. "The Aftermath of Financial Crises." *American Economic Review* 99 (2): 466–72.

Reinhart, C. M., and K. S. Rogoff. 2010. "Growth in a Time of Debt." *American Economic Review: Papers & Proceedings* 100 (May): 573–78.

Reynaerts, J., and J. Vanschoonbeek. 2018. "The Economics of State Fragmentation: Assessing the Economic Impact of Secession." Working Paper, University of Leuven, Belgium.

Ritchie, H., and M. Roser. 2020. "Natural Disasters." *Our World in Data*. https://ourworldindata.org/natural-disasters.

Rodrik, D. 1999. "Where Did All the Growth Go? External Shocks, Social Conflict, and Growth Collapses." *Journal of Economic Growth* 4 (4): 385–412.

Sandri, D. 2015. "Dealing with Systemic Sovereign Debt Crises: Fiscal Consolidation, Bail-Ins or Official Transfers?" IMF Working Paper 17/223, International Monetary Fund, Washington, DC.

Sawada, Y. 2007. "The Impact of Natural and Manmade Disasters on Household Welfare." *Agricultural Economics* 37 (S1): 59–73.

Sawada, Y., K. Tomoaki, and R. Bhattacharyay. 2011. "Aggregate Impacts of Natural and Human-Made Disasters in the Global Economy." Working Paper, University of Tokyo, Tokyo.

Schnitzer, M. 2002. "Debt v. Foreign Direct Investment: The Impact of Sovereign Risk on the Structure of International Capital Flows." *Economica* 69 (273): 41–67.

Singer, J. D., and M. Small. 1994. "Correlates of War Project: International and Civil War Data, 1816–1992." Inter-University Consortium for Political and Social Research, University of Michigan.

Skidmore, M., and H. Toya. 2002. "Do Natural Disasters Promote Long-Run Growth?" *Economic Inquiry* 40 (4): 664–87.

Strand, J., and M. Toman. 2010. "Green Stimulus, Economic Recovery, and Long-Term Sustainable Development," Policy Research Working Paper 5163, World Bank, Washington, DC.

Strobl, E. 2011. "The Economic Growth Impact of Hurricanes: Evidence from U.S. Coastal Countries." *Review of Economics and Statistics* 93 (2): 575–89.

Strömberg, D. 2007. "Natural Disasters, Economic Development, and Humanitarian Aid." *Journal of Economic Perspectives* 21 (3): 199–222.

Teulings, C. N., and N. Zubanov. 2014. "Is Economic Recovery a Myth? Robust Estimation of Impulse Responses." *Journal of Applied Econometrics* 29 (3): 497–514.

Thomas, V., and R. López. 2015. "Global Increase in Climate-Related Disasters." ADB Economics Working Paper 466, Asian Development Bank, Manila.

UNCTAD (United Nations Conference on Trade and Development). 2020. "Impact of the COVID-19 Pandemic on Global FDI and GVCs. Updated Analysis." United Nations Conference on Trade and Development, Washington, DC.

UNHCR (United Nations High Commissioner for Refugees). 2018. "Global Trends: Forced Displacement in 2017." https://www.unhcr.org/5b27be547.pdf.

Voigt, S., T. Kemper, T. Riedlinger, R. Kiefl, K. Scholte, and H. Mehl. 2007. "Satellite Image Analysis for Disaster and Crisis-Management Support." *IEEE Transactions on Geoscience and Remote Sensing* 45 (6): 1520–28.

Von Peter, G., S. Von Dahlen, and S. Saxena. 2012. "Unmitigated Disasters? New Evidence on the Macroeconomic Cost of Natural Catastrophes." BIS Working Paper 394, Bank for International Settlements, Basel.

World Bank. 2020a. "COVID-19: Potential Channels of Impact and Mitigating Policies." Unpublished paper, World Bank, Washington, DC.

World Bank. 2020b. *The COVID-19 Pandemic: Shocks to Education and Policy Responses*. Washington, DC: World Bank.

World Bank. 2020c. *Global Economic Prospects: Slow Growth, Policy Challenges*. January. Washington, DC: World Bank.

World Bank. 2020d. "Pandemic, Recession: The Global Economy in Crisis." In *Global Economic Prospects*, June. Washington, DC: World Bank.

Over a long period of time; the main force in favor of greater equality has been the diffusion of knowledge and skills.

Thomas Piketty (2014)

Professor, Paris School of Economics

The future has arrived—it's just not evenly distributed yet.

William Gibson (1999)

Author

CHAPTER 4

Productivity Convergence: Is Anyone Catching Up?

Labor productivity in emerging market and developing economies (EMDEs) is just under 20 percent of the advanced economy average, whereas in low-income countries it is a mere 2 percent. Average productivity growth in EMDEs has picked up rapidly since 2000, renewing interest in the convergence hypothesis, which predicts that economies with low productivity should close productivity gaps over time. Yet the average rate of convergence remains low, with current growth differentials halving the productivity gap only after more than 100 years. Behind the low average pace of convergence lies considerable diversity among groups of countries converging toward different productivity levels—so-called convergence clubs. Many EMDEs have moved into higher-level productivity convergence clubs since 2000, with 16 countries joining the highest club that is primarily composed of advanced economies. These transitioning EMDEs have been characterized by systematically better initial education levels, greater institutional quality, and high or deepening economic complexity relative to their income level, and are frequently aided by policies to encourage participation in global value chains. However, countries seeking to replicate successes, or continue along rapid convergence paths, face a range of headwinds, including a more challenging environment to gain market share in manufacturing production as well as to increase global value chain integration. The global recession due to COVID-19 (coronavirus disease 2019) may amplify many of these headwinds.

Introduction

Labor productivity in emerging market and developing economies (EMDEs) is less than 20 percent of the level in advanced economies; in low-income countries (LICs), it is just 2 percent of advanced economy levels. The unconditional convergence hypothesis states that productivity catch-up growth will tend to occur where productivity differentials exist and that these differentials will decline over time. However, this type of convergence may fail to occur for reasons such as the existence of international barriers to technology transfer and differences in saving and investment behavior.[1] Conditional convergence is more restrictive, because catch-up productivity growth may depend on characteristics of economies beyond their initial productivity levels. For example, only economies with characteristics such as high institutional quality or education levels may be able to converge to the frontier.

The large productivity gap between EMDEs and the frontier implies that there is a potential for substantial income gains in EMDEs if either of these two hypotheses

---

Note: This chapter was prepared by Gene Kindberg-Hanlon and Cedric Okou. Research assistance was provided by Khamal Clayton and Xinyue Wang.

[1] See annex 4A for further details of the theoretical underpinnings of the convergence hypothesis, implied by the models of Solow (1956) and Swan (1956).

holds.[2] Historically, productivity gaps have remained stubbornly ingrained, with the bulk of evidence pointing away from unconditional convergence (Johnson and Papageorgiou 2020). However, falling global poverty rates in recent decades have been an encouraging sign that economies near the bottom of the distribution have made productivity and income gains, helping reduce the proportion of the world's population living in extreme poverty from 36 percent in 1990 to 10 percent in 2015 (World Bank 2018b). Most of the fall is concentrated in East Asia and Pacific (EAP) and South Asia (SAR), the two regions with the highest rates of productivity growth among EMDEs (see chapter 1).[3]

Faster EMDE productivity growth in recent decades does not itself imply convergence toward the advanced economy frontier, which has also continued to expand. In addition, if the unconditional convergence hypothesis holds, the gains in productivity should be broad-based. More complex dynamics of productivity growth could instead support the convergence club hypothesis, with different clubs of economies converging toward different productivity levels depending on their characteristics.

Finally, productivity growth has slowed following the global financial crisis (GFC) in EMDEs and faces headwinds from the COVID-19 crisis. The COVID-19-driven global recession is occurring during a period of heightened debt vulnerabilities, and previous pandemics and other major natural disasters were followed by prolonged declines in labor productivity growth and investment. Commodity prices have also collapsed, adding negative pressure on investment in the large number of commodity-reliant EMDEs, and will remain weak in the event the global recovery is drawn out. There are further risks to EMDE convergence if countries adopt inward-looking policies that result in the fragmentation of global trade—integration into global value chains has been a key vehicle for the adoption of more advanced production processes in EMDEs.

Against this backdrop, this chapter examines the following questions.

- How has productivity convergence evolved over the past five decades?

- Are there "clubs" of economies following different convergence trajectories?

- What separates those economies in successful and unsuccessful clubs?

- What are the policy implications?

Contributions

This chapter makes several contributions to the literature. First, it expands a reinvigorated literature on *income per capita* convergence by examining *labor productivity*

---

[2] Cross-country differences in per capita income, which account for two-thirds of global income equality, largely reflect differentials in labor productivity (World Bank 2018a, 2020a).

[3] Over the same time frame as the productivity-driven reduction in global poverty, global infant mortality has halved and secondary school enrollment has increased by 14 percentage points.

convergence. The existing literature, which began empirically assessing income convergence in the mid-1980s, has generally found broad-based support for convergence that is conditional on country characteristics, but has found little support for the unconditional convergence hypothesis. The surge in EMDE growth in the 2000s has re-ignited this debate (Patel, Sandefur, and Subramanian 2018). Most of the literature has focused on convergence in income per capita (Barro 2015; Caselli 2005; Mankiw, Romer, and Weil 1992). In contrast, the focus in this chapter is on labor productivity convergence, the main driver of lasting per capita income convergence.

Second, this chapter highlights important nonlinearities captured by "convergence clubs" following different convergence paths. The existing literature on convergence clubs thus far has not taken account of the large increase in EMDE productivity growth since 2000 (Battisti and Parmeter 2013; Pesaran 2007; Phillips and Sul 2009). This chapter updates that literature and identifies important changes in the membership of convergence clubs that have occurred in recent decades.

Third, this chapter utilizes multiple methodologies and common data sets—previous studies have been hampered by data differences that have made conclusions noncomparable (Johnson et al. 2013). It is also the only recent study of convergence that measures labor productivity at market exchange rates as opposed to measures adjusted by purchasing power parity (PPP), noting that the latter can be problematic in assessing club convergence (annex 4F).

Fourth, this chapter is one of the few studies examining the drivers of convergence club membership and *transitions*, and the only one applied to a global set of economies. Existing studies focus on either regions in the European Union (Bartkowska and Riedl 2012; Von Lyncker and Thoennessen 2017) or regions within China (Tian et al. 2016) and do not assess the causes of changing club membership over time. In contrast, this study identifies the drivers of convergence club membership and transitions between clubs among 97 economies during 1970-2018.

Main findings

The following findings emerge from the analysis in this chapter.

- *Large productivity gaps.* The gap between advanced economy and EMDE labor productivity levels is large. On average since 2010, labor productivity in EMDEs was just under 20 percent of that in advanced economies, and in LICs it is a mere 2 percent. EMDE productivity gaps relative to advanced economies widened during the 1970s, 1980s, and 1990s but began to narrow in the 2000s.

- *Convergence since 2000.* Examples of economies converging from low levels of labor productivity all the way to the frontier were rare in the latter half of the twentieth century. Since 2000, productivity growth has exceeded the advanced economy average in about 60 percent of EMDEs. However, the productivity gap declined at just 0.5 percent per year, on average, and convergence rates have begun to slow. Even at this peak rate, it would take nearly 140 years to halve the initial productivity gap between economies. Although the average rate of convergence has been low, convergence rates for economies with good characteristics are substantially higher— new evidence suggests that the conditional convergence rate has accelerated in recent decades.

- *Convergence clubs.* Since 1970, countries have fallen into five distinct convergence clubs. The first club of countries, converging to the highest-productivity levels, includes all advanced economies and several middle-income EMDEs that have experienced sustained long periods of robust growth since the 1990s. The second club includes the majority of upper-middle-income EMDEs; the third through fifth clubs include lower-middle- and low-income countries.

- *Transition to higher-productivity convergence clubs: successful policies.* Increasing numbers of EMDEs have moved into the highest-level productivity club in recent decades, in contrast to older assessments of club convergence that found few positive convergence club transitions. These countries are found to have had a foundation of systematically better initial education levels and greater political stability, which has helped them deepen the complexity of their economies, with diversified production across a broad range of sectors outside of their original comparative advantage. Several country case studies highlight the importance of export promotion, global value chain integration, and foreign direct investment (FDI) in transitioning to higher-productivity convergence clubs.

- *Challenging environment for convergence models.* EMDEs that have successfully shifted into higher-level productivity clubs have often relied upon manufacturing-led development—efforts to enhance the complexity and diversity of exports can prove to have high rewards but have also frequently been costly failures. This strategy faces increasing challenges due to falling global manufacturing employment and slower trade growth (chapter 7). In addition, a weak outlook for commodity prices and slow improvements in many key covariates of productivity growth, such as institutional quality, urbanization, and educational attainment, pose further headwinds to both new and continuing transitions to high productivity levels (chapter 2). The global recession due to COVID-19 has the potential to amplify many of these headwinds. Risks include persistently subdued commodity prices, global value chain fragmentation if governments pursue inward-looking policies, and lasting damage to human capital development from the widespread closure of education institutions due to social distancing measures and erosion of skills due to unemployment.

Definitions and data. This chapter examines convergence in labor productivity, defined as output per worker (at 2010 prices and exchange rates; annex 4B). Labor productivity data are available for 103 countries since 1970, consisting of 29 advanced economies and 74 EMDEs.[4] Labor productivity is more readily measured than total factor

---

[4] This sample is expanded to 126 EMDEs for recent years in order to help understand the current distribution of productivity levels, but data back to 1970 are available for just 74 of these economies. The sample is subsequently shrunk in order to ensure consistency over time for convergence tests.

productivity (TFP), which can be estimated only on the basis of special assumptions. Labor productivity is also conceptually closer to per capita income, the variable of primary interest in discussions of global average living standards and the global income distribution. The data set is constructed from national accounts, the World Bank's World Development Indicators, The Conference Board, and the Penn World Table 9.1 (annex 4B).

The next section discusses the evolution of convergence over time, then the third section estimates the speed of convergence, both regardless of country characteristics and conditional on country characteristics. The fourth section provides evidence for the presence of club convergence and assesses the characteristics of EMDEs that have demonstrated faster degrees of convergence. The final section concludes and discusses policy implications.

How has productivity convergence evolved?

Productivity gaps. The gap between advanced economy and EMDE labor productivity levels is large. On average since 2010, labor productivity in EMDEs was just 16 percent, and in LICs just 2 percent, of the advanced economy average (figure 4.1, panel A). Even the top decile of EMDE output per worker was just 70 percent of the lowest decile of advanced economy labor productivity levels.

Among EMDE regions, labor productivity is highest in the Middle East and North Africa (MNA), Latin America and the Caribbean (LAC), and Europe and Central Asia (ECA); it is lowest in Sub-Saharan Africa (SSA) and SAR (figure 4.1, panel B). On average, MNA produced 41 percent of the output per worker of advanced economies, and output per worker in SSA and SAR was well below the EMDE average, at just 8 and 7 percent, respectively, of advanced economy productivity. Other regional features are as follows.

- *EAP.* EAP economies are characterized by a relatively low dispersion of productivity levels compared to other EMDE regions, ranging from 2-25 percent of the level in the average advanced economy. This may partly reflect the close economic integration of the region's economies.

- *ECA.* Close trade integration with the euro area, strong growth since the deep recessions following the collapse of the Soviet Union, and relatively high initial productivity levels in some cases have led economies in the ECA region to have the second-highest average labor productivity level among EMDE regions. However, there is significant variation, with output per worker in nonoil commodity exporters in the region averaging just one-quarter of the output per worker relative to commodity-importing economies.

- *LAC.* In LAC, the labor productivity gap with advanced economies has widened since the 1970s, with labor productivity falling from 23 to 20 percent of the levels in the average advanced economy.

FIGURE 4.1 **Labor productivity gaps**

On average, labor productivity in EMDEs is 16 percent of the advanced economy average, and in LICs it is just 2 percent. Within EMDEs, oil exporters, concentrated in MNA, have the highest average level of output per worker, whereas metals and agricultural exporters have the lowest. Regional heterogeneity among EMDEs is small compared to the large gap between EMDEs and advanced economies, which has led to a polarized global distribution of productivity, with EMDEs concentrated at the bottom of the distribution, and a range of significantly higher advanced economy productivity levels.

A. Labor productivity by country group, 2010-18 average

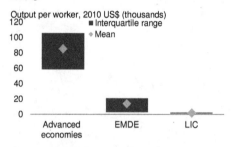

B. Labor productivity by EMDE region, 2010-18 average

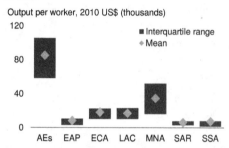

C. Labor productivity in EMDEs by commodity exporter status, 2010-18 average

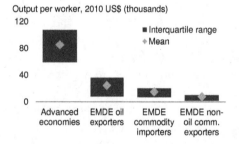

D. Distribution of labor productivity, 2010-18 average

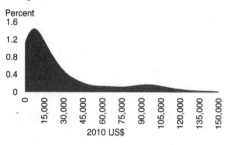

Sources: Conference Board; Penn World Table; World Bank, World Development Indicators.
Note: Productivity defined as output per worker in U.S. dollars (at 2010 prices and exchange rates). Sample of 35 advanced economies and 126 EMDEs, of which 27 are LICs. AEs = advanced economies; EMDEs = emerging market and developing economies; LICs = low-income economies; EAP = East Asia and Pacific; ECA = Europe and Central Asia; LAC = Latin America and the Caribbean; MNA = Middle East and North Africa; SAR = South Asia; SSA = Sub-Saharan Africa.
C. Sample includes 35 advanced economies, 27 EMDE oil exporters, 47 commodity-importing EMDEs, and 52 nonoil commodity-exporting EMDEs.
D. Smoothed distribution of output per worker estimates using a Gaussian kernel.

- *MNA.* Although the region has the highest average labor productivity, it also has an exceptionally wide range of labor productivity levels. They range from 10 percent of the advanced economy average in the Arab Republic of Egypt and in Morocco to over 100 percent of the advanced economy average in oil-exporting economies such as Qatar (figure 4.1, panel C).[5]

---

[5] For example, Qatar and Saudi Arabia have labor productivity levels that are close to that of the United States, but TFP levels are just half those of the United States as measured in the Penn World Table.

- *SAR.* Despite relying on commodity imports in aggregate, South Asian economies are heavily reliant on the agricultural sector. Agriculture has accounted for 18 percent of value added since 2010, compared to the EMDE average of 10 percent. In addition, SAR is the region with the largest number of informal workers (World Bank 2019a). These two factors may help to account for uniformly low labor productivity in EMDEs in the region.

- *SSA.* Labor productivity in SSA is among the lowest across EMDE regions. There is a degree of heterogeneity: in its most productive non-energy-exporting economy, South Africa, labor productivity has been just 32 percent of the advanced economy average since 2010. However, fragile and conflict-affected economies—14 out of the 45 SSA economies in the sample—had less than half of the labor productivity level of the SSA average.

The stark divide between advanced economy and EMDE labor productivity levels significantly exceeds regional variations among EMDEs—a polarization exists in the distribution of productivity levels, with EMDEs concentrated at the bottom of the distribution while advanced economies occupy a wide range of significantly higher productivity levels (figure 4.1, panel D; Quah 1996, 1997). On average during 2010-18, EMDE productivity was concentrated around $7,000 of output per worker per year, and advanced economies were clustered around a high level of productivity peaking at $95,000, below the United States ($109,000) but above lower-productivity advanced economies such as the Republic of Korea ($48,000). The fact that EMDEs and advanced economies cluster around these highly differential productivity levels is strong evidence both for convergence being conditional and for the presence of multiple points of attraction for productivity.

Average productivity gaps over time. Following a steep decline in EMDE productivity growth in the 1980s and early 1990s, caused by a series of financial crises in LAC and SSA, and the collapse of the Soviet Union, growth rose sharply in the late 1990s (chapter 1). For the first time since the data set began in 1970, average EMDE productivity growth exceeded that of advanced economies on a nearly continuous basis starting in 2000 (figure 4.2, panel A). The improvement in performance was broad-based, with over 60 percent of EMDEs growing faster than the average advanced economy over the past two decades (figure 4.2, panel B; Rodrik 2011). Nevertheless, on average, the productivity gap between advanced economies and EMDEs has closed only modestly since the 1990s.

Progress in closing the productivity gap occurred mainly in commodity-importing EMDEs; commodity exporters, on average, moved further away from the frontier (figure 4.2, panel C). Among the regions, EAP, ECA, and SAR had average productivity growth in 2010-18 that exceeded that of advanced economies by a significant margin. In other regions, many of which have large numbers of commodity exporters, productivity growth was similar to, or below, that of advanced economies (figure 4.2, panel D).

Convergence across countries and populations. The faster pace of productivity growth since 2000 has shifted the distribution of productivity levels to the right but has yet to

FIGURE 4.2 **Evolution of labor productivity gaps**

EMDE productivity gaps with the advanced economy average widened in the 1970s, 1980s, and 1990s but narrowed from 2000 onward. Convergence in the 2000s was broad-based but most pronounced in regions consisting primarily of commodity-importing EMDEs (EAP and SAR). Faster productivity growth has led to a large fall in the number of low-income EMDEs concentrated at the lowest levels of productivity.

A. Average annual labor productivity growth (five-year moving average)

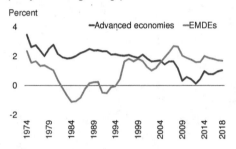

B. Share of EMDEs with a narrowing productivity gap vs. advanced economies

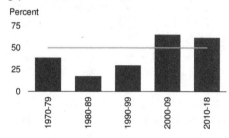

C. EMDE labor productivity, percent of advanced economy average

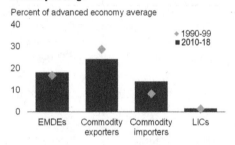

D. Productivity growth by region, 2010-2018 average

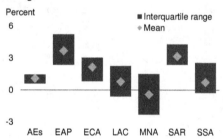

E. Share of EMDEs with narrower productivity gap in 2010-18 than in the 1970s, by region

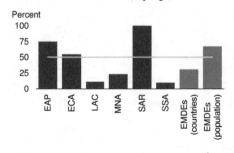

F. Distribution of productivity: 1990s and 2010s

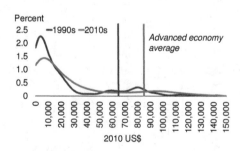

Sources: Conference Board; Penn World Table; World Bank, World Development Indicators.
Note: Productivity is output per worker in U.S. dollars (at 2010 prices and market exchange rates). Based on a sample of 35 advanced economies and 123 EMDEs for a consistent sample since 1990, and 29 advanced economies and 74 EMDEs for a consistent sample since 1970. AEs = advanced economies; EMDEs = emerging market and developing economies; LICs = low-income economies; EAP = East Asia and Pacific; ECA = Europe and Central Asia; LAC = Latin America and the Caribbean; MNA = Middle East and North Africa; SAR = South Asia; SSA = Sub-Saharan Africa.
A. Simple average of productivity growth in advanced economies and EMDEs.
B. Share of EMDEs with average productivity growth that exceeds the average productivity growth of advanced economies.
C. GDP-weighted average gap across EMDE groups relative to average advanced economy productivity level by decade.
D. Mean and interquartile range of productivity growth during 2010-18.
E. Proportion of economies in each region, proportion of all EMDE economies, and proportion of EMDE total population that live in economies with smaller productivity gap with advanced economies during 2010-18 than during the 1970s on average.
F. Smoothed distribution of output per worker estimates using a Gaussian kernel during 1990-99 and 2010-18.

lead to a material proportion of EMDEs reducing the income gap with advanced economies relative to the 1970s, particularly given the lackluster growth experienced in the 1980s and early 1990s. SAR, EAP, and ECA are the only regions where a material proportion of EMDEs have a smaller gap today than in the 1970s (figure 4.2, panel E). Only one-third of EMDEs have narrowed their productivity gaps over the past 50 years. However, the economies where productivity gaps have narrowed since the 1970s account for about 70 percent of the population of EMDEs: a clear majority of the population of EMDEs lives in economies where the productivity gap has narrowed.

Absolute improvements in productivity. Despite the slow progress in closing productivity gaps, absolute productivity levels have improved in many of the poorest economies. Like the productivity distribution in the 2010s, the productivity distribution in the 1990s featured a concentration of countries around low productivity levels and another concentration close to the average advanced economy productivity level. However, since the 1990s, the share of economies in the lowest productivity region (<$10,000) has almost halved (figure 4.2, panel F). Using the World Bank's income classifications, about half of the economies classified as low-income economies in 1990 are now classified as lower-middle- or upper-middle-income economies (see also World Bank 2019b, Special Focus 2.1). And 60 percent of economies are now classified as high-income or upper-middle-income economies, compared to just 35 percent in 1990. However, World Bank income thresholds are adjusted only for inflation—the threshold for the high-income classification has remained unchanged in real terms since 1990. Therefore, they do not imply convergence to the frontier but rather a broad-based absolute improvement.

Historical episodes of convergence toward the frontier are rare (Durlauf, Johnson, and Temple 2005; Johnson and Papageorgiou 2020; Rodrik 2011). Full convergence to the frontier requires sustained high productivity growth over many decades.[6] Just nine economies transitioned into the top quartile of incomes between the 1950s and the post-GFC period. Of these, Equatorial Guinea and Oman benefited from oil and gas exploration; Cyprus, Japan, and Portugal were already close to the highest quartile in 1950. Hong Kong SAR, China; Korea; and Singapore were "Asian Miracle" economies, with their success attributed to a number of factors, including high education levels, strong governance, and industrial policies that included export promotion (Jeong 2019; Leipziger and Thomas 1993).

In summary, productivity growth improved for a broad set of EMDEs starting around 2000 but has not yet led to a material reduction in productivity gaps with advanced economies. In some cases, these improvements only partially unwound previous

---

[6] This statement relies on income per capita instead of labor productivity, allowing a sample of 137 economies since 1950, compared to 103 since 1970 for labor productivity. The Maddison Project database of income per capita for 137 economies since 1950 provides much wider coverage than the labor productivity database used throughout this chapter; the productivity data set falls to 49 economies for the same period of data. Output per capita provides a less precise measure of productivity, not accounting for changes in labor force participation or the share of working-age population.

productivity growth underperformance, such that a minority of economies, but a majority of the population, has seen productivity gaps decline since the 1970s. Since the GFC, this surge in productivity growth has declined in several EMDE regions. In addition, historically, sustained convergence to the frontier is rare.

In the following section, formal statistical tests of the convergence hypothesis are undertaken to assess the speed of convergence, before delving into more complex examinations of club convergence.

Testing for convergence and its pace

Countries with lower initial levels of productivity have only recently begun to outperform productivity growth in high-productivity economies on a broad basis, suggesting the presence of *unconditional* convergence. This has occurred in recent decades at a slow pace but does not hold over the entire sample. Convergence potential may be hindered by unfavorable characteristics in some economies that hold back productivity growth, such as poor human capital or lack of infrastructure, a phenomenon dubbed "conditional convergence" (Barro and Sala-i-Martin 1992). This section explores the pace of unconditional and conditional convergence in a more formal statistical framework.

Unconditional convergence

Unconditional convergence can be assessed using a beta-convergence regression, which posits that productivity growth depends on its initial level:

$$y_{iT} - y_{i0} = c + \beta y_{i0} + \epsilon_{iT},$$

where y is the natural log of output per worker at both time T and the initial period 0 under consideration and the disturbance term ϵ_{iT} captures shocks to productivity in country i that are unrelated to convergence drivers of productivity growth. The hypothesis that $\beta < 0$ implies that lower initial productivity produces faster cumulative growth (between time 0 and time T). When all countries have access to the same technology, those with higher marginal returns to capital—in other words, capital-scarce poorer economies—should benefit from greater capital accumulation and higher growth. The coefficient β can then be converted to an annual rate of convergence, the percent fall in the average productivity gap that is estimated to have occurred each year.[7]

Literature. Early estimates of β-convergence found little evidence of its existence, often instead finding that initial income was positively related to the subsequent rate of growth (Barro 1991; Baumol 1986; Dowrick 1992).[8] More recent tests for unconditional

---

[7] This is computed as $(-1) * \ln(\beta + 1)/T$, where T is the number of years under consideration, as in Barro and Sala-i-Martin (1992).

[8] Barro (1991) and Barro and Sala-i-Martin (1992) apply the unconditional convergence testing procedure to U.S. states and the Organisation for Economic Co-operation and Development; Sala-i-Martin (1996) applies the procedure to Japanese prefectures and regions in five European Union countries. All studies have found little evidence of unconditional convergence.

convergence show tentative evidence in support of the hypothesis. In tests on data from the late 1990s onward, a statistically significant negative coefficient on initial income has been found (Patel, Sandefur, and Subramanian 2018; Roy, Kessler, and Subramanian 2016). Additionally, in manufacturing, evidence in support of statistically significant unconditional convergence has also been found, although tests on an expanded set of economies have cast doubt on this finding (chapter 7; Rodrik 2013).

Results. Globally, there has been little evidence of systematic unconditional productivity convergence until last two decades, during which the negative coefficient on initial productivity becomes statistically significant (figure 4.3, panel A, and table 4C.1).[9] Although statistically significant in recent decades, the estimated pace of convergence is slow, with the average economy closing just 0.5 percent of the productivity gap since 2010.[10] At this rate, it would take nearly 140 years to close just half of the initial productivity gap between economies on average. In contrast, within the group of advanced economies, unconditional convergence is statistically significant and there is a clear relationship between initial labor productivity and subsequent growth (figure 4.3, panels B and C; annex 4C). Within advanced economies, labor productivity converged at a rate of 2 percent per year in the 1980s and 1990s, requiring less than 40 years to close half of the outstanding productivity gaps, although the rate of convergence has declined in recent decades as residual gaps became smaller. Even among EMDEs, a modest rate of convergence (0.3 percent) is detected over the last decade. This is evidence that, within groups with similar characteristics, economies tend to converge toward a similar productivity level.

Conditional convergence

Much of the literature has found evidence that, once country characteristics are controlled for, the coefficient on initial income becomes negative and statistically significant. Tests for conditional convergence use a similar regression specification as tests for unconditional convergence but control for country characteristics:

$$y_{it} - y_{i0} = c + \beta y_{i0} + \gamma X_i + \epsilon_{iT},$$

where X_i is a set of country characteristics. These country characteristics include the initial levels and changes in variables relating to factors such as educational attainment, trade openness, natural resources, demographics, population health, and governance.

Covariates of convergence. Controlling for the level of human capital, as measured by average years of education, has been found to result in statistically significant convergence (Barro and Lee 1994; Mankiw, Romer, and Weil 1992). Other than direct inputs into the production function, various additional factors have also been found to

---

[9] These results are also consistent with regressions using output per capita instead of productivity.

[10] Barro and Sala-i-Martin (1992) show that the speed of convergence can be calculated from a beta-test coefficient using the formula $\beta = e^{-\lambda T} - 1$, where λ is the annual speed of convergence and T is the number of years over which the β coefficient has been estimated.

FIGURE 4.3 **Conditional and unconditional convergence**

Since the late 1990s, productivity growth has been higher in those economies with lower initial levels of productivity. However, the implied pace of convergence is small, suggesting that on average the productivity gap will halve only after more than 100 years. Within advanced economies, the pace of convergence is slightly higher, suggesting that economies with common characteristics are more likely to converge. When controlling for country characteristics, such as average educational attainment and institutional quality, the pace of convergence is higher still and has been increasing in recent decades.

A. Convergence rate implied by β-regression

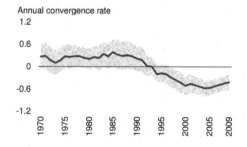

B. Initial log labor productivity and growth, 1970-2018

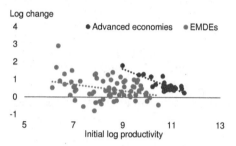

C. Unconditional annual convergence rate *within* advanced economies and EMDEs

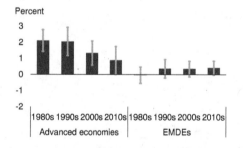

D. Conditional annual convergence rate: All economies

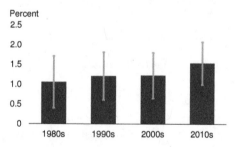

Sources: Conference Board; Penn World Table; World Bank, World Development Indicators.
Note: Based on data for 98 economies, consisting of 29 advanced economies and 69 EMDEs. Sample excludes 6 EMDE oil exporters with productivity levels above those of the United States in the 1970s. EMDEs = emerging market and developing economies.
A. Gray shaded area indicates 95 percent confidence intervals. Estimation performed over 10-year rolling windows in the specification $\Delta \log Y_t = c + \beta \log Y_{t-10} + \epsilon_t$, where Y_t is output per worker. The x-axis indicates start year of regression sample. Negative value indicates productivity gaps are declining at rate indicated. Regression coefficient converted to a convergence rate using the transformation $\beta = e^{-\lambda T} - 1$, where λ is the annual convergence rate and T is the number of years over which the regression is estimated.
B. Dotted lines indicate a fitted relationship between initial log productivity level (log of labor productivity measured in 2010 U.S. dollars) and subsequent change in the log productivity level.
C. Annual percent decline in productivity gaps, derived from a β-regression containing only advanced economies or EMDEs. Convergence rate indicated is based on productivity growth since the previous decade.
D. Annual convergence rate implied by a β-regression that controls for a number of country features, including average years of education, a commodity-exporter dummy, economic complexity (Hidalgo and Hausman 2009 measure), trade openness, investment as a share of GDP, and a measure of political stability (annex 4C).

be important controls for assessing convergence. These have included trade openness and export orientation (Dollar and Kraay 2003; Frankel and Romer 1999; Sachs and Warner 1995), strong institutions (Rodrik, Subramanian, and Trebbi 2004), natural resources and other geographical factors (Easterly and Levine 2001, 2003; Sachs and Warner 2001), and economic or export complexity (Hausmann, Hwang, and Rodrik 2007; Hidalgo and Hausmann 2009).

Pace of conditional convergence. Consistent *rates* of convergence have also been found when controlling for country characteristics. The "rule of 2 percent" was coined after a common rate of annual income convergence across U.S. states, and separately countries, was identified when controls for factors such as educational levels and political stability were included (Barro and Sala-i-Martin 1992). Most studies have found results within a range of 1 to 3 percent per annum (Durlauf, Johnson, and Temple 2005). An annual convergence rate of 2 percent implies that half of any initial difference in productivity levels will disappear after 35 years.

Evolution of conditional convergence rate. The results of a conditional convergence regression, containing typical country characteristics used in the literature, show that lower initial incomes were associated with higher productivity growth in each decade since the 1980s.[11] The convergence rate is estimated to have increased over time, peaking at 1.5 percent per year over the past decade, which if sustained would halve the productivity gap in just under 50 years (figure 4.3, panel D). Previous studies, including recent tests for club convergence, have documented similar rates of conditional convergence but have yet to document the acceleration in pace in recent decades (Johnson and Papageorgiou 2020). The panel specification, covering all decades, shows an annual convergence rate of 1.3 percent, within the range of 1-3 percent found in surveys of the literature of growth regressions on income per capita (annex 4C).[12]

Conditional or unconditional convergence rates? Unconditional convergence rates have recently turned positive but remain very low, requiring over 100 years to close just half of the average productivity gap. Estimates conditional on other characteristics, such as the level of education and investment, suggest that convergence rates have been much faster and rising in recent decades. However, the conditional convergence concept is less useful as a generalized measure of convergence progress among EMDEs, because it suggests that economies may be on many different productivity paths dependent on their characteristics. A deeper examination of *which* economies are experiencing fast rates of convergence because of their characteristics can be explored through club convergence analysis.

Convergence clubs

Club convergence definition. In general, the β-convergence framework underlying the unconditional and conditional convergence results faces limitations in distinguishing between multiple attraction points that may exist for productivity levels in different economies. Even in cases where the coefficient is negative, economies may not be

---

[11] See annex 4C for further details. Regression includes controls for average levels of education, trade openness, the Economic Complexity Index of Hidalgo and Hausmann (2009), commodity exporter status, the level of investment as a share of output, and a measure of political stability.

[12] Most of these studies have performed these exercises on PPP-adjusted measures of income per capita. This alternative measure results in estimates of a convergence rate of 1.7 percent using the same specification. However, PPP adjustment may be inappropriate for measuring growth in output per worker. Many economies have substantially faster productivity growth rates measured using time-varying PPP adjustments compared to national accounts measures (annex 4F).

converging to a common level of productivity, and there may not even be a reduction in the dispersion of productivity levels (Bernard and Durlauf 1996; Phillips and Sul 2007; Quah 1993b).[13] Therefore, the analysis of convergent behavior across economies is better explored in an alternative framework. Tests for convergence clubs—groups of economies that are converging to one of a range of attraction points and that likely share common characteristics—are less prone to the failings of the β-convergence framework (Durlauf and Johnson 1995; Quah 1993a, 1997).

Literature. The early literature on the existence of convergence clubs extended the β-convergence framework to assess whether different groups of economies converged at different values for β, finding evidence that this parameter was not stable between groups (Canova 2004; Durlauf and Johnson 1995). The literature then extended into two primary categories of approaches, which are both applied in this chapter.

- *Distributional analysis: commonalities in levels.* Studies conducting distributional analysis have explored whether economies can be subdivided into statistically distinct distributions (mixture modeling), with much of the literature focusing on the distribution of per capita income and not productivity. Countries' per capita income levels appeared to fall into two to four different distributions, with limited transitions between them(see Battisti and Parmeter 2013; Henderson, Parmeterm and Russell 2008; Pittau and Zelli 2006). A study that included additional variables to help inform the clustering of labor productivity—TFP, human capital, or physical capital—similarly identified two to three clusters during the decades 1960-2000 (Battisti and Parmeter 2013). The gap between different clusters appears to have widened since the 1970s (Pittau, Zelli, and Johnson 2010). Distributional analysis has more generally found evidence of increasing divergence between groups of economies.

- *Time series analysis: commonalities in trajectories.* Studies conducting time series analysis have typically tested for cointegration and more recently used factor model structures to test for convergence. Cointegration tests of output per capita have tended to find little evidence for convergence of income per capita in either advanced economies or wider samples of 140 advanced economies and EMDEs between 1950 and 2000 (Bernard and Durlauf 1995, 1996; Pesaran 2007). However, evidence is found for convergence in per capita income *growth* rates in the cointegration testing framework, suggesting that income gaps do not increase over time. More recently, a factor model framework for club convergence testing has been proposed that is less liable to make false rejections of the formation of convergence clubs than previous time series approaches. In a data set spanning 1970-2003 for income per capita in 152 economies, evidence was found for the

---

[13] Even simple modifications to the standard β-convergence framework expose some of its weaknesses. For example, an additional squared measure of initial income suggests that those with an initial income below one-sixth of that of the United States exhibit different behavior than do those economies above this level (Chatterji 1992). Separately, in a partially linear regression model, no evidence has been found of convergence for countries with income below $1,800 per annum (Liu and Stengos 1999).

existence of five convergence clubs, with the first dominated by advanced economies (Phillips and Sul 2007, 2009).

Commonalities in productivity levels

The first strand of the literature can identify clubs of economies well in an ex post sense: those economies that have converged over time toward common attraction points will have similar productivity levels and thus be found to have been in a convergence club. Updating the distributional analysis literature to the post-2000 period, when EMDE productivity growth has picked up substantially relative to earlier decades, results in a similar number of clubs relative to earlier estimates (four in the most recent period). However, relative to earlier studies, 10 faster-growing EMDEs have separated from the lowest-productivity club over the past decade to join a convergence club consisting of many middle-income EMDEs (annex 4D). The period of faster productivity growth in EMDEs has resulted in new convergence club dynamics—a more comprehensive examination in the following subsection of both the level of productivity and the *trajectory* of productivity over time provides greater clarity over the development of convergence clubs in recent decades.

Commonalities in productivity trajectories

Common productivity trajectories. The clubs identified above capture common productivity levels at different points in time. However, these same productivity levels can be achieved along very different trajectories—a low-productivity economy may be on a growth path that is convergent with high-productivity economies in the future but may not be considered to be in a similar convergence club on the basis of a snapshot of productivity levels alone. This subsection identifies commonalities in the *trajectories* of productivity over time: countries in the same convergence club are on paths that converge toward similar productivity levels, even if productivity differentials are high in the period under examination.

Methodology. Labor productivity (in logs) is modeled as a country-specific weighting on a common factor, which reflects the common productivity attraction point that club members are drawn to (Phillips and Sul 2009):

$$y_{it} = b_{it}\mu_t.$$

Countries in the same convergence club will initially feature different coefficients b_{it}, reflecting their varying distance from a common attraction point. For a group of economies to form a convergence club, their deviations from the common attraction point should fall over time. Using an iterative procedure, the methodology tests combinations of economies for common convergence dynamics; economies that do not display falling productivity gaps are discarded until groups are found that do (annex 4E). Data are available for 29 advanced economies and 69 EMDEs for 1970-2018.[14]

---

[14] Six EMDE oil exporters with output per worker above that of the United States in 1970 are excluded from the analysis. Real oil prices increased fivefold between 1970 and 1980, due in part to the 1973 oil crisis and 1979 energy crisis.

FIGURE 4.4 **Convergence club memberships**

During 1970-2018, there were five clubs of countries with declining productivity differentials. Sixteen EMDEs have transitioned to the highest-productivity convergence club since the 2000s, and 22 have transitioned to the second highest.

A. Convergence clubs, 1970-2018 and transitions relative to the early-sample estimation of convergence clubs (1970-2000)

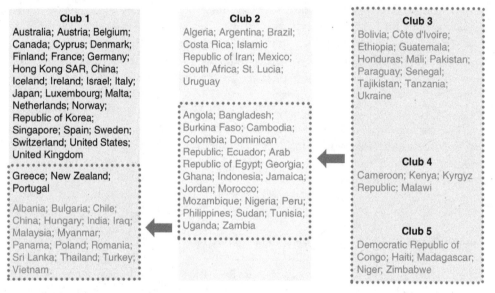

Source: World Bank.
Note: Based on convergence clubs estimated as in Phillips and Sul (2009). EMDEs = emerging market and developing economies.
A. The figures show the club composition when estimated over the whole sample (1970-2018). The red dotted boxes show economies that were in a lower convergence club in the first half of the sample 1970-2000 (for example, moved from Club 2 to Club 1). Black text indicates advanced economies, and blue text are EMDEs.

Results. Since 1970, countries have fallen into five distinct convergence clubs in which productivity moved along a similar trajectory and productivity differentials were decreasing over time. Several countries have moved into faster-productivity clubs since 2000 (figure 4.4).

- *Clusters during 1970-2018.* The first club (Club 1) consists of economies converging toward the highest-productivity level. It includes all advanced economies, several upper-middle-income EMDEs that have sustained long periods of robust growth, and three low-income or lower-middle-income economies with rapid productivity growth (figure 4.5, panel A). This club initially had a broad range of productivity levels in 1970, which had narrowed by 2010 as low-productivity economies caught up. The second club includes the majority of upper-middle-income, or near upper-middle-income EMDEs, converging toward an intermediate level of productivity. Lower clubs consist primarily of lower-middle- and low-income economies that have persisted in a low-productivity low-growth state (figure 4.5). Advanced economy members of the high-productivity Club 1 have achieved average productivity growth of about 2 percent since 1970, rising to 3 percent for EMDE Club 1 members—

FIGURE 4.5 **Convergence clubs of productivity trajectories**

EMDEs that have transitioned into the highest-productivity convergence club have increased productivity levels relative to the 1970s by significantly more than EMDEs in lower-productivity convergence clubs. Many EMDEs remain in convergence Clubs 4 and 5 where productivity growth has stagnated in recent decades.

A. Productivity, by convergence club, 1970s-2010s

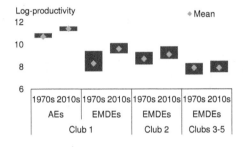

B. Average productivity level, by convergence club

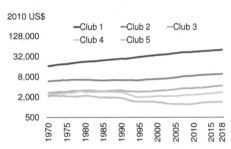

C. Average productivity growth, by convergence club, 1970-2018

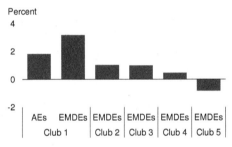

D. Average productivity growth and number of EMDEs transitioning to higher-productivity clubs

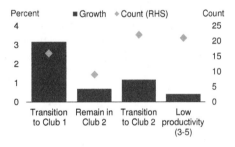

Source: World Bank.
Note: Based on convergence clubs estimated as in Phillips and Sul (2009). AEs = advanced economies; EMDEs = emerging market and developing economies.
A. Unweighted average log-productivity levels during 1970-79 and 2010-18. Blue bars show interquartile range.
B. Unweighted average productivity level in each identified convergence club.
C. Simple average of productivity growth over the sample 1970-2018. All members of Clubs 2 to 5 are EMDEs.
D. "Transition to Club 1" group includes EMDEs that have joined convergence Club 1 during the whole-sample estimation relative to the early-sample estimation (1970-2000). "Remain in Club 2" economies are those that are in Club 2 in both estimations. "Transition to Club 2" economies joined Club 2 from lower clubs in the 1970-79 estimation, and "Low productivity (3-5)" economies are estimated to be in lower clubs in both samples.

over twice the average productivity growth of EMDEs in Clubs 2 and 3 and in contrast to stagnant productivity levels in lower-productivity convergence Clubs 4 and 5. The economies in each club tend to be geographically diverse.[15]

- *Changes over time.* When estimating convergence clubs separately for the period 1970-2000, the decades during which average EMDE productivity growth fell short of the advanced economy average, no EMDEs were estimated to be in a

---

[15] The Moran I-statistic, a measure of geographical clustering that can range between -1 and 1, is 0.14, suggesting a low correlation between club allocation and geographical proximity.

convergence club with advanced economies. In this earlier period, the second club included a combination of advanced economies and middle-income EMDEs (figure 4.4, panel A). Three advanced economies (Greece, New Zealand, and Portugal) and 16 middle-income EMDEs (including China, India, and Turkey) in this club have since moved to Club 1, converging toward the highest-productivity levels, and 22 middle-income EMDEs (including Indonesia) have moved to the second-highest-productivity club. Earlier studies using the same methodology to 2003 found that just four of the economies identified as transitioning to Club 1 in this study had done so on the basis of the earlier sample (Phillips and Sul 2009).

- Alternatively, using PPP-adjusted measures of labor productivity levels, as opposed to labor productivity measured at market exchange rates, results in an additional five EMDEs being estimated to have joined the highest-productivity level convergence club. However, large discrepancies with national accounts measures of productivity growth suggest some caution should be used in interpreting these PPP-adjusted results (annex 4F).

Country characteristics associated with convergence club membership

Several country characteristics—including higher levels of education, greater economic complexity, and greater political stability—have been systematically associated with more favorable long-term productivity trajectories.[16] This is consistent with findings in the literature that have associated higher productivity or per capita income with a better-educated labor force (Rodrik 1994), greater diversification and complexity of industrial production and exported goods (Hausmann and Hidalgo 2010; Hausmann, Hwang, and Rodrik 2007), and better institutions, governance, and stability (Hall and Jones 1999; Rodrik, Subramanian, and Trebbi 2004).[17]

Group averages. On average, members of Club 1 had significantly higher levels of education, greater economic complexity, higher initial labor productivity, and stronger perceptions of political stability than members of other clubs (figure 4.6). In contrast, there were significant overlaps between the interquartile range of clubs for trade openness and the ratio of investment to gross domestic product (GDP), suggesting that these characteristics were less decisive in determining club membership.

---

[16] Similar results are found for the determinants of the convergence clubs from the distributional clustering approach. The results are available in annex 4E. In this case, many transitions to higher clubs are also found over recent decades, with many similar economies transitioning as in the Phillips and Sul routine. The covariates associated with transitioning economies are estimated to be the same for both clustering algorithms.

[17] Economic complexity is a measure of two concepts: the diversity and ubiquity of the products an economy is able to produce. Diversity reflects the range of products the economy in question produces, and ubiquity reflects the number of other economies producing those products. For example, an economy specializing in just food products (produced by many other economies) will score poorly in the Economic Complexity Index (ECI), whereas an economy producing a large range of high-value-added information and communication technologies (ICTs) and automobile products will score highly.

FIGURE 4.6 **Key characteristics of convergence clubs**

Members of Club 1 had significantly higher levels of education, greater economic complexity, higher initial productivity, and stronger perceptions of political stability than members of other clubs. There is more overlap between levels of trade openness and investment between Clubs 1 and 2, suggesting that those factors are less important in determining club membership.

A. Average years of education

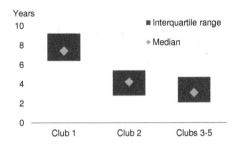

B. Economic Complexity Index

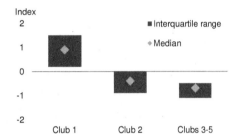

C. Initial productivity

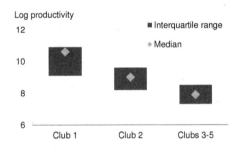

D. Trade openness

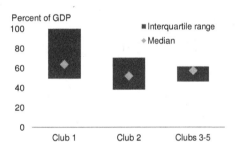

E. Perceptions of government effectiveness

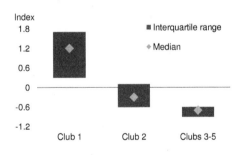

F. Investment

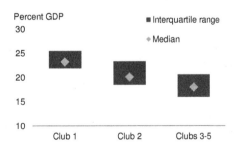

Sources: Barro and Lee (2015); Hidalgo and Hausmann (2009); World Bank, Worldwide Governance Indicators.

Note: Average of data available between 1970 and 2017, with the exception of panel C, which uses 1970-80 data for initial productivity, and panel E, which is only available from 1995 (1995-2017 average used instead).

A. Average years of schooling for males and females from Barro and Lee (2015).

B. Economic Complexity Index of Hidalgo and Hausmann (2009).

C. Log of labor productivity measured in U.S. dollars at 2010 prices and exchange rates.

D. Exports and imports in percent of GDP.

E. Government effectiveness survey from the World Bank's Worldwide Governance Indicators. Measures include perceptions of the quality of public services, the quality of the civil service and the degree of its independence from political pressures, the quality of policy formulation and implementation, and the credibility of the government's commitment to such policies.

F. Gross fixed capital formation in percent of GDP.

Logit analysis. The determinants of club membership are more formally examined in a multinomial logit model (annex 4E). In this approach, the conditional probability of membership in a particular club relative to the highest-productivity Club 1 is estimated for Club 2 and an amalgamation of Clubs 3 to 5 to ensure sufficiently consistent club sizes. A one-year increase in the average length of education, a one-standard-deviation increase in the Economic Complexity Index (ECI), or a unit increase in the index of government effectiveness perceptions substantially reduces the probability of membership in Clubs 2 to 5 relative to Club 1; the ratio of the probability of being a member of Clubs 2 to 5 relative to Club 1 more than halves (figure 4.7). Higher initial productivity levels increase the probability of membership in a lower-productivity convergence club, once other country characteristics are controlled for. That is, countries with high levels of initial productivity but median levels of the other characteristics are more likely to be in a lower convergence club.[18]

Country characteristics associated with transitioning to higher convergence clubs

In this section, the preconditions for transitioning to a higher convergence club are examined, using the 16 EMDEs that transitioned to Club 1 as informative examples. In this exercise, the problem of endogeneity is less of a concern than in the previous exercise when examining the determinants of club membership.[19] However, the results are consistent with the country features associated with membership in a higher-productivity club. Multiple approaches suggest that better initial education, deepening economic complexity, and stronger institutions were associated with successful transitions.

Group averages. EMDEs that switched into the higher-productivity convergence club were not initially more productive than other EMDEs, and their productivity levels only overtook other EMDEs in the early 1990s on average (figure 4.8). Their education levels were initially higher but did not accelerate at a faster pace than in other EMDEs. In contrast, economic complexity increased continuously among the EMDEs that transitioned into the high-productivity club but has stagnated in nonconvergent EMDEs. Measures of institutional quality, such as perceptions of government effectiveness, were initially higher in those countries that transitioned. Trade openness and levels of investment have also significantly overlapped between the two groups for much of the sample—although trade openness did accelerate in transitioning economies from 2000 onward.

---

[18] This finding is consistent with the concept of the "middle income trap" (Aiyar et al. 2013; Eichengreen, Park, and Shin 2013; Im and Rosenblatt 2015). Economies that have progressed to productivity levels consistent with middle-income status risk stagnating if they do not continue to improve educational outcomes, expand to more complex industries, or improve governance.

[19] Examining the determinants of transitioning economies *before* or *during* the transition to faster productivity growth trajectories reduces the endogeneity problem between productivity growth and the drivers of productivity growth.

FIGURE 4.7 **Characteristics associated with convergence club membership**

A one-year increase in the average length of education, a one-standard-deviation increase in the Economic Complexity Index, or a one unit increase in the index of government effectiveness perceptions reduces the chance of membership in Clubs 2-5 relative to Club 1 by 50 percent or more. Increasing log productivity by one unit raises the probability of being in a lower-trajectory convergence club; therefore, higher initial productivity levels alone do not imply fast rates of productivity growth, and must be accompanied by strong fundamentals to ensure convergence to the frontier.

A. Odds ratio of one additional year of average education

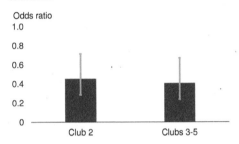

B. Odds ratio of one-unit increase in economic complexity

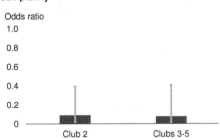

C. Odds ratio of one-unit increase in government effectiveness

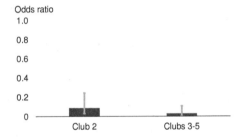

D. Odds ratio of higher initial productivity (one log productivity unit)

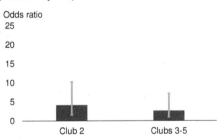

Sources: Barro and Lee (2015); Hidalgo and Hausmann (2009); World Bank.
Note: Covariates are calculated as their average value during 1970-90 in the multinomial logit estimation, with the exception of the measure of government effectiveness from the Worldwide Governance Indicators, which uses the 1990s average because of data availability. "Odds ratio" measures the impact of a one-unit increase in each covariate on the probability of membership in each convergence club relative to Club 1. An odds ratio of more than 1 implies that the characteristic makes membership of Clubs 2-5 more likely relative to membership in Club 1. A ratio of less than one implies than an increase in the covariate reduces the likelihood of being in Clubs 2 or 3-5 relative to Club 1. Orange lines show 95 percent confidence interval.

Logit analysis. A logit model estimates the probability of transitioning into a higher-productivity club on the basis of country characteristics (annex 4E, tables 4E.3 and 4E.4). The logit model was estimated over two separate time periods, 1980-90, just before the transitioning EMDEs overtook the nontransitioning EMDEs, and 1990-2000, just after the transitioning EMDEs began to display accelerating growth relative to other EMDEs. This allows an examination of the conditions in transitioning economies at key junctures in their development.

1980-90 covariates. Higher initial education, greater economic complexity, institutional quality (measured using the World Bank's Worldwide Governance Indicator metric on

FIGURE 4.8 Characteristics of EMDEs transitioning to the highest convergence club

EMDEs that were able to shift to the highest-productivity convergence club were not initially more productive than other EMDEs but had better-educated workforces and greater government effectiveness. Their economic complexity increased continuously, whereas it stagnated elsewhere. There were initially large overlaps in the degree of trade openness and level of investment early in the sample with nontransitioning economies. Club 1 EMDEs subsequently accelerated above other EMDEs in these measures, particularly after 2000.

A. Log productivity

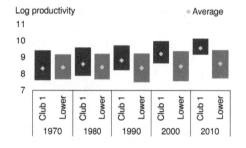

B. Average years of education

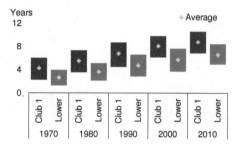

C. Economic complexity

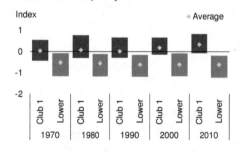

D. Trade openness

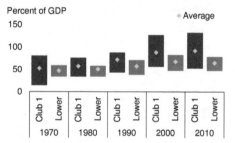

E. Perceptions of government effectiveness

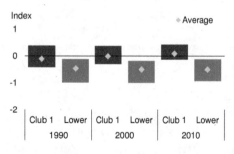

F. Investment

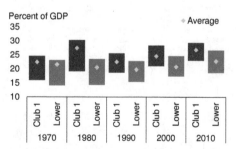

Sources: Barro and Lee (2015); Hidalgo and Hausmann (2009); World Bank (World Development Indicators, Worldwide Governance Indicators).

Note: Bars show interquartile range of each group for average values in each decade. Club 1 are EMDEs that transitioned into the high-productivity convergence club after 2000 (16 economies), "lower" indicates EMDEs that remained in a lower club. EMDEs = emerging market and developing economies.

B. Average years of schooling for males and females from Barro and Lee (2015).

C. Economic Complexity Index of Hidalgo and Hausmann (2009).

D. Exports and imports in percent of GDP.

E. Government effectiveness survey from the World Bank's Worldwide Governance Indicators. Measures include perceptions of the quality of public services, the quality of the civil service and the degree of its independence from political pressures, the quality of policy formulation and implementation, and the credibility of the government's commitment to such policies.

F. Gross fixed capital formation in percent of GDP.

government effectiveness), and lower initial productivity levels are consistently associated with a higher probability of switching into a higher-productivity club between 1980 and 1990.[20] As with the results of the multinomial logit estimation on club membership, there is less evidence that the share of investment in GDP or openness to trade is a key determinant of transitioning to higher convergence clubs. A one-standard-deviation increase in either the ECI or Worldwide Governance Indicator measure of government effectiveness results in an increase of about 30 percent in the probability of joining the highest convergence club (figure 4.9, panel A).

1990-2000 covariates. In the 1990s, institutional quality became less decisive in determining whether a country transitions to Club 1, becoming statistically insignificant in the logit results (figure 4.9 and table 4E.5). Here, education, economic complexity, and FDI are significant covariates, the latter only at the 10 percent significance level. One interpretation of this difference from the results for 1980-90 is that a foundation of high governance quality is required for EMDEs to transition to higher convergence clubs, but further success is often dependent on attracting FDI and introducing new and more complex production capabilities into an economy.

Successful transitions: Chile, Poland, and Thailand

These countries are among those that successfully transitioned from a lower-productivity club to the highest-productivity Club 1. Since the 1980s, labor productivity in Chile and Poland has increased from about 25 to 35 percent of the advanced economy average. Thailand's labor productivity has increased from 5 to 10 percent of advanced economy levels over the same period. Poland and Thailand exemplify successful transitions to higher productivity trajectories through the attraction of FDI and engagement with global supply chains, maintaining or increasing economic complexity through these channels. Chile has taken another path, maintaining a concentration in the agricultural products and primary production sectors while pursuing quality upgrading within existing sectors and still attracting significant FDI inflows.

In Thailand, a sharp increase in economic complexity relative to the EMDE average was in part achieved by encouraging inward FDI and a focus on export promotion (Kohpaiboon 2003; figure 4.9, panel B). Having previously been concentrated in agriculture, with over 70 percent of employment in this sector in 1980, Thailand was able to cultivate successful electronics and automobile exporting sectors through a concerted effort to integrate into regional and global supply chains (Hobday and Rush 2007; Wad 2009).[21] Tax exemptions and subsidized lending for export-focused

---

[20] The Worldwide Governance Indicators indicators for government effectiveness and political stability are available only from 1995 onward. Therefore, an average of their values between 1995 and 2000 is used. A range of other variables that proxy for governance (for example, black market currency premium, inflation level, and level of government debt) are used that extend to earlier time periods. None is found to be statistically significant.

[21] This was in part driven by large Japanese FDI inflows, promoting agglomeration effects and encouraging further inflows (Milner, Reed, and Talerngsri 2006). In addition, Thailand established domestic content requirements for automotive parts before World Trade Organization membership, restricting FDI that would have prevented the creation of sufficient value-added intermediate products domestically (Natsuda and Thoburn 2013).

FIGURE 4.9 Covariates of EMDEs joining top-tier convergence club

A one-unit increase in the ECI boosts the likelihood that an EMDE will join Club 1 by about 40 percent, and improvements in education, increasing inflows of FDI, and higher institutional quality all boost the probability of transitioning in some time periods. Not all economies have followed a similar pattern to achieve faster productivity convergence. For example, Chile has low economic complexity but high education and institutional quality, and has focused on upgrading the quality of its agricultural and food exports.

A. The marginal effect of covariates on the probability of EMDE joining convergence Club 1

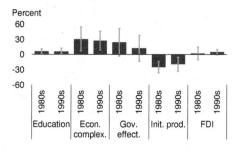

B. Output per worker

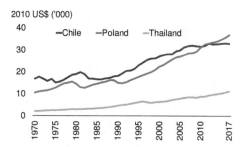

C. Economic complexity

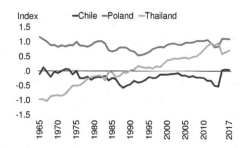

D. FDI inflows

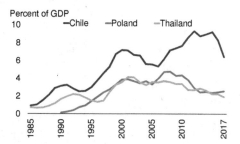

E. Education

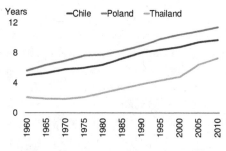

F. WGI: Government effectiveness

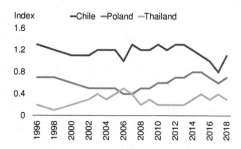

Sources: Barro and Lee (2015); Hidalgo and Hausmann (2009); World Bank, World Development Indicators.
Note: ECI = Economic Complexity Index; EMDE = emerging market and developing economy; FDI = foreign direct investment; WGI = Worldwide Governance Indicators.
A. Marginal effect of a one-unit increase in the covariates on the probability of an EMDE joining the fast productivity growth convergence Club 1. Derived using a logit model. Detailed results in annex 4E.
B-F. Average years of schooling for males and females from Barro and Lee (2015). Economic Complexity Index of Hidalgo and Hausmann (2009). FDI is measured in percent of GDP. Government effectiveness survey from the World Bank's Worldwide Governance Indicators. Measures include perceptions of the quality of public services, the quality of the civil service and the degree of its independence from political pressures, the quality of policy formulation and implementation, and the credibility of the government's commitment to such policies.
D. Five-year moving average.

manufacturers were also introduced in the 1980s and 1990s, whereas policies restricting foreign ownership and imports were gradually reduced (Herderschee 1993; Urata and Yokota 1994). These are thought to have reduced distortions that had previously been present. Despite great strides in rapidly enhancing domestic production capabilities, there remain significant challenges to transitioning further to domestic, rather than FDI-led, innovation and increasing production at more advanced stages of the manufacturing supply chain (Busser 2008; Ohno 2009; World Bank 2018b).

In Poland, industrial complexity was high even before joining the Club 1 convergence cluster. However, integration into the European Union's supply chains, particularly with Germany, enabled a larger export market and facilitated quality upgrading of Polish automobile and electronic goods production (Baldwin and Lopez-Gonzalez 2015; Kaminski and Smarzynska 2001). Polish firms that were foreign-owned or export-focused were found to be significantly more productive than their domestically owned or focused counterparts as markets became more liberalized from the mid-1990s (Hagemejer and Kolasa 2011). Poland and other former Warsaw Pact economies that received the largest inflows of FDI in the 1990s and 2000s saw the most rapid integration into European trade networks—these inflows allowed a rapid transition from low-wage garment manufacturing to higher stages of the supply chain (World Bank 2005). As in Thailand and Chile, Poland has rapidly increased its stock of human capital, reflected by increasing average years of education of adults in each economy (figure 4.9, panel E). In addition, Poland experienced a wave of progressive institutional reforms in the 1990s following the collapse of the Soviet Union, followed by a second wave on accession to the European Union, which would have supported domestic investment strength and aided in attracting FDI (Georgiev, Nagy-Mohacsi, and Plekhanov 2018).

Both Poland and Thailand have expanded into industries more closely associated with more developed economies.[22] They illustrate how increasing industrial complexity and quality can improve productivity through a range of channels. For example, the existence of more complex industries can begin a chain reaction of further development as the fixed costs associated with developing a domestic skill-base are spread more widely (Hausmann, Hwang, and Rodrik 2007). A substantial literature explains the benefits of network and agglomeration effects that can foster the development of increasingly specialized, complex, and productive industries (Fujita, Krugman, and Venables 1999; Porter 1990). In many convergence success stories, active government intervention has been used to establish production capabilities beyond an economy's immediate comparative advantage (Cherif and Hasanov 2019; Hausmann, Hwang, and Rodrik 2007; Rodrik 2004). An important channel through which advanced technologies and production methodologies can be imported is through participation in global value

---

[22] Imbs and Wacziarg (2003) find that industrial diversification occurs as part of the standard development process through per capita income increases. So, when controlling for income per capita, the significance of the ECI variable in driving convergence suggests that transition have expanded beyond their immediate comparative advantage for a given level of development.

chains (World Bank 2020c). However, policies to encourage and promote new industries and workforce capabilities, including those to encourage new "hubs" of sophisticated industries in particular regions, have been met with mixed success (UNCTAD 2019; World Bank 2019c).

Not all strongly performing EMDEs have achieved success by increasing the complexity of their industrial capabilities. Some economies, such as Chile, have displayed fast productivity growth relative to other EMDEs while remaining concentrated in the production of primary commodities. Copper alone accounts for 20 percent of total exports in 2017 and agricultural products for about 33 percent. Therefore, Chile is an important, albeit rare, counterexample of a commodity exporter that has experienced robust productivity growth. Expanded export markets and increasing value-added content have been accomplished through quality upgrading of food exports (Herzer and Nowak-Lehnmann 2007; IADB 2007). Chile has also benefited from high levels of education, institutional quality, and a macroeconomic policy framework that has provided stability and certainty for the private sector, boosting productivity growth (figure 4.9, panels E and F; Kalter et al. 2004). Therefore, with high levels of human capital and institutional certainty, productivity can still rapidly grow while remaining concentrated in a subset of traditionally low-productivity sectors and pursuing quality upgrading and diversity within existing sectors. Economies such as Chile that are less concentrated in manufacturing production have also been able to benefit from technology transfer and investment financing through high FDI inflows (figure 4.9, panel D).

The future of convergence

Existing convergence models do not guarantee continued success in those economies that have made progress in reducing productivity gaps or provide a clear route for progress in those that have not. A range of headwinds to EMDE productivity convergence should be considered.

Increasing barriers to manufacturing-led strategies. Adjustments to the traditional manufacturing-led model of productivity enhancement are particularly important in light of concerns over premature deindustrialization. A limited market for manufactured goods and falling global prices for them have, in recent years, led to declines in the share of manufacturing output in many low- and middle-income economies at lower per capita income levels than have occurred historically (EBRD 2019; Rodrik 2016). Increasingly, there are risks that further automation in the manufacturing sector will shrink opportunities to increase productivity growth by expanding into complex manufacturing production, because this will require an increasingly high-skilled labor force out of reach for many EMDEs, and provide fewer jobs (Hallward-Driemeier and Nayyar 2017). Finally, the COVID-19 pandemic has severely disrupted some supply chains, particularly in the automobile sector (World Bank 2020b). A key risk to manufacturing and value chain-led development will be if the pandemic leads to more inward-looking trade policies that seek to fragment current production processes and onshore activity.

Transitioning from foreign to domestically led innovation. Early success in diversifying sectoral employment and increasing economic complexity can be met with subsequent stagnation. Initially, low-wage and proximity advantages can provide a route to increasingly complex and higher-value-added production processes through engagement in global supply chains and the attraction of FDI in the "flying geese" model of development (Kojima 2000). As productivity and wages grow, the comparative advantage of economies in attracting these forms of production, often reliant on foreign technology transfer and investment flows, may fade (Mahon 1992). In the past, many economies have previously struggled to transition from the rapid-growth phase that has benefited from the adoption of technologies to the development of domestic innovation (Im and Rosenblatt 2015). Middle-income economies have been found to be vulnerable to growth slowdowns, particularly those economies with lower levels of tertiary education and where high-technology exports are low (Eichengreen, Park, and Shin 2013).

Commodity reliance and the outlook for commodity prices. Several upper-middle-income economies such as Argentina, Brazil, and South Africa have remained Club 2 members over the entire sample (1970-2018) and not transitioned to Club 1. In many cases, commodity-exporting upper-middle-income economies have fallen further away from the productivity frontier since the 1980s. In addition to risks facing economies taking a manufacturing-led approach to development, economies with a high degree of commodity reliance, even those such as Chile where quality upgrading has been pursued, face a larger obstacle to growth as they contend with the challenge that the precrisis period of rapidly rising commodity prices has ended. The COVID-19-driven recession in 2020 may generate a prolonged reduction in demand for commodities. For example, changing consumer preferences for transportation, travel, and fuel may result; and demand for industrial metals may be persistently weaker if the recovery is drawn out.

Slowing fundamental drivers of convergence. Furthermore, a range of additional headwinds to EMDE productivity growth could pose additional challenges to the development model of rapidly growing economies. As educational systems mature in many fast-growing EMDEs, there will be fewer high-return gains to education. EMDEs in EAP and ECA currently have workforces whose average years of education are within one year of those of advanced economies (World Bank 2020a). There is an additional danger of human capital development being set back in EMDEs because of COVID-19. The majority of schools and universities have been closed for some period during 2020 because of social distancing measures. EMDEs may be less able to conduct remote learning, and large negative income shocks have also been found to increase school dropout rates in EMDEs (World Bank 2020b). In addition, progress in improving institutional quality has stagnated in many EMDEs: measures of government effectiveness (Worldwide Governance Indicators) have not improved on average since the 1990s (chapter 2).

Conclusion and policy implications

This chapter is the first comprehensive study of long-term labor productivity convergence trends to take account of the EMDE productivity growth increase that began in 2000. It implements a range of methodologies, including newer techniques for estimating club convergence with a sample that reaches into the post-GFC period. In doing so, it highlights a shift in the pace of productivity convergence since 2000 among a subset of EMDEs. Specifically, the chapter documents the following findings.

Main findings. On average since 2010, labor productivity in EMDEs was just 16 percent of the advanced economy average and, in LICs, was only 2 percent. Despite only limited evidence of broad-based productivity convergence until 2000, EMDE economies are now closing the gap with advanced economies, on average, following a broad-based increase in EMDE productivity growth. However, the pickup in productivity growth in EMDEs is unlikely to reduce productivity disparities materially for EMDEs on average—productivity gaps were declining by just 0.5 percent annually in the post-GFC period, and the pace has begun to decline. Even at the peak rate of convergence, for the average EMDE to reduce the productivity gap with advanced economies by half would take nearly 140 years.

The results in this chapter suggest that weak or nonexistent average rates of convergence to the productivity frontier in EMDEs partly reflect the presence of multiple productivity attraction points to which different groups of EMDEs are drawn. Over the past five decades, multiple methodologies find that countries have fallen into distinct convergence clubs in which productivity moved toward a similar long-term productivity level. In contrast to previous studies, problems associated with PPP-adjusted output levels that could bias estimates of productivity convergence rates are avoided; this study uses productivity levels adjusted by market exchange rates as an alternative.

Many EMDEs have separated from lower-productivity clubs and moved into higher-productivity clubs since 2000. These countries have been characterized by systematically better initial education levels, greater political stability and governance, and greater or deepening economic complexity, producing in sectors beyond their immediate comparative advantage. EMDEs in lower-productivity clubs have made little progress in catching up to advanced economy productivity levels over the past 50 years.

Policy implications. These findings highlight the critical importance of policies and institutions that are conducive to productivity growth. EMDEs that have made significant progress in rising to higher convergence trajectories have often had a strong foundation of high education levels with which to enhance production efficiency and incorporate new technologies. However, educational reforms should focus on learning outcomes rather than simply years of attainment (World Bank 2018d). A highly educated and well-trained workforce will be better placed to adopt new technologies and attract FDI, which is also associated with faster rates of productivity convergence. Commitment to effective governance and ensuring legal and institutional stability has been found to be important in creating the optimal conditions for investment and innovation (World Bank 2017).

In addition, this chapter finds a key role for policies that can enhance the complexity of an economy beyond its immediate comparative advantage. Expanding the diversity of an economy to a broader set of increasingly complex industries to benefit from innovation spillovers and network effects is an attractive proposition, but one which is difficult to implement. New technologies that are likely to be introduced into the manufacturing sector will also mean that the bar for maintaining competitiveness with other economies in complex sectors will be increasingly difficult (Hallward-Driemeier and Nayyar 2017). Countries should consider their proximity and connectedness to existing supply chains in more developed economies to judge how they can most readily benefit from technological spillovers. In addition, future risks from automation should be considered when expanding into new complex and higher-productivity sectors. Alternatively, various high-productivity service sectors, such as finance, offer alternatives to industrial-led development, but often require a costly investment in skillsets that are difficult to attain (chapter 7). Finally, countries can also focus on quality upgrading and diversity within existing sectors to enhance production capabilities and generate knowledge spillovers (Brenton, Newfarmer, and Walkenhorst 2009).

Specific country examples demonstrate that various possible development approaches are shown to have been important in driving membership of the most rapidly growing productivity convergence club. These have included integration into regional supply chains, through the attraction of FDI and trade liberalization. Export-promotion policies have been used to increase engagement in value chains in order to promote knowledge transfer. Alternative strategies have consisted of maintaining a concentration in primary product production but pursuing quality upgrading and diversification among these products. However, both strategies face challenges as global trade volumes and commodity prices stagnate. And in many cases the promotion of new industries or production capabilities by governments has failed or has not driven the same level of growth as observed in Club 1 economies. Notably, Club 1 economies have had a stronger foundation of higher-than-average education levels and institutional quality than other economies, which may have increased the likelihood of success for policies that have aimed to promote certain industries. These features are likely to have been associated with high levels of government capacity, which is key to delivering successful industrial policies (Maloney and Nayyar 2018).

Future research. Understanding the drivers of transitions of economies into convergence clubs with higher-productivity convergence trajectories can provide useful insights for policy makers about the conditions necessary for faster productivity growth. However, methodologies to isolate the period of transition, currently used in this chapter, are currently underdeveloped and generally rely on comparing results over different estimation samples. Future research should place more focus on estimating more precise transition points. In addition, further work should be performed to identify the strategies that could be used by EMDEs to develop capabilities in more advanced and complex sectors in light of challenges presented by increasing automation. The next chapter examines the regional dimensions of productivity.

ANNEX 4A Solow-Swan growth model

One of the implications of the Solow-Swan growth model (Solow 1956; Swan 1956) is that countries with low levels of productivity should catch up to those at the frontier. In an economy characterized by the standard production function, consisting of technology (A_t), capital (K_t), and labor (L_t): [23]

$$Y_t = F(K_t, A_t L_t)$$
$$= K_t^{\alpha} (A_t L_t)^{1-\alpha}$$
,

the rate of growth in the capital stock per worker (g_k), and therefore output per worker, is decreasing in $k_t = K_t / L_t$ (capital per worker). Formally,

$$g_k = \frac{s}{k_t^{1-\alpha}} - (\delta + n + g),$$

where s is the fraction of output that is saved, δ denotes the depreciation rate of capital, n is the growth rate of population, and g is the growth rate of technology.[24] Countries with lower initial capital should, therefore, grow faster, converging to the productivity level of high-income economies. However, this is contingent on several assumptions: that there are decreasing returns to capital intensity, saving rates (s) are homogenous across economies (Mankiw, Romer, and Weil 1992), and technology (A) is costless to replicate across borders regardless of country characteristics.

ANNEX 4B Data

Throughout the document, productivity is measured as output per worker, measured at 2010 prices and exchange rates to the U.S. dollar. Labor productivity measured as output per worker can mismeasure output per unit of labor input when workers or employers adjust their working hours. Total hours worked is a more accurate measure of labor input than the number of workers, but data are available for only 30 EMDEs. As a result, sizable changes in hours worked over the business cycle can generate cyclical swings in measured labor productivity per worker.[25] Data on other macroeconomic aggregates such as GDP are from the World Bank's World Development Indicators (WDI) database, with data on employment from the Conference Board's Total Economy Database (TED), complemented by data from the International Labour Organization (ILO) where TED data are incomplete. Data are available on a consistent

---

[23] See Romer (2011) and Barro and Sala-i-Martin (2004) for a detailed treatment of the Solow-Swan model of growth.

[24] A zero saving rate $(s = 0)$ implies that the capital stock per worker declines at the effective rate $(\delta + n)$, reflecting both capital depreciation and population increase.

[25] Hours worked per employee can fluctuate over time. For example, average number of hours per worker has fallen by 6 percent in the average Organisation for Economic Co-operation and Development (OECD) country since 1990. Within the OECD, average hours per worker ranged from 1,363 in Germany to 2,148 in Mexico in 2015.

basis since 1970 for a sample consisting of 29 advanced economies and 74 EMDEs. Six oil-exporting EMDEs that had productivity levels above those of the United States in the 1970s are excluded from the statistical analysis of beta and club convergence. For the initial overview of the current distribution of productivity levels, the sample is expanded to 126 EMDEs and 35 advanced economies.

ANNEX 4C Beta-convergence testing

This annex shows the results of the conditional and unconditional beta-convergence tests described in the third section of the main text in more detail.

The simple unconditional beta-convergence regression includes no covariates of productivity growth except the initial level of productivity. Productivity growth is calculated as log difference between the average level of productivity in one decade relative to the preceding decade. The coefficient on initial productivity levels becomes statistically significant only in the post-2000 period. Converting the coefficient to the rate at which the productivity gap declines annually, as in Barro and Sala-i-Martin (1992), shows a decline of 0.5 percent per year in this final period (table 4C.1). Performing the same exercise on a sample containing only advanced economies shows a statistically significant rate of convergence in each decade. In EMDEs, the coefficient is statistically significant only in the final decade of the sample.

TABLE 4C.1 Beta-convergence

Dependent = 10-year log change in productivity	1970-1980s (1)	1980-1990s (2)	1990-2000s (3)	2000-2010s (4)	Panel (5)
All economies					
Initial productivity	0.028*	0.03*	-0.01	-0.05***	0
Convergence rate (annual)	-0.28%*	-0.33%*	0.13%	0.53%***	0.03%
EMDEs					
Initial productivity	0.00	-0.03	-0.03	-0.05*	-0.03**
Convergence rate (annual)	-0.02%	0.31%	0.33%	0.46%*	0.27%**
Advanced economies					
Initial productivity	-0.19***	-0.19***	-0.13***	-0.08*	-0.16***
Convergence rate (annual)	2.12%***	2.04%***	1.34%***	0.82%*	1.74%***
Observations (all)	98	98	98	98	392
Observations (EMDEs)	69	69	69	69	276
Observations (AEs)	29	29	29	29	116
*p<0.1; **p<0.05; ***p<0.01					

Source: World Bank.

Note: Decade dummies are used in the panel specification but country fixed effects are not. Initial productivity is the average of log productivity over the 10 years in the preceding decade, measured in U.S. dollars at 2010 prices and exchange rates. Productivity growth calculated as the change in average log productivity between the two decades (10-year average growth). Productivity is assumed to grow at its average rate between 2010 and 2018 for the final year of the decade (that is, 2019). AEs = advanced economies; EMDEs = emerging market and developing economies.

TABLE 4C.2 **Conditional beta-convergence**

Dependent = 10-year log change in productivity	1970-1980s (2)	1980-1990s (3)	1990-2000s (4)	2000-2010s (5)	Panel (6)
All economies					
Initial productivity	-0.101***	-0.12***	-0.12***	-0.14***	-0.12***
Convergence rate (annual)	1.06%***	1.29%***	1.24%***	1.46%***	1.33%***
Schooling (years)	0.00	0.01	0.01	0.02	0.01
Economic complexity	0.08**	0.09*	0.07*	0.04	0.07***
Commodity exporter	-0.13*	-0.11*	-0.09	-0.02	-0.09***
Trade (% GDP)	0.08	0.04	-0.02	-0.01	0.02
Investment (% of GDP)	0.01	0.41*	0.68*	0.72**	0.08*
Law and order	0.04*	0.04*	0.03	0.03	0.04***
Adj-R^2	0.34	0.34	0.27	0.38	0.30
Observations (all)	62	68	78	79	287

*p<0.1; **p<0.05; ***p<0.01

Source: World Bank.
Note: Time effects are used in the panel specification but country fixed effects are not. Initial productivity is the average of log productivity over the 10 years in the preceding decade, measured in U.S. dollars at 2010 prices and exchange rates. Productivity growth calculated as the change in average log productivity between the two decades (10-year average growth). Productivity is assumed to grow at its average rate between 2010 and 2018 for the final year of the decade (that is, 2019). All conditioning variables are lagged decadal averages. Data availability of these covariates affects the sample size in each decade.

Tests for conditional convergence are also performed by including controls for average years of schooling, economic complexity (index of Hidalgo and Hausmann 2009), commodity exporter status, trade openness, the ratio of investment to GDP, and an index of law and order.[26] The regression uses lagged values of each control variable to reduce endogeneity concerns. The coefficient on initial productivity level is negative and statistically significant in each decade and in the panel specification (which includes decade fixed effects). The peak annual rate of convergence implied by the conditional convergence regression is 1.5 percent (table 4C.2).

ANNEX 4D **Estimating convergence clubs: Commonalities in productivity levels**

The mixture model analysis allows the detection of convergence clubs using snapshots of the cross-country distribution of productivity levels (Battisti and Parmeter 2013; Grün and Leisch 2008; Henderson, Parmeter, and Russell 2008). Countries fall into the same convergence club when their productivity levels gravitate toward the same long-term productivity level. In contrast, countries fall into distinct convergence clubs when their productivity levels are pulled toward different attraction points.

---

[26] To control for governance and political stability across economies, the "Law and Order" rating from the PRS Group's International Country Risk Guide is used. This provides a longer sample of data than the subsequently used Worldwide Governance Indicators.

Methodology. A finite mixture model with K components takes the form

$$h(Y|Z,\psi) = \sum\nolimits_{k=1}^{K} \pi_k(Z,\gamma) f_k(Y|\theta_k),$$
$$\pi_k(Z,\gamma) \geq 0, \sum\nolimits_{k=1}^{K} \pi_k(Z,\gamma) = 1, \tag{4D.1}$$

where Y is a (possibly multivariate) dependent variable with conditional density h, π_k is the prior probability of membership component k, θ_k is the component-specific parameter vector for the component-specific density function f_k, and $\psi = (\pi_k, \theta_k)_{k=1,\ldots,K}$ denotes the vector of all parameters for the mixture density h. In the Gaussian case, the component-specific parameter vector contains the mean and the standard deviation, $\theta_k = (\mu_k, \sigma_k)$.

The prior probability (weight) of each component $\pi_k(Z,\gamma)$ can be fixed ($Z = 1$, a vector of ones) or depend on associated (exogenous) variables Z. In the latter case, one can incorporate a multinomial logit model to map the exogenous variables to the prior probability of inclusion in each subdistribution:[27]

$$\pi_k(Z,\gamma) = \frac{e^{Z\gamma_k}}{\sum_{j=1}^{K} e^{Z\gamma_j}} \forall j, with \ \gamma_1 = 0. \tag{4D.2}$$

Estimation strategy. Mixture models are commonly estimated using an expectation-maximization (EM) approach. The EM algorithm (Dempster et al. 1977) is the most common method for maximum likelihood estimation of finite mixture models where the number of components K is fixed. In practice, the number of components K is unknown and can be determined using information criteria. The EM algorithm relies on a missing data augmentation scheme. It is assumed that a latent variable $\varepsilon_{nk} \in \{0,1\}^K$ exists for each observation $n = 1, 2, \ldots, N$, which indicates the component membership, that is, $\varepsilon_{nk} = 1$ if the nth observation comes from component k and 0 otherwise. In the EM algorithm, these unobserved component memberships ε_{nk} of the observations are treated as missing values and the data are augmented by estimates of the component membership, that is, the estimated a posteriori probabilities $\hat{\lambda}_{nk}$. For a sample of N observations $(Y_n, Z_n)_{n=1,\ldots,N}$ the two-step EM algorithm is as follows (Dempster et al. 1977; Grün and Leisch 2008).

1. *The expectation steps.* Given the current parameter estimates $\hat{\psi}^{(i)}$ in the ith iteration, estimate the posterior class probability of each observation n (which amounts to replacing the missing data ε_{nk}) using the function:

$$\Pr(k|Y_n, Z_n, \hat{\psi}^{(i)}) := \hat{\lambda}_{nk} = \frac{\pi_k(Z_n, \hat{\gamma}^{(i)}) f_k(Y_n|\hat{\theta}_k^{(i)})}{\sum_{j=1}^{K} \pi_j(Z_n, \hat{\gamma}^{(i)}) f_j(Y_n|\hat{\theta}_j^{(i)})}, \tag{4D.3}$$

and back out the prior class probabilities as $\hat{\pi}_k = \frac{1}{N} \sum_{n=1}^{N} \hat{\lambda}_{nk}$.

---

[27] Alternative specifications can be used to model component weights as a function of concomitant variables (Dayton and Macready 1988).

2. *The maximization steps.* Maximize the log likelihood for each component separately using the posterior probabilities as weights:

$$\max_{\theta_k} \sum_{n=1}^{N} \hat{\lambda}_{nk} \log f_k (Y_n | \theta_k). \qquad (4D.4)$$

The procedure iterates between these steps until the improvement in the overall likelihood becomes marginal (falls under a fixed threshold).[28]

Economies are divided into clubs using snapshots of (the log of) labor productivity at 10-year intervals, as described above (Battisti and Parmeter 2013). The sample includes data for 29 advanced economies and 69 EMDEs and for the period 1970-2018. Therefore, this approach extends earlier studies to include data from the 2000s onward, the period of fastest EMDE productivity growth during the past five decades.

Results. Since 1980, countries have fallen into two to four distinct productivity clusters that have pulled apart over time (figure 4D.1). This finding is consistent with previous studies in some respects, but also demonstrates the existence of a new "breakout" cluster of EMDE economies away from the lowest-productivity club in recent decades (Battisti and Parmeter 2013). Since the early 2000s, when EMDE productivity growth picked up sharply, 10 economies have transitioned to the intermediate-productivity cluster. This "breakout" cluster of EMDEs left behind mostly low-income economies primarily based on agricultural activities with widespread informal activity. Except for the lowest-productivity club, the countries in each cluster are geographically diverse but similar in per capita income and productivity levels.[29]

- In the 1980s, labor productivity fell into two clusters: a high-productivity cluster and a low-productivity cluster. The low-productivity cluster included not only most of today's EMDEs but also several more productive Latin American and Central European EMDEs and South Africa. All of today's advanced economies fell into the high-productivity cluster.

- By 2000, a third cluster had emerged, reflecting a new frontier cluster, composed of a few advanced economies (including Luxembourg, Norway, and Switzerland).

- After the GFC, a fourth cluster emerged with many EMDEs previously in the lowest income cluster moving into an intermediate Club 3, between the low-income cluster and the advanced economy cluster. This occurred shortly after the surge in EMDE growth that began in 2000.

---

[28] For cases where the weighted likelihood estimation in equation (4D.4) is not feasible because of analytical or computational challenges, variants of the EM procedure use hard (Celeux and Govaert 1992) or random (Diebolt and Ip 1996) assignment of the observations to disjoint classes.

[29] The Moran I-statistic, a measure of geographical clustering that can range between -1 and +1, is 0.22. This suggests a relatively weak spatial correlation of club members.

FIGURE 4D.1 Convergence clubs at specific points in time

Since 1980, countries have fallen into two to four distinct productivity clusters that have pulled apart over time. On average, the productivity level in the high club has more than doubled, whereas it has halved in the low club over the period 1980-2018 because of composition effects. Since 2007, 10 faster-growing EMDEs split from the lowest convergence club, breaking away from the primarily low-income economies.

A. Convergence clubs in 1980

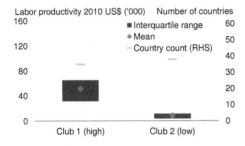

B. Convergence clubs in 2000

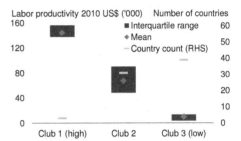

C. Convergence clubs in 2007

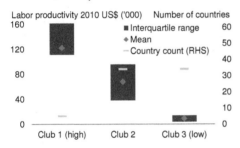

D. Convergence clubs in 2018

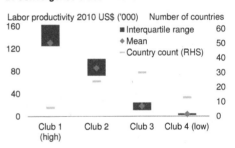

Source: World Bank.
Note: Convergence clubs estimated using mixture model clustering of labor productivity. Red diamonds are average labor productivity expressed in thousands of 2010 U.S. dollars for high- and low-productivity clubs. Blue bars show corresponding interquartile ranges. Orange dashes are the number of countries in each club. The number of clubs and membership of clubs varies over time. EMDEs = emerging market and developing economies.

By using productivity levels to identify convergence clubs, a subset of EMDEs has been identified as making progress in separating from the lowest-productivity groups—at the same time, it is clear that a low-income grouping has made little progress and remains at very low levels of productivity.

Characteristics of club membership. On average, frontier economies (Clubs 1 and 2) in the mixture model analysis tend to have a significantly higher Economic Complexity Index and higher average years of education relative to lagging economies (Clubs 3 and 4). Initial productivity, trade openness, political stability, and investment share seem to play a secondary role in explaining the different groupings in the mixture model approach (figure 4D.2).

FIGURE 4D.2 Characteristics of convergence clubs (mixture model)

On average, frontier economies (Clubs 1 and 2) in the mixture model analysis tend to have a significantly higher Economic Complexity Index and better education relative to lagging economies (Clubs 3 and 4). Initial productivity, trade openness, political stability, and investment share seem to play a secondary role in explaining the different groupings in the mixture model approach.

A. Average years of education

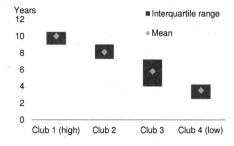

B. Economic Complexity Index

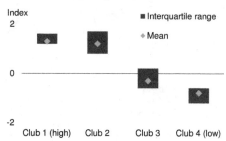

C. Initial productivity

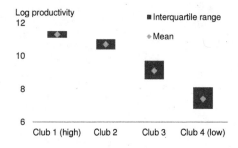

D. Trade openness

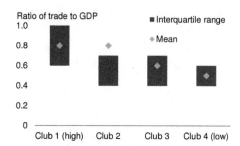

E. Perceptions of political stability

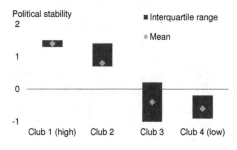

F. Ratio of investment to GDP

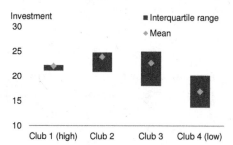

Sources: Barro and Lee (2015); Center for International Development, Harvard University; National Accounts; World Bank (World Development Indicators, Worldwide Governance Indicators).

Note: Average of data available between 1970 and 1990, with the exception of panel E, which reflects data available only from 1995 (1995-2000 average used instead).

A. Average years of schooling for males and females from Barro and Lee (2015).

B. Economic Complexity Index of Hidalgo and Hausmann (2009).

D. The ratio of exports and imports to GDP.

E. Political stability and absence of violence survey from the World Bank's Worldwide Governance Indicators. This indicator measures perceptions of the likelihood of political instability or politically motivated violence, including terrorism. Estimate gives the country's score on the aggregate indicator, in units of a standard normal distribution, that is, ranging from approximately -2.5 to 2.5.

F. The ratio of gross fixed capital formation to GDP.

ANNEX 4E Convergence clubs with common productivity trajectories

This time series analysis follows Phillips and Sul (2007, 2009) in proposing a simple factor model structure for log labor productivity developments in which each economy is attracted to a common steady-state $\log \widetilde{y}_1^*$, but also can follow an idiosyncratic transition path to that attractor:

$$\log y_{it} = \underbrace{\log \widetilde{y}_i^* + \log A_{i0} + \left[\log \widetilde{y}_{i0} - \log \widetilde{y}_i^*\right] e^{-\beta_0 t} + x_{it} t}_{a_{it}}.$$

Initial conditions, such as the distance to the steady-state $(\log \widetilde{y}_{i0} - \log \widetilde{y}_i^*)$, affect the pace of growth. In addition, the rate of technological progress can vary across countries (x_{it}). This growth path of productivity for each economy can be considered in relative terms to a common growth path, μ_t:

$$\log y_{it} = \left(\frac{a_{it} + x_{it} t}{\mu_t}\right) \mu_t = b_{it} \mu_t.$$

For b_{it} to converge across economies, the contribution of a_{it} will decline to 0 as $t \to \infty$, were μ_t to be a simple linear trend. The dynamics of y_{it} would be subsequently determined by x_{it}. As such, convergence in productivity levels requires that x_{it} converges across countries:

$$b_{it} = x_{it} + \frac{a_{it}}{t} \to x_{it}.$$

Estimation. Phillips and Sul advocate modeling the transition parameter b_{it} using a relative scaling of the data:

$$h_{it} = \frac{\log y_{it}}{N^{-1}\Sigma_{i=1}^N \log y_{it}} = \frac{b_{it}}{N^{-1}\Sigma_{i=1}^N b_{it}}.$$

Here, divergences from the common growth path (μ_t) are reflected by h_{it}. Effectively, the mean productivity level is assumed to be the common growth path, with deviations from that growth path reflected by each economy's divergence from that path their relative productivity level to the mean. b_{it} will converge to 1 if the convergence hypothesis holds.

In order to test the hypothesis that $b_{it} = h_{it} \to b = h$, or $b_{it} = h_{it}$, or that countries are on a trajectory to steady-state values, Phillips and Sul propose a form for a test statistic of convergence:

$$H_t = N^{-1} \sum_{i=1}^N (h_{it} - 1)^2,$$

and a functional form for b_{it} if it were, in fact, a declining function of time:

$$b_{it} = b_i + \frac{\sigma_i \xi_{it}}{L(t) t^\alpha},$$

where ξ is independent and identically distributed (i.i.d.) but may be weakly time-dependent. $L(t)$ is a slowly increasing function of t, and $\alpha > 0$ ensures that $b_{it} \rightarrow b_i$ over time. In conjunction with this requirement, if $b_i = b$ across countries, the convergence hypothesis holds. There may also be multiple points of homogeneity $b = b_1, b_2, \ldots$ serving as attractors for groups of countries.

Phillips and Sul (2007) show that, under this specification, for b_{it}, the hypothesis statistic has the limiting form

$$H \sim \frac{A}{L(t)^2 t^{2\alpha}},$$

for some constant A. By letting $L(t) = \log t$, the following log-regression model can be specified

$$\log \frac{H_1}{H_t} - 2\log(\log t) = a + \gamma \log t + u_t.$$

Here, γ is equivalent to 2α, and must be positive for convergence to hold. Under the hypothesis of convergence, γ is more than 0, so the dispersion of productivity levels falls as a function of time. Because of the penalty term $2\log(\log t)$, the t-statistic will converge to $-\infty$ where the hypothesis of convergence is rejected. A one-sided t-test of $\alpha \geq 0$ will assess the hypothesis for a given sample.

In addition to the significance of the coefficient, the magnitude of γ shows the degree of convergence in effect. For $0 < \gamma < 2$, convergence in growth rates but not levels will occur. For $\gamma > 2$, convergence in levels will hold.

The above convergence test is appropriate to test for convergence within a particular group but must be combined with an additional algorithm to test for club convergence among multiple potential clubs of economies. Phillips and Sul propose the following procedure to establish the presence of club convergence:

1. Order economies according to income in the final period (or average in last half).

2. Choose a core group G_k of k economies and compute the test statistic $t_k = t(G_k)$. Choose group size k to maximize the test statistic t_k, subject to the constraint $\min t_k > -1.65$ (the 5 percent critical value for the t-test). Where the minimum test statistic is not met with $k = 2$, drop the first economy and proceed to maximize t_k.

3. Add one country at a time to group k and include in the group if the t-statistic exceeds the criterion c*.

4. Form a new group for those countries not included in the initial three steps. If the remaining countries have $t_k > 1.65$, then there are two groups. Otherwise, repeat steps 1-3. It may be the case that the remaining economies are divergent and that there is no additional club.

5. If $c* = 0$, then the requirement to be added to an existing group will be very conservative (relative to -1.65, 5 percent critical value).

Converging in levels vs. growth rates. Applying the Phillips and Sul (PS) routine to our market exchange rate-adjusted data produces five convergence clubs (table 4E.1). The parameter $\gamma = 2\beta$ is between 0 and 1 in most cases. This suggests that the convergence clubs uncovered show a tendency for relative convergence, or the reduction of the size of the gap in relative productivity levels over time, but not necessarily full convergence to the same level of output per worker. However, this does not rule out a substantial closure of productivity gaps over time—instead, it implies that over time productivity growth rates will align, alongside smaller productivity gaps between members of clubs. Full convergence in levels is a very strict condition not met even by advanced economies, where productivity gaps have declined considerably over the past 50 years, but persistent smaller gaps remain (figure 4.3, panel B). Applying the PS test to advanced economies yields a γ of just 0.15, in line with the results for many of the convergence clubs identified for in table 4E.1.

Estimated over the period 1970-2000, there are considerably fewer members of the two highest convergence clubs (table 4E.1), which as noted in the main text is a result of fewer EMDEs displaying fast-convergence characteristics in this period.

Determinants of club membership. As noted in the main text, initial productivity, governance quality, education, and economic complexity are all statistically significant drivers of club membership in a multinomial logit regression. Further details of these regressors are provided in table 4E.2. To preserve degrees of freedom, Clubs 3-5 are considered to be a single group (Club 3-5). The coefficients in table 4E.3 are directionally informative around the probability of being a member of either Club 2 or Club 3-5 relative to the fast-converging Club 1. A positive coefficient implies an increased probability of being in either club relative to Club 1. These are converted to odds ratios in figure 4.8, which converts the coefficients into the change in probability of membership in Clubs 2-5 relative to Club 1 for a one-unit increase in the variable under consideration.

Determinants of transitioning to Club 1. Tables 4E.4 and 4E.5 show additional covariate regressors to the ones shown in assessing the determinants of an EMDE joining the fast-growing Club 1 economies (figure 4.9, panel A). As in the main text, the averages of each covariate are taken separately for the period 1980-89 and for 1990-99 given the uncertainty of the period in which these economies transitioned to Club 1.

TABLE 4E.1 Output per worker at market exchange rates, PS results

Club 1970-2017 [members]	Convergence rate (γ) (SE)	Club 1970-2000 [members]	Convergence rate (γ) (SE)
Club 1 [45]	0.18 (0.04)	Club 1 [26]	0.19 (0.04)
Club 2 [31]	0.06 (0.03)	Club 2 [21]	0.08 (0.04)
Club 3 [10]	0.09 (0.04)	Club 3 [18]	0.12 (0.06)
Club 4 [6]	0.06 (0.09)	Club 4 [25]	-0.03 (0.05)
Club 5 [5]	0.06 (0.09)	Club 5 [7]	0.74 (0.13)

Source: World Bank.
Note: PS = Phillips and Sul; SE = standard error.

TABLE 4E.2 List of determinants of club membership, PS results

	Description	Source
Education (years)	Average years of education by economy; the data are comprehensive, covering 80 economies since 1960. This a key indicator of the level of human capital in the economy and is widely used in the conditional convergence literature.	Barro and Lee (2015)
Economic Complexity Index	This index is a measure of two concepts: the diversity and the ubiquity of the products an economy is able to produce. For example, an economy specializing in just food products (produced by many other economies) will score poorly in the ECI. An economy producing a wide range of manufactured products, many of which are not widely produced (because of complexity) will score highly. This measure is a relative index, measured in standard deviations from the mean.	The Observatory of Economic Complexity (see also Hidalgo and Hausmann 2009)
Initial productivity	As in the β-convergence case, it is important to control for the initial level of productivity; it may be that club convergence groups are determined by the starting level of productivity. This is measured as the log of initial productivity.	WDI
Trade openness	Trade is also often cited as an important factor enabling technological diffusion and improving competitive forces to enhance productivity. The measure is the sum of exports and imports as a proportion of GDP.	WDI
WGI perceptions of political stability and violence and of government effectiveness	Much of the conditional convergence literature has pointed to the importance of institutional quality for convergence. We control for this using survey measures from the World Bank's WGI measures of both government effectiveness and perceptions of political stability and violence. These measures did not start being produced until 1995, much later than the other indicators.	WGI
Investment ratio	The ratio of investment to output is not a structural determinant of convergence per se. However, it can also reflect convergence via "perspiration" or investment, rather than TFP catch-up. It is measured as the ratio of gross fixed capital formation to GDP.	WDI

Sources: Barrol and Lee (2015); Hidalgo and Hausmann (2009); World Bank (World Development Indicators, Worldwide Governance Indicators).
Note: ECI = Economic Complexity Index; PS = Phillips and Sul; TFP = total factor productivity; WDI = World Development Indicators; WGI = Worldwide Governance Indicators.

TABLE 4E.3 **Determinants of club membership, multinomial logit**

	Dependent variable: Membership of Clubs 2 and 3-5 relative to Club 1			
	(1)	(2)	(3)	(4)
2: Years of education	-0.80***	-0.92***	-0.82***	-0.88***
3-5: Years of education	-0.94***	-1.08***	-0.90 **	-1.10***
2: Economic Complexity Index	-2.59***	-2.93***	-2.34**	-3.07***
3-5: Economic Complexity Index	-2.9***	-3.20***	-2.18***	-3.52***
2: Initial productivity	1.24***	1.45**	2.30***	1.64***
3-5: Initial productivity	0.80	0.56	1.89**	1.31**
2: Trade openness		2.08		
3-5: Trade openness		0.11		
2: WGI – political stability			-2.45**	
3-5: WGI – political stability			-3.58***	
2: Investment (% of GDP)				-5.56**
3-5: Investment (% of GDP)				-10.00
Observations	78	73	78	76
Pseudo-R^2	0.42	0.44	0.47	0.43
$p<0.1$; **$p<0.05$; ***$p<0.01$				

Source: World Bank.
Note: Unadjusted coefficients from multinomial logit. Intercept included in estimation but omitted in results. Each variable reflects averages during 1970-90, except for WGI measures of political stability, which is calculated as the average 1990s value because of data limitations. WGI = Worldwide Governance Indicators.

TABLE 4E.4 **Determinants of transition into Club 1, 1980-90**

	Dependent variable: EMDE membership of highest-productivity convergence Club 1			
	(1)	(2)	(3)	(4)
Years of education	0.10***	0.09**	0.06***	0.09***
Economic Complexity Index	0.20**	0.33***	0.30**	0.32**
Initial productivity	-0.17***	-0.22***	-0.24***	-0.22***
Trade openness		0.15		
WGI: Government effectiveness			0.24*	
Investment in percent of GDP				-0.68
FDI in percent of GDP			0.02	0.06
Observations	54	47	53	48
Pseudo-R^2	0.39	0.46	0.54	0.49
$p<0.1$; **$p<0.05$; ***$p<0.01$				

Sources: Barro and Lee (2015); Hidalgo and Hausmann (2009); World Bank, Worldwide Governance Indicators.
Note: Marginal effects of a one-unit increase in each variable on the probability of an EMDE joining convergence Club 1 relative to other EMDEs. Derived from a logit model, with standard errors and significance levels calculated using the delta method. Average years of schooling for males and females from Barro and Lee (2015). Economic Complexity Index of Hidalgo and Hausmann (2009). Exports and imports as a percent of GDP. Government effectiveness survey from the World Bank's WGI. Measures include perceptions of the quality of public services, the quality of the civil service and the degree of its independence from political pressures, the quality of policy formulation and implementation, and the credibility of the government's commitment to such policies. Estimate gives the country's score on the aggregate indicator, in units of a standard normal distribution, that is, ranging from approximately -2.5 to 2.5. A higher index value indicates greater political stability. Gross fixed capital formation and FDI are measured in percent of GDP. Each covariate reflects averages during 1980-90. EMDEs = emerging market and developing economies; FDI = foreign direct investment; WGI = Worldwide Governance Indicators.

TABLE 4E.5 Determinants of transition into Club 1, 1990-2000

	Dependent variable: EMDE membership of highest-productivity convergence Club 1				
	(1)	(2)	(3)	(4)	(5)
Years of education	0.07**	0.06**	0.05*	0.05*	0.05**
Economic Complexity Index	0.29**	0.29***	0.27***	0.26***	0.25***
Initial productivity	-0.18***	-0.18***	-0.19***	-0.16***	-0.17***
Trade openness		0.10			
WGI: Government effectiveness			0.12		0.06
Investment in percent of GDP				1.87**	1.76*
FDI in percent of GDP			0.05*	0.06**	0.05*
Observations	54	54	54	54	54
Pseudo-R^2	0.32	0.33	0.41	0.42	0.46
*p<0.1; **p<0.05; ***p<0.01					

Sources: Barro and Lee (2015): Hidalgo and Hausmann (2009): World Bank, Worldwide Governance Indicators.
Note: Marginal effects of a one-unit increase in each variable on the probability of an EMDE joining convergence Club 1 relative to other EMDEs. Derived from a logit model, with standard errors calculated using the delta method. Average years of schooling for males and females from Barro and Lee (2015). Economic Complexity Index of Hidalgo and Hausmann (2009). Exports and imports as a percent of GDP. Government effectiveness survey from the World Bank's WGI, defined as perceptions of the quality of public services, the quality of the civil service and the degree of its independence from political pressures, the quality of policy formulation and implementation, and the credibility of the government's commitment to such policies. Estimate gives the country's score on the aggregate indicator, in units of a standard normal distribution, that is, ranging from approximately -2.5 to 2.5. A higher index value indicates greater political stability. Gross fixed capital formation and FDI are measured in percent of GDP. Each covariate reflects averages during 1990-2000. EMDEs = emerging market and developing economies; FDI = foreign direct investment; WGI = Worldwide Governance Indicators.

ANNEX 4F Productivity measurement: PPP vs. market exchange rates

EMDEs produce 34 percent of the average advanced economy output per worker when measured at PPP but produce just 16 percent of advanced economy output when measured in U.S. dollars converted at market exchange rates. In theory, the PPP adjustment of output corrects for lower average prices of nontradable goods in EMDEs and serves as a more accurate measurement of output. However, additional issues are associated with PPP adjustment. Productivity growth measured using the Penn World Table's PPP-adjusted output series has considerably exceeded growth in national accounts-based measures of productivity and may in part reflect methodological differences and flaws in historical cross-country price comparison surveys. Faster growth rates in PPP-adjusted output series may be biasing estimated convergence rates to be higher and also result in implausible club convergence allocations.

Aggregation

In the analysis of productivity growth and differentials in this chapter, cross-country comparisons are made using productivity measured in U.S. dollars at 2010 prices and exchange rates. Often, studies of convergence have used cross-country comparisons of income per capita calculated at PPP. This annex addresses the following questions:

- How do measures of productivity at market exchange rates and PPP differ conceptually?

- What are the cross-country differences in productivity levels using PPP measures, and how do these differ from the market exchange rate-based measures in the main text?

- Do any of the key unconditional convergence tests or club convergence analyses change when using PPP measures of productivity?

PPP vs. market exchange rates

Concepts. PPP calculates the rate at which the currency of one country would have to be converted into another to buy the same assortment of goods and services. Market exchange rates are the rates at which goods and services are actually traded in international markets. Because PPP reflects the fact that goods and services that are not traded internationally tend to be cheaper in lower-income countries, the purchasing power of lower-income country currencies tends to be higher at PPP exchange rates than at market exchange rates.

Purposes. Transactions in global trade, financial markets, and commodity markets are all conducted at market exchange rates; hence, for aggregating output, market exchange rates (as used by the World Bank) are frequently an appropriate weighting scheme. In contrast, for measuring living standards and aggregating welfare, PPP weights would be appropriate because they capture the consumption affordable to households for comparable consumption baskets.

Pros and cons. Although the theoretical purposes of the weighting schemes are clearly distinct, they also have different features in practice. First, PPP exchange rates are subject to greater measurement challenges. Because they are constructed from prices of the same baskets of goods and services, they rely on price surveys by the World Bank's International Comparison Program (Callen 2007). These are conducted infrequently and not available for all countries, hence subject to considerable measurement error and extrapolation to countries and years with missing data.[30] PPP exchange rates tend to be more stable than market exchange rates (Schnatz 2006). Hence, for weighting purposes, market exchange rates are typically fixed at the value of a specific year or period by the World Bank, and can therefore be influenced by short-term fluctuations that occurred in the chosen period.

Data. The majority of convergence studies have used versions of the Penn World Table (PWT) as a data source of PPP-adjusted income per capita because of its large coverage of both the time and country coverage dimensions (Feenstra, Inklaar, and Timmer 2015; Johnson et al. 2013). In recent iterations, the PPP adjustment is estimated on a time-varying basis, rather than simply using survey-based evidence from a particular year. The PWT version 9.1 is used in this annex as a source of PPP-adjusted labor productivity levels and growth rates.

---

[30] The last comprehensive International Comparison Program survey was conducted in 2017.

FIGURE 4F.1 **PPP-adjusted productivity gaps**

On average, labor productivity in EMDEs is about 33 percent of the advanced economy average when measured in PPP-adjusted terms, and in LICs it is 4 percent of the advanced economy average. Measured at market exchange rates, labor productivity levels in EMDEs are less than 20 percent of advanced economy levels, but 2 percent of advanced economy levels in LICs.

A. Productivity by country group, 2010-17 average

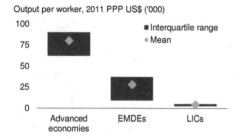

B. Productivity by EMDE region, 2010-17 average

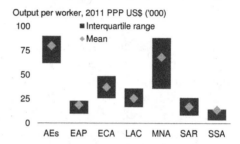

C. EMDEs by commodity producer status, 2010-17 average

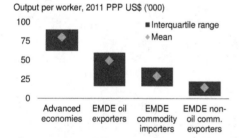

D. Distribution of productivity, 2010-17 average

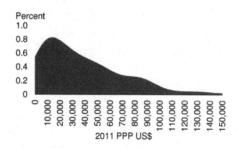

Sources: Penn World Table; World Bank.
Note: Output-measured real GDP at PPP-adjusted 2011 U.S. dollars ("rgdpo" in the PWT data set) per worker. AEs = advanced economies; EMDEs = emerging market and developing economies; LICs = low-income countries; PPP = purchasing power parity; EAP = East Asia and Pacific; ECA = Europe and Central Asia; LAC = Latin America and the Caribbean; MNA = Middle East and North Africa; SAR = South Asia; SSA = Sub-Saharan Africa.

PPP-adjusted cross-country productivity differences

The productivity gap between advanced economies and EMDEs is substantially smaller once productivity is measured at PPP-adjusted exchange rates (figure 4F.1, panel A). The average EMDE worker produces 34 percent (16 percent at market exchange rates) of the output of the average advanced economy worker, and workers in LICs produce 4 percent (2 percent when measured at market exchange rates) of the advanced economy average. Although the scale of productivity differentials relative to advanced economies is smaller under PPP measurement, the relative ordering of productivity levels between EMDE commodity exporters and importers, and EMDE regions, is largely unchanged. Oil-exporting EMDEs continue to have the smallest gap with advanced economies, followed by EMDE commodity importers; MNA has the highest output per worker among EMDE regions (figure 4F.1, panels B and C). In addition, the distribution of productivity retains its polarized structure, although the advanced economy and EMDE regions are significantly closer together.

To the extent that PPP adjustments can accurately account for nontradable pricing differentials between economies, productivity gaps are significantly lower. However, EMDEs still face a substantial productivity gap with advanced economies, requiring sustained high productivity growth to close.

Unconditional and conditional β-convergence results using PPP measures of labor productivity

Measuring labor productivity at PPP-adjusted levels suggests a modest increase in the pace of unconditional convergence relative to market exchange rate-based measures. Consistent with the market exchange rate results in table 4C.2, tests of unconditional convergence are insignificant before 2000 (table 4F.1). The pace of convergence is higher, however, rising from 0.5 percent per annum at market exchange rates to 0.7 percent at PPP-adjusted rates after 2000. At this rate, it would still take about 90 years to close half of the productivity gap.

Conditional convergence results also show higher rates of convergence than when using market exchange rate-based estimates. As with the market exchange rate estimates, most decades show evidence of conditional convergence (table 4F.2). In each decade, convergence rates are higher when productivity is measured using PPP-adjusted dollars relative to those estimated in dollars converted at market exchange rates. The PPP panel specification, covering all decades since 1970, shows a convergence rate of 1.7 percent per year, close to the "rule of 2 percent" established in the literature, compared to 1.3 in the market exchange rate panel specification. In part, the faster convergence rates using the PPP measurement reflect smaller estimated productivity gaps. However, productivity growth also differs in the PPP estimates of productivity relative to those implied by the market exchange rates—because the exchange rates applied in this chapter are fixed at 2010 levels, the growth of the MER series is equivalent to growth rates implied by the national accounts for each economy.

PPP effects on productivity growth

To establish the effects of differences in relative prices on the level of output across economies, the PWTs draw on multiple years of data from the World Bank's International Comparison Program (ICP), with data beginning in 1970. Because their PPP adjustments are updated across multiple years, their impact is not just on the level of output per worker but also on the growth rate of output per worker. The PPP-adjusted growth rate of output in each economy often differs substantially from the national accounts growth rate used in the market exchange rate approach (where exchange rates are fixed in one year). This occurs for two reasons, both of which cause the prices recorded by the ICP to differ from the price deflator recorded in national accounts (Feenstra, Inklaar, and Timmer 2015):

1. The basket of goods under consideration by the ICP can differ from the goods produced by an economy.

2. Measurement error in the ICP or national accounts could cause them to diverge.

FIGURE 4F.2 **PPP-adjusted growth differentials**

PPP-measured productivity growth has substantially exceeded productivity growth measured at market exchange rates for nearly all economies. This difference is a result of discrepancies between the change in prices over time in the ICP and the change in prices in national accounts. Five additional EMDE economies are found to be in the top-tier productivity convergence club when using PPP-adjusted data compared to productivity measured at market exchange rates. These economies display significantly faster growth rates under the PPP measure.

A. Cumulative growth 1990-2017, PPP vs. adjusted MER

B. Cumulative growth rate differences for PPP vs. market exchange rates (1990-2017): convergence club changes

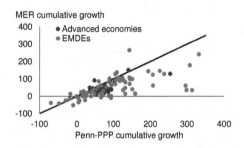

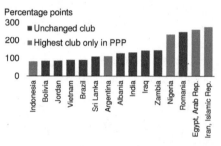

Sources: Penn World Table; World Bank, International Comparison Program.
Note: Output-measured real GDP at PPP-adjusted 2011 U.S. dollars ("rgdpo" in the PWT data set) per worker relative to output measured at 2010 U.S. dollars at 2010 exchange rates. EMDEs = emerging market and developing economies; ICP = International Comparison Program; MER = market exchange rate; PPP = purchasing power parity; PWT = Penn World Table.
A. Percent productivity growth between 1990 and 2017 under the PPP and market exchange rate measures of productivity.
B. Percentage point difference in cumulative productivity growth in the 15 countries with the largest growth differential between both measures of productivity. Five of these economies are found to be in the highest-productivity club under the Phillips and Sul (2007) convergence algorithm (in red) when labor productivity is measured in PPP-adjusted U.S. dollars but are found to be in lower clubs when labor productivity is measured at 2010 market exchange rates.

Since 1990, the cumulative growth of output per worker in PPP terms has systematically exceeded the growth registered in the national accounts across nearly all economies under consideration (figure 4F.2, panel A). That could suggest that the ICP measure of prices has fallen more than the national accounts measure of prices. The faster rates of growth contribute to the faster rates of estimated convergence listed above and may provide a modest exaggeration of the pace of productivity convergence.

In addition, certain economies are affected more than others by the discrepancy in the evolution of national accounts-based growth and PPP-adjusted productivity growth. This also leads to different results in the club convergence clustering algorithms. For the Phillips and Sul approach, 7 EMDEs join the highest convergence Club 1 than when the algorithm is applied to the market exchange rate measure of productivity (figure 4F.2, panel B). The size of the discrepancy between PPP and national accounts measures of growth in these economies suggests a degree of caution in interpreting these results. For example, the cumulative growth rates of the Islamic Republic of Iran and of Nigeria since 1990 are over 200 percentage points higher in the PPP measure. In Argentina and Brazil, cumulative growth rates are over 75 percent higher.

Several studies have found flaws in the price-surveying methodologies used before the 2011 ICP exercise. These flaws may be an important driver of the discrepancy between the price deflator in the ICP and the deflator used in the national accounts. Methodological changes in the 2011 ICP survey have resulted in substantial re-estimations of the size of many economies relative to the 2005 ICP (Deaton and Aten 2017; Inklaar and Prasada Rao 2017). Some of the discrepancies between national accounts-based measures of labor productivity and PPP-based estimates may also be due to inconsistent sampling methodologies for prices over time.

TABLE 4F.1 **Beta-convergence, PPP-adjusted**

Dependent = 10-year productivity growth	1970-1980s (2)	1980-1990s (3)	1990-2000s (4)	2000-2010s (5)	Panel (6)
All economies					
Initial productivity	0.022	0.078**	-0.028	-0.066***	-0.005
Convergence rate (annual)	-0.22%	-0.75%**	0.28%	0.68%***	0.05%
EMDEs					
Initial productivity (PPP)	-0.026	-0.003	-0.067	-0.019	-0.030
Convergence rate (annual)	0.26%	0.03%	0.69%	0.19%	0.30%
Advanced economies					
Initial productivity (PPP)	-0.310***	-0.420***	-0.237**	0.092	-0.294***
Convergence rate (annual)	3.71%***	5.45%***	2.71%**	-0.88%	3.48%***
Observations (All)	98	98	98	98	392
Observations (EMDEs)	68	68	68	68	268
Observations (AEs)	30	30	30	30	116

Source: World Bank.
Note: AEs = advanced economies; EMDEs = emerging market and developing economies; PPP = purchasing power parity.

TABLE 4F.2 **Conditional beta-convergence: Labor productivity, PPP-adjusted**

Dependent = 10-year productivity growth	1970-1980s (2)	1980-1990s (3)	1990-2000s (4)	2000-2010s (5)	Pooled (6)
All economies					
Initial productivity	-0.129**	-0.134**	-0.170***	-0.150***	-0.169***
Convergence rate PPP (annual)	1.38%	1.43%**	1.86%***	1.62%***	1.79%***
Convergence rate market exchange rates for comparison (table 4C.2)	1.06%***	1.29%***	1.24%***	1.46%***	1.33%***
Schooling (years)	0.007	0.025	0.022	0.014	0.016*
Economic complexity	0.093*	0.135*	-0.024	-0.021	0.034
Commodity exporter	0.030	-0.065	-0.124	-0.052	-0.077*
Trade (% GDP)	0.134*	0.123	-0.033	-0.009	0.055
Investment (% of GDP)	-0.208	-1.109**	2.133***	1.010***	-0.153
Law & order	0.033	0.010	0.052	0.011	0.046***
Adj-R^2	0.22	0.26	0.25	0.31	0.23
Observations (All)	62	70	77	78	287

Source: World Bank.
Note: PPP = purchasing power parity.

References

Aiyar, S., R. Duval, D. Puy, Y. Wu, and L. Zhang. 2013. "Growth Slowdowns and the Middle-Income Trap." IMF Working Paper 13/71, International Monetary Fund, Washington, DC.

Baldwin, R., and J. Lopez-Gonzalez. 2015. "Supply-Chain Trade: A Portrait of Global Patterns and Several Testable Hypotheses." *World Economy* 38 (11): 1682–721.

Barro, R. J. 1991. "Economic Growth in a Cross Section of Countries." *Quarterly Journal of Economics* 106 (2): 407–43.

Barro, R. J. 2015. "Convergence and Modernisation." *Economic Journal* 125 (585): 911–42.

Barro, R. J., and J-W. Lee. 1994. "Sources of Economic Growth." Carnegie-Rochester Conference Series on Public Policy 40, Cambridge, MA.

Barro, R. J., and J.-W. Lee. 2015. *Education Matters: Global Schooling Gains from the 19th to the 21st Century.* New York: Oxford University Press.

Barro, R. J., and X. Sala-i-Martin. 1992. "Convergence." *Journal of Political Economy* 100 (2): 223–51.

Barro, R. J., and X. Sala-i-Martin. 2004. *Economic Growth.* Cambridge, MA: MIT Press.

Bartkowska, M., and A. Riedl. 2012. "Regional Convergence Clubs in Europe: Identification and Conditioning Factors." *Economic Modelling* 29 (1): 22–31.

Battisti, M., and C. F. Parmeter. 2013. "Clustering and Polarization in the Distribution of Output: A Multivariate Perspective." *Journal of Macroeconomics* 35 (March): 144–62.

Baumol, W. J. 1986. "Growth, Convergence, and Welfare: What the Long-Run Data Show." *American Economic Review* 76 (5): 1072–85.

Bernard, A. B., and S. N. Durlauf. 1995. "Convergence in International Output." *Journal of Applied Econometrics* 10 (2): 97–108.

Bernard, A. B., and S. N. Durlauf. 1996. "Interpreting Tests of the Convergence Hypothesis." *Journal of Econometrics* 71 (1–2): 161–73.

Brenton, P., R. Newfarmer, and P. Walkenhorst. 2009. "Avenues for Export Diversification: Issues for Low-Income Countries." MPRA Paper 22758, University Library of Munich.

Busser, R. 2008. "'Detroit of the East'? Industrial Upgrading, Japanese Car Producers and the Development of the Automotive Industry in Thailand." *Asia Pacific Business Review* 14 (1): 29–45.

Callen, T. 2007. "Back to Basics—PPP versus the Market: Which Weight Matters?" *Finance and Development,* Volume 44, International Monetary Fund, Washington, DC.

Canova, F. 2004. "Testing for Convergence Clubs in Income Per Capita: A Predictive Density Approach." *International Economic Review* 45 (1): 49–77.

Caselli, F. 2005. "Accounting for Cross-Country Income Differences." In *Handbook of Economic Growth 1A,* edited by P. Aghion and S. N. Durlauf, 679–741. Amsterdam: North-Holland.

Celeux, G., and G. Govaert. 1992. "A Classification EM Algorithm for Clustering and Two Stochastic Versions." *Computational Statistics and Data Analysis* 14 (3): 315–32.

Chatterji, M. 1992. "Convergence Clubs and Endogenous Growth." *Oxford Review of Economic Policy* 8 (2): 57–69.

Cherif, R., and F. Hasanov. 2019. "The Return of the Policy That Shall Not Be Named: Principles of Industrial Policy." IMF Working Paper 19/74, International Monetary Fund, Washington, DC.

Dayton, C. M., and G. M. Macready. 1988. "Concomitant-Variable Latent-Class Models." *Journal of the American Statistical Association* 83 (401): 173–78.

Deaton, A., and B. Aten. 2017. "Trying to Understand the PPPs in ICP 2011: Why Are the Results so Different." *American Economic Journal: Macroeconomics* 9 (1): 243–64.

Dempster, A. P. P., N. M. Laird, and D. B. Rubin. 1977. "Maximum Likelihood from Incomplete Data via the EM Algorithm." *Journal of the Royal Statistical Society* 39 (1): 1–38.

Diebolt, J., and E. H. S. Ip. 1996. *Stochastic EM: Method and Application*. In *Markov Chain Monte Carlo in Practice*, edited by W. R. Gilks, S. Richardson, and D. J. Spiegelhalter, Chapter 15. London: Chapman & Hall.

Dollar, D., and A. Kraay. 2003. "Institutions, Trade, and Growth." *Journal of Monetary Economics* 50 (1): 133–62.

Dowrick, S. 1992. "Technological Catch Up and Diverging Incomes: Patterns of Economic Growth 1960-88." *The Economic Journal* 102 (412): 600–10.

Durlauf, S. N., and P. A. Johnson. 1995. "Multiple Regimes and Cross-Country Growth Behaviour." *Journal of Applied Econometrics* 10 (4): 365–84.

Durlauf, S. N., P. A. Johnson, and J. R. W. Temple. 2005. "Growth Econometrics." In *Handbook of Economic Growth 1A*, edited by P. Aghion and S. N. Durlauf, 555–677. Amsterdam: North-Holland.

Easterly, W., and R. Levine. 2001. "What Have We Learned from a Decade of Empirical Research on Growth? It's Not Factor Accumulation: Stylized Facts and Growth Models." *World Bank Economic Review* 15 (2): 177–219.

Easterly, W., and R. Levine. 2003. "Tropics, Germs, and Crops: How Endowments Influence Economic Development." *Journal of Monetary Economics* 50 (1): 3–39.

EBRD (European Bank for Reconstruction and Development). 2019. *Middle Income Transitions*. London: EBRD.

Eichengreen, B., D. Park, and K. Shin. 2013. "Growth Slowdowns Redux: New Evidence on the Middle-Income Trap." NBER Working Paper 18673, National Bureau of Economic Research, Cambridge, MA.

Feenstra, R. C., R. Inklaar, and M. P. Timmer. 2015. "The Next Generation of the Penn World Table." *American Economic Review* 105 (10): 3150–82.

Frankel, J. A., and D. Romer. 1999. "Does Trade Cause Growth?" *American Economic Review* 89 (3): 397–98.

Fujita, M., P. R. Krugman, and A. Venables. 1999. *The Spatial Economy: Cities, Regions and International Trade*. Cambridge, MA: MIT Press.

Georgiev, Y., P. Nagy-Mohacsi, and A. Plekhanov. 2018. "Structural Reform and Productivity Growth in Emerging Europe and Central Asia." ADB Economics Working Paper 523, Asian Development Bank, Manila.

Gibson, W. 1999. "Interview at National Public Radio." http://quoteinvestigator.com/2012/01/24/future-has-arrived/.

Grün, B., and F. Leisch 2008. "FlexMix Version 2: Finite Mixtures with Concomitant Variables and Varying and Constant Parameters." *Journal of Statistical Software* 28 (4): 1–35.

Hagemejer, J., and M. Kolasa. 2011. "Internationalisation and Economic Performance of Enterprises: Evidence from Polish Firm-Level Data." *World Economy* 34 (1): 74–100.

Hall, R. E., and C. I. Jones. 1999. "Why Do Some Countries Produce So Much More Output per Worker than Others?" *Quarterly Journal of Economics* 114 (1): 83–116.

Hallward-Driemeier, M., and G. Nayyar. 2017. *Trouble in the Making? The Future of Manufacturing-Led Development.* Washington, DC: World Bank.

Hausmann, R., and C. Hidalgo. 2010. "Country Diversification, Product Ubiquity, and Economic Divergence." CID Working Paper 201, Harvard Kennedy School, Cambridge, MA.

Hausmann, R., J. Hwang, and D. Rodrik. 2007. "What You Export Matters." *Journal of Economic Growth* 12 (1): 1–25.

Henderson, D. J., C. F. Parmeter, and R. R. Russell. 2008. "Modes, Weighted Modes, and Calibrated Modes: Evidence of Clustering Using Modality Tests." *Journal of Applied Econometrics* 23 (5): 607–38.

Herderschee, H. 1993. "Incentives for Exports: The Case of Thailand." *ASEAN Economic Bulletin* 9 (3): 348–63.

Herzer, D., and F. Nowak-Lehnmann 2007. "What Does Export Diversification Do for Growth? An Econometric Analysis." *Applied Economics* 38 (15): 1825–38.

Hidalgo, C., and R. Hausmann. 2009. "The Building Blocks of Economic Complexity." *Proceedings of the National Academy of Sciences of the United States of America* 106 (26): 10570–75.

Hobday, M., and H. Rush. 2007. "Upgrading the Technological Capabilities of Foreign Transnational Subsidiaries in Developing Countries: The Case of Electronics in Thailand." *Research Policy* 36 (9): 1335–56.

IADB (Inter-American Development Bank). 2007. "The Emergence of New Successful Export Activities in Latin America: The Case of Chile." Research Network Working Paper R-552, Inter-American Development Bank, Washington, DC.

Im, F. G., and D. Rosenblatt. 2015. "Middle-Income Traps: A Conceptual and Empirical Survey." *Journal of International Commerce, Economics and Policy* 6 (3): 1–39.

Imbs, J., and R. Wacziarg. 2003. "Stages of Diversification." *American Economic Review* 93 (1): 63–86.

Inklaar, R., and D. S. Prasada Rao. 2017. "Cross-Country Income Levels over Time: Did the Developing World Suddenly Become Much Richer?" *American Economic Journal: Macroeconomics* 9 (1): 265–90.

Jeong, H. 2019. "Productivity Growth and Efficiency Dynamics of Korea's Structural Transformation." Seoul National University Working Paper, Graduate School of International Studies, Seoul.

Johnson, P., and C. Papageorgiou. 2020. "What Remains of Cross-Country Convergence?" *Journal of Economic Literature* 58 (1): 129–75.

Johnson, S., W. Larson, C. Papageorgiou, and A. Subramanian. 2013. "Is Newer Better? Penn World Table Revisions and Their Impact on Growth Estimates." *Journal of Monetary Economics* 60 (2): 255–74.

Kalter, E., S. Phillips, M. A. Espinosa-Vega, R. Luzio, M. Villafuerte, and M. Singh. 2004. "Chile: Institutions and Policies Underpinning Stability and Growth." International Monetary Fund, Washington, DC.

Kaminski, B., and B. K. Smarzynska. 2001. "Integration into Global Production and Distribution Networks through FDI: The Case of Poland." Policy Research Working Paper 2646, World Bank, Washington, DC.

Kohpaiboon, A. 2003. "Foreign Trade Regimes and the FDI–Growth Nexus: A Case Study of Thailand." *Journal of Development Studies* 40 (2): 55–69.

Kojima, K. 2000. "The 'Flying Geese' Model of Asian Economic Development: Origin, Theoretical Extensions, and Regional Policy Implications." *Journal of Asian Economics* 11 (4): 375–401.

Leipziger, D. M., and V. Thomas. 1993. "The Lessons of East Asia: An Overview of Country Experience." World Bank, Washington, DC.

Liu, Z., and T. Stengos. 1999. "Non-Linearities in Cross-Country Growth Regressions: A Semiparametric Approach." *Journal of Applied Econometrics* 14 (5): 527–38.

Mahon, J. E. 1992. "Was Latin America Too Rich to Prosper? Structural and Political Obstacles to Export-Led Industrial Growth." *Journal of Development Studies* 28 (2): 241–63.

Maloney, W. F., and G. Nayyar. 2018. "Industrial Policy, Information, and Government Capacity." *World Bank Research Observer* 33 (2): 189–217.

Mankiw, N. G., D. Romer, and D. N. Weil. 1992. "A Contribution to the Empirics of Economic Growth." *Quarterly Journal of Economics* 107 (2): 407–37.

Milner, C., G. Reed, and P. Talerngsri. 2006. "Vertical Linkages and Agglomeration Effects in Japanese FDI in Thailand." *Journal of the Japanese and International Economies* 20 (2): 193–208.

Natsuda, K., and J. Thoburn. 2013. "Industrial Policy and the Development of the Automotive Industry in Thailand." *Journal of the Asia Pacific Economy* 18 (3): 413–37.

Ohno, K. 2009. "Avoiding the Middle-Income Trap: Renovating Industrial Policy Formulation in Vietnam." *ASEAN Economic Bulletin* 26 (1): 25–43.

Patel, D., J. Sandefur, and A. Subramanian. 2018. "Everything You Know about Cross-Country Convergence Is (Now) Wrong." Center for Global Development, October 15. https://www.cgdev.org/blog/everything-you-know-about-cross-country-convergence-now-wrong.

Pesaran, H. 2007. "A Pair-Wise Approach to Testing for Output and Growth Convergence." *Journal of Econometrics* 138 (1): 312–55.

Phillips, P., and D. Sul. 2007. "Transition Modeling and Econometric Convergence Tests." *Econometrica* 75 (6): 1771–855.

Phillips, P., and D. Sul. 2009. "Economic Transition and Growth." *Journal of Applied Econometrics* 24 (7): 1153–85.

Piketty, T. 2014. *Capital in the Twenty-First Century*. Harvard University Press.

Pittau, M. G., and R. Zelli. 2006. "Empirical Evidence of Income Dynamics across EU Regions." *Journal of Applied Econometrics* 21 (5): 605–28.

Pittau, M. G., R. Zelli, and P. A. Johnson. 2010. "Mixture Models, Convergence Clubs, and Polarization." *Review of Income and Wealth* 56 (1): 102–22.

Porter, M. E. 1990. *The Competitive Advantage of Nations: With a New Introduction*. New York: Free Press.

Quah, D. T. 1993a. "Empirical Cross-Section Dynamics in Economic Growth." *European Economic Review* 37 (2–3): 426–34.

Quah, D. T. 1993b. "Galton's Fallacy and Tests of the Convergence Hypothesis." *Scandinavian Journal of Economics* 95 (4): 427.

Quah, D. T. 1996. "Twin Peaks: Growth and Convergence in Models of Distribution Dynamics." *Economic Journal* 106 (437): 1045–55.

Quah, D. T. 1997. "Empirics for Growth and Distribution: Stratification, Polarization, and Convergence Clubs." *Journal of Economic Growth* 2 (1): 27–59.

Rodrik, D. 1994. "King Kong Meets Godzilla: The World Bank and the East Asian Miracle." CEPR Discussion Papers 944, Centre for Economic Policy Research, London, U.K.

Rodrik, D. 2004. "Industrial Policy for the Twenty-First Century." KSG Faculty Research Working Paper Series RWP04-047, John F. Kennedy School of Government, Harvard University, Cambridge, MA.

Rodrik, D. 2011. "The Future of Economic Convergence." NBER Working Paper 17400, National Bureau of Economic Research, Cambridge, MA.

Rodrik, D. 2013. "Unconditional Convergence in Manufacturing." *Quarterly Journal of Economics* 128 (1): 165–204.

Rodrik, D. 2016. "Premature Deindustrialization." *Journal of Economic Growth* 21 (1): 1–33.

Rodrik, D., A. Subramanian, and F. Trebbi. 2004. "Institutions Rule: The Primacy of Institutions over Geography and Integration in Economic Development." *Journal of Economic Growth* 9 (2): 131–65.

Romer, D. 2011. *Advanced Macroeconomics*. New York: McGraw-Hill.

Roy, S., M. Kessler, and A. Subramanian. 2016. "Glimpsing the End of Economic History? Unconditional Convergence and the Missing Middle Income Trap." Center for Global Development Working Paper 438, Center for Global Development, Washington, DC.

Sachs, J. D., and A. Warner. 1995. "Economic Convergence and Economic Policies." NBER Working Paper Series 5039, National Bureau of Economic Research, Cambridge, MA.

Sachs, J. D., and A. Warner. 2001. "Natural Resources and Economic Development: The Curse of Natural Resources." *European Economic Review* 45 (2001): 827–38.

Sala-i-Martin, X. 1996. "The Classical Approach to Convergence Analysis." *Economic Journal* 106 (437): 1019–36.

Schnatz, B. 2006. "Is Reversion to PPP in Euro Exchange Rates Non-Linear?" ECB Working Paper 682, European Central Bank, Frankfurt.

Solow, R. 1956. "A Contribution to the Theory of Economic Growth." *Quarterly Journal of Economics* 70 (1): 65–94.

Swan, T. W. 1956. "Economic Growth and Capital Accumulation." *Economic Record* 32 (2): 334–61.

Tian, X., X. Zhang, Y. Zhou, and X. Yu. 2016. "Regional Income Inequality in China Revisited: A Perspective from Club Convergence." *Economic Modelling* 56 (August): 50–58.

UNCTAD (United Nations Conference on Trade and Development). 2019. *World Investment Report 2019: Special Economic Zones.* Geneva: United Nations.

Urata, S., and K. Yokota. 1994. "Trade Liberalization and Productivity Growth in Thailand." *Developing Economies* 32 (4): 444–56.

Von Lyncker, K., and R. Thoennessen. 2017. "Regional Club Convergence in the EU: Evidence from a Panel Data Analysis." *Empirical Economics* 52 (2): 525–53.

Wad, P. 2009. "The Automobile Industry of Southeast Asia: Malaysia and Thailand." *Journal of the Asia Pacific Economy* 14 (2): 172–93.

World Bank. 2005. *From Disintegration to Reintegration: Eastern Europe and the Former Soviet Union in International Trade.* Washington, DC: World Bank.

World Bank. 2017. *World Development Report 2017: Governance and the Law.* Washington, DC: World Bank.

World Bank. 2018a. *Global Economic Prospects: Broad-Based Upturn, but for How Long?* January. Washington, DC: World Bank.

World Bank. 2018b. *Piecing Together the Poverty Puzzle.* Washington, DC: World Bank.

World Bank. 2018c. "Thailand Economic Monitor: Beyond the Innovation Paradox." World Bank, Washington, DC.

World Bank. 2018d. *World Development Report 2018: Learning to Realize Education's Promise.* Washington, DC: World Bank.

World Bank. 2019a. *Global Economic Prospects: Darkening Skies.* January. Washington, DC: World Bank.

World Bank. 2019b. *Global Economic Prospects: Heightened Tensions, Subdued Investment.* June. Washington, DC: World Bank.

World Bank. 2019c. "Jobs and Economic Transformation (JET)—Drivers, Policy Implications and World Bank Group Support." World Bank, Washington, DC.

World Bank. 2020a. "Fading Promise: How to Rekindle Productivity Growth?" In *Global Economic Prospects: Slow Growth, Policy Challenges*, January. Washington, DC: World Bank.

World Bank. 2020b. "Pandemic, Recession: The Global Economy in Crisis." In *Global Economic Prospects*, June. Washington, DC: World Bank.

World Bank. 2020c. *World Development Report 2020: Trading for Development in the Age of Global Value Chains.* Washington, DC: World Bank.

PART II

Regional Dimensions of Productivity

Divergence in relative productivity levels and living standards is the dominant feature of modern economic history.

Lant Pritchett (1997)
Visiting Scholar, Blavatnik School of Government,
University of Oxford

In the search for the secrets of long-run economic growth, a high priority should go to rigorously defining TFP [total factor productivity], empirically dissecting it, and identifying the policies and institutions most conducive to its growth.

William Easterly and Ross Levine (2001)
Professor of Economics and Co-Director of the NYU
Development Research Institute, New York University

William H. Booth Chair in Banking and Finance, Haas School of
Business, University of California, Berkeley

CHAPTER 5
Regional Productivity: Trends, Explanations, and Policies

Even before the COVID-19 (coronavirus disease 2019) pandemic delivered a severe shock to emerging market and developing economies, a broad-based labor productivity growth slowdown had been under way since the 2007-09 global financial crisis. The slowdown was particularly severe in East Asia and Pacific, Europe and Central Asia, and Sub-Saharan Africa amid slowing investment growth, financial market disruptions, and a postcrisis commodity price slide. Productivity growth in Latin America and the Caribbean and the Middle East and North Africa, already sluggish before the global financial crisis, stagnated thereafter, reflecting political uncertainty, episodes of financial stress in major economies, falling commodity prices, and market distortions. In several regions, the productivity gap with advanced economies has widened. The shocks related to COVID-19 may exacerbate the productivity growth slowdown in emerging market and developing economies. A well-targeted reform agenda is needed to reignite productivity, in particular to address key obstacles, such as lack of economic diversification, weak governance and institutions, widespread informality, shortcomings in education, and lack of integration through trade.

Introduction

Even before the COVID-19 (coronavirus disease 2019) pandemic, emerging market and developing economies (EMDEs) had experienced a broad-based slowdown in labor productivity growth. In the years following the global financial crisis (GFC), the slowdown was most pronounced in regions that are closely integrated into advanced economy supply chains and those with a large number of commodity exporters. In several regions, the slowdown occurred in the context of already sluggish productivity growth. Weaker productivity growth has resulted in a widening productivity gap with advanced economies in some EMDE regions and made achieving the Sustainable Development Goals more difficult. A well-targeted reform agenda is needed to reignite productivity growth, especially in light of the possible persistent economic effects of COVID-19.

This chapter draws out differences in regional productivity trends and policy priorities.[1] Specifically, it addresses the following questions:

- How has the evolution of productivity varied across the six EMDE regions?

- What factors have been associated with productivity growth?

- What policies should be prioritized in order to boost productivity growth?

Note: This chapter was prepared by Dana Vorisek, Gene Kindberg-Hanlon, Rudi Steinbach, Temel Taskin, Ekaterine T. Vashakmadze, Collette M. Wheeler, and Lei Sandy Ye. Research assistance was provided by Yi Li, Vasiliki Papagianni, Shijie Shi, Kaltrina Temaj, and Xinyue Wang.

[1] For the purposes of this chapter, productivity is defined as labor productivity—that is, real GDP per worker (at 2010 prices and exchange rates).

Contributions

The chapter makes several contributions to the literature and policy debate on productivity at the regional level.

- *EMDE focus.* The chapter uses a larger, more diverse sample of EMDEs relative to previous studies and to other chapters in this book.[2] It starts with a discussion of the evolution and sources of, and bottlenecks to, productivity growth and challenges across the six EMDE regions.

- *Factor decomposition.* For each of the six regions, the chapter decomposes productivity growth into contributions from human capital, physical capital, and total factor productivity (TFP). For some regions, this analysis is extended to include natural capital.

- *Sectoral decomposition.* Using a nine-sector database, the chapter measures the within-sector and between-sector contributions to productivity growth in each of the six regions and calculates the contribution of each of the sectors to productivity growth, employment, and value added.

- *Policy options.* The chapter contains a detailed discussion of the policy options for boosting productivity growth, including some of the policies that may be effective in offsetting the adverse effects of the COVID-19 pandemic on productivity.

Main findings

The chapter offers several key findings.

- *Heterogeneous productivity slowdown across regions.* Although the post-GFC productivity slowdown affected all EMDE regions, it was most pronounced in East Asia and Pacific (EAP), Europe and Central Asia (ECA), and Sub-Saharan Africa (SSA) amid slowing investment growth, financial market disruptions, and a major commodity price slide. The recent productivity growth slowdown occurred in the context of already weak productivity growth in some regions. Productivity growth in Latin America and the Caribbean (LAC) and the Middle East and North Africa (MNA), already sluggish before the GFC, was stagnant in the post-GFC period, reflecting political uncertainty, episodes of financial stress in major economies, falling commodity prices, and ongoing market distortions.

- *Slowing pace of productivity catch-up to advanced economy levels.* As a result of the productivity growth slowdown during the post-GFC period, the pace of catch-up to advanced economy productivity levels slowed in most EMDE regions, and fell further behind advanced economy levels in LAC, MNA, and SSA. This means that in these regions it will now take longer to reach the level of productivity, or real

---

[2] To be as representative of each region as possible, this chapter uses a broader sample (129 EMDEs) than the other chapters (74 EMDEs), resulting in a shorter time horizon under consideration. Unless otherwise stated, regional productivity statistics are averages weighted by gross domestic product (GDP).

gross domestic product (GDP) per worker, observed in advanced economies, all else equal. In MNA, labor productivity averaged 40 percent of the advanced economy level in the post-GFC period, down from 49 percent before the GFC. In SSA, productivity relative to that in advanced economies dropped to 12 percent, from 13 percent before the GFC, and in LAC stalled at 22 percent.

- *Fading support from TFP growth.* Although the contribution of human capital to productivity growth was relatively stable, capital deepening contributed less to productivity growth in the post-GFC period compared to the pre-GFC period in all regions except SSA. All regions experienced a weaker contribution from TFP— especially LAC and SSA, where TFP contracted after the GFC.

- *Declining gains from sectoral reallocation.* Productivity gains from the reallocation of labor between sectors faded in four regions (EAP, ECA, LAC, and SSA) during the post-GFC period. LAC and SSA were particularly affected. Within-sector productivity enhancements also slowed. Only one region, EAP, achieved within-sector productivity gains during the post-GFC period.

- *Need for well-targeted policies to boost productivity growth.* A well-targeted reform agenda is needed to reignite productivity growth, especially in light of the possible persistent effects of COVID-19 on productivity. In particular, policies are needed to address key obstacles common across multiple regions, such as lack of economic diversification, weak governance and institutions, widespread informality, shortcomings in education, and lack of integration through trade.

Evolution of productivity across regions

Slowing labor productivity growth across EMDE regions. Before the GFC, EMDEs experienced an exceptional and broad-based surge in productivity, with productivity growing faster than the advanced economy average in more than 50 percent of economies in all regions except MNA (figure 5.1; Rodrik 2011; Roy, Kessler and Subramanian 2016). In the period following the GFC (2013-18), productivity growth slowed from pre-GFC (2003-08) rates in all EMDE regions. The COVID-19 pandemic may lead to a significant further setback in productivity growth.

The post-GFC slowdown was particularly steep in ECA, and to a lesser degree in EAP and SSA. In these regions, investment growth declined sharply from pre-GFC levels amid financial system disruptions associated with the euro area debt crisis (affecting ECA), policy-guided public investment slowdown in China (EAP), and the commodity price collapse of 2014-16 (ECA and SSA). However, in all three regions, there were important exceptions to the sharp slowdown. In EAP, the slowdown was concentrated in China whereas productivity and investment growth continued to be robust in other major economies, such as the Philippines and Vietnam. In ECA, the slowdown was muted in agricultural economies in Central Asia that shifted their economic ties toward China and in Central European economies that continued to integrate into Western European supply chains and benefited from investment financed

FIGURE 5.1 Evolution of regional productivity in EMDE regions

The slowdown in productivity growth following the GFC affected all regions but was particularly severe in EAP, ECA, and SSA. Productivity levels fell further behind advanced economy levels in some regions during the post-GFC period. In all regions, TFP contributed less to productivity growth in the post-GFC period.

A. Productivity growth

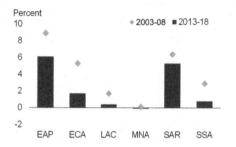

B. Share of economies with faster productivity growth than the average advanced economy

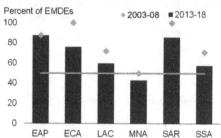

C. Rate of convergence to advanced economy productivity levels

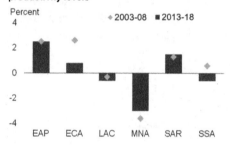

D. Productivity levels

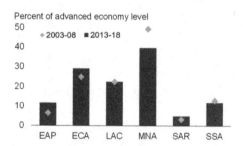

E. Factor contributions to regional productivity growth: EAP, ECA, and LAC

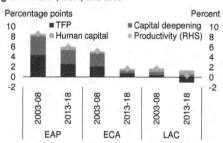

F. Factor contributions to regional productivity growth: MNA, SAR, and SSA

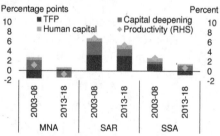

Sources: Barro and Lee (2015); The Conference Board; Groningen Growth Development Center database; Haver Analytics; International Labour Organization, ILOSTAT; International Monetary Fund; Organisation for Economic Co-operation and Development, Structural Analysis Database; Penn World Table; United Nations (Human Development Reports); Wittgenstein Centre for Demography and Global Human Capital; World KLEMS; World Bank (World Development Indicators).

Note: Productivity is defined as real GDP per worker (at 2010 market prices and exchange rates). Country group aggregates for a given year are calculated using constant 2010 U.S. dollar GDP weights. Data for multiyear spans show simple averages of the annual data. EMDEs = emerging market and developing economies; GFC = global financial crisis; TFP = total factor productivity; EAP = East Asia and Pacific; ECA = Europe and Central Asia; LAC = Latin America and the Caribbean; MNA = Middle East and North Africa; SAR = South Asia; SSA = Sub-Saharan Africa.

A.-D. Sample includes 35 advanced economies and 129 EMDEs.

B. Horizontal line indicates 50 percent.

C. Rate of convergence is calculated as the difference in productivity growth rates with the average advanced economy divided by the log difference in productivity levels with the average advanced economy.

E.F. Productivity growth is computed as log changes. Sample includes 93 EMDEs, including 8 in EAP, 21 in ECA, 20 in LAC, 12 in MNA, 2 in SAR, and 30 in SSA.

by European Union structural funds. In SSA, productivity growth accelerated in agricultural commodity exporters.

Productivity growth in LAC and MNA was sluggish even before the GFC, and slowed further in the post-GFC period as investment collapsed amid political uncertainty, episodes of financial stress in major economies, and falling commodity prices. The slowdown was mildest in MNA, where productivity in energy exporters was contracting in the pre-GFC period and productivity picked up moderately in energy importers. The South Asia (SAR) region experienced the second-mildest slowdown, in part because the region is the least open EMDE region to global trade and finance, has urbanized rapidly, and, as a commodity-importing region, benefited from the commodity price slide in 2014-16.

Slower convergence to advanced economy levels in most regions. As a result of the slide in productivity growth during the post-GFC period, the pace of catch-up to advanced economy productivity levels slowed in ECA, and productivity fell further behind advanced economy levels in LAC, MNA, and SSA. The COVID-19 crisis is likely to further weaken productivity growth as the crisis delivers a decisive blow to regions grappling with large domestic outbreaks (ECA, LAC, and SAR), the dual shock of the pandemic and collapse in industrial commodity prices (ECA, LAC, MNA, and SSA), and severe disruptions to international trade, particularly for those dependent on global value chains (EAP and ECA) and tourism (ECA and LAC; World Bank 2020a).

Among EMDE regions, productivity was highest in MNA (40 percent of the advanced economy average), followed by ECA and LAC (29 and 22 percent, respectively), and lowest in EAP and SSA (both 12 percent) and SAR (5 percent). However, there was wide disparity within some regions, especially MNA, ECA, and SSA. In some Gulf Cooperation Council (GCC) countries, for example, productivity was 60 percent or more of the advanced economy average in 2013-18, whereas, in heavily agricultural economies such as the Arab Republic of Egypt and Morocco, it amounted to less than 9 percent of the advanced economy average. Within ECA, deepening global trade integration and major reforms after the collapse of the Soviet Union helped raise the productivity level to the second highest among EMDE regions. Yet, whereas productivity in Poland was 36 percent of the advanced economy average in 2013-18, in some agricultural economies in Central Asia, it was just 3 or 4 percent. Low-income countries (LICs), most of which are in SSA, had productivity of less than 2 percent of the advanced economy average in 2013-18; however, Gabon, an oil exporter, reached 36 percent.

Progress on convergence in productivity levels is likely to be interrupted by the COVID-19 pandemic as attempts to limit the spread of the virus disrupt activity around the world. The pandemic is projected to push 71 million to 100 million people into extreme poverty in 2020, with a large share of the new extreme poor expected to be concentrated in SAR and SSA, the regions that already accounted for the majority of extreme poverty (Lakner et al. 2020).

Capital deepening vs. TFP growth, by region. Productivity growth can be decomposed into factor inputs (human and physical capital) and the effectiveness of their use (TFP; figure 5.1). In EAP and ECA, the post-GFC slowdown in productivity growth reflected both a slower pace of capital deepening and weaker TFP growth, albeit to varying degrees. Two-fifths of the slowdown in EAP reflected slowing capital deepening, and the remainder the result of slowing TFP growth. In EAP, a policy-guided move toward more sustainable growth in China and trade weakness weighed on investment and capital deepening. In ECA, about two-thirds of the productivity growth slowdown reflected a collapse in investment growth as conflict erupted in parts of the region, sanctions were imposed on the Russian Federation, political and economic shocks unfolded in Turkey, financial systems transformed after the euro area debt crisis, and the commodity price collapse hit commodity exporters (Arteta and Kasyanenko 2019).

The slowdown in labor productivity was the least pronounced in MNA and SAR. In SAR, TFP continued growing at roughly the pre-GFC pace, but capital deepening slowed sharply. Persistent post-GFC investment weakness—in part due to disruptive policy changes and a slowing pace of foreign direct investment (FDI) inflows—was offset by productivity-enhancing sectoral reallocation, as labor moved out of agriculture into more productive sectors amid rapid urbanization. In MNA, TFP stabilized after earlier contractions, whereas capital deepening reversed. The oil price collapse of 2014-16 weighed heavily on investment in oil exporters, and political tensions discouraged investment in commodity importers. However, macroeconomic stabilization and structural reform efforts helped stem pre-GFC contractions in TFP.

Conversely, in LAC and SSA, TFP contracted during the post-GFC period. In major LAC economies, continued credit extension or intensifying economic distortions (such as trade restrictions and price controls) allowed unproductive firms to survive to a greater extent than before the GFC. In SSA, the contraction in TFP was partly offset by accelerating capital deepening as a number of countries invested heavily in public infrastructure. Across EMDE regions, the COVID-19 pandemic is likely to erode investment prospects further amid substantial uncertainty and, for energy exporters, the unprecedented collapse in oil demand and prices (IEA 2020; World Bank 2020a).

Sources of, and bottlenecks to, regional productivity growth

Various factors have weighed on productivity growth since the GFC, but their relative roles differ across regions. In most regions, productivity gains from reallocation from low-productivity (usually agriculture) sectors to high-productivity sectors slowed, as did the pace of improvement in various aspects of the supporting environment for productivity growth. Productivity levels in all regions remained less than half of those in advanced economies, providing significant scope for faster productivity growth. Significant bottlenecks to productivity convergence remain, many of which differ across regions and are expected to be exacerbated by the COVID-19 pandemic.

Sectoral reallocation

Declining gains from sectoral reallocation. Switching employment from low-productivity sectors to sectors with above-average productivity levels supported between-sector productivity growth during the pre-GFC period in all regions except MNA, especially in EAP, ECA, and SSA (figure 5.2). In SSA, the transition of employment between sectors accounted for nearly three-quarters of productivity growth in the median economy during 2003-08 (Diao, McMillan, and Rodrik 2017).

After the GFC, productivity gains from sectoral reallocation faded in all regions except MNA. In commodity-reliant regions such as LAC and SSA, this in part reflected lower absorption of labor by services and construction sectors as real income losses in resource sectors spilled over into weaker demand. In EAP, it reflected slowing labor reallocation as overcapacity was gradually unwound. In ECA, high-productivity manufacturing, financial, and mining sectors suffered during the euro area debt crisis and the post-GFC commodity price collapse. In SAR, however, the movement of labor out of low-productivity agriculture into more productive sectors accelerated as rapid urbanization continued and strong consumption growth fueled employment in higher-productivity trade services. At the same time, within-sector productivity enhancements also slowed after the GFC. Only one region, EAP, achieved within-sector productivity gains during the post-GFC period.

Looking ahead, further sectoral reallocation continues to have the potential to lift productivity growth in SAR and SSA, where low-productivity agriculture accounts for about 50 percent of employment but less than 20 percent of output. Substantial gaps in productivity between sectors remain, offering the potential for further aggregate productivity gains from resource reallocation between sectors. In the short term, however, the mobility restrictions implemented as part of the policy response to COVID-19 may hinder sectoral reallocation.

Bottlenecks to productivity growth

Several bottlenecks to higher productivity are shared, to varying degrees, by multiple EMDE regions. These include commodity reliance, widespread informality, poor education, and weak governance. Other bottlenecks are more region-specific.

Lack of diversification. In LAC, MNA, and SSA, commodities account for over 20 percent of exports on average. In ECA, they account for 30 percent of exports, because in Russia about 60 percent of exports are (mostly energy) commodities. Widespread subsistence agriculture in SSA holds back productivity in SSA's large agricultural sector. Economies that are highly reliant on a narrow range of commodity exports can also suffer from misallocation and procyclical trends for productivity growth (Frankel 2010). Conversely, producing across a broad range of sectors can insulate economies from external shocks and can facilitate knowledge transfer to strengthen productivity (Kraay, Soloaga, and Tybout 2002; Schor 2004). In EAP, for example, high pre-GFC productivity growth was spurred by rapid integration into global supply chains and

FIGURE 5.2 Sectoral contributions to regional productivity growth in EMDE regions

Since the global financial crisis, productivity gains from reallocation of labor between sectors have faded in most regions. In SAR and SSA, about half of employment is in the agricultural sector, which accounts for less than one-fifth of output, reflecting low productivity in this sector. The wide dispersion of sectoral productivity levels within regions demonstrates the importance of introducing measures to reduce misallocation and boost productivity in the weakest sectors.

A. Within- and between-sector contributions to regional productivity growth: EAP, ECA, and LAC

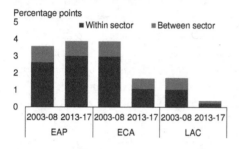

B. Within- and between-sector contributions to regional productivity growth: MNA, SAR, and SSA

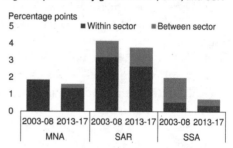

C. Composition of employment, by sector, 2017

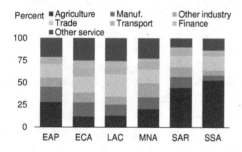

D. Composition of value added, by sector, 2017

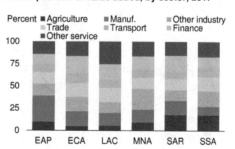

E. Sectoral contribution to aggregate productivity growth, 2013-17

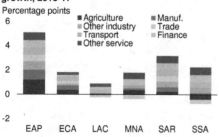

F. Sectoral productivity levels disparity within regions, 2017

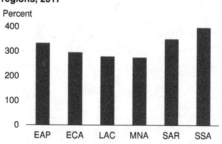

Sources: Asia Productivity Organization, Productivity Database; Expanded African Sector Database; Groningen Growth Development Center Database; Haver Analytics; International Labour Organization, ILOSTAT; Organisation for Economic Co-operation and Development, Structural Analysis Database; United Nations; World KLEMS; World Bank.

Note: Sample includes 69 EMDEs, of which 9 are in EAP, 11 in ECA, 17 in LAC, 6 in MNA, 4 in SAR, and 22 in SSA. EMDEs = emerging market and developing economies; EAP = East Asia and Pacific; ECA = Europe and Central Asia; LAC = Latin America and the Caribbean; MNA = Middle East and North Africa; SAR = South Asia; SSA = Sub-Saharan Africa.

A.B. Median contribution for each region. "Within-sector" shows the contribution of initial real value added-weighted productivity growth rate of each sector, and "between sector" shows the contribution arising from changes in sectoral employment shares.

C-E. "Other industry" includes mining, utilities, and construction; "other service" includes government and personal services. "Manuf." indicates manufacturing.

E. Median contribution to productivity growth.

F. Range of (regional averages of) sector-specific productivity levels relative to advanced economy average productivity. The range for MNA excludes sectoral productivity for mining, which is more than 1,000 percent of the advanced economy average.

inflows of FDI, which enabled a substantial increase in the range and sophistication of production in the region (Wei and Liu 2006). The COVID-19 pandemic and subsequent plunge in oil prices present an opportunity for the revival of diversification efforts to reduce reliance on the energy sector and spur private sector development, which could yield productivity gains because employment in energy exporters tends to be concentrated in lower-productivity jobs (OECD 2020a; World Bank 2020a).[3]

Weak governance and institutions. In most EMDE regions, governance and business climates are less favorable than in advanced economies. The most business-friendly climates are in LAC, SAR, and SSA, but also in pockets of ECA (Central Asia and Eastern Europe). In all regions, a large majority of EMDEs falls below the global average for tackling corruption. Poor institutions have been associated with weak firm productivity and inefficient government investment in productivity-augmenting infrastructure (Cirera, Fattal-Jaef, and Maemir 2020).

Informality. Informality is pervasive in EMDEs, although there are large differences in the productivity of informal sectors across regions. Across EMDE regions, the informal sector accounts for 22-40 percent of official GDP, but it accounts for a much wider range of employment (22-62 percent), in part reflecting heterogeneity in productivity (World Bank 2019a). Informal firms are less productive than those in the formal sector and, by competing on more favorable terms, can deter investment and erode the productivity of formal firms (Amin, Ohnsorge, and Okou 2019). Moreover, several of the key vulnerabilities linked to informality, such as lack of access to financial systems, weak social safety nets, and deficient medical resources, have amplified the economic shock of COVID-19 (World Bank 2020a). These aspects may make an acceleration of productivity growth more challenging in EMDEs with high informality.

Limited human capital. With schools closed in an unprecedented number of countries for a prolonged period as part of the policy response to COVID-19, learning progress is expected to be set back, while dropout rates are likely to rise, and students may face adverse effects on their lifetime education achievement and earnings (Armitage and Nellumns 2020; Azevedo et al. 2020; Burgess and Sievertsen 2020; Wang et al. 2020; World Bank 2020b). Disruptions to school feeding programs could also lower long-term productivity, because malnutrition early in life can permanently impair learning abilities. The education shocks related to the pandemic build on existing vulnerabilities in education in EMDEs. In EAP and ECA, expected years of schooling for children are now within one year of advanced economies on average, but SAR and SSA lag more than three years behind the advanced economy average (figure 5.3). Even where years of schooling are on par with advanced economies, education can be ineffective when

---

[3] Following the 2014-16 oil price plunge, many energy exporters embarked on efforts to boost macroeconomic resilience and diversify their economies by putting in place measures that reduce labor market rigidities (Oman, Qatar, and Saudi Arabia), support foreign and private investment (Saudi Arabia), expand infrastructure investment (Malaysia), improve the business environment (Algeria, Brunei Darussalam, the GCC countries, Kazakhstan, Nigeria, and Russia), expand deeper trade integration within the Eurasian Economic Union (Russia), and increase strategic investment plans in renewables energy (Azerbaijan and the GCC countries). See World Bank (2020a) for further details.

FIGURE 5.3 **Potential bottlenecks to productivity growth in EMDE regions**

Several bottlenecks to higher productivity are shared, to varying degrees, by EMDE regions. They include undiversified economies, weak governance, widespread informality, poor learning outcomes, low trade and financial openness, and poor business environments.

A. Share of commodities in total exports, 2013-18

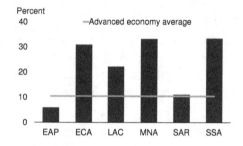

B. Government effectiveness, 2013-18

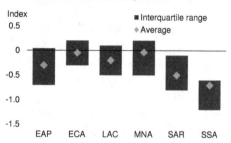

C. Informality, 2016

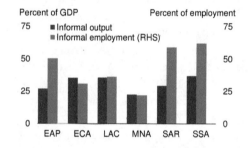

D. Educational attainment, 2017

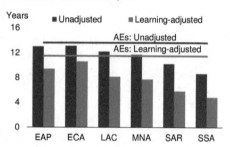

E. Trade and financial openness, 2013-18

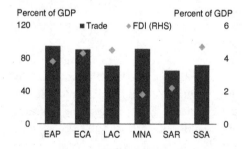

F. Business climate, 2020

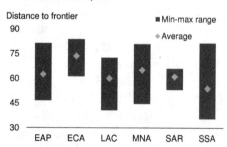

Sources: United Nations; World Bank (Doing Business, Human Capital Project, World Development Indicators, Worldwide Government Indicators).

Note: AEs = advanced economies; DGE = dynamic general equilibrium (model); EMDEs = emerging market and developing economies; FDI = foreign direct investment; EAP = East Asia and Pacific; ECA = Europe and Central Asia; LAC = Latin America and the Caribbean; MNA = Middle East and North Africa; SAR = South Asia; SSA = Sub-Saharan Africa.

A. Exports of metals, agricultural and energy products in percent of total exports. GDP-weighted average for each region for each year. Simple average during 2013-18.

B. The government effectiveness index captures perceptions of the quality of public services, quality of the civil service and the degree of its independence from political pressures, quality of policy formation and implementation, and credibility of the government's commitment to such policies. Index is on a scale of -2.5 (weak) to 2.5 (strong).

C. Average informal output (DGE-based estimates, percent of official GDP) and employment estimate (self-employment, percent of total employment) in each region. Based on World Bank (2019a).

D. Expected years of schooling and learning-adjusted years of schooling from the World Bank's Human Capital Project. Learning-adjusted years of schooling use harmonized cross-country test scores to adjust average years of schooling.

E. Unweighted average of trade (exports plus imports) in percent of GDP and net foreign direct investment inflows in percent of GDP.

F. Unweighted average distance to frontier measure of the ease of doing business score from the 2020 Doing Business Indicators. A higher value indicates a business climate that is closer to best practices.

learning outcomes are poor (World Bank 2018a). In learning-adjusted terms, which controls for the quality of education in addition to years of attainment, SAR and SSA lag substantially (six or more learning-adjusted years) behind advanced economies. Higher-skilled and better-educated labor forces tend to adopt new technologies, including new information and communication and manufacturing technologies, more readily and more effectively (World Bank 2019b).

Trade integration. LAC, SAR, and SSA could receive a productivity boost from more participation in global trade, particularly through deeper integration into global value chains (GVCs). EAP, meanwhile, faces maturing supply chains and has the challenge of maintaining the productivity gains it achieved through rapid trade integration in the 2000s. Regions deeply integrated into GVCs (EAP and ECA) may also experience weaker productivity should companies reassess the existing production networks, or even re-shore production, in the context of COVID-19 (Freund 2020; World Bank 2020a).

East Asia and Pacific

Before the COVID-19 pandemic, EAP had the fastest productivity growth of the six regions, averaging 6.1 percent a year in 2013-18. Nevertheless, productivity levels remain below the EMDE average in most EAP economies. Factor reallocation toward more productive sectors, high levels of investment, and trade integration promoted above-average productivity growth. Most of these drivers are expected to become less favorable in the future, however, and the pandemic could further weaken investment and the supply chain linkages that have been an important conduit for productivity gains in the region over the past decade. A comprehensive set of reforms to liberalize services sectors, improve corporate management, level the playing field for private firms, enhance human capital, facilitate urban development, foster innovation, and build resilience against future unexpected shocks is needed to support robust productivity growth.

Evolution of regional productivity

Rapid productivity growth. Labor productivity growth in EAP rose from an average of 4.3 percent a year in the 1980s to 6.3 percent in the 1990s and 8.9 percent in 2003-08 (figures 5.4 and 5.5).[4] Although productivity growth in the region remained the highest of the six EMDE regions, it slowed decisively following the GFC, averaging 6.1 percent per year during 2013-18.[5] The post-GFC productivity growth slowdown was also

---

[4] Productivity data are available for 16 EAP countries: Cambodia, China, Fiji, Indonesia, Lao People's Democratic Republic, Malaysia, Mongolia, Myanmar, Papua New Guinea, the Philippines, Samoa, the Solomon Islands, Thailand, Tonga, Vanuatu, and Vietnam. EAP averages are heavily influenced by China, which accounts for 80 percent of EAP output in 2013-18. That said, even the median productivity level in EAP is below that of the median EMDE region.

[5] For studies using country-level data, see APO (2018); IMF (2006, 2017); and World Bank (2018b, 2019a). For studies using firm-level data, see Di Mauro et al. (2018); de Nicola, Kehayova, and Nguyen (2018); OECD (2016); and World Bank and DRCSC (2019). For studies of how product and labor market reforms have increased output and productivity, see Adler et al. (2017); Bouis, Duval, and Eugster (2016); Chen (2002); Nicoletti and Scarpetta (2005); and Timmer and Szirmai (2000).

FIGURE 5.4 Productivity in EAP in regional comparison

EAP remains the region with the fastest productivity growth, at 6.1 percent a year in 2013-18, notwithstanding the second-largest post-GFC slowdown among EMDE regions. Nevertheless, productivity levels in most EAP economies remain below the EMDE average.

A. Productivity growth relative to other EMDE regions

B. Productivity levels and rate of productivity convergence

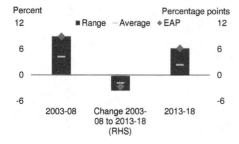
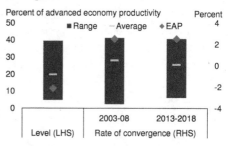

Sources: The Conference Board; Penn World Table; World Bank (World Development Indicators).
Note: Productivity is defined as real GDP per worker (at 2010 market prices and exchange rates). Country group aggregates for a given year are calculated using constant 2010 U.S. dollar GDP weights. Data for multiyear spans show simple averages of the annual data. EMDEs = emerging market and developing economies; GFC = global financial crisis; EAP = East Asia and Pacific; ECA = Europe and Central Asia; LAC = Latin America and the Caribbean; MNA = Middle East and North Africa; SAR = South Asia; SSA = Sub-Saharan Africa.
A. Blue bars show the range of average productivity across the six EMDE regions. Yellow dashes denote the average of the six EMDE regional aggregates. Red diamonds denote simple average of EAP economies. Sample includes 16 EAP economies and 129 EMDEs.
B. Rate of convergence is calculated as the difference in productivity growth rates over the log difference in productivity levels between EAP and advanced economies. Blue bars and yellow dashes show the range and average of the six EMDE regional aggregates. "Level" of productivity refers to the GDP-weighted average of regional productivity as a share of the average advanced economy during 2013-18. LHS refers to left-hand side. RHS refers to right-hand side. Sample includes 16 EAP economies, 129 EMDEs, and 35 advanced economies.

accounted for largely by China, in particular that country's policy-guided move toward more sustainable growth after a period of exceptionally rapid expansion of investment and exports. Productivity growth in the region's other major economies was broadly stable. About two-thirds of EAP economies in 2013-18 were still experiencing labor productivity growth above their long-run average.

Within-region productivity growth trends. Relative to other EAP countries, China had particularly fast productivity growth during the post-GFC period, followed by several large Association of Southeast Asian Nations (ASEAN) economies, including Vietnam. Several of these countries were among the 10 percent of EMDE economies with the fastest productivity growth in the period. They benefited from improvements in human capital and trade, and investment openness, technology transfer and adaptation, high investment rates, and an industrial base that was rapidly becoming more sophisticated (Andrews, Criscuolo, and Gal 2015). Productivity growth was slowest among EAP economies in some Pacific Islands, partly reflecting their exposure to periodic natural disasters and their relatively undiversified economies. Still, productivity growth was more homogeneous within EAP than within other EMDE regions, possibly reflecting particularly close regional integration, including through regional supply chains.

Low productivity levels. Notwithstanding rapid productivity growth, average productivity levels in EAP (12 percent of the advanced economy average in 2013-18),

FIGURE 5.5 **Evolution of productivity in EAP**

The post-GFC slowdown in EAP's productivity growth reflects slowing TFP growth, especially in China. Slowing TFP growth accounted for two-thirds of the post-GFC slowdown in the region's labor productivity growth, compared to about half in all EMDEs. Notwithstanding still rapid productivity growth, average productivity levels in EAP remain below the EMDE average.

A. Productivity growth

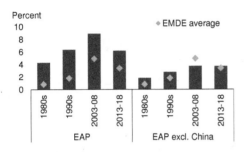

B. Economies with 2013-18 average productivity growth below long-run and pre-GFC averages

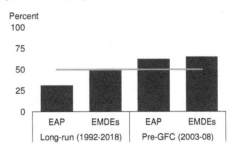

C. Factor contributions to productivity growth

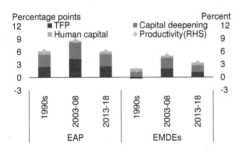

D. Factor contributions to productivity growth, by subregions

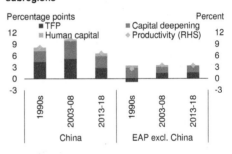

E. Productivity levels relative to advanced economy average

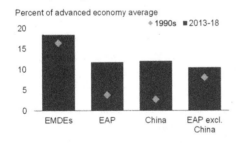

F. Labor force growth

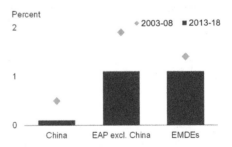

Sources: Barro and Lee (2015); Haver Analytics; International Labour Organization, ILOSTAT; International Monetary Fund; Penn World Table; United Nations; Wittgenstein Centre for Demography and Global Human Capital; World Bank (World Development Indicators).

Note: EAP = East Asia and Pacific; EMDEs = emerging market and developing economies; GFC = global financial crisis; TFP = total factor productivity.

A.-E. Productivity is defined as real GDP per worker (at 2010 market prices and exchange rates). Country group aggregates for a given year are calculated using constant 2010 U.S. dollar GDP weights. Data for multiyear spans show simple averages of the annual data.

A.B. Sample includes 16 EAP economies and 129 EMDEs.

B. Orange line denotes 50 percent.

C.D. Productivity growth is computed as log changes. Sample includes 8 EAP economies and 93 EMDEs.

E. Sample includes 16 EAP economies, 129 EMDEs, and 35 advanced economies.

including China, remained below the EMDE average of 18 percent of the advanced economy average (APO 2018; Di Mauro et al. 2018). Malaysia, with the highest productivity level in EAP (24 percent of the post-GFC advanced economy average), has benefited from several decades of sustained high growth rates reflecting its diversified production and export base and sound macroeconomic policies (Munoz et al. 2016).

Labor productivity convergence. Whereas convergence of productivity toward advanced economy levels in most other EMDE regions slowed following the GFC, it remained robust in EAP. The sustained productivity growth in EAP was supported by macroeconomic stability, strong fundamentals, still high investment rates, and diversified and competitive production bases in the region's major economies. About two-fifths of economies in the region are still on course to halve their productivity gap relative to advanced economy averages over the next 40 years, assuming regional productivity growth swiftly recovers from the fallout of the pandemic and is sustained around its post-GFC rates. Historically, countries in the region that have successfully converged, such as Singapore and the Republic of Korea, experienced high and sustained productivity growth differentials relative to established advanced economies over several decades.

Sources of productivity growth

Decomposing productivity growth into factor accumulation (human and physical capital) and increases in the efficiency of factor use (TFP) shows that slowing TFP growth accounted for two-thirds of the post-GFC slowdown in labor productivity growth in EAP, compared to about half in the average EMDE. This followed a decade of surging TFP growth in EAP, when China's accession to the World Trade Organization in 2001 was followed by rapid trade integration, large FDI inflows into the region, and rapid technological adaptation (Mason and Shetty 2019; Tuan, Ng, and Zhao 2009; Xu and Sheng 2012). These reforms were accompanied by improvements in macroeconomic policies, strengthening institutions, and higher investment in infrastructure and human capital in several countries (China, Indonesia, Malaysia, the Philippines and Vietnam). The post-GFC slowdown in the region's TFP growth partly reflected a moderation in the pace of global integration (Ruta, Constantinescu, and Mattoo 2017). About another one-third of the slowdown in labor productivity growth in EAP was accounted for by weaker investment, which subsided in the immediate wake of the crisis, especially in response to policy-guided moderation in China (Kose and Ohnsorge 2019).

The slowdown in EAP productivity growth was not universal across the region. Whereas TFP growth and capital deepening slowed in China between 2003-08 and 2013-18 amid a policy-guided investment slowdown, it accelerated elsewhere, especially in some ASEAN countries (the Philippines and Vietnam), reflecting high rates of investment partly financed by significant FDI inflows. The decline in China's TFP growth was attributed to both the slowdown in investment growth and its associated embodied technical progress, as well as to fading gains from global trade integration and institutional reforms (Subramanian and Kessler 2013; World Bank 2019a; and World Bank and DRCSC 2014).

Productivity growth through sectoral reallocation. Strong pre-GFC productivity growth in EAP was supported by policies that encouraged resource reallocation from low- to high-productivity sectors, as well as within-sector productivity growth (IMF 2006). During the post-GFC period, as in other EMDE regions, EAP gains from factor reallocation toward more productive sectors slowed sharply, as the pace of urbanization decelerated (in most cases well before reaching average levels for Organisation for Economic Co-operation and Development countries) and overcapacity in China weighed on the efficiency of investment. During 2013-17, sectoral reallocation accounted for less than one-quarter of EAP productivity growth, slightly less than in 2003-08 (figure 5.6).

In East Asia, structural transformation, in the form of the movement of people and capital from agriculture to manufacturing and services, was a key driver of productivity growth as countries rose from low- to middle-income status. Once countries reached middle-income levels, within-sector productivity gains became a more important driver of productivity growth and cross-sectoral shifts less important (de Nicola, Kehayova, and Nguyen 2018; Mason and Shetty 2019). However, there was considerable heterogeneity across the region. In recent years, sectoral reallocation stalled in Thailand, proceeded slowly in Malaysia, and continued apace in Indonesia, the Philippines, and Vietnam (World Bank 2018c). In Vietnam, intersectoral reallocation continued to account for approximately half of labor productivity growth, with no sign of deceleration (World Bank and MPIV 2016).

Productivity growth in the manufacturing sector was a major driving force behind overall productivity growth in most EAP countries (figure 5.6; APO 2018). Since the 2000s, the contribution of services to productivity growth increased, albeit from a low base, as innovations in this sector took hold (APO 2018; ADB 2019; Cirera and Maloney 2017; Kinda 2019). For example, e-commerce accelerated sharply in China, with e-commerce firms having 30 percent higher productivity, as well as being more export-oriented than other firms (Kinda 2019). Recent advances in information and communication technology bolstered productivity growth in wholesale and retail trade, hotels, and restaurants; transport, storage, and communications; and finance, real estate, and business activities. It is likely that the growth in value added generated by intangible services is underestimated to the extent such services are incorporated in the production of manufactured goods (ADB 2019).

In contrast to other EMDE regions, EAP achieved within-sector productivity gains in the post-GFC period. China was an exception: there, within-sector productivity growth slowed amid increased overcapacity, declining firm dynamism, and increasing financial constraints, including as a result of rising leverage (IMF 2018a). This was notwithstanding considerable in-house research and development (R&D) and domestic and foreign technology transfers (Hu, Jefferson, and Jinchang 2005).

Drivers of productivity. Fundamental drivers of productivity have improved more rapidly in EAP than in the average EMDE (figure 5.7). Favorable initial conditions, such as strong human capital, allowed China and Vietnam to achieve higher productivity

FIGURE 5.6 Factors underlying productivity growth in EAP

Factor reallocation toward more productive sectors, high investment, trade integration with product upgrading, and rapid innovation have all contributed to productivity growth in EAP that is above the average for EMDEs. Productivity growth in the manufacturing sector has been a driving force behind overall productivity growth in most EAP countries.

A. Within- and between-sector contributions to regional productivity growth

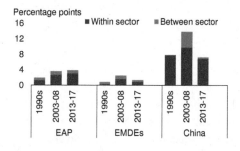

B. Sectoral productivity growth, 2017

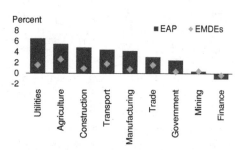

C. Sectoral contribution to aggregate productivity growth

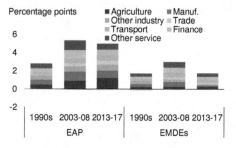

D. Composition of value added, by sector

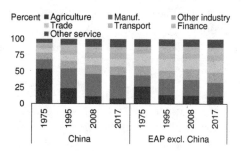

Sources: Asian Productivity Organization, Productivity Database; Expanded African Sector Database; Groningen Growth Development Center Database; Haver Analytics; International Labour Organization, ILOSTAT; Organisation for Economic Co-operation and Development, Structural Analysis Database; United Nations; World Bank; World KLEMS.
Note: Productivity is defined as real GDP per worker (at 2010 market prices and exchange rates). Medians of country-specific contributions. Sample includes 69 EMDEs, of which 9 are EAP economies. EAP = East Asia and Pacific; EMDEs = emerging market and developing economies.
A. Within-sector contribution shows the contribution to overall productivity growth of initial real value added-weighted sectoral productivity growth; between-sector contribution shows the contribution of intersectoral changes in employment shares.
C.D. "Other industry" includes mining, utilities, and construction; "other service" includes government and personal services. "Manuf." indicates manufacturing.
D. Values are calculated using constant U.S. dollars at constant 2010 market exchange rates.

growth than other economies in the region. Productivity in EAP economies also benefited from high investment (IMF 2006; World Bank 2019c). Other supporting factors were trade integration, including through global supply chains; foreign investment, which supported rapid technology adoption from abroad; and progress toward more complex products with higher value added (World Bank 2019d).[6]

---

[6] In EAP, 35 percent of firms are large (compared with 25 percent in the average EMDE) and 16 percent are exporters (compared with 12 percent). Exporting firms tend to have higher productivity because they are exposed to frontier knowledge and best managerial practices that help them make better decisions regarding investment, input selection, and production processes (Hallward-Driemeier, Iarossi, and Sokoloff 2002).

FIGURE 5.7 **Drivers of productivity growth in EAP**

Fundamental drivers of productivity have improved more rapidly in EAP than in the average EMDE. Compared to many other EMDEs, productivity growth in EAP economies benefited from high investment and trade integration.

A. Index of productivity drivers

B. Drivers of productivity growth, 2017

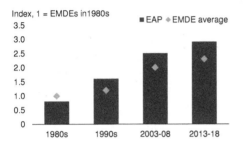

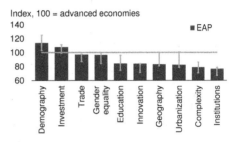

Sources: Freedom House; Haver Analytics; International Country Risk Guide (ICRG); Organisation for Economic Co-operation and Development; Observatory of Economic Complexity; Penn World Table; United Nations Educational, Scientific, and Cultural Organization (Institute for Statistics); United Nations Population Prospects; World Integrated Trade Solution; World Bank (Doing Business, Enterprise Surveys, and Global Financial Development Database).

Note: EAP = East Asia and Pacific; EMDEs = emerging market and developing economies.

A. For each country, index is a weighted average of the normalized value of each driver of productivity. Refer to chapter 2 for weights. Drivers include the ICRG rule of law index, patents per capita, nontropical share of land area, investment as percent of GDP, ratio of female average years of education to male average years, share of population in urban area, Economic Complexity Index, years of schooling, share of working-age population, and inflation. Regional and EMDE indexes are GDP-weighted averages. Sample includes 7 EAP economies and 54 EMDEs.

B. Unweighted average levels of drivers normalized as an average of advanced economies as 100 and standard deviation of 10. Blue bars represent average within EAP economies. Orange whiskers represent the range of the average drivers for the six EMDE regions. Horizontal line indicates 100. Variables are defined as follows: Education = years of education, Urbanization = share of population living in urban areas, Investment = investment as share of GDP, Institutions = government effectiveness, Complexity = Economic Complexity Index of Hidalgo and Hausmann (2009), Gender equality = share of years of schooling for females to males, Demography = share of population under age 14, Innovation = log patents per capita, and Trade = (exports+imports)/GDP. Sample includes 7-16 EAP economies and 65-127 EMDEs, depending on the driver, and 32 advanced economies.

Macroeconomic stability encouraged investment, while trade and investment openness and R&D above the EMDE average supported innovation (Kim and Loayza 2019).

Growth of the drivers most strongly associated with productivity growth, including labor force growth and investment, slowed in EAP after 2008. The slowdown in investment growth in the largest EAP economies was policy-led and aimed at moderating credit expansion. In addition, earlier favorable demographic trends in China, Thailand, and Vietnam have waned as populations have started to age. Other factors that previously helped to spur EAP productivity growth have also deteriorated since the GFC. For example, the trend toward broadening production to a more diverse range of products at more upstream stages of the value chain slowed partly because of a stagnation in GVCs after 2008 (World Bank 2019c).

Prospects for productivity growth. Productivity gaps were still substantial between advanced economies and EAP countries in 2018, suggesting potential for further significant productivity gains. However, although EAP productivity growth remained solid in 2013-18 relative to long-run historical rates, it is likely to soften further in the future as some fundamental drivers of productivity become less favorable (figure 5.8).

FIGURE 5.8 **Prospects for productivity growth in EAP**

Being less able to rely on export growth than in the past, EAP countries need to unleash domestic sources of productivity growth. Priority areas include reforms to enhance human capital, address informality, foster innovation, and facilitate urban development. In addition, achieving long-term sustainable development calls for debt overhangs to be addressed and excessive leverage to be avoided.

A. Contribution of export growth to GDP growth

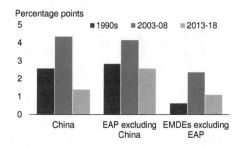

B. Human capital index and productivity growth

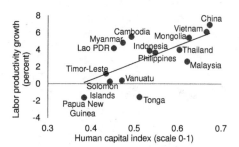

C. Informality

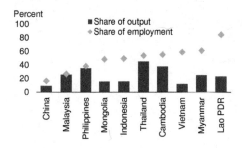

D. Research and development expenditure

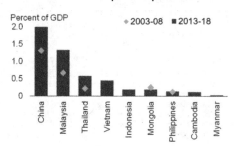

E. Urbanization

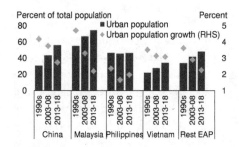

F. Debt and labor productivity

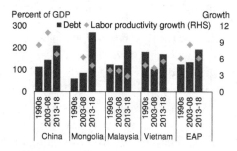

Sources: Elgin et al. (forthcoming); Haver Analytics; World Bank (Human Capital Project, World Development Indicators).

Note: EAP = East Asia and Pacific; EMDEs = emerging market and developing economies.

A.B.F. Productivity is defined as real GDP per worker (at 2010 market prices and exchange rates).

A. Exports include goods and nonfactor services.

B. The Human Capital Index calculates the contributions of health and education to worker productivity. The final index score ranges from zero to one and measures the productivity as a future worker of a child born today relative to the benchmark of a child with full health care and complete education. Human Capital Index data are for 2017. Labor productivity growth data are for 2018.

C. Blue bars show the share of informal output in total output based on the dynamic general equilibrium (DGE) model. The diamonds show the share of informal employment in total employment.

E. Urbanization levels denote share of urban population in total population.

F. Total debt comprises bank credit to households, nonfinancial corporations, and general government debt (broad definition).

Thus, trade and investment growth are expected to continue to ease in an environment of weakening global demand, heightened global policy uncertainty, and a continued policy-guided slowdown in investment growth in China. Slowing global trade growth may also lower incentives to innovate or upgrade products and processes (World Bank 2019c). Structural declines in working-age populations in major economies will also weaken growth momentum (World Bank 2016a, 2018a). In addition, the pandemic will likely further slow productivity growth in the region by weakening investment and supply chain linkages (World Bank 2020a). The negative impact is expected to be broad-based and will add to the long-term slowdown from deteriorating demographic and other structural trends (World Bank 2020a).

Policy options

A comprehensive set of policy efforts can help countries in EAP swiftly recover from the pandemic fallout and accelerate their productivity growth and their income convergence with advanced economies. These policies fall into four broad categories: improving factors of production, including through human capital development; encouraging productivity at the firm level, including by leveling the playing field for private relative to state-owned firms and improving corporate governance; removing obstacles to between-sector reallocation, including through continued urban development; and fostering a productivity-friendly business environment. Specific policies within these four broad categories depend on country-specific circumstances (Kim and Loayza 2017; Munoz et al. 2016; World Bank 2018d).

Improving factors of production

Improve public investment. A range of policy efforts is needed to lift investment, especially in countries with particularly large investment needs (Cambodia, Indonesia, the Lao People's Democratic Republic, and, Myanmar; World Bank 2018a). Access to adequate infrastructure in EAP remains fragmented, particularly in water and sanitation and transport, and in several lower-middle-income economies (World Bank 2018a). In these countries, strengthening the efficiency of public investment management and fiscal transparency could boost productive public investment (World Bank 2018d).

Remove obstacles to private investment. Private investment could be spurred by higher FDI inflows that could offer knowledge and technology transfers, deeper regional trade integration, and better institutional environments (World Bank 2018d, 2019c). In China, private investment could be lifted by improved market access, increased competition, policies that provide a more level playing field relative to state-owned enterprises (SOEs), greater financial discipline, stronger intellectual property rights, lower barriers to entry, and a gradual opening of China's financial system to international investors (World Bank 2018a, 2018e; World Bank and DRCSC 2019). Other major economies in the region, including Indonesia, Malaysia, Thailand, and Vietnam, could boost private investment by increasing private sector participation in major infrastructure projects and by changing their funding policies to provide more opportunities for international and domestic private investors.

Increase human capital. Children born in EAP today are expected, by age 18, to be only 53 percent as productive as they would be in the presence of best practices in education and health (World Bank 2019c). Several economies, such as Cambodia and Lao PDR, have below-average educational attainment. Reforms that augment human capital through strengthening the quality and flexibility of education systems and improving education outcomes are critical to achieving and sustaining high productivity growth.

Boosting firm productivity

Reduce market distortions, and level the playing field for private firms. A gradual transfer from public to private firm ownership in many cases, greater involvement of international firms, and reforms to lower entry costs and encourage fair competition, including in trade and innovation, can help level the playing field for private firms and SOEs. Curbing preferential lending agreements with SOEs and easing the access of private firms to long-term funding can improve the allocative efficiency of capital and raise productivity. Greater product market competition would spur innovation (Cusolito and Maloney 2018).

Encourage innovation. Effective policies to promote innovation begin with strengthening managerial and organizational practices (Cirera and Maloney 2017). Strengthening the effectiveness of R&D spending and measures to raise productivity in the services sectors are also key (World Bank 2016b). Fiscal incentives for R&D are in place in some EAP countries (China and Malaysia), but in many others R&D spending is small relative to GDP (figure 5.8). Strengthening intellectual property rights while avoiding undue limitations on competition could encourage R&D. These reforms could be complemented by efforts to facilitate moving up the value chain through innovation, especially in R&D-intensive sectors, and enabling new business processes, including through digitization and energy efficiency.

Address informality. The share of informal output in the EAP region is below the EMDE average, whereas the share of informal employment is above average (World Bank 2019a). Within the region, informality is higher in lower-income countries. However, even higher-income economies in EAP have urban informality (China, Malaysia, and Thailand). To address challenges associated with informality, higher-income countries can prioritize urban planning along with the provision of essential social protection to informal workers. Lower-income countries can focus on policies that encourage investment and reduce costs of regulatory compliance.

Encouraging sectoral reallocation

Liberalize service markets, and shift out of agriculture. A gradual liberalization of service sectors, including education, health care, the financial sector, communications, transport, and utilities, could encourage job creation in these sectors (Beverelli, Fiorini, and Hoekman 2017). It could also boost manufacturing productivity because services sectors provide important inputs into manufacturing.

Design policy to support labor mobility. The reallocation of factors, especially labor, from low-productivity agricultural activities to higher-productivity manufacturing and services could accelerate the convergence of EAP to the productivity frontier. Clarification of land ownership rights and transferable social benefits could encourage such labor movement (Fuglie et al. 2020). Urban planning can encourage a reallocation of labor toward more productive sectors by improving access to jobs, affordable housing, public transportation, health care, education, and other services (World Bank 2015a). Urban planning can also reduce road congestion, which is a major problem in many large cities, and may discourage job switching (World Bank 2018f, 2019a). Accelerated productivity growth will also require improved management of country and regional transportation, telecommunications, and utility infrastructure in urban areas.

Creating a growth-friendly environment

Safeguard macroeconomic stability. In the long term, strong and sustained productivity gains require financial stability. Elevated corporate debt, especially in China, weighs on investment and productivity in exposed corporations. Policy measures to rein in financial risks are therefore critical. The region will need to strengthen its resilience to future unexpected shocks, including pandemic preparedness (World Bank 2020a).

Europe and Central Asia

Before the COVID-19 pandemic, productivity growth in ECA suffered the steepest decline of any EMDE region following the GFC, falling to an average of 1.7 percent in 2013-18, from 5.3 percent during 2003-08. There was wide heterogeneity within the region, however, with productivity growth below zero over 2013-18 in the Western Balkans and above 2.5 percent in Central Europe. The productivity slowdown in ECA predominantly reflected weaker within-sector productivity growth and weaker TFP growth in Eastern Europe, the South Caucasus, and the Western Balkans. Weakness in private investment and schooling disruptions at all levels during the pandemic will likely further weigh on productivity. The policy response to COVID-19 can be complemented with a comprehensive reform agenda to boost investment in physical and human capital, address continuing demographic pressures, and raise innovation. Reforms are also needed to improve business climates and governance, reduce the role of the state in the economy, and promote the diversification of commodity-dependent economies.

Evolution of regional productivity

Sharp post-GFC productivity growth slowdown. Before the COVID-19 pandemic, productivity growth in ECA fell from a pre-GFC (2003-08) rate of 5.3 percent, above the EMDE average, to a below-average post-GFC (2013-18) rate of 1.7 percent—the steepest decline of any EMDE region (figure 5.9).[7] This slowdown was broad-based

---

[7] Productivity data are available for 23 ECA economies. Central Europe includes Bulgaria, Croatia, Hungary, Poland, and Romania. Western Balkans includes Albania, Bosnia and Herzegovina, Kosovo, Montenegro, North Macedonia, and Serbia. Eastern Europe includes Belarus, Moldova, Russia, and Ukraine. South Caucasus includes Armenia, Azerbaijan, and Georgia. Central Asia includes Kazakhstan, the Kyrgyz Republic, Tajikistan, Turkmenistan, and Uzbekistan. Kosovo, Turkmenistan, and Uzbekistan are excluded in some of the analysis because of limited data availability.

FIGURE 5.9 Productivity in ECA in regional comparison

Productivity growth in ECA fell from a pre-GFC rate of 5.3 percent, above the EMDE average, to a post-GFC rate of 1.7 percent—the steepest decline of any EMDE region. Convergence toward advanced economies slowed in the post-GFC period, after having been the fastest among EMDE regions in the pre-GFC period. Productivity levels in ECA were still above the EMDE average in the post-GFC period.

A. Productivity growth relative to other EMDE regions

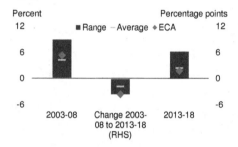

B. Productivity levels and rate of productivity convergence

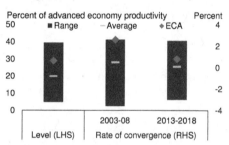

Sources: The Conference Board; Penn World Table; World Bank (World Development Indicators).
Note: Productivity is defined as real GDP per worker (at 2010 market prices and exchange rates). Country group aggregates for a given year are calculated using constant 2010 U.S. dollar GDP weights. Data for multiyear spans show simple averages of the annual data. ECA = Europe and Central Asia; EMDEs = emerging market and developing economies; GFC = global financial crisis.
A. Blue bars show the range of average productivity across the six EMDE regions. Yellow dashes denote the average of the six EMDE regional aggregates. Red diamonds denote simple average of ECA economies. Sample includes 21 ECA economies and 129 EMDEs.
B. Rate of convergence is calculated as the difference in productivity growth rates over the log difference in productivity levels between ECA and advanced economies. Blue bars and yellow dashes show the range and average of the six EMDE regional aggregates. "Level" of productivity refers to the GDP-weighted average of regional productivity as a share of the average advanced economy during 2013-18. LHS refers to left-hand side. RHS refers to right-hand side. Sample includes 21 ECA economies, 129 EMDEs, and 35 advanced economies.

across the region, affecting nearly all economies, with post-GFC productivity growth below longer-term (1992-2018) averages in roughly two-thirds of the region's economies (figure 5.10).

The COVID-19 crisis is likely to exacerbate the weakness in regional productivity growth because the pandemic has dented private investment, particularly foreign direct investment inflows, and has disrupted the education of nearly 90 million schoolchildren (Shmis et al. 2020; World Bank 2020a). The pandemic could also pose medium-term risks, especially if GVC linkages are lost or if protracted flights of safety or ratings downgrades trigger cascading debt defaults and financial stress. A more subdued outlook for commodity prices could also weigh on extractive investment and activity in the region's commodity exporters.

Within-region trends following the GFC (2013-18). The post-GFC productivity growth slowdown was particularly steep in Russia and the South Caucasus, as well as in the Western Balkans. The slowdown reflected bouts of conflict and violence (Eastern Europe and the South Caucasus), a plunge in commodity prices (Russia and the South Caucasus), and disruptions to financial intermediation during the euro area debt crisis of 2010-12 (Western Balkans) amid already elevated unemployment rates. In contrast, the deceleration was milder in Central Europe, which is well integrated into Western

FIGURE 5.10 **Evolution of productivity in ECA**

The post-GFC slowdown in productivity growth affected nearly all the economies in ECA. There was wide heterogeneity within the region, however, with productivity growth below zero in the post-GFC period in the Russian Federation and the Western Balkans but above 2.5 percent in Central Asia and Central Europe. The post-GFC productivity growth slowdown reflected a sharp deceleration in TFP growth in Eastern Europe, the South Caucasus, and the Western Balkans but investment weakness in Russia and Central Europe.

A. Productivity growth in nonmajor ECA economies and Central Europe

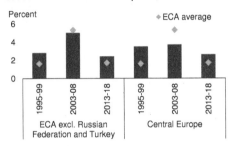

B. Productivity growth in Central Asia, the South Caucasus, and the Western Balkans

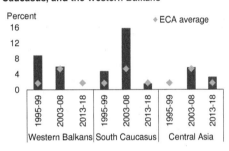

C. Productivity levels relative to advanced economy average, 2013-18

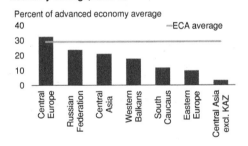

D. Economies with 2013-18 average productivity growth below long-run and pre-GFC averages

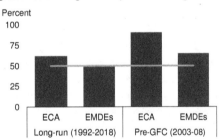

E. Factor contributions to productivity growth

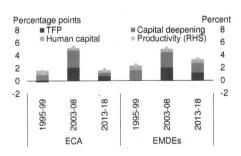

F. Factor contributions to productivity growth, by subregion

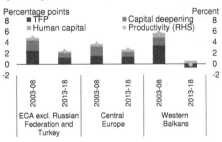

Sources: Barro and Lee (2015); Haver Analytics; International Monetary Fund; Penn World Table; United Nations; Wittgenstein Centre for Demography and Global Human Capital; World Bank (World Development Indicators).
Note: Productivity is defined as real GDP per worker (at 2010 market prices and exchange rates). Country group aggregates for a given year are calculated using constant 2010 U.S. dollar GDP weights. Data for multiyear spans show simple averages of the annual data. ECA = Europe and Central Asia; EMDEs = emerging market and developing economies; GFC = global financial crisis; KAZ = Kazakhstan; TFP = total factor productivity.
C. Figure shows subregional productivity levels as a share of 2013-18 advanced economy weighted average. Sample includes 35 advanced economies and 21 ECA economies.
D. Sample includes 129 EMDEs, of which 21 are ECA economies.
E.F. Productivity growth is computed as log changes. Samples are unbalanced because of data availability, and include up to 21 ECA economies and 93 EMDEs.

European supply chains, and Central Asia, which insulated itself somewhat from the impact of the oil price slump of 2014-16 and recession in Russia during 2015-16 by pivoting its exports toward China.

High productivity levels relative to EMDEs, but with a wide range. Partly as a result of rapid productivity growth in 2003-08, the average productivity level in ECA in 2013-18 was nearly 30 percent of the advanced economy average—roughly one-half above the EMDE average. However, there was wide divergence across subregions. Agricultural commodity exporters, most of which are in Central Asia (excluding Kazakhstan) and Eastern Europe, had the lowest productivity levels, ranging from 3 to 14 percent of the advanced economy average over 2013-18. In contrast, productivity in Poland and Turkey was more than 35 percent of the advanced economy average over 2013-18, reflecting integration into GVCs and roles as regional financial centers (World Bank 2014, 2019e). Central Europe, which is deeply embedded in Western European supply chains and where countries have benefited from the absorption of European Union (EU) structural funds, had the highest productivity of the ECA subregions. Following the GFC, the pace of convergence to advanced economy productivity levels in the ECA region slowed sharply, to average 0.8 percent per year over 2013-18—about one-third of the rate in 2003-08.

Sources of regional productivity growth

Decomposing labor productivity growth into factor accumulation (human and physical capital) and advances in the efficiency of factor use (TFP) indicates that about two-thirds of the post-GFC slowdown in productivity growth in ECA was due to slowing capital accumulation—partly reflecting weak investment amid lower FDI inflows and declining commodity prices—and one-third to slowing TFP growth, compared with about equal contributions in all EMDEs.

In Russia and in Central Europe, particularly Bulgaria and Romania, slowing capital accumulation accounted for most (about three-quarters) of the slowdown in productivity growth in the post-GFC period. In Russia, international sanctions, combined with the 2014-16 oil price plunge, deterred investment (Russell 2018). Although EU structural funds buoyed overall investment in Central Europe, they did not fully offset weakness in machinery and equipment investment, which was due partly to reduced commercial credit supply (Gradzewicz et al. 2018; Levenko, Oja, and Staehr 2019).

In contrast, reduced TFP growth accounted for most (about three-quarters) of the productivity growth slowdown in Eastern Europe, the South Caucasus, and the Western Balkans, reflecting pockets of conflict and violence (Armenia, Georgia, and Ukraine) and weak private and public investment. As a result of weak investment, these subregions face large infrastructure gaps, particularly in transport and telecommunications, limiting the capacity for regional integration and, in energy-reliant economies, for diversification (IMF 2014). Private sector shortcomings, such as corporate overindebtedness and market concentration in the Western Balkans, also constrained TFP in these subregions (EBRD 2018a). In Turkey and Central Asia, the sources of the productivity deceleration were broad-based, reflecting a slowdown in physical capital deepening and human capital improvements, as well as in TFP growth. Reform momentum slowed in Central Asia, Eastern Europe, and the Western Balkans, where many economies did not completely transition to competitive and inclusive markets.

Post-GFC productivity slowdown across all sectors. Pre-GFC productivity growth in ECA was mostly driven by shifts of resources from agriculture and industry to higher-productivity services sectors, partly as a result of reforms to address resource misallocation inherited from central planning (World Bank 2008). The decade that followed the GFC, however, was marked by weakness of growth across all sectors as a slowdown in manufacturing, exacerbated by dwindling global trade growth and a collapse in commodity prices, affected the services sector (figure 5.11; Orlic, Hashi, and Hisarciklilar 2018).

Sectoral reallocation as a source of productivity growth in ECA. Resource reallocation toward more productive sectors accounted for one-third of ECA's productivity growth in the 1990s, as output of the region's services sectors increased by nearly 15 percentage points of GDP (Arnold, Javorcik, and Mattoo 2011; World Bank 2008, 2015b). In contrast, the surge in productivity growth of 2003-08 mostly reflected within-sector growth, as firms in Central Europe became integrated into euro area supply chains, technology transfer accelerated, and the services sectors were liberalized (Bartelsman and Scarpetta 2007; Brown and Earle 2007; Georgiev, Nagy-Mohacsi, and Plekhanov 2017; Shepotylo and Vakhitov 2015; World Bank 2008).

After the GFC, within-sector productivity growth slowed sharply, to less than one-third of the pre-GFC average. This may have reflected investment declines in physical capital, particularly in commodity exporters amid the collapse of commodity prices, as well as stalled structural reforms to improve business environments (EBRD 2018b; Georgiev, Nagy-Mohacsi, and Plekhanov 2017). Between-sector shifts in resources to productivity growth also declined in ECA. The fall may have partly reflected a larger shift out of agriculture into lower-productivity sectors after the GFC (trade services) than before the GFC (manufacturing), such as was the case in Kazakhstan (World Bank 2019f). More broadly, spillovers from the euro area debt crisis, slowing global trade growth, and the oil price plunge dampened growth in sectors with higher levels of productivity—finance, manufacturing, and mining—limiting their ability to continue to absorb additional labor from other sectors with lower productivity (ILO 2017).

Continued differences in productivity levels across sectors imply scope for further overall productivity gains from resource reallocation. In sectors such as agriculture, mining, and utilities, ECA's productivity lagged about 50 percent behind advanced economy averages over 2013-17, and in mining it lagged even EMDE averages. On average in ECA, productivity in agriculture was about two-thirds of productivity in other low-skilled sectors such as construction and trade and about one-quarter of productivity in high-skilled services such as finance.

Waves of reform momentum. Two waves of reform spurred productivity growth in ECA before the GFC. During the first wave, in the wake of the collapse of the Soviet

FIGURE 5.11 Factors supporting productivity growth in ECA

Within-sector productivity growth—the main driver of pre-GFC productivity growth in ECA—fell sharply in the post-GFC period, and productivity gains from sectoral reallocation halved as economies moved to services sectors with relatively low productivity levels.

A. Within- and between-sector contributions to regional productivity growth

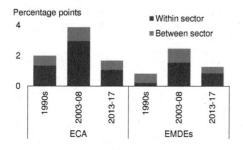

B. Sectoral productivity levels, 2017

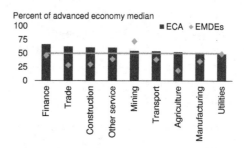

C. Sectoral contribution to productivity growth

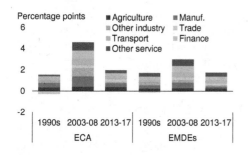

D. Composition of value added, by sector

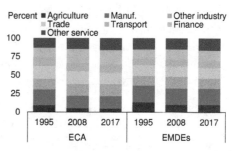

Sources: Asian Productivity Organization, Productivity Database; Expanded African Sector Database; Groningen Growth Development Center Database; Haver Analytics; International Country Risk Guide; International Labour Organization, ILOSTAT; Observatory of Economic Complexity; Organisation for Economic Co-operation and Development Structural Analysis Database; Penn World Table; United Nations; World Bank; World KLEMS.

Note: ECA = Europe and Central Asia; EMDEs = emerging market and developing economies; GFC = global financial crisis.

A.B. Productivity is defined as real GDP per worker (at 2010 market prices and exchange rates). Data for multiyear spans show simple averages of the annual data.

A-D. The sample includes 69 EMDEs, of which 11 are ECA economies.

A.D. Aggregates calculated using GDP weights at 2010 prices and market exchange rates.

A. Growth "within sector" shows the contribution to aggregate productivity growth of each sector holding employment shares fixed. The "between sector" effect shows the contribution arising from changes in sectoral employment shares.

B. Figure shows the median of country groups. Horizontal line indicates 50 percent.

C.D. "Other industry" includes mining, utilities, and construction; "other service" includes government and personal services. "Manuf." indicates manufacturing.

Union in the early 1990s, central planning was dismantled and replaced by more market-based approaches (Falcetti, Lysenko, and Sanfey 2006). ECA economies were opened up to international trade and capital markets, prices and interest rates were liberalized, and SOEs were privatized to a degree (Georgiev, Nagy-Mohacsi, and Plekhanov 2017). These reforms helped boost productivity growth in the mid-1990s, particularly in the South Caucasus (World Bank 2018g).

In the early 2000s, a second wave of reforms related to Central European countries' accession to the EU accelerated international integration and propelled institutional improvements, privatization, and capital market deepening (Bruszt and Campos 2016). FDI and private investment surged as reforms were anchored externally, with many ECA economies rapidly becoming integrated into GVCs with Western Europe, accelerating the adoption of new technologies and practices (Aiyar et al. 2013; EBRD 2014). The growing international integration of financial and banking systems helped deepen capital markets, particularly in Central Europe.[8]

In the decade that followed the GFC, ECA faced multiple headwinds to productivity-enhancing reforms, including the legacy of the crisis, the collapse of oil prices in 2014-16, heightened geopolitical tensions, and international sanctions on Russia. Continued progress on reforms are needed, particularly in Central Asia and Eastern Europe—which are not anchored to an EU accession process—and the Western Balkans (EBRD 2013; Lehne, Mo, and Plekhanov 2014; Georgiev, Nagy-Mohacsi, and Plekhanov 2017; Rovo 2019; World Bank 2019g). Many commodity exporters in the region continue to suffer from structural constraints, including a lack of export diversification, large state presence in firms, unfavorable business environments, and weak international competitiveness (EBRD 2017; Funke, Isakova, and Ivanyna 2017).

Post-GFC slowdown in drivers of productivity. The key drivers of productivity in ECA were decreasingly supportive during the post-GFC period of 2013-18 (figure 5.12). Demographic pressures intensified in nearly all ECA economies. Working-age population growth had long lagged the average for EMDEs as a result of significant migration to Western European countries in the EU and to Russia and sharp declines in fertility rates. Particularly in Central Europe, Eastern Europe, and the Western Balkans, there were declines in the urban population, in turn discouraging dissemination of knowledge and technologies that lift TFP (World Bank 2017a, 2018h).

Additionally, more than four-fifths of ECA economies experienced post-GFC slowdowns in investment rates, reflecting adverse shifts in investor sentiment amid conflicts and financial pressures in the region, as well as weak external economic growth. Low innovation rates—which partly stem from weak competitiveness, inadequate control of corruption, and a high presence of SOEs—continued to dampen the business environment and hinder investment in the region, particularly in the absence of progress with other reforms (EBRD 2018a, 2019). Finally, the rate of extraction of natural capital (such as oil, metals, and agricultural land) declined in some economies following the boom and as commodity prices fell, dampening TFP growth. This followed a pre-GFC boost to productivity growth in ECA from increased natural capital extraction during the commodity price boom (Khan et al. 2016).

The COVID-19 pandemic is likely to amplify the slowdown in investment in ECA, particularly FDI. The most vulnerable economies are expected to be those that suffered from large domestic outbreaks or supply chain disruptions, as well as those with a heavy

---

[8] A rise in foreign currency borrowing, however, increased exposure to external vulnerabilities, such as capital flow reversals, and deepened the recession following the GFC as economies faced a credit crunch and a period of deleveraging (de Haas et al. 2015; de Haas and van Lelyveld 2006; Zettelmeyer et al. 2010).

FIGURE 5.12 **Drivers of productivity growth in ECA in regional comparison**

Decelerating productivity in ECA reflects slowing improvements in a broad range of fundamental drivers in recent years. ECA performs poorly relative to other EMDE regions in measures of demography and investment but favorably in terms of drivers such as trade and education.

A. Share of EMDEs with slowing post-GFC improvement in underlying drivers of productivity

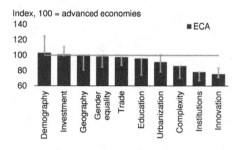

B. Drivers of productivity growth, 2017

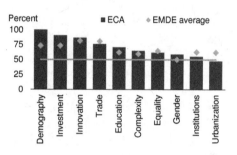

Sources: Freedom House; Haver Analytics; International Country Risk Guide; Organisation for Economic Co-operation and Development; Observatory of Economic Complexity; Penn World Table; United Nations Educational, Scientific, and Cultural Organization (Institute for Statistics); United Nations Population Prospects; World Integrated Trade Solution; World Bank (Doing Business, Enterprise Surveys, and Global Financial Development Database).
Note: ECA = Europe and Central Asia; EMDE = emerging market and developing economy.
A.B. Variables are defined as follows: Education = years of education, Urbanization = share of population living in urban areas, Investment = investment as share of GDP, Institutions = government effectiveness, Complexity = Economic Complexity Index of Hidalgo and Hausmann (2009), Equality = income equality defined as (-1)*Gini, Gender equality = share of years of schooling for females to males, Demography = share of population under age 14, Innovation = log patents per capita, and Trade = (exports + imports)/GDP.
A. Post-GFC slowdown defined as a decline in the growth of each variable during 2008-17 compared to growth in the pre-GFC period, defined as 1998-2007. The blue bars represent the share of 21 economies in ECA where improvements in each driver of productivity were lower during 2008-17 than in 1998-2007 or changes in 2008-17 were below zero. Orange diamond is the corresponding value for EMDE countries. Horizontal line indicates 50 percent. Sample includes 17-21 ECA economies, depending on the driver, and 79-128 EMDEs.
B. Unweighted average levels of drivers normalized as an average of advanced economies as 100 and standard deviation of 10. Blue bars represent average within ECA economies. Orange whiskers represent the range of the average drivers for the six EMDE regions. Horizontal line indicates 100. Sample includes 16-21 ECA economies and 65-127 EMDEs, depending on the driver, and 32 advanced economies.

presence of travel and transport industries and capital-intensive sectors, such as energy and high-value manufacturing industries (World Bank 2020a). Many multinational enterprises have issued profit warnings. This is expected to dampen reinvested earnings—an important source of FDI for ECA economies. The impact could also weigh on the labor market, particularly in Central Europe where foreign-owned firms can account for a quarter of jobs in the private sector.

Policy options

Although confronting the COVID-19 pandemic is the primary focus of policy efforts, these measures can be complemented by structural reforms to rekindle productivity growth. A four-pronged policy approach is needed to improve the provision and quality of factors of production, boost firm productivity, promote productivity-enhancing sectoral reallocation, and improve business environments. Some policies, such as changes in SOE ownership and improvements in the investment climate, would offer relatively short-term productivity gains; but others, such as efforts to improve human capital or adjust migration policies, would lay the foundation for longer-term gains. Policy priorities need to be tailored to country-specific circumstances, however.

Improving factors of production

Address investment and infrastructure gaps. Investment growth fell sharply in ECA in the post-GFC period as commodity prices declined sharply and investor sentiment deteriorated amid conflict, international sanctions, and financial pressures (figure 5.13). In response to the COVID-19 pandemic, investment prospects in ECA have further deteriorated. Reforms to boost private sector development and transition to competitive and inclusive markets are needed to attract private investment and capital flows to ECA, particularly to economies outside the EU (EBRD 2018a; World Bank 2019g).

Public investment was also constrained over the past decade as many governments faced a collapse in commodity revenues amid the sustained decline in commodity prices over 2011-16. The COVID-19-related downturn in oil prices, however, provides a window of opportunity to put in place mechanisms that permanently eliminate costly and poorly targeted energy subsidies, including in Central Asia and Eastern Europe (World Bank 2020a). Fiscal savings generated by lower subsidies could instead fund productivity-enhancing investment in education and infrastructure, or be directed toward medium-term measures that build climate resilience, such as investment in technology to improve agricultural productivity and increase food security during years of severe drought.

In some subregions within ECA, particularly Central Asia, removing key bottlenecks to private sector development, such as inadequate infrastructure, is key to accelerating the absorption of technology and lifting productivity growth (Gould 2018). Insufficient infrastructure, particularly transport and electricity, remains a critical constraint in some of the region. Although the percentage of firms experiencing electrical outages is lower in ECA than in other EMDE regions, related losses for affected firms in Central Asia can exceed 9 percent of annual sales (Blimpo and Cosgrove-Davies 2019; IMF 2019a). In surveyed manufacturing firms in Uzbekistan, for instance, smaller firms report more interruptions of electricity, gas, and water supply than do larger firms (Trushin 2018). Appropriate land use planning and urbanization policies can substantially reduce the cost of meeting transport needs while minimizing carbon footprints (ITF 2018; Rozenberg and Fay 2019). The COVID-19 pandemic, however, threatens to further disrupt critical infrastructure sectors in ECA as the sharp decline in firm revenues has generated unprecedented financial pressures.

Raise human capital. Boosting human capital investment, including through education and health, could help remove bottlenecks to productivity growth. In a few economies in ECA, particularly in Central Asia, inadequate investment in human capital left parts of the workforce poorly equipped for rapid technological change even before the COVID-19 pandemic (Flabbi and Gatti 2018). Although ECA has on average the highest years of schooling among the EMDE regions, educational attainment and skills acquisition are lower in some ECA economies than expected given the level of school enrollment and the average years of schooling (Altinok, Angrist, and Patrinos 2018). Low educational attainment among the workforce, large gender gaps in education, and inadequate skills are often cited as constraints to doing business, firm growth, job creation, and innovation in ECA (Brancatelli, Marguerie, and Brodmann 2020; World Bank 2019a).

FIGURE 5.13 Drivers of productivity growth in ECA

Investment growth in ECA has fallen in the post-GFC period, reflecting external headwinds, such as a commodity price plunge, and idiosyncratic factors, including conflict in pockets of the region and financial pressures in large economies. The workforce is aging, and the working-age share of the population is declining. The role of the state remains large, and control of corruption weak.

A. Investment growth: Actual vs. Consensus Economics forecasts

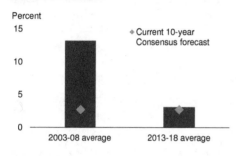

B. Share of regional GDP accounted for by economies with growing working-age populations

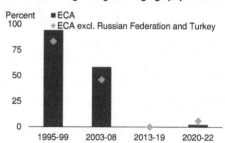

C. Assessment of transition to a competitive market economy, 2019

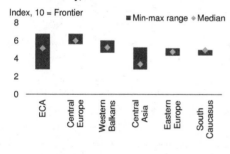

D. Control of corruption, 2017

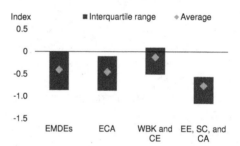

Sources: Consensus Economics; European Bank for Reconstruction and Development; Kraay (2018); United Nations; World Bank.

Note: CA = Central Asia; CE = Central Europe; ECA = Europe and Central Asia; EE = Eastern Europe; EMDEs = emerging market and developing economies; GFC = global financial crisis; SC = South Caucasus; WBK = Western Balkans.

A. Investment is measured as gross fixed capital formation. Actual growth aggregate calculated using GDP weights at 2010 prices and market exchange rates. Consensus forecasts aggregate calculated as a simple average of surveys for periods indicated based on data availability. Unbalanced sample includes 8 ECA economies because of data availability.

B. The working-age population is defined as people ages 15-64. Unbalanced sample includes 23 ECA economies.

C. Figure shows the distance to the frontier for achieving a full transition to a competitive market economy, as measured by EBRD (2019). Economies with higher index levels are closer to the frontier, where scores range from 1 to 10, with 10 denoting the synthetic frontier. Sample includes 24 ECA economies.

D. The indicator reflects perceptions of the extent to which public power is exercised for private gain, including both petty and grand forms of corruption, as well as "capture" of the state by elites and private interests, as measured by the Worldwide Governance Indicators. Index is on a scale of -2.5 (weak) to 2.5 (strong). Sample includes 23 ECA economies and 150 EMDEs.

Human capital development in ECA, however, is likely to slide as a result of the COVID-19 pandemic because of severe disruption to schooling at all levels, which has affected nearly 90 million schoolchildren. In previous crises, the number of out-of-school children doubled in some ECA countries despite declining demographic trends, and income disparities increased as vulnerable groups faced higher rates of dropout and depressed skills development (Shmis et al. 2020). Extended school closures are expected to reduce the learning-adjusted years of schooling in ECA from 10.4 years to between

9.3 and 10.1 years—the steepest reduction among EMDE regions—which, combined with the de-skilling associated with prolonged unemployment, could also lead to sizable future earnings losses (Azevedo et al. 2020). The COVID-19 crisis underscores the critical need for investment in digital skills and technology to ensure educational continuity, as well as for resources to upgrade information and communication technology infrastructure to support virtual learning, particularly for more vulnerable households.

On the health front, the pandemic has laid bare the need to detect rapidly and respond to public health emergencies (World Bank 2020c). Aging populations in the region and the greater vulnerability of the elderly to many infectious diseases make this an even greater priority. Addressing and minimizing the health risks of high rates of obesity, smoking, and heavy drinking in the region are also important, not only for limiting the impact of noncommunicable diseases but also for minimizing the loss of lives associated with major outbreaks of infectious diseases.

Counteract unfavorable demographic trends. An aging workforce, a declining working-age population share, and high emigration rates among young and skilled workers in ECA highlight the need for education to help workers adapt to new job requirements and technologies (Aiyar, Ebeke, and Shao 2016; Hallward-Driemeier and Nayyar 2018; World Bank 2018a). Generating stronger productivity growth will require measures to mitigate the decline in skilled workforces. Implementing more flexible immigration policies could help relieve skilled labor shortages by attracting skilled foreign workers in an orderly way (Delogu, Docquier, and Machado 2014; World Bank 2019g).

Boosting firm productivity

Level the playing field. In Central Asia and Eastern Europe, and to some extent in Russia, the state's presence in the economy remains large, with state ownership accounting for more than 10 percent of firms surveyed in some cases. In terms of state ownership, ECA ranks second overall among EMDE regions, after SSA (World Bank 2019h). In Ukraine, firms with at least partial state presence account for roughly 20 percent of total turnover by firms and over 25 percent of firms' assets (Balabushko et al. 2018). SOEs also have a large presence in Moldova, accounting for one-third of GDP (World Bank 2019i). Yet efficiency in SOEs is lower than in private firms, suggesting that restructuring or privatizing SOEs therefore still presents an opportunity to raise economy-wide productivity in several countries across the region, if such restructuring or privatization is accompanied by effective regulation and improvements in management, corporate governance, and the business environment (Brown, Earle, and Telegdy 2006; EBRD 2019; Funke, Isakova, and Ivanyna 2017; World Bank 1995). For some economies, including in Eastern Europe, the removal of price controls for various goods could improve competition and productivity.

Improve market development and financial inclusion. Small and medium enterprises (SMEs) have the largest potential for productivity catch-up with advanced economies. Yet growth of SMEs in ECA continues to be hindered by insufficient access to finance and regulatory barriers, among other factors (Ayyagari, Demirgüç-Kunt, and Maksimovic 2017; Cusolito, Safadi, and Taglioni 2017; Wang 2016). The largest gaps in financial inclusion for SMEs in ECA are in Central Asia and the South Caucasus (excluding Georgia), where access to financial services is nearly as limited as in MNA, SAR, and SSA (IMF 2019b).

Policies that promote more widespread adoption of digital technologies, including in the delivery of financial and public sector services, could bolster financial inclusion and boost productivity by helping spread innovation and improving private sector and government efficiency (Baldwin 2019). In economies with large informal sectors, more widespread adoption of these technologies could also help expand tax bases through the fiscalization of informal sector transactions (World Bank 2019a). Increasing SMEs' access to finance could help these firms increase their average size and reduce their reliance on retained earnings to fund investment, which in turn would support job creation (Ayyagari, Demirgüç-Kunt, and Maksimovic 2017; Ayyagari et al. 2016).

The COVID-19 pandemic, however, is likely to intensify the challenges as the crisis generates cashflow issues for SMEs, which are more vulnerable to financing fluctuations. In turn, this could render the banking sector vulnerable, especially in economies with rising levels of nonperforming loans (World Bank 2020c). In the immediate term, ensuring liquidity during the COVID-19 crisis could help banks provide relief to sound borrowers via loan restructuring, debt service deferment, or bridge financing. Strengthening the frameworks to bolster resilience in the financial system, such as having measures to identify stressed assets and support a smooth insolvency process, could also help avert serious impairment to future balance sheets and ensure a smooth recovery.

Encouraging sectoral reallocation

Diversify economies. Before the COVID-19 pandemic and subsequent plunge in oil prices, hydrocarbon activity represented more than one-third of GDP in some ECA energy exporters (World Bank 2020a). Energy-exporting economies, including those in ECA, are characterized by generally low levels of diversification in terms of exports and fiscal revenue (Grigoli, Herman, and Swiston 2017; World Bank 2020a).[9] Although energy sector production tends to be capital-intensive, with relatively high labor productivity, productivity growth was more tepid in ECA's energy-exporting countries than in the region overall, with post-GFC (2013-18) growth at 0.7 percent vs. 1.7 percent, reflecting weaker TFP growth (Aslam et al. 2016; Danforth, Medas, and Salins 2016; Stocker et al. 2018). Diversification presents an opportunity to boost TFP and productivity growth, as well as macroeconomic stability (Brenton, Newfarmer, and Walkenhorst 2009; Papageorgiou and Spatafora 2012). Diversification, combined with private sector development, could also help support higher-productivity job creation because the bulk of employment tends to be concentrated in low-productivity sectors in

---

[9] However, on the fiscal front, Russia has made strides in anchoring fiscal policy by implementing a fiscal rule that targets a primary balance of zero at the benchmark oil price of $40 per barrel. Any excess fiscal reserves that are generated from higher oil prices are saved in the National Welfare Fund.

some of ECA's energy exporters (OECD 2020a). Diversification of resource-based economies can be promoted by reforms that increase capital and skill accumulation, encourage innovation, and reduce transaction costs (Beck 2018; Gylfason 2018; Hesse 2008; IMF 2016a; Lederman and Maloney 2007).

Enhancing a growth-friendly environment

Improve governance. Over the long term, institutional quality is one of the most important determinants of productivity growth. In ECA, productivity catch-up to advanced economies was particularly pronounced in Central Europe during the pre-GFC period, reflecting the anchoring of structural and institutional reforms to the EU accession process (Rodríguez-Pose and Ketterer 2019). ECA continued to face governance challenges before the COVID-19 crisis, however, with over 75 percent of the countries below the global average in terms of control of corruption in 2017, including almost all of the economies of Central Europe, Eastern Europe, and the South Caucasus (Kaufmann, Kraay, and Mastruzzi 2010).

Structural reforms to improve governance can lead to sizable productivity gains, particularly in countries that are farthest from best practices (Acemoglu, Johnson, and Robinson 2005; Cusolito and Maloney 2018). Major governance and business reforms in EMDEs have been associated with higher growth rates in output, TFP, and investment (Divanbeigi and Ramalho 2015; Hodge et al. 2011; World Bank 2018a). The detrimental effects of corruption on firm productivity can be exacerbated by excess or complex regulation (Amin and Ulku 2019). Anticorruption campaigns, as well as reductions in the number of regulations and tax complexity, have helped some economies tackle corruption (IMF 2019c).

Improve business climates. Lack of exposure to international competition—including from nontariff barriers and complex trade rules—as well as restrictive product market and services regulation, remain structural bottlenecks in the region, hindering the ability to attract domestic and foreign investment in Kazakhstan, Russia, and Ukraine (Shepotylo and Vakhitov 2015; World Bank 2016c). Although significant improvements in business environments in Central Europe, the South Caucasus, and the Western Balkans have occurred over the past decade, Central Asia and Eastern Europe lag the ECA average, with the former trailing the EMDE average in access to electricity and the ease of trading across borders (World Bank 2019f). For example, in Ukraine, the largest economy in Eastern Europe, the average worker takes one year to produce the same output that the average worker in Germany produces in 17 days (World Bank 2019j). At current growth trends, Ukraine is unlikely to converge to Poland's per capita income, despite having had similar income levels in 1990; this partly reflects Ukraine's relatively low ratio of capital stock to GDP. Removing market distortions and improving resource allocation could triple manufacturing productivity and help improve prospects in Ukraine (Ryzhenkov 2016). Although Turkey has high productivity levels, it lags well behind the ECA average for resolving insolvency, which could dampen overall productivity because less productive firms are more likely to remain in the market

(World Bank 2019e). To address this, Turkey has recently introduced a more streamlined procedure that focuses on business continuation instead of liquidation.

Latin America and the Caribbean

Even before LAC was hit by severe health and economic impacts from COVID-19, labor productivity growth there had stalled. Productivity growth in the region averaged 0.4 percent in 2013-18, the second lowest of the six EMDE regions, and well below 1.7 percent in the lead-up to the GFC, in 2003-08. In more than one-third of LAC economies, productivity growth was negative during 2013-18. Sluggish productivity growth during 2013-18 reflects negative TFP growth in some large LAC economies, as the commodity price slump and market distortions allowed unproductive firms to continue operating. Although the level of productivity in LAC remains higher than the EMDE average, this is a legacy of gains made decades ago. Shocks related to COVID-19 are likely to further set back productivity growth in the region. To boost productivity, targeted policy actions are needed to improve competition and innovation, deepen trade linkages, improve the quality of education, reduce labor market inefficiencies, strengthen institutional quality, and raise infrastructure investment.

Evolution of regional productivity

Post-GFC productivity growth slowdown to near zero. For decades, productivity growth in LAC has been anemic (Fernández-Arias and Rodríguez-Apolinar 2016). After a burst during the pre-GFC period (2003-08), the second-longest period of positive productivity growth since 1980, productivity growth fizzled out again during the post-GFC years. Relative to a pre-GFC (2003-08) average of 1.7 percent, productivity growth in the region dropped to 0.4 percent during 2013-18—a slowdown broadly in line with the EMDE average but from a lower starting rate (figure 5.14).[10]

The productivity growth slowdown in the post-GFC period was broad-based, affecting three-fifths of LAC countries. In 10 of 26 countries, nearly all of which are in the Caribbean and South America, productivity growth contracted in 2013-18. In most cases, productivity growth was also lower than both the pre-GFC and long-term averages, as major economies in the region struggled with poor business climates, political tensions, regulatory burdens, and plunging commodity prices. Over the course of the past four decades, troughs in productivity growth have broadly coincided with major adverse economic events, including a series of severe debt crises in the 1980s that spawned the region's "lost decade," the GFC, and periodic commodity price slumps.

Within-region productivity growth trends. Notwithstanding weak labor productivity growth at the aggregate level in LAC during 2013-18, there was considerable

---

[10] Labor productivity data are available for 9 EMDEs in South America (Argentina, Bolivia, Brazil, Chile, Colombia, Ecuador, Paraguay, Peru, and Uruguay), 7 EMDEs in North and Central America (Costa Rica, El Salvador, Guatemala, Honduras, Mexico, Nicaragua, and Panama), and 10 EMDEs in the Caribbean (the Bahamas, Barbados, Belize, the Dominican Republic, Guyana, Haiti, Jamaica, St. Lucia, St. Vincent and the Grenadines, and Suriname).

FIGURE 5.14 **Productivity in LAC in regional comparison**

Productivity growth in LAC fell from 1.7 percent in 2003-08 to 0.4 percent in 2013-18. The level of productivity in LAC is still higher than that in other EMDE regions, yet sluggish productivity growth in the post-GFC period has caused the region to lose ground in converging toward the level of productivity in advanced economies.

A. Productivity growth relative to other EMDE regions

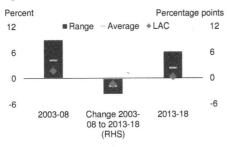

B. Productivity levels and rate of productivity convergence

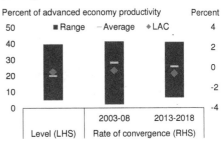

Sources: The Conference Board; Penn World Table; World Bank (World Development Indicators).
Note: Productivity is defined as real GDP per worker (at 2010 market prices and exchange rates). Country group aggregates for a given year are calculated using constant 2010 U.S. dollar GDP weights. Data for multiyear spans show simple averages of the annual data. EMDEs = emerging market and developing economies; GFC = global financial crisis; LAC = Latin America and the Caribbean.
A. Blue bars show the range of average productivity across the six EMDE regions. Yellow dashes denote the average of the six EMDE regional aggregates. Red diamonds denote simple average of LAC economies. Sample includes 26 LAC economies and 129 EMDEs.
B. Rate of convergence is calculated as the difference in productivity growth rates over the log difference in productivity levels between LAC and advanced economies. Blue bars and yellow dashes show the range and average of the six EMDE regional aggregates. "Level" of productivity refers to the GDP-weighted average of regional productivity as a share of the average advanced economy during 2013-18. LHS refers to left-hand side. RHS refers to right-hand side. Sample includes 26 LAC economies, 129 EMDEs, and 35 advanced economies.

heterogeneity across countries (figure 5.15). Bolivia, Costa Rica, the Dominican Republic, and Paraguay featured the highest labor productivity growth, measuring well above pre-GFC and long-term regional averages. The improvement in the Dominican Republic reflects greater contribution from capital deepening and higher TFP growth; this arose from increased FDI inflows that were encouraged by reforms that opened most sectors to foreign investment, and by tax incentives for foreign investment (World Bank 2018i). Bolivia and Paraguay benefited from population migration from rural to urban areas, which coincided with a shrinking share of agriculture as a share of employment (IMF 2016b; World Bank 2018j). In Costa Rica, continued policy reforms and positive spillovers from FDI inflows supported a broad-based rise in productivity growth across sectors (OECD 2018a). Four of the six LAC economies with the highest productivity growth during 2013-18 (Bolivia, the Dominican Republic, Panama, and Peru) benefited from the steepest declines in the share of informal activity in the region during the decade to 2016 (World Bank 2019a).

Higher productivity level than the EMDE average but slowing convergence with advanced economies. The level of productivity in LAC (22 percent of the advanced economy average) was slightly higher in 2013-18 than the EMDE average (18 percent of the advanced economy average). However, this outcome is a legacy of productivity growth advances made in the region decades ago. Since the 1980s, labor productivity in

FIGURE 5.15 Evolution of labor productivity growth in LAC

Despite weak aggregate productivity growth in the region, some countries, including Bolivia, Costa Rica, the Dominican Republic, and Paraguay, achieved productivity growth in line with the EMDE average during 2013-18.

A. Economies with 2013-18 average productivity growth below long-run and pre-GFC averages

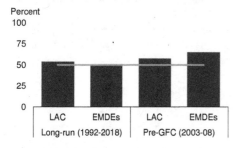

B. Productivity growth, by year

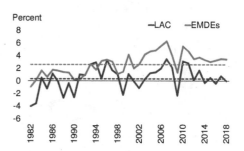

C. Productivity growth, by country

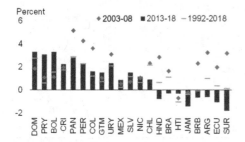

D. Productivity levels, 2013-18

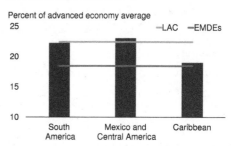

Sources: The Conference Board; Penn World Table; World Bank (World Development Indicators).

Note: Productivity is defined as real GDP per worker (at 2010 market prices and exchange rates). Country group aggregates for a given year are calculated using constant 2010 U.S. dollar GDP weights. Data for multiyear spans show simple averages of the annual data. Sample includes 26 LAC countries and 129 EMDEs. EMDEs = emerging market and developing economies; GFC = global financial crisis; LAC = Latin America and the Caribbean.

A. Orange line represents a 50 percent threshold.

B. Dotted lines show 1981-2018 averages.

C. DOM = the Dominican Republic; PRY = Paraguay; BOL = Bolivia; CRI = Costa Rica; PAN = Panama; PER = Peru; COL = Colombia; GTM = Guatemala; URY = Uruguay; MEX = Mexico; SLV = El Salvador; NIC = Nicaragua; CHL = Chile; HND = Honduras; BRA = Brazil; HTI = Haiti; JAM = Jamaica; BRB = Barbados; ARG = Argentina; ECU = Ecuador; SUR = Suriname.

D. Sample includes 9 economies in South America; 7 in Mexico and Central America; 10 in the Caribbean; and 129 EMDEs.

LAC relative to the level in advanced economies has fallen (Fernández-Arias and Rodríguez-Apolinar 2016; Ferreira, de Abreu Pessoa, and Veloso 2013). The pre-GFC rise in productivity growth halted this divergence only briefly. This is in stark contrast to the narrowing labor productivity gap between the broader group of EMDEs and advanced economies since the 1990s.

Sources of regional productivity growth

Decomposing labor productivity into factor accumulation and the efficiency with which labor and capital are used during production (TFP) shows that the post-GFC productivity growth slowdown predominantly reflected a return to negative TFP growth rates, as had prevailed in LAC during the 1990s (figure 5.16; Busso, Madrigal, and Pagés 2013). However, the post-GFC (2013-18) average disguises a steep slowdown in investment growth during 2016-18, as Brazil struggled to exit a deep recession, the effects of the commodity price slump rippled through the region's many commodity-reliant economies, and numerous economies experienced bouts of policy uncertainty.

With the region experiencing its deepest economic contraction in decades in 2020, productivity growth is likely to weaken further in the short term. The region experienced severe capital outflows in the first half of the year, which together with deep uncertainty about the trajectory of the pandemic will contribute to a sharp investment contraction, and labor markets have been severely disrupted (World Bank 2020a). Widespread school and workplace closures may adversely affect productivity in the medium term because of lost learning opportunities and setbacks in workforce skill development.

- *South America.* The post-GFC labor productivity slowdown was most pronounced in South America, where productivity growth averaged only 0.1 percent, compared to 2.1 percent in the pre-GFC period. The subregion was deeply affected by the commodity price slump and country-specific constraints in large economies. TFP growth in South America was continually negative during 2013-18, in part reflecting growing directed credit in Brazil (Calice, Ribiero, and Byskov 2018; Dutz 2018). It also reflected intensifying economic distortions (such as trade restrictions and price controls) in Argentina during the early part of the period, which allowed unproductive firms to survive.

- *Mexico and Central America.* The early impacts of the GFC in 2007 and 2008 weighed on TFP in Mexico during 2003-08. Although post-GFC TFP growth was subdued, and capital deepening weakened during this period in the context of the repeated bouts of policy uncertainty, the removal of the crisis effects in Mexico allowed slightly higher productivity growth of 1.0 percent in the Mexico and Central America subregion during 2013-18, vs. 0.7 percent in 2003-08.

- *The Caribbean.* In the Caribbean, TFP growth accelerated during the post-GFC period, to 1.5 percent, from 1.0 percent in 2003-08, largely reflecting capital deepening in the largest economy in the subregion, the Dominican Republic.

Post-GFC productivity growth slowdown across sectors. As in most other EMDE regions, manufacturing made a sizable sectoral contribution to productivity growth in LAC during the pre-GFC period. The post-GFC period in LAC was marked by a broad-based slowdown in productivity growth across sectors, particularly in the trade sector.

Stalling between-sector labor productivity growth. For most large LAC economies with available sectoral data, within-sector productivity gains have historically been greater than between-sector gains from labor reallocation from low-productivity to higher-productivity sectors (figure 5.17). This is consistent with other studies of the region (Brown et al. 2016; Diao, McMillan, and Rodrik 2017). During the 1990s, a substantial

FIGURE 5.16 Sources of productivity growth in LAC

Sluggish productivity growth in LAC during the post-GFC period predominantly reflected a negative contribution from TFP. The TFP contraction was especially pronounced in South America. In recent years, capital deepening has made a slowing contribution to productivity growth.

A. Factor contributions to productivity growth

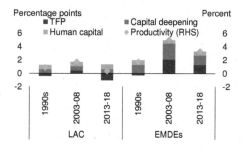

B. Factor contributions to productivity growth, by subregion

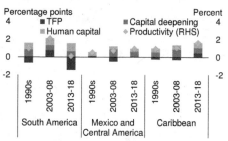

Sources: Barro and Lee (2015); International Monetary Fund; Penn World Table; United Nations (Human Development Reports), Wittgenstein Centre for Demography and Global Human Capital; World Bank.
Note: EMDEs = emerging market and developing economies; GFC = global financial crisis; LAC = Latin America and the Caribbean; TFP = total factor productivity.
A.B. Productivity is defined as real GDP per worker (at 2010 market prices and exchange rates). Country group aggregates for a given year are calculated using constant 2010 U.S. dollar GDP weights. Data for multiyear spans show simple averages of the annual data.
A.B. Productivity growth is computed as log changes. Sample includes 20 LAC economies and 93 EMDEs.
B. Sample includes 9 economies in South America, 6 in Mexico and Central America, and 16 in the Caribbean.

part of labor productivity growth was due to within-sector growth as LAC countries liberalized trade policy in the second half of the 1980s and the early 1990s (Rodrik 2016). The 1990s and early 2000s were a period of significant change in LAC's manufacturing industry. Faced with increasing foreign competition as the result of globalization, domestic manufacturing firms implemented more efficient processes that required less labor, and uncompetitive firms ceased operating. As workers were displaced from manufacturing, they shifted toward lower-productivity services and informal activities (McMillan, Rodrik, and Verduzco-Gallo 2014; Pagés-Serra 2010).

As the manufacturing sector in LAC transformed during the 1990s and early 2000s, the agricultural sector became more productive relative to other sectors, with a shrinking share of agricultural employment accounting for a stable share of output between 1995 and 2008. The trade sector, however, became less productive, accounting for a growing share of employment and the same share of output.

Since 2013, between-sector productivity gains have stalled in the two largest regional economies, Brazil and Mexico. Within-sector productivity growth at the region level collapsed to near zero as multiple structural constraints (for example, inefficient provision of credit in Brazil and trade restrictions and price controls in Argentina) were compounded by an inability to adjust to adverse events, including unfavorable policy choices, a commodity price collapse, and financial stress episodes. In the short term, changes in consumer behavior and mobility restrictions implemented as part of the policy response to COVID-19 may hinder sectoral reallocation.

FIGURE 5.17 **Sectoral productivity in LAC**

Within-sector productivity growth, the main driver of productivity growth in LAC during the pre-GFC period, was much lower during the post-GFC period in several large economies, while between-sector productivity growth slowed in all economies with available sectoral data.

A. Within- and between-sector contributions to productivity growth

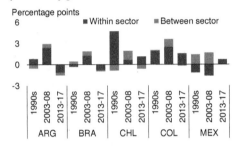

B. Composition of employment, by sector

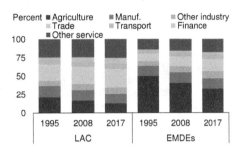

C. Composition of value added, by sector

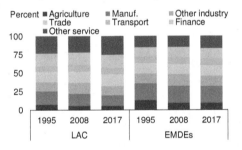

D. Sectoral productivity levels, 2017

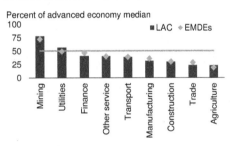

Sources: Groningen Growth Development Center database; Haver Analytics; International Labour Organization, ILOSTAT; Organisation for Economic Co-operation and Development, Structural Analysis Database; United Nations; World KLEMS; World Bank.

Note: EMDEs = emerging market and developing economies; GFC = global financial crisis; LAC = Latin America and the Caribbean.

A.D. Productivity is defined as real GDP per worker (at 2010 market prices and exchange rates). Country group aggregates for a given year are calculated using constant 2010 U.S. dollar GDP weights. Data for multiyear spans show simple averages of the annual data.

A. The within-sector productivity contribution shows the initial real value added-weighted productivity growth; the between-sector contribution measures the productivity growth from a cross-sectoral shift of employment. ARG = Argentina; BRA = Brazil; CHL = Chile; COL = Colombia; MEX = Mexico.

B.C. "Other industry" includes mining, utilities, and construction; "other service" includes government and personal services. "Manuf." indicates manufacturing. Sample includes 69 EMDEs, of which 17 are LAC economies.

D. Horizontal line indicates 50 percent.

Sectoral productivity levels in LAC relative to EMDEs. In most sectors, productivity levels in LAC are close to the EMDE average, although productivity in trade and finance lags that in all EMDEs slightly. Removing productivity barriers in these sectors would benefit aggregate regional productivity.

Key drivers of productivity. LAC has long lagged other EMDE regions in several key drivers of productivity—investment, innovation, and trade—and performs only about average in other drivers (figure 5.18). Over time, the drivers of productivity in LAC have improved, but the improvement has not kept pace with that in EMDEs. Cyclical factors, such as weak investment in large economies in the region and gyrations in global

FIGURE 5.18 Drivers of productivity growth in LAC in regional comparison

Multiple structural constraints contribute to low productivity growth in LAC. The region performs particularly poorly relative to other EMDE regions in measures of investment, innovation, and trade. In other drivers, LAC is a mediocre performer relative to other regions. The drivers of productivity growth have become more supportive over time but at a slower pace than the EMDE average.

A. Drivers of productivity growth, 2017

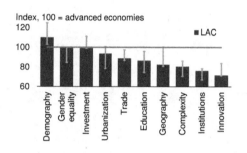

B. Index of productivity drivers

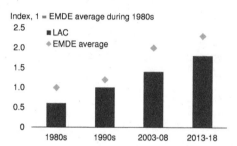

Sources: Freedom House; Haver Analytics; International Country Risk Guide (ICRG); Organisation for Economic Co-operation and Development; Observatory of Economic Complexity; Penn World Table; United Nations Educational, Scientific, and Cultural Organization (Institute for Statistics); United Nations Population Prospects; World Integrated Trade Solution; World Bank (Doing Business, Enterprise Surveys, and Global Financial Development Database).

Note: EMDEs = emerging market and developing economies; LAC = Latin America and the Caribbean.

A. Unweighted average levels of drivers normalized as an average of advanced economies as 100 and standard deviation of 10. Blue bars represent average within LAC economies. Orange whiskers represent the range of the average drivers for the six EMDE regions. Variables are defined as follows: Education = years of education, Urbanization = share of population living in urban areas, Investment = investment as share of GDP, Institutions = government effectiveness, Complexity = Economic Complexity Index of Hidalgo and Hausmann (2009), Gender equality = share of years of schooling for females to males, Demography = share of population under age 14, Innovation = log patents per capita, and Trade = (exports+imports)/GDP. Sample includes 16-25 LAC economies and 65-127 EMDEs, depending on the driver, and 32 advanced economies.

B. For each country, index is a weighted average of the normalized value of each driver of productivity. Refer to chapter 2 for weights. Drivers include the ICRG rule of law index, patents per capita, nontropical share of land area, investment as percent of GDP, ratio of female average years of education to male average years, share of population in urban area, Economic Complexity Index of Hidalgo and Hausmann (2009), years of schooling, working-age share of population, and inflation. Regional and EMDE indexes are GDP-weighted averages for single years and simple averages for time periods. Sample includes 18 LAC economies and 54 EMDEs.

commodity price trends, are also linked to weak productivity growth in LAC. Investment growth weakened substantially in the post-GFC period (figure 5.19).

Limited innovation and technology adoption. Innovation, achieved through dedicating resources to R&D or through introducing new processes or products, has been a key driver of labor and firm productivity in LAC (Crespi and Zuniga 2011; Grazzi and Jung 2016). Likewise, adoption of new technologies can reduce information costs and facilitate market access, thereby increasing productivity and expanding output in the region (Dutz, Almeida, and Packard 2018). LAC has missed key opportunities to raise productivity through these channels. R&D expenditure as a share of GDP is low in LAC relative to that in comparator EMDEs, as is the likelihood of firms in LAC introducing product innovations (Lederman et al. 2014).

Weak trade linkages. In three large economies in the region (Argentina, Chile, and Mexico), deeper participation in GVCs is associated with positive effects on firm productivity (Montalbano, Nenci, and Pietrobelli 2018). Yet nearly all LAC economies trade less (as a share of their GDP) than EMDEs overall, and GVC participation is lower

FIGURE 5.19 **Drivers of productivity growth in LAC**

A sustained period of contracting investment growth in LAC has held back productivity gains in recent years. Lower R&D spending relative to other regions, weak trade linkages in several large economies, and inadequately educated workers also hinder productivity growth.

A. Investment growth

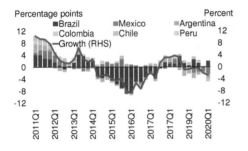

B. Research and development spending

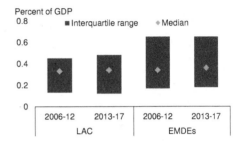

C. Trade, 2015-17

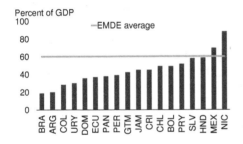

D. Firms indicating inadequately educated workers as their biggest obstacle

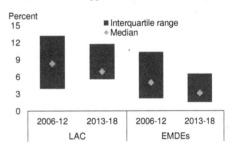

Sources: Haver Analytics; World Integrated Trade Solution; World Bank (Doing Business, Enterprise Surveys, and Global Financial Development Database).

Note: EMDEs = emerging market and developing economies; LAC = Latin America and the Caribbean; R&D = research and development.

A. Bars show investment-weighted averages. Last observation is 2020Q1. Investment growth is year-on-year.

B. Sample includes 16 economies for LAC and 94 for EMDEs.

C. Bars show 2015-17 average of exports plus imports as a share of GDP. Sample includes 96 EMDEs. BRA = Brazil; ARG = Argentina; COL = Colombia; URY = Uruguay; DOM = the Dominican Republic; ECU = Ecuador; PAN = Panama; PER = Peru; GTM = Guatemala; JAM = Jamaica; CRI = Costa Rica; CHL = Chile; BOL = Bolivia; PRY = Paraguay; SLV = El Salvador; HND = Honduras; MEX = Mexico; NIC = Nicaragua.

D. Sample includes 30 LAC economies and 113 EMDEs.

than in the EAP and ECA regions. Even the LAC countries most integrated in GVCs (Chile, Costa Rica, and Mexico) are not among the most integrated EMDEs and may suffer the economic consequences of GVC disruptions as a result of COVID-19 (OECD 2018b; World Bank 2020a). The opportunity for regional productivity gains through trade is further hindered by the structure of intra- and extraregional trade relationships. Although LAC countries are party to numerous trade agreements, there is little harmonization of rules of origin and nontariff measures across agreements, and there is no region-wide agreement. These characteristics result in fragmentation of trading priorities and, together with weak diversification of traded goods in many countries, limit the development of intraregional GVCs. Rules of origin imposed under preferential trade agreements in the region are estimated to negate more than 15 percent of the positive trade effect of the agreements, while the costs of nontariff measures imposed by LAC countries are estimated to equate to a 15 percent tariff for intermediate goods (Cadestin, Gourdon, and Kowalski 2016).

Poor-quality education and labor market constraints. At a median of 9.2 years in 2018, the duration of schooling in LAC compares favorably with 7.7 years in the average EMDE, and the gap between the median years of schooling in LAC and advanced economies narrowed from 3.5 years in 2008 to 2.9 years in 2018. However, learning outcomes in LAC fall short of their potential, as indicated by international standardized test results and high dropout rates at the tertiary level (World Bank 2017b). Moreover, in most LAC countries, education outcomes are highly correlated with socioeconomic conditions, a scenario reinforced by persistently elevated income inequality (World Bank 2018a). The prolonged, widespread school closures during the COVID-19 pandemic may set back long-term education achievement and earnings, and unequal access to technology may exacerbate existing education inequalities (Azevedo et al. 2020).

Ultimately, skills deficiencies and mismatches and low-quality education have negative implications for labor productivity and labor market functioning. The incidence of youth who are neither in school nor working is high (de Hoyos, Rogers, and Székely 2016). An estimated half of firms are unable to find local workers with the skills they need and consequently turn to foreign labor (OECD 2018b). Firm-level survey data for 2013-18 indicate that 7 percent of firms in LAC perceive an inadequately educated workforce as their biggest obstacle, more than double the share in all EMDEs. The poor functioning of labor markets due to skills deficiencies is compounded by longstanding regulatory rigidities that prevent efficient worker allocation and mobility (Kaplan 2009).

High informality. The informal sector in LAC averages about one-third of GDP, higher than in all other EMDE regions except Sub-Saharan Africa (World Bank 2019a). Informality in LAC is associated with lower aggregate and firm-level productivity (Chong, Galdo, and Saavedra 2008; de Paula and Sheinkman 2011; Loayza, Servén, and Sugawara 2010). In Paraguay, for example, informal firms are not only less productive than formal firms but also have negative productivity spillovers on formal firms (Vargas 2015). Importantly, informality is considered a key vulnerability that made LAC susceptible to the health and economic effects of COVID-19 (OECD 2020b).

Policy options

A range of options, targeted to country experiences, can be pursued to boost productivity in LAC and put the region on a path toward closing the productivity gap with advanced economies. Productivity in the region stands to benefit most from policy reforms to boost TFP, rather than to improve factors of production.

Improving factors of production

Increase the volume and efficiency of infrastructure investment. Relative to the pre-GFC period, capital deepening was the main source of productivity growth in large parts of the region during the post-GFC period. However, it has slowed sharply in the most recent years, and large infrastructure gaps remain. Although access to water and electricity in LAC is high relative to all EMDEs, the region underperforms in transportation and sanitation (Fay et al. 2017). To address this, transport network development is under way in several countries, such as Colombia. In addition, across the region, there is significant capacity to reduce infrastructure gaps by improving infrastructure spending efficiency—in particular, through improvements at the appraisal and evaluation stages of public investment projects and in public procurement systems.

Boosting firm productivity

Pursue well-targeted competition and innovation policies. Reducing barriers to entry for firms and easing the rigidity of labor regulations, on which LAC performs poorly compared to other EMDE regions and which encourage informal operation, are critical for promoting entrepreneurship and productivity. In Peru, for example, the elimination of subnational barriers to entry is found to have boosted firm productivity (Schiffbauer and Sampi 2019). Boosting low R&D spending and low technology-related innovations can also improve financial inclusion through development of secure digital payment systems and financial technology (fintech) regulatory frameworks (World Bank 2017c). Improving the speed of uptake of new technologies in LAC, where firms adopt new technologies with a significant lag relative to the United States, would also boost productivity (Eden and Nguyen 2016).

Deepen trade linkages, and reduce trade barriers. Trade relationships can boost productivity by facilitating knowledge exchange and innovation for the participating firms (Bown et al. 2017). Significant productivity gains could be made by reducing barriers to trade in LAC. The landmark European Union-Mercosur trade agreement, finalized by negotiators in June 2019 but not yet ratified, holds significant promise for decreasing trade barriers and deepening trade flows between Latin America and Europe. In addition, there have been some recent efforts to reduce trade barriers within the region; for instance, the Pacific Alliance eliminated tariffs among its members (Chile, Colombia, Mexico, and Peru) in May 2016. With global trade linkages disrupted by the COVID-19 pandemic, now may be a particularly good time to undertake structural reforms that would allow the region to better integrate into GVCs (World Bank 2020a).

Boost quality of education, and implement labor market reforms. In the short term, the use of technologies and innovative, offline solutions may help offset human capital losses and reduce education inequalities stemming from prolonged school closures in the region due to COVID-19 (Cobo, Hawkins, and Rovner 2020).

With the working-age share of the population on the cusp of the downward trajectory that EAP and ECA regions have already begun, the contribution of additional labor to productivity growth in LAC will fade. Advancing human capital through education and skills development will become increasingly important in the medium term. On-the-job training is an important element of boosting worker productivity, especially in the context of rapidly changing technologies. Programs that engage youth who are neither working nor studying are also critical (Almeida and Packard 2018). Skills training programs such as Jovenes en Acción in Colombia and ProJoven in Peru have had positive impacts on employment and productivity among the target populations and could be replicated. (Attanasio et al. 2015; Diaz and Rosas 2016). Apprenticeship programs also hold potential. For many countries, including Brazil, adapting labor markets to shifting economic opportunities in the strongly integrated global economy requires revision of dated labor market regulation (Dutz 2018). This could include reducing restrictions on use of term contracts, not allowing minimum wages above market equilibrium, and reducing penalties for redundancy.

Encouraging sectoral reallocation

Given that within-sector productivity gains in several large economies in LAC have stalled since the GFC, and may be further held back by shocks stemming from the COVID-19 pandemic, policy makers in the region should rekindle efforts to implement policies that reallocate capital and labor toward more productive firms within the sectors. Policies could aim to strengthen competition, including through trade, and reform labor markets to facilitate the movement and productivity of labor. The longstanding weakness in the region's between-sector productivity growth calls for policies that reduce misallocation of capital and labor toward sectors with low productivity. In particular, with limited opportunity for further industrialization, LAC countries should target lack of competition in services industries, including transport, finance, trade, and technology, and ensure that workers have sufficiently strong skills to thrive in occupations being transformed by technology (Araujo, Vostroknutova, and Wacker 2017; World Bank 2019k).

Creating a growth-friendly environment

Implement supportive governance and business climate reforms. Institutional quality is a key driver of productivity over the long term. For instance, fair contract enforcement, straightforward and transparent legal processes, and contained political risk have all been shown to support productivity gains (Acemoglu et al. 2019; Rodrik 1999; Rodrik, Subramanian, and Trebbi 2004). Relative to other regions, however, LAC is a mediocre performer on measures of governance. Moreover, the region's performance has deteriorated during the post-GFC period in measures of government effectiveness, control of corruption, and regulatory quality (Kaufmann, Kraay, and Mastruzzi 2010). Especially when the burden of regulation is high, as it tends to be in LAC, corruption is detrimental for productivity (Amin and Ulku 2019). On measures of doing business, no country in LAC is among the top 50 performers in the world (World Bank 2020d). Business environment reforms can also help reduce the size of the informal sector, where productivity is lower than in the formal sector. The process of institutional reforms could be spearheaded through productivity commissions such as those created in Chile, Colombia, and Mexico. Colombia, for example, is implementing a series of structural reforms as part of its Productive Development Policy 2016-2025.

Middle East and North Africa

Labor productivity growth in MNA was the weakest among EMDE regions before and after the GFC. It averaged –0.1 percent between 2013-18, although with wide heterogeneity across economies within the region. Weak productivity growth has widened the region's productivity gap with advanced economies. Large public sectors, underdeveloped private sectors, and lack of economic diversification hold back productivity growth. Although recent reform initiatives in many countries in the region are promising, the COVID-19 pandemic may hinder productivity in the short and medium term. A multipronged policy effort is needed to reliably raise productivity growth in the region, including raising the quality of human capital and boosting private sector investment, increasing firm productivity, removing obstacles to sectoral reallocation, and creating business-friendly environments.

Evolution of regional productivity

Low labor productivity growth. From an already weak pre-GFC rate (0.1 percent during 2003-08), labor productivity growth in MNA decelerated further, to about –0.1 percent during 2013-18, the weakest among EMDE regions (figure 5.20).[11] This slowdown affected more than half of EMDEs in the region and was strongest among energy exporters, where productivity growth has been severely constrained by weak investment (figure 5.21). Moreover, continued reliance on commodity exports in many economies means that they have not experienced the diversification or expansion of other sectors that helped drive high productivity growth in regions such as EAP. Weak post-GFC productivity growth in the region continues a long-standing trend that featured productivity growth below the EMDE average for the past two decades. The disruptions spurred by the COVID-19 pandemic put the productivity prospects of the region at substantial risk, especially combined with the negative oil price shock.

Within-region heterogeneity. Within-region productivity trends differ considerably. Energy-exporting economies experienced a 0.5 percent productivity contraction in 2013-18, amid a 50 percent plunge in oil prices from a mid-2014 peak. In energy importers, productivity growth rose to 1.9 percent in 2013-18, from 1.3 percent in 2003-08.

Wide dispersion in labor productivity levels. At two-fifths of advanced economy productivity, MNA has the highest productivity level of any EMDE region. Yet, relative to the advanced economy average, the level was lower in 2013-18 than in 2003-08. Moreover, productivity levels in MNA differ widely within the region, with substantially higher levels in the Gulf Cooperation Council (GCC) economies than in energy importers. This disparity reflects the variation in natural resource endowments between lower-middle-income energy importers such as Egypt, Morocco, and Tunisia, and high-income energy exporters such as Saudi Arabia and the United Arab Emirates.

---

[11] The primary sample under which regional labor productivity trends are discussed is based on 14 MNA economies: Algeria, Bahrain, the Arab Republic of Egypt, the Islamic Republic of Iran, Iraq, Jordan, Kuwait, Lebanon, Morocco, Oman, Qatar, Saudi Arabia, Tunisia, and the United Arab Emirates.

FIGURE 5.20 **Productivity in MNA in regional comparison**

Labor productivity growth in MNA has been the weakest among EMDE regions, before and after the GFC, averaging –0.1 percent during 2013-18. Despite a high average productivity level relative to other EMDE regions, weak productivity growth has recently widened MNA's productivity gap with advanced economies.

A. Productivity growth relative to other EMDE regions

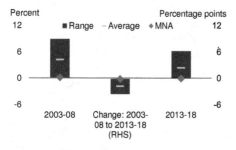

B. Productivity levels and rate of productivity convergence

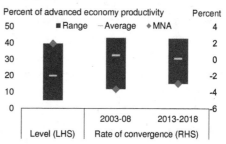

Sources: The Conference Board; Penn World Table; World Bank (World Development Indicators).
Note: Productivity is defined as real GDP per worker (at 2010 market prices and exchange rates). Country group aggregates for a given year are calculated using constant 2010 U.S. dollar GDP weights. Data for multiyear spans show simple averages of the annual data. EMDEs = emerging market and developing economies; GFC = global financial crisis; MNA = Middle East and North Africa.
A. Blue bars show the range of average productivity across the six EMDE regions. Yellow dashes denote the average of the six EMDE regional aggregates. Red diamonds denote simple average of MNA economies. Sample includes 14 MNA economies and 129 EMDEs. The 14 MNA economies in the sample are Algeria, Bahrain, the Arab Republic of Egypt, the Islamic Republic of Iran, Iraq, Jordan, Kuwait, Lebanon, Morocco, Oman, Qatar, Saudi Arabia, Tunisia, and the United Arab Emirates.
B. Rate of convergence is calculated as the difference in productivity growth rates over the log difference in productivity levels between MNA and advanced economies. Blue bars and yellow dashes show the range and average of the six EMDE regional aggregates. "Level" of productivity refers to the GDP-weighted average of regional productivity as a share of the average advanced economy during 2013-18. LHS refers to left-hand side. RHS refers to right-hand side. Sample includes 14 MNA economies, 129 EMDEs, and 35 advanced economies.

Sources of labor productivity growth. In the two decades before the oil price collapse of 2014-16, labor productivity growth in the region was primarily supported by capital deepening, driven by capital investment by energy exporters (IMF 2012, 2015; Malik and Masood 2018). In an alternative decomposition that also incorporates natural resources (similar to Brandt, Schreyer, and Zipperer 2017), natural resource activity appears to drive MNA productivity growth significantly. Its average contribution to productivity growth shrank from about 1.2 percentage points during 2003-08 to essentially zero during 2013-14.

The commodity sector is capital intensive. As a result, oil prices and capital expenditures are closely linked in the MNA region (Albino-War et al. 2014; IMF 2018b). FDI is also highly undiversified and heavily concentrated in the commodity sector (World Bank 2003). After the GFC, investment growth in the region slowed sharply. Among energy exporters, this slower growth has been attributed to tight financial constraints associated with lower oil prices. Among energy importers, the legacies of the Arab Spring movements led many economies to increase investment on defense at the expense of infrastructure and other productivity-enhancing projects and initiatives (Ianchovichina 2017).

FIGURE 5.21 **Evolution of labor productivity growth in MNA**

The post-GFC productivity growth slowdown was concentrated in energy exporters and affected about half of the region's economies. Productivity contracted by 0.5 percent in energy exporters and grew by 1.9 percent in energy importers. Falling productivity growth in the region has been largely driven by shrinking capital stock, especially in energy exporters. Productivity levels in exporters remain much higher than in importers, however. The contribution of natural capital to productivity growth fell significantly relative to the pre-GFC period.

A. Productivity growth

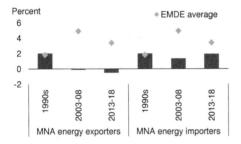

B. Economies with 2013-18 average productivity growth below long-run and pre-GFC averages

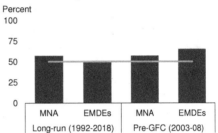

C. Productivity levels relative to advanced economies

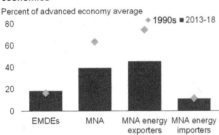

D. Factor contributions to productivity growth

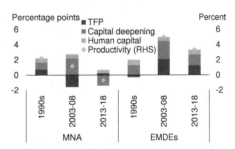

E. Factor contributions to productivity growth, MNA energy exporters and importers

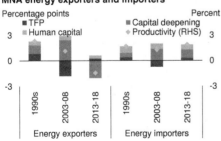

F. Factor contributions to productivity growth, including natural capital

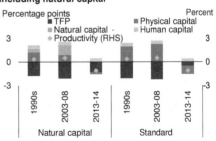

Sources: Barro and Lee (2015); Haver Analytics; International Monetary Fund; Penn World Table; United Nations (Human Development Reports), Wittgenstein Centre for Demography and Global Human Capital; World Bank.

Note: Productivity is defined as real GDP per worker (at 2010 market prices and exchange rates). Country group aggregates for a given year are calculated using constant 2010 U.S. dollar GDP weights. Data for multiyear spans show simple averages of the annual data. EMDEs = emerging market and developing economies; GFC = global financial crisis; MNA = Middle East and North Africa; TFP = total factor productivity.

A-C. The sample includes 14 MNA economies (Algeria, Bahrain, the Arab Republic of Egypt, the Islamic Republic of Iran, Iraq, Jordan, Kuwait, Lebanon, Morocco, Oman, Qatar, Saudi Arabia, Tunisia, and the United Arab Emirates) and 129 EMDEs.

B. Horizontal line indicates 50 percent.

D-F. Productivity growth is computed as log changes.

D.E. Sample includes 12 MNA economies (same as in A but excluding Algeria and the United Arab Emirates) and 93 EMDEs.

F. Sample includes 10 MNA economies with data for natural capital: Bahrain, Egypt, Jordan, Kuwait, Lebanon, Morocco, Oman, Qatar, Saudi Arabia, and Tunisia. The post-GFC time period differs from E and F because of natural capital data availability.

Pre-GFC capital deepening was partly offset by contractionary TFP growth, the long-standing weakness of which has been widely documented.[12] The inverse relationship between capital accumulation and TFP growth suggests inefficient investment and may be attributed to two factors. First, predominantly public investment combined with the large economic role of SOEs crowds out private investment and job creation. Second, fiscal policy tends to be procyclical—just like public investment—as countries often pursue expansionary fiscal policy during oil price booms (Abdih et al. 2010). During periods of high capital investment and oil price booms, the momentum of reform oriented toward enhancing technology tends to be weaker, weighing on TFP growth. Negative TFP growth in MNA before the global financial crisis stands in sharp contrast to the robust pre-GFC TFP growth in the broader group of EMDEs. TFP growth started to pick up as oil prices bottomed out in 2016, however.[13]

Heterogeneity in sources of labor productivity growth. Although labor productivity growth in the MNA region as a whole has long been anemic and continues to be weak, there is wide divergence in the driving forces. For energy exporters, productivity growth decelerated markedly from 2003-08 to the post-GFC period of 2013-18 because of sharply declining investment activity. For energy importers, productivity growth improved modestly from a weak base, largely because of the recovery from negative average TFP growth rates during 2003-08 to slightly above zero percent during 2013-18.

Sources of regional productivity growth

High barriers to factor reallocation. Factor reallocation toward more productive activity has played a limited role in driving productivity growth in MNA. This reflects high barriers to entry and distortions such as the lack of competitive markets (Arezki et al. 2019a). Small exporting firms are hesitant to scale up their operations and benefit little from GVC integration (World Bank 2016d). In the North Africa subregion, evidence from Egypt and Morocco suggests that within-sector productivity gains have been the main source of productivity growth for their economies, both before and after the GFC (figure 5.22). In Saudi Arabia, employment appears to have moved toward sectors with relatively low productivity in the past (Fayad and Rasmussen 2012). These trends imply the existence of distortions in the economy that prevent more efficient reallocation of resources across sectors. High capital intensity of the commodity sector accounted for high average productivity levels in MNA, and scope for productivity improvement in the private sector remains large. Moreover, employment is concentrated in the services sector, reflecting an exceptionally high proportion of the workforce (about one-fifth) employed in the public sector (Tamirisa and Duenwald 2018).

---

[12] Weak or negative TFP growth is found to be a prevalent feature in the MNA region during the past three decades. For regional and country-specific studies that highlight TFP growth in MNA, see Baier, Dwyer, and Tamura (2006); Bisat, El-Erian, and T. Helbling (1997); Callen et al. (2014); IMF (2012); Keller and Nabli (2002); Malik and Masood (2018); World Bank (2017d); and Yousef (2004).

[13] TFP growth can be affected by nontechnology factors, such as capital and labor utilization. Hence, TFP growth estimates may overstate or understate the true change in the influence of technology on productivity (Dieppe, Kindberg-Hanlon, and Kilic Celik, forthcoming).

FIGURE 5.22 **Factors supporting productivity growth in MNA**

Productivity levels relative to advanced economies are the highest in MNA's capital-intensive mining sector. Evidence for the Arab Republic of Egypt and for Morocco suggests that productivity growth in North Africa has been largely limited to within-sector productivity gains.

A. Sectoral productivity levels, 2017

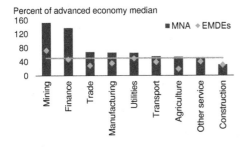

B. Within- and between-sector contributions to productivity growth

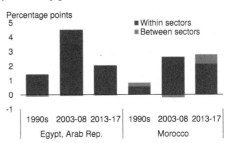

Sources: Groningen Growth Development Center Database; Haver Analytics; International Labour Organization; Penn World Table; World Bank.
Note: Productivity is defined as real GDP per worker (at 2010 market prices and exchange rates). Country group aggregates for a given year are calculated using constant 2010 U.S. dollar GDP weights. Data for multiyear spans show simple averages of the annual data. EMDEs = emerging market and developing economies; MNA = Middle East and North Africa.
A. Medians across economies in each sector. Horizontal line indicates 50 percent. Sample includes 12 MNA economies.
B. The within-sector productivity contribution shows the initial real value added-weighted productivity growth contribution, holding employment share fixed; the between-sector contribution measures the productivity growth from a cross-sectoral shift of employment.

Other drivers of labor productivity growth. Weak productivity in the MNA region has been associated with underdevelopment of the private sector, overreliance on the public sector, and lack of economic diversification (Devarajan and Mottaghi 2015).

- *Large public sector.* On average, about one-fifth of the region's workforce is employed in the public sector, and public-private sector wage gaps are among the highest in the world (Purfield et al. 2018; Tamirisa and Duenwald 2018). The education system is targeted toward government employment, with few high-quality private sector jobs (World Bank 2018k). These dynamics hold back the adoption of technology from abroad (Mitra et al. 2016; Raggl 2015; Samargandi 2018). In the GCC, weak productivity growth has been associated with low mobility of high-skilled foreign workers (Callen et al. 2014).

- *Restrictive business climate.* Poor governance quality, large informal sectors, and cumbersome tax policy and administration hampered the reallocation of resources from low-productivity to higher-productivity firms (Nabli 2007; World Bank 2016d). Non-GCC economies in MNA rank especially low in the World Bank's Worldwide Governance Indicators, such as regulatory quality and government effectiveness. Private firms often face challenges in access to finance, yet providing access to formal finance is associated with labor productivity growth being 2 percentage points higher in MNA firms (Blancher, Bibolov, and Fouejieu 2019).

- *Anemic private sector.* Firm productivity in MNA has been restricted by low firm turnover and creation. Only six limited liability companies were created annually for every 10,000 working-age people in MNA during 2009-12—considerably less than in other EMDEs (Schiffbauer et al. 2015).

- *Lack of diversification.* Trade openness and export diversification remain low among MNA economies. Lack of diversification is partly the result of exchange rate misalignments associated with high reliance on extractive industries or low technological content of exports (Benhassine et al. 2009). In the region's large economies, low export diversification has been found to hinder productivity growth (IMF 2013, 2015; Morsey, Levy, and Sanchez 2014; Samargandi 2018). Although R&D, as measured by the number of patent applications per capita, is above the EMDE average, it is well below advanced economy averages, holding back productivity growth and diversification (Rahmati and Pilehvari 2017; Samargandi 2018).

- *Conflict.* Armed conflicts in countries such as Syria and the Republic of Yemen continue to prevent productivity gains domestically and within the region.

In the GCC, a series of reforms includes measures to improve productivity and diversify away from the energy sector. Efforts to boost SMEs and to encourage private sector development include the establishment of an SME agency in Saudi Arabia and SME delicensing in the United Arab Emirates. Among energy importers, measures to improve the business and private sector climate have been enacted in Egypt, Morocco, and Tunisia (World Bank 2019l). Initial market responses to these developments suggest that efficiency gains have been generated. Many GCC economies have implemented policies to relax foreign investment restrictions (for example, the United Arab Emirates' relaxation of restriction in 13 sectors in 2019). These changes have been associated with foreign investment inflows, which in EMDEs often catalyze productivity-enhancing private investment (Henry 2007).

Policy reforms have also made it easier to raise international capital, which has already helped finance fiscal and balance-of-payments needs in MNA (IMF 2019d). Egypt's macroeconomic reforms since 2016, including the liberalization of the exchange rate, business climate reforms, and energy subsidy reforms, have been perceived positively by investors and may have raised the country's export and investment prospects (Youssef et al. 2019). In some cases, however, reforms are subject to high risk of implementation delay, especially in non-GCC economies, where political fragmentation and budget irresolution frequently hold back multiyear reform plans and social tensions underscore the fragility associated with reform progress. Moreover, the COVID-19 pandemic has also created higher uncertainty about the pace of reforms, and their prospects are contingent on how reform initiatives are integrated with COVID-19 policy responses.

Policy options

Concerted and multipronged efforts are required to reliably raise productivity growth. Policies need to be directed at raising the quality of human capital and boosting private sector investment, increasing firm productivity, removing obstacles to sectoral reallocation, and creating business-friendly environments. Within these broad themes, specific policies need to be tailored to a country's specific circumstances.

In practice, the effectiveness of reform is contingent on the health of each economy and the timing of political events (Alesina et al. 2019). In some circumstances, a targeted approach that leverages synergies may be warranted. Deep institutional reforms to raise market contestability, for example, may bring a variety of collateral benefits, such as higher technological progress (Arezki et al. 2019a). Well-designed deployment of fintech could help garner broad-based support for institutional reforms (World Bank 2019l).

Improving factors of production

Boost private investment. Although capital deepening has been a main driver of productivity growth in MNA, it has been primarily supported by large public spending (for example, the commodity sector in the GCC; IMF 2018b). This suggests large scope to boost private investment. A wide range of reforms is needed to encourage private investment, including expanding access to finance, improving business climates and governance, reducing the wage premium of government employment, and leveling the playing field with state-controlled enterprises (Arezki et al. 2019a).

Raise human capital. The contribution of human capital to labor productivity growth has been modest in the past two decades, amounting to only about half a percentage point. The region's human capital challenge is to improve educational access for youth and women, improve the connection between educational attainment and private sector jobs, and shift its bias in educational training away from the public sector (World Bank 2018k). These measures would help the productivity potential of MNA's large youth population. More educational programs to improve the skills match between workers and employers can enhance the quality of jobs in MNA (Gatti et al. 2013).

Boosting firm productivity

Improve access to finance. Access to finance is a large obstacle for firms in MNA, particularly for non-GCC economies, because lack of financing hinders their ability to invest and innovate (figure 5.23). Better access to credit, supported by broader credit bureau coverage and stronger insolvency resolution regimes, appears to yield sizable benefits to productivity growth in MNA (Ghassibe, Appendino, and Mahmoudi 2019). New insolvency resolution laws adopted in Djibouti, Egypt, Jordan, and Saudi Arabia are promising for facilitating debt resolution between creditors and debtors. New minority investor protection regulation in Egypt aims to improve corporate governance and investor confidence.

Address informality. Informality, although low by average EMDE standards, presents a challenge to businesses in non-GCC economies. Competition from the informal sector is a major obstacle for formal sector businesses in several large economies (such as Morocco and Tunisia), and a higher share of informal workers in SMEs is associated with lower wages and more limited export potential (Elbadawi and Loayza 2008). Aligning tax systems to international best practices (for example, harmonized electronic filing systems

FIGURE 5.23 **Policy challenges in MNA**

Multipronged and sustainable reforms that improve governance and boost private sector development are crucial in MNA. Reforms could lift the potential of its young population and relieve constraints to firm productivity, such as access to finance.

A. Firms indicating access to finance as a major obstacle

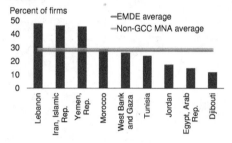

B. Youth not in education or employment

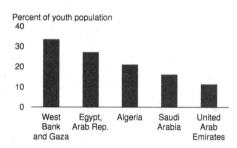

Source: World Bank.
Note: EMDE = emerging market and developing economy; GCC = Gulf Cooperation Council; MNA = Middle East and North Africa.
A. Based on World Bank's Enterprise Surveys. Latest available survey year for each economy denoted. Non-GCC MNA denotes average of all economies shown in the figure.
B. Share of youth not in education, employment, or training, as a percent of youth population. Latest available data since 2015.

in Morocco) and reducing regulatory hurdles for firms can help attract informal firms to more productive formal activity while raising revenue collection.

Encouraging efficient resource reallocation

Diversify through trade. Reforms in investment, trade, and tariff policies could help MNA move up the export value chain and encourage greater product variety, in which MNA currently lags behind international benchmarks. Regional integration efforts (for example, Compact with Africa) could help promote diversification and raise productivity.

Diversify away from commodity dependence. For energy exporters, including the GCC economies, stronger fiscal management could help promote diversification by broadening the revenue base (Diop and Marotta 2012; World Bank 2019m). For energy importers, options for diversification may include investment in renewable energies via public-private partnerships (for example, Egypt; Vagliasindi 2013), or initiatives to boost the private services sector (for example, tourism initiatives in oil importers). Efforts to expand the reach of firms to the global market can also help boost productivity growth (World Bank 2016d).

Creating a growth-friendly environment

Improve business climates. Business climate reforms, such as the reduction of regulatory hurdles to start businesses or the removal of particularly distortionary taxes, can help boost private investment and productivity. They can also provide firms easier access to critical inputs, such as improved electricity supply. They can support productivity through better allocation of resources (for example, more efficient taxation systems) and stronger entrepreneurship activities (for example, lower cost to start a business). In MNA, reforms that move an economy one unit higher in the Global Competitiveness Index have been estimated to have raised productivity potential significantly (Mitra et al. 2016). Many MNA economies have adopted broad-based business climate reforms recently, including improved electricity connection in Bahrain, enhanced electronic tax filing in Jordan, and easier property registration in Kuwait.

Improve governance. Governance quality in MNA, especially in non-GCC economies, lags behind other EMDEs and has improved little over the past decade. Weak governance has discouraged private sector activity and investment (Nabli 2007). Reforms such as streamlining public service delivery and strengthening legal frameworks in areas like procurement laws can increase productivity growth by encouraging more efficient allocation of resources. They can also increase investment prospects through improved investor confidence. Reforms for SOEs in telecom industries can also enhance productivity via higher efficiency (Arezki et al. 2019b).

Improve gender equality. Women account for only about one-fifth of the labor force in MNA. Bridging the gender gap in a number of areas, including workforce development and access to digital and financial services, is especially relevant for MNA. Closing these gaps can raise productivity growth through more vibrant entrepreneurship and private sector participation. Legislation to reduce economic discrimination against women in Tunisia is an example of a recent reform in this area.

South Asia

In contrast to other regions, labor productivity growth in SAR slowed only mildly after the GFC. During 2013-18, SAR's productivity growth remained the second fastest among the six EMDE regions, at 5.3 percent a year. Although this has helped reduce the region's wide productivity gap with the advanced economy average, the level of productivity in SAR remains the lowest among EMDE regions, in part reflecting widespread informal economic activity and struggling manufacturing sectors. Low human capital, poor business environments, inefficient resource allocation, and limited exposure to foreign firms and foreign investment also weigh on productivity. Moreover, SAR economies are likely to face a broad-based decline in labor productivity growth because of the COVID-19 shock. Increasing openness, by enhancing FDI inflows and participation in global and regional value chains, could support technology and information transfer to the region and boost productivity growth. Promoting access to finance and improving infrastructure could lift firm-level productivity in the region.

Evolution of regional productivity

Robust productivity growth. In contrast to other EMDE regions, productivity growth in SAR slowed only mildly after the GFC, to 5.3 percent a year during 2013-18, from

6.4 percent in 2003-08 (figure 5.24).[14] This followed a steady rise from anemic rates in the mid-1980s when heavily state-directed economic policy strategies dampened investment and innovation. In the post-GFC period, a slight moderation in India's productivity growth was partially offset by pickups in Bangladesh and Pakistan. The region's resilience reflected three main elements: SAR's limited exposure to external headwinds, continued rapid urbanization, and an improving business environment that supported productivity gains from the continuing shift away from agriculture toward more productive services sectors (APO 2018; World Bank 2016e). As a result, in the post-GFC period, the share of economies with productivity growth below long-run and pre-GFC averages was lower than in other EMDEs. However, the COVID-19 shock and the related plunge in global forecasts present a substantial risk of slowing productivity growth in the region (World Bank 2020a, 2020e).

- In *India*, disruptions to economic activity due to cash shortages in 2016 and transitional costs related to the introduction of the new Goods and Services Tax (GST) system in 2017 contributed to a slowing of productivity growth to 5.6 percent a year during 2013-18, from the 2003-08 average of 7.1 percent a year. Nevertheless, India's post-GFC productivity growth remained in the highest decile among EMDEs. It was supported by investment in the energy and transport sectors, improvement in the ease of doing business, and ongoing structural reforms.

- In *Pakistan*, annual productivity growth picked up from a pre-GFC average of 2.5 percent to 3.5 percent during 2013-18. During the post-GFC period, productivity growth benefited from strong FDI inflows and infrastructure projects that supported private sector activity.

- In *Bangladesh*, post-GFC productivity growth benefited from improved macro-economic and political stability that supported both public and private fixed investment. As a result, productivity growth in Bangladesh was robust during 2013-18, at 5.1 percent, slightly above the pre-GFC average of 4.7 percent and in the top decile of EMDEs.

- Productivity growth in the rest of the region either stalled or declined in the post-GFC period in line with the global trend. The factors behind the slowdown included natural disasters, macroeconomic and political instability, and weaker growth of global trade and manufacturing activity.

SAR's robust productivity growth through the 2000s is in stark contrast to its weakness during the 1980s and 1990s, even though in those decades also it was mostly stronger than in other EMDEs. In the 1980s, India's state-directed economy generated minimal productivity growth as heavy regulation and widespread corruption (the "license raj")

---

[14] Data for labor productivity at the national level, as well as for the three main production sectors (agriculture, manufacturing and mining, and services), are available for seven EMDEs in SAR: Bangladesh, Bhutan, India, Maldives, Nepal, Pakistan, and Sri Lanka.

FIGURE 5.24 **Evolution of productivity growth in SAR**

Productivity in SAR expanded by 5.3 percent a year during 2013-18, substantially higher than the EMDE average but lower than in 2003-08. The catch-up to advanced economy productivity levels starts from a low base; productivity levels in the region were about 5 percent of the advanced economy average in 2013-18. Although productivity growth is high in several large economies, there is significant disparity across the region.

A. Productivity growth relative to other EMDE regions

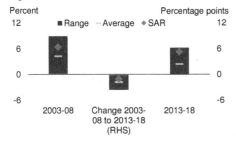

B. Productivity levels and rate of productivity convergence

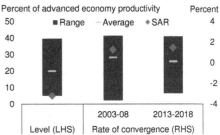

C. Productivity growth, by year

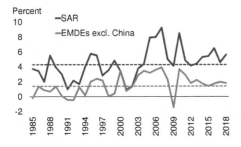

D. Productivity growth, by country

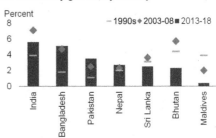

E. Share of economies with 2013-18 average productivity growth below long-run and pre-GFC averages

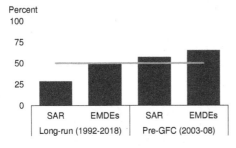

F. Productivity level relative to advanced economy average, by country

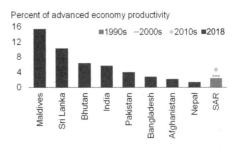

Sources: The Conference Board; Haver Analytics; Penn World Table; World Bank (World Development Indicators).
Note: Productivity is defined as real GDP per worker (at 2010 market prices and exchange rates). Country group aggregates for a given year are calculated using constant 2010 U.S. dollar GDP weights. Data for multiyear spans show simple averages of the annual data. Sample includes 7 SAR economies and 129 EMDEs unless otherwise indicated. EMDEs = emerging market and developing economies; GFC = global financial crisis; SAR = South Asia.
A.B. Blue bars show the range of average productivity across the six EMDE regions. Yellow dashes denote the average of the six EMDE regional aggregates. Red diamonds denote simple average of SAR economies.
B. Rate of convergence is calculated as the difference in productivity growth rates over the log difference in productivity levels between SAR and advanced economies. Blue bars and yellow dashes show the range and average of the six EMDE regional aggregates. "Level" of productivity refers to the GDP-weighted average of regional productivity as a share of the average advanced economy during 2013-18. Sample includes 7 SAR economies, 129 EMDEs, and 35 advanced economies.
C. Dashed lines indicate 1981-2018 averages.
E. Horizontal line indicates 50 percent.

stifled manufacturing, investment, and technology adoption. Following India's 1991 balance-of-payments crisis, major reforms reduced restrictions on product and factor markets and allowed more trade, catalyzing a surge in productivity growth (Rodrik and Subramanian 2004; Virmani and Hashim 2011). In Pakistan, productivity growth was limited by macroeconomic instability (Amjad and Awais 2016; Lopez-Calix, Srinivasan, and Waheed 2012).

Low productivity levels. Despite strong productivity growth over the past three decades, the average level of labor productivity in SAR during 2013-18 was still only 5 percent of the advanced economy average, and the lowest among EMDE regions, compared to about 18 percent of the advanced economy average in all EMDEs. In contrast to other EMDE regions, though, the pace of convergence has picked up since the GFC. At the recent rate of convergence (2013-18), however, only one-eighth of economies in SAR would halve their productivity gap with advanced economies over the next 40 years.

Within-region disparity of productivity levels. Productivity differences across countries are very large in SAR. Nepal had the lowest productivity levels in 2013-18, at about 1 percent of the advanced economy average, partly reflecting natural disasters. Bhutan, Maldives, and Sri Lanka have higher productivity levels, in the range of 6 to 15 percent of the advanced economy average, reflecting the benefit of relatively large service sectors, in particular tourism activity. Productivity levels in the three largest economies of SAR—India, Bangladesh, and Pakistan—are lower, ranging between 3 and 5 percent of the advanced economy average, reflecting their relatively large informal sectors, low urbanization rates, and weak financial development.

Slowing contribution from capital deepening. Decomposing labor productivity growth into contributions from increases in other factors of production and efficiency with which the factors are used (TFP) shows that nearly all of the productivity growth slowdown in SAR during the post-GFC period was due to less accumulation of capital. This decomposition is possible only for India and Sri Lanka, however. The contributions to labor productivity growth of TFP growth and human capital growth remained approximately the same as in the pre-GFC period (figure 5.25). Weakening investment growth in part reflected the economic disruptions in India around the currency exchange of 2016 and the introduction of the GST in 2017. Slower global trade in the most recent years has weighed further on investment. The slowdown of investment growth was from high pre-GFC rates that were fueled partly by large FDI inflows after financial liberalization reforms in the 1990s (Fujimori and Sato 2015; Park 2010).

Sources of regional productivity growth

The slight deceleration in SAR's post-GFC productivity growth was accounted for mainly by India and by weaker growth in the industrial sector. The median productivity level of the industrial sector in SAR was less than two-thirds of the EMDE median in 2017. In part, manufacturing productivity reflects limited integration into international trade networks and GVCs, which has limited the region's interaction with more productive foreign firms and reduced opportunities to benefit from technology transfer.

FIGURE 5.25 Sectoral productivity and employment in SAR

Productivity gains in SAR benefited from improvements in TFP growth and capital deepening, albeit from low levels. Productivity levels in the services sector are higher than in the industrial sector and have grown significantly over the past decade. Within-sector productivity growth has accounted for a much larger share of aggregate productivity growth than between-sector productivity growth. The share of employment in trade and other services sectors has increased over time as workers have shifted away from low-productivity agricultural production to these sectors.

A. Factor contributions to productivity growth

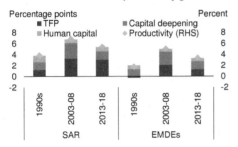

B. Sectoral productivity levels in SAR

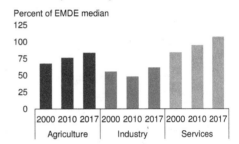

C. Sectoral productivity levels, 2017

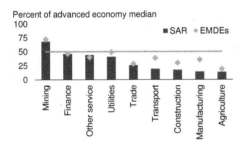

D. Within- and between-sector contributions to productivity growth

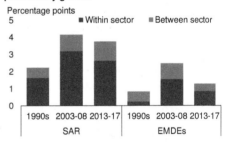

E. Composition of employment, by sector

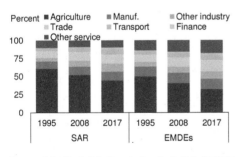

F. Sectoral contribution to aggregate productivity growth

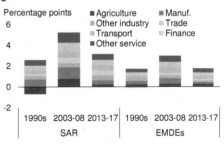

Sources: Asian Productivity Organization, Productivity Database; Expanded African Sector; Groningen Growth Development Center database; International Labour Organization, ILOSTAT; Organisation for Economic Co-operation and Development, Structural Analysis Database; United Nations; World KLEMS.

Note: Productivity is defined as real GDP per worker (at 2010 market prices and exchange rates). EMDEs = emerging market and developing economies; SAR = South Asia; TFP = total factor productivity.

A. Country group aggregates for a given year are calculated using constant 2010 U.S. dollar GDP weights. Data for multiyear spans show simple averages of the annual data. SAR sample includes India and Sri Lanka. EMDE sample includes 93 economies. Productivity growth is computed as log changes.

C.D. Sample includes 3 SAR economies (India, Pakistan, Sri Lanka) and 129 EMDEs.

C. Horizontal line indicates 50 percent.

D. Growth within sector shows the contribution of initial real value added-weighted productivity growth rate of each sector, holding employment shares fixed, and "between sector" effect shows the contribution arising from changes in sectoral employment shares. Median of the country-specific contributions.

E.F. "Other industry" includes mining, utilities, and construction; "other service" includes government and personal services. "Manuf." indicates manufacturing. Sample includes 69 EMDEs, of which 5 are SAR economies (Bangladesh, India, Nepal, Pakistan, Sri Lanka).

However, post-GFC productivity growth in this sector remained higher than the EMDE average, reflecting improvements in the business environment as well as ongoing public investment in transportation and energy infrastructure.

Most productivity gains from within-sector reallocation. Factor reallocation from low-productivity to high-productivity sectors and firms has historically not been an important source of productivity gains in SAR, accounting for less than one-fifth of productivity growth (Goretti, Kihara, and Salgado 2019; Mallick 2017; World Bank 2017e). However, this has shifted since the GFC. Between-sector reallocation accounted for about 30 percent of productivity growth in 2013-17, up from less than 25 percent in 2003-08. Meanwhile, the contribution of within-sector productivity growth slowed.

Most of the post-GFC productivity gains from sectoral reallocation reflected a shift from agriculture, which accounted for less than one-fifth of SAR GDP in 2017 but almost half of employment, into services, which accounted for more than half of GDP but roughly one-third of employment. Agriculture, the region's lowest-productivity sector (with median productivity 13 percent that of advanced economies), has less than one-third the productivity of financial services (46 percent of the average for advanced economies) in the region. In the post-GFC period, the contribution of services sectors to productivity in SAR has declined along with that of agriculture and manufacturing.

Other drivers of productivity. In SAR, the contributions of most of the long-run drivers of productivity to productivity growth have remained low compared to other EMDEs and advanced economies (figure 5.26). Measures of gender equality and trade openness are below other EMDE regions, as demonstrated by very low female participation rates and weak integration with GVCs. In the post-GFC period, the pace of improvement in several of the long-run determinants of productivity slowed, including average years of schooling, labor force participation, investment, urbanization, and economic complexity. Nonetheless, improvements in these drivers continued. Despite a slowdown in the post-GFC period, investment continued to contribute to productivity growth more than in other EMDEs and advanced economies. By contrast, limited global integration, weakness in control of corruption, low R&D activity, and pervasive informality continued to weigh on productivity growth.

- *Limited global integration.* Export-oriented firms in SAR are more productive than nonexporters (figure 5.27). However, the largest regional economies are less open to trade than the average EMDE. Moreover, although FDI inflows have grown, they remain below the EMDE average. Both of these trends limit the potential for technology and information transfer that could boost regional productivity growth (Fujimori and Sato 2015; Maiti 2019; Topalova and Khandelwal 2011).

- *Lack of supporting infrastructure.* Many firms cite infrastructure gaps as important obstacles to their business activities. In Pakistan and Bangladesh, these firms are found to be less productive than others (Fernandes 2008; Grainger and Zhang 2017). The environment has also become decreasingly supportive in terms of access to finance with state-owned banks dominating banking system assets (for example,

FIGURE 5.26 **Drivers of productivity growth in SAR**

Many of the drivers of productivity in SAR remain at the low end of the EMDE regional range, suggesting scope for further improvements. The labor force dedicated to R&D lags significantly behind that in other regions.

A. Drivers of productivity growth, 2017

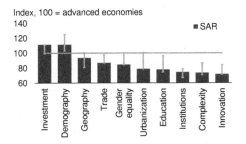

B. Research and development, 2017

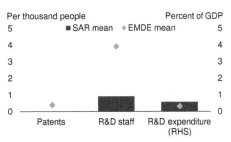

Sources: Freedom House; Haver Analytics; International Country Risk Guide; Organisation for Economic Co-operation and Development; Observatory of Economic Complexity; Penn World Table; United Nations Educational, Scientific, and Cultural Organization (Institute for Statistics); United Nations Population Prospects; World Integrated Trade Solution; World Bank (Doing Business, Enterprise Surveys, and Global Financial Development Database).
Note: EMDEs = emerging market and developing economies; R&D = research and development; SAR = South Asia.
A. Unweighted average levels of drivers normalized as an average of advanced economies as 100 and standard deviation of 10. Blue bars represent average within SAR economies. Orange whiskers represent the range of the average drivers for the six EMDE regions. Horizontal line indicates 100. Variables are defined as follows: Education = years of education, Urbanization = share of population living in urban areas, Investment = investment as share of GDP, Institutions = government effectiveness, Complexity = Economic Complexity Index of Hidalgo and Hausmann (2009), Gender equality = share of years of schooling for females to males, Demography = share of population under age 14, Innovation = log patents per capita, and Trade = (exports+imports)/GDP. Sample includes 4-7 SAR economies and 65-127 EMDEs, depending on the driver, and 32 advanced economies.
B. Aggregates are calculated using constant 2010 U.S. dollar GDP weights.

roughly 70 percent in India) and their balance sheets encumbered by elevated nonperforming loan ratios (usually about 10 percent).

- *Firm characteristics.* Heavy regulatory restrictions have prevented firms from becoming more productive in SAR (Cirera and Cusolito 2019; Kanwar and Sperlich 2019). Complicated tax systems, labor regulations, and licensing requirements have been factors containing the productivity of smaller firms and have encouraged widespread informality. The informal sector accounts for roughly one-third of GDP and 70 percent of total employment in SAR (World Bank 2019a). The potential for productivity gains from resource reallocation from less productive to more productive firms stands to be large (Lall, Shalizi, and Deichmann 2004).[15]

- *Weak human capital.* SAR has lagged most EMDE regions in educational enrollment and attainment, as well as in mortality indicators. In addition, poor

---

[15] For example, equalizing the efficiency of capital and labor allocation across firms to the level of the United States would have increased TFP in India as much as 50 percent in the 1990s (Hsieh and Klenow 2009). Similarly, a one-standard-deviation decrease in the misallocation of land and buildings in India was estimated to have improved labor productivity by 25 percent between 1989 and 2010 (Duranton et al. 2016). The direct and indirect contribution of services to the total value added of the manufacturing sector varies between 33 and 50 percent in SAR as of 2017 (Mercer-Blackman and Ablaza 2018).

FIGURE 5.27 **Policy challenges in SAR**

Low trade openness remains a major constraint to productivity growth in SAR. Low FDI inflows hold back positive spillovers from productive foreign firms. Low productivity among state banks weighs on financial sector productivity. Small firms face obstacles in accessing finance, and their TFP is lower relative to large firms.

A. Exporter status, location, and TFP

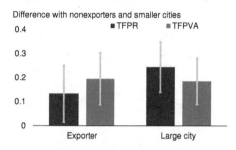

B. Trade openness

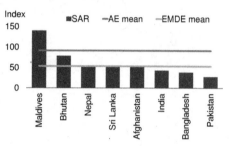

C. FDI inflows

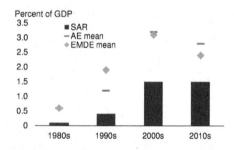

D. Firm ownership status and TFP

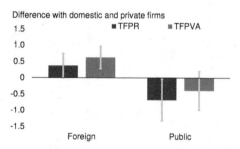

E. Access to finance

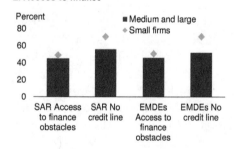

F. Firm size and TFP

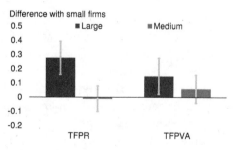

Sources: World Bank.

Note: Firm-level TFP is computed using a Cobb-Douglas production function, assuming elasticities of output with respect to inputs are the same across countries in a given income group. AE = advanced economy; EMDEs = emerging market and developing economy; FDI = foreign direct investment; SAR = South Asia; TFP = total factor productivity; TFPR = log TFP based on revenues; TFPVA = log TFP based on value added.

A.D.E.F. Calculations are based on World Bank Enterprise Surveys. The bars represent estimated coefficients of dummy variables for "exporter," "located in a city with population larger than 1 million," "foreign owner," and "public enterprise" in a regression where dependent variable is log TFP and independent variables are the aforementioned dummy variable, country dummy variables, and year dummy variables. Survey weights are used in all calculations. Sample includes 15,248 firms in 109 EMDEs, including 20 low-income countries, for 2007-17.

B. Trade openness index is defined as the ratio of imports plus exports to GDP. Aggregates are calculated using constant 2010 U.S. dollar GDP weights. Sample includes 155 EMDEs and 35 AEs.

C. Aggregates are calculated using constant 2010 U.S. dollar GDP weights. Sample includes 155 EMDEs and 35 AEs.

E. The vertical axis shows the percentage of responses indicating access to finance as a moderate/major/very severe obstacle.

operations and human resource management quality has reduced firm productivity (Bloom et al. 2013).

• *Gender gaps.* SAR's female labor force participation rate is far below comparable economies, and progress in this area is mixed across the region (Goretti, Kihara, and Salgado 2019). Gender gaps in workforce participation, education, and financial inclusion restrain the region's long-term growth potential (Khera 2018).

Productivity outlook. The forecast plunge in global output due to COVID-19 presents a heightened risk globally and in SAR economies of a broad-based productivity slowdown if the global recession is prolonged (World Bank 2020a). The COVID-19 shock is particularly disappointing given the region's already large productivity gaps with advanced economies and other EMDE regions.

Many of the drivers of productivity in SAR are at the low end of the EMDE range, indicating scope for substantial improvements. Increasing rates of school enrollment would lift human capital and improve productivity (figure 5.28). In the long term, urbanization in the region is set to rise, potentially bringing productivity benefits that other regions have experienced. Recent reforms, such as the new GST system in India and the Inland Revenue Act in Sri Lanka, are expected to broaden the tax base and make resources available for human capital and infrastructure investments. Various business reforms implemented in recent years, such as shortening approval times for trademarks and patents, lowering restrictions on FDI, and accelerating investment in energy and transport infrastructure, are expected to yield productivity benefits over time (World Bank 2017f). At the same time, the region is highly vulnerable to natural disasters, and environmental deterioration and climate change risks weigh on the productivity growth outlook. An improved productivity outlook will require the resolution of financial sector issues to unlock credit for investment, along with further business environment improvements.

The working-age share of the population is expected to increase in SAR until 2045, providing a larger and more prolonged demographic dividend than in all other regions except SSA. Against the backdrop of improving human capital and continued urbanization, this increase in the labor force is expected to lift productivity growth.

Policy options

The post-GFC productivity slowdown in SAR was milder than in other EMDE regions. The COVID-19 shock poses a significant risk for productivity growth, however. A range of policy actions could prevent persistent negative effects. Notwithstanding the potential significant benefits from productivity-enhancing reforms, such policies need to be well directed. Key areas of focus should be improving the quality and quantity of human and physical capital, increasing firm productivity, encouraging efficient sectoral reallocation, and creating business-friendly environments.

FIGURE 5.28 Productivity prospects in SAR

Increasing urbanization, accompanied by sectoral reallocation, could support productivity in the region. However, the region is highly vulnerable to natural disasters, and environmental deterioration and climate change risks weigh on the productivity growth outlook.

A. Urbanization projections

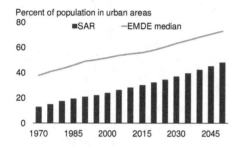

B. Impact of natural disasters

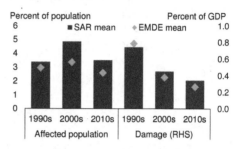

Sources: United Nations; World Bank.
Note: Aggregates are calculated using constant 2010 U.S. dollar GDP weights. EMDE = emerging market and developing economy; SAR = South Asia.
A. Sample includes 8 SAR economies and 159 EMDEs. Last projection year is 2050.
B. Simple average during year spans of aggregate regional damages per year.

Improving factors of production

Support physical capital accumulation, especially infrastructure investment. The post-GFC slowdown in SAR productivity growth mostly reflected weaker capital accumulation. A large share of firms cites infrastructure gaps as their biggest obstacle (figure 5.29). In Bangladesh and Pakistan, firms facing infrastructure obstacles have been found to be less productive than others (Fernandes 2008; Grainger and Zhang 2017). Improved infrastructure in the energy and transportation sectors, as well as technology-oriented capital accumulation, can promote productivity growth and boost international competitiveness (Calderón, Moral-Benito, and Servén 2015).

Strengthen investment in human capital. Although the region has benefited from raising life expectancy, reducing mortality, and expanding access to education over the past three decades, there is still significant capacity for further human capital development. With the increasing working-age share of the population in the region, delivering strong output growth and improvements in human capital will be key to progress in productivity growth (Goretti, Kihara, and Salgado 2019). A better-educated and healthier workforce can have better and more stable jobs and be more productive (World Bank 2018a). Policies to expand school attendance and support nutrition programs for early childhood development can boost educational outcomes in SAR (Beteille 2019; Torlese and Raju 2018; World Bank 2018l).

Reduce gender gaps. Addressing constraints on economic opportunities for women can provide significant gains in long-term growth (Khera 2018). Key policies such as increasing access to childcare, improving financial inclusion, and ensuring public safety

FIGURE 5.29 **Constraints to productivity growth in SAR**

Many firms experience obstacles in their operations due to infrastructure gaps and political instability. The region is behind other EMDEs in terms of some business environment indicators, as well as human capital development, limiting opportunities to improve productivity. Financial development is also weaker compared to other EMDEs, which is reflected in low credit-to-GDP ratios. Many of these obstacles to doing business contribute to the high levels of informality in the region.

A. Obstacles to firm operations

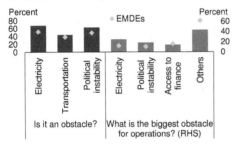

B. Human capital

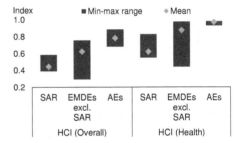

C. Informality

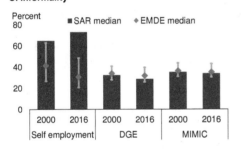

D. Domestic credit

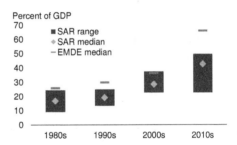

E. Obstacles related to regulations

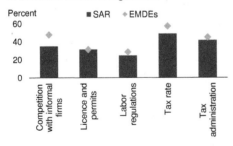

F. Doing business, distance to frontier

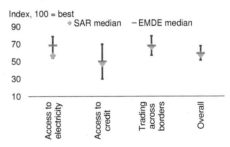

Sources: Elgin and Oztunali (2012); United Nations; World Bank.

Note: AEs = advanced economies; EMDEs = emerging market and developing economies; HCI = Human Capital Index; SAR = South Asia.

A. Calculations are based on World Bank Enterprise Surveys. Survey weights are used in calculations. Left section represents the responses to "How much of an obstacle?" The vertical axis shows the percentage of responses that indicate moderate/major/very severe obstacle. Right section represents the responses to "What is the biggest obstacle affecting the operations of this establishment?" Vertical axis shows the percentage of responses.

B. Range reflects the minimum and maximum of the distribution across countries. Higher values of the index reflect better human capital development. See World Bank (2018b) for methodology. Aggregates are calculated using U.S. dollar GDP weights at 2010 prices and exchange rates.

C. Both DGE (dynamic general equilibrium) and MIMIC (multiple indicators multiple causes) model estimates measure the informal output in percent of official GDP.

E. Calculations are based on World Bank Enterprise Surveys and represent responses to "How much of an obstacle?" The vertical axis shows the percentage of responses that indicate moderate/major/very severe obstacle.

F. Sample includes 8 SAR economies and 159 EMDEs. The blue whiskers indicate interquartile range of EMDEs.

and sanitation can promote gender equality and boost productivity in SAR (Sharafudheen 2017; World Bank 2016f).

Enhancing firm productivity

Increase the region's integration into the global economy. SAR's participation in international trade remains substantially less than that of other regions (Gould, Tan, and Emamgholi 2013), and the COVID-19 shock poses risk of further deterioration in the region's integration to GVCs. Although both imports and exports in SAR, relative to GDP, are lower than in comparable economies, the gap in exports—both within and outside the region—is much larger (World Bank 2019n). The empirical evidence on positive productivity spillovers from international trade and FDI inflows indicates that measures to foster FDI and participation in global and regional value chains can lift productivity in SAR. SAR may benefit from shifting FDI flows in the context of recent shifts in global manufacturing activity.

Bangladesh's apparel sector benefited substantially from tailored policies during the 1990s and 2000s, which lifted barriers to international trade and investment and enhanced participation in GVCs. The interaction with foreign firms lifted productivity of local suppliers through the demand for inputs with higher standards and quality. Similarly, Bangladesh's duty-free access to the EU from 2001 boosted knitwear exports to the EU between 2000 and 2004, enhanced the productivity of producers, and helped them expand to other export markets (World Bank 2019d).

Improve corporate management practices. Lack of information and training on best management practices seems to limit progress in productivity at the firm level. Governments can help improve the quality of management in the region through training programs and dissemination of information on best management practices. In India, for example, productivity in firms that provided management training increased by 17 percent in the first year of the intervention (Bloom et al. 2013). The low number of patents granted and the limited number of staff engaged in R&D in SAR firms have also been in part attributed to limited management capacity (Cirera and Maloney 2017). Policies that ensure property rights and create technology hubs can increase firms' participation in product innovation and expand their business in foreign markets.

Address informality. Self-employment accounts for about 70 percent of employment in SAR, which could amplify the economic effects of COVID-19 (World Bank 2020a). The level of output informality (as determined by dynamic general equilibrium and multiple indicators multiple causes models) and some obstacles related to business operations are comparable to other EMDEs. This sector is associated with lower productivity and weaker access to finance, a barrier to productive investment and a constraint on firms. Encouraging participation in GVCs and enhancing a business-friendly regulatory and tax environment can promote resource reallocation from less productive informal activities to more productive formal ones in SAR (Amin, Ohnsorge, and Okou 2019; Artuc et al. 2019).

With sizable rural populations employed informally in agriculture and large shares of self-employment in the workforce, productivity in the region could benefit significantly from improvements in the productivity of the informal sector. Policies to promote such improvements could include efforts to improve labor force skills and enhance the functioning of agricultural markets (Goretti, Kihara, and Salgado 2019).

Promoting efficient sectoral reallocation of resources

Optimize between- and within-sector allocation of resources. SAR has continued to be supported by intersectoral reallocation of resources since the GFC. A policy challenge will be to maintain this momentum. The productivity gains from sectoral reallocation from agriculture to more productive sectors can be increased if accompanied by improved local services and urban planning (Ellis and Roberts 2016; World Bank 2019o). Such policies should be complemented by measures to increase agriculture sector productivity (Cusolito and Maloney 2018).

The contribution of within-sector productivity growth has weakened substantially since the GFC. This calls for a renewed effort to promote the reallocation of capital and labor to more productive firms within sectors. By one estimate, such interfirm reallocation could unlock productivity gains of 40-60 percent in India (Hsieh and Klenow 2009). Productivity-enhancing interfirm reallocation could be encouraged by policies to foster competition and by reducing regulatory burdens that discourage firm growth (Duranton et al. 2016).

Encourage intersectoral linkages. Intersectoral linkages play an important role in improving productivity through value chains in SAR. For instance, information and communication technology progress provides positive productivity spillovers to broader services sectors (Krishna et al. 2016). Reducing barriers to trade and encouraging intersectoral and regional linkages can lift productivity through technology spillovers. For example, in Bangladesh, India, and Sri Lanka, special economic zones have helped expand exports and product diversification (Aggarwal, Hoppe, and Walkenhorst 2019).

Creating a growth-friendly environment

Unlock access to finance. Infrastructure spending in recent years has eased supply-side bottlenecks in SAR. However, poor access to finance remains a hindrance for the region, particularly given the weaknesses on corporate and financial sector balance sheets. Weak access to finance constrains small- and medium-sized firms—especially women-owned businesses—and holds back firm-level productivity gains in India (Schiantarelli and Srivastava 1997; World Bank 2013a).

Improve business environments. Despite improvements in recent years, SAR is still among the least business-friendly EMDE regions. India's economic reforms during the early 1990s enhanced openness and eased regulatory burdens in the services sector, and were followed by a significant expansion in domestic and foreign investment. The entry of foreign service providers in India was associated with more competitive business services, which supported productivity gains in the manufacturing sector (Arnold et al. 2016).

Ensure macroeconomic and political stability. Economic and financial crises have proven to hold back productivity in the region, as observed after the GFC and in economic downturns in India and Pakistan in the 1990s. Political instability seems to be a more severe obstacle to the operations of South Asian firms than in other EMDE regions (World Bank 2013b, 2013c). Strengthening economic policy institutions, improving monetary and fiscal policy frameworks, and enhancing financial regulation and supervision can help to provide a stable macroeconomic framework for firms, reduce uncertainty, and boost productivity.

Sub-Saharan Africa

Before the COVID-19 pandemic, SSA had already experienced a broad-based slowdown in labor productivity growth. In the pre-GFC period, productivity growth benefited from strengthening institutions, stronger investment, infrastructure development, improving human capital, and better macroeconomic policy frameworks. By 2013-18, productivity in the region was less than two-thirds that of the EMDE regional average and roughly one-tenth that of advanced economies, amid a commodity price plunge, weakening external demand, and growing domestic fragilities. The COVID-19 pandemic will most likely weigh further on productivity. Ambitious policy efforts will be needed to generate the productivity growth required for per capita incomes in SSA to reach those of other EMDE regions, let alone those of advanced economies. To stimulate labor productivity growth, policies are needed to boost agricultural productivity, increase resilience to climate change, diversify economies, accelerate adoption of digital technologies, and continue human capital development.

Evolution of regional productivity

Stalling post-GFC productivity. Labor productivity growth slowed sharply in SSA after the GFC, to 0.8 percent during 2013-18, from about 2.9 percent during the pre-GFC period of 2003-08 (figure 5.30).[16] TFP growth, which accounted for more than half of pre-GFC productivity growth, contracted in the post-GFC period; and the contribution of TFP to productivity growth shrank by more than in any other region during the post-GFC period. Oil- and metal-exporting countries experienced the steepest slowdown, amid the commodity price slump of 2014-16, as productivity growth fell to 0.4 percent in the post-GFC period, from 3.2 percent growth before the GFC. The COVID-19 pandemic is likely to have markedly accelerated this slowing trend, with activity in the

---

[16] Data are available for 45 EMDEs in SSA, of which 21 are oil or metals exporters, 19 are exporters of agricultural commodities, and 6 are commodity importers. An economy is defined as a commodity exporter when, on average in 2012-14, either (1) total commodities exports accounted for 30 percent or more of total goods exports or (2) exports of any single commodity accounted for 20 percent or more of total goods exports. Economies for which these thresholds are met as a result of re-exports are excluded. Commodity importers are economies not classified as commodity exporters. Chad is classified as both an oil and an agricultural-commodity exporter.

FIGURE 5.30 **Productivity in SSA in regional comparison**

Productivity growth in SSA averaged 2.9 percent in the pre-GFC period, reflecting a favorable external environment and improvements in key drivers of productivity. After the GFC, productivity growth in the region slowed to 0.8 percent. The region's productivity levels have, on average, diverged from advanced economy levels during the post-GFC period.

A. Productivity growth relative to other EMDE regions

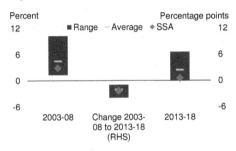

B. Productivity levels and rate of productivity convergence

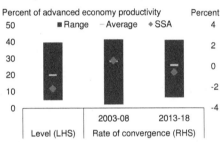

Sources: The Conference Board; Penn World Table; World Bank (World Development Indicators).
Note: Productivity is defined as real GDP per worker (at 2010 market prices and exchange rates). Country group aggregates for a given year are calculated using constant 2010 U.S. dollar GDP weights. Data for multiyear spans show simple averages of the annual data. Blue bars show the range of average productivity across the six EMDE regions. Yellow dashes denote the average of the six EMDE regional aggregates. Red diamonds denote simple average of SSA economies. Sample includes 45 SSA economies and 129 EMDEs. EMDEs = emerging market and developing economies; GFC = global financial crisis; SSA = Sub-Saharan Africa.
B. Rate of convergence is calculated as the difference in productivity growth rates over the log difference in productivity levels between SSA and advanced economies. "Level" of productivity refers to the GDP-weighted average of regional productivity as a share of the average advanced economy during 2013-18. LHS refers to left-hand side. RHS refers to right-hand side. Sample includes 45 SSA economies,129 EMDEs, and 35 advanced economies.

region expected to contract sharply in 2020 and remain well below its prepandemic trend in 2021 (World Bank 2020a).

Post-GFC productivity growth in agricultural commodity exporters and commodity importers was more resilient, particularly among the former, where it strengthened to 2.2 percent. Despite the sharp fall in agricultural commodity prices during the commodity price slump—albeit less severe than the drop in industrial commodity prices—sustained productivity growth was supported by improving macroeconomic policy frameworks, investment in infrastructure, and continuous efforts to improve business environments. Country-specific trends also helped lift productivity among agricultural commodity exporters. In Rwanda, for example, productivity growth was boosted by continued reforms to strengthen institutions and governance, upgrade infrastructure, increase access to education, and improve the business environment to attract private investment (World Bank 2019p). In Côte d'Ivoire, a return to stability following the end, in 2011, of decade-long civil strife has since enabled a sharp rise in productivity, amid increased public investment, recovering FDI inflows, an improving business environment, and rising export activity (Klapper, Richmond, and Tran 2013; World Bank 2015c).

The post-GFC productivity slowdown in SSA follows a favorable pre-GFC trend, when productivity benefited from a supportive external environment, including a commodity price boom that fueled foreign capital inflows and unprecedented investment, and benefited the region's low-income countries (figure 5.31; Khan et al. 2016; Steinbach 2019; World Bank 2019a). Improvements in education, health care, infrastructure, financial access, and trade openness also played a role (Calderón and Servén 2010; Cole and Neumayer 2006; Shiferaw et al. 2015; World Bank 2018a, 2019q).

Low productivity levels. The level of productivity in SSA is the second lowest of all EMDE regions but is still roughly twice that of SAR. However, if the five most productive economies are excluded (Equatorial Guinea, Gabon, Mauritius, Seychelles, and South Africa), productivity in SSA is on par with that in SAR, at about 5 percent of the advanced economy average in 2013-18. The average of the higher productivity levels in these five economies—at 28 percent of the advanced economy average—is roughly 50 percent higher than the EMDE average. Their better performance than other SSA economies is in part due to significant oil wealth (Equatorial Guinea and Gabon), dominant tourism sectors in island states (Mauritius and Seychelles), and mineral wealth along with a considerably higher capital stock (South Africa). Absent major policy efforts to lift productivity growth, stagnation in productivity levels suggests dim prospects for the nearly 60 percent of the global extreme poor who currently reside in SSA. With the number of extreme poor in SSA expected to rise sharply because of the COVID-19 pandemic, while potential growth is expected to slow, wide-ranging policy actions to lift productivity growth have become even more urgent (Lakner et al. 2020; World Bank 2020a). If recent rates of productivity growth persist, less than 5 percent of economies in SSA will halve their productivity gap with advanced economies over the next 40 years.

Post-GFC TFP decline. The slowdown in SSA's productivity growth following the GFC reflected less effective use of factor inputs, as captured by TFP.[17] TFP growth, which accounted for more than half of pre-GFC productivity growth, contracted in the post-GFC period. The sharp post-GFC decline in TFP was pronounced in industrial commodity exporters, following the commodity price collapse of 2014-16 and the accompanying collapse in investment, FDI inflows, and exports, compounded by somewhat weaker business environments. In Liberia and Sierra Leone, the post-GFC fall in TFP was exacerbated by the devastating Ebola outbreak of 2014-16 (World Bank 2019r).

In contrast, TFP has remained resilient, or even strengthened, among some exporters of agricultural commodities and commodity importers during 2013-18 (Côte d'Ivoire, Kenya, Mauritius, and Togo). Agricultural commodity prices fell less steeply, on average, than industrial commodity prices during the 2011-16 commodity price slump, and beneficial terms of trade supported activity among commodity importers. Faster TFP

---

[17] From a long-term perspective, World Bank (2019u) finds that the significant difference between productivity in SSA and that of the productivity frontier (United States) largely reflected weak factor accumulation between 1960 and the 1990s, as the index of human capital in SSA relative to that of the United States declined sharply from 1960 to 1980, while the relative accumulation of physical capital remained subdued. In contrast, from 2000, the gap in efficiency (or TFP) became the major contributor to difference in productivity between SSA and the frontier. This TFP gap widened further from 2010 onward.

FIGURE 5.31 **Evolution of labor productivity growth in SSA**

The sharp slowdown in SSA's productivity growth during the post-GFC period was concentrated among exporters of industrial commodities. Rapid productivity growth in the lead-up to the global financial crisis reflected improvements in human capital, deepening physical capital, and rising TFP. Following the commodity price slump, TFP slowed sharply among industrial commodity exporters. TFP has contracted in recent years, but the decline was less severe when accounting for the contribution from slowing extraction of natural capital.

A. Labor productivity growth

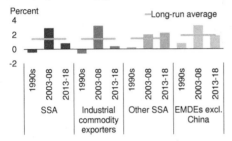

B. Productivity levels

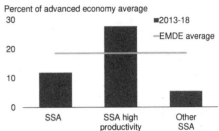

C. Factor contributions to productivity growth

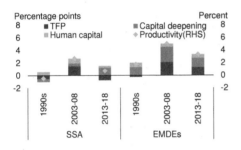

D. Factor contributions to productivity growth, by export composition

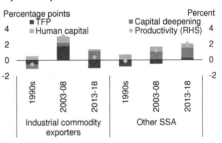

E. Factor contributions to productivity growth in Nigeria

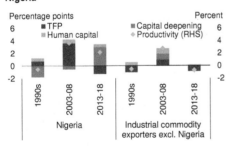

F. Factor contributions to SSA productivity growth, with and without natural capital

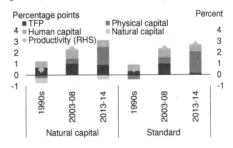

Sources: Barro and Lee (2015); International Monetary Fund; Penn World Table; United Nations (Human Development Reports); Wittgenstein Centre for Demography and Global Human Capital; World Bank.

Note: Productivity is defined as real GDP per worker (at 2010 market prices and exchange rates). Country group aggregates for a given year are calculated using constant 2010 U.S. dollar GDP weights. Data for multiyear spans show simple averages of the annual data. EMDEs = emerging market and developing economies; SSA = Sub-Saharan Africa; TFP = total factor productivity.

A. Long-run averages are 1981-2018 for SSA and 1990-2018 for EMDEs excluding China. "Other SSA" includes agriculture exporters and commodity importers. Sample includes 45 SSA economies and 129 EMDEs.

B. "SSA high productivity" includes Equatorial Guinea, Gabon, Mauritius, Seychelles, and South Africa. Sample includes 45 SSA economies and 129 EMDEs.

C-F. Productivity growth is computed as log changes. Sample includes 30 SSA economies and 93 EMDEs.

D. Industrial commodity exporters includes metals and oil exporters. "Other SSA" includes agricultural commodity exporters and commodity importers.

F. For comparability, the sample for both the natural and standard decomposition includes 22 SSA economies.

growth in these economies was also underpinned by sustained public investment in infrastructure, continued efforts to improve business environments, and more robust macroeconomic policy frameworks.

Post-GFC acceleration of capital deepening. The contraction in TFP growth offset the post-GFC boost to productivity growth generated from capital deepening. Labor productivity in agricultural commodity exporters benefited from heavy public investment. In Nigeria, investment was fueled by large FDI inflows into the energy, banking, manufacturing, and telecommunications sectors (although investment slowed sharply after 2014 as oil prices collapsed; World Bank 2019s). In contrast, investment has fallen sharply in other industrial commodity exporters in SSA—by 7 percentage points of GDP in the median economy—following the 2014-16 commodity price slump, compounding the already slowing TFP growth.

Impact of natural resource extraction on productivity measurement. Standard productivity decompositions subsume the extraction of natural capital (such as oil, metals, and agricultural land) into TFP and, to a lesser extent, physical capital, biasing their estimated contributions to productivity growth (Brandt, Schreyer, and Zipperer 2017; Calderón and Cantu 2019; World Bank 2019q). During the pre-GFC commodity price boom, the increased extraction of natural capital lifted productivity growth in SSA (Khan et al. 2016). As the boom ended, natural capital extraction declined accordingly, and its contribution detracted from overall productivity growth. When considering natural capital, it appears that the post-GFC fall in TFP was likely less severe than the standard decomposition suggests.[18]

Sources of regional productivity growth

Productivity growth through sectoral reallocation. The post-GFC slowdown in productivity growth from pre-GFC rates reflects slowing gains due to reallocation of labor from low-productivity sectors (mostly agriculture) to higher-productivity sectors. In contrast, within-sector productivity growth has continued apace (figure 5.32).[19]

Productivity differs widely across sectors in SSA. Productivity in agriculture—the least productive sector that employs more than half of the workforce and accounts for less than 20 percent of GDP—is between 3 and 5 percent of the productivity in mining and finance, the two most productive sectors at the nine-sector level. Relative to the wider EMDE sample, agricultural productivity in SSA is about three times lower, on average. Low agricultural productivity in SSA reflects the prevalence of subsistence farming, sub-optimal crop selection, poor land quality amid unfavorable climates, limited uptake of modern technologies and production methods to improve yields, and small farm sizes

---

[18] Direct comparisons between the standard decomposition and the decomposition including natural capital are complicated, however, by different country samples. In the natural capital decomposition, the sample includes 22 countries (72 percent of SSA GDP), compared to 30 countries (83 percent of SSA GDP) in the standard decomposition. Furthermore, the decline in natural capital may capture a lower valuation of natural capital.

[19] Sectoral productivity data are available for only about half the SSA economies with data for aggregate productivity, however.

FIGURE 5.32 **Sectoral productivity growth in SSA**

The sectoral reallocation of labor in SSA has been an important driver of regional productivity growth; however, its contribution dwindled during 2013-18 relative to 2003-08. Agriculture in SSA has the lowest productivity, whereas productivity is highest in mining and finance. Low aggregate productivity in the region is partly explained by the agricultural sector's significant contribution to value added, combined with the disproportionate share of employment devoted to the sector.

A. Within- and between-sector contributions to regional productivity growth

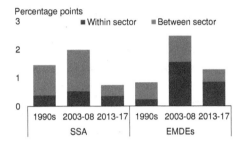

B. Sectoral productivity levels, 2017

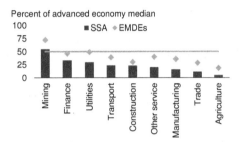

C. Composition of employment, by sector

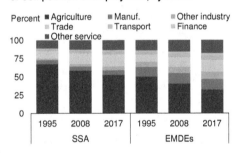

D. Composition of value added, by sector

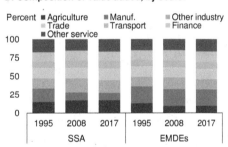

Sources: Asian Productivity Organization, Productivity Database; de Vries, Timmer, and de Vries (2013); Expanded Africa Sector Database; Groningen Growth Development Center database; Haver Analytics; International Labour Organization, ILOSTAT; Mensah and Szirmai (2018); Mensah et al. (2018); Organisation for Economic Co-operation and Development, Structural Analysis Database; United Nations; World Bank; World KLEMS.

Note: EMDEs = emerging market and developing economies; SSA = Sub-Saharan Africa.

A.B. Productivity is defined as real GDP per worker (at 2010 market prices and exchange rates).

A. Growth within sector shows the contribution of initial real value added-weighted productivity growth rate of each sector and between sector effect shows the contribution arising from changes in sectoral employment shares. Median of the country-specific contributions. Sample includes 69 EMDEs, of which 22 are SSA economies.

B. Figure shows the median of country groups. Horizontal line indicates 50 percent. The sample includes 19 SSA economies and 46 EMDEs.

C.D. "Other industry" includes mining, utilities, and construction; "other service" includes government and personal services. "Manuf." indicates manufacturing. Sample includes 69 EMDEs, of which 22 are SSA economies.

(Adamopoulos and Restuccia 2014, 2018; Caselli 2005; Sinha and Xi 2018). Moreover, the use of price controls—a widespread practice particularly across low-income countries in the region—often distorts the allocation of resources and adversely affects incentives to invest in human capital or adopt new technologies (Chen 2017; Chen and Restuccia 2018; World Bank 2019q). The agricultural sector's significant contribution to value added, combined with the disproportionate share of employment devoted to the sector, helps explain SSA's low aggregate productivity relative to other EMDE regions.

Other drivers of productivity growth. Although SSA has long lagged well behind other EMDEs in some key drivers of productivity, rapid improvements during the pre-GFC period supported productivity growth until the GFC; since then, the pace of improvement has lost momentum. Productivity drivers with particularly prominent slowdowns in improvements include innovation, gender equality, education, health, trade openness, institutional quality, and investment (figure 5.33).

Institutional quality and the business environment. Although various aspects of governance and institutional quality improved in the region from the late 1990s into the pre-GFC period, this progress has mostly stalled, and even deteriorated in some instances. On average, business climates have also regressed during the post-GFC period; today, almost two-thirds of SSA countries still rank in the lowest quartile of countries by business climates, and one-half do so for poor governance. Poor business climates and governance, as well as distortions caused by price controls, have not only constrained productivity by distorting the efficient allocation of resources but also deterred private sector investment (Cirera, Fattal-Jaef, and Maemir 2020; World Bank 2019q).

Integration with the global economy. Between the mid-1990s and 2008, the region's openness to trade—that is, the sum of imports and exports relative to the size of the economy—rose 16 percentage points to 81 percent of GDP, helping to boost productivity. However, as commodity prices fell and external demand from SSA's largest trading partners (China and the euro area) slowed, trade integration partially unwound, with openness falling to 74 percent of GDP by 2017. The region's heavy dependence on commodity extraction sectors manifests in a smaller share of exporting firms compared to the EMDE average. Although the share of foreign-owned firms—which are generally more productive than their domestically owned counterparts—is high, such firms tend to cluster in extractives sectors with limited links to other sectors (Liu and Steenbergen 2019; World Bank 2018m). Greater manufacturing sector participation in international trade and GVCs has been constrained by the sector's relative lack of international competitiveness, in part because of high productivity-adjusted labor costs (Gelb et al. 2017) and an array of nontariff barriers, including the region's disadvantageous geography (Christ and Ferrantino 2011; Raballand et al. 2012).

Prospects for productivity growth slowdown. Although wide sectoral productivity differentials offer ample potential for productivity gains through sectoral reallocation away from agriculture, headwinds to productivity growth are substantial and expected to persist. SSA's agricultural sector faces increasing productivity constraints as mean temperatures rise and extreme weather events occur more frequently (IPCC 2014; Steinbach 2019; World Bank 2019a, 2019t). Moreover, commodity demand growth is expected to moderate in the long term as growth in China—the largest source of commodity demand—slows and shifts toward less resource-intensive sectors (World Bank 2018n). Widespread school closures and disruptions to school feeding programs amid the COVID-19 pandemic are also expected to have lasting adverse impacts on human capital formation, particularly for vulnerable groups (Azevedo et al. 2020; World Bank 2020a). Before the pandemic, a 20-percentage-point rise in government indebtedness between 2013 and 2019, on average, to 60 percent of GDP, had already

FIGURE 5.33 **Drivers of productivity growth in SSA**

Despite significant improvements, key productivity drivers remain significantly below those of advanced economies and EMDEs. Moreover, their pace of improvement has slowed in recent years. On average, business environments in SSA are more challenging than in other regions.

A. Index of productivity drivers

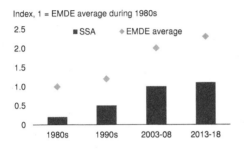

B. Share of EMDEs with a post-GFC slowdown in improvement of underlying drivers of productivity

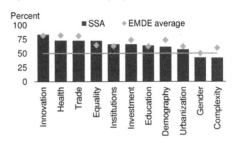

C. Levels of drivers across regions, 2017

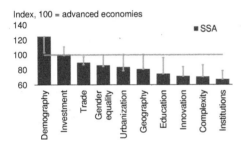

D. Obstacles to doing business

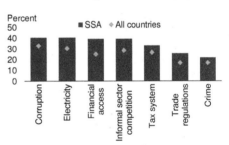

Sources: Freedom House; Haver Analytics; International Country Risk Guide (ICRG); Organisation for Economic Co-operation and Development; Observatory of Economic Complexity; Penn World Table; United Nations Educational, Scientific, and Cultural Organization (Institute for Statistics); United Nations Population Prospects; World Integrated Trade Solution; World Bank (Doing Business, Enterprise Surveys, and Global Financial Development Database).

Note: EMDEs = emerging market and developing economies; GFC = global financial crisis; SSA = Sub-Saharan Africa.

A. For each country, index is a weighted average of the normalized value of each driver of productivity. Refer to chapter 2 for weights. Drivers include the ICRG rule of law index, patents per capita, nontropical share of land area, investment as a percent of GDP, share of years of schooling for females to males, share of population in urban areas, Economic Complexity Index of Hidalgo and Hausmann (2009), years of schooling, share of working-age population, and inflation. Regional and EMDE indexes are GDP-weighted averages. Samples include 11 SSA economies and 54 EMDEs.

B. Blue bars represent share of 48 SSA economies where improvements in each driver of productivity were lower during 2013-17 than in the pre-GFC period 1998-2007, or changes in 2008-17 were below zero. Orange diamond is the corresponding value for 152 EMDE countries. Horizontal line indicates 50 percent. Variables are defined as follows: Institutions = government effectiveness; Innovation = patents per capita; Investment = investment to GDP ratio; Equality = income equality defined as (-1)*Gini; Urbanization = share of population in urban areas; Complexity = Economic Complexity Index of Hidalgo and Hausmann (2009) ; Education = years of schooling; Demography = share of working-age population; and Gender equality = share of years of schooling for females to males. Samples include 26-48 SSA economies.

C. Unweighted average levels of drivers normalized as an average of advanced economies as 100 and standard deviation of 10. Blue bars represent average within SSA economies. Orange whiskers represent the range of the average drivers for the six EMDE regions. Horizontal line indicates 100. Variables are defined as follows: Education = years of education; Urbanization = share of population living · in urban areas; Investment = investment as share of GDP; Institutions = government effectiveness; Complexity = Economic Complexity Index of Hidalgo and Hausmann (2009); Gender equality = share of years of schooling for females to males; Demography = share of population under age 14; Innovation = log patents per capita; and Trade = (exports+imports)/GDP. Sample includes 10-44 SSA economies and 65-127 EMDEs, depending on the driver, and 32 advanced economies.

D. Unweighted averages. Variables corresponding to the concepts are as follows: Corruption = percent of firms identifying corruption as a major constraint; Electricity = percent of firms identifying electricity as a major constraint; Financial access = percent of firms identifying access to finance as a major constraint; Informal sector competition = percent of firms identifying practices of competitors in the informal sector as a major constraint; Tax system is the average of tax rates (percent of firms identifying tax rates as a major constraint) and tax administration (percent of firms identifying tax administration as a major constraint); Trade regulations = percent of firms identifying customs and trade regulations as a major constraint; Crime = percent of firms identifying crime, theft and disorder as a major constraint.

reduced fiscal space for productivity-enhancing infrastructure, health, and education initiatives, and for R&D. The significant fiscal burden of the pandemic will further reduce the fiscal space needed for growth-enhancing spending (World Bank 2020a). The pandemic is also expected to weigh heavily on potential growth prospects. In addition, high levels of informality—about 40 percent of official GDP and 90 percent of total employment—may inhibit faster productivity growth, because productivity among informal firms is only one-seventh of that in their formal counterparts (La Porta and Shleifer 2014; World Bank 2019a). The challenges faced by informal firms have been exacerbated by the COVID-19 pandemic (World Bank 2020a).

Policy options

Coordinated policy efforts are required to achieve stronger productivity growth, reduce poverty, and narrow the significant income gap with the rest of the world. Four strands of policies could support more robust productivity growth.

Improving factors of production

Boost human capital, and leverage demographic dividends. Continued investment and increased spending on health care, including greater provision of treatment for highly prevalent conditions such as malaria and HIV/AIDS, could raise productivity of the labor force and life expectancy in general (figure 5.34; Asiki et al. 2016; Barofsky, Anekwe and Chase 2015; Ferreira, Pessoa and Dos Santos 2011). The COVID-19 pandemic has underscored the need for and importance of investing in health sector capacity (World Bank 2020a, 2020f). Increased life expectancy due to improved health care also generates incentives to invest in education (Cervellati and Sunde 2011). In Ethiopia, a rapid decline in fertility rates between 1995 and 2015, rising incomes, and falling poverty rates reflected an approach combining improvements in education and health, family planning, and increased economic opportunity (World Bank 2019u). Harnessing the region's potential demographic dividend from declining fertility rates and falling dependency ratios requires policies that support female empowerment, including education, health care, and greater labor market access for women (Bloom, Kuhn and Prettner 2017; Groth and May 2017; Kalemli-Ozcan 2003). As the youth dependency ratio declines in SSA, resources could be freed up to invest in the health and education of the young, boosting the productivity of the future labor force and spurring per capita growth (Ashraf, Weil, and Wilde 2013).

Narrow the gender gap. Although the gender gap in labor force participation has been narrowing, on average, significant gaps in earnings of women relative to men persist (World Bank 2012). This reflects gender disparity in secondary and tertiary education, differing occupations, and greater time devoted by women to housework and childcare (World Bank 2019u). Moreover, improvements in the ratio of average years of education of females to males have been slowing in the post-GFC period. This is reflected by lower productivity of females in agriculture and of female entrepreneurs (Campos et al. 2019; O'Sullivan et al. 2014). Widespread school closures amid the COVID-19 pandemic could exacerbate gender inequality in the region; evidence from the Ebola epidemic in

FIGURE 5.34 **Prospects for productivity growth in SSA**

Continued improvements in health care could raise life expectancy and the overall productivity of the labor force, because rising life expectancy also generates incentives to invest in education. Owing to limited access to resources and training, crops tended by women yield one-third less per hectare than those of men; a similar margin applies to profits earned by female entrepreneurs. Meeting the infrastructure-related Sustainable Development Goals will require investment spending of about 7 percent of GDP per year. Reducing trade costs would accelerate regional and global integration.

A. Human capital development

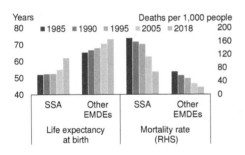

B. Shortfalls in profits and agricultural output of females relative to males

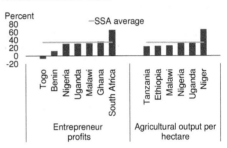

C. Infrastructure spending needs

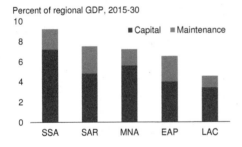

D. Import and export compliance costs

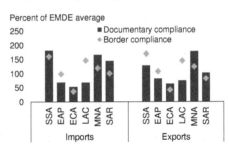

Sources: Armed Conflict Location and Event Data Project database; Campos et al. (2019); O'Sullivan et al. (2014); Rozenberg and Fay (2019); United Nations; World Bank (Doing Business).

Note: EAP = East Asia and Pacific; ECA = Europe and Central Asia; EMDEs = emerging market and developing economies; LAC = Latin America and the Caribbean; MNA = Middle East and North Africa; SAR = South Asia; SSA = Sub-Saharan Africa.

A. Unweighted averages. "Mortality rate" refers to under-five mortality.

B. "Entrepreneur profits" measures the extent to which profits for male-owned firms exceed those of female-owned firms using data from impact evaluations. "Agricultural output per hectare" measures the extent to which agricultural output per hectare of male-managed plots exceeds that of female-managed plots. Entrepreneur profits in Ghana reflect the average of the Grants for Micro-Enterprises Survey and the Tailoring Survey; Entrepreneur profits in Nigeria reflect the average of both the Growth and Employment Survey and the Business Plan Competition Survey. Agricultural output per hectare accounts for differences in plot size and geographic factors. Agricultural output in Nigeria reflects a simple average of gaps for northern Nigeria (46 percent) and southern Nigeria (17 percent).

C. Bars show average annual spending needs during 2015-30. Estimates are generated using policy assumptions that cap investment needs at 4.5 percent of lower- and middle-income countries' GDP per year.

D. Unweighted averages. Sample includes 156 EMDEs and 47 SSA economies. EMDE average excludes SSA.

West Africa in 2014 suggests that school closures were associated with wider gender gaps in educational attainment (UNDP 2015; World Bank 2020a). Policies to empower women and boost their productivity include promoting skills building beyond traditional training programs, such as through a greater focus on developing an entrepreneurial mindset; this approach has been found to lift sales and profits in Togo (Campos et al. 2017; World Bank 2019u). Relieving capital constraints faced by females and addressing social norms that constrain women's economic opportunities and earnings, such as perceptions about the type of work that is suitable for men or women, may also help.

Close infrastructure gaps. Capital deepening has slowed considerably among most industrial commodity exporters, and severe infrastructure deficiencies remain throughout the region. Meeting the infrastructure-related Sustainable Development Goals in 2030 will require additional investment spending between 2015 and 2030 of roughly 7 percent of GDP per year in SSA (excluding maintenance spending)—the highest of all EMDE regions (Rozenberg and Fay 2019). Stronger productivity growth—through both capital-deepening investment and improved TFP—is contingent on boosting the availability of electricity and improving access in a sustainable manner that strikes a balance between affordable provision for consumers, particularly the poor, and cost recovery for utilities (Blimpo and Cosgrove-Davies 2019; Vorisek and Yu 2020). In addition to closing infrastructure gaps, improvements to the resilience of existing infrastructure are needed to limit frequent disruptions, particularly in power, water and sanitation, transport, and telecommunications (World Bank 2019v). These efforts should be supported by public investment management frameworks that include strong cash management and procurement processes.

Boosting firm productivity

Boost productivity in agriculture. Given the large share of activity and employment accounted for by agriculture, measures to raise agricultural productivity—especially in staple crops—can yield significant development gains (Beegle and Christiaensen 2019). These include ensuring secure land tenures, better access to markets and finance, better crop choices, more effective and increased use of fertilizers, improved irrigation, diffusion and adoption of new technologies, and targeted training to help small farmers reap the benefits of cutting-edge knowledge and practices (Chen 2017; Fuglie et al. 2020; Sinha and Xi 2018; World Bank 2019u). For example, text messages providing information to sugarcane farmers in Kenya helped boost fertilizer use and crop yields (Casaburi et al. 2019; Fuglie et al. 2020). Ensuring gender equality in access to resources could further boost agricultural productivity; giving women in Ghana and Malawi the same access to fertilizers and other inputs as men could boost maize yields by one-sixth (World Bank 2012). Gains from faster productivity growth in agriculture will free up workers to transition to other, more productive, sectors.

Address informality. Informal firms in SSA often brim with potential, and the transition to formality is found to be shorter than in other EMDEs (World Bank 2019a). Policies to unlock informal firms' potential include upgrading skills of workers and ensuring better access to financial services, transport and communications connectivity, health services, land and property rights, and product markets (Oosthuizen et al. 2016). Removing barriers to enter the formal sector can further accelerate the transition out of informality: lowering registration costs by half could double the share of formal enterprises through formalization of informal firms and new entrants (Nguimkeu 2015; World Bank 2019u). Regulatory and institutional reforms to build public trust and support youth entrepreneurship can strengthen incentives for firms to operate formally and reduce youth unemployment. In Rwanda, entrepreneurship has been introduced as a secondary school subject to help prepare youth to be successful entrepreneurs or to compete in the formal labor market (Choi, Dutz, and Usman 2020).

Leverage digital technologies. Firm productivity in SSA could benefit significantly from the proliferation of digital technologies (Choi, Dutz, and Usman 2020; Hjort and Poulsen 2019). SSA's comparatively low levels of human capital and high degree of informality are ideally suited for the adoption and development of productivity-enhancing, low-skill-biased digital technologies. In some countries, the use of digital technologies has been found to boost firm productivity by facilitating process and product innovation (as in the Democratic Republic of Congo and in Tanzania; Cirera, Lage, and Sabetti 2016). Digital technologies can also support financial inclusion. Kenya's mobile money service, M-Pesa, boosted the financial savings of female-headed households and enabled women to move out of agriculture into more productive sectors (Suri and Jack 2016). Digital loans offered through mobile money platforms, which are growing in popularity, may help individuals without credit scores or sufficient collateral access financing because digital loan providers use alternative credit scores based on telecommunications data (Cook and McKay 2015; Francis, Blumenstock, and Robinson 2017; World Bank 2019u). With digital solutions enabling some industries to quickly adapt to working from home, investments in these technologies have become even more critical as the region adjusts to the COVID-19 shock and builds greater resilience to possible future pandemics (Choi, Dutz, and Usman 2020).

Accelerate trade openness and global integration. The African Continental Free Trade Area (AfCFTA) has the potential to boost regional trade and bolster firm productivity by facilitating investment, international competitiveness, the transfer of technology and new innovations, and participation in regional and global value chains (Berg and Krueger 2003; Calderon and Cantú 2019; Del Prete, Giovannetti, and Marvasi 2017; Laget et al. 2018; World Bank 2020g). To maximize the potential productivity gains from the AfCFTA, infrastructure—particularly transport networks—must be expanded and business climates improved. Productivity gains from AfCFTA also depend on the implementation of trade facilitation measures and addressing significant nontariff barriers to trade (World Bank 2019d).

Encouraging sectoral reallocation

Enable factor mobility. Productivity gains from sectoral reallocation of labor in the region can be reignited by policies aimed at reducing the barriers to factor mobility. These barriers include low human capital of the labor force, weak infrastructure (such as inadequate transport systems in urban areas), low access to finance, and disadvantageous trade policies. In Nigeria, tariff structures have been shown to reduce incentives for sectoral reallocation to higher-productivity sectors, because tariffs systematically boosted profitability of the least productive sectors but not the most productive sectors (World Bank 2017g).

Enable diversification. Policies aimed at shifting the production base toward a wider and more complex array of export goods, across a range of manufacturing and services sectors, will enable greater participation in value chains and help insulate economic activity from the destabilizing effects of large international commodity price swings. In Côte d'Ivoire—the world's largest supplier of cocoa beans—diversification along the cocoa value chain through the expansion of domestic grinding and processing facilities has allowed the country to also produce a diverse array of value-added cocoa products and overtake the Netherlands as the world's leading cocoa-processing country (World Bank 2016g). AfCFTA could also contribute to economic diversification if it leads to the establishment of regional value chains. However, successful diversification requires several supporting measures, including improved human capital, better infrastructure, stronger governance, and deeper financial markets (Fosu and Abass 2019).

Creating a growth-friendly environment

Strengthen protection from climate change. The adverse effects of climate change could be partially mitigated through land-use planning and investment in climate-smart infrastructure (Collier, Conway, and Venables 2008; World Bank 2019a). Effective social protection policies, possibly financed with energy taxes or the removal of fuel subsidies, could provide resources to support livelihoods during extreme events (Hallegatte et al. 2015). Climate adaptation could be strengthened by building capacity in policy implementation, boosting access to adaptation financing, and raising public awareness of climate change (Adenle et al. 2017; World Bank 2019w).

Reduce violence. SSA has experienced many conflicts, particularly between the 1970s and early 2000s. These not only took heavy human tolls but also shook the stability of the affected countries by weakening institutions and severely damaging or destroying infrastructure. Conflicts in Burundi, the Democratic Republic of Congo, Liberia, Rwanda, and Sierra Leone inflicted losses of human life equivalent to between 1 and 10 percent of their populations (Steinbach 2019; World Bank 2019a). In recent years, violence against civilians has increasingly weighed on activity in several countries and forcibly displaced large populations. Efforts to achieve lasting peace can strengthen growth and boost productivity through stronger investment and increased TFP (Chen, Loayza, and Reynal-Querol 2008).

Strengthen institutional quality and business environments. Limited access to reliable electricity, poor transport infrastructure, and high levels of corruption are often cited as key constraints to business in SSA. High noninfrastructure costs, such as high prices of transport goods within countries and across borders, tend to exacerbate the burden of weak infrastructure. In many instances, high road-transport costs reflect excessive market power of trucking companies. Competition-enhancing deregulation can help alleviate this business constraint and boost productivity. For example, in landlocked Rwanda, deregulation in the transport sector led to an abrupt fall in transport costs (Barrett et al. 2017). Business environment deficiencies can be further addressed by increasing access to finance, simplifying tax systems, reducing regulatory burdens and compliance requirements, addressing corruption, and liberalizing labor and product markets (Bah and Fang 2015; World Bank 2019a). Strengthening institutional quality by improving judicial systems can help address corruption—a leading obstacle to doing business—and strengthen contract enforcement. Such structural reforms can bolster firm productivity (Kouamé and Tapsoba 2018). Reforms aimed at improving the business environment can also help reduce the size of the informal economy, which tends to have lower productivity than the formal economy.

Conclusion

Even before the severe global recession induced by COVID-19, productivity growth was slowing across the six EMDE regions. The slowdown in productivity growth was particularly severe in EAP, ECA, and SSA; productivity growth in LAC and MNA, which had already been low before the GFC, fell to near zero in the post-GFC period amid political uncertainty, episodes of financial stress in major economies, and falling commodity prices. As a result, catch-up to advanced economy productivity levels has slowed in most regions and, in some regions, the gap with advanced economies has widened.

Productivity levels in EMDEs were about 18 percent of those in advanced economies in 2013-18 (using GDP-weighted averages), pointing to significant scope for faster productivity growth. In all regions, productivity levels remain less than half of those in advanced economies, although there is significant disparity across and within regions. Whereas productivity in MNA is 40 percent of that in advanced economies, in EAP and SSA it is only 12 percent, and in SAR it is a mere 5 percent.

In five of the six EMDE regions—all except MNA—a slowdown in TFP growth contributed to slowing productivity during the post-GFC period. Slowing capital deepening contributed to weaker productivity growth in all regions except SSA.

The sectoral analysis in the chapter finds that productivity gains from the reallocation of labor from low-productivity to higher-productivity sectors slowed sharply during the post-GFC period relative to the pre-GFC period in all most regions, and particularly so in LAC and SSA. Falling gains from sectoral reallocation have been accompanied by weaker within-sector productivity gains during the post-GFC period in all regions except EAP, most severely in ECA and LAC.

Alongside this failure to reap within- and between-sector productivity gains, a range of other long-standing factors has weighed on productivity growth in recent years. Continued heavy reliance on commodities in some EMDEs, weak governance and institutions, widespread informality in some regions, poor education and job skills, and lack of integration into GVCs are some of the most common bottlenecks. Future analysis should focus on identifying, describing, and quantifying the types of reform that EMDEs can implement to boost productivity growth, especially in the context of possible long-lasting negative effects of COVID-19 on human capital development, investment in physical capital, and trade linkages.

References

Abdih, Y., P. Lopez-Murphy, A. Roitman, and R. Sahay. 2010. "The Cyclicality of Fiscal Policy in the Middle East and Central Asia: Is the Current Crisis Different?" IMF Working Paper 10/68, International Monetary Fund, Washington, DC.

Acemoglu, D., S. Johnson, and J. Robinson. 2005. "Institutions as a Fundamental Cause of Long-Run Growth." In *Handbook of Economic Growth 1A,* edited by P. Aghion and S. Durlauf, 385–472. Amsterdam: North-Holland.

Acemoglu, D., S. Naidu, P. Restrepo, and J. Robinson. 2019. "Democracy Does Cause Growth." *Journal of Political Economy* 127 (1): 47–100.

Adamopoulos, T., and D. Restuccia. 2014. "The Size Distribution of Farms and International Productivity Differences." *American Economic Review* 107 (10): 1667–97.

Adamopoulos, T., and D. Restuccia. 2018. "Geography and Agricultural Productivity: Cross–Country Evidence from Micro Plot-Level Data." NBER Working Paper 24532, National Bureau of Economic Research, Cambridge, MA.

ADB (Asian Development Bank). 2019. *The Servicification of Manufacturing in Asia: Redefining the Sources of Labor Productivity.* Manila: Asian Development Bank.

Adenle, A. A., J. D. Ford, J. Morton, S. Twomlow, K. Alverson, A. Cattaneo, R. Cervigni, et al. 2017. "Managing Climate Change Risks in Africa—A Global Perspective." *Ecological Economics* 141 (November): 190–201.

Adler, G., R. A. Duval, D. Furceri, S. K. Celik, K. Koloskova, and M. Poplawski-Ribeiro. 2017. "Gone with the Headwinds: Global Productivity." IMF Staff Discussion Note 17/04, International Monetary Fund, Washington, DC.

Aggarwal, A., M. Hoppe, and P. Walkenhorst. 2019. *Special Economic Zones in South Asia: Industrial Islands or Vehicles for Diversification?* Washington, DC: World Bank.

Aiyar, S., B. Augustyniak, C. Ebeke, E. Ebrahimy, S. Elekdag, N. Klein, S. Lall, H. Zhao, and D. Muir. 2013. "German-Central European Supply Chain–Cluster Report." IMF Country Report 13/263, International Monetary Fund, Washington, DC.

Aiyar, S., C. Ebeke, and X. Shao. 2016. "The Impact of Workforce Aging on European Productivity." IMF Working Paper 16/238, International Monetary Fund, Washington, DC.

Albino-War, M., S. Cerovic, F. Grigoli, J.C. Flores, J. Kapsoli, H. Qu, Y. Said, B. Shukurov, M. Sommer, and S. Yoon. 2014. "Making the Most of Public Investment in MENA and CCA Oil Exporting Countries." IMF Staff Discussion Note 14/10, International Monetary Fund, Washington, DC.

Alesina, A., D. Furceri, J. Ostry, C. Papageorgiou, and D. Quinn. 2019. "Structural Reforms and Election: Evidence from a World-wide New Dataset." Harvard University Working Paper, Cambridge, MA.

Almeida, R., and T. Packard. 2018. "Competências e Empregos: uma Agenda para a Juventude." World Bank, Washington, DC.

Altinok, N., N. Angrist, and H. A. Patrinos. 2018. "Global Data Set on Education Quality (1965–2015)." Policy Research Working Paper 8314, World Bank, Washington, DC.

Amin, M., F. Ohnsorge, and C. Okou. 2019. "Casting a Shadow Productivity of Formal Firms and Informality." Policy Research Working Paper 8945, World Bank, Washington, DC.

Amin, M., and H. Ulku. 2019. "Corruption, Regulatory Burden and Firm Productivity." Policy Research Working Paper 8911, World Bank, Washington, DC.

Amjad, R., and N. Awais. 2016. "Pakistan's Productivity Performance and TFP Trends, 1980–2015: Cause for Real Concern." *Lahore Journal of Economics* 21 (SE): 33–63.

Andrews, D., C. Criscuolo, and P. N. Gal. 2015. "Frontier Firms, Technology Diffusion and Public Policy: Micro Evidence from OECD Countries." In *The Future of Productivity. Main Background Papers.* Paris: Organisation for Economic Co-operation and Development.

APO (Asian Productivity Organization). 2018. *Asian Productivity Databook.* Tokyo: Asian Productivity Organization.

Araujo, J. T., E. Vostroknutova, and K. Wacker. 2017. "Productivity Growth in Latin America and the Caribbean: Exploring the Macro-Micro Linkages." MFM Global Practice Discussion Paper 19, World Bank, Washington, DC.

Arezki, R., M. Ait Ali Slimane, A. Barone, K. Decker, D. Detter, R. Fan, H. Nguyen, G. Miralles, and L. Senbet. 2019a. *MENA Economic Update: Reaching New Heights: Promoting Fair Competition in the Middle East and North Africa.* October. Washington, DC: World Bank.

Arezki, R., D. Lederman, A. Harb, R. Fan, and H. Nguyen. 2019b. *MENA Economic Update: Reforms and External Imbalances: The Labor-Productivity Connectivity Connection in the Middle East and North Africa.* April. Washington, DC: World Bank.

Armitage, R., and L. Nellumns. 2020. "Considering Inequalities in the School Closure Response to COVID19." *Lancet Global Health 2020: Correspondence.*

Arnold, J. M., B. S. Javorcik, M. Lipscomb, and A. Mattoo. 2016. "Services Reform and Manufacturing Performance: Evidence from India." *Economic Journal* 126 (590): 1–39.

Arnold, J. M., B. S. Javorcik, and A. Mattoo. 2011. "Does Services Liberalization Benefit Manufacturing Firms? Evidence from the Czech Republic." *Journal of International Economics* 85 (1): 136–46.

Arteta, C., and S. Kasyanenko. 2019. "Financial Market Developments." In *A Decade after the Global Recession: Lessons and Challenges for Emerging and Developing Economies,* edited by M. A. Kose and F. Ohnsorge. Washington, DC: World Bank.

Artuc, E., G. Lopez-Acevedo, R. Robertson, and D. Samaan. 2019. *Export to Jobs: Boosting the Gains from Trade in South Asia. South Asia Development Forum.* Washington, DC: World Bank.

Ashraf, Q. H., D. N. Weil, and J. Wilde. 2013. "The Effect of Fertility Reduction on Economic Growth." *Population and Development Review* 39 (1): 97–130.

Asiki, G., G. Reniers, R. Newton, K. Baisley, J. Nakiyingi-Miiro, E. Slaymaker, and I. Kasamba et al. 2016. "Adult Life Expectancy Trends in the Era of Antiretroviral Treatment in Rural Uganda (1991–2012)." *Aids* 30 (3): 487–93.

Aslam, A., S. Beidas-Strom, R. Bems, O. Celasun, S. K. Celik, and Z. Koczan. 2016. "Trading on Their Terms? Commodity Exporters in the Aftermath of the Commodity Boom." IMF Working Paper 16/27, International Monetary Fund, Washington, DC.

Attanasio, O., A. Guarin, C. Medina, and C. Meghir. 2015. "Long Term Impacts of Vouchers for Vocational Training: Experimental Evidence in Colombia." NBER Working Paper 21390, National Bureau of Economic Research, Cambridge, MA.

Ayyagari, M., A. Demirgüç-Kunt, and V. Maksimovic. 2017. "SME Finance." Policy Research Working Paper 8241, World Bank, Washington, DC.

Ayyagari, M., P. F. Juarros, M. S. Martinez Peria, and S. Singh. 2016. "Access to Finance and Job Growth: Firm-Level Evidence across Developing Countries." Policy Research Working Paper 7604, World Bank, Washington, DC.

Azevedo, J. P., A. Hasan, D. Goldemberg, S. A. Iqbal, and K. Geven. 2020. "Simulating the Potential Impacts of COVID-19 School Closures on Schooling and Learning Outcomes: A Set of Global Estimates." Policy Research Working Paper 9284, World Bank, Washington, DC.

Baffes, J., M. A. Kose, F. Ohnsorge, and M. Stocker. 2015. "The Great Plunge in Oil Prices: Causes, Consequences, and Policy Responses." Policy Research Note 1, World Bank, Washington, DC.

Bah, E., and L. Fang. 2015. "Impact of the Business Environment on Output and Productivity in Africa." *Journal of Development Economics* 114 (May): 159–71.

Baier, S. L., G. P. Dwyer, and R. Tamura. 2006. "How Important Are Capital and Total Factor Productivity for Economic Growth." *Economic Inquiry* 44 (1): 23–49.

Balabushko, O., O. Betliy, V. Movchan, R. Piontkivsky, and M. Ryzhenkov. 2018. "Crony Capitalism in Ukraine: Relationship between Political Connectedness and Firms' Performance." Policy Research Working Paper 8471, World Bank, Washington, DC.

Baldwin, R. 2019. *The Globotics Upheaval: Globalization, Robotics and the Future of Work.* New York: Oxford University Press.

Baldwin, R., and J. Lopez-Gonzalez. 2013. "Supply-Chain Trade: A Portrait of Global Patterns and Several Testable Hypotheses." *The World Economy* 38 (11): 1682–721.

Barofsky, J., T. D. Anekwe, and C. Chase. 2015. "Malaria Eradication and Economic Outcomes in Sub-Saharan Africa: Evidence from Uganda." *Journal of Health Economics* 44 (December): 118–36.

Barrett, C. B., L. Christiaensen, M. Sheahan, and A. Shimeles. 2017. "On the Structural Transformation of Rural Africa." Policy Research Working Paper 7938, World Bank, Washington, DC.

Barro, R. J., and J. W. Lee. 2015. *Education Matters: Global Schooling Gains from the 19th to the 21st Century.* New York: Oxford University Press.

Bartelsman, E. J., and S. Scarpetta. 2007. "Reallocation and Productivity in Transition and Integration Phases." Policy Research Working Paper 6572, World Bank, Washington, DC.

Beck, T. 2018. "Finance and Resource Booms: A Complicated Relationship." In *Rethinking the Macroeconomics of Resource-Rich Countries,* edited by A. Arezki, J. Boucekkine, J. Frankel, M. Laksaci, and R. van der Ploeg. London: CEPR Press.

Beegle, K., and L. Christiaensen. 2019. *Accelerating Poverty Reduction in Africa.* Washington, DC: World Bank.

Benhassine, N., S. H. Youssef, P. Keefer, A. Stone, and S. N. Wahba. 2009. *From Privilege to Competition: Unlocking Private-led Growth in the Middle East and North Africa. MENA Development Report.* Washington, DC: World Bank.

Berg, A., and A. O. Krueger. 2003. "Trade, Growth, and Poverty: a Selective Survey." *Annual World Bank Conference on Development Economics,* 47–91. World Bank, Washington, DC.

Beteille, T. 2019. *Ready to Learn, Ready to Thrive: Before School, in School and beyond School in South Asia.* Washington, DC: World Bank.

Beverelli, C., M. Fiorini, and B. Hoekman. 2017. "Services Trade Policy and Manufacturing Productivity: The Role of Institutions." *Journal of International Economics* 104 (January): 166–82.

Bisat, A., M. A. El-Erian, and T. Helbling. 1997. "Growth, Investment, and Saving in the Arab Economies." IMF Working Paper 97/85, International Monetary Fund, Washington, DC.

Blancher, N., A. Bibolov, and A. Fouejieu. 2019. "Financial Inclusion of Small and Medium-Sized Enterprises in the Middle East and Central Asia." IMF Working Paper 19/02, International Monetary Fund, Washington, DC.

Blimpo, M. P., and M. Cosgrove-Davies. 2019. *Electricity Access in Sub-Saharan Africa: Uptake, Reliability, and Complementary Factors for Economic Impact.* Africa Development Forum. Washington, DC: World Bank.

Bloom, D. E., M. Kuhn, and K. Prettner. 2017. "Africa's Prospects for Enjoying a Demographic Dividend." *Journal of Demographic Economics* 83 (1): 63–76.

Bloom, N., B. Eifert, A. Mahajan, D. McKenzie, and J. Roberts. 2013. "Does Management Matter? Evidence from India." *Quarterly Journal of Economics* 128 (1): 1–51.

Bouis, R., R. Duval, and J. Eugster. 2016. "Product Market Deregulation and Growth: New Country-Industry-Level Evidence." IMF Working Paper 16/114, International Monetary Fund, Washington, DC.

Bown, C., D. Lederman, S. Pienknagura, and R. Robertson. 2017. *Better Neighbors: Toward a Renewal of Integration in Latin America.* Washington, DC: World Bank.

Brancatelli, C., A. Marguerie, and S. Brodmann. 2020. "Job Creation and Demand for Skills in Kosovo: What Can We Learn from Job Portal Data?" Policy Research Working Paper 9266, World Bank, Washington, DC.

Brandt, N., P. Schreyer, and V. Zipperer. 2017. "Productivity Measurement with Natural Capital." *Review of Income and Wealth* 63 (s1): s7–s21.

Brenton, P., R. Newfarmer, and P. Walkenhorst. 2009. "Avenues for Export Diversification: Issues for Low-Income Countries." MPRA Paper 22758, University Library of Munich, Munich.

Brown, J. D., G. A. Crespi, L. Iacovone, and L. Marcolin. 2016. "Productivity Convergence at Firm Level: New Evidence from the Americas." In *Understanding the Income and Efficiency Gap in Latin America and the Caribbean,* edited by J. T. Araujo, E. Vostroknutova, K. Wacker, and M. Clavijo. Washington, DC: World Bank.

Brown, J. D., and J. S. Earle. 2007. "Firm-Level Components of Aggregate Productivity Growth in ECA Economies." Background Paper, World Bank, Washington, DC.

Brown, J. D., J. S. Earle, and Á. Telegdy. 2006. "The Productivity Effects of Privatization: Longitudinal Estimates from Hungary, Romania, Russia, and Ukraine." *Journal of Political Economy* 114 (1): 61–99.

Bruszt, L., and N. Campos. 2016. "Deep Economic Integration and State Capacity: The Case of the Eastern Enlargement of the European Union." ADP Working Paper, Asian Development Bank, Manila.

Burgess, S., and H. H. Sievertsen. 2020. "Schools, Skills, and Learning: The Impact of COVID-19 on Education." Vox CEPR Policy Portal, April 1, 2020. https://voxeu.org/article/impact-covid-19-education.

Busso, M., L. Madrigal, and C. Pagés. 2013. "Productivity and Resource Misallocation in Latin America." *B. E. Journal of Macroeconomics* 13 (1): 903–32.

Cadestin, C., J. Gourdon, and P. Kowalski. 2016. "Participation in Global Value Chains in Latin America: Implications for Trade and Trade-Related Policy." Trade Policy Paper 192, Organisation for Economic Co-operation and Development, Paris.

Calderón, C., and C. Cantú. 2019. "Trade Integration and Growth: Evidence from Sub-Saharan Africa." Policy Research Working Paper 8859, World Bank, Washington, DC.

Calderón, C., E. Moral-Benito, and L. Servén. 2011. "Is Infrastructure Capital Productive? A Dynamic Heterogeneous Approach." *Journal of Applied Econometrics* 30 (2): 177–98.

Calderón, C., and L. Servén. 2010. "Infrastructure and Economic Development in Sub-Saharan Africa." *Journal of African Economies* 19 (S1): i13–i87.

Calice, P., E. P. Ribiero, and S. Byskov. 2018. "Efficient Financial Allocation and Productivity Growth in Brazil." Policy Research Working Paper 8479, World Bank, Washington, DC.

Callen, T., R. Cherif, F. Hasanov, A. Hegazy, and P. Khandelwal. 2014. "Economic Diversification in the GCC: Past, Present, and Future." IMF Staff Discussion Note, International Monetary Fund, Washington, DC.

Campos, F., R. Coleman, A. Conconi, A. Donald, M. Gassier, M. Goldstein, and Z. Chavez et al. 2019. *Profiting from Parity: Unlocking the Potential of Women's Business in Africa.* Washington, DC: World Bank.

Campos, F., M. Frese, M. Goldstein, L. Iacovone, H. Johnson, D. McKenzie, and M. Mensmann. 2017. "Teaching Personal Initiative Beats Traditional Training in Boosting Small Business in West Africa." *Science* 357 (6357): 1287–90.

Casaburi, L., M. Kremer, S. Mullainathan, and R. Ramrattan. 2019. "Harnessing ICT to Increase Agricultural Production: Evidence from Kenya." Harvard University, Cambridge, MA.

Caselli, F. 2005. "Accounting for Cross-country Income Differences." In *Handbook of Economic Growth Volume 1A,* edited by P. Aghion and S. N. Durlauf, 679–741. Amsterdam: Elsevier.

Cervellati, M., and U. Sunde. 2011. "Life Expectancy and Economic Growth: The Role of the Demographic Transition." *Journal of Economic Growth* 16 (2): 99–133.

Chen, C. 2017. "Technology Adoption, Capital Deepening, and International Productivity Differences." Department of Economics Working Paper 584, University of Toronto.

Chen, C., and D. Restuccia. 2018. "Agricultural Productivity Growth in Africa." Background paper prepared for the AFRCE project "Boosting Productivity in Sub-Saharan Africa," World Bank, Washington, DC.

Chen, E. 2002. "The Total Factor Productivity Debate: Determinants of Economic Growth in East Asia." *Asian-Pacific Economic Literature* 40 (1): 18–38.

Chen, S., N. V. Loayza, and M. Reynal-Querol. 2008. "The Aftermath of Civil War." *World Bank Economic Review* 22 (1): 63–85.

Choi, J., M. Dutz, and Z. Usman. 2020. *The Future of Work in Africa: Harnessing the Potential of Digital Technologies for All.* Washington, DC: World Bank.

Chong, A., J. Galdo, and J. Saavedra. 2008. "Informality and Productivity in the Labor Market in Peru." *Journal of Economic Policy Reform* 11 (4): 229–45.

Christ, N., and M. J. Ferrantino. 2011. "Land Transport for Export: The Effects of Cost, Time, and Uncertainty in Sub-Saharan Africa." *World Development* 39 (10): 1749–59.

Cirera, X., and A. P. Cusolito. 2019. "Innovation Patterns and Their Effects on Firm-Level Productivity in South Asia." Policy Research Working Paper 8876, World Bank, Washington, DC.

Cirera, X., R. N. Fattal-Jaef, and H. Maemir. 2020. "Taxing the Good? Distortions, Misallocation, and Productivity in Sub-Saharan Africa." *World Bank Economic Review* 34 (1): 75–100.

Cirera, X., F. Lage, and L. Sabetti. 2016. "ICT Use, Innovation, and Productivity: Evidence from Sub-Saharan Africa." Policy Research Working Paper 7868, World Bank, Washington, DC.

Cirera, X., and W. F. Maloney. 2017. *The Innovation Paradox: Developing-Country Capabilities and the Unrealized Promise of Technological Catch-Up*. Washington, DC: World Bank.

Cobo, C., R. Hawkins, and H. Rovner. 2020. "How Countries in Latin America Use Technology during COVID-19 Driven School Closures." *Education for Development* (blog), March 31, 2020. https://blogs.worldbank.org/education/how-countries-across-latin-america-use-technology-during-covid 19-driven-school-closures.

Cole, M. A., and E. Neumayer. 2006. "The Impact of Poor Health on Total Factor Productivity." *Journal of Development Studies* 42 (6): 918–38.

Collier, P., G. Conway, and T. Venables. 2008. "Climate Change and Africa." *Oxford Review of Economic Policy* 24 (2): 337–53.

Cook, T., and C. McKay. 2015. "How M-Shwari Works: The Story So Far." Consultative Group to Assist the Poor (CGAP) and FSD (Financial Sector Deepening) Kenya.

Crespi, G., and P. Zuniga. 2011. "Innovation and Productivity: Evidence from Six Latin American Countries." *World Development* 40 (2): 273–90.

Cusolito, A. P., and W. F. Maloney. 2018. *Productivity Revisited: Shifting Paradigms in Analysis and Policy*. Washington, DC: World Bank.

Cusolito, A. P., R. Safadi, and D. Taglioni. 2017. "Inclusive Global Value Chains: Policy Options for Small and Medium Enterprises and Low-Income Countries." A co-publication of the World Bank Group and the Organization for Economic Co-operation and Development.

Danforth, J., P. A. Medas, and V. Salins. 2016. *How to Adjust to a Large Fall in Commodity Prices*. Washington, DC: International Monetary Fund.

De Haas, R., A. Britta, H. Harmgart, and C. Meghir. 2015. "The Impacts of Microcredit: Evidence from Bosnia and Herzegovina." *American Economic Journal: Applied Economics* 7 (1): 183–203.

De Haas, R., and I. van Lelyveld. 2006. "Foreign Banks and Credit Stability in Central and Eastern Europe. A Panel Data Analysis." *Journal of Banking & Finance* 30 (7): 1927–52.

de Hoyos, R., H. Rogers, and M. Székely. 2016. *Out of School and Out of Work: Risk and Opportunities for Latin America's Ninis*. Washington, DC: World Bank.

De Nicola, F., V. V. Kehayova, and H. M. Nguyen, 2018. "On the Allocation of Resources in Developing East Asia and Pacific (English)." Policy Research Working Paper 8634, World Bank, Washington, DC.

de Paula, A., and J. A. Scheinkman. 2011. "The Informal Sector: An Equilibrium Model and Some Empirical Evidence from Brazil." *Review of Income and Wealth* 57 (s1): s8–s26.

de Vries, G. J., M. P. Timmer, and K. de Vries 2013. "Structural Transformation in Africa: Static Gains, Dynamic Losses." GGDC Research Memorandum 136, Groningen Growth and Development Centre, University of Groningen, Netherlands.

Del Prete, D., G. Giovannetti, and E. Marvasi. 2017. "Global Value Chains Participation and Productivity Gains for North African Firms." *Review of World Economics* 153 (4): 675–701.

Delogu, M., F. Docquier, and J. Machado. 2014. "The Dynamic Implications of Liberalizing Global Migration." CESifo Working Paper 4596, CESifo Group, Munich.

Devarajan, S., and L. Mottaghi. 2015. *MENA Economic Monitor: Towards a New Social Contract*. April. Washington, DC: World Bank.

Di Mauro, F., H. Duy, A. Feng, S. J. Ong, and J. Pang. 2018. "Productivity Was Not that Sluggish in Developing Asia, Afterall: A Firm Level Perspective Using a Novel Dataset." Productivity Research Network, National University of Singapore.

Diao, X., M. McMillan, and D. Rodrik. 2017. "The Recent Growth Boom in Developing Economies: A Structural Change Perspective." NBER Working Paper 23132, National Bureau of Economic Research, Cambridge, MA.

Diaz, J. J., and D. Rosas. 2016. "Impact Evaluation of the Job Youth Training Program Projoven." IDB Working Paper 693, Inter-American Development Bank, Washington, DC.

Dieppe, A., G. Kindberg-Hanlon, and S. Kilic Celik. Forthcoming. "Global Productivity Trends: Looking Through the Turbulence." In *Productivity in Emerging and Developing Economies.* Washington, DC: World Bank.

Diop, N., and D. Marotta. 2012. *Natural Resource Abundance, Growth, and Diversification in the Middle East and North Africa: The Effects of Natural Resources and the Role of Policies.* Washington, DC: World Bank.

Divanbeigi, R., and R. Ramalho. 2015. "Business Regulations and Growth." Policy Research Working Paper 7299, World Bank, Washington, DC.

Duranton, G., E. Ghani, A. G. Goswami, and W. Kerr. 2016. "A Detailed Anatomy of Factor Misallocation in India." Policy Research Working Paper 7547, World Bank, Washington, DC.

Dutz, M. A. 2018. *Jobs and Growth: Brazil's Productivity Agenda.* Washington, DC: World Bank.

Dutz, M. A., R. K. Almeida, and T. G. Packard. 2018. *The Jobs of Tomorrow: Technology, Productivity, and Prosperity in Latin America and the Caribbean.* Washington, DC: World Bank.

Easterly, W., and R. Levine. 2001. *It's Not Factor Accumulation: Stylized Facts and Growth Models.* Washington, DC: World Bank.

EBRD (European Bank for Reconstruction and Development). 2014. *Transition Report 2013: Stuck in Transition?* London: EBRD.

EBRD (European Bank for Reconstruction and Development). 2017. *Transition Report 2017-18: Sustaining Growth.* London: EBRD.

EBRD (European Bank for Reconstruction and Development). 2018a. "The Western Balkans in Transition: Diagnosing the Constraints on the Path to a Sustainable Market Economy." Background paper for the EBRD Western Balkans Investment Summit, February 26, London.

EBRD (European Bank for Reconstruction and Development). 2018b. *Transition Report 2018-19: Work in Transition.* London: EBRD.

EBRD (European Bank for Reconstruction and Development). 2019. *Transition Report 2019-20: Better Governance, Better Economies.* London: EBRD.

Eden, M., and H. Nguyen. 2016. "Reconciling Micro and Macro-Based Estimates of Technology Adoption Lags in a Model of Endogenous Technology Adoption." In *Understanding the Income and Efficiency Gap in Latin America and the Caribbean,* edited by J. T. Araujo, E. Vostroknutova, K. Wacker, and M. Clavijo. Washington, DC: World Bank.

Elbadawi, I., and N. Loayza. 2008. "Informality, Employment and Economic Development in the Arab World." *Journal of Development and Economic Policies* 10 (2): 27–75.

Elgin, C., M. A. Kose, F. Ohnsorge, and S. Yu. Forthcoming. "Measuring the Informal Economy and Its Business Cycles." World Bank, Washington, DC.

Elgin, C., and O. Oztunali. 2012. "Shadow Economies around the World: Model Based Estimates." Working Paper 2012/05, Department of Economics, Boğaziçi University, Istanbul.

Ellis, P., and M. Roberts. 2016. *Leveraging Urbanization in South Asia: Managing Spatial Transformation for Prosperity and Livability: South Asia Development Matters.* Washington, DC: World Bank.

Falcetti, E., T. Lysenko, and P. Sanfey. 2006. "Reforms and Growth in Transition: Re-examining the Evidence." *Journal of Comparative Economics* 34 (3): 421–45.

Fay, M., L. Andres, C. Fox, U. Narloch, S. Straub, and M. Slawson. 2017. *Rethinking Infrastructure in Latin America and the Caribbean: Spending Better to Achieve More.* Washington, DC: World Bank.

Fayad, G., and T. Rasmussen. 2012. "Realizing Growth Objectives: Transitioning from Factor Accumulation to Productivity Improvement." In "Saudi Arabia: Selected Issues." IMF Country Report 12/272, International Monetary Fund, Washington, DC.

Fernandes, A. M. 2008. "Firm Productivity in Bangladesh Manufacturing Industries." *World Development* 36 (10): 1725–44.

Fernández-Arias, E., and S. Rodríguez-Apolinar. 2016. "The Productivity Gap in Latin America: Lessons from 50 Years of Development." Working Paper 692, Inter-American Development Bank, Washington, DC.

Ferreira, P. C., S. de Abreu Pessoa, and F. Veloso. 2013. "On the Evolution of Total Factor Productivity in Latin America." *Economic Inquiry* 51 (1): 16–30.

Ferreira, P. C., S. Pessoa, and M. R. Dos Santos. 2011. "The Impact of AIDS on Income and Human Capital." *Economic Inquiry* 49 (4): 1104–16.

Flabbi, L., and R. Gatti. 2018. "A Primer on Human Capital." Policy Research Working Paper 8309, World Bank, Washington, DC.

Fosu, A. K., and A. F. Abass. 2019. "Domestic Credit and Export Diversification: Africa from a Global Perspective." *Journal of African Business* 20 (2): 160–79.

Francis, E., J. Blumenstock, and J. Robinson. 2017. "Digital Credit in Emerging Markets: A Snapshot of the Current Landscape and Open Research Questions." Digital Credit Observatory, Center for Effective Global Action, University of California, Berkeley.

Frankel, J. 2010. "The Natural Resource Curse: A Survey." NBER Working Paper 15836, National Bureau of Economic Research, Cambridge, MA.

Freund, C. 2020. "Governments Could Bring Supply Chains Home. It Would Defy Economic Rationality." *Barron's.* May 1, 2020. https://www.barrons. com/articles/will-supply-chains-come-home-after-thecoronavirus-recession-51588327200.

Fuglie, K., M. Gautam, A. Goyal, and W. Maloney. 2020. *Harvesting Prosperity: Technology and Productivity Growth in Agriculture.* Washington, DC: World Bank.

Fujimori, A., and T. Sato. 2015. "Productivity and Technology Diffusion in India: The Spillover Effects from Foreign Direct Investment." *Journal of Policy Modeling* 37 (4): 630–51.

Funke, N., A. Isakova, and M. Ivanyna. 2017. "Identifying Structural Reform Gaps in Emerging Europe, the Caucasus, and Central Asia." IMF Working Paper 17/82, International Monetary Fund, Washington, DC.

Gatti, R., M. Morgandi, E. Grun, S. Brodmann, D. Angel-Urdinola, J. M. Moreno, D. Marotta, M. Schiffbauer, and E. Mata Lorenzo. 2013. *Jobs for Shared Prosperity: Time for Action in the Middle East and North Africa.* Washington, DC: World Bank.

Gelb, A., C. J. Meyer, V. Ramachandran, and D. Wadhwa. 2017. "Can Africa Be a Manufacturing Destination? Labor Costs in Comparative Perspective." CGD Working Paper 466, Center for Global Development, Washington, DC.

Georgiev, Y., P. Nagy-Mohacsi, and A. Plekhanov. 2017. "Structural Reform and Productivity Growth in Emerging Europe and Central Asia." ADB Economics Working Paper 532, Asian Development Bank, Manila.

Ghassibe, M., M. Appendino, and S. E. Mahmoudi. 2019. "SME Financial Inclusion for Sustained Growth in the Middle East and Central Asia." IMF Working Paper 19/209, International Monetary Fund, Washington, DC.

Goretti, M., D. Kihara, and R. Salgado. 2019. "Is South Asia Ready for Take Off? A Sustainable and Inclusive Growth Agenda." Asia and Pacific Department Paper 19/18, International Monetary Fund, Washington, DC.

Gould, D. 2018. *Critical Connections: Promoting Economic Growth and Resilience in Europe and Central Asia.* Europe and Central Asia Studies. Washington, DC: World Bank.

Gould, D. M., C. Tan, and A. S. S. Emamgholi. 2013. "Attracting Foreign Direct Investment: What Can South Asia's Lack of Success Teach Other Developing Countries?" Policy Research Working Paper 6696, World Bank, Washington, DC.

Gradzewicz, M., J. Growiec, M. Kolasa, Ł. Postek, and P. Strzelecki. 2018. "Poland's Uninterrupted Growth Performance: New Growth Accounting Evidence." *Post-Communist Economies* 30 (4): 1–35.

Grainger, C. A., and F. Zhang. 2017. "The Impact of Electricity Shortages on Firm Productivity: Evidence from Pakistan." Policy Research Working Paper 8130, World Bank, Washington, DC.

Grazzi, M., and J. Jung. 2016. "ICT, Innovation, and Productivity." In *Firm Innovation and Productivity in Latin America and the Caribbean: The Engine of Economic Development,* edited by M. Grazzi and C. Pietrobelli, 103–36. Washington, DC: Inter-American Development Bank.

Grigoli, F., A. Herman, and A. J. Swiston. 2017. "A Crude Shock: Explaining the Impact of the 2014-16 Oil Price Decline across Exporters." IMF Working Paper 17/160, International Monetary Fund, Washington, DC.

Groth, H., and J. F. May, eds. 2017. *Africa's Population: In Search of a Demographic Dividend.* Cham, Switzerland: Springer International.

Gylfason, T. 2018. "From Economic Diversification to Growth. Two Proposals." In *Rethinking the Macroeconomics of Resource-Rich Countries,* edited by A. Arezki, R. Boucekkine, J. Frankel, M. Laksaci, and R. van der Ploeg. https://voxeu.org/content/rethinking-macroeconomics-resource-rich-countries.

Hallegatte, S., M. Bangalore, L. Bonzanigo, M. Fay, T. Kane, U. Narloch, J. Rozenberg, D. Treguer, and A. Vogt-Schilb. 2015. *Shock Waves: Managing the Impacts of Climate Change on Poverty.* Washington, DC: World Bank.

Hallward-Driemeier, M., G. Iarossi, and K. L. Sokoloff. 2002. "Exports and Manufacturing Productivity in East Asia: A Comparative Analysis with Firm-Level Data." NBER Working Paper 8894, National Bureau of Economic Research, Cambridge, MA.

Hallward-Driemeier, M., and G. Nayyar. 2018. *Trouble in the Making? The Future of Manufacturing-Led Development.* Washington, DC: World Bank.

Henry, P. 2007. "Capital Account Liberalization: Theory, Evidence, and Speculation." *Journal of Economic Literature* 45 (4): 887–935.

Hesse, H. 2008. "Export Diversification and Economic Growth." Commission on Growth and Development Working Paper 21, World Bank, Washington, DC.

Hidalgo, C., and R. Hausmann. 2009. "The Building Blocks of Economic Complexity." CID Working Paper 186, Harvard Kennedy School, Cambridge, MA.

Hjort, J., and J. Poulsen. 2019. "The Arrival of Fast Internet and Employment in Africa." *American Economic Review* 109 (3): 1032–79.

Hodge, A., S. Shankar, D. S. Prasada Rao, and A. Duhs. 2011. "Exploring the Links Between Corruption and Growth." *Review of Development Economics* 15 (3): 474–90.

Hsieh, C., and P. J. Klenow. 2009. "Misallocation and Manufacturing TFP in China and India." *Quarterly Journal of Economics* 124 (4): 1403–48.

Hu, A. G. Z., G. H. Jefferson, and Q. Jinchang. 2005. "R&D and Technology Transfer: Firm-Level Evidence from Chinese Industry." *Review of Economics and Statistics* (87) 4: 780–86.

Ianchovichina, E. 2017. *Eruptions of Popular Anger: The Economics of the Arab Spring and Its Aftermath.* MENA Development Report. Washington, DC: World Bank.

IEA (International Energy Agency). 2020. "Oil Market Report." June. International Energy Agency, Paris.

ILO (International Labour Office). 2017. *What Future for Decent Work in Europe and Central Asia: Opportunities and Challenges.* Geneva: International Labour Office.

IMF (International Monetary Fund). 2006. "Asia Rising: Patterns of Economic Development and Growth. In *World Economic Outlook. Financial Systems and Economic Cycles,* Chapter 3. Washington, DC: International Monetary Fund.

IMF (International Monetary Fund). 2012. "Saudi Arabia Article IV Consultation." IMF Country Report 12/271, International Monetary Fund, Washington, DC.

IMF (International Monetary Fund). 2014. "The Caucasus and Central Asia: Transitioning to Emerging Markets." International Monetary Fund, Washington, DC.

IMF (International Monetary Fund). 2015. "Islamic Republic of Iran Consultation." IMF Country Report 15/349, International Monetary Fund, Washington, DC.

IMF (International Monetary Fund). 2016a. "Economic Diversification in Oil-Exporting Arab Countries." Annual Meeting of Arab Ministers of Finance.

IMF (International Monetary Fund). 2016b. "Bolivia: 2016 Article IV Staff Report." IMF Country Report 16/387, International Monetary Fund, Washington, DC.

IMF (International Monetary Fund). 2017. *Asia and Pacific: Preparing for Choppy Seas.* Regional Economic Outlook. May. Washington, DC: International Monetary Fund.

IMF (International Monetary Fund). 2018a. "Productivity Growth in Asia: Boosting Firm Dynamism and Weeding out the Zombies." In *Asia and Pacific: Asia at the Forefront: Growth Challenges for the Next Decade and Beyond.* Regional Economic Outlook. October. Washington, DC: International Monetary Fund.

IMF (International Monetary Fund). 2018b. *Middle East and Central Asia.* Regional Economic Outlook. November. Washington, DC: International Monetary Fund.

IMF (International Monetary Fund). 2019a. *Promoting Inclusive Growth in the Caucasus and Central Asia.* Washington, DC: International Monetary Fund.

IMF (International Monetary Fund). 2019b. "Financial Inclusion of Small and Medium-Sized Enterprises in the Middle East and Central Asia." IMF Departmental Paper 19/02, International Monetary Fund, Washington, DC.

IMF (International Monetary Fund). 2019c. *Fiscal Monitor: Curbing Corruption.* April. Washington, DC: International Monetary Fund.

IMF (International Monetary Fund). 2019d. *Middle East and Central Asia.* Regional Economic Outlook. October. Washington, DC: International Monetary Fund.

IPCC (Intergovernmental Panel on Climate Change). 2014. "Climate Change 2014: Impacts, Adaptation, and Vulnerability." IPCC Working Group II, Intergovernmental Panel on Climate Change, Geneva.

ITF (International Transport Forum). 2018. "The Billion Dollar Question: How Much Will It Cost to Decarbonise Cities' Transport Systems?" Discussion Paper, ITF, Paris.

Kalemli-Ozcan, S. 2003. "A Stochastic Model of Mortality, Fertility, and Human Capital Investment." *Journal of Development Economics* 70 (1): 103–18.

Kanwar, S., and S. Sperlich. 2019. "Innovation, Productivity and Intellectual Property Reform in an Emerging Market Economy: Evidence from India." *Empirical Economics* 59 (May): 933–50.

Kaplan, D. 2009. "Job Creation and Labor Reform in Latin America." *Journal of Comparative Economics* 37 (1): 91–105.

Kaufmann, D., A. Kraay, and M. Mastruzzi. 2010. "The Worldwide Governance Indicators: Methodology and Analytical Issues." Policy Research Working Paper 5430, World Bank, Washington, DC.

Keller, J., and M. K. Nabli. 2002. "The Macroeconomics of Labor Market Outcomes in MENA over the 1990s: How Growth Has Failed to Keep Pace with a Burgeoning Labor Market." Working Paper 71, Egyptian Center for Economic Studies, Cairo.

Khan, T., T. Nguyen, F. Ohnsorge, and R. Schodde. 2016. "From Commodity Discovery to Production." Policy Research Working Paper 7823, World Bank, Washington, DC.

Khera, P. 2018. "Closing Gender Gaps in India: Does Increasing Women's Access to Finance Help?" IMF Working Paper 18/212, International Monetary Fund, Washington, DC.

Kim, Y. E., and N. V. Loayza. 2017. "Productivity Determinants: Innovation, Education, Efficiency, Infrastructure, and Institutions." Policy Research Paper, World Bank, Washington, DC.

Kim, Y. E., and N. V. Loayza. 2019. "Productivity Growth: Patterns and Determinants across the World." Policy Research Working Paper 8852, World Bank, Washington, DC.

Kinda, T. 2019. "E-commerce as a Potential New Engine for Growth in Asia." IMF Working Paper 19/135, International Monetary Fund, Washington, DC.

Klapper, L., C. Richmond, and T. Tran. 2013. "Civil Conflict and Firm Performance: Evidence from Côte d'Ivoire." Policy Research Working Paper 6640, World Bank, Washington, DC.

Kose, M. A., and F. Ohnsorge, eds. 2019. *A Decade after the Global Recession: Lessons and Challenges for Emerging and Developing Economies.* Washington, DC: World Bank.

Kouamé, W., and S. Tapsoba. 2018. "Structural Reforms and Firms' Productivity: Evidence from Developing Countries." Policy Research Working Paper 8308, World Bank, Washington, DC.

Kraay, A. 2018. "Methodology for a World Bank Human Capital Index." Policy Research Working Paper 8593, World Bank, Washington, DC.

Kraay, A., I. Soloaga, and J. Tybout. 2002. "Product Quality, Productive Efficiency, and International Technology Diffusion: Evidence from Plant-Level Panel Data." Policy Research Working Paper 2759, World Bank, Washington, DC.

Krishna, K. L., D. K. Das, A. A. Erumdan, S. Aggarwal, and P. C. Das. 2016. "Productivity Dynamics in India's Service Sector: An Industry-Level Perspective." Working Paper 261, Center for Development Economics, Delhi School of Economics, Delhi.

La Porta, R., and A. Scheifler. 2014. "Informality and Development." *Journal of Economic Perspectives* 28 (3): 109–26.

Laget, E., A. Osnago, N. Rocha, and M. Ruta. 2018. "Deep Trade Agreements and Global Value Chains." Policy Research Working Paper 8491, World Bank, Washington, DC.

Lakner, C., D. G. Mahler, M. Negre, and E. B. Prydz. 2020. "How Much Does Reducing Inequality Matter for Global Poverty?" Global Poverty Monitoring Technical Note 13, World Bank, Washington, DC.

Lall, S., Z. Shalizi, and U. Deichmann. 2004. "Agglomeration Economies and Productivity in Indian Industry." *Journal of Development Economics* 73 (2): 643–73.

Lederman, D., and W. F. Maloney. 2007. *Natural Resources: Neither Curse nor Destiny.* Palo Alto, CA: Stanford University Press.

Lederman, D., J. Messina, S. Pienknagura, and J. Rigolini. 2014. *Latin American Entrepreneurs: Many Firms but Little Innovation.* Washington, DC: World Bank.

Lehne, J., J. Mo, and A. Plekhanov. 2014. "What Determines the Quality of Economic Institutions? Cross-Country Evidence." EBRD Working Paper 171, European Bank for Reconstruction and Development, London.

Levenko, N., K. Oja, and K. Staehr. 2019. "Total Factor Productivity Growth in Central and Eastern Europe before, during and after the Global Financial Crisis." *Post-Communist Economies* 31 (2): 137–60.

Liu, Y., and V. Steenbergen. 2019. "The Role of FDI in Global Value Chains (GVCs): Implications for Sub-Saharan Africa." Unpublished working paper, World Bank, Washington, DC.

Loayza, N. V., L. Servén, and N. Sugawara. 2010. "Informality in Latin America and the Caribbean." In *Business Regulation and Economic Performance,* edited by N. Loayza and L. Servén, 157–96. Washington, DC: World Bank.

Lopez-Calix, J., T. G. Srinivasan, and M. Waheed. 2012. "What Do We Know About Growth Patterns in Pakistan?" Policy Paper Series 05/12, World Bank, Washington, DC.

Maiti, D. 2019. "Trade, Labor Share, and Productivity in India's Industries." ADBI Working Paper 926, Asian Development Bank Institute, Tokyo.

Malik, M., and T. Masood. 2018. "Economic Growth, Productivity and Convergence of the Middle East and North African Countries." MPRA Working Paper 87882, Munich Personal RePEc Archive, Munich.

Mallick, J. 2017. "Structural Change and Productivity Growth in India and the People's Republic of China." ADBI Working Paper 656, Asian Development Bank Institute, Tokyo.

Mason, A. D., and S. Shetty. 2019. *A Resurgent East Asia: Navigating a Changing World.* East Asia and Pacific Regional Report. Washington, DC: World Bank.

McMillan, M., D. Rodrik, and I. Verduzco-Gallo. 2014. "Globalization, Structural Change, and Productivity Growth, with an Update on Africa." *World Development* 63 (C): 11–32.

Mensah, E. B., S. Owusu, N. Foster-McGregor, and A. Szirmai. 2018. "Structural Change, Productivity Growth and Labor Market Turbulence in Africa." UNU-MERIT Working Paper 2018-25, Maastricht University, Netherlands.

Mensah, E. B., and A. Szirmai. 2018. "Africa Sector Database (ASD): Expansion and Update." UNUMERIT Working Paper 2018-20, Maastricht University, Netherlands.

Mercer-Blackman, V., and C. Ablaza. 2018. "The Servicification of Manufacturing in Asia: Redefining the Sources of Labor Productivity." ADBI Working Paper 902, Asian Development Bank Institute, Tokyo.

Mitra, P., A. Hosny, G. Minasyan, M. Fischer, and G. Abajyan. 2016. "Avoiding the New Mediocre: Raising Long-Term Growth in the Middle East and Central Asia." Middle East and Central Asia Departmental Paper 16/1, International Monetary Fund, Washington, DC.

Montalbano, P., S. Nenci, and C. Pietrobelli. 2018. "Opening and Linking Up: Firms, GVCs, and Productivity in Latin America." *Small Business Economics* 50 (4): 917–35.

Morsy, H., A. Levy, and C. Sanchez. 2014. "Growing without Changing: A Tale of Egypt's Weak Productivity Growth." EBRD Working Paper 172, European Bank for Reconstruction and Development, London.

Munoz, M. R., V. Perotti, J. Revilla, N. V. Loayza, T. Sharifuddin, S. Binti, J. Kunicova, et al. 2016. "The Quest for Productivity Growth." *Malaysia Economic Monitor.* Washington, DC: World Bank.

Nabli, M. 2007. *Breaking the Barriers to Higher Economic Growth: Better Governance and Deeper Reforms in the Middle East and North Africa.* Washington, DC: World Bank.

Nguimkeu, P. E. 2015. "An Estimated Model of Informality with Constrained Entrepreneurship." Working Paper, Georgia State University.

Nicoletti, G., and S. Scarpetta. 2005. "Regulation and Economic Performance: Product Market Reforms and Productivity in the OECD." OECD Economics Department Working Paper 460, Organisation for Economic Co-operation and Development, Paris.

O'Sullivan, M., A. Rao, R. Banerjee, K. Gulati, and M. Vinez. 2014. "Levelling the Field: Improving Opportunities for Women Farmers in Africa." World Bank and ONE Campaign, Washington, DC.

OECD (Organisation for Economic Co-operation and Development). 2016. "The Best versus the Rest: The Global Productivity Slowdown, Divergence across Firms and the Role of Public Policy." OECD Productivity Working Paper 5, Organisation for Economic Co-operation and Development, Paris.

OECD (Organisation for Economic Co-operation and Development). 2018a. *OECD Economic Survey of Costa Rica: Research Findings on Productivity.* Paris: OECD Publishing.

OECD (Organisation for Economic Co-operation and Development). 2018b. *Boosting Productivity and Inclusive Growth in Latin America.* Paris: OECD Publishing.

OECD (Organisation for Economic Co-operation and Development). 2020a. "COVID-19 Crisis Response in Central Asia." OECD Policy Responses to Coronavirus (COVID-19), OECD, Paris.

OECD (Organisation for Economic Co-operation and Development). 2020b. "COVID-19 in Latin America and the Caribbean." OECD Policy Responses to Coronavirus (COVID-19), OECD, Paris.

Oosthuizen, M., K. Lilenstein, F. Steenkamp, and A. Cassim. 2016. "Informality and Inclusive Growth in Sub-Saharan Africa." ELLA Regional Evidence Paper, ELLA Network, Lima.

Orlic, E., I. Hashi, and M. Hisarciklilar. 2018. "Cross Sectoral FDI Spillovers and Their Impact on Manufacturing Productivity." *International Business Review* 27 (4): 777–96.

Pagés-Serra, C., ed. 2010. *The Age of Productivity: Transforming Economies from the Bottom Up.* Washington, DC: Inter-American Development Bank.

Papageorgiou, C., and N. Spatafora. 2012. "Economic Diversification in LICs: Stylized Facts and Macroeconomic Implications." IMF Staff Discussion Note 12/13, International Monetary Fund, Washington, DC.

Park, J. 2010. "Projection of Long-Term Total Factor Productivity Growth for 12 Asian Economies." ADB Economics Working Paper 227, Asian Development Bank, Manila.

Pritchett, L. 1997. "Divergence, Big Time." *Journal of Economic Perspectives* 11 (3): 3–17.

Purfield, C., H. Finger, K. Ongley, B. Baduel, C. Castellanos, G. Pierre, V. Stepanyan, and E. Roos. 2018. "Opportunity for All: Promoting Growth and Inclusiveness in the Middle East and North Africa." IMF Departmental Paper 18/11, International Monetary Fund, Washington, DC.

Raballand, G., S. Refas, M. Beuran, and G. Isik. 2012. *Why Does Cargo Spend Weeks in Sub-Saharan African Ports? Lessons from Six Countries.* Washington, DC: World Bank.

Raggl, A. 2015. "Determinants of Total Factor Productivity in the Middle East and North Africa." *Review of Middle East Economic and Finance* 11 (2): 119–43.

Rahmati, M., and A. Pilehvari. 2017. "The Productivity Trend in Iran: Evidence from Manufacturing Firms." *Economics of Transition and Institutional Change* 27 (1): 395–408.

Rodríguez-Pose, A., and T. Ketterer. 2019. "Institutional Change and the Development of Lagging Regions in Europe." *Regional Studies:* 54 (7): 1–13.

Rodrik, D. 1999. "Where Did All the Growth Go? External Shocks, Social Conflict, and Growth Collapses." *Journal of Economic Growth* 4 (4): 385–412.

Rodrik, D. 2011. "The Future of Economic Convergence." NBER Working Paper 17400, National Bureau of Economic Research, Cambridge, MA.

Rodrik, D. 2016. "Premature Deindustrialization." *Journal of Economic Growth* 21 (1): 1–33.

Rodrik, D., and A. Subramanian. 2004. "From 'Hindu Growth' to Productivity Surge: The Mystery of the Indian Growth Transition." IMF Working Paper 04/77, International Monetary Fund, Washington, DC.

Rodrik, D., A. Subramanian, and F. Trebbi. 2004. "Institutions Rule: The Primacy of Institutions over Geography and Integration in Economic Development." *Journal of Economic Growth* 9 (2): 131–65.

Rovo, N. 2020. "Structural Reforms to Set the Growth Ambition." Policy Research Working Paper 9175, World Bank, Washington, DC.

Roy, S., M. Kessler, and A. Subramanian. 2016. "Glimpsing the End of Economic History? Unconditional Convergence and the Missing Middle Income Trap." CGD Working Paper 438, Center for Global Development, Washington, DC.

Rozenberg, J., and M. Fay. 2019. *Beyond the Gap: How Countries Can Afford the Infrastructure They Need while Protecting the Planet.* Washington, DC: World Bank.

Russell, M. 2018. "Seven Economic Challenges for Russia: Breaking Out of Stagnation?" European Parliament Research Service, In-Depth Analysis Series, Brussels.

Ruta, M., I. C. Constantinescu, and A. Mattoo. 2017. "Does Vertical Specialization Increase Productivity?" Policy Research Working Paper 7978, World Bank, Washington, DC.

Ryzhenkov, M. 2016. "Resource Misallocation and Manufacturing Productivity: The Case of Ukraine." *Journal of Comparative Economics* 44 (1): 41–55.

Samargandi, N. 2018. "Determinants of Labor Productivity in MENA Countries." *Emerging Markets Finance and Trade* 54 (5): 1063–81.

Schiantarelli, F., and V. Srivastava. 1997. "Debt Maturity and Firm Performance: A Panel Study of Indian Companies." Policy Research Working Paper 1724, World Bank, Washington, DC.

Schiffbauer, M., and J. Sampi. 2019. "Enforcing Competition and Firm Productivity: Evidence from 1,800 Peruvian Municipalities." Policy Research Working Paper 8714, World Bank, Washington, DC.

Schiffbauer, M., A. Sy, S. Hussain, H. Sahnoun, and P. Keefer. 2015. *Jobs or Privileges: Unleashing the Employment Potential of the Middle East and North Africa.* MENA Development Report. Washington, DC: World Bank.

Schor, A. 2004. "Heterogeneous Productivity Response to Tariff Reduction: Evidence from Brazilian Manufacturing Firms." *Journal of Development Economics* 75 (2): 373–96.

Sharafudheen, T. 2017. *South Asia Gender Initiative.* Washington, DC: World Bank.

Shepotylo, O., and V. Vakhitov. 2015. "Services Liberalization and Productivity of Manufacturing Firms: Evidence from Ukraine." *Economics of Transition* 23 (1): 1–44.

Shiferaw, A., M. Söderbom, E. Siba, and G. Alemu. 2015. "Road Infrastructure and Enterprise Dynamics in Ethiopia." *Journal of Development Studies* 51 (11): 1541–58.

Shmis, T., A. Sava, J. E. N. Teixeira, and H. A. Patrinos. 2020. "Response Note to COVID-19 in Europe and Central Asia: Policy and Practice Recommendations." World Bank, Washington, DC.

Sinha, R., and X. Xi. 2018. "Agronomic Endowment, Crop Choice and Agricultural Productivity." Background paper prepared for the AFRCE project Boosting Productivity in Sub-Saharan Africa. World Bank, Washington, DC.

Steinbach, M. R. 2019. "Growth in Low-Income Countries: Evolution, Prospects, and Policies." Policy Research Working Paper 8949, World Bank, Washington, DC.

Stocker, M., J. Bayes, Y. Some, D. Vorisek, and C. Wheeler. 2018. "The 2014-16 Oil Price Collapse in Retrospect: Sources and Implications." Policy Research Working Paper 8419, World Bank, Washington, DC.

Subramanian, A., and M. Kessler. 2013. "The Hyperglobalization of Trade and Its Future." PIIE Working Paper 13-6, Peterson Institute for International Economics, Washington, DC.

Suri, T., and W. Jack. 2016. "The Long-Run Poverty and Gender Impacts of Mobile Money." *Science* 354 (6317): 1288–92.

Tamirisa, N., and C. Duenwald. 2018. "Public Wage Bills in the Middle East and North Africa." IMF Departmental Paper. International Monetary Fund, Washington, DC.

Timmer, M. P., and A. Szirmai. 2000. "Productivity Growth in Asian Manufacturing: The Structural Bonus Hypothesis Examined." *Structural Change and Economic Dynamics* 11 (4): 371–92.

Topalova, P., and A. Khandelwal. 2011. "Trade Liberalization and Firm Productivity: The Case of India." *The Review of Economics and Statistics* 93 (3): 995–1009.

Torlese, H., and D. Raju. 2018. "Feeding of Infants and Young Children in South Asia." Policy Research Working Paper 8655, World Bank, Washington, DC.

Trushin, E. 2018. "Growth and Job Creation in Uzbekistan: An In-Depth Diagnostic." World Bank, Washington, DC.

Tuan, C., L. F. Y. Ng, and B. Zhao. 2009. "China's Post-Economic Reform Growth: The Role of FDI and Productivity Progress." *Journal of Asian Economics* 20 (3): 280–93.

UNDP (United Nations Development Programme). 2015. "Confronting the Gender Impact of Ebola Virus Disease in Guinea, Liberia, and Sierra Leone." *UNDP Africa Policy Note* 2 (1): 1–9.

Vagliasindi, M. 2013. *Revisiting Public-Private Partnerships in the Power Sector.* Washington, DC: World Bank.

Vargas, M. 2015. "Informality in Paraguay: Macro-Micro Evidence and Policy Implications." IMF Working Paper 15/245, International Monetary Fund, Washington, DC.

Virmani, A., and D. Hashim. 2011. "J-Curve of Productivity and Growth: Indian Manufacturing Post-Liberalization." IMF Working Paper 11/163, International Monetary Fund, Washington, DC.

Vorisek, D., and S. Yu. 2020. "Understanding the Cost of Achieving the Sustainable Development Goals: The World Bank Group's Contributions." Policy Research Working Paper 9146, World Bank, Washington, DC.

Wang, G, Y. Zhang, J. Zhao, J. Zhang, and F. Jiang. 2020. "Mitigate the Effects of Home Confinement on Children during the COVID-19 Outbreak." *Lancet: Correspondence* 395 (10228): 945–47.

Wang, Y. 2016. "What Are the Biggest Obstacles to Growth of SMEs in Developing Countries? – An Empirical Evidence from an Enterprise Survey." *Borsa Istanbul Review* 16 (3): 167–76.

Wei, Y., and X. Liu. 2006. "Productivity Spillovers from R&D, Exports and FDI in China's Manufacturing Sector." *Journal of International Business Studies* 37 (4): 544–57.

World Bank. 1995. *Bureaucrats in Business: The Economics and Politics of Government Ownership.* World Bank Policy Research Report. Washington, DC: World Bank.

World Bank. 2003. *Trade, Investment and Development in the Middle East and North Africa: Engaging with the World.* Washington, DC: World Bank.

World Bank. 2008. *Unleashing Prosperity: Productivity Growth in Eastern Europe and the Former Soviet Union.* Washington, DC: World Bank.

World Bank. 2012. *World Development Report 2012: Gender Equality and Development.* Washington, DC: World Bank.

World Bank. 2013a. *Micro, Small, and Medium Enterprise Finance: Women-Owned Business in India.* Washington, DC: World Bank.

World Bank. 2013b. "Enterprise Surveys: Nepal Country Highlights 2013." Washington, DC: World Bank.

World Bank. 2013c. "Enterprise Surveys: Bangladesh Country Highlights 2013." Washington, DC: World Bank.

World Bank. 2014. *Turkey's Transition.* Washington, DC: World Bank.

World Bank. 2015a. *East Asia's Changing Urban Landscape: Measuring a Decade of Spatial Growth.* Washington, DC: World Bank.

World Bank. 2015b. *Golden Aging: Prospects for Healthy, Active, and Prosperous Aging in Europe and Central Asia.* Europe and Central Asia Studies Series. June. Washington, DC: World Bank.

World Bank. 2015c. "Côte d'Ivoire: Systematic Country Diagnostic; From Crisis to Sustained Growth—Priorities for Ending Poverty and Boosting Shared Prosperity." World Bank, Washington, DC.

World Bank. 2016a. *Thailand Economic Monitor. Aging Society and Economy.* Washington, DC: World Bank.

World Bank. 2016b. *World Development Report 2016: Digital Dividends.* Washington, DC: World Bank.

World Bank. 2016c. "Russian Federation—Systematic Country Diagnostic: Pathways to Inclusive Growth." World Bank, Washington, DC.

World Bank. 2016d. *What's Holding Back the Private Sector in MENA? Lessons from the Enterprise Survey.* Washington, DC: World Bank.

World Bank. 2016e. *Global Economic Prospects: Spillovers amid Weak Growth.* January. Washington, DC: World Bank.

World Bank. 2016f. "South Asia Regional Gender Action Plan (RGAP): FY16–FY21, June 2016." World Bank, Washington, DC.

World Bank. 2016g. *Africa's Pulse: An Analysis of Issues Shaping Africa's Economic Future.* October. Washington, DC: World Bank.

World Bank. 2017a. "Cities in Eastern Europe and Central Asia: A Story of Urban Growth and Decline." World Bank, Washington, DC.

World Bank. 2017b. *At a Crossroads: Higher Education in Latin America and the Caribbean.* Washington, DC: World Bank.

World Bank. 2017c. *The Global Findex Database 2017: Measuring Financial Inclusion and the Fintech Revolution.* Washington, DC: World Bank.

World Bank. 2017d. *Gulf Economic Monitor: Sustaining Fiscal Reforms in the Long Term.* June. Washington, DC: Washington, DC.

World Bank. 2017e. *South Asia's Turn: Policies to Boost Competitiveness and Create the Next Export Powerhouse.* South Asia Development Matters Series. Washington, DC: World Bank.

World Bank. 2017f. *Doing Business 2018: Reforming to Create Jobs.* Washington, DC: World Bank.

World Bank. 2017g. "Nigeria Bi-Annual Economic Update: Fragile Recovery." April. World Bank, Washington, DC.

World Bank. 2018a. *World Development Report 2018: Learning to Realize Education's Promise.* Washington, DC: World Bank.

World Bank. 2018b. *Global Economic Prospects: Broad-Based Upturn, but for How Long?* January. Washington, DC: World Bank.

World Bank. 2018c. *Growth and Productivity in the Philippines: Winning the Future.* Washington, DC: World Bank.

World Bank. 2018d. *East Asia and Pacific Economic Update: Enhancing Potential.* April. Washington, DC: World Bank.

World Bank. 2018e. "China: Systematic Country Diagnostic: Towards a More Inclusive and Sustainable Development." World Bank, Washington, DC.

World Bank. 2018f. "Productivity Unplugged: The Challenges of Malaysia's Transition into a High-Income Country." Malaysian Development Experience Series, World Bank, Washington, DC.

World Bank. 2018g. *Europe and Central Asia Economic Update: Cryptocurrencies and Blockchain.* May. Washington, DC: World Bank.

World Bank. 2018h. *Jobs in the Kyrgyz Republic.* Washington, DC: World Bank.

World Bank. 2018i. "Dominican Republic: Systemic Country Diagnostic." World Bank, Washington, DC.

World Bank. 2018j. "Paraguay: Systemic Country Diagnostic." World Bank, Washington, DC.

World Bank. 2018k. *Expectations and Aspirations: A New Framework for Education in the Middle East and North Africa.* Washington, DC: World Bank.

World Bank. 2018l. *India Gender Portfolio Review 2018.* Part-2: Sectoral Findings Vol. 2. Washington, DC: World Bank.

World Bank. 2018m. *Global Investment Competitiveness Report 2017/2018: Foreign Investor Perspectives and Policy Implications.* Washington, DC: World Bank.

World Bank. 2018n. *Global Economic Prospects: The Turning of the Tide.* June. Washington, DC: World Bank.

World Bank. 2019a. *Global Economic Prospects: Darkening Skies.* January. Washington, DC: World Bank.

World Bank. 2019b. "Growth in Low-Income Countries: Evolution, Prospects, and Policies." In Global Economic Prospects, Heightened Tensions, Subdued Investment. Washington, DC: World Bank.

World Bank. 2019c. *East Asia and Pacific Economic Update: Weathering Growing Risks.* October. Washington, DC: World Bank.

World Bank. 2019d. *World Development Report 2020: Trading for Development in the Age of Global Value Chains.* Washington, DC: World Bank.

World Bank. 2019e. "Firm Productivity and Economic Growth in Turkey." Country Economic Memorandum, World Bank, Washington, DC.

World Bank. 2019f. "Kazakhstan: Reversing Productivity Stagnation." Country Economic Memorandum, World Bank, Washington, DC.

World Bank. 2019g. *Europe and Central Asia Economic Update: Migration and Brain Drain.* Fall. Washington, DC: World Bank.

World Bank. 2019h. "Enterprise Surveys." Data page (accessed on November 4, 2020). https://www.enterprisesurveys.org.

World Bank. 2019i. *Moldova: Rekindling Economic Dynamism.* Washington, DC: World Bank.

World Bank. 2019j. *Ukraine Growth: Faster, Lasting and Kinder.* Washington, DC: World Bank.

World Bank. 2019k. "Economic Transformation and the Future of Work in LAC." World Bank, Washington, DC.

World Bank. 2019l. *The Middle East and North Africa: From Transition to Transformation.* Washington, DC: World Bank.

World Bank. 2019m. *Gulf Economic Monitor: Economic Diversification for a Sustainable and Resilient GCC.* Washington, DC: World Bank.

World Bank. 2019n. *South Asia Economic Focus: Exports Wanted.* Spring. Washington, DC: World Bank.

World Bank. 2019o. *South Asia Economic Focus: Making Decentralization Work.* Fall. Washington, DC: World Bank.

World Bank. 2019p. "Rwanda: Systematic Country Diagnostic." World Bank, Washington, DC.

World Bank. 2019q. *Boosting Productivity in Sub-Saharan Africa.* Washington, DC: World Bank.

World Bank. 2019r. "Liberia Growth and Economic Diversification Agenda: Productivity-Driven Growth and Diversification." World Bank, Washington, DC.

World Bank. 2019s. "Nigeria Bi-Annual Economic Update: Jumpstarting Inclusive Growth—Unlocking the Productive Potential of Nigeria's People and Resource Endowments." Fall. World Bank, Washington, DC.

World Bank. 2019t. *Global Economic Prospects: Heightened Tensions, Subdued Investment.* June. Washington, DC: World Bank.

World Bank. 2019u. *Africa's Pulse: An Analysis of Issues Shaping Africa's Economic Future.* October. Washington, DC: World Bank.

World Bank. 2019v. *Lifelines: The Resilient Infrastructure Opportunity.* Washington, DC: World Bank.

World Bank. 2019w. *The World Bank Group's Action Plan on Climate Change Adaptation and Resilience.* Washington, DC: World Bank.

World Bank. 2020a. *Global Economic Prospects.* June. Washington, DC: World Bank.

World Bank. 2020b. *The COVID-19 Pandemic: Shocks to Education and Policy Responses.* Washington, DC: World Bank.

World Bank. 2020c. *Europe and Central Asia Economic Update: Fighting COVID-19.* Spring. Washington, DC: World Bank.

World Bank. 2020d. *Doing Business 2020. Comparing Business Regulation in 190 Economies.* Washington, DC: World Bank.

World Bank. 2020e. *South Asia Economic Focus: The Cursed Blessing of Public Banks.* Spring. Washington, DC: World Bank.

World Bank. 2020f. *Africa's Pulse: Assessing the Economic Impact of COVID-19.* April. Washington, DC: World Bank.

World Bank. 2020g. *World Development Report 2020: Trading for Development in the Age of Global Value Chains.* Washington, DC: World Bank.

World Bank and DRCSC (Development Research Center of the State Council, the People's Republic of China). 2014. *Urban China: Toward Efficient, Inclusive, and Sustainable Urbanization.* Washington, DC: World Bank.

World Bank and DRCSC (Development Research Center of the State Council, the People's Republic of China). 2019. *Innovative China: New Drivers of Growth.* Washington, DC: World Bank. https://openknowledge.worldbank.org/handle/10986/32351.

World Bank and MPIV (Ministry of Planning and Investment of Vietnam). 2016. *Vietnam 2035: Toward Prosperity, Creativity, Equity, and Democracy.* Washington, DC: World Bank.

Xu, X., and Y. Sheng. 2012. "Productivity Spillovers from Foreign Direct Investment: Firm-Level Evidence from China." *World Development* 40 (1): 62–74.

Yousef, T. 2004. "Development, Growth and Policy Reforms in the Middle East and North Africa." *Journal of Economic Perspectives* 18 (3): 91–116.

Youssef, H., S. Alnashar, J. Erian, A. Elshawarby, and C. Zaki. 2019. *Egypt Economic Monitor: From Floating to Thriving–Taking Egypt's Exports to New Levels.* Washington, DC: World Bank.

Zettelmeyer, J., E. Berglöf, L. Bruynooghe, H. Harmgart, P. Sanfey, and H. Schweiger. 2010. "European Transition at Twenty: Assessing Progress in Countries and Sectors." UNU-WIDER Working Paper 91, United Nations University—World Institute for Development Economics Research, Helsinki, Finland.

PART III

Technological Change and Sectoral Shifts

We are being afflicted with a new disease of which some readers may not yet have heard the name, but of which they will hear a great deal in the years to come—namely, technological unemployment. This means unemployment due to our discovery of means of economising the use of labour outrunning the pace at which we can find new uses for labour.

J. M. Keynes (1932)
Economist

Labor, no matter how inexpensive, will become a less important asset for growth and employment expansion, with labor-intensive, process-oriented manufacturing becoming a less effective way for early-stage developing countries to enter the global economy.

Michael Spence (2014)
Nobel Laureate and Professor at New York University

CHAPTER 6
Productivity: Technology, Demand, and Employment Trade-Offs

Lasting per capita income growth and poverty reduction depend on sustained growth in labor productivity, which is driven by technological progress, often embedded in new investment, capital deepening, and structural change. The productivity growth slowdown over the past decade reflects weakening in all these drivers. The consequences of the COVID-19 (coronavirus disease 2019) pandemic including the current deep recession, suggest negative repercussions for labor productivity. However, COVID-19 could catalyze rapid technological innovation and structural change. Nonetheless, the resulting income gains might not be equitably distributed, partly because of the possible effects of innovation on employment. Following technological improvements during 1980-2018, employment declined in 70 percent of emerging market and developing economies and 90 percent of advanced economies. The largest negative effects occurred in economies where employment was concentrated in industry, which tends to be more amenable to labor-saving innovation than other sectors. Cyclical fluctuations in activity can also have persistent effects on productivity, particularly in countries with weak fiscal positions. These findings indicate the importance of retraining programs and effective social safety nets to lower transition costs for workers displaced by technology advancements, as well as the strengthening of fiscal positions to ensure adequate space for stabilization policy.

Introduction

Productivity growth in advanced economies and emerging market and developing economies (EMDEs) has undergone many surges and declines in recent decades, usually coinciding with economic upswings and slowdowns, respectively. In the four largest surges since 1980, annual labor productivity growth in EMDEs rose by at least 3 percentage points, and it fell by nearly 2 percentage points in the subsequent slowdowns (figure 6.1). Productivity growth has been less volatile in advanced economies but has followed a similar pattern of rapid growth gains in upswings followed by slowdowns. Such short-term swings reflect cyclical fluctuations in labor and capacity utilization (Basu, Fernald, and Kimball 2006; Fernald and Wang 2016).[1]

The COVID-19 (coronavirus disease 2019) pandemic has likely dealt a severe blow to labor productivity by triggering the deepest global recession since World War II. If past recessions are any guide, labor productivity is likely to rebound in a cyclical upturn as the global economy recovers but to remain below the prepandemic trend for many years to come.[2] However, the global recession resulting from shocks related to COVID-19

Note: This chapter was prepared by Alistair Dieppe, Neville Francis, and Gene Kindberg-Hanlon. Research assistance was provided by Aygul Evdokimova and Yi Li.

[1] In the United States, one-half of total factor productivity growth variability has been attributed to demand-driven factors (Basu, Fernald, and Kimball 2006).

[2] Many studies have documented the persistent negative output effects of financial, currency, and political crises (Cerra and Saxena 2008; Jordà, Schularick, and Taylor 2013; Reinhart and Rogoff 2009).

FIGURE 6.1 Global labor productivity surges and declines

Over the past 40 years, labor productivity growth in advanced economies and EMDEs has undergone several cycles of surges and subsequent declines. Surges in labor productivity growth have tended to occur during cyclical upswings and declines in downturns. The most recent surge and decline in productivity growth, and the largest in EMDEs since 1980, occurred in the run-up to, and following, the global financial crisis.

A. Advanced economy and EMDE labor productivity growth

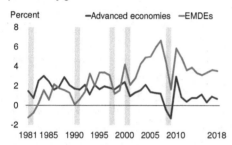

B. Labor productivity surges and declines following global slowdowns

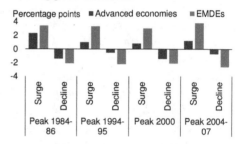

Sources: Conference Board; Kose and Terrones (2015); Penn World Table; World Bank, World Development Indicators.
Note: EMDEs = emerging market and developing economies.
A. Labor productivity growth in advanced economies and EMDEs constructed as GDP-weighted average growth rates, measured at 2010 prices and market exchange rates. Shaded regions indicate global recessions and slowdowns (1982, 1991, 1998, 2001, 2009), as defined in Kose and Terrones (2015).
B. Each surge in productivity shows the increase in productivity growth from its lowest point to its peak rate in advanced economies and EMDEs, with the lowest point being the weakest rate of growth in the five years preceding its peak. The decline is calculated as the decline to the lowest rate of growth in the five years following the peak of productivity growth. Peaks do not always occur in the same year in advanced economies and EMDEs. The range over which these peaks occur is indicated on the x axis.

may drive a larger decline in productivity growth even than experienced during the global financial crisis (World Bank 2020, chapter 2).

Yet lasting per capita income growth and poverty reduction depend on sustained labor productivity growth, stripped of such short-lived swings. Sustained labor productivity growth may be driven by capital-deepening (growth of capital per unit of labor input) or by technological and organizational changes, including the adoption of more efficient methods of production, in some cases incorporated through capital investment (Hulten 1992).

The COVID-19 pandemic may trigger lasting organizational and technological changes to the way businesses operate. These could be adverse to productivity growth if they erode capital or disrupt the accumulation of physical or human capital (chapter 2). However, pandemic-induced structural changes could also have productivity-enhancing effects, such as a "cleansing" effect, eliminating the least efficient firms and encouraging the adoption of more efficient production technologies (Caballero and Hammour 1994).[3] Although such effects could result in faster overall per capita income gains, they may also displace workers from their current roles, increasing income inequality.

---

[3] The threat of labor shortages because of social distancing could foster a wave of automation in certain industries (Leduc and Liu 2020).

Against this backdrop, this chapter disentangles long-term productivity changes from short-term, cyclical productivity fluctuations using structural vector auto-regressions (SVARs). Throughout this chapter, the long-term drivers of productivity growth will be referred to as "technology," as is common in the literature.[4] Changes in technology, in this sense, occur not only as a result of technical innovations but also when there are organizational or institutional changes to the production process.[5]

This chapter addresses the following questions:

- How much do long-term changes and business cycle fluctuations each contribute to changes in labor productivity growth?

- What are the effects of long-term changes in labor productivity growth on employment and other variables?

- What are the lasting effects of demand-driven cyclical fluctuations in labor productivity growth?

- What are the policy implications?

Contributions

This chapter makes multiple contributions to a literature that has primarily focused on advanced economies. First, this chapter is the first study to identify "technology" drivers of labor productivity growth in a comprehensive cross-country sample of 30 advanced economies and 96 EMDEs.[6] Other studies have restricted themselves to a decomposition of labor productivity growth into its growth accounting components, or have only examined the role of cyclically adjusted total factor productivity (TFP) growth or econometrically identified measures of changes in technology in a small number of advanced economies. (Coibion, Gorodnichenko, and Ulate 2017; Fernald 2014; Goodridge, Haskel, and Wallis 2018; OECD 2015; World Bank 2018b).

Second, this chapter is the first study to estimate the effects of technological change on aggregate employment across a broad range of EMDEs and advanced economies. It is also the first to examine the extent of technology-driven job losses outside the Group of Seven (G7) economies and to determine the correlates of their scale and persistence, in contrast to earlier studies that focused on a narrower set of advanced economies (box 6.1).[7]

---

[4] More specifically, they are referred to as "technology shocks," or unanticipated changes in labor productivity. These may include investment-specific technologies. See also Chen and Wemy (2015), Fisher (2006), and Francis and Ramey (2005).

[5] A survey of the SVAR literature has found that technology shocks account for between 1 and 55 percent of variations in output in the United States (Ramey 2016).

[6] Previous studies have focused on a small subset of advanced economies. For example, Galí (1999) and Rujin (2019) apply long-run restriction-identified SVARs to G7 economies only.

[7] Some studies have examined the link between productivity growth and employment growth in a reduced-form framework in a broad set of economies including some EMDEs, but have not separately identified the differential impact of technology- and demand-driven changes in productivity (Beaudry and Collard 2003; Boulhol and Turner 2009). G7 countries are Canada, France, Germany, Italy, Japan, the United Kingdom, and the United States.

Third, this chapter is the first study to illustrate the persistent effects of demand shocks on labor productivity and its components in a wide range of EMDEs and advanced economies. Previous studies have examined a smaller subset of productivity growth drivers over shorter time horizons or have used data for fewer and mostly advanced economies (Aslam et al. 2016; Dabla-Norris et al. 2015; Fornero, Kirchner, and Andres 2014). This complements the analysis in chapter 3, which explores a set of specific adverse events, some of which also constitute demand shocks.

Main findings

The chapter reports several novel findings. First, long-term, "technological" drivers of productivity accounted for a large portion of labor productivity variation in the period 1980-2018: for about 40 percent of the 1-year-ahead forecast error variance of labor productivity and 60-75 percent of the 5- to 10-year-ahead forecast error variance of labor productivity. The cyclical, nontechnological component of productivity growth accounts for the remainder and largely reflects volatile TFP growth.

Second, in about 70 percent of EMDEs and 90 percent of advanced economies, employment fell initially after technology-driven productivity improvements. These employment losses were larger but less persistent in advanced economies than in EMDEs. Such employment losses were also larger in economies with larger increases in industry's share of employment since the 1990s, possibly because industry is particularly amenable to labor-saving innovations such as automation.

Third, this chapter highlights the persistent effects that cyclical developments driven by demand shocks can have on productivity. Although such developments may unwind faster than technology shocks, their impact on productivity can last well beyond the typical two- to eight-year duration of a business cycle. Demand-driven fluctuations in productivity growth have historically been considered to be neutral in the long run, with rising efficiency of production in cyclical upswings reversed in downswings. This chapter's contrasting finding is in line with a growing literature uncovering persistent effects on productivity in advanced economies from a range of demand-side developments.[8]

Fourth, policy options are available to promote the equitable sharing across the economy of gains from technology-driven productivity growth. These include measures to ensure that technological change does not lead to prolonged unemployment and measures that encourage diversification of skills. Training and retraining can encourage the accumulation of worker skills that complement new technologies, including in sectors conducive to automation. Adequate social protection provisions can help temporarily displaced workers transition to new sectors.

---

[8] Bachmann and Sims (2012) and Jordà, Singh, and Taylor (2020) find evidence that monetary and fiscal policy-induced expansions and contractions have had long-lasting effects on advanced economy productivity, in contrast to traditional assumptions of neutrality at long horizons.

Methodology. A new SVAR approach, before now applied only in studies of a few advanced economies, allows a decomposition of labor productivity into long-term drivers and drivers that operate at business cycle frequencies (Angeletos, Collard, and Dellas 2018a; Dieppe, Francis, and Kindberg-Hanlon 2019). The SVAR includes the log level of labor productivity, the log of employment per capita, consumption as a share of GDP, investment as a share of gross domestic product (GDP), consumer price inflation, and monetary policy interest rates where available (Francis et al. 2014).[9] For illustrative purposes, TFP is also included to show how labor productivity and TFP individually react to a technology shock.[10] Panel estimations for advanced economies and EMDEs were run with country fixed effects as well as a series of country-specific estimations. Technology shocks are defined as shocks that explain the largest share of the variance of labor productivity at the horizon of more than 10 years; demand shocks are those that explain the largest share at horizons of 2-8 years (annex 6A).[11] Chapter 3 offers some examples of such demand shocks.

Data. This chapter uses a data set broad enough to capture global productivity developments. Data on capital services and human capital are taken from the Penn World Table 9.1, and data on other macroeconomic aggregates such as GDP and employment are from the World Bank's World Development Indicators (WDI) database and The Conference Board's Total Economy Database (TED). Consistent annual data are available for 1980-2018 for 103 economies, of which 74 are EMDEs and 29 are advanced economies, for labor productivity and as a basis for estimates for TFP and capital services (chapter 1). Labor productivity is measured as output per worker. Data requirements to estimate SVAR technology shocks require additional variables, resulting in an unbalanced, but broader, panel of 30 advanced economies and 96 EMDEs.[12] The average sample length is 40 years for EMDEs and 45 years for advanced economies.

Drivers of productivity: Technology vs. demand shocks

The productivity surge that peaked in 2004 and 2007 in advanced economies and EMDEs, respectively, was the largest since at least 1980 in EMDEs (World Bank 2020).

---

[9] Checks on robustness to the inclusion of exchange rate and cyclically adjusted primary balance are shown in annex 6A. They do not materially affect impulse response functions (IRFs) but do result in shorter and more unbalanced data.

[10] TFP estimates are taken from chapter 1. An alternative approach to identify the long-run drivers of productivity takes into account changes in the utilization of labor and capital in the calculation of TFP growth. Basu, Fernald, and Kimball (2006), Comin et al. (2019), Duval et al. (2020), and Levchenko and Pandalai-Nayar (2018) have implemented this approach for advanced economies other than the United States, but not for EMDEs.

[11] Typically, business cycles are assumed to last two to eight years (Christiano and Fitzgerald 2003; Sargent 1987).

[12] Typically, technology-identifying SVARs have been applied to quarterly data sets. Data shortcomings for EMDEs—with typically less than 20 years of quarterly data on employment or productivity—impose severe constraints. Hence, annual data are used to estimate the SVARs. This choice significantly lengthens the time period over which the SVAR is estimated for many EMDEs.

FIGURE 6.2 **Decomposition of labor productivity variation**

In EMDEs, 60 percent of the variation of labor productivity growth since 1980 is estimated to have consisted of business cycle fluctuations, with just 40 percent being longer-lasting technological changes. Over longer horizons, however, in part by construction, technology shocks become more important. At the 5- or 10-year horizon, technology shocks account for 60-75 percent of the forecast error variance decomposition of labor productivity, both for advanced economies and EMDEs.

A. Variance of labor productivity growth

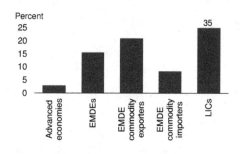

B. Share of long-term and business cycle variation in labor productivity growth

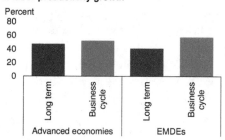

C. Forecast error variance of labor productivity: Share explained by technology

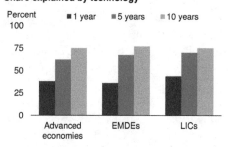

D. Forecast error variance of employment: Share explained by technology

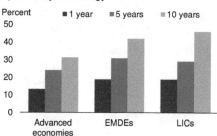

Sources: Conference Board; Penn World Table; World Bank, World Development Indicators.
Note: EMDEs = emerging market and developing economies; LICs = low-income countries.
A. Median variance of labor productivity in each group of economies. Y axis cropped at 25, but median LIC labor productivity is 35.
B. Applying spectral decomposition, the variance of each series is decomposed into components that reflect long-term and business cycle frequencies. Here, business cycle frequencies are classified as those lasting between 2 and 8 years; long-term frequencies include the variance contributed by fluctuations at frequencies longer than 8 years. Frequencies at 2 years are negligible and excluded (annual data cannot be decomposed into frequencies higher than 2 years).
C.D. Median of forecast error variance contribution to labor productivity or employment at the 1-, 5-, and 10-year horizon.

It was followed by the steepest and most prolonged decline in EMDE productivity growth since 1980 (chapter 1).

The methodology described above is used to decompose variations in labor productivity growth into business cycle fluctuations and longer-term trends. In EMDEs, 60 percent of the variation of labor productivity growth between 1980 and 2018 consisted of business cycle fluctuations (of between 2 and 8 years), with just 40 percent representing longer-lasting changes (figure 6.2). Over longer horizons, however, in part by construction, technology shocks become more important drivers of labor productivity. Thus at the 5- or 10-year horizon, technology shocks accounted for 60-75 percent of the forecast error variance decomposition of labor productivity, both for advanced economies and EMDEs.

FIGURE 6.3 **Contribution of cyclicality to labor productivity slowdown**

Cyclical factors such as changes in aggregate demand pressures and factor utilization explain less than one-half of the longer-term postcrisis slowdown in labor productivity growth. A "technology" measure of labor productivity growth, which removes these cyclical factors, has declined significantly since the global financial crisis but by different magnitudes across EMDE regions, suggesting different degrees of scarring from the crisis.

A. Slowdown 2013-18 relative to precrisis period: Advanced economies and EMDEs

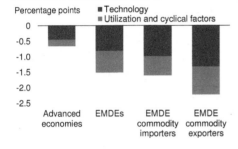

B. Productivity growth 2013-18 relative to precrisis period: EMDE regions

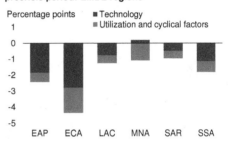

Source: World Bank.
Note: The "technology" contribution to labor productivity growth consists of the contribution of the Spectral SVAR-identified technology shock in addition to the contribution from the constant and initial condition in the SVAR, which can also be considered long-term processes. Utilization and cyclical factor contributions are defined as the residual of the contribution of "technology" and labor productivity growth. See annex 6A for further details. EAP = East Asia and Pacific; ECA = Europe and Central Asia; EMDEs = emerging market and developing economies; LAC = Latin America and the Caribbean; MNA = Middle East and North Africa; SAR = South Asia; SSA = Sub-Saharan Africa; SVAR = structural vector autoregression.
A.B. Precrisis period defined as 2003-07 for advanced economies and 2003-08 for EMDEs.

At least half of the immediate slowdown in productivity growth in EMDEs after the 2008 global financial crisis was attributable to cyclical factors such as weaker investment and reduced factor utilization (chapter 1). Over the longer term, most of the slowdown in EMDEs is structural, reflecting weaker technological development and adoption (figure 6.3). In advanced economies, two-thirds of the slowdown is explained by structural factors. The contributions vary across EMDE regions.

Effects of technology shocks

Response of productivity to technology shocks. The impulse responses suggest an economically meaningful and statistically significant effect of technology shocks on labor productivity growth over the long term (figure 6.4). Initially, almost all of the boost to labor productivity in both EMDEs and advanced economies is accounted for by TFP.[13] The proportion accounted for by TFP falls over time as investment rises, increasing the capital stock per worker.

Short-term macroeconomic responses to a technology shock. Alongside a sustained improvement in labor productivity and TFP, the levels of consumption and investment

---

[13] The labor productivity and TFP responses are scaled to the initial impact on each variable, respectively. The scaling of the IRFs obscures the substantial difference in the size of the shocks in advanced economies compared to EMDEs. A one-standard-deviation technology shock raises the level of productivity by about 1.5 percent over 10 years in advanced economies and about 4.5 percent in EMDEs.

FIGURE 6.4 Productivity effects of technology shocks

Labor productivity and TFP increase following a positive technology shock, but employment initially falls, with the effects in EMDEs fading away only after 10 years. Investment adjusts rapidly to a positive technology shock, as higher returns increase the incentive to boost the capital stock, whereas consumption increases more gradually. Inflation falls following a positive technology shock, as an improvement in the efficiency of production reduces costs and increases supply.

A. Scaled impulse response of labor productivity to a technology shock

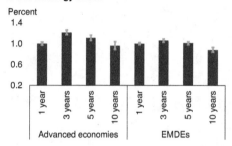

B. Scaled impulse response of TFP to a technology shock

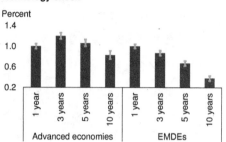

C. Scaled impulse response of employment to a technology shock

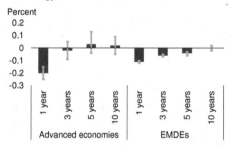

D. Scaled impulse response of investment to a technology shock

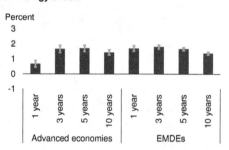

E. Scaled impulse response of consumption to a technology shock

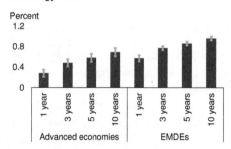

F. Scaled impulse response of consumer price inflation to a technology shock

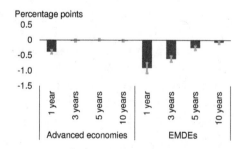

Source: World Bank.
Note: Panel VAR estimates of impulse responses from a technology shock identified using the Spectral VAR methodology. Panel estimations with fixed effects are performed separately for advanced economies and EMDEs. All impulse responses except TFP are scaled to the size of the impact on labor productivity. Therefore, each IRF can be viewed as the response of the variable for each 1 percent increase in labor productivity. The labor productivity and TFP responses are scaled to the initial impact on each variable respectively. The scaling of the IRFs obscures the substantial difference in the size of the shocks in advanced economies compared to EMDEs. A one-standard-deviation technology shock raises the level of productivity by about 1.5 percent over 10 years in advanced economies and about 4.5 percent in EMDEs. Consumption and investment responses are calculated as the sum of the impact on labor productivity and employment (which approximates to output) added to the impulse on the share of consumption or investment in GDP (measured in logs). EMDEs = emerging market and developing economies; IRF = impulse response function; TFP = total factor productivity; VAR = vector autoregression.

are found to rise, whereas consumer price inflation and employment are found to fall initially.[14] Employment falls by 0.1-0.2 percent in the next year in response to a technology shock, which boosts labor productivity by 1.0 percent.[15] These initial employment losses are statistically significant in the panel estimations, in one-half of individual country estimations for advanced economies and in one-third of those for EMDEs. In EMDEs, investment initially responds twice as strongly as in labor productivity to a technology shock, suggesting that technological change in these economies may often be capital-embodied or introduced into the production process alongside new investment (Hulten 1992). This contrasts with the response in advanced economies, where the investment response builds over time. Consumption rises significantly, by 0.3 percent (advanced economies) to 0.5 percent (EMDEs), after the technology shock as incomes grow and consumer price inflation declines.

Long-term macroeconomic response to a technology shock. Over time, the adverse employment effects of the technology shock taper off whereas the consumption gains continue to build. Employment in advanced economies is no longer economically or statistically significantly different from before the technology shock after three years and in EMDEs for longer. The more persistent employment losses in EMDEs may reflect difficulties in finding new roles for workers following a labor-substituting productivity shock. Meanwhile, consumption continues to grow until it reaches 0.7 percent (advanced economies) to 0.9 percent (EMDEs) above the preshock level after 10 years. Disinflation unwinds in less than a decade (figure 6.4).[16]

Channels for technology-induced employment losses. The literature has identified a variety of channels through which advances in production technology can result in changes in employment (box 6.1). Technology can be either a substitute or a complement for labor, and therefore can boost job opportunities as well as reduce them (Autor 2015). New technologies may substitute for labor, for example, where the costs of updating existing production technologies with the existing workforce become prohibitively high relative to the cost of automating capital (Acemoglu and Autor 2011; Acemoglu and Restrepo 2018). Employment losses are more likely in sectors where tasks are easily automated. Several studies of advanced economies have found evidence of increased employment in recent decades in service sector occupations involving tasks that are less easily automated, such as professional services and creative roles (Acemoglu 1999; Autor et al. 2013; Goos, Manning, and Salomons 2014).

---

[14] Overall, the IRFs for both advanced economies and EMDEs are consistent with theory and similar to typical responses in previous findings for positive technology shocks in advanced economies (Ramey 2016). The more persistent fall in inflation in EMDEs is likely to be a result of less well anchored inflation expectations (Kose et al. 2018).

[15] The finding that technology-driven improvements in labor productivity reduce employment in the short run is well-established for the United States and some economies in Europe (Basu, Fernald, and Kimball 2006; Francis and Ramey 2005; Galí 1999).

[16] Each IRF is scaled to the response of labor productivity to an improvement in technology (figure 6.4). The IRFs can therefore be interpreted as the impact on each variable for each 1 percent boost to labor productivity. For the labor productivity and TFP IRFs, the scaling is relative to the initial impact on each variable, respectively.

FIGURE 6.5 Employment effects of technology developments

Technology-induced employment losses were larger in economies with higher productivity (advanced economies), larger increases in the share of employment in industry, less openness to trade, and smaller FDI inflows.

A. Covariates of employment impact in year 1

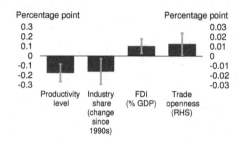

B. Covariates of employment impact in year 10

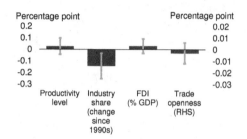

C. Advanced economies: Employment impact of a technology shock

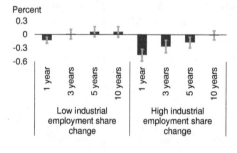

D. EMDEs: Employment impact of a technology shock

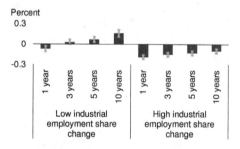

Source: World Bank.

Note: FDI = foreign direct investment; IRF = impulse response function; VAR = vector autoregression.

A. B. Coefficient estimated in a regression of the correlates of the employment impact of a technology innovation at the 1-year and 10-year horizon. Productivity level is measured in log units of output per worker measured in US dollars at 2010 prices and exchange rates, industry share shows the effect of a 10-percentage-point increase in the share of industrial sector employment between 1990-99 and 2010-18, FDI is the average net inflow relative to GDP during 1990-2018 (showing the effect of a 10-percentage-point increase), and trade openness is exports and imports as a share of GDP during 1990-2018, also scaled to show the effect of a 10-percentage-point increase. Orange lines show the 95 percent confidence interval.

C. D. Panel VAR estimation of the employment impact of a technology innovation in two separate groups. "High industrial employment share change" are those in the top quartile of changes in employment share in industry between 1990-9 and 2010-2018. "Low industrial employment share change" includes economies in the bottom quartile of changes in the share of industrial employment over the same time horizon. IRFs are scaled to reflect the employment impact per percentage point increase in labor productivity at each horizon.

Country characteristics associated with larger technology-induced employment losses. Economies with larger increases in the share of employment in the industrial sector since the 1990s have tended to suffer larger and more prolonged aggregate job losses from new productivity-enhancing technologies (figure 6.5).[17] This may reflect a failure to reallocate workers who have lost jobs to sectors in which automation has been less prevalent.

---

[17] Evidence from the United States suggests that technological displacement leads unemployed workers to stop seeking work as well as directly reducing employment, and also results in smaller flows of new workers into the labor force (Cortes et al. 2020).

Technology-induced employment losses were also more severe in countries with smaller foreign direct investment (FDI) inflows and, in the short term, in higher-productivity countries and those less open to global trade.

Effects of demand shocks

Although demand shocks are, by construction, short-lived, their effects can be long-lived. Over a 10-year horizon, demand shocks accounted for about one-quarter to one-third of labor productivity variation between 1980 and 2018.

Demand shocks can be caused by changes in expectations about the returns to investment, changes in government spending or taxes, changes in monetary conditions, externally driven changes in commodity prices and terms of trade, or changes in "animal spirits" affecting investment behavior (Justiniano, Primiceri, and Tambalotti 2010; Keynes 1936).[18] Although the methodology used here does not explicitly distinguish demand shocks from other factors that can drive business cycle fluctuations, the resulting characteristics are consistent with those associated with a typical demand shock.[19] Below we consider changes in animal spirits as a determinant of investment behavior and show that their productivity effects can be highly persistent through the capital-deepening channel. Annex 6B examines as a second example the effects of commodity price fluctuations, a key demand-driven determinant of productivity developments in EMDE commodity exporters.

Response of labor productivity to demand shocks. In advanced economies, a positive demand shock raises labor productivity only for a couple of years, after which the effect fades. In contrast, in EMDEs, positive demand shocks are associated with sustained productivity gains (figure 6.6): a decade after a one-standard-deviation positive demand shock, labor productivity remains about 1 percent higher.

Long-term responses to demand shocks. In advanced economies, the rapid reversal of labor productivity gains arising from positive demand shocks largely reflects a contraction of TFP and fading investment after an initial boost. Initial employment gains fade, in less than a decade, as do gains in consumption and the initial surge in inflation. In EMDEs, however, the effects of demand shocks are more persistent. TFP and employment gains fade, but investment remains 4 percent higher and consumption about 1 percent higher a decade after a positive demand shock that generates a 1 percent increase in labor productivity (figure 6.6).

---

[18] Changing expectations ("news") about future technological innovations have also been cited as a key driver of the business cycle, resulting in large swings in investment growth (Beaudry and Portier 2014). Demand-side factors have been found to dominate the short-run volatility of output in the G7 economies (den Haan and Sumner 2004).

[19] Angeletos, Collard, and Dellas (2018a) identify a common driver of unemployment, investment, consumption, and output at business cycle frequencies in the United States using the same technique. They find similar characteristics to those identified in the panel VAR framework here across advanced economies and EMDEs. They attribute the resulting responses to "confidence" shocks, which cause comovement of investment and consumption at the targeted frequencies (Angeletos, Collard, and Dellas 2018b).

FIGURE 6.6 **Effects of demand shocks**

In advanced economies, positive demand shocks lifted labor productivity, investment, consumption, and employment only temporarily. In EMDEs, positive demand shocks lifted labor productivity, investment, and consumption (but not employment) for a decade.

A. Scaled response of labor productivity to demand shock

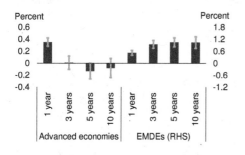

B. Scaled response of TFP to a demand shock

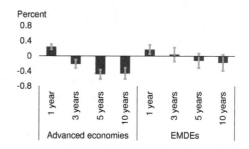

C. Scaled response of employment to demand shock

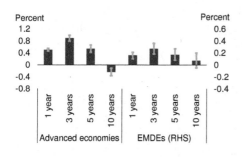

D. Scaled response of investment to demand shock

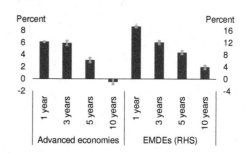

E. Scaled response of consumption to demand shock

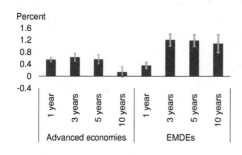

F. Scaled response of consumer price inflation to demand shock

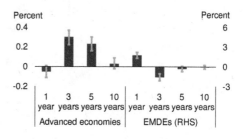

Source: World Bank.
Note: Panel VAR estimation of the impulse responses to the shock driving the largest proportion of business cycle variation in investment, identified using the Spectral methodology. See annex 6A for further details. Responses show each variable in levels, except for inflation, which shows the percentage point change in the growth of consumer prices. Consumption and investment responses are calculated as the sum of the impact on labor productivity and employment (which approximates to output) added to the impulse on the share of consumption or investment in GDP (measured in logs). EMDEs = emerging market and developing economies; TFP = total factor productivity; VAR = vector autoregression.

FIGURE 6.7 Negative demand shocks, labor productivity, and fiscal space

In both advanced economies and EMDEs, negative demand shocks have had more persistent effects on labor productivity in those economies with weaker fiscal positions, higher government debt, and wider primary deficits.

A. High and low average primary balances: Advanced economies

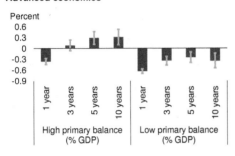

B. High and low average primary balances: EMDEs

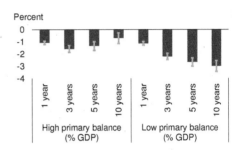

C. High and low debt: Advanced economies

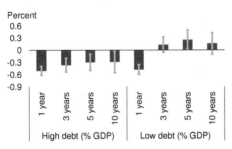

D. High and low debt: EMDEs

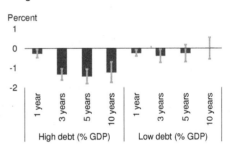

Source: World Bank.
Note: Panel VAR estimation of the impulse responses to the shock driving the largest proportion of business cycle variation in investment, identified using the Spectral methodology. See annex 6A for further details. IRFs are a response to a negative one-standard-deviation shock. EMDEs = emerging market and developing economies; IRF = impulse response function; VAR = vector autoregression.
A.B. Thirty advanced economies and 50 EMDEs are grouped into the top half and bottom half of the distribution of their average primary balances during 1990-2018.
C.D. Thirty advanced economies and 95 EMDEs are grouped into a top and bottom quartile by their average government debt-to-GDP ratio during 1990-2018.

Country characteristics associated with larger demand-driven productivity losses. One reason for less persistent effects on productivity from demand shocks in advanced economies than in EMDEs may be the presence of more robust fiscal frameworks. EMDEs have historically been more likely to accommodate demand booms, spending revenue gains and conducting more procyclical fiscal policy: countercyclical frameworks have been introduced in many EMDEs only in the past two decades (Abiad et al. 2012; Frankel, Vegh, and Vuletin 2013). In both advanced economies and EMDEs with weak fiscal positions (government debt in the top quartile or above-median primary deficits), negative demand shocks significantly lowered labor productivity whereas the effect either dissipated or was much weaker in advanced economies and EMDEs with strong fiscal positions (figure 6.7). The persistent decline in labor productivity largely reflected lower capital accumulation, not TFP, in countries with weaker fiscal positions.

BOX 6.1 Do productivity-enhancing improvements in technology threaten jobs?

New technologies can both substitute for, and complement, labor. Evidence from a large global sample of economies suggests that the substitution effect dominates in the short run. A typical 1.0 percent technology-driven improvement in labor productivity reduces employment in the first year by 0.2 percent in advanced economies and 0.1 percent in emerging and developing economies (EMDEs). Advanced economies have been more affected in the short run by employment-displacing technological change, but the disruption in the labor market in EMDEs has been more persistent. Economies where the share of industrial employment has increased the most (or decreased the least) in recent decades have been more subject to employment-displacing technologies and have experienced larger and more persistent negative effects on employment. Trends toward greater automation and digitalization are growing in EMDEs, increasing the importance of measures to improve the labor force skill base to better complement the introduction of new technologies while ensuring adequate social safety nets for transitioning workers.

Introduction

Productivity-enhancing technological innovation is key for reducing poverty and raising living standards. However, concerns are frequently raised about how the gains from new technologies are shared and about their impact on employment. Currently, concerns are perhaps highest around the automation of manufacturing jobs and digitalization of repetitive tasks, but historically many innovations have been accompanied by the threat of job losses (World Bank 2019). In the early industrialization of the United Kingdom, the Luddites famously destroyed newly invented machines such as the Spinning Jenny, used to improve the efficiency of textile production in the early nineteenth century (Mantoux 2006). Over the long run, the benefits from industrialization through improved productivity have outweighed transition costs, and the actions of the Luddites look misplaced. Technological progress can be both a substitute and a complement for labor, and can also boost real incomes, so that it can boost job opportunities as well as reduce them (Autor 2015). However, certain segments of the labor market can be harmed by technological change, suffering losses of real incomes or jobs, at least temporarily. And where the skills needed to accompany new technologies are unavailable, or demand for new labor tasks does not rise sufficiently, aggregate employment can be persistently lower for a long period.

A large literature has attempted to assess the impact of technological change on employment within affected sectors, but so far the effects on aggregate

---

Note: This box was prepared by Gene Kindberg-Hanlon, with research assistance from Aygul Evdokimova.

BOX 6.1 Do productivity-enhancing improvements in technology threaten jobs? *(continued)*

employment have been underexplored, particularly in EMDEs. This box reviews the literature and employs recently developed statistical techniques using structural vector autoregressions (SVARs) to assess the impact of technology improvements on aggregate employment. This is the first exercise to employ these techniques on EMDE data, estimating effects across 96 EMDEs and 30 advanced economies. The scale of the sample also allows for an exploration of the factors that explain cross-economy differences in the effects of new technologies on employment.

This box addresses the following questions:

• Is there evidence from the literature that new production technologies can reduce employment?

• What is the estimated effect of productivity-enhancing technological change on employment, and how does this effect vary between advanced economies and EMDEs?

• How should policy makers respond?

Literature

Theory. Productivity-improving technologies generate two opposing forces on employment: first a substitution effect, by which new technologies can replace the need for workers; and, second, an income effect, by which increases in the profitability of production increase the demand for labor in the affected or other sectors (Aghion and Howitt 1994). The extent to which the income effects offset the automation effect will depend crucially on the type of tasks required to complement new technologies and associated capital assets, and the supply of workers with the appropriate skills for these tasks (Acemoglu and Autor 2011; Acemoglu and Restrepo 2018). Search-and-matching models have been used to show that new technologies can increase unemployment when the costs of updating existing technology become prohibitively high, labor market flexibility is low, or the skills required to accompany new technologies become increasingly novel (Mortensen and Pissarides 1998; Restrepo 2015).

Sectoral evidence. A large body of evidence has shown that jobs have become increasingly polarized into low- and high-skill occupations in the United States and Europe in recent decades as a combination of automation and offshoring has reduced demand for middle- and low-skilled workers performing routine and codifiable jobs (Acemoglu 1999; Autor et al. 2013; Goos, Manning, and

BOX 6.1 Do productivity-enhancing improvements in technology threaten jobs? *(continued)*

Salomons 2014).[a] Many of these lost occupations were in the industrial sector, even as value added produced by the sector remained resilient—in the United States, employment of machine operators, assemblers, and other production employees fell by over one-third every 10 years between 1980 and 2005 (Autor and Dorn 2013). In a study of 16 European economies during 1993-2010, the share of employment accounted for by industrial sector occupations fell by nearly 10 percentage points (Goos, Manning, and Salomons 2014). In the United States and France, the increased use of robotics is found to be inversely related to industrial employment levels since 1990 and 2010, respectively (Acemoglu, LeLarge, and Restrepo 2020; Acemoglu and Restrepo 2020). Some service sector occupations are also found to have been negatively affected by this trend in both regions, notably middle-skill jobs such as office clerks. However, codifiable middle- and low-skill jobs have been (at least partially) replaced by higher demand for both low-skill service sector jobs, which are less easy to automate, and higher-skill jobs that complement new technologies. SVAR analysis of sectoral manufacturing data for advanced economies has also found negative effects on total hours worked of developments that have driven persistent positive TFP growth (Chang and Hong 2006; Khan and Tsoukalas 2013; Park 2012).

General equilibrium impacts of technological progress on employment. Several studies of the U.S. economy have found that technological progress has caused *aggregate* and not just sectoral employment to fall. During the so-called jobless recoveries in the United States after the recessions of 1991, 2001, and 2008, during which the employment rate fell overall, declines in employment were concentrated in middle-skill and automatable jobs, particularly in the manufacturing sector (Charles, Hurst, and Notowidigdo 2016; Jaimovich and Siu 2020). It has been further argued that even high-skilled workers have been replaced by newer technologies and pushed into lower-skill positions (Beaudry, Green, and Sand 2016). There remains controversy over the net effect on total employment of technological change. In some advanced economy studies, the fall in employment in the sector where innovation occurs is offset by employment gains in other sectors (Autor and Salomons 2018).

EMDE evidence. There have been few studies of the effects of technological change on employment in EMDEs. In part this is because EMDEs have been large beneficiaries of outsourcing from advanced economies: many manufacturing and "codifiable" service sector jobs have moved to EMDEs

---

a. Although offshoring is a separate phenomenon from the technological displacement of workers, technological advances have lowered the costs of offshoring both information-based tasks and manufacturing jobs (Blinder and Krueger 2013).

BOX 6.1 Do productivity-enhancing improvements in technology threaten jobs? *(continued)*

(Maloney and Molina 2016).[b] What technology-influenced change does appear to be occurring has increased the share of routine middle-skill jobs in many EMDEs, in contrast to the fall in the share of these types of jobs in advanced economies (World Bank 2019). That said, large increases in manufacturing productivity have resulted in "premature deindustrialization" in EMDEs, with the shares of employment in the industrial sector rising by less, or falling at much lower levels of income per capita than has occurred in the past, particularly in the development of today's advanced economies (Rodrik 2016). That could suggest that productivity-enhancing technology in the manufacturing sector has reduced employment relative to a counterfactual, which would have been otherwise higher still.

Estimating the effects of technology shocks on employment

Many of the recent studies of the effects of productivity-improving technological change on employment have concerned the effects of progress in information technology (IT) and manufacturing technology in the United States and Europe on codifiable jobs in recent decades. There has been no broader assessment of the effects of technological progress on employment in a wide range of countries. To assess the effects of technical progress on employment in a range of countries, we turn to SVAR techniques, which have already been used extensively to estimate the relationship between technology shocks and total hours worked in the United States and some European economies, finding a negative impact on total hours worked (see table 6A.2 for a summary of published findings). In some cases, the loss of jobs in the United States following an SVAR-identified technology shock has been attributed to creative destruction, with labor tasks being replaced by new technologies (Canova, Lopez-Salido, and Michelacci 2013; Michelacci and Lopez-Salido 2007).

Methodology. Here, productivity-enhancing developments in technology are identified as developments that bring persistent changes in labor productivity and that drive most of the variation in long-run productivity (annex 6A).[c] The implicit assumption in this exercise is that technological innovations are the dominant long-run driver of improvements in labor productivity. The SVAR has

---

b. The term "codifiable jobs" generally refers to those consisting of repetitive tasks that are vulnerable to automation.

c. Specifically, the SVAR identifies a "technology" shock as the shock that drives the largest proportion of low-frequency variation in labor productivity (frequencies below 10 years). This has been found to be more robust than traditional long-run restrictions in identifying technology shocks (Dieppe, Francis, and Kindberg-Hanlon 2019).

BOX 6.1 Do productivity-enhancing improvements in technology threaten jobs? *(continued)*

the same specification as that used in the main chapter text and contains output per worker, employment per capita, consumption and investment as shares of GDP, the short-term interest rate (where available), and consumer price inflation. The SVARs are estimated across 30 advanced economies and 96 EMDEs. Panel VAR estimations are performed to show general impulse responses for groups of economies, whereas individual estimations are used to examine the extent to which findings are broad-based.

Effects of productivity-enhancing technologies on employment

For both the average advanced economy and the average EMDE, an SVAR-identified positive technology development results in a sustained increase in labor productivity over a 10-year horizon (figure B6.1.1).[d] Although productivity and output increase, the short-term impact on employment is negative and statistically significant in both advanced economies and EMDEs. Employment falls by 0.2 percent in the first year in advanced economies for each 1.0 percent boost to labor productivity, before returning to its original level by year 3 (figure B6.1.1). In EMDEs, employment falls by 0.1 percent initially, but the fall is more persistent and employment remains below its original level at the 5-year horizon. Therefore, although on average technological change in EMDEs seems to have had a smaller initial negative impact on employment, EMDEs have been less successful at restoring employment levels over long horizons.[e] The smaller negative employment effect in EMDEs is consistent with the finding in the literature that the displacement of low- and middle-skilled workers has primarily been an advanced economy phenomenon.

The finding of falling employment following technological improvements is broad-based across advanced economies, EMDEs, and regions. Estimates for individual economies show that 90 percent of advanced economies have experienced a negative impact on employment in year 1, with statistically significant falls in 50 percent of them. In EMDEs, 70 percent of economies experienced a fall in the first year, statistically significant in 30 percent of cases.

---

d. The larger impact of technology shocks on productivity in EMDEs reflects higher average EMDE productivity growth over the past 20 years as well as the higher volatility of the data.

e. For robustness, the same specification is estimated for advanced economies using data on total hours worked instead of employment (for EMDEs, data for hours worked are available for only one-quarter of the sample and frequently show little deviation from labor input measured by employment). The average of the median impacts on total hours worked following a technology shock very closely matches the impact on employment. In addition, despite using annual data in our VAR exercises, a statistically significant negative impact on hours is found for the United States, which lasts for one year, matching the results of the U.S. literature (using quarterly data).

BOX 6.1 Do productivity-enhancing improvements in technology threaten jobs? *(continued)*

FIGURE B6.1.1 **Impact of a positive technology innovation**

Technology improvements result in a sustained increase in labor productivity in advanced economies and EMDEs. Employment declines in nine-tenths of advanced economies and three-quarters of EMDEs, although the fall is statistically significant in only one-third of EMDEs. The estimated impact on employment of a technology shock that boosts productivity by 1.0 percent is -0.1 to -0.2 percent in the first year—it is smaller in EMDEs but persists there for longer.

A. Labor productivity impact of technology shocks

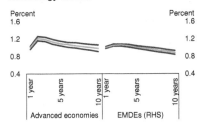

B. Change in employment per 1 percent productivity gain

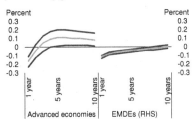

C. Proportion of economies with negative employment impact in year 1: advanced economies and EMDEs

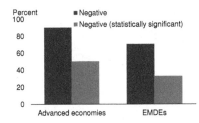

D. Proportion of economies with negative employment impact in year 1: EMDE regions

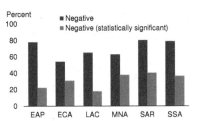

Source: World Bank.
Note: EAP = East Asia and Pacific; ECA = Europe and Central Asia; EMDEs = emerging market and developing economies; IRF = impulse response function; LAC = Latin America and the Caribbean; MNA = Middle East and North Africa; SAR = South Asia; SSA = Sub-Saharan Africa; VAR = vector autoregression.
A.B. Based on a separate panel VAR estimation for 30 advanced economies and 96 EMDEs, including fixed effects for each economy. Error bars show 16th to 84th percentiles.
A. Impact on labor productivity is scaled to the side of the initial impact—because of the higher variation of labor productivity in EMDEs, a one-standard-deviation technology shock boosts productivity by 5 percent, relative to 1.7 percent in advanced economies (annex 6A).
B. Impact on employment per 1 percent increase in labor productivity driven by the identified technology shock.
C.D. Based on individual VAR estimations. The proportion of economies where the median of the IRF is negative in the dark blue bars, and proportion where the 84th percentile is below zero in year 1 in the red bars.

BOX 6.1 Do productivity-enhancing improvements in technology threaten jobs? *(continued)*

The finding is also consistent in all EMDE regions: more than half of the economies in each region experienced negative employment impacts.

What country features are associated with prolonged technology-driven employment losses?

Both advanced economies and EMDEs are thus found to have experienced job losses following advances in technology. Of primary concern for policy makers are first, the scale of initial losses and, second, whether employment recovers quickly, including through the movement of labor to new activities, or whether there are long-lasting scarring effects on the labor force, such as a long-lasting decline in participation rates. The degree and duration of labor market disruption in each economy may depend on multiple factors. These include the types of technologies introduced over the sample period and the degree to which they substitute for, or complement, skilled or unskilled labor, and the policies implemented by the governments to facilitate labor mobility, including the promotion of training and retraining.

A regression is performed on the size of the estimated employment impact and a range of covariates that could determine the size and persistence of job losses. First, higher average productivity levels over the estimation sample are found to be negatively related to the employment impact of technology shocks: more productive economies seem to have been more subject to labor-displacing technologies (figure B6.1.2). Second, the change in the share of industrial employment since 1990 (when these data begin for a broad range of countries) is also negatively related to the employment impact, both in the short term (after 1 year) and long term (at the 10-year horizon). Third, higher average degrees of trade openness and foreign direct investment (FDI) inflows are associated with fewer job losses following a technology shock. These findings are further explored below.

Growth of industrial employment shares. The change in the share of employment in industry since the 1990s is a key correlate of both the size of the employment impact from the SVAR-identified technology shock and its persistence (figure B6.1.2). A panel VAR is used to estimate employment losses following positive technology developments in economies in the top and bottom quartiles of growth in industrial sector employment since the 1990s. In advanced economies, the share of employment in industry has declined since the 1990s. However, those economies where the declines have been smallest (including France, Germany, and the United States) have experienced negative employment impacts of technological advances four times larger than the economies where the

BOX 6.1 Do productivity-enhancing improvements in technology threaten jobs? *(continued)*

FIGURE B6.1.2 **Covariates of the impact of technology on employment**

Economies with a larger increase in the share of workers in industry since the 1990s have experienced larger and more persistent job losses from productivity-enhancing technology developments. Trade openness and FDI inflows are positively related to the employment impact in year 1 but do not affect the persistence of the employment impact.

A. Covariates of employment impact in year 1

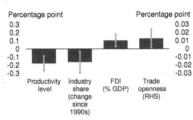

B. Covariates of employment impact in year 10

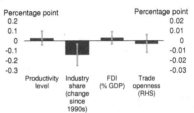

C. Advanced economies: High and low change in industrial employment share, employment IRFs

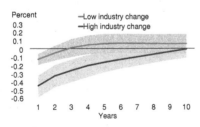

D. EMDEs: High and low increase in industrial employment share, employment IRFs

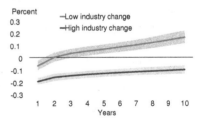

Source: World Bank.
Note: IRFs from panel VAR estimations with fixed effects. EMDEs = emerging market and developing economies; FDI = foreign direct investment; IRF = impulse response function; VAR = vector autoregression.
A.B. Coefficients estimated in a regression of the correlates of the employment impact of a technology innovation at the 1-year and 10-year horizons. Productivity level is measured in log units of output per worker measured in U.S. dollars at 2010 prices and exchange rates; industry share shows the effect of a 10-percentage-point increase in the share of industrial sector employment between 1990-99 and 2010-18; FDI is the average net inflow relative to GDP during 1990-2018 (showing the effect of a 10-percentage-point increase); and trade openness is exports plus imports as a ratio to GDP during 1990-2018, also scaled to show the effect of a 10-percentage-point increase.
C.D. These show panel VAR estimations of the employment impact of a technology innovation in two separate groups. "High industry change" economies are those in the top quartile of changes in industry's share of employment between 1990-9 and 2010-2018. "Low industry change" are economies in the bottom quartile of changes in the share of industrial employment over the same time horizon. Quartiles calculated for advanced economies and EMDEs separately. IRFs are scaled to reflect the employment impact per percentage point increase in labor productivity at each horizon. Shaded areas reflect 68 percent confidence bands.

BOX 6.1 Do productivity-enhancing improvements in technology threaten jobs? *(continued)*

declines have been largest (including Singapore, Spain, and the United Kingdom). In EMDEs, the industrial share of employment has risen since the 1990s in half of those in the sample. In those EMDEs with the largest increases (including China, India, and Vietnam), declines in employment in response to positive productivity developments were three times larger than in those with the largest declines (including Argentina, Romania, and South Africa).[f] However, as indicated earlier, the scale of job losses was significantly smaller in EMDEs than in advanced economies.

These findings link directly to much of the literature on the effects of new technologies on employment; that literature has found that routine manufacturing jobs (and routine service sector jobs) have been at the highest risk of being lost through changes in technology, including automation. Those economies with increasing industrial employment shares in the industrial sector since the 1990s will have been at the highest risk from automation. In addition, those economies with increasing employment shares in this sector may have had the least success in increasing employment in other sectors following job losses in the industrial sector. For example, the share of employment in industry will fall if jobs are replaced by new technologies in that sector. It will fall by even more if affected workers are reemployed in sectors that are less affected by automation. Countries that successfully redeploy workers to new roles will see stronger aggregate employment growth and a smaller share of workers in sectors such as industry, where workers may be most at risk of technology-driven displacement. On average, those economies where industrial employment as a proportion of the total workforce has fallen by more have experienced larger increases in aggregate employment and the labor force since 1990 (figure B6.1.3).

International trade and investment. A regression of the employment impact of changes in technology on a range of covariates finds that trade openness and FDI inflows are *positively* correlated with the employment impact in year 1: higher levels of both variables are associated with fewer job losses or more gains in employment from productivity-enhancing changes in technology (figure B6.1.2). FDI, particularly when it is export-focused, has been associated with job generation (Waldkirch, Nunnenkamp, and Bremont 2009). More generally, in a range of studies, FDI has been found to be associated with increased employment and skill-upgrading in the host country in EMDEs (Hale and Xu 2016).

---

f. The industrial sector is defined as including mining and construction as well as manufacturing, so it includes production of some commodities.. The share of primary commodities in total exports shows no relationship with the scale of job losses following an SVAR-identified technology shock, however, suggesting that manufacturing is the primary driver of the results for the industrial sector.

BOX 6.1 Do productivity-enhancing improvements in technology threaten jobs? *(continued)*

FIGURE B6.1.3 **Share of workers in industry and aggregate employment**

Employment growth since 1990 is negatively correlated across economies with the increase in the industrial sector's share of employment. This is likely to reflect differences in success with the redeployment of technology-displaced workers into sectors that have been less affected by automation.

A. Employment growth in economies with high and low growth in the industrial sector's share of employment

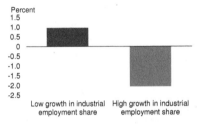

B. High and low growth in the share of employment in industry and aggregate labor force growth

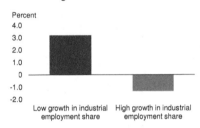

Sources: World Bank, World Development Indicators.
Note: Sample of 100 advanced economies and EMDEs. The y axis shows the percentage point change in the ratio of employment to the working-age population (ages 15-64) and the change in the ratio of the labor force to the working-age population between 1990-99 and 2010-18. The labor force includes those who are employed and unemployed. Those economies with above-median growth in the share of workers in industry between 1990-99 and 2010-18 are classified as "high growth," whereas those with below-median growth are classified as "low growth." EMDEs = emerging market and developing economies.

Future risks and policy options

Technology-driven employment losses have been found to be larger but less persistent in advanced economies than in EMDEs. Increases in the industrial sector's share of employment are key correlates of larger and more persistent falls in employment. As EMDEs have continued to gain an increasing share of global industrial activity and reached higher income levels, they may have become more exposed to risks of employment dislocation from new technologies. This section considers these risks and policies that can help manage them.

Estimates of jobs at risk. The analysis in this chapter is backward-looking, New trends toward digitalization of tasks and automation could accelerate the adoption of labor-replacing technologies. For advanced economies, there are wide-ranging of estimates of the proportion of jobs at risk of automation. Arntz, Gregory, and Zierahn (2016) find that 9 percent of jobs across 21 Organisation for Economic Co-operation and Development economies are at high risk of automation. A broader study of 32 economies, including several EMDEs, finds

BOX 6.1 Do productivity-enhancing improvements in technology threaten jobs? *(continued)*

FIGURE B6.1.4 **Risks of future employment disruption in EMDEs**

Some estimates suggest that 14 percent of jobs in OECD economies, including some EMDEs, are at high risk of automation and that a further 32 percent are at risk of significant change because of automation. The jobs at risk are primarily in the manufacturing and agricultural sectors, although increasingly service sector roles such as food preparation and transportation are at risk. As EMDE employment increasingly shifts toward the industrial sector, jobs in these economies may be increasingly at risk from automation.

A. OECD estimates of jobs at risk of automation

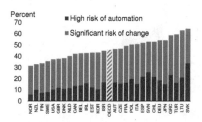

B. Share of employment in industry

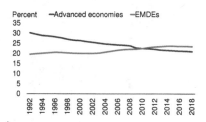

Sources: Nedelkoska and Quintini (2018); World Bank, World Development Indicators.
Note: EMDEs = emerging market and developing economies; OECD = Organisation for Economic Co-operation and Development.
A. Estimates from Nedelkoska and Quintini (2018). "High risk" reflects an estimated probability of over 70 percent that the role will be automated. "Significant risk of change" estimates a probability of between 50 and 70 percent that the role will subject to significant change because of automation.
B. Share of employment in industry in 17 advanced economies and 105 EMDEs, weighted by total employment in each economy.

that on average 14 percent of jobs are at high risk of automation, with a further 32 percent at risk of significant change because of new technologies (figure B6.1.4). The jobs found to be at risk in this study are primarily in manufacturing (the largest component of industry). However, other sectors are also at risk, including agriculture and increasingly the service sector, including food services, transport, and middle-skill office clerk positions (Nedelkoska and Quintini 2018; OECD 2019).[g] This literature does not take into account new jobs that could be created by the introduction of new technologies given that those jobs represent gross, rather than net, effects. However, as shown in this box, the net impact of new technologies on jobs tends to be negative in the short run and can be persistent in EMDEs. So far, no studies have estimated the likely impact of

---

g. Frey and Osborne (2017) find that 47 percent of occupations in the United States are at risk of automation.

BOX 6.1 Do productivity-enhancing improvements in technology threaten jobs? *(continued)*

expected future technological change on a large sample of EMDE labor markets. As EMDEs acquire an increasing share of global industrial employment, it is likely that they will increasingly face similar challenges from automation (figure B6.1.4, panel B).

Policies to manage technology-driven labor market disruption. A more highly educated and trained workforce will reduce the fall in employment following the adoption of skill-biased production processes. Many EMDEs need to make improvements at early stages of education to build a foundation for more advanced levels of education and training (World Bank 2018a, 2019). Education at the early stages of childhood development is currently underprovided in many EMDEs and is critical to the development of language and cognitive skills that are crucial for further education. Many EMDEs also suffer from an underprovision of universities, apprenticeships, other facilities for training and re-training, and continuing adult education. Government efforts to expand provision in these areas can bring high social returns as well as large private returns, in terms of wage premiums, to the workers who take advantage of them, in addition to enabling better adaptation to changing production technologies.

Different sectors, or even different industries within manufacturing, may be more or less exposed to risks of automation. For those economies seeking to expand the scale of their manufacturing sector because of its historic role in driving rapid productivity gains, textiles, garments, and footwear production may seem attractive options because they have been less affected by automation so far (Hallward-Driemeier and Nayyar 2017). However, the risk of future automation in such industries may be high. Economies may also focus on service sectors that support the manufacturing process but are less vulnerable to automation, such as designing, selling, and supporting the production of manufactured goods.

Adequate social protection should be provided to ensure that those who are displaced from their employment can increase their opportunities to transition to new industries. In low-income countries, less than 20 percent of workers are covered by social insurance, in part because of large informal sectors (World Bank 2019). Encouraging both private savings and social insurance schemes for unemployment can provide a safety net for displaced workers and encourage workers to take advantage of new employment opportunities that may entail risks for them.

Conclusion and policy implications

This chapter offers several novel findings. First, long-term, "technological" drivers of productivity have accounted for a considerable portion of labor productivity variation since 1980: for about 40 percent of the 1-year-ahead forecast error variance of labor productivity and 60-75 percent of the 5- to 10-year-ahead forecast error variance. Second, employment has typically fallen, at least initially, after technology-driven productivity improvements. These employment losses were larger but less persistent in advanced economies than in EMDEs. Third, although demand shocks may unwind faster than technology shocks, their impact on productivity can be long-lasting. These findings point to two policy priorities.

Although technological progress is generally beneficial in the long term, it may initially be disruptive to employment (Arntz, Gregory, and Zierahn 2016; Autor 2015; World Bank 2019). The appropriate policy response is three-pronged: first, policies to encourage and support the training and retraining of workers to equip them with the skills required by new technologies; second, policies to mitigate the negative effects on transitioning workers; and, third, demand management to maintain full employment. The COVID-19 pandemic and resulting global recession may trigger another wave of restructuring and technological innovation, as firms adjust to social distancing and new restrictions on doing business or search for efficiency savings to remain competitive. EMDEs, in particular, will need to ensure that workers are equipped with skills to complement new technologies, rather than be replaced by them (World Bank 2018a).

Universities, vocational training facilities, on-the-job training, and continued learning are often underprovided in many EMDEs, and there are potentially high social returns to their expansion. Many EMDEs also need to make improvements at earlier stages of education in order to build a foundation for the more advanced education that will enable workers to adapt to skill requirements associated with new technologies (World Bank 2018a, 2019). Adequate social protection can help those displaced by technological change to transition into new industries. For example, in LICs, fewer than 20 percent of workers are covered by social insurance, in part because of large informal sectors in these economies (World Bank 2019). Encouraging private savings, including through initiatives that expand financial inclusion, and expanding unemployment insurance programs in the formal and informal sectors can strengthen the safety net.

The lasting productivity damage that even short-term demand shocks can cause calls for room to allow active deployment of fiscal and monetary policy to support activity. This will require the shoring up of fiscal positions once economic recovery from the pandemic is well established, a strengthening of monetary and fiscal policy frameworks, and effective supervision and regulation to ensure a resilient financial system (chapter 1; Kose et al. 2020). For commodity exporters, the creation or expansion of sovereign wealth funds, as well as better prioritization of spending, could help avoid procyclical spending in response to commodity price fluctuations (Mohaddes and Raissi 2017).

The findings above point to two directions for future research. First, future studies could examine peak and trough episodes in individual countries to see whether and how they correspond with significant technology- and demand-driven events. The analysis could also examine in greater depth the types of employment that are most vulnerable to disruption from technology and demand shocks, especially in EMDEs. Second, this chapter points to important differences in the long-term effects of shocks, and future research could explore which characteristics of EMDEs cause these differences, for example, differences in institutional factors like educational and legal systems; economic differences in monetary and fiscal policies, trading partners, and trade compositions; and development differences like the sophistication of stock markets and levels of industrialization. Finally, the sectoral dimension could be further explored.

This chapter has focused on the role of short- and long-term shocks in driving labor productivity. However, the literature has also identified sectoral reallocation as an important driver of labor productivity. This is examined in the next chapter.

ANNEX 6A **SVAR identification of technology drivers of productivity**

This annex describes the Spectral technology SVAR procedures in greater detail.

Spectral identification

Supply-side technology shocks are identified as those that explain the majority of productivity fluctuations at frequencies longer than 10 years—this approach disregards fluctuations at higher (shorter) frequencies and is, therefore, robust to contamination in economies where productivity is affected by many other factors. This approach identifies long-lasting innovations to labor productivity, assuming that these highly persistent changes are likely to be driven by structural factors such as new production technologies. Historically, long-run restrictions have been used to identify technology shocks; however, this type of restriction has been found to perform poorly in short samples and in volatile data compared to the spectral identification used in this chapter.[20]

A Fourier transform is used to estimate the contributions of potential structural shocks at various frequencies. Effectively this involves the application of a band-pass filter (Christiano and Fitzgerald 2003) to the reduced form coefficients of a VAR, identifying the spectral density of the variables within a particular frequency band. The technology shock is then identified as the shock that explains the largest share of variance of productivity at the desired frequency.

---

[20] Long-run restrictions imposed on a finite sample can lead to biased and inefficient estimates (Chari, Kehoe, and McGrattan 2008; Erceg, Guerrieri, and Gust 2005; Francis et al. 2014), especially around structural breaks (Fernald and Wang 2016), and have been shown to perform poorly except in situations in which technology shocks explain the large majority of productivity developments (Chari, Kehoe, and McGrattan 2008; Dieppe, Francis, and Kindberg-Hanlon 2019).

Identifying technology shocks through restrictions that explain the majority of low (long-term) frequency volatility of productivity is a novel approach. However, this methodology has been used to assess the types of shocks that drive the business cycle; for example, Angeletos, Collard, and Dellas (2018a) find that a single shock drives the majority of the variance of a range of macroeconomic variables at business cycle frequencies. And DiCecio and Owyang (2010) use a similar methodology to identify technology shocks.

A VAR representation of the spectral density of Y is generated using the Wold representation of the VAR (assuming it is invertible):

$$Y_t = [I - (A_1 L + A_2 L^2 + \ldots A_p L^p)]^{-1} \mu_t = D\mu_t = D_0 \mu_t + D_1 \mu_{t-1} \ldots,$$

where A is the reduced-form VAR coefficients and D are the moving average (MA) coefficients on the reduced form innovations (μ) at each horizon. Post-multiplying Y_t by $Y_{t-\tau}$ generates a series of autocorrelations, which in turn can generate the spectral density of the endogenous variables at frequency ω, based on the reduced-form VAR coefficients:

$$S_{YY}(\omega) = D(e^{-i\tau\omega})\Sigma_\mu D(e^{i\tau\omega})' = \sum_{\tau=-\infty}^{\infty} \gamma(\tau)e^{-i\tau\omega}.$$

To assess the spectral density within a frequency band, the spectrum can be summed within the band of interest:

$$S_{YY}(band) = \sum_{Lower\,bound}^{Upper\,bound} S_{YY}(\omega).$$

To identify technology, the band of interest is restricted to frequencies that are longer than 10 years, in order to exclude business cycle frequencies. In the exercise identifying the primary business cycle driver of investment, frequencies of 2-8 years are chosen. The shock that maximizes the variance of labor productivity over the desired frequency is the eigenvector associated with the largest eigenvalue of S_{YY} (Uhlig 2003).

Given the limited sample size under consideration, the MA coefficient matrix D is constrained to the 1-10 year horizon, which has been shown to reduce estimation bias (Dieppe, Francis, and Kindberg-Hanlon 2019; Francis et al. 2014).

Estimation

Each VAR is estimated using annual data. Table 6A.1 provides summary statistics on the data length available in each income group.

TABLE 6A.1 Median sample periods

	Spectral SVAR
AEs	1973-2018
EMDEs	1981-2018
LICs	1981-2018

Source: World Bank.
Note: AEs = advanced economies; EMDEs = emerging market and developing economies; LICs = low-income countries; SVAR = structural vector autoregression.

Panel VAR framework for IRFs

A panel VAR is used to estimate the IRFs shown in several figures. Here, advanced economies and EMDEs are separately estimated in panel estimations to illustrate the typical effects of technology and primary business cycle shocks on economies in both groups, and also for some subgroups (for example, high and low industrial employment share change economies).

The estimation takes the form $\quad Y_t^n = C^n + \sum_{\tau=1}^{k} B_\tau Y_{t-1}^n + u_t,$

where C^n, the constant, varies across countries, n, while B and the variance-covariance matrix of residuals Σ_u are assumed to be common across economies. Additional dummy variables are included in certain economies during periods when inflation exceeds 20 percent. The estimated parameters B and Σ_u can then be used to identify the effects of technology shocks using the Spectral identification for each group.

Robustness of lag length. In the standard specification, two lags of the endogenous variables are included in the VAR estimations. This is the minimum number of lags required to account for cyclical processes (which can be described as a second-order autoregressive [AR(2)] process). Results, including the employment impact of SVAR-identified technology shocks, are robust to including four lags (accounting for four years of data).

Robustness to additional variables. Including additional variables does not materially change impulse responses but does reduce data availability. For advanced economies, including the log change in the exchange rate and the cyclically adjusted primary balance estimated by the International Monetary Fund results in similar employment effects to the core specification used in figure 6.4. In EMDEs, data availability for cyclically adjusted primary balances is poor before 2000, so only the log change in the exchange rate is included. Once again, IRFs are largely the same as in the core specification, with the exception of the inflation response, which is smaller.

Robustness to sample time period. Results for both the technology shock and the demand shock are robust to changing time periods. Using data for just the past 25 years results in a technology shock that reduces employment by 0.1 percent for each 1.0 percent boost to labor productivity in EMDEs, and by 0.2 percent in advanced economies. Excluding the financial crisis and postcrisis periods in the panel estimation of the demand shock for EMDEs continues to result in a persistent impact on labor productivity (but not TFP), whereas the advanced economy impulse response for labor productivity fades within the 10-year horizon, as in the whole sample estimation.

TABLE 6A.2 SVAR literature summary of technology shocks on employment

Study	Coverage	Methodology and measure of labor input	Finding—Sign of effect on labor input	Finding—Persistence
Galí (1999); Galí (2005)	G7	Long-run identifications. Effect on hours worked.	Negative initial impact in all economies except Japan.	Persistent negative impact to three years in France, Germany, Italy, and the U.K. Less than one year in Canada and the U.S. No significance levels are shown.
Christiano, Eichenbaum, and Vigfusson (2003)	U.S.	Long-run. Effect on hours. In contrast to many other long-run identifications, hours are measured in log levels, not log differences.	Positive.	Not persistent.
Francis and Ramey (2005)	U.S.	Long-run. Effect on hours worked.	Negative.	Persistent in some specifications but not statistically significant.
Francis (2009)	U.K.	Long-run. Effect on hours worked.	Negative.	Negative impact for one year.
Collard and Dellas (2007)	U.S.	Long-run. Effect on hours worked.	Negative.	Persistent in some specifications to the five-year horizon but not statistically significant.
Dupaigne and Fève (2009)	G7	Long-run. Effect on employment.	Negative except for the U.S. Positive for aggregated data for G7.	Persistently negative in France, Italy, and the U.K. for three years. Only statistically significant persistence in Italy.
Francis et al. (2014)	U.S.	Max-share. Effect on hours worked.	Negative.	Negative impact for less than two years.
Fisher (2006)	U.S.	Long-run, with separate identifications for neutral technology shocks and investment-specific technology shocks.	Negative for both neutral and investment-specific technology shock.	Effects fade in less than two years.
Canova, Lopez-Salido, and Michelacci (2010)	U.S.	Long-run, with separate identifications for neutral technology shocks and investment-specific technology shocks. Effect on hours.	Negative for neutral technology shocks. Positive for investment-specific technology shocks.	Neutral technology shocks have persistent effects for five to six years.
Canova, Lopez-Salido, and Michelacci (2013)	U.S.	Long-run, with separate identifications for neutral technology shocks and investment-specific technology shocks. Effect on hours and unemployment, job separation rates and job-finding rates.	A rise in job separation rate drives unemployment higher.	Unemployment rate persistently higher for over five years in response to neutral technology shock, because of the slow recovery of the job-finding rate.
Rujin (2019)	G7	Long-run identification. Effects on hours and employment.	Negative effects on employment and hours in Canada, France, Germany, Italy, and the U.S. Neutral effects on employment in France and Japan but negative effects on hours.	Persistent negative effects in Canada, France, Germany, Italy, the U.K., and the U.S.

Source: World Bank.

Note: G7 = Group of Seven (Canada, France, Germany, Italy, Japan, the United Kingdom, and the United States); SVAR = structural vector autoregression. U.K. = United Kingdom; U.S.A = United States.

ANNEX 6B Commodity-driven productivity developments

Two-thirds of EMDEs depend significantly on agriculture or mining (including oil drilling) and quarrying for export revenues, and more than half of the world's poor live in such commodity-exporting EMDEs. Therefore, externally driven fluctuations in commodity demand and prices have potentially important implications for productivity growth in EMDEs. Beginning in 2000, commodity prices surged in the run-up to the global financial crisis, then began declining in 2011. A 50 percent fall in energy prices in 2014-15 weighed on prospects for returns on investment in commodity exporters. These price changes have driven large fluctuations in productivity growth (Kose et al. 2017).

Most energy price fluctuations historically have been attributed to global demand rather than to supply-side factors (Kilian 2009; Kilian and Hicks 2013; Kilian and Murphy 2014). A large proportion of movements in agricultural and metals prices in recent decades has also been estimated to have been related mainly to common global demand factors such as the increasing consumption of these products in Asia, particularly China (Chiaie, Ferrara, and Giannone 2017; Gervais, Kolet, and Lalonde 2010).

Previous analysis has generally found that commodity price changes explain over half of the volatility of investment in commodity-exporting EMDEs (Fernández, González, and Rodríguez 2018; Kose 2002).[21] The evidence on the impact of commodity price changes on TFP growth is varied, with some studies finding little evidence of any short-term or long-term effect of commodity price changes on TFP in exporters (Aslam et al. 2016). Other studies find some synchronization of TFP with commodity prices (Kataryniuk and Martínez-Martín 2018).

Methodology. The local projection methodology of Jordà (2005) is used to assess the impact of commodity price changes on a range of productivity measures. The local projection is estimated up to a horizon of 10 years and controls for developments in global demand that could be driving commodity price changes by using export-weighted GDP growth for each economy (annex 6C). The estimation is performed on the components of labor productivity growth in the growth accounting framework—the contributions of capital deepening and TFP growth—thus allowing a deeper examination of the transmission of commodity price fluctuations to productivity. The local projection estimates are obtained separately for exporters of agricultural products and exporters of metals and energy using the World Bank's Pink Sheet measures of real commodity prices for each category.

Effects of commodity price shocks on agricultural exporters. Commodity price changes have had highly persistent effects on labor productivity in EMDE agricultural exporters (figure 6B.1). Following a 10 percent agricultural price rise in real terms, labor

---

[21] Drechsel and Tenreyro (2018) find, for Argentina, that up to 60 percent of the variance of investment growth could be explained by commodity price fluctuations.

productivity and GDP in EMDE agricultural exporters have tended to be 2.0-2.5 percent higher after 10 years.[22] This rise is accounted for by capital deepening and TFP growth in similar proportions.

Metals exporters. In metals exporters, the effect on labor productivity, reaching 1.1 percent after five years, is smaller than for agricultural exporters and less persistent. In this case, most of the rise is accounted for by increased capital deepening, and the effects fade after five years.[23] The effect on TFP growth is neutral in the long term.

Oil exporters. For oil exporters, oil price rises boost GDP growth temporarily and capital deepening persistently but do not improve labor productivity because of a corresponding fall in TFP growth. Following a 10.0 percent rise in oil prices, GDP is 0.8 percent higher after five years, with a similar increase in the contribution of capital deepening to labor productivity growth. However, TFP falls by 0.8 percent after 5 years and 1.5 percent after 10 years.

Persistent effects on TFP in agriculture. Rising agricultural prices can trigger structural improvements in labor productivity through several channels. The agriculture sector generally has the lowest productivity level across sectors, often significantly lower than mining-related activities, and so may benefit from higher demand to implement newer technologies and more capital into the production process where producers are often finance-constrained (chapter 7). In addition, rising incomes in the agricultural sector can facilitate reallocation to more productive and efficient sectors by increasing demand for manufacturing and service sector products (Emerick 2018).

Capital deepening dominates in extractive commodity producers. Sectoral analysis has also found that rising commodity prices are often accompanied by declining within-sector TFP in the extractives sector, along with rising capital deepening and muted effects on sectoral reallocation (Aslam et al. 2016). One reason for the decline in TFP in response to rising prices is that they incentivize the extraction of increasingly capital-intensive and low-return land resources, reducing the efficiency of production (Byrne, Fernald, and Reinsdorf 2016; Dabla-Norris et al. 2015).[24] SVAR evidence for a range of metals exporters finds effects of metals price changes on GDP of a similar magnitude to the local projection estimates in this chapter (Fornero, Kirchner, and Andres 2014). These are also found to operate primarily through the investment channel (not affecting TFP) and to begin to fade near the five-year horizon.

---

[22] Examining the effects of commodity price shocks at the seven-year horizon, Aslam et al. (2016) find similar evidence of persistent productivity and output effects in agricultural goods exporters, and less evidence of persistence in a combined sample of metals and oil exporters.

[23] This is consistent with previous analysis of the effects of changing metals prices in Chile, a major copper exporter, with the effects of price changes on labor productivity fading after five years and no effect on TFP (Eyraud 2015).

[24] In the United States, TFP in the mining sector has tended to decrease following oil price increases because it has become economic to drill in less-accessible sources. Byrne, Fernald, and Reinsdorf (2016) estimate that TFP growth measures are understated by about five basis points per year in the years following the introduction of fracking in the Unites States, not accounting for the changing quality of natural resources used in production.

FIGURE 6B.1 **Effects of commodity prices on productivity in EMDEs**

Commodity price shocks are key drivers of productivity growth in commodity-exporting EMDEs. In agricultural and metal exporters, labor productivity is estimated to rise by 1-2 percent after 5 years following a 10 percent rise in commodity prices, with the effect lasting for 10 years and rising further in agricultural goods exporters. Most of the effect is accounted for by capital deepening in the case of metals exporters, whereas agricultural goods exporters experience persistently higher TFP growth. In oil exporters, GDP rises sharply following a 10 percent rise in oil prices, and there is also a significant increase in the contribution of capital deepening; however, productivity is relatively unchanged, with a statistically significant decline in TFP offsetting these gains.

A. Agriculture exporters: GDP and labor productivity

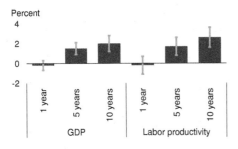

B. Agriculture exporters: TFP and capital deepening

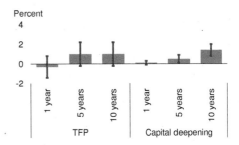

C. Metals exporters: GDP and labor productivity

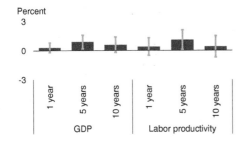

D. Metals exporters: TFP and capital deepening

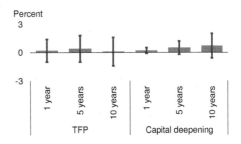

E. Oil exporters: GDP and labor productivity

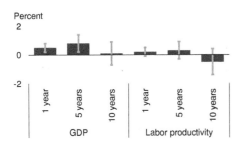

F. Oil exporters: TFP and capital deepening

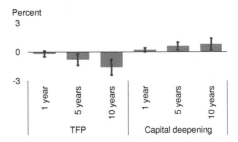

Sources: World Bank, Penn World Table, Haver Analytics.

Note: Local projection estimates of commodity price shock on the level of GDP, productivity growth accounting components. The response is the cumulative change in the level of each variable to a 10 percent rise in real commodity prices. The commodity price is measured as the log change in the World Bank's Pink Book real commodity price series for agricultural goods, metals, and energy products for each group of economies respectively. The specification controls for external demand and lags of the endogenous variable and shock. "Capital deepening" reflects the contribution of capital deepening to labor productivity. Local projections are performed on 15 agricultural exporters, 10 metals exporters, and 14 oil exporters with all measures available since at least 1990. Further details are available in annex 6C. EMDEs = emerging market and developing economies; TFP = total factor productivity.

To summarize, demand drivers can have smaller, but still important, longer-term effects on labor productivity, particularly in economies with little fiscal space and in commodity exporters. Historically, with the exception of agricultural goods exporters, these longer-run effects have occurred primarily through capital deepening, with evidence of some negative effects of positive demand shocks on the overall efficiency of production (TFP).

ANNEX 6C Commodity-driven productivity developments: Methodology

A local projection model was used to estimate the effects of commodity price changes on GDP, labor productivity, capital deepening, and TFP. The model follows Jordà (2005) in estimating impulse responses over a series of horizons, in this case from 1 to 10 years. Agricultural, metals, and energy exporters are separately estimated in panel specifications using fixed effects. Commodity price (real U.S. dollar indexes) changes are assumed to be exogenous to each country in the specification. However, this property may be violated when individual economies are associated with the price change, for example, because of supply disruptions in individual economies that are large enough to influence global commodity prices.

In addition, the local projection specification controls for changes in global demand conditions that may be driving the commodity price change, including those that occur before and after the commodity price shock under examination. This control is constructed as an export-weighted aggregate of global GDP growth of each country under consideration.

The outcome variable y_t reflects the log level of GDP, labor productivity, the cumulative contribution of capital deepening to labor productivity growth, and the log level of TFP. In addition to controlling for global demand (D_t), the specification controls for lagged values of the growth of the outcome variable (dy_{t-1}) and lagged values of the commodity price series (Δp_{t-1}^{com}) to reduce bias associated with serial correlation of commodity price changes and the productivity variables. The estimation is performed for each period h from 1 to 10 years.

$$y_{t+h} - y_{t-1} = \alpha_h^i + \beta_h \Delta p_t^{com} + \gamma_h^p \Delta p_{t-1}^{com} + \gamma_h^y dy_{t-1} + \sum_{i=0}^{1} \gamma_i^d D_{t-i} + \sum_{j=0}^{h} \gamma_i^d D_{t+j} + \epsilon_{t+h}$$

It has been argued that, for a true IRF representation, subsequent developments in the shock of interest should be controlled for (Alloza, Gonzalo, and Sanz 2019). Including leading changes in commodity price changes results in larger impacts but does not alter the qualitative channels through which price shocks operate, or the qualitative differences between the transmission channels in each type of commodity exporter.

References

Abiad, A., J. Bluedorn, J. Guajardo, P. Topalova, P. by Abdul Abiad, O. Blanchard, J. Decressin, T. Helbling, J. de Gregorio, and R. Duval. 2012. "The Rising Resilience of Emerging Market and Developing Economies" IMF Working Paper 12/300, International Monetary Fund, Washington, DC.

Acemoglu, D. 1999. "Changes in Unemployment and Wage Inequality: An Alternative Theory and Some Evidence." *American Economic Review* 89 (5): 1259–78.

Acemoglu, D., and D. Autor. 2011. "Skills, Tasks and Technologies: Implications for Employment and Earnings." In *Handbook of Labor Economic, Vol. 4*, edited by D. Card and O. Ashenfelter, 1043–171. Amsterdam: Elsevier.

Acemoglu, D., C. LeLarge, and P. Restrepo. 2020. "Competing with Robots: Firm-Level Evidence from France." NBER Working Paper 26738, National Bureau of Economic Research, Cambridge, MA.

Acemoglu, D., and P. Restrepo. 2018. "The Race between Man and Machine: Implications of Technology for Growth, Factor Shares, and Employment." *American Economic Review* 108 (6): 1488–542.

Acemoglu, D., and P. Restrepo. 2020. "Robots and Jobs: Evidence from US Labor Markets." *Journal of Political Economy* 128 (6): 2188–244.

Aghion, P., and P. Howitt. 1994. "Growth and Unemployment." *The Review of Economic Studies* 61 (3): 477–94.

Alloza, M., J. Gonzalo, and C. Sanz. 2019. "Dynamic Effects of Persistent Shocks." Banco de España Working Paper 1944, Banco de España, Madrid.

Angeletos, G.-M., F. Collard, and H. Dellas. 2018a. "Business Cycle Anatomy." NBER Working Paper 24875. National Bureau of Economic Research, Cambridge, MA.

Angeletos, G.-M., F. Collard, and H. Dellas. 2018b. "Quantifying Confidence." *Econometrica* 86 (5): 1689–726.

Arntz, M., T. Gregory, and U. Zierahn. 2016. "The Risk of Automation for Jobs in OECD Countries: A Comparative Analysis." OECD Social, Employment and Migration Working Papers 189, Organisation for Economic Co-operation and Development, Paris.

Aslam, A., S. Beidas-Strom, R. Bems, O. Celasun, S. Kilic Celik, and Z. Koczan. 2016. "Trading on Their Terms? Commodity Exporters in the Aftermath of the Commodity Boom." IMF Working Paper 16/27, International Monetary Fund, Washington, DC.

Autor, D. H. 2015. "Why Are There Still So Many Jobs? The History and Future of Workplace Automation." *Journal of Economic Perspectives* 29 (3): 3–30.

Autor, D. H., and D. Dorn. 2013. "The Growth of Low-Skill Service Jobs and the Polarization of the U.S. Labor Market." *American Economic Review* 103 (5): 1553–97.

Autor, D. H., G. H. Hanson, D. Acemoglu, A. Costinot, D. Donaldson, R. Lawrence, I. Mbiti, et al. 2013. "The China Syndrome: Local Labor Market Effects of Import Competition in the United States." *American Economic Review* 103 (6): 2121–68.

Autor, D. H., and A. Salomons. 2018. "Is Automation Labor-Displacing? Productivity Growth, Employment, and the Labor Share." NBER Working Paper 24871, National Bureau of Economic Research, Cambridge, MA.

Bachmann, R., and E. R. Sims. 2012. "Confidence and the Transmission of Government Spending Shocks." *Journal of Monetary Economics* 59 (3): 235–49.

Basu, S., J. G. Fernald, and M. S. Kimball. 2006. "Are Technology Improvements Contractionary?" *American Economic Review* 96 (5): 1418–48.

Beaudry, P., and F. Collard. 2003. "Recent Technological and Economic Change among Industrialized Countries: Insights from Population Growth." *Scandinavian Journal of Economics* 105 (3): 441–63.

Beaudry, P., D. A. Green, and B. M. Sand. 2016. "The Great Reversal in the Demand for Skill and Cognitive Tasks." *Journal of Labor Economics* 34 (S1): S199–247.

Beaudry, P., and F. Portier. 2014. "News-Driven Business Cycles: Insights and Challenges." *Journal of Economic Literature* 52 (4): 993–1074.

Blinder, A. S., and A. B. Krueger. 2013. "Alternative Measures of Offshorability: A Survey Approach." *Journal of Labor Economics* 31 (S1): S97–128.

Boulhol, H., and L. Turner. 2009. "Employment-Productivity Trade-Off and Labour Composition." OECD Economics Department Working Paper 698, Organisation for Economic Co-operation and Development, Paris.

Byrne, D. M., J. G. Fernald, and M. B. Reinsdorf. 2016. "Does the United States Have a Productivity Slowdown or a Measurement Problem?" *Brookings Papers on Economic Activity*, Spring, 109–82.

Caballero, R. J., and M. L. Hammour. 1994. "The Cleansing Effect of Recessions." *American Economic Review* 84 (5): 1350–68.

Canova, F., D. Lopez-Salido, and C. Michelacci. 2010. "The Effects of Technology Shocks on Hours and Output: A Robustness Analysis." *Journal of Applied Econometrics* 25 (5): 755–73.

Canova, F., D. Lopez-Salido, and C. Michelacci. 2013. "The Ins and Outs of Unemployment: An Analysis Conditional on Technology Shocks." *The Economic Journal* 123 (569): 515–39.

Cerra, V., and S. C. Saxena. 2008. "Growth Dynamics: The Myth of Economic Recovery." *American Economic Review* 98 (1): 439–57.

Chang, Y., and J. H. Hong. 2006. "Do Technological Improvements in the Manufacturing Sector Raise or Lower Employment?" *American Economic Review* 96 (1): 352–68.

Chari, V. V., P. J. Kehoe, and E. R. McGrattan. 2008. "Are Structural VARs with Long-Run Restrictions Useful in Developing Business Cycle Theory?" *Journal of Monetary Economics* 55 (8): 1337–52.

Charles, K. K., E. Hurst, and M. J. Notowidigdo. 2016. "The Masking of the Decline in Manufacturing Employment by the Housing Bubble." *Journal of Economic Perspectives* 30 (2): 179–200.

Chen, K., and E. Wemy. 2015. "Investment-Specific Technological Changes: The Source of Long-Run TFP Fluctuations." *European Economic Review* 80 (November): 230–52.

Chiaie, S. D., L. Ferrara, and D. Giannone. 2017. "Common Factors of Commodity Prices." ECB Working Paper Series 2112, European Central Bank, Frankfurt.

Christiano, L., M. Eichenbaum, and R. Vigfusson. 2003. "What Happens after a Technology Shock?" NBER Working Paper 9819, National Bureau of Economic Research, Cambridge, MA.

Christiano, L. J., and T. J. Fitzgerald. 2003. "The Band Pass Filter." *International Economic Review* 44 (2): 435–65.

Coibion, O., Y. Gorodnichenko, and M. Ulate. 2017. "The Cyclical Sensitivity in Estimates of Potential Output." NBER Working Paper 23580, National Bureau of Economic Research, Cambridge, MA.

Collard, F., and H. Dellas. 2007. "Technology Shocks and Employment." *Economic Journal* 117 (523): 1436–59.

Comin, D., J. Quintana, T. Schmitz, and A. Trigari. 2019. "A New Measure of Utilization-Adjusted TFP Growth for European Countries." FRAME Final Policy Conference, Centre for Economic Policy Research, London.

Cortes, G. M., C. J. Nekarda, N. Jaimovich, and H. E. Siu. 2020. "The Dynamics of Disappearing Routine Jobs: A Flows Approach." *Labour Economics* 65 (August): 101823.

Dabla-Norris, E., S. Guo, V. Haksar, M. Kim, K. Kochhar, K. Wiseman, and A. Zdzienicka. 2015. "The New Normal: A Sector-Level Perspective on Productivity Trends in Advanced Economies." IMF Staff Discussion Note 15/03, International Monetary Fund, Washington, DC.

den Haan, W. J., and S. W. Sumner. 2004. "The Comovement between Real Activity and Prices in the G7." *European Economic Review* 48 (6): 1333–47.

DiCecio, R., and M. Owyang. 2010. "Identifying Technology Shocks in the Frequency Domain." Working Paper 2010-025A, Federal Reserve Bank of St. Louis.

Dieppe, A., N. Francis, and G. Kindberg-Hanlon. 2019. "New Approaches to the Identification of Low-Frequency Drivers: An Application to Technology Shocks." Policy Research Working Paper 9047, World Bank, Washington, DC.

Drechsel, T., and S. Tenreyro. 2018. "Commodity Booms and Busts in Emerging Economies." *Journal of International Economics* 112 (May): 200–18.

Dupaigne, M., and P. Fève. 2009. "Technology Shocks around the World." *Review of Economic Dynamics* 12 (4): 592–607.

Duval, R., D. Furceri, S. K. Celik, and M. Poplawski-Ribeiro. 2020. "Productivity Spillovers in Advanced Economies." IMF Working Paper Series, International Monetary Fund, Washington, DC.

Emerick, K. 2018. "Agricultural Productivity and the Sectoral Reallocation of Labor in Rural India." *Journal of Development Economics* 135 (November): 488–503.

Erceg, C. J., L. Guerrieri, and C. Gust. 2005. "Can Long-Run Restrictions Identify Technology Shocks?" *Journal of the European Economic Association* 3 (6): 1237–78.

Eyraud, L. 2015. "End of the Supercycle and Growth of Commodity Producers: The Case of Chile." IMF Working Paper 15/242, International Monetary Fund, Washington, DC.

Fernald, J. G. 2014. "Productivity and Potential Output before, during, and after the Great Recession." *NBER Macroeconomics Annual* 29 (1): 1–51.

Fernald, J., and J. C. Wang. 2016. "Why Has the Cyclicality of Productivity Changed? What Does It Mean?" *Annual Review of Economics* 8 (1): 465–96.

Fernández, A., A. González, and D. Rodríguez. 2018. "Sharing a Ride on the Commodities Roller Coaster: Common Factors in Business Cycles of Emerging Economies." *Journal of International Economics* 111 (March): 99–121.

Fisher, J. D. M. 2006. "The Dynamic Effects of Neutral and Investment-Specific Technology Shocks." *Journal of Political Economy* 114 (3): 413–51.

Fornero, J., M. Kirchner, and Y. Andres. 2014. "Terms of Trade Shocks and Investment in Commodity-Exporting Economies." Series on Central Banking Analysis 22, Central Bank of Chile, Santiago.

Francis, N. 2009. "The Source of U.K. Historical Economic Fluctuations: An Analysis Using Long-Run Restrictions." *B.E. Journal of Macroeconomics* 9 (1): 1–20.

Francis, N., M. T. Owyang, J. E. Roush, and R. DiCecio. 2014. "A Flexible Finite-Horizon Alternative to Long-Run Restrictions with an Application to Technology Shocks." *Review of Economics and Statistics* 96 (4): 638–47.

Francis, N., and V. A. Ramey. 2005. "Is the Technology-Driven Real Business Cycle Hypothesis Dead? Shocks and Aggregate Fluctuations Revisited." *Journal of Monetary Economics* 52 (8): 1379–99.

Frankel, J. A., C. A. Vegh, and G. Vuletin. 2013. "On Graduation from Fiscal Procyclicality." *Journal of Development Economics* 100 (1): 32–47.

Frey, C. B., and M. A. Osborne. 2017. "The Future of Employment: How Susceptible Are Jobs to Computerisation?" *Technological Forecasting and Social Change* 114 (January): 254–80.

Galí, J. 1999. "Technology, Employment, and the Business Cycle: Do Technology Shocks Explain Aggregate Fluctuations?" *American Economic Review* 89 (1): 249–71.

Galí, J. 2005. "Trends in Hours, Balanced Growth, and the Role of Technology in the Business Cycle." NBER Working Paper 11130, National Bureau of Economic Research, Cambridge, MA.

Gervais, O., I. Kolet, and R. Lalonde. 2010. "A Larger Slice of a Growing Pie: The Role of Emerging Asia in Forecasting Commodity Prices." *Money Affairs* XXIII (1): 75–95.

Goodridge, P., J. Haskel, and G. Wallis. 2018. "Accounting for the UK Productivity Puzzle: A Decomposition and Predictions." *Economica* 85 (339): 581–605.

Goos, M., A. Manning, and A. Salomons. 2014. "Explaining Job Polarization: Routine-Biased Technological Change and Offshoring." *American Economic Review* 104 (8): 2509–26.

Hale, G., and M. Xu. 2016. "FDI Effects on the Labor Market of Host Countries." Federal Reserve Bank of San Francisco Working Paper Series 01–26, Federal Reserve Bank of San Francisco.

Hallward-Driemeier, M., and G. Nayyar. 2017. *Trouble in the Making? The Future of Manufacturing-Led Development.* Washington, DC: World Bank.

Hulten, C. R. 1992. "Growth Accounting When Technical Change Is Embodied in Capital." *American Economic Review* 82 (4): 964–80.

Jaimovich, N., and H. E. Siu. 2020. "Job Polarization and Jobless Recoveries." *Review of Economics and Statistics* 102 (1): 129–47.

Jordà, Ò. 2005. "Estimation and Inference of Impulse Responses by Local Projections." *American Economic Review* 95 (1): 161–82.

Jordà, Ò., M. Schularick, and A. M. Taylor. 2013. "When Credit Bites Back." *Journal of Money, Credit and Banking* 45 (S2): 3–28.

Jordà, Ò., S. R. Singh, and A. M. Taylor. 2020. "The Long-Run Effects of Monetary Policy." FRBSF Working Paper 2020-01, Federal Reserve Bank of San Francisco.

Justiniano, A., G. E. Primiceri, and A. Tambalotti. 2010. "Investment Shocks and Business Cycles." *Journal of Monetary Economics* 57 (2): 132–45.

Kataryniuk, I., and J. Martínez-Martín. 2018. "What Are the Drivers of TFP Growth? An Empirical Assessment." In *International Macroeconomics in the Wake of the Global Financial Crisis,* edited by L. Ferrara, H. Ignacio, and D. Marconi. New York: Springer International Publishing.

Keynes, J. M. 1932. "Economic Possibilities for our Grandchildren." In *Essays in Persuasion,* 358–73. New York: Harcourt Brace.

Keynes, J. M. 1936. *The General Theory of Employment, Interest, and Money.* London: Macmillan.

Khan, H., and J. Tsoukalas. 2013. "Effects of Productivity Shocks on Hours Worked: U.K. Evidence." *B.E. Journal of Macroeconomics* 13 (1): 549–79.

Kilian, L. 2009. "Not All Oil Price Shocks Are Alike: Disentangling Demand and Supply Shocks in the Crude Oil Market." *American Economic Review* 99 (3): 1053–69.

Kilian, L., and B. Hicks. 2013. "Did Unexpectedly Strong Economic Growth Cause the Oil Price Shock of 2003-2008?" *Journal of Forecasting* 32 (5): 385–94.

Kilian, L., and D. P. Murphy. 2014. "The Role of Inventories and Speculative Trading in the Global Market for Crude Oil." *Journal of Applied Econometrics* 29 (3): 454–78.

Kose, M. A. 2002. "Explaining Business Cycles in Small Open Economies 'How Much Do World Prices Matter?'" *Journal of International Economics* 56 (2): 299–327.

Kose, M. A., H. Matsuoka, U. Paniza, and D. Vorisek. 2018. "Inflation Expectations: Review and Evidence." In *Inflation in Emerging and Developing Economies*, edited by J. Ha, M. A. Kose, and F. Ohnsorge, 205–70. Washington, DC: World Bank.

Kose, M. A., P. Nagle, F. Ohnsorge, and N. Sugawara. 2020. *Global Waves of Debt*. Washington, DC: World Bank.

Kose, M. A., F. Ohnsorge, L. S. Ye, and E. Islamaj. 2017. "Weakness in Investment Growth: Causes, Implications and Policy Responses." Policy Research Working Paper 7990, World Bank, Washington, DC.

Kose, M. A., and M. E. Terrones. 2015. *Collapse and Revival: Understanding Global Recessions and Recoveries.* Washington, DC: International Monetary Fund.

Leduc, S., and Z. Liu. 2020. "Can Pandemic-Induced Job Uncertainty Stimulate Automation?" FRBSF Working Paper 2020–19, Federal Reserve Bank of San Francisco.

Levchenko, A., and N. Pandalai-Nayar. 2018. "Technology and Non-Technology Shocks: Measurement and Implications for International Comovement." Conference proceedings, ECB-CBRT Conference, the Federal Reserve Board, UT-Austin, and the NBER-IFM, Cambridge, MA.

Maloney, W. F., and C. Molina. 2016. "Are Automation and Trade Polarizing Developing Country Labor Markets, Too?" Policy Research Working Paper 7922, World Bank, Washington, DC.

Mantoux, P. 2006. *The Industrial Revolution in the Eighteenth Century: An Outline of the Beginnings of the Modern Factory System in England.* London: Routledge.

Michelacci, C., and D. Lopez-Salido. 2007. "Technology Shocks and Job Flows." *The Review of Economic Studies* 74 (4): 1195–227.

Mohaddes, K., and M. Raissi. 2017. "Do Sovereign Wealth Funds Dampen the Negative Effects of Commodity Price Volatility?" *Journal of Commodity Markets* 8 (December): 18–27.

Mortensen, D. T., and C. A. Pissarides. 1998. "Technological Progress, Job Creation, and Job Destruction." *Review of Economic Dynamics* 1 (4): 733–53.

Nedelkoska, L., and G. Quintini. 2018. "Automation, Skills Use and Training." OECD Social, Employment and Migration Working Papers 202, Organisation for Economic Co-operation and Development, Paris.

OECD (Organisation for Economic Co-operation and Development). 2015. *The Future of Productivity.* Paris: OECD.

OECD (Organisation for Economic Co-operation and Development). 2019. *OECD Employment Outlook 2019*. Paris: OECD.

Park, K. 2012. "Employment Responses to Aggregate and Sectoral Technology Shocks." *Journal of Macroeconomics* 34 (3): 801–21.

Ramey, V. A. 2016. "Macroeconomic Shocks and Their Propagation." In *Handbook of Macroeconomics*, edited by J. B. Taylor and H. Uhlig, 71–162. Amsterdam: Elsevier.

Reinhart, C. M., and K. S. Rogoff. 2009. "The Aftermath of Financial Crises." *American Economic Review* 99 (2): 466–72.

Restrepo, P. 2015. "Skill Mismatch and Structural Unemployment." Job Market Paper. http://pascual.scripts.mit.edu/research/01/PR_jmp.pdf.

Rodrik, D. 2016. "Premature Deindustrialization." NBER Working Paper 20935, National Bureau of Economic Research, Cambridge, MA.

Rujin, S. 2019. "What Are the Effects of Technology Shocks on International Labor Markets?" Ruhr Economic Paper 806, RWI—Leibniz Institute for Economic Research, Germany.

Sargent, T. J. 1987. *Macroeconomic Theory*. New York: Academic Press.

Spence, M. 2014. "Labor's Digital Displacement." Project Syndicate, May 22, 2014.

Uhlig, H. 2003. "What Moves Real GNP?" Working paper, Humboldt University, Berlin. http://fmwww.bc.edu/repec/esNAWM04/up.2923.1054309431.pdf.

Waldkirch, A., P. Nunnenkamp, and J. E. A. Bremont. 2009. "Employment Effects of FDI in Mexico's Non-Maquiladora Manufacturing." *Journal of Development Studies* 45 (7): 1165–83.

World Bank. 2018a. *World Development Report 2018: Learning to Realize Education's Promise*. Washington, DC: World Bank.

World Bank. 2018b. *Africa's Pulse: An Analysis of Issues Shaping Africa's Economic Future*. October. Washington, DC: World Bank.

World Bank. 2019. *World Development Report 2019: The Changing Nature of Work*. Washington, DC: World Bank.

World Bank. 2020. "Fading Promise: How to Rekindle Productivity Growth?" In *Global Economic Prospects: Slow Growth, Policy Challenges*, January. Washington, DC: World Bank.

You can see the computer age everywhere but in the productivity statistics.

Robert Solow (1987)
Emeritus Institute Professor of Economics
at Massachusetts Institute of Technology (MIT)

CHAPTER 7

Sectoral Sources of Productivity Growth

Sectoral reallocation—the shift of labor from low- to high-productivity sectors—accounted for about two-fifths of overall labor productivity growth in emerging market and developing economies between 1995 and 2017. Over 2013-17, productivity gains from reallocation slowed as productivity gaps narrowed between different sectors. The disruptions caused by the COVID-19 (coronavirus disease 2019) pandemic may exacerbate this slowdown. Over the medium term, policy measures to improve agricultural productivity, such as actions to improve infrastructure and strengthen land property rights, and steps to facilitate the reallocation of workers to other sectors, can raise productivity.

Introduction

Factor reallocation toward higher-productivity sectors has long been recognized as one of the most powerful drivers of overall productivity growth (Baumol 1967). It has been identified as an important driver of productivity growth in many emerging market and developing economies (EMDEs), including in regions as diverse as Sub-Saharan Africa (SSA) and East Asia and Pacific (EAP; Cusolito and Maloney 2018; de Vries, Timmer, and de Vries 2015). The transfer of labor out of agriculture into higher-productivity industry has long been recognized as a major source of productivity growth in the industrialization process, and in recent decades the shift of labor from agriculture into manufacturing and services has been credited as a major contributor to rapid productivity growth, especially in East Asia, including China (Helble et al. 2019).

After several decades of reallocation out of agriculture, the sector in 2017 accounts for 30 percent of employment in EMDEs—compared with 50 percent less than two decades ago—and less than 10 percent of value added. In low-income countries (LICs), however, agriculture still accounts for over 60 percent of employment, partly explaining the low overall productivity observed in these countries (Caselli 2005; Restuccia, Yang, and Zhu 2008).

After rapid growth of services sectors in EMDEs over the preceding two decades, in 2017 they accounted for about 40 percent of employment, still below their 75 percent share in advanced economies. Productivity growth in services sectors was the main source of overall productivity growth in EMDEs in the period following the global financial crisis (GFC), accounting for almost two-thirds of overall productivity growth in the average EMDE (compared with one-fifth accounted for by industry) and more than nine-tenths in the average LIC.

Note: This chapter was prepared by Alistair Dieppe, and Hideaki Matsuoka. Cedric Okou authored the box. Bala Bhaskar, Naidu Kalimili, and Charles Yao Kouadio Kouame helped compile the sectoral database. Research assistance was provided by Xinyue Wang.

Productivity gains through factor reallocation slowed after 2008, after contributing to the steepest and most prolonged slowdown in EMDE productivity growth since the 1980s (chapter 1).[1] The COVID-19 (coronavirus disease 2019) pandemic may slow reallocation further. The widespread restrictions on physical interaction and mobility that have been introduced by governments to combat the COVID-19 pandemic, together with self-imposed restraints with similar effects, may not only damage within-sector productivity through its effects on health, business models, and workplace practices but also reduce between-sector factor mobility and the associated gains in productivity growth (World Bank 2020).

Against this backdrop, this chapter addresses the following questions:

• How large are productivity gaps across sectors?

• What has been the role of sectoral reallocation in overall labor productivity growth?

• How might government policies help raise sectoral productivity growth?

Contributions

This chapter extends the literature in two dimensions.

First, the chapter employs the most comprehensive data set of sectoral labor productivity available, with data for nine sectors.[2] Past analysis had limited country or time coverage.[3] The updated data set includes sufficient recent data to allow an analysis of developments following the GFC.

Second, the rich sectoral detail allows an analysis of the heterogeneity of industrial and services subsectors within and across countries, as well as within-sector and between-sector developments that are sensitive to aggregation bias (de Vries et al. 2012; Üngör 2017). This sectoral analysis is complemented by firm-level analysis that points to drivers of within-sector productivity growth (box 7.1).

Main findings

The chapter offers several novel findings.

First, the chapter documents large productivity gaps across the nine sectors and also across countries within each of the nine sectors. In the average EMDE, productivity in agriculture, the lowest-productivity sector, is 85 percent lower than the average productivity. In advanced economies, the corresponding difference is considerably

---

[1] Unless otherwise indicated, productivity is defined in this chapter as value added per worker.

[2] The nine sectors distinguished in the data set are agriculture, mining, manufacturing, utilities, construction, trade services, transport services, financial and business services, and government and personal services. Annex 7A provides additional details.

[3] McMillan, Rodrik, and Verduzco-Gallo (2014) and Diao, McMillan, and Rodrik (2017) employ 38 and 39 countries; Martins (2019) uses 7 sectors and 169 countries; International Monetary Fund (2018) uses 10 sectors and 62 countries; and McCullough (2017) has 16 sectors for the United States and EU10 (10 countries that joined the European Union in 2004).

narrower. Agriculture accounts for less than 10 percent of value added and about 30 percent of employment in EMDEs. The gap between EMDE and advanced economy productivity is particularly wide in agriculture, with EMDEs less than 20 percent of advanced economies. This partly reflects slow technology adoption in the agriculture sector in some of the poorest EMDEs. Within manufacturing, productivity is highest among firms with a high share of exports in output. Those that operate in a conducive business environment are also closer to the global technology frontier (box 7.1).

Second, sectoral reallocation accounted for two-fifths of overall productivity gains between 1995 and 2017. This shift lost momentum after the GFC. This slowing sectoral reallocation accounted for two-fifths of the productivity growth slowdown in EMDEs between 2013 and 2017. By curtailing labor mobility as well as economic activity, the COVID-19 pandemic may further slow sectoral reallocation.

Third, policies can both rekindle sectoral reallocation and boost productivity in low-productivity sectors. Policies to support labor mobility and capital investment include improving the quality of, and access to, education; promoting good governance and reducing the costs of doing business; strengthening institutional and managerial capabilities; reducing distortions, such as anticompetitive regulations and subsidies; supporting research and development; and removing infrastructure bottlenecks. Given the low productivity of EMDE agricultural sectors and agriculture's role as the primary employer in LICs, policies to raise productivity in this sector, such as actions to strengthen infrastructure and improve land property rights, could pay particularly significant dividends.

Methodology. The chapter estimates a "shift-share" decomposition of overall labor productivity growth in an economy into within- and between-sector components (Padilla-Pérez and Villarreal 2017; Wong 2006; see annex 7A for details). Within-sector productivity growth captures that part of overall labor productivity growth that is due to productivity improvements within sectors. This may reflect the effects of improvements in human capital, investments in physical capital, technological advances, and the reallocation of resources from the least to the most productive firms within each sector. Between-sector productivity growth captures the part of overall labor productivity growth that is driven by the reallocation of resources between sectors—both between sectors with different productivity levels (static sectoral effect) and between sectors with different productivity growth rates (dynamic sectoral effect).

Data. The database includes value added and employment for nine sectors during 1975-2017 in 103 countries: 34 advanced economies and 69 EMDEs, of which 9 are LICs. For 94 countries, of which 60 are EMDEs, the database is balanced for 1995-2017. The nine sectors include agriculture; four industrial sectors (construction, manufacturing, mining, and utilities), and four services sectors (financial and business, trade, transport, and other services). The database combines data from the World Bank's World Development Indicators database, the Organisation for Economic Co-operation and Development Structural Analysis Database, KLEMS, the Groningen Growth Development Center database (de Vries, Timmer, and de Vries 2015), and the

Expanded Africa Sector Database (Mensah and Szirmai 2018). The Asian Productivity Organization Productivity Database, United Nations data, International Labour Organization ILOSTAT, and national sources are used for supplementary purposes. Following Wong (2006), local currency value added is converted to U.S. dollars using the 2011 purchasing power parity (PPP) exchange rate obtained from Penn World Table for international comparisons of productivity levels.[4]

Sectoral productivity gaps

Continuing wide productivity differentials across sectors. Productivity differs widely across sectors, offering large potential productivity gains by factor reallocation across sectors (figure 7.1; Gollin, Lagakos, and Waugh 2014; Rodrik 2013). Productivity in mining is usually high because the sector is highly capital intensive and dominated by major global companies. Productivity in agriculture tends to be lowest, in part because of the proportion of smallholder ownership and family farms (Cusolito and Maloney 2018; Fuglie et al. 2020; Lowder, Skoet, and Raney 2016).[5] But there are also some services subsectors, such as trade services, with productivity below that of manufacturing.

In the average EMDE, productivity in the lowest-productivity sector—agriculture, which accounts for 10 percent of value added and 32 percent of employment—is 85 percent lower than the average productivity.[6] In advanced economies, the corresponding difference is considerably narrower.

Over time, the productivity gap between the agricultural sector and other higher-productivity sectors has narrowed. Thus productivity in higher-productivity sectors, relative to productivity in agriculture, declined in the average EMDE from 350 percent in 1995 to 310 percent in 2017 and, in the average LIC, from 500 percent in 1995 to 400 percent in 2017.

Wide sectoral productivity differentials across countries. Productivity in all sectors is lower in EMDEs than in advanced economies, and lower again in LICs. Agriculture productivity in EMDEs is 20 percent of advanced economy productivity. In part, this gap reflects slow technology adoption in the agriculture sector in some of the poorest EMDEs, which tend to be characterized by smallholder ownership and family farms

---

[4] van Biesebroeck (2009) builds expenditure-based sector-specific PPP estimates for Organisation for Economic Co-operation and Development countries, using detailed price data.

[5] Mechanization tends to increase agricultural labor productivity through both capital deepening and embodied new technology, but mechanization in LICs is often hindered by frictions such as untitled land (Chen 2017). Also, Restuccia, Yang, and Zhu (2008) show that agricultural labor productivity is positively associated with the use of relatively advanced intermediate inputs (for example, modern fertilizers and high-yield seeds) and argue that certain distortions in factor markets may severely dampen the incentives for their use.

[6] This is consistent with findings by Bartelsman and Doms (2000) and Levchenko and Zhang (2016). Because agricultural workers often do not work full time in agriculture, the sectoral gap is diminished if productivity is measured per hours worked instead of per worker (Gollin, Lagakos, and Waugh 2014). However, even after taking into account hours worked and human capital per worker, a large sectoral gap remains for a large number of countries (Hicks et al. 2017).

FIGURE 7.1 **Sectoral labor composition and productivity gaps**

EMDEs are characterized by large, albeit narrowing, productivity gaps across sectors. Gaps are larger in EMDEs than advanced economies. The share of agricultural employment in advanced economies has been small for several decades and continues to decline, whereas the services sector continues to increase. In EMDEs, the share of the agriculture sector has nearly halved since 1975 but remains large in LICs.

A. Productivity gap relative to cross-sector average, 2017

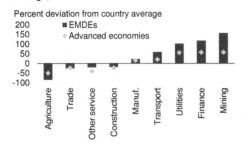

B. Productivity gap relative to advanced economy median, 2017

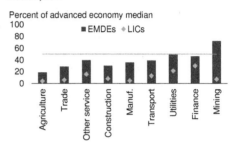

C. Composition of employment, by sector

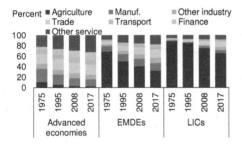

D. Composition of value added, by sector

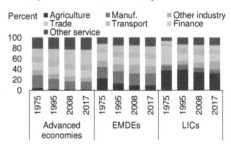

Sources: Asian Productivity Organization; Expanded Africa Sector Database; Groningen Growth Development Center; International Labour Organization; KLEMS; national sources; Organisation for Economic Co-operation and Development; United Nations; World Bank.
Note: Based on samples of 94 countries during 1995-99 and 103 countries during 2003-17. Median of the country-specific productivity within indicated country groupings. "Finance" includes business services; "Other service" includes government and personal services. EMDEs = emerging market and developing economies; LICs = low-income countries.
A.B. Average labor productivity is value added per worker based on 2017 data. Horizontal line indicates 50 percent.

(Lowder, Skoet, and Raney 2016). In mining, where production is dominated globally by a few large companies, the productivity gap is considerably narrower (about 70 percent). Productivity gaps between advanced economies and EMDEs have narrowed only a little or have actually widened in agriculture, manufacturing, and utilities.

Sectoral productivity growth

Heterogeneous sectoral productivity growth. In the most recent subperiod examined, 2013-17, the sectors with the fastest-growing productivity in the average EMDE were agriculture, trade, and transport services, with annual growth rates between 1.5 and 3.0 percent (figure 7.2). This differs from the period before the GFC, 2003-08, when manufacturing was the sector with strong productivity growth. Productivity growth was

FIGURE 7.2 Sectoral labor productivity growth

In EMDEs, labor productivity growth slowed in most sectors following the global financial crisis, most markedly in manufacturing and nonfinancial services. In LICs, slower productivity growth in agriculture accounted for most of the overall productivity growth slowdown after the global financial crisis.

A. Advanced economies: Sectoral productivity growth

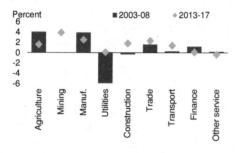

B. EMDEs: Sectoral productivity growth

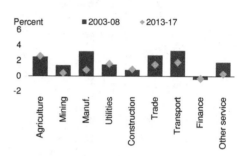

C. Sectoral contributions to productivity growth

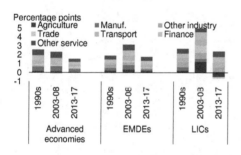

D. Change in sectoral contribution to productivity growth between 2003-08 and 2013-17

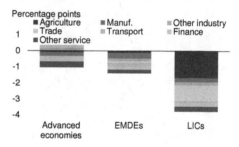

Sources: Asian Productivity Organization; Expanded Africa Sector Database; Groningen Growth Development Center; International Labour Organization; KLEMS; national sources; Organisation for Economic Co-operation and Development; United Nations; World Bank.
Note: "Other industry" includes mining, utilities, and construction; "Finance" includes business services; "Other service" includes government and personal services. All medians. EMDEs = emerging market and developing economies; LICs = low-income countries.

near zero or negative in both subperiods in finance and in the more recent subperiod in mining and other services. In advanced economies, post-2013 productivity growth was strongest in mining and manufacturing, notwithstanding a slowdown in manufacturing, and near zero in utilities, finance, and other services.

Sectoral productivity growth slowdown. In EMDEs, productivity growth slowed after the crisis (2013-17) from its precrisis (2003-08) rates in one-half of the sectors. The sector with the steepest slowdown, of over 2 percentage points, was manufacturing. The regions that experienced the sharpest slowdown were Latin American and the Caribbean (LAC) and South Asia (SAR). In SAR and SSA, and in the LICs, the productivity slowdown in agriculture was particularly marked as commodity prices collapsed. In contrast, EMDE productivity growth increased slightly in 2013-17 in construction and utilities. In the advanced economies, productivity growth strengthened after the GFC in sectors such as trade, transport, utilities, and construction.

Sectoral contributions to postcrisis productivity growth slowdown. Overall labor productivity growth in EMDEs accelerated ahead of the GFC but subsequently slowed (chapter 1).[7] More than one-third of the post-GFC slowdown in overall productivity growth in the average EMDE is accounted for by slower growth in the manufacturing sector and another one-third by the finance and trade services sectors combined.[8] This partly reflects the persistent weakness of global trade after the GFC as well as the disruptions to global finance wrought by the financial crisis itself. From 2010 to 2017, services accounted for two-thirds of productivity growth in EMDEs compared with one-fifth in the case of manufacturing.

Roles of between- and within-sector productivity gains. Between 1995 and 2017, advanced economy productivity growth was almost entirely driven by within-sector productivity gains, whereas two-fifths of EMDE productivity growth, and more than one-half of LICs' productivity growth, was driven by sectoral reallocation (figure 7.3).

In advanced economies, within-sector productivity growth in this period occurred mainly in the manufacturing, trade, and finance sectors.[9] Overall within-sector productivity growth slowed to 0.9 percent a year during 2013-17. This was compounded by slower reallocation-driven productivity gains (Duernecker, Herrendorf, and Valentinyi 2017).

In EMDEs, within-sector productivity growth accounted for about three-fifths of overall productivity growth after 1995. Within-sector growth was broad-based across sectors, reflecting gains in agriculture as well as trade, transport, and government and personal services. Between-sector productivity gains mainly reflected moves out of agriculture and manufacturing into services. The share of workers employed in agriculture fell from about 70 percent in 1975 to about 30 percent in 2017. The effect of sectoral reallocations was particularly large in SSA but also important in SAR and EAP (Diao, McMillan, and Rodrik 2017; McMillan, Rodrik, and Verduzco-Gallo 2014). In the post-GFC period, productivity gains from sectoral reallocation declined across most EMDE regions compared to the pre-GFC period. In the EMDE, slowing sectoral reallocation accounted for two-fifths of the slowdown in productivity growth between 2003-08 and 2013-17.

In LICs, sectoral reallocation accounted for more than one-half of overall productivity growth between 1995 and 2017 but, as in other EMDEs, it lost momentum after the GFC. The contribution of sectoral reallocation to productivity growth declined from 2.7 percentage points a year during 2003-08 to 0.8 percentage points during 2013-17. Whereas between-sector productivity gains in LICs in the pre-GFC period reflected a broad-based shift out of agriculture, in the post-GFC period the shift was mainly into

---

[7] This finding is broadly in line with the evidence in Hallward-Driemeier and Nayyar (2017).

[8] Sectoral productivity contributions are calculated by the difference between sectoral value added contributions and sectoral employment contributions.

[9] In addition, prior to the GFC, productivity growth was boosted by shifts of factors of production to financial and business services, offsetting the negative effect of the decline in the share of employment in the manufacturing sector.

FIGURE 7.3 Between- and within-sector sources of productivity growth

Although overall productivity growth in advanced economies has predominantly originated within sectors, between-sector gains have accounted for a sizable portion of both EMDE productivity growth and its post-GFC slowdown. In EMDEs, between-sector productivity gains have involved shifts out of agriculture into higher-productivity sectors that have differed over time .

A. Within- and between-sector contributions to productivity growth

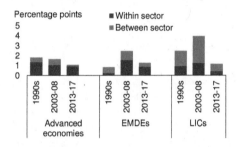

B. Within- and between-sector contributions to productivity growth: Regions

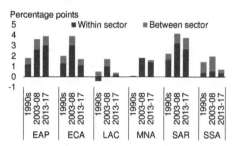

C. Contributions of within-sector growth

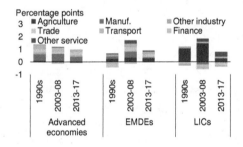

D. Contributions of within-sector growth: Regions

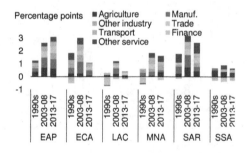

E. Contributions of between-sector growth

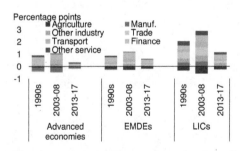

F. Contributions of between-sector growth: Regions

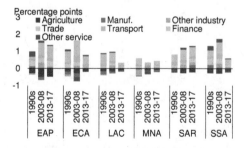

Sources: Asian Productivity Organization; Expanded Africa Sector Database; Groningen Growth Development Center; International Labour Organization; KLEMS; national sources; Organisation for Economic Co-operation and Development; United Nations; World Bank.

Note: Based on samples of 94 countries during 1995-99 and 103 countries during 2003-17. Median of the country-specific productivity. EAP = East Asia and Pacific; ECA = Europe and Central Asia; EMDEs = emerging market and developing economies; GFC = global financial crisis; LAC = Latin America and the Caribbean; LICs = low-income countries; MNA = Middle East and North Africa; SAR = South Asia; SSA = Sub-Saharan Africa.

A-F. Growth within sector shows the contribution of initial real value added weighted productivity growth rate and between sector growth effect give the contribution arising from changes in the change in employment share. Median of the country-specific contributions. "Other industry" includes mining, utilities, and construction; "Finance" includes business services; "Other service" includes government and personal services.

services such as trade services and finance, with only limited shifts into manufacturing. The slowdown in between-sector productivity gains was compounded by a slowdown in the contribution of within-sector productivity gains from 1.2 percentage point a year in 2003-08 to 0.4 percentage point in 2013-17.

Sources of fading sectoral reallocation. In some commodity exporters, especially in LAC and SSA, the slowdown in sectoral reallocation after the GFC partly reflected lower absorption of labor by the services and construction sectors as weaker global commodity prices weighed on domestic demand (Diao, McMillan, and Rodrik 2017). In EAP, it also reflected slower economic growth as productive overcapacity was gradually unwound.[10] In Europe and Central Asia (ECA), higher-productivity manufacturing, financial, and mining sectors suffered during the euro area debt crisis and the commodity price collapse in 2014-16. Meanwhile, in SAR, the move of labor out of low-productivity agriculture into more productive sectors accelerated as rapid urbanization continued and strong consumption growth fueled employment growth in higher-productivity trade services. Although labor has continued to move out of agriculture in EMDEs, this process has slowed in all EMDE regions other than SAR.[11]

The COVID-19 pandemic has inflicted a severe shock on the global economy. Economic and financial disruptions like those that have resulted from the pandemic can increase sectoral reallocation, as workers shift from sectors most adversely affected to those less adversely, or favorably, affected (Foster, Grim, and Haltiwanger 2016). But the constraints on mobility resulting from the pandemic, together with the failure, at least in the short term, of job creation to keep pace with job destruction, seem likely to slow the process of reallocation (Barrero, Bloom, and Davis 2020; Chodorow-Reich and Wieland 2020).[12] If the COVID-19 pandemic discourages mobility out of agriculture into urban centers, productivity gains from sectoral reallocation may well slow, particularly in LICs (Hale et al. 2020; World Bank 2020). During the 2014-16 Ebola outbreak in West Africa, for example, the movement of labor out of agriculture slowed in Liberia and Sierra Leone.

Leapfrogging and deindustrialization. In decades past, the economic development of advanced economies typically involved a period of industrialization, as labor moved out of the agricultural sector into manufacturing, and a subsequent period of de-

---

[10] As highlighted in chapter 6, this suggests a risk that productivity growth may slow in these regions as demand loses momentum.

[11] Alvarez-Cuadrado and Poschke (2011); Duarte and Restuccia (2007, 2010); Herrendorf, Rogerson, and Valentinyi (2013); Imrohoroğlu, A., S. IImrohoroğlu, and M. Üngör (2014); and Üngör (2013, 2017) show that productivity improvements in the agricultural sector, along with low income elasticity of demand for food, explain most of the declines in agriculture's employment share in a closed economy. The move out of agriculture also depends on the extent of economic integration of the domestic economy and global markets as well as the degree of subsidization and other barriers to reallocation (Barrett et al. 2017; Dercon and Christiaensen 2011; Rodrik 2016). In an open economy context, Uy, Yi, and Zhang (2013) argue the role of international trade is quantitatively important for explaining sectoral re-allocation.

[12] Foster, Grim, and Haltiwanger (2016) found in the United States that reallocation effects increased in recessions prior to the GFC.

industrialization, as labor moved into the services sector.[13] However, in some EMDEs, labor has recently shifted directly from agriculture into services, a phenomenon dubbed "leapfrogging" (Rodrik 2016). In three EMDE regions (ECA, LAC, and MNA), labor has moved not only out of agriculture (as a share of labor) but also out of industry— another case of "deindustrialization" (Rodrik 2016). In these regions, employment has largely shifted into construction (MNA), finance (ECA and LAC), and trade services (ECA and MNA). Because some of these sectors, especially construction and trade services, have lower productivity than manufacturing, this has resulted in a sharply lower (ECA) or even negative (LAC and MNA) contribution of between-sector sources of productivity growth.

Leapfrogging has been encouraged by rapid growth in demand for services and slower growth in demand for labor-intensive manufactured goods (Eichengreen and Gupta 2013). In LICs, leapfrogging has primarily consisted of growth in traditional (personal) services. Especially in commodity-reliant countries, the increase in incomes arising from the commodity price boom during the 2000s may have boosted the demand for services, along with services employment (Rodrik 2016, 2018).[14] Leapfrogging has included the growth of modern services (financial, communication, computer, technical, legal, advertising, and business) that have benefited from the application of information technologies as well as the ability to trade across borders.[15] In the past, labor-intensive manufacturing traditionally absorbed significant quantities of unskilled labor (Stiglitz 2018).[16] The scope for unskilled labor to move into manufacturing has diminished because of rising global competition, robotization, and artificial intelligence (Bernard and Jones 1996; Eichengreen and Gupta 2013; Matsuyama 2009).

Policy implications

The redistribution of labor across sectors has been an important engine of productivity growth in EMDEs in recent decades. The sizable productivity gaps between different sectors that remain indicate that this source of growth still has significant potential. Yet there are obstacles. For example, the increasing complexity and automation of manufacturing processes, with their increased requirements of skilled labor, may make it increasingly difficult for countries to achieve gains in overall productivity from shifts in employment to high-productivity sectors. This is among the considerations that point to the need for policies to support productivity growth across three dimensions.

---

[13] Manufacturing increases during low stages of development as capital is accumulated. At the next stage higher incomes drive up demand for services, while rising labor costs make domestic manufacturing less competitive (Boppart 2014; Buera and Kaboski 2009; Duarte and Restuccia 2010; Herrendorf, Rogerson, and Valentinyi 2013, 2014).

[14] After the commodity boom, the contribution of between-sector growth in LAC and SSA fell in 2013-17.

[15] Those services industries with the fastest productivity growth tend to be among the most intensive users of information and communication technologies (Stiroh 2002). Recent advances in those technologies are likely to have played an important role in boosting the productivity in the sectors that use them (Bosworth and Triplett 2003, 2007; Duernecker, Herrendorf, and Valentinyi 2017; Jorgenson and Timmer 2011). This second wave has occurred also in those LICs that are democracies and have high trade and financial openness (Rodrik 2016).

[16] It should be noted that refining and processing of extractives are sometimes classified as manufacturing in resource-rich countries.

FIGURE 7.4 **Policies to reallocate employment and boost growth, Vietnam**

Vietnam's agricultural reform shifted employment toward manufacturing, trade, and other services, providing a significant boost to overall productivity growth.

A. Sectoral contributions to productivity growth in Vietnam

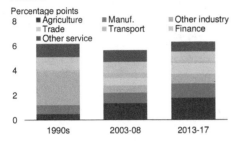

B. Within- and between-sector contributions to productivity growth in Vietnam

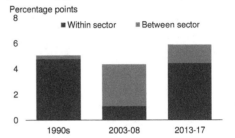

C. Sectoral employment shares in Vietnam

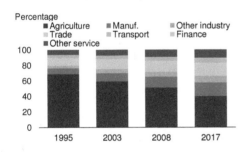

D. Productivity increase in sectoral reallocation scenario

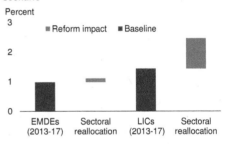

Sources: Asian Productivity Organization; Expanded Africa Sector Database; Groningen Growth Development Center; International Labour Organization; KLEMS; national sources; Organisation for Economic Co-operation and Development; United Nations; World Bank.
Note: EMDEs = emerging market and developing economies; LICs = low-income countries.
D. The reform scenario assumes that the sectoral reallocation reform is calibrated for China and Vietnam, which experienced successful structural change during 2003-08. More specifically, it assumes a decrease in the share of employment in the agriculture sector by 15 percent, a corresponding increase in the share of manufacturing and trade sectors.

Improving agricultural productivity. Although productivity in agriculture has been improving in EMDEs and LICs, it is still well below levels in advanced economies. Given that agriculture remains the primary employer in most LICs, raising productivity in this sector is key to boosting employment in other sectors, raising overall productivity, and reducing poverty. The experience of countries such as Vietnam suggests that agricultural productivity can be improved through targeted measures that improve the infrastructure that serves the sector, ensure secure land tenures, and promote access to finance (figure 7.4).[17] If other EMDEs replicated the reallocation of

---

[17] Agricultural reforms in Vietnam have included the legalization of private economic activity, giving farms greater exposure to markets and competition by eliminating price controls and the state procurement system, strengthened household land property rights, and relaxed restrictions on external and internal trade of agricultural goods and inputs, such as fertilizers. Vietnam succeeded with the expansion of manufacturing employment partly also through the liberalization of foreign investment. Foreign-owned firms, mainly labor-intensive manufacturing, accounted for over half of all exports by 2010, up from about a quarter in 1995 (McCaig and Pavcnik 2013).

BOX 7.1 Patterns of total factor productivity: A firm-level perspective

There is substantial variation in firm-level total factor productivity (TFP) across industries and across regions. Weak firm productivity in emerging markets and developing economies (EMDEs) partly reflects the divergence between a few highly productive firms and a large number of firms that operate far from the productivity frontier. The difference between frontier and laggard firms is, on average, larger in EMDEs than in advanced economies. Among EMDE firms, large firms tend to be more productive than small firms. Firms in technology-intensive industries, mainly located in East Asia and Pacific, Europe and Central Asia, and South Asia, tend to be more productive than firms in more traditional sectors. Measures to promote exports and improve business climates can help close the observed TFP gap.

Introduction

Firm-level productivity in emerging markets and developing economies (EMDEs) has been low relative to advanced economies, and growth has lost momentum over the past decade. This has diminished prospects among many EMDEs to catch up with the advanced economies (Andrews, Criscuolo, and Gal 2016; Bloom et al. 2010; Cusolito and Maloney 2018).

Numerous factors have been identified as underlying the low firm-level productivity observed in EMDEs: weak institutions and pervasive informality, slow technology innovation and adoption, subdued investment and poor quality infrastructure, low human capital and poor firm management practices, protectionist trade policies, and weak economic integration (Cusolito and Maloney 2018; World Bank 2019a, 2019b).[a] Moreover, outdated technologies, lagging innovation, misallocation of labor to inefficient sectors, and market rigidities weigh on productivity and contribute to dispersion in total factor productivity (TFP) across countries (Araujo, Vostroknutova, and Wacker 2017; Bahar 2018; Syverson 2011). In some EMDEs, low participation in global value chains, or lack of openness to foreign direct investment and migration, has resulted in missed opportunities for a productivity boost through the transfer of innovative processes and managerial capabilities (Goldberg et al. 2010; Wolitzky 2018).

This box undertakes a cross-sectional study to analyze firm-level TFP patterns, and maps these to firm characteristics in EMDEs to address the following questions:

- How does firm-level TFP vary across EMDE sectors and regions?

Note: This box was prepared by Cedric Okou.

a. Many studies focus on labor productivity, which depends on both TFP and capital per worker—also known as capital deepening.

BOX 7.1 Patterns of total factor productivity: A firm-level perspective (continued)

- What firm characteristics account for the dispersion in TFP?

TFP variation across sectors and regions

Productivity varies across firms, within sectors, and across regions (Bloom et al. 2010; Goñi and Maloney 2017). By focusing on TFP, differences due to capital deepening or other factor inputs can be abstracted from. This allows the identification of where TFP dispersion and gaps are the largest, and where steps are needed to improve productivity. Firm-level TFP data are obtained from surveys conducted by the World Bank from 2007 to 2017 (Cusolito et al. 2018). The database of survey results contains TFP for 15,181 manufacturing firms in 108 EMDEs, including 20 low-income countries (LICs). A cross-sectional analysis of the firm-level TFP database is undertaken, which complements longitudinal studies that use micro-level panel data, but with a smaller country coverage (Dall'Olio et al. 2014; Di Mauro et al. 2018).[b] Two measures of TFP are constructed: output and value added revenue TFP measures. The latter is obtained by subtracting the value of intermediate inputs (materials, electricity, and so on) from output before computing TFP (Cusolito and Maloney 2018; Cusolito et al. 2018). TFP measurement challenges are discussed in annex 7C.

TFP across sectors. Differences in firm-level TFP across sectors have been frequently emphasized in the literature (for example, Bahar 2016; Bartelsman and Doms 2000; Levchenko and Zhang 2016; Restuccia and Rogerson 2013). On average, firms in technology-intensive industries have higher TFP than those in other sectors (figure B7.1.1, panels A and B). Technology-intensive industries, denoted by TINT (as in Fernald 2015), include computing and electrical machinery, precision equipment, electronics, information, and communication sectors (table 7C.1). One explanation for this observation is that firms operating in a technology-intensive industry rely more on research and development (R&D) and network linkages than physical assets, and as such can reap the benefits of technology to boost productivity (Chevalier, Lecat, and Oulton 2012; Vaaler and McNamara 2010).

Distance to TFP frontier across sectors. TFP dispersion may signal rigidities in the generation, transfer, and acquisition of technology across firms in a sector (Bahar 2018; Cette, Corde, and Lecat 2018). To assess within-sector productivity

---

b. This analysis does not explore the time series dimension because World Bank firm output and input data used to construct TFP estimates were collected at different times in different countries. For example, these firm surveys were conducted in 2007 in South Africa and in 2017 in Ecuador. Moreover, the number of surveyed firms in many countries is small, which does not allow for conducting robust within- and cross-country comparisons.

BOX 7.1 Patterns of total factor productivity: A firm-level perspective *(continued)*

FIGURE B7.1.1 Firm TFP and distance to frontier in EMDEs, by industry

Firms in technology-intensive industry have higher average TFP. These technology-intensive firms are also more tightly clustered around their industry-specific frontier than firms in other sectors.

A. Output TFP estimates, by industry

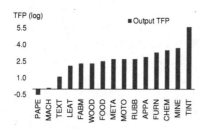

B. Value added TFP estimates, by industry

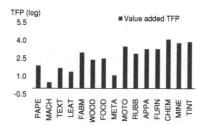

C. Distance to frontier and average output TFP, by industry

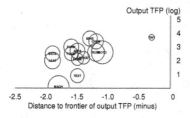

D. Distance to frontier and average value added TFP, by industry

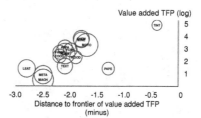

Source: World Bank Enterprise Surveys.

Note: Firm-level TFP is computed using a Cobb-Douglas production function, assuming that elasticities of output with respect to inputs are the same across countries in a given income group. The distance to frontier of TFP is computed within each industry, excluding the top 2.5 percent of firms. For each sector, the location shows the average, and the size of the marker (circle) is proportional to one standard deviation of distance to frontier of TFP. Averages and standard deviations are computed using survey weights. Sample includes 15,181 firms in 108 EMDEs, including 20 LICs, for the period 2007-17. Table 7C.1 contains a description of each industry. TINT includes firms in computing and electrical machinery, precision equipment, electronics, information, and communication sectors. APPA = apparel; CHEM = chemicals; FABM = fabricated metals; FOOD = food; FURN = furniture; LEAT = leather; MACH = nonelectrical machinery; META = metals; MINE = nonmetallic minerals; MOTO = motor vehicles; PAPE = paper; RUBB = rubber; TEXT = textiles; TFP = total factor productivity; TINT = technology-intensive industry; WOOD = wood.

A.B. In the manufacture of paper (PAPE) industry, the value added TFP is positive and much higher than the corresponding (negative) output TFP due to a relatively high elasticity of output with respect to intermediate inputs.

C.D. Distance to frontier of firm-level TFP (minus) and TFP (log), by industry. The right-hand-side y-axes represent the frontier.

BOX 7.1 Patterns of total factor productivity: A firm-level perspective
(continued)

dispersion, a firm's distance to an industry-specific TFP frontier is computed.[c] Firms in basic manufacturing industries, such as nonelectrical machinery (MACH), textiles (TEXT), leather (LEAT), and basic metals (META), are not only on average less productive than firms in other sectors but also relatively far from their industry-specific frontiers (figure B7.1.1, panels C and D). By contrast, firms in technology-intensive industries (TINT) are more tightly clustered around their industry-specific frontiers and are more productive.[d]

TFP across regions. Across regions, firms in East Asia and Pacific (EAP) are, on average, more productive than those in other regions (figure B7.1.2, panel A). EAP also has the highest proportion of large firms and firms exporting more than half of their sales (figure B7.1.2, panels C and D). Most firms in technology-intensive industries are located in EAP, Europe and Central Asia (ECA), and South Asia (SAR) (figure B7.1.2, panel B). Perceptions of corruption and licensing as obstacles for firm operation seem to correlate negatively with TFP (figure B7.1.2, panels E and F).

Robustness of TFP dispersion. Substantial TFP dispersion may signal misallocation of factor inputs or rigidities in the generation, transfer, and acquisition of technology across firms (Bahar 2016; Hsieh and Klenow 2009; Restuccia and Rogerson 2008). However, commonly used dispersion metrics can also reflect mismeasurements, quality differences, adjustment costs, markups, and investment risks, among other factors. Recent evidence shows that half of the dispersion is unrelated to misallocation, and driven rather by markups and technology wedges (Cusolito and Maloney 2018). Thus, dispersion results should be interpreted with caution. Nonetheless, the variation in distance to frontier in technology-intensive industries is less than one-fifth of that in basic manufacturing industries (leather, metals, and machinery), suggesting that firms in technology-intensive industries are much closer to their sector-specific frontier.

Firm characteristics associated with higher TFP growth

Heterogeneous characteristics related to entering, incumbent, and exiting firms can explain the observed patterns of TFP dispersion (Bartelsman and Doms 2000). A large and expanding literature points to three broad categories of correlates of sectoral TFP dispersion in EMDEs: within-firm upgrading, spillovers, and regulatory environment.

---

c. For a given firm i, the distance to an industry-specific TFP frontier (97.5th quantile) is computed as $DTF_i = TFP_{0.975} - TFP_{i \leq 0.975}$. The top 2.5 percent firm-level TFP values are dropped to minimize the impact of extreme values. Results are robust to alternative 1 and 5 percent cutoffs of top firm TFP values.

d. This finding is broadly in line with the evidence in Hallward-Driemeier and Nayyar (2017).

BOX 7.1 Patterns of total factor productivity: A firm-level perspective *(continued)*

FIGURE B7.1.2 **Firm TFP, by region**

Firms in EAP are more productive than those located in other EMDE regions. EAP also has the highest share of large firms and those exporting more than half of their sales. Most firms in technology-intensive industry are located in EAP, ECA, and SAR. Perceptions of corruption and licensing as obstacles for firm operation seem to correlate negatively with TFP.

A. Firm-level TFP, by region

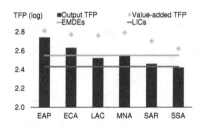

B. Percentage of firms in each region, by industry

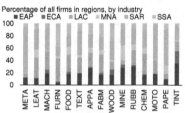

C. Firm size, by region

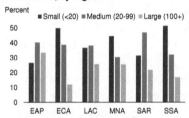

D. Exporting firms, by region

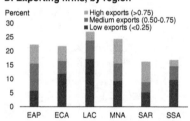

E. Perception of corruption, by region

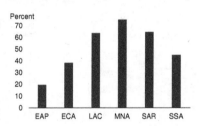

F. Perception of licensing obstacle, by region

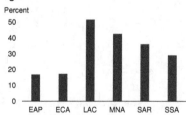

Source: World Bank Enterprise Surveys.
Note: Sample includes 15,181 firms in 108 EMDEs, including 20 LICs, for the period 2007-17. EAP = East Asia and Pacific; ECA = Europe and Central Asia; EMDE = emerging market and developing economy; LAC = Latin America and the Caribbean; LIC = low-income country; MNA = Middle East and North Africa; SAR = South Asia; SSA = Sub-Saharan Africa; TFP = total factor productivity.
A. Solid lines are averages of output TFP (log) for EMDEs (orange) and LICs (red).
B. Bars show in each industry the percentage of firms in each region, by industry (see also table 7C.1).
APPA = apparel; CHEM = chemicals; FABM = fabricated metals; FOOD = food; FURN = furniture; LEAT = leather; MACH = nonelectrical machinery; META = metals; MINE = nonmetallic minerals; MOTO = motor vehicles; PAPE = paper; RUBB = rubber; TEXT = textiles; TINT = technology-intensive industry; WOOD = wood.
C.D. Firm size in terms of number of employees (D) and share of exporting firms (C). High, medium, and low exports firms export more than 75 percent, between 50 and 75 percent, and up to 25 percent of their sales, respectively.
E. Share of firms that perceive corruption as an obstacle for their operations.
F. Share of firms that perceive licensing and permits as an obstacle for their operations.

BOX 7.1 Patterns of total factor productivity: A firm-level perspective (continued)

Within-firm upgrading and technology spillovers. Controlling for both size and exports, firms in the technology-intensive industries are on average much closer to the TFP frontier than firms in traditional industries such as nonelectric machinery, food, and nonmetallic minerals industries (figure B7.1.3, panels A and B). Knowledge, experience, R&D, and information technology can raise TFP through improvements in product quality and production process upgrading within firms (Atkin, Khandelwal, and Osman 2017; Brynjolfsson and Hitt 1995; Goldberg et al. 2010). Firms with a large number of employees are significantly closer to the TFP frontier, because larger firms can invest more in R&D and bring together a richer set of ideas. On average, the productivity of a firm in the highest quartile of size is about 12 and 22 percent closer to output and value added TFP frontiers relative to a firm in the lowest quartile of size (figure B7.1.3, panel C). Moreover, technology in frontier firms can have positive spillovers for productivity in other firms through agglomeration linkages and cross-border flows of goods, capital, and people. Firms can reap agglomeration benefits by emulating the best production practices and organization structures of "nearby" highly productive firms (Dercon et al. 2004; Syverson 2011). Knowledge is also transferred through contacts with other firms, courtesy of trade, foreign direct investment, and migration (De Loecker 2007; Foster-McGregor, Isaksson, and Kaulich 2016). Firms with a high share of exports are significantly closer to the TFP frontier. A firm in the top quartile of exports, measured as a share of exports in total sales, is about 4 and 6 percent closer to output and value added TFP frontiers relative to a firm in the lowest quartile of exports (figure B7.1.3, panel C). Enabling effective innovation policies appears critical to boosting innovation gains (Cirera and Maloney 2017).

Regulatory environment. Institutions reflect political and legal forces that shape social and economic environments. Regulations and policies affect firms' productivity through incentives to acquire human capital, physical capital, and technology (Bartelsman and Doms 2000; Kouamé and Tapsoba 2018). Firm productivity tends to drop in poorly regulated markets because of adverse incentives and the lack of creative destruction (Goldberg et al. 2010). In contrast, improvements in the business environment are associated with lower distance to TFP frontier, even after controlling for firm characteristics. Conducive regulatory practices—reflected in highest quartile values of the business freedom index—may entail up to 9 percent reduction in the distance to frontier of TFP relative to firms in the lowest quartile. Similarly, high quality governance—proxied by the top quartile estimates of the control of corruption index—is associated with up to 12 percent drop in the distance to TFP frontier relative to firms in the bottom quartile (figure B7.1.3, panel D).

BOX 7.1 Patterns of total factor productivity: A firm-level perspective (continued)

FIGURE B7.1.3 Distance to frontier of TFP, firm characteristics, and regulations

On average, a firm in the technology-intensive industry is significantly closer to the frontier than a firm in the nonelectric machinery, food, and nonmetallic minerals industries. As firms increase their number of employees and ratios of exports to sales, they move closer to the TFP frontier. A conducive business environment supports TFP. Improvements in business freedom and control of corruption tend to reduce the distance to frontier of TFP.

A. Distance to output TFP frontier differential between traditional industries and the technology-intensive industry

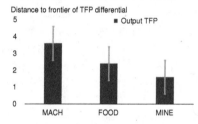

B. Distance to value added TFP frontier differential between traditional industries and the technology-intensive industry

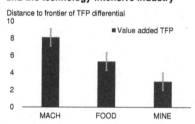

C. Distance to TFP frontier differential between firms in lowest and highest quartile of firm size and exports

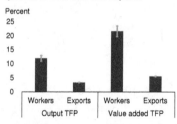

D. Distance to TFP frontier differential between firms in lowest and highest quartile of business environment

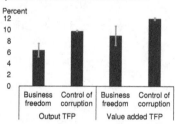

Source: World Bank Enterprise Surveys.

Note: The distance to frontier (DTF) of TFP is computed within each industry (see also table 7C.1), excluding the top 2.5 percent of firms. Sample includes 15,181 firms in 108 EMDEs, including 20 LICs, for the period 2007-17. Based on ordinary least squares regressions of the DTF of TFP (dependent variable) on industry dummies (panels A-C) and business environment quality (panel D), controlling for firm characteristics and using the technology-intensive industry as the base category (annex 7C). EMDEs = emerging market and developing economies; LICs = low-income countries; TFP = total factor productivity.

A.B DTF of TFP differential between traditional industries, such as manufacturing of nonelectric machinery (MACH), food (FOOD), and nonmetallic minerals (MINE), and the technology-intensive industry, controlling for firm characteristics (firm size and exports).

C. Distance to TFP frontier differential between the median firm in the lowest quartile and highest quartile of firms in terms of firm size (number of workers) and exports (share of exports in total sales). A positive DTF differential implies that firms in the lowest quartile in terms of size and exports are far from the frontier relative to firms in the highest quartile. The lowest quartile of exports is zero, as more than half of firms have no exports.

D. Distance to TFP frontier differential between the median firm in the lowest quartile and highest quartile of firms in terms of business freedom and control of corruption index, controlling for firm characteristics. A positive DTF differential implies that firms in the lowest quartile in terms of business freedom and control of corruption are far from the frontier relative to firms in the highest quartile.

**BOX 7.1 Patterns of total factor productivity: A firm-level perspective
(continued)**

Conclusion

The dispersion of firm-level TFP within and across industries in EMDEs is
associated with various firm characteristics. TFP dispersion correlates negatively
with firm size, partly because large firms can invest more in R&D to innovate.
Exports also facilitate the transfer and adoption of new technologies and,
therefore, can help close the gap between laggards and frontier firms. Moreover, a
conducive business climate characterized by greater freedom in entrepreneurship
and less corruption can support TFP improvements. Undertaking policies to
support R&D and innovation, promote exports, combat corruption, and increase
the ease of doing business appears critical to boosting productivity.

---

labor from agriculture to manufacturing and services that occurred in China and
Vietnam during 2003-08, it is estimated that this would lift their overall productivity
growth by 0.1 percentage point a year (and by 1.0 percentage point a year in LICs).

Opportunities in services. Such secular trends as the declining employment share in
manufacturing and the rise of automation may make manufacturing-led development
increasingly challenging (Hallward-Driemeier and Nayyar 2017; Sinha 2016). At the
same time, many high-value-added services sectors such as finance, information and
communication technology, accounting, and legal services provide opportunities for
rapid productivity catch-up growth (Maloney and Nayyar 2018). However,
governments have found it difficult to identify which sectors might play this role. The
complexity and scale of interventions to foster new areas have often challenged their
capacity to manage risks such as political capture by special interests (Hsieh and Klenow
2009).

Reduce barriers to reallocations. Supporting the efficient allocation of resources through
the removal of market distortions can yield significant productivity gains—some
estimates suggest that productivity in firms in China and India may be 30 to 60 percent
lower than it could be if misallocation of capital and labor across sectors were eliminated
(Hsieh and Klenow 2009). Reducing regulatory complexity and burdens, as well as
reassessing the role of state-owned enterprises, can improve the ability of new firms to
enter and compete in high-productivity sectors. Reducing subsidies, including energy
subsidies, can also reduce the misallocation of resources into low-productivity and
inefficient energy-intensive sectors. Many high-productivity manufacturing and service
sectors activities are becoming increasingly skill intensive. Significant investment in
human capital, including at the tertiary education level, would increase the ability of
workers to be mobile across sectors and to work with new and more productive

technologies (chapter 2). Firms in EMDEs can update and improve their management styles and benefit from technology spillovers by participating in global value chains (box 7.1). Furthermore, removing barriers to migration can help facilitate structural transformation.[18]

Future research. This chapter's findings point to three new directions for future research. First, the data set used would allow a more granular assessment of the impact of the GFC, other major economic shocks, and country-specific recessions on the pace of labor reallocation and within-sector productivity growth. This could include differentiation between the nine sectors by their sensitivity to macroeconomic or financial stress. Second, the data set could be used to assess whether countries that "leap-frogged" the manufacturing sector benefited from stronger productivity growth over long periods or during times of economic stress. Third, future research could tackle the endogeneity of sectoral reallocation. For example, an improvement in agricultural productivity could allow a reduction in agriculture's share of employment and facilitate between-sector productivity growth. In this case the causal contribution of agriculture productivity growth to overall productivity growth could be found to be larger (and that of sectoral reallocation smaller) than simple growth accounting suggests.

ANNEX 7A **Data and methodology**

Data. The database consists of sectoral and aggregate labor productivity statistics for 103 countries and nine sectors covering the period up to 2017 (tables 7A.1 and 7A.2). Compared with the literature using nine-sector data, it employs a large and diverse sample of countries (table 7A.3). The database combines data from World Bank World Development Indicators, the Organisation for Economic Co-operation and Development's Structural Analysis Database, KLEMS, the Groningen Growth Development Center (GGDC) database (de Vries, Timmer, and de Vries 2015), and the Expanded Africa Sector Database (EASD; Mensah and Szirmai 2018) for value added data and employment. The Asian Productivity Organization's Productivity Database, United Nations data, the International Labour Organization's ILOSTAT, and national sources are used for supplementary purposes. Following Wong (2006), local currency value added is converted to U.S. dollars using 2011 PPP exchange rate obtained from Penn World Table for the international comparison of productivity levels.[19]

---

[18] Restuccia, Yang, and Zhu (2008) argue that obstacles to migration reduce labor flows out of agriculture. Artuc, Lederman, and Porto (2015) estimate, from data for eight major sectors, that the labor mobility costs of labor market frictions are larger in EMDEs than those in advanced economies. Bryan and Morten (2019), using Indonesian data, show that reducing migration costs to the U.S. level, a high-mobility benchmark, leads to a 7-percentage-point increase in productivity growth.

[19] Van Biesebroeck (2009) builds an expenditure-based sector-specific PPP in Organisation for Economic Co-operation and Development countries, using detailed price data.

Shift-share analysis. Following Wong (2006), this chapter employs a shift-share-analysis that decomposes aggregate labor productivity into the growth within a sector and shifts between sectors:

$$
\underbrace{\frac{\Delta y}{y}}_{\substack{Aggregate \\ productivity \\ growth}} = \underbrace{\sum_{j=1}^{k} \frac{Y_j}{Y} \left[\frac{\Delta y_j}{y_j} \right]}_{\substack{Within \\ sectoral \\ effect}} + \underbrace{\underbrace{\sum_{j=1}^{k} \left[\frac{y_j}{y} \right] \Delta s_j}_{\substack{Static \\ sectoral \\ effect}} + \underbrace{\sum_{j=1}^{k} \left[\frac{y_i}{y} \right] \left[\frac{\Delta y_j}{y_j} \right] \Delta s_j}_{\substack{Dynamic \\ sectoral \\ effect}}}_{\substack{Between \\ sectoral \\ effect}},
$$

where y is aggregate labor productivity, y_j is labor productivity of sector j, Y_j is initial value added of sector j, s_j is the employment share of sector j. Between sector effects are driven by the change in employment share. They are further decomposed into those that are due to the reallocation of sources to sectors with higher productivity levels (*static sectoral effect*) and those due to reallocation toward sectors with higher productivity growth (*dynamic sectoral effect*).

TABLE 7A.1 **Sample coverage (nine-sector labor productivity)**

Advanced economies			
Economy	Group	Period	Source
Australia	AEs	1975-2018	OECD/APO/ILO
Austria	AEs	1970-2017	OECD/KLEMS/ILO
Belgium	AEs	1975-2017	OECD/ILO
Canada	AEs	1970-2018	OECD/ILO/World Bank estimates
Cyprus	AEs	1995-2018	OECD/KLEMS/ILO
Czech Republic	AEs	1993-2017	OECD/ILO
Denmark	AEs	1970-2017	OECD/ILO
Estonia	AEs	1995-2017	OECD/KLEMS
Finland	AEs	1975-2017	OECD/ILO
France	AEs	1970-2017	OECD/ILO
Germany	AEs	1970-2017	OECD/ILO
Greece	AEs	1995-2017	OECD/ILO

TABLE 7A.1 Sample coverage (nine-sector labor productivity) *(continued)*

Advanced economies			
Economy	Group	Period	Source
Hong Kong SAR, China	AEs	1974-2018	GGDC/APO/Haver/ILO
Iceland	AEs	1994-2018	OECD/Haver/World Bank estimates
Ireland	AEs	1995-2018	OECD/ILO
Italy	AEs	1970-2017	OECD/GGDC/ILO
Korea, Rep.	AEs	1963-2018	OECD/GGDC/ILO
Japan	AEs	1973-2017	OECD/Haver/ILO
Latvia	AEs	1995-2017	OECD/KLEMS/ILO
Lithuania	AEs	1995-2018	OECD/ILO
Luxembourg	AEs	1970-2018	OECD/KLEMS/ILO
Netherlands	AEs	1970-2017	OECD/KLEMS/ILO
New Zealand	AEs	1990-2018	OECD/Haver/World Bank estimates
Norway	AEs	1970-2017	OECD/ILO
Portugal	AEs	1995-2017	OECD/ILO
Singapore	AEs	1970-2018	GGDC/APO
Slovakia	AEs	1995-2017	OECD
Slovenia	AEs	1995-2018	OECD/ILO
Spain	AEs	1970-2018	OECD/KLEMS/ILO
Sweden	AEs	1970-2018	OECD/KLEMS/ILO
Switzerland	AEs	1992-2018	OECD/ILO
Taiwan	AEs	1963-2018	GGDC/APO/ILO/National source
United Kingdom	AEs	1960-2017	OECD/GGDC/ILO
United States	AEs	1950-2017	OECD/KLEMS/ILO

Emerging market and developing economies			
Economy	Group	Period	Source
China	EAP	1952-2017	GGDC/APO/Haver/ILO/World Bank estimates
Fiji	EAP	1977-2018	APO/UN/ILO/National source
Indonesia	EAP	1971-2018	GGDC/APO/UN/ILO/National source
Lao PDR	EAP	1990-2017	APO/UN/ILO
Malaysia	EAP	1975-2018	GGDC/APO/UN/ILO/National source
Mongolia	EAP	1970-2018	APO/UN/ILO/National source
Philippines	EAP	1971-2018	GGDC/APO/UN/ILO/National source
Thailand	EAP	1960-2018	GGDC/APO/UN/ILO/National source
Vietnam	EAP	1990-2017	APO/UN/ILO
Azerbaijan	ECA	2001-2018	ILO/National source
Bulgaria	ECA	1995-2017	ILO/National source
Croatia	ECA	1995-2017	ILO/National source
Georgia	ECA	2003-2018	ILO/National source
Hungary	ECA	1995-2017	ILO/National source
Montenegro	ECA	2000-2018	ILO/National source
Poland	ECA	1995-2018	ILO/National source
Romania	ECA	1995-2018	ILO/National source
Russian Federation	ECA	1995-2018	KLEMS/Haver/ILO/National source
Serbia	ECA	1995-2018	ILO/National source
Turkey	ECA	1988-2018	OECD/APO/ILO/National source
Argentina	LAC	1990-2018	GGDC/KLEMS/WDI/Haver
Belize	LAC	1991-2018	ILO/National source
Bolivia	LAC	1991-2018	ILO/National source
Brazil	LAC	1970-2018	GGDC/KLEMS/Haver/ILO/National source
Chile	LAC	1950-2018	GGDC/UN/ILO/National source
Colombia	LAC	1950-2018	GGDC/KLEMS/UN/ILO/National source

TABLE 7A.1 Sample coverage (nine-sector labor productivity) *(continued)*

Emerging market and developing economies			
Economy	**Group**	**Period**	**Source**
Costa Rica	LAC	1950-2018	OECD/GGDC/ILO/National source
Dominican Republic	LAC	1991-2018	ILO/National source
Ecuador	LAC	1991-2017	ILO/National source
Guatemala	LAC	2001-2018	ILO/National source
Honduras	LAC	1991-2018	ILO/National source
Jamaica	LAC	1993-2018	ILO/National source
Mexico	LAC	1950-2018	GGDC/KLEMS/ILO/National source
Paraguay	LAC	1991-2017	ILO/National source
Saint Lucia	LAC	1991-2018	ILO/National source
St. Vincent and the Grenadines	LAC	1991-2018	ILO/National source
Uruguay	LAC	1997-2018	ILO/National source
Algeria	MNA	1999-2018	ILO/National source
Egypt, Arab Rep.	MNA	1960-2018	GGDC/Haver/ILO/National source
Iran, Islamic Rep.	MNA	1991-2017	ILO/National source
Jordan	MNA	1992-2018	ILO/National source
Morocco	MNA	1970-2018	GGDC/Haver/ILO
Qatar	MNA	1986-2018	APO/UN/ILO/National source
Bangladesh	SAR	1991-2018	ILO/National source
India	SAR	1960-2017	GGDC/APO/ILO/National source
Nepal	SAR	2001-2018	ILO/National source
Pakistan	SAR	1970-2018	APO/UN/ILO/National source
Sri Lanka	SAR	1971-2018	APO/UN/ILO/National source
Angola	SSA	2002-2017	ILO/National source
Botswana	SSA	1964-2017	EASD/ILO/National source
Burkina Faso	SSA	1970-2017	EASD/ILO/World Bank estimates
Cameroon	SSA	1965-2018	EASD/ILO/Haver
Eswatini	SSA	1991-2018	UN/ILO/National source
Ethiopia	SSA	1961-2017	EASD/ILO/National source
Ghana	SSA	1960-2018	EASD/ILO/National source
Kenya	SSA	1969-2018	EASD/ILO/National source
Lesotho	SSA	1970-2018	EASD/ILO/National source
Malawi	SSA	1966-2017	EASD/ILO/World Bank estimates
Mauritius	SSA	1970-2018	EASD/ILO/National source
Mozambique	SSA	1970-2018	EASD/ILO/National source
Namibia	SSA	1960-2018	EASD/ILO/National source
Nigeria	SSA	1960-2018	EASD/ILO/National source
Rwanda	SSA	1970-2018	EASD/ILO/National source
Senegal	SSA	1970-2017	EASD/ILO/World Bank estimates
Sierra Leone	SSA	2001-2018	ILO/National source
South Africa	SSA	1960-2018	EASD/ILO/National source
Tanzania	SSA	1960-2017	EASD/ILO/National source
Uganda	SSA	1990-2018	EASD/ILO/National source
Zambia	SSA	1965-2018	EASD/Haver/ILO

Source: World Bank.
Note: APO = Asian Productivity Organization; EASD = Expanded Africa Sector Database; GGDC = Groningen Growth Development Center database (de Vries, Timmer, and de Vries 2015); Haver = Haver Analytics; ILO International Labour Organization ILOSTAT; KLEMS = World KLEMS (Russian Federation, European Union, and Latin America and the Caribbean); OECD = Organisation for Economic Co-operation and Development Structural Analysis Database; AEs = advanced economies; EAP = East Asia and Pacific; ECA = Europe and Central Asia; LAC = Latin America and the Caribbean; MNA = Middle East and North Africa; SAR = South Asia; SSA = Sub-Saharan Africa.

TABLE 7A.2 **Nine-sector categories**

Sector	Description
1.Agriculture	Agriculture, forestry, and fishing
2.Mining	Mining and quarrying
3.Manufacturing	Manufacturing
4.Utilities	Electricity, gas, steam and air conditioning supply
5.Construction	Construction
6.Trade services	Wholesale and retail trade; repair of motor vehicles and motorcycles; Accommodation and food service activities
7.Transport services	Transportation and storage; Information and communication
8.Financial and business services	Financial and insurance activities; Real estate activities; Professional, scientific and technical activities; Administrative and support service activities
9.Other services	Public administration and defense; compulsory social security; Education; Human health and social work activities; Arts, entertainment and recreation; Other service activities; Activities of households as employers; undifferentiated goods- and services-producing activities of households for own use; Activities of extraterritorial organizations and bodies

Sources: Asian Productivity Organization; Expanded Africa Sector Database; Groningen Growth Development Center; International Labour Organization; KLEMS; national sources; Organisation for Economic Co-operation and Development; United Nations; World Bank.

TABLE 7A.3 **Comparison with other studies using nine-sector labor productivity**

	Period	Country coverage	Group coverage
This study	2003-2017	103	34 AEs 69 EMDEs 9 LICs
	1995-2017	94	34 AEs 60 EMDEs 7 LICs
	1975-2017	54	21 AEs 33 EMDEs 6 LICs
IMF (2018)	1965-2010	62	19 AEs 43EMDEs 2 LICs
	(1965-2015)	(39)	(19 AEs 20 EMDEs 0 LICs)
McMillan, Rodrik, and Verduzco-Gallo (2014)	1990-2005	38	13 AEs 25 EMDEs 2 LICs
Diao, McMillan, and Rodrik (2017)	2000-2010	39	13 AEs 26 EMDEs 3 LICs

Source: World Bank.
Note: AEs = advanced economies; EMDEs = emerging market and developing economies; LICs = low-income countries.

ANNEX 7B Marginal productivity gap

Large productivity gaps do not necessarily imply inefficiencies in the allocation of resources across sectors or potential gains from the reallocation of workers. Even if average productivity were the same across sectors, there could still be gains from reallocation if the labor shares of value added vary across sectors. Under the assumption that labor markets are competitive, efficiency implies the equalization of marginal labor productivities across sectors (Fuglie et al. 2020; Sinha 2016; Vollrath 2009). That is, employment should shift across sectors until the marginal productivity of hiring an extra employee is equalized. If marginal labor productivities differ significantly, there can be gains from sectoral reallocation.

FIGURE 7B.1 **Marginal productivity gaps**

Marginal productivity gaps are broadly similar to average productivity gaps. Negative gaps in agriculture, construction, and trade services, along with positive gaps in the finance and utilities sectors may be signs of allocative inefficiencies. They suggest that reforms to increase intersectoral mobility might substantially improve aggregate labor productivity and incomes.

A. Marginal productivity gap: Advanced economies and EMDEs

B. Average productivity gap: Advanced economies and EMDEs

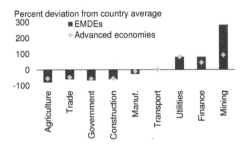
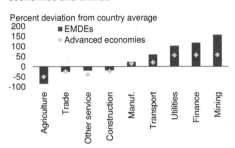

Sources: Asian Productivity Organization; Expanded Africa Sector Database; Groningen Growth Development Center; International Labour Organization; KLEMS; national sources; Organisation for Economic Co-operation and Development; United Nations; World Bank.
Note: EMDEs = emerging market and developing economies.
A. Marginal productivity is calculated by the average labor productivity multiplied by the value added labor share. Setting distortions in transport services at zero gives the relative distortion in eight sectors, although transport service is not assumed to be undistorted.
B. Average labor productivity is value added per worker based on 2017 data. "Finance" includes business services; "Other service" includes government and personal services. Based on 2017 data.

Marginal productivity gaps, "distortions," are calculated as average productivity multiplied by the estimated value added labor shares following Sinha (2016).[20] To compute these gaps across sectors, the transport services sector is used as the reference sector relative to which marginal productivity gaps are normalized to zero for that sector (this does not imply that the transport service sector itself is undistorted).[21] The calculated gaps are indicative of (relative) distortions: a negative value of the marginal productivity gap can be interpreted as a subsidy or support to that sector, whereas a positive gap reflects barriers such as taxes, entry regulations, and access to credit.

The marginal productivity gaps for the agriculture, construction, trade, government services, and manufacturing sectors are negative (figure 7B.1). This in part likely reflects protections such as price interventions in the agricultural sector, which have often been large—for example, in LAC (Üngör 2017). The manufacturing sector in EMDEs too has been supported in many countries with tax concessions, relatively low tariffs, price controls, regulations on foreign trade, and foreign currency regulations (Tybout 2000). Finance and utilities are quite heavily regulated. Overall, the estimated marginal productivity gaps are broadly in line with the average productivity gaps, and larger in

---

[20] Based on the first-order condition from the firm's optimization.

[21] This normalization is done purely in order to simplify the quantitative results. The allocations remain independent of any normalization.

EMDEs than in advanced economies. Furthermore, the distortions in the finance sector in LICs are particularly large. These findings are in line with the literature.[22]

ANNEX 7C Firm TFP data, estimates, and methodology

Data. The World Bank Enterprise Surveys (ES) collect firm-level data from surveys conducted with more than 129,000 firms in 127 countries, including 71,000 manufacturing firms, over a period spanning 2007 to 2017. This annex uses revenue TFP constructed for 15,181 manufacturing firms for which output, input, and firm characteristics data are available (Cusolito et al. 2018). The sample covers 108 EMDEs.

TFP estimates. The underlying assumption is that sector-specific elasticities of output with respect to inputs are the same across economies in a given income group.[23] Firm-level revenue TFP estimates are computed in each sector s by pooling all firms i across economies c.[24] The weighted regressions, using survey weights, exploit the log transform of a Cobb-Douglas production function and, therefore, TFP estimates can assume negative and positive values. The ES data set provides two estimates of firm-level TFP, output TFP and value added TFP.

Output TFP is estimated as

$$TFPR_{sci}^{YKNM} = ln(Y_{sci}) - \left[\begin{array}{l} \alpha_{s,K} \ ln(K_{sci}) + \alpha_{s,N} \ ln(N_{sci}) + \alpha_{s,M} \ ln(M_{sci}) \\ + interaction \ \& \ quadratic \ terms \end{array} \right].$$

Value added TFP is estimated as

$$TFPR_{sci}^{VAKN} = ln(VA_{sci}) - \left[\begin{array}{l} \alpha_{s,K} \ ln(K_{sci}) + \alpha_{s,N} \ ln(N_{sci}) \\ + interaction \ \& \ quadratic \ terms \end{array} \right],$$

where Y is the firm's output, K is the input capital, N is the input labor, M is intermediate materials, and VA is the firm's value added (Cusolito et al. 2018).[25] Two-

---

[22] Vollrath (2009) shows that the ratio of marginal product of labor in industry to that of agriculture ranges from a low of a low of 1.67 in Australia to a high of 16.84 in Kenya. Moreover, Dennis and Işcan (2011) find that the rate of structural change (that is, the reallocation of labor from low- to high-productivity sectors) is slow in countries with large distortions in agriculture; and Restuccia, Yang, and Zhu (2008) find that wage wedges, measured as differences in average wage across sectors, significantly slow the process of structural change.

[23] This assumption implies that firm-level TFP are not directly comparable to aggregate TFP from macro panel data.

[24] Firms are grouped in two-digit ISIC code industries for the estimation. To allow for comparison, values (collected in local currency units) are converted to U.S. dollars using the corresponding exchange rate and then deflated using the 2009 gross domestic product deflator for the United States [$LCU/(FX \ x \ defl_{2009}^{US})$].

[25] The value of (log) intermediate inputs (materials, electricity) is subtracted from the (log) output to obtain the (log) value added. Thus, output and value added TFP are the same when elasticities of intermediate inputs with respect to output ($\alpha_{s,M}$ in equation 1) is equal to one, but different otherwise. Interaction and quadratic terms are included to control for possible nonlinearities. Because of the lack of information on self-reported inputs in the World Bank ES data set, TFP values are not available for some firms in the manufacturing sector. Extreme observations are also removed in the upper tail of the firm-level TFP distribution in Sub-Saharan Africa.

digit ISIC codes are used to define 15 industries (table 7C.1). Firms in electrical machinery, precision equipment, electronics, information, and communication sectors are grouped into a single technology-intensive industry denoted by TINT.

Measurement challenges. TFP captures the efficiency in production not explained by shifts in inputs—capital, labor, and intermediate materials. At least four key issues arise when estimating TFP at the firm level. First, a large negative productivity shock may lead a firm to reduce input quantities (simultaneity) or to liquidate (selection).[26] Basic ordinary least squares estimates are therefore biased due to the potential correlation between inputs and productivity. To alleviate the endogeneity problem of input choices and selection bias, existing techniques use firm-specific fixed effects (Pavcnik 2002), instrumental variables (Wooldridge 2009), or two-stage estimation schemes with auxiliary variables (Imrohoroğlu and Tuzel 2014; Levinsohn and Petrin 2003; Olley and Pakes 1996; Satpathy, Chatterjee, and Mahakud 2017). Second, common firm-level TFP measures are based on revenues and line item costs rather than physical outputs and inputs. Revenue-based TFP (TFPR) measures conflate productivity and market power, especially in a context of imperfect competition in input markets (Andrews, Criscuolo, and Gal 2016; Foster, Haltiwanger, and Syverson 2008). TFPR estimates are biased when output prices are correlated with inputs choice. Markups-corrected or physical TFP (TFPQ) estimates, obtained by deflating firm-level sales by corresponding prices, can help purge the confounding price effects (Cusolito and Maloney 2018; Van Beveren 2012). Third, a given firm may produce various products using distinct technologies (Bernard, Redding, and Schott 2010; Goldberg et al. 2010). Thus, specifying a single production function for a multiple-product firm is rather restrictive and yields biased TFP estimates. Using granular product-level data, if available, to back out firm-level TFP can help account for the diversity in a firm's production mix. Fourth, young, small, and less productive establishments can be underrepresented in the sample of firms due to a lack of information. A limited sample representativeness may distort the distribution of firm-level TFP and restrict what can be inferred from the evidence (Andrews, Criscuolo, and Gal 2016). Particular caution is warranted when interpreting the evidence of TFP dispersion among firms.

Methodology. The fitted specification is

$$DTF_i^g = \theta_0 + \sum_g \rho_g I(g \in G \setminus \{ref\}) + \sum_{j=1}^J \gamma_j X_{ij} + \upsilon_i$$

where DTF_i^g is the distance to frontier of TFP for firm i in industry g, θ_0 stands for the constant term, $ref = TINT$ is the reference industry, and coefficients ρ_g are interpreted relatively to the reference group. X_{ij} is firm i's j^{th} characteristic such as gross domestic product per capita (in 2009 U.S. dollars per worker), size (number of employees), exports (as a proportion of total sales), and business climate (control of corruption, business freedom). The error term is denoted by υ_i.

---

[26] Selection and simultaneity problems occur when a firm's decision regarding continuation of operations and quantities of inputs is guided by its productivity.

TABLE 7C.1 **Definitions of industries**

Two-digit ISIC	Label	Description	Sample
15 and 16	FOOD	Manufacturing of food products and beverages, and manufacturing of tobacco products	3,552
17	TEXT	Manufacturing of textiles	1,074
18	APPA	Manufacture of wearing apparel; dressing and dyeing of fur	1,912
19	LEAT	Tanning and dressing of leather; manufacture of luggage, handbags, saddlery, harness and footwear	397
20	WOOD	Manufacturing of wood and of products of wood and cork, except furniture; manufacturing of articles of straw and plaiting materials	368
21	PAPE	Manufacturing of paper and paper products	132
22, 30, 31, 32, and 33	TINT= MEDI +OFFI	Publishing, printing and reproduction of recorded media, Manufacturing of office, accounting and computing machinery, manufacturing of electrical machinery and apparatus n.e.c., manufacturing of radio, television and communication equipment and apparatus, and manufacturing of medical, precision and optical instruments, watches and clocks	177
23 and 24	CHEM	Manufacturing of coke, refined petroleum products and nuclear fuel, and manufacturing of chemicals and chemical products	1,250
25	RUBB	Manufacturing of rubber and plastics products	1,174
26	MINE	Manufacturing of other nonmetallic mineral products	1,007
27	META	Manufacturing of basic metals	475
28	FABM	Manufacturing of fabricated metal products, except machinery and equipment	1,519
29	MACH	Manufacturing of machinery and equipment not elsewhere classified	844
34 and 35	MOTO	Manufacturing of motor vehicles, trailers and semi-trailers, and manufacturing of other transport equipment	367
36	FURN	Manufacturing of furniture; manufacturing not elsewhere classified	933
		Total	15,181

Source: Cusolito et al. (2018); World Bank Enterprise Surveys.
Note: ISIC = International Standard Industrial Classification of all Economic Activities.

References

Alvarez-Cuadrado, F., and M. Poschke. 2011. "Structural Change Out of Agriculture: Labor Push versus Labor Pull." *American Economic Journal: Macroeconomics* 3 (3): 127–58.

Andrews, D., C. Criscuolo, and P. Gal. 2016. "The Best versus the Rest: The Global Productivity Slowdown, Divergence across Firms and the Role of Public Policy." OECD Productivity Working Paper 05, Organization for Economic Co-operation and Development, Paris.

Araujo, J. T., E. Vostroknutova, and K. Wacker. 2017. "Productivity Growth in Latin America and the Caribbean: Exploring the Macro-Micro Linkages." Discussion Paper 19, World Bank, Washington, DC.

Artuc, E., D. Lederman, and G. Porto. 2015. "A Mapping of Labor Mobility Costs in the Developing World." *Journal of International Economics* 95 (1): 28–41.

Atkin, D., A. K. Khandelwal, and A. Osman. 2017. "Exporting and Firm Performance: Evidence from a Randomized Experiment." *Quarterly Journal of Economics* 132 (2): 551–615.

Bahar, D. 2016. "Using Firm-Level Data to Study Growth and Dispersion in Total Factor Productivity." Brookings and Center for International Development, Washington, DC.

Bahar, D. 2018. "The Middle Productivity Trap: Dynamics of Productivity Dispersion." *Economics Letters* 167: 60–66.

Barrero, J. M., N. Bloom, and S. J. Davis. 2020. "COVID-19 Is Also a Reallocation Shock." *SSRN Electronic Journal.* SSRN: https://ssrn.com/abstract=3592953.

Barrett, C. B., L. Christiaensen, M. Sheahan, and A. Shimeles. 2017. "On the Structural Transformation of Rural Africa." *Journal of African Economies* 26 (1): 11–35.

Bartelsman, E. J., and M. Doms. 2000. "Understanding Productivity: Lessons from Longitudinal Microdata." *Journal of Economic Literature* 38 (3): 569–94.

Baumol, W. J. 1967. "Macroeconomics of Unbalanced Growth: The Anatomy of Urban Crisis." *American Economic Review* 57 (3): 415–26.

Bernard, A. B., and C. I. Jones. 1996. "Technology and Convergence Author." *Economic Journal* 106 (437): 1037–44.

Bernard, A. B., S. J. Redding, and P. K. Schott. 2010. "Multiple-Product Firms and Product Switching." *American Economic Review* 100 (1): 70–97.

Bloom, N., A. Mahajan, D. McKenzie, and J. Roberts. 2010. "Why Do Firms in Developing Countries Have Low Productivity?" *American Economic Review* 100 (2): 619–23.

Boppart, T. 2014. "Structural Change and the Kaldor Facts in a Growth Model with Relative Price Effects and Non-Gorman Preferences." *Econometrica* 82 (6): 2167–96.

Bosworth, B. P., and J. E. Triplett. 2003. "Productivity Measurement Issues in Services Industries: 'Baumol's Disease' Has Been Cured." *Economic Policy Review* 9 (3): 23–33.

Bosworth, B. P., and J. E. Triplett. 2007. "The Early 21st Century U.S. Productivity Expansion Is Still in Services." *International Productivity Monitor* 14: 3–19.

Bryan, G., and M. Morten. 2019. "The Aggregate Productivity Effects of Internal Migration: Evidence from Indonesia." *Journal of Political Economy* 127 (5): 2229–68.

Brynjolfsson, E., and L. Hitt. 1995. "Information Technology as a Factor of Production: The Role of Differences among Firms." *Economics of Innovation and New Technology* 3 (3–4): 183–99.

Buera, F. J., and J. P. Kaboski. 2009. "Can Traditional Theories of Structural Change Fit The Data?" *Journal of the European Economic Association* 7 (2–3): 469–77.

Caselli, F. 2005. "Accounting for Cross-Country Income Differences." In *Handbook of Economic Growth*, edited by Philippe Aghion and Steven N. Durlauf, 679–741. Amsterdam: Elsevier.

Cette, G., S. Corde, and R. Lecat. 2018. "Firm-Level Productivity Dispersion and Convergence." *Economics Letters* 166: 76–78.

Chen, C. 2017. "Untitled Land, Occupational Choice, and Agricultural Productivity." *American Economic Journal: Macroeconomics* 9 (4): 91–121.

Chevalier, P. A., R. Lecat, and N. Oulton. 2012. "Convergence of Firm-Level Productivity, Globalisation and Information Technology: Evidence from France." *Economics Letters* 116 (2): 244–46.

Chodorow-Reich, G., and J. Wieland. 2020. "Secular Labor Reallocation and Business Cycles." *Journal of Political Economy* 128 (6): 2245–87.

Cirera, X., and W. F. Maloney. 2017. *The Innovation Paradox: Developing-Country Capabilities and the Unrealized Promise of Technological Catch-Up*. Washington, DC: World Bank.

Cusolito, A. P., D. C. Francis, N. Karalashvili, and J. R. Meza. 2018. "Firm Level Productivity Estimates." Methodological Note, World Bank, Washington, DC.

Cusolito, A. P., and W. F. Maloney. 2018. *Productivity Revisited: Shifting Paradigms in Analysis and Policy*. Washington, DC: World Bank.

Dall'Olio, A., M. Iootty, N. Kanehira, and F. Saliola. 2014. "Enterprise Productivity a Three-Speed Europe." ECB Working Paper 1748, European Central Bank, Frankfurt.

De Loecker, J. 2007. "Do Exports Generate Higher Productivity? Evidence from Slovenia." *Journal of International Economics* 73 (1): 69–98.

de Vries, G. J., A. A. Erumban, M. P. Timmer, I. Voskoboynikov, and H. X. Wu. 2012. "Deconstructing the BRICs: Structural Transformation and Aggregate Productivity Growth." *Journal of Comparative Economics* 40 (2): 211–27.

de Vries, G., M. Timmer, and K. de Vries. 2015. "Structural Transformation in Africa: Static Gains, Dynamic Losses." *Journal of Development Studies* 51 (6): 674–88.

Dennis, B. N., and T. B. Işcan. 2011. "Agricultural Distortions, Structural Change, and Economic Growth: A Cross-Country Analysis." *American Journal of Agricultural Economics* 93 (3): 881–901.

Dercon, S., and L. Christiaensen. 2011. "Consumption Risk, Technology Adoption and Poverty Traps: Evidence from Ethiopia." *Journal of Development Economics* 96 (2): 159–73.

Dercon, S., M. Fafchamps, C. Pattillo, R. Oostendorp, J. Willem Gunning, P. Collier, A. Zeufack, et al. 2004. "Do African Manufacturing Firms Learn from Exporting?" *Journal of Development Studies* 40 (3): 115–41.

Diao, X., M. McMillan, and D. Rodrik. 2017. "The Recent Growth Boom in Developing Economies: A Structural Change Perspective." NBER Working Paper 23132, National Bureau of Economic Research, Cambridge, MA.

Di Mauro, F., B. Mottironi, G. Ottaviano, and A. Zona-Mattioli. 2018. "Living with Lower Productivity Growth: Impact on Exports." Working Paper 18-10, Peterson Institute for International Economics, Washington, DC.

Duarte, M., and D. Restuccia. 2007. "The Structural Transformation and Aggregate Productivity in Portugal." *Portuguese Economic Journal* 6 (1): 23–46.

Duarte, M., and D. Restuccia. 2010. "The Role of the Structural Transformation in Aggregate Productivity." *Quarterly Journal of Economics* 125 (February): 129–73.

Duernecker, G., B. Herrendorf, and A. Valentinyi. 2017. "Structural Change within the Service Sector and the Future of Baumol's Disease." CEPR Discussion Paper DP12467, Center for Economic Policy Research, London.

Eichengreen, B., and P. Gupta. 2013. "The Two Waves of Service-Sector Growth." *Oxford Economic Papers* 65 (1): 96–123.

Fernald, J. 2015. "Productivity and Potential Output before, during, and after the Great Recession." Working Paper Series 01-51, Federal Reserve Bank of San Francisco.

Foster, L., C. Grim, and J. Haltiwanger. 2016. "Reallocation in the Great Recession: Cleansing or Not?" *Journal of Labor Economics* 34 (S1): S293–331.

Foster, L., J. Haltiwanger, and C. Syverson. 2008. "Reallocation, Firm Turnover, and Efficiency: Selection on Productivity or Profitability?" *American Economic Review* 98(1): 394–425.

Foster-McGregor, N., A. Isaksson, and F. Kaulich. 2016. "Importing, Productivity and Absorptive Capacity in Sub-Saharan African Manufacturing and Services Firms." *Open Economies Review* 27 (1): 87–117.

Fuglie, K., M. Gautam, A. Goyal, and W. F. Maloney. 2020. *Harvesting Prosperity: Technology and Productivity Growth in Agriculture*. Washington, DC: World Bank.

Goldberg, P. K., A. K. Khandelwal, N. Pavcnik, and P. Topalova. 2010. "Multi-Product Firms and Product Turnover in the Developing World: Evidence from India." *Review of Economic Statistics* 92 (4): 1042–49.

Gollin, D., D. Lagakos, and M. E. Waugh. 2014. "The Agricultural Productivity Gap." *Quarterly Journal of Economics* 129 (2): 939–93.

Goñi, E., and W. F. Maloney. 2017. "Why Don't Poor Countries Do R&D? Varying Rates of Factor Returns across the Development Process." *European Economic Review* 94 (May): 126–47.

Hale, T., A. Petherick, T. Phillips, and S. Webster. 2020. "Variation in Government Responses to COVID-19." BSG Working Paper 2020/31, Blavatnik School of Government, University of Oxford, U.K.

Hallward-Driemeier, M., and G. Nayyar. 2017. *Trouble in the Making? The Future of Manufacturing-Led Development*. Washington, DC: World Bank.

Helble, M., L. Q. Trinh, T. T. Le, T. Long, and T. T. Le. 2019. "Sectoral and Skill Contributions to Labor Productivity in Asia." ADBI Working Paper 929, Asian Development Bank Institute, Manila.

Herrendorf, B., R. Rogerson, and Á. Valentinyi. 2013. "Two Perspectives on Preferences and Structural." *American Economic Review* 103 (7): 2752–89.

Herrendorf, B., R. Rogerson, and Á. Valentinyi. 2014. "Growth and Structural Transformation." In *Handbook of Economic Growth Vol. 2*, edited by P. Aghion and S. Durlauf, 855–941. Amsterdam: Elsevier.

Hicks, J. H., M. Kleemans, N. Y. Li, E. Miguel, D. Albouy, J. Alvarez, L. Beaman, et al. 2017. "Reevaluating Agricultural Productivity Gaps with Longitudinal Microdata." NBER Working Paper 23253, National Bureau of Economic Research, Cambridge, MA.

Hsieh, C.-T., and P. J. Klenow. 2009. "Misallocation and Manufactring TFP in China and India." *Quarterly Journal of Economics* 124 (4): 1403–48.

IMF (International Monetary Fund). 2018. *World Economic Outlook: Cyclical Upswing, Structural Change*. Washington, DC: International Monetary Fund.

Imrohoroğlu, A., S. Imrohoroğlu, and M. Üngör. 2014. "Agricultural Productivity and Growth in Turkey." *Macroeconomic Dynamics* 18 (5): 998–1017.

Imrohoroğlu, A., and S. Tuzel. 2014. "Firm-Level Productivity, Risk, and Return." *Management Science* 60 (8): 2073–90.

Jorgenson, D. W., and M. P. Timmer. 2011. "Structural Change in Advanced Nations: A New Set of Stylised Facts." *Scandinavian Journal of Economics* 113 (1): 1–29.

Kouamé, W. A., and S. J. Tapsoba. 2018. "Structural Reforms and Firms' Productivity: Evidence from Developing Countries." IMF Working Paper 18/63, International Monetary Fund, Washington, DC.

Levchenko, A., and J. Zhang. 2016. "The Evolution of Comparative Advantage: Measurement and Welfare Implications." *Journal of Monetary Economics* 78 (April): 96–111.

Levinsohn, J., and A. Petrin. 2003. "Estimating Production Function Using Inputs to Control for Unobservables." *Review of Economic Studies* 70: 317–41.

Lowder, S. K., J. Skoet, and T. Raney. 2016. "The Number, Size, and Distribution of Farms, Smallholder Farms, and Family Farms Worldwide." *World Development* 87 (November): 16–29.

Maloney, W. F., and G. Nayyar. 2018. "Industrial Policy, Information, and Government Capacity." *The World Bank Research Observer* 33 (2): 189–217.

Martins, P. M. G. 2019. "Structural Change: Pace, Patterns and Determinants." *Review of Development Economics* 23 (1): 1–32.

Matsuyama, K. 2009. "Structural Change in an Interdependent World: A Global View of Manufacturing Decline." *Journal of the European Economic Association* 7 (2–3): 478–86.

McCaig, B., and N. Pavcnik. 2013. "Moving out of Agriculture: Structural Change in Vietnam." NBER Working Paper 19616, National Bureau of Economic Research, Cambridge, MA.

McCullough, E. B. 2017. "Labor Productivity and Employment Gaps in Sub-Saharan Africa." *Food Policy* 67 (February): 133–52.

McMillan, M., D. Rodrik, and Í. Verduzco-Gallo. 2014. "Globalization, Structural Change, and Productivity Growth, with an Update on Africa." *World Development* 63 (2014): 11–32.

Mensah, E. B., and A. Szirmai. 2018. "Africa Sector Database (ASD): Expansion and Update." UNU-MERIT Working Paper 020, Maastricht, Netherland.

Olley, G. S., and A. Pakes. 1996. "The Dynamics of Productivity in the Telecommunications Equipment Industry." *Econometrica* 64 (6): 1263–97.

Padilla-Pérez, R., and F. G. Villarreal. 2017. "Structural Change and Productivity Growth in Mexico, 1990–2014." *Structural Change and Economic Dynamics* 41 (March): 53–63.

Pavcnik, N. 2002. "Trade Liberalization, Exit, and Productivity Improvements: Evidence from Chilean Plants." *Review of Economic Studies* 69 (1): 245–76.

Restuccia, D., and R. Rogerson. 2008. "Policy Distortions and Aggregate Productivity with Heterogeneous Establishments." *Review of Economic Dynamics* 11 (4): 707–20.

Restuccia, D., and R. Rogerson. 2013. "Misallocation and Productivity." *Review of Economic Dynamics* 16 (1): 1–10.

Restuccia, D., D. T. Yang, and X. Zhu. 2008. "Agriculture and Aggregate Productivity: A Quantitative Cross-Country Analysis." *Journal of Monetary Economics* 55 (2): 234–50.

Rodrik, D. 2013. "Unconditional Convergence in Manufacturing." *Quarterly Journal of Economics* 128 (1): 165–204.

Rodrik, D. 2016. "Premature Deindustrialization." *Journal of Economic Growth* 21 (1): 1–33.

Rodrik, D. 2018. "An African Growth Miracle?" *Journal of African Economies* 27 (1): 10–27.

Satpathy, L. D., B. Chatterjee, and J. Mahakud. 2017. "Firm Characteristics and Total Factor Productivity: Evidence from Indian Manufacturing Firms." *Journal of Applied Economic Research* 11 (1): 77–98.

Sinha, R. 2016. "Sectoral Productivity Gaps and Aggregate Productivity." Policy Research Working Paper 7737, World Bank, Washington, DC.

Solow, R. M. 1987. "We'd Better Watch Out." Book review of *The Myth of the Post-Industrial Economy*, by S. S. Cohen and J. Zysman. *New York Times*, July 12.

Stiglitz, J. E. 2018. "From Manufacturing-Led Export Growth to a Twenty-First-Century Inclusive Growth Strategy: Explaining the Demise of a Successful Growth Model and What to Do about It." WIDER Working Paper Series 2018/176, UNU-WIDER, Maastricht, Netherland.

Stiroh, K. 2002. "Information Technology and the U.S. Productivity Revival: What Do the Industry Data Say?" *American Economic Review* 92 (5): 1559–76.

Syverson, C. 2011. "What Determines Productivity?" *Journal of Economic Literature* 49 (2): 326–65.

Tybout, J. R. 2000. "Manufacturing Firms in Developing Countries: How Well Do They Do, and Why?" *Journal of Economic Literature* 38 (1): 11–44.

Üngör, M. 2013. "De-Agriculturalization as a Result of Productivity Growth in Agriculture." *Economics Letters* 119 (2): 141–45.

Üngör, M. 2017. "Productivity Growth and Labor Reallocation: Latin America versus East Asia." *Review of Economic Dynamics* 24 (March): 25–42.

Uy, T., K. M. Yi, and J. Zhang. 2013. "Structural Change in an Open Economy." *Journal of Monetary Economics* 60 (6): 667–82.

Vaaler, P. M., and G. McNamara. 2010. "Are Technology-Intensive Industries More Dynamically Competitive? No and Yes." *Organization Science* 21 (1): 271–89.

Van Beveren, I. 2012. "Total Factor Productivity Estimation: A Practical Review." *Journal of Economic Surveys* 26 (1): 98–128.

van Biesebroeck, J. 2009. "Disaggregate Productivity Comparisons: Sectoral Convergence in OECD Countries." *Journal of Productivity Analysis* 32 (2): 63–79.

Vollrath, D. 2009. "How Important Are Dual Economy Effects for Aggregate Productivity?" *Journal of Development Economics* 88 (2): 325–34.

Wolitzky, A. 2018. "Learning form Others' Outcomes." *American Economic Review* 108 (10): 2763–801.

Wong, W.-K. 2006. "OECD Convergence: A Sectoral Decomposition Exercise." *Economics Letters* 2 (93): 210–14.

Wooldridge, J. M. 2009. "On Estimating Firm-Level Production Functions Using Proxy Variables to Control for Unobservables." *Economics Letters* 104 (3): 112–14.

World Bank. 2019a. *Global Economic Prospects: Darkening Skies*. January. Washington, DC: World Bank.

World Bank. 2019b. *Global Economic Prospects: Heightened Tensions, Subdued Investment*. June. Washington, DC: World Bank.

World Bank. 2020. *Africa's Pulse: An Analysis of Issues Shaping Africa's Economic Future*. Spring. Washington, DC: World Bank.